1595

SOCIAL SUPPORT NETWORKS

Informal Helping in the Human Services

CONTRIBUTORS TO THIS VOLUME

ELLIOT ASP, *Pennsylvania State University*
ANTHONY D'AUGELLI, *Pennsylvania State University*
RICHARD BARTH, *University of California, Berkeley*
BETTY J. BLYTHE, *University of Washington*
MARK W. FRASER, *University of Utah*
J. DAVID HAWKINS, *University of Washington*
NANCY HOOYMAN, *University of Washington*
FLORENCE LONG, *Pennsylvania State University*
CAROL PFEIFFENBERGER, *Pennsylvania State University*
RHONDA RICHARDSON, *Pennsylvania State University*
ROBERT F. SCHILLING, *University of Washington*
STEVEN PAUL SCHINKE, *University of Washington*

SOCIAL SUPPORT NETWORKS

Informal Helping in the Human Services

James K. Whittaker, James Garbarino,
and Associates

ALDINE PUBLISHING COMPANY
New York

ABOUT THE AUTHORS

JAMES K. WHITTAKER is Professor of Social Work at the University of Washington. Dr. Whittaker is author of CARING FOR TROUBLED CHILDREN, SOCIAL TREATMENT, CHILDREN AWAY FROM HOME (with A. E. Trieschman), and THE OTHER 23 HOURS (with A. E. Trieschman and L. K. Brendtro).

JAMES GARBARINO is Associate Professor of Human Development at Pennsylvania State University. Dr. Garbarino is author of PROTECTING CHILDREN FROM ABUSE AND NEGLECT (with S. Stocking), UNDERSTANDING ABUSIVE FAMILIES (with G. Gilliam), SUCCESSFUL SCHOOLS AND COMPETENT STUDENTS, and CHILDREN AND FAMILIES IN THE SOCIAL ENVIRONMENT.

Aldine Publishing Company
200 Saw Mill River Road
Hawthorne, New York 10532

Library of Congress Cataloging in Publication Data

Social support networks.

  Bibliography: p.
  Includes index.
  1. Social service.   2. Helping behavior.
3. Friendship.   4. Interpersonal relations.   I. Whittaker,
James K.   II. Garbarino, James.
HV40.S617   1983   362   83-11761
ISBN 0-202-36031-8
ISBN 0-202-36032-6 (pbk.)

Printed in the United States of America
10 9 8 7 6 5 4 3 2

Contents

Part II: Services for Mental Health, Health Care, and the Elderly

Part III: Child and Family Services

Part IV: Services to Adolescents

Part V: Services to the Chemically Dependent

Part VI: Services to the Developmentally Disabled

Chapter 13   *Robert F. Schilling and Steven Paul Schinke*

SOCIAL SUPPORT NETWORKS IN DEVELOPMENTAL DISABILITIES

Preface

This is a book about a quiet revolution currently taking place in the human service field. It concerns, essentially, two fundamentally different but equally powerful types of helping: the "formal" aid offered by the traditional helping professions through remedial, educational, counseling, and advocacy services, and that offered by "informal," or lay helpers—*networks* of family, friends, and neighbors—through the provision of primary *social support*. The basic purpose of the book is to suggest some tentative ways in which these formal and informal caregivers can join together in new and creative alliances to offer a more effective and compassionate response to people in need of help. Specifically, the book will provide human service professionals, social workers, psychologists, nurses, educators, and others with practical suggestions for understanding, identifying, creating, and using *social support networks* as a complementary strategy to professional helping.

The use of social support networks—extended family, friends, neighbors, and other "informal" helpers—is an idea whose time has come in the human service field. This is so for two fundamental reasons. At the same time that spiraling inflation and popular sentiment weigh against any major expansion of services, it is also becoming apparent that a service strategy based primarily on the notion of professional helping delivered on a case-by-case basis, usually in a one-to-one relationship, has built-in limitations of its own. For these and related reasons, the seminal contributions of such early investigators as Urie Bronfenbrenner (1979), Gerald Caplan (1974; 1976), Speck and Attneave (1973), and Collins and Pancoast (1976) have taken root in an ever-increasing number of service fields through the extension of such concepts as "support systems," "mutual aid," "family network therapy," and "informal helping networks." Such developments signal the beginning of a new partnership between professional and lay helpers that will better serve the needs of children and families, the aged, the developmentally disabled, and many other citizen groups that turn to the human services for help and support.

We do not subscribe to the simplistic view that informal helping can, or should, totally supplant the valuable help presently offered by social workers, clinical and community psychologists, nurses, psychiatrists, and other professionals in the broad human service field. Nor do we assume that formal and informal helping strategies are necessarily antagonistic to each other. Rather, we believe that professional services will be strengthened and clients better served if ways can be found to link both formal and informal helping in an overall framework of human services.

As social worker and developmental psychologist, respectively, we undertook this project well aware of our own limitations, as well as the limitations imposed by this newly emerging field of knowledge. We did feel and continue to feel that much is to be gained from bridging the gap between human development research and human service practice. In short, we feel that social support strategies in human service practice make as much sense on developmental grounds as they do on the basis of service effectiveness. In the process, we learned much from each other and from our respective disciplines.

Early on, we decided against sole authorship—the "waterfront" we sought to cover was simply too expansive. Similarly, we chose not to solicit contributions from the seminal contributors to the social support network literature, since their own substantive published contributions stand preeminent. That said, we are greatly in the debt of those pioneering scholars already mentioned, as well as other investigators like Charles Froland (1981), Ben Gottlieb (1981), Dave Biegel, and Arthur Naparstek (1982), whose recent excellent contributions do much to extend the concept of social support networks from the realm of theory to the crucible of practice. As is evident in our text, we profited greatly from their ideas as well as those of others.

We turned, instead, to younger scholars in our respective institutions— the University of Washington, School of Social Work, and the Pennsylvania State University, College of Human Development—who had substantive expertise and, in many instances, substantial research and experience in one or another area of human service practice. Moreover, all of our contributors possessed a keen interest in extending the concept and strategy of social support networks to their respective area of practice. Working collaboratively and from a common outline, we sought to answer basic questions regarding the state of the art:

—What problems in various areas of human services practice appear to lend themselves to combined formal and informal helping strategies?

—What research and practice demonstration projects currently exist and in what direction are they leading us?

—What barriers and incentives exist in various subfields of practice to implementing social support strategies?

—What practical suggestions may be gleaned from current efforts at combined helping that will aid future practice applications?

—What are the *potential* applications for social support interventions in the various subfields of human services?

In brief, we see this volume as an effort to provide a clear conception of what social support networks are, why they are important, how they are identified and sustained, where they fit in an overall framework of human services, and what their limits and potential consist of in selected fields of practice. Chapter 1 provides a working definition of social support networks; it reviews its origins in research and theory from the broader context of the ecology of human development. Chapter 2 offers a conceptual framework for integrating social support strategies within the multiple roles that human service practitioners fulfill: therapist, counselor, advocate, teacher, service broker, and consultant. The remaining eleven chapters build on this common conceptual base and review the current use of social support strategies in: mental health, health, services to the elderly, child welfare, day care and early childhood development, services to divorced and stepfamilies, schools, youth services, delinquency services, services to the chemically dependent, and developmental disabilities.

A word of caution must be added: social support networks offer no panacea or quick solution to the problems faced by human service practitioners. Social networks can be destructive as well as supportive, and an improper infusion of professional expertise can quickly eliminate what is most vital in all social support strategies: their informality, mutuality, and reciprocity. We are well aware of these risks, as well as the need to test empirically, refine, and develop many of the ideas contained in this book. We offer, at best, a series of snapshots of work in progress.

With this in mind, we believe that this volume will serve as a valuable source book for social workers, psychologists, nurses, physicians, and other human service providers. It offers a clear conceptual framework for identifying and using a variety of social support networks with different age groups and in different practice settings. It relates the use of social support networks to such other helping approaches as direct and indirect treatment, advocacy, and social brokerage. It contains a wealth of practical information on current best uses of social support networks in such fields as child and youth services, day care, family services, mental health and mental retardation, schools, aging, and health care delivery. We also see the book as a complementary text in practice methods courses in social work, clinical and community psychology, psychosocial nursing, family medicine, and human services.

Finally, we acknowledge, in a general way, the numerous pioneering investigators and contemporary contributors to the literature of social support networks whose collective efforts, provide evidence that ours, indeed, is a field of a "thousand flowers" rather than a single blossom. Closer at hand, we are deeply grateful to our colleagues in Seattle and University Park who contributed to this present effort: Tony D'Augelli, Betty Blythe, Nancy Hooyman, Florence Long, Rhonda Richardson, Carol Pfeiffenberger, Eliott Asp, Rick Barth, Dave Hawkins, Mark Fraser, Steve Schinke, and Rob Schilling. Their attention to detail, critical feedback, and willingness to share materials made the book a joy to work on. We are most grateful to Rolf Olsen for his comments on social support networks from a British perspective. We also acknowledge Dean Scott Briar, School of Social Work, University of Washington, and Dean Evan Pattishall, College of Human Development, the Pennsylvania State University, for creating and maintaining a climate supportive of scholarship and research. We are similarly grateful to the Editorial Director of Aldine, Kyle Wallace. Nan Garbarino provided us with superb "in-house" editing and critical review—we are much in her debt. Special thanks are due to Alice Saxion for her help in preparing the manuscript.

Our families—Kathleen and Nan, Matthew, Patrick, Abby, Josh, and Joanna—as well as our many friends offer tangible, constant, and, to us, compelling evidence for what social support means in day-to-day living. We are part of an evolving experiment.

James K. Whittaker and
James Garbarino

Foreword: Social Support Networks from a British Perspective

M. Rolf Olsen *

This collection of papers, which describe and evaluate the utilisation of social support networks, appears at a significant moment for the personal social services, both in the United States and Britain. It offers fresh insights and practical solutions at a time of alleged frustration and disenchantment with many of the efforts and outcomes of social work and the social services; when for the first time in almost 50 years we are faced with the social and personal consequences of world recession and high unemployment; and when the preferred political and economic strategies have worsened the chronic lack of resources long suffered by the personal social services. The senior authors, James Whittaker and James Garbarino, and their colleagues at the University of Washington, School of Social Work and the Pennsylvania State University, College of Human Development do not offer up social support networks as a panacea for the many social ills spawned by these problems. Rather, they suggest in their review of research and practice, how such social support strategies can be utilised in an overall network of personal social services. That the field of social services on both sides of the Atlantic is ready for such an infusion may be seen in an analysis of recent British experience.

I have shown elsewhere (1980)[1] that in recent years the question of social work—how to define it, its objectives, and how to determine its worth and effectiveness—has become the centre of professional and public debate. In Britain, perhaps the most important and significant discontent relates to the discrepancy between society's expectation of social work, what the public presumes, and what is actually possible. Throughout the 1970's the prolif-

*M. ROLF OLSEN is Director of Social Work Courses at the University of Birmingham, UK, where he holds the first chair in Social Work.

Dr. Olsen has published over 60 articles and comments, is a contributor to numerous books, and is a member of the board of the *British Journal of Social Work*. He is currently the general editor of the *Library of Social Work Practise*. He is editor of "Differential Approaches in Social Work with the Mentally Disabled" and co-author of "Community Care for the Mentally Disabled."

eration of statutory responsibilities in this country, together with the growth in the duty of social work "to provide services to the people," and the ever-increasing demand for services, have not been matched by either a sufficient increase in resources or in demonstrated social work effectiveness. This has led to public disapproval, to a degree unknown since the Poor Law, which has shown itself in a hostile media, critical of what it sees as the failure of social work to socialise the delinquent, restrain parents who abuse their children, prevent old people from dying alone, and to provide a satisfactory level of community care for the mentally disordered and the chronically handicapped. Some have gone so far as to call for a Royal Commission to review the working of the local authority social services departments.

In part, the seeds of this discontent in Britain also lie in the reorganisation of our social work services in 1970. Throughout the 1960's the adverse consequences of the fragmented organisation of our personal social services, with their exclusive concern with individuals and what seemed to be an undue interest in their psychological functioning rather than with their relationships and the social systems within which they functioned, were increasingly recognised. Critics advocated the replacement of the compartmentalised service and social work practice which defined need according to age and the type of problem, with a unified service which provided care based on the family and multiple systems of helping. The Seebohm Report, published in 1968,[2] gave shape to these aspirations and with its key recommendation, incorporated into the Local Authorities Social Services Act, 1970,[3] that the personal social services be redesigned so that the needs were met "on the total requirements of the individual or family, rather than on the basis of limited set of symptoms" (¶ 111). Whilst the reorganising principles contained within the Act were generally welcomed, the decision to transform the social services was taken largely in ignorance of a number of problems which have since conspired to confound social work and result in the criticism referred to above. Not least were the complexity of the organisational change, the adverse effects of creating large bureaucratic departments, the disruption caused by rapid promotion, the failure to anticipate the extent of the growth in demand for services as a result of increased public awareness, the lack of a model in which generic social work might be organised and practiced, and the inability to demonstrate therapeutic effectiveness. The overall result is that social workers were caught wrong-footed when faced with the huge task of redesigning and delivering services which fulfilled the prophecies and aspirations of a conceptual revolution in social care.

In September 1980, Patrick Jenkin, the then Secretary of State for Social Services, announced an inquiry, under the Chairmanship of Peter Barclay, to "secure an authoritative and agreed view of the role of social workers in social services departments."[4]

The report of the Barclay Committee, published in April 1982,[5] constitutes a major statement about the future direction of social work in the UK, and the recommendations have considerable implications for its theory, practice, and organisation. Its proposals are sympathetic to the conclusions offered by Whittaker, Garbarino, and their colleagues in this volume. These argue a return to the use of social support networks or informal helpers, pioneered by the social reformers of the nineteenth century, but which in our antipathy to laisse-faire and belief in the State and professionalism, have been largely disregarded since the last great war.

The Report concludes that social workers have two main areas of responsibility: first, a continuing duty to provide the traditional services of counselling and casework help to individuals and families; second, they have a responsibility to undertake what the Committee have termed ameliorative and preventive community care, which includes the promotion of strategies to provide effective community support, including community development and the necessary social and political action. Throughout the Report there is a strong emphasis on decentralisation of power downward to the individual worker, and outward to the community. To achieve this the Report stresses the need for greater community orientation and the utilisation of community networks. It is suggested that at present the voluntary sector tends to stand in the same relation to the statutory social services as a servant to a master, and argues that it is time for a change in attitude and the establishment of a more equal partnership based upon a realistic assessment of what social support networks can provide.

The Report outlines the measures which are necessary to bring these aspirations nearer to reality. These include a recognition of the amount of support and help which is provided by informal careers, mutual aid groups, and volunteers, and an acceptance of the fact that the services provided by social services departments are but a drop in the bucket compared with the caring given by families day and night, and year in and year out. It makes ten proposals to improve the partnership and effectiveness of this closer collaboration. This must start with joint planning and analysis of needs; service delivery must be based on consultative and collaborative machinery to ensure that decisions are fully informed; agency arrangements for allocating grants should be fully understood by volunteers; two-way secondment of staff and helpers should be promoted; proper joint training arrangements should be instituted; and the development of "purchase of service contracting," used in the USA, should be developed, particularly to release the service-providing potential of local community groups. Above all, it recognises that social support networks—the subject of this present volume—are an essential part of the fabric of social work services, and have a distinctive contribution to make. It is becoming increasingly evident that such networks should not be regarded as anything less than fully engaged in meeting those needs which until now have been regarded as the prerogative and responsibility of the statutory services and the professional worker.

The Report puts its weight wholeheartedly behind the expansion of community work, which it sees not only as a technique but also as a guiding philosophy. It believes this to be an essential, but not the only, element in the process of bringing social work and community networks closer together. It defines "community" as "a network or networks of informal relationships between people connected with each other by kinship, common interests, geographical proximity, friendship, occupation, or the giving or receiving of services—or various combinations of these" (¶ 13.6). In the words of the Seebohm Report[2] ". . . a network of reciprocal relationships which, among other things ensure mutual aid and give those who experience it a sense of wellbeing" (¶ 476).

As part of a community work approach the Committee urged the utilisation of residential establishments as resource centres for the local communities in which they are situated. These would provide a calling point and offer facilities for the use of individuals and groups.

It is argued that the reasons for now promoting such an approach are practical, political and economic—practical in that the community is both the provider and the recipient of social services; political in the general disenchantment with centralism and professional organisations, and in the belief that social workers may now be ready to pursue a community approach; and economic in the light of the financial situation.

These proposals have considerable implications for the style and responsibility of social work management. Bamford (1983),[6] in a forthcoming book, identifies the manager's pivotal role in social care planning, the entrepreneurial skills in bargaining over resources for teams and community groups, negotiating skills in linking with voluntary agencies and self-help groups, and planning skills to ensure that the views of the team and the surrounding community are taken into account in agency planning. The manager must also ensure the participation of stigmatised groups who command little prestige and often fail to receive their fair share of resources.

It is naive to assume that community networks will operate in harmony, and that interests will not sometimes be in conflict. Therefore utilisation of complex networks will require managers to have knowledge of the local community, its organisations, and its leaders. This knowledge must be accompanied by sensitivity to community and group needs, a readiness to listen and to enable them to identify their problems and work out their solutions, and an ability to relate particular needs and aspirations to the total situation.

But perhaps the most important implications for managers relates to the organisational structure and decision-making processes which have emerged in British social work since the Seebohm reorganisation. The proliferation of management tiers has resulted in a high level of professional accountability, and causes undue delay in reaching decisions by those who often have no personal knowledge of the situation. Bamford considers four likely consequences of implementing consumer participation, delegation and decentralisation. "First, it removes full control over resource allocation from central management. Second, it can lead to marked differences in practice and level of provision. Third, it runs against the tide of events in Social Services departments which has pushed important decisions up to senior managers. Fourth, it may leave managers in the unenviable position of having responsibility without power." He goes on to argue that it is important to retain a strong central planning and policy-making capacity in order to meet the first two problems and ensure equitable resource allocation. The third and fourth problems will require managers to "exercise responsibility by participatory influence rather than control, by natural authority rather than formal status. Embarking upon the progressive relinquishment of control demands considerable managerial self-confidence. It requires a commitment to ideas of delegation, and a readiness on occasion to accept risks. But it is necessary if agencies are to become more open to influences from the community, and more creative in their approach."

Before concluding this foreword to this volume in praise of community networks, it is worth briefly restating the limits to their expected and potential roles. The high value which we now place on this system of care runs the risk that we will ask too much of it, and in so doing compound the misery and deprivation of those it seeks to help, and waste the creative resource at our disposal. As Whittaker and Garbarino point out, there is a real danger of ideological naiveté and of falsely implying that a more firm embrace of voluntary effort will provide the solution to most, if not all, of our social problems—a view which is held by many politicians. Deakin (1982),[7] after reviewing the changing nature of the relationship between the statutory and voluntary sectors, argued "There seems to be a real risk in the present situation of encouraging the voluntary sector to do what it does worst—that is, turn itself into a rather smudgy carbon-copy of statutory (and professional) agencies, with all their faults of over-bureaucratisation (from which the voluntary sector is not in any case immune) and excessive deference to professional susceptibilities, and few of their very real virtues." We must ensure that the swing to voluntarism does not result in government and professional abdication of their responsibilities to provide resources, services, and coherent welfare policies. Community networks must not be expected to provide life-belts for the victims of the government's economic policies. For example, there is no question there is a substantial role for community networks in helping individuals and families to cope with the demoralising and economic effects of unemployment. But to believe that it can make a substantial difference to the employment situation in the severely affected areas of our inner cities is quite unrealistic. We must carefully distinguish the respective and complementary roles of the professional and community network sectors. This relationship should not be set in concrete, but be dynamic and innovative, a relationship in which there is mutual accountability but sufficient distance to enable each to remain the severest critic of the other.

An American observer once claimed that social work has "champagne pretensions but a root beer performance" (1955),[8] giving credence to the suppositions that, first, there is nothing particularly difficult about social work and that anyone with a kind heart can do it; and second, by professionalising the activity a great number of people are prevented from contributing—in so doing depriving them of personal satisfaction and the opportunity to contribute to the well-being of others. Nearly 30 years later, Whittaker, Garbarino and their colleagues redress this imbalance, and state the case for the utilisation of community networks by defining the areas where formal and informal support might combine; relating the findings of research which support this view; looking at the organisational barriers against such collaboration; demonstrating the outcome to current efforts; and pointing the directions for further initiatives. There is no doubt that such an approach requires of social workers changes in attitude toward their professional responsibilities; increased understanding of the interactions of people in groups and communities; and a capacity to negotiate and bring people together. It will also make new demands on committees and managers, in particular, the need to ensure the greatest possible delegation of decision-making to social workers, and to make policy-making less remote. It will mean the formalisation of clients' rights through appeals and grievance procedures.

In stating the importance of developing community networks, the authors stress that this cannot replace professional social work, or substitute for inadequate government policies. Neither will it be cheaper. Social work cannot be considered in isolation from political reality. There is no endless pool of financial resources for the personal social services, but social work must hold fast to its commitment to the disadvantaged, and strive to ensure their fair share of increasingly scarce resources. It is also clear that there is greater scope for the more effective use of social support networks.

REFERENCES

1. Olsen, M. R. (1980). *The Question of Social Work*, Inaugural Lecture, publ. Birmingham University, PO Box 363, Birmingham B15 2TT, England.

2. *Report of the Committee on Local Authority and Allied Personal Social Services*, Cmnd. 3703, HMSO, London, England, 1968.

3. Local Authority Social Services Act, 1971, HMSO, London, England.

4. *Social Work Today* (1980). Vol. 12, No. 4, 23.9.80, p. 2.

5. Report of Barclay Committee (1982). Bedford Sq. Press, 26 Bedford Sq., London, WC1B 3HU, England.

6. Bamford, T. (1983). *Managing Social Work*, Tavistock, Methuen Inc., NY.

7. Deakin, N. D. (1982). *The Voluntary Sector in the Eighties*, publ. Birmingham Settlement, Birmingham B19 3RL, England.

8. Gladstone, I. (1955). "How social is social work?", quoted in Rapoport, L. *in* "In Defence of Social Work," FWA, *Social Work*, April 1962, p. 12.

PART I

An Introduction to
Social Support Networks
in the Human Services

CHAPTER 1
Social Support Networks: Rx for the Helping Professions

James Garbarino

INTRODUCTION TO SOCIAL SUPPORT NETWORKS

Sally is a social worker in a medium-sized city. Her current caseload includes a family which was referred to her because of the 11-year-old's truancy; the case is driving her crazy. Obtaining information from the mother is like pulling teeth—the woman won't volunteer anything and seems reluctant to answer Sally's questions. Moreover, the 11-year-old has missed three of the four clinic appointments which were arranged for academic and medical assessment. The mother insists that everything is okay with her child and that she does not need Sally's help. Every time Sally visits the home she finds her client in the company of a couple of friends or relatives, even when she has requested a private meeting. Sally has discussed this with her co-worker and friend Louise at the office and with her husband, but not with her supervisor—he seems too cool and impersonal. She does not feel that he sees things from her point of view even though he seems to know that something is wrong and says he wants to help. Sally has managed to find excuses for missing the last two regularly scheduled staff conferences (always with good reasons) to avoid having to deal with her supervisor's questions. Her supervisor has finally hit upon a solution to *his* problem. He has spoken to Louise and persuaded her to act as an intermediary to reach Sally.

To whom do most people turn for help with their day-to-day problems? Social workers? Physicians? Psychologists? Nurses? Counselors? Therapists? These professionals are part of the picture, but they are not the primary or first-line sources of assistance for most people most of the time. Research by community psychologists and others has shown that most people usually turn for help to friends, relatives, neighbors, co-workers, and even acquaintances (Gottlieb, 1980). When professional assistance is sought, clergy, teachers, and physicians rank highest on the list; however, beauticians, bartenders, and the like also rank high (Eddy, Paap, & Glad, 1970; Turner, Kimbaugh, & Traynhano, 1977). The formal social service system

3

and its representatives typically rank relatively low on the list. This situation is unfortunate, in some ways, because these professionals and the agencies they represent have much to offer.

Even Sally turned first to family and friends for assistance, rather than to her immediate supervisor, the "professional helper" in this case. Ironically, of course, she was adopting the same approach in dealing with *her* problem (the client) as her client was in dealing with hers (her truant 11-year-old). Like her client, she found ways to resist official channels when the informal channels seemed more supportive and useful. Unlike her supervisor, however, she has not yet found an alternative route to her target. The emphasis in this volume is helping the thousands of human service professionals like Sally find and make use of these alternative routes as a way of enhancing and complementing existing services.

Many terms exist to refer to the people in one's life who provide the "meat and potatoes" of social existence, whose presence, concern, and feedback are a valued part of day-to-day life. Although considerable time will be spent defining terms (and the alternatives), what we need to begin with is a working definition. "Social support networks" conveys something about the *processes* of support [". . . a range of interpersonal exchanges that provide an individual with information, emotional reassurance, physical or maternal assistance, and a sense of the self as an object of concern," according to Pilisuk and Parks, (1980, p. 158)] as well as the *structures* and *regular patterns* of support. Networks are interconnected relationships, durable patterns of interaction, and interpersonal threads that comprise a social fabric.

Our use of "social support networks" derives from an extensive sociological and anthropological literature on social networks. Certainly one of the modern pioneering efforts in this field was Mitchell's 1969 volume. The root concept of network as "a collection of points, partially connected with each other" (Polister, 1980, p. 71) has been incorporated into the concept of social networks as the links among a group of individuals (or even families). Thus developed, social network is seen as the relational structure through which people request support and make demands. The network becomes a series of communication links. When viewed in this light (e.g., Craven & Wellman, 1974), network size and density–intensity become key issues. How many people are involved? How interconnected are they? A large body of literature has examined the role of social networks in providing access to tangible and intangible resources (e.g., Craven & Wellman, 1974), in shaping child development (e.g., Cochran & Brassard, 1979), and in many other domains of concern to human service professionals.

Cochran and Brassard (1979) suggest several dimensions for classifying and categorizing social networks. These dimensions have been formulated out of a concern for qualitatively facilitating human development (specifically child development); they are therefore of use to us in our discussions.

The first dimension concerns the network's dyadic characteristics: the content of interactions, the diversity of network membership types, the reciprocity of interactions, the intensity of the relationship, and the geographic proximity of the dyad. The second broad dimension is the cumulative character of the network: size and interconnectedness.

A social support network is a set of interconnected relationships among a group of people that provides enduring patterns of nurturance (in any or all forms) and provides contingent reinforcement for efforts to cope with life on a day-to-day basis. As shall see, these social support networks often grow out of other groups (e.g., when co-workers become a social resource for each other or when co-residents in a residential area engage in neighboring), but they may be created deliberately (e.g., groups formed by and for women who have had mastectomies or groups initiated by a health professional for parents of handicapped children). Our emphasis throughout this book is on social support networks that a professional can find or initiate, become part of or at least connected to, and then collaborate with in achieving human service missions. We are concerned with social support networks as enhancing, complementing, and offering alternatives to conventional human service approaches that rely on the dyadic relationship between individual client and professional helper. One form of these support networks is the support group, of which there are at least two kinds.

Pilisuk and Parks (1980) studied 28 support groups of two basic types. One type was described as "contrived extended families." Some were residential, some were not, but all either had set out to become analogous to kin groups or had spontaneously and serendipitously grown in that direction after starting out as something else. These may have been a purely convenient residential situation. The second type consisted of "common life situation or crisis groups." All groups of this type were generated by private individuals or professionals who saw a need for a mutual-help approach to some problem, stress, or challenge, such as coping with job changes, reentering college, breastfeeding, alcoholism, and teaching. Formal groups of these two types do not exhaust the range of social support networks. Social support networks that function informally merit consideration. Cochran and Brassard (1979) reviewed evidence dealing with social networks—the informal, interpersonal relationships that exist outside or beyond formal groups. They cited friendship groups as primary resources, particularly for single women. Garbarino and Sherman (1980a) studied two neighborhoods chosen to represent economically similar settings that had very different rates of child maltreatment, and found very different patterns of neighboring; the low-neighboring area was characterized by more stress and more family disruption. Stack (1974) examined the reliance of impoverished Blacks upon each other in a community setting and found an elaborate network of exchanges. Froland and his colleagues (1979) have undertaken a national compilation of programs that relate to social support networks of all types. Garbarino, Stocking, and associates (1980) have outlined a strategy for professionals to recognize and use social support networks as a complement, supplement, and, in some cases, as an alternative to conventional child protective services. All of these efforts build upon the classic notions of social networks as interconnected sets of relationships that provide an information system (Bott, 1957; Mitchell, 1969; Wellman, 1981).

The first step in finding and making use of these sources of helping is to take a close look at ourselves. Some of what we may interpret as unreasonable client resistance becomes much more comprehensible when we put ourselves in the client's shoes, when we empathize with him or her. Would we turn to strangers for help? Do we? Would we resist or reject help when it seemed to be delivered in a condescending or patronizing manner? Do we? Once we realize that our client's behavior is not radically different from our own, we have taken the first step in identifying and making use of social support networks as a way to enhance professional helping.

In an effort to understand and improve the lives of our clients, we would do well to remember Harry Stack Sullivan's conclusion that "people are more simply human than otherwise." In other words, in trying to understand the behavior of others we should always assume that the same basic motives and goals exist. The same is true in understanding social support systems: *the human commonalities* are likely to outweigh the particularities of groups and individuals. For example, we all need acceptance. Anthropologist Ronald Rohner's cross-cultural study (1975) demonstrates the universal negative influence of rejection on mental health and personality development. Also, trust figures prominently as a releasor of intimacy and help-seeking behavior. Too often, we forget this once we don the mantle of professional helper. We may expect clients to respond to strangers as we ourselves probably never would if we were receiving rather than providing the help. We must start affectively with empathy, and cognitively with a realistic picture of how day-to-day helping really works. An ecological perspective on human behavior and development provides such a realistic picture of the world, and that is a good place to start.

AN ECOLOGICAL PERSPECTIVE ON THE SOCIAL ENVIRONMENT

Look around you. What do you see? Do you see the social environment? Now "think" around you. What do you know is there? People physically present or absent? Rules and expectations governing or at least shaping your conduct? Institutions, small and large? To understand the social context of human services we need a set of cognitive lenses to see beyond the immediate causes of our behavior to the complex historical and environmental influences that operate on us directly as well as indirectly through others. We need to share an understanding of how the social environment directs us and how we shape that environment. In short, we need a broad perspective on the relationship between the individual (child or adult) and the various environmental systems that impinge upon and that are, in turn, shaped by the individual. This perspective allows us to see where and how social support networks arise, how they function, and what role the professional helper can play in and with them.

The individual brings both his personal and his species' biology ("nature") to each situation. The environment shapes the individual through reinforcement and modeling ("nurture"). Nature and nurture can work together or in opposition, and the level of risk or opportunity experienced by an individual depends on the interplay of these two forces. In extreme cases, facts of nature can all but overwhelm environmental differences. Likewise, environmental conditions can be so extreme (either in a positive or negative way) as to override all but the most powerful conditions of biology. This is human nature, to be whatever conditions encourage.

Understanding the interaction between nature and nurture is difficult. Most researchers do not even try to handle both parts of the equation at once. Rather, they tend to let one side vary while they hold the other constant—as in studying genetically identical twins reared apart to learn about the role of nature and nurture in intelligence, or in seeing how different newborns respond to a constant stimulus, such as a smiling face. Another method is to vary one side systematically while letting the other vary randomly—as in presenting school-age children with three different teaching styles and observing the overall effect of each. It is rare that a researcher is able really to look at the interplay of nature and nurture in development. This is extremely unfortunate where social risk is concerned, because the inevitable issues of policy making and service delivery *need* a science of the costs and benefits of alternative experiences to the individual and to the society. In computing these costs and benefits, we must understand where history fits into individual and cultural development.

In a sense, our interest in development is really an interest in biography. We must discover how the lives of individuals, families, and societies are interdependent. Events taking place at the level of nations (the big picture) can reverberate down into the day-to-day life of the individual and the family (the little picture). One example is when the actions of an oil-producing cartel result in unemployment that affects family dynamics, and deprives a child of a nurturant relationship with his or her parents. Conversely, millions of individual decisions can add up to major social changes, as when millions of women decide to delay childbearing so that they can pursue careers. Understanding this interplay of biography and history is at the heart of understanding human development. One important aid in applying this concept practically is an emerging ecological perspective on development.

The word *ecological* is used here to convey an interest in the way the organism and its immediate environment (the ecological niche) affect and respond to each other. The process of mutual adaptation and accommodation that takes place causes the terms of the equation that produce behavior to shift, sometimes subtly and sometimes drastically. Because of this process, we cannot account for or understand intimate relationships without understanding how the conditions surrounding the social interaction affect interaction between individuals, and how these conditions shape and "press" patterns of interaction.

"Environmental press" refers to the combined influence of forces working in an environment to shape the behavior and development of individuals in that setting. It arises from the circumstances confronting and surrounding an individual that generate psychosocial momentum, which tend to guide that individual in a particular direction. Thus, the individual's environment is multifaceted and multileveled—a complex network of forces that affect the individual through behavior settings.

From the perspective ecological psychology, "behavior settings are coercive of behavior. People who enter a setting are pressed to help enact its program (while at the same time using the setting for their own purposes)" (Gump & Adelberg, 1978, p. 174). Over time, individual behavior tends to become congruent with the situational demands of the environment. Environmental press implements this "principle of progressive conformity" (Moos, 1976).

However, environmental press is not a single or unitary force, but the influence of all forces interacting within an environment. Various elements of a setting generate behavior-modifying forces that contribute to environmental press. A setting's physical characteristics may facilitate or impede access to desired destinations or alternate uses of existing space. For example, one can promote enduring patterns of interaction at work by providing convenient sites for lunch. Social patterns also may reward or punish particular values or attitudes or encourage or discourage various actions, such as neighboring in residential areas or socializing in work settings. Further, these various influences interact with and modify each other, so that physical attributes affect social variables and vice versa.

The presence, strength, and dynamic balance among environmental forces differ, of course, across contrasting settings. Contrasting environments therefore press toward different forms of behavior or directions for development. For example, small social environments (towns, groups, or institutions) are associated with patterns of behavior which differ from large ones (Barker & Gump, 1964). Large secondary schools tend to discourage participation by students, whereas small schools tend to encourage it (Barker & Gump, 1964; Garbarino, 1980b). The same is true of other organizations as well. Environments that separate residential concentrations of children from recreational settings with busy streets lined on both sides by parked cars generate both injuries to children and pressure on parents to provide regulation (Aldrich, 1979; Michelson & Roberts, 1979). High-rise appartments discourage informal interaction among parents.

The balance of environmental forces is not the sole determinant of outcomes for an organism, of course. The individual organism figures significantly as well. While environmental press is the environment's contribution to individual–environment transactions, the individual brings to the situation an arrangement of personal resources and a level of development. Different people thus may react differently to the same environment. The big school–little school findings cited above, for instance (Barker & Gump, 1964; Garbarino, 1980b), applied most significantly to academically marginal students. Further, the same environment may interact differently with the same person at different times. For example, the same busy street that is life-threatening to a child of 4 may be a developmentally appropriate challenge for a 9-year-old, a mild inconvenience for a teenager, go unnoticed by a 30-year-old single, and be an impenetrable barrier to a feeble elder.

Interindividual differences and intraindividual change require that we consider individual characteristics if we are attempting to predict outcomes of individual–environment interactions. All environments contain forces that support or undermine the processes of personal development. These forces may work for or against fulfillment of the individual's basic survival needs; for or against provision of emotional nurturance and continuity; for or against developmentally appropriate attempts at self-determination—in short, for or against the creation of a positive environment for growth and development across the life span. Forces that support people represent opportunities for adequate, or even enhanced, developmental experiences, whereas the absence of such characteristics or the presence of threatening forces presents environmental risks to the developing individual. Throughout this book we shall be looking at these forces in relation to social support networks.

To study the ecology of human development is to undertake the scientific study of how the individual develops interactively with the immediate social and physical environment, and how aspects of the larger social context affect what goes on in the individual's immediate settings. This distinguishes an ecological perspective on human development (see Bronfenbrenner, 1979; Garbarino & Gilliam, 1980), from both ecological psychology (see Barker & Schoggen, 1973) and traditional human ecology (see Hawley, 1950). Although there is little value to a "my ecological perspective is better than yours" argument, there are significant differences among these approaches. Both of the latter ecological approaches focus on environmental systems without really attending to the role of the developing organism. As Devereux (1977) so aptly observed, ecological psychology examines the inner life of human settings with inadequate attention to how the primary economy of the community produces, maintains, and terminates those settings. Traditional human ecology, on the other hand, focuses on precisely that community role without really attending to how the settings themselves function (let alone the organisms in them). The principal contribution of recent ecological initiatives in human development is to bring Kurt Lewin's classic formulation of human behavior ("Behavior is a function of Person and Environment") to fruition.

This framework establishes the individual as a developing person who plays an active role in an ever-widening world. Indeed, the very definition of development itself reflects this theme. Bronfenbrenner defines human development as "the process through which the growing person acquires a more extended, differentiated, and valid conception of the ecological environment, and becomes motivated and able to engage in activities that reveal the properties of, sustain, or restructure that environment at levels of similar or greater complexity in form and content" (1979, pp. 27–28). This definition has important implications for understanding social support networks. It suggests that an individual's social field increases concomitantly with his or her overall development. Optimal development thus has a strong social component. As Aristotle put it, "He who is unable to live in society or who has no need because he is sufficient for himself, must be either a beast or a god" (*Politics*). Development entails an ever-expanding and deepening set of social networks. The newborn shapes the feeding behavior of its mother but is confined largely to a crib or a lap and has limited means of communicating its needs and wants. The 10-year-old, on the other hand, influences many adults and other children located in many different settings, and has many means of communicating. The world of adolescents is larger and more diverse, as is their ability to influence it. Adults can have a set of social networks that stretches across continents.

The individual and the environment negotiate their relationship over time. Neither is constant; each depends on the other in this reciprocal process. One cannot predict the future of one without knowing something about the other. Does a handicapped child stand a greater risk of being abused? It depends. Some environments are more "vulnerable" to the stresses of caring for such a child than are others (see Young & Kopp, 1980). Does economic deprivation harm development? It depends on how old one is when it hits, what sex one is, what the future brings in the way of vocational opportunity, what the quality of family life was in the past, what one's economic expectations and assumptions are, and whether an investigator looks at the short-term or the long-term effects (Elder, 1974; Elder & Rockwell, 1977).

In addition to recognizing the transactive nature of development, an ecological framework also considers the multiple levels at which environmental influences originate (Garbarino & Plantz, 1981). Bronfenbrenner describes the individual's environment as "a set of nested structures, each inside the next, like a set of Russian dolls" (1979, p. 22). As we ask and answer questions about development at one level, this ecological framework reminds us to look at the next levels beyond and within the immediate setting for questions to ask and answer. For example, if we see husbands and wives in conflict over lost income we need to look outward to the economy that puts the husbands out of work and welcomes the wives into the labor force, and to the culture that defines personal worth in monetary terms and blames the victims of economic dislocation for their own losses. In addition, we must look inward to the parent–child relationships that are affected by the changing roles and status of the parents and to temperamental characteristics of the individuals involved (Elder, 1974). Further, we must look "across" to see how the several systems involved (family, social networks, workplace, and economy) adjust to new conditions over time. These swirling social forces are the stuff of which ecological analyses are made, namely, interlocking social systems.

Bronfenbrenner's framework posits four general types of environmental systems, categorized by their proximity to and immediacy of effects on individuals. The following discussion presents the four levels of environmental systems, their distinctive relationships to the developing person, and the crucial issue of the risks and opportunities these environments can represent (Garbarino & Plantz, 1981). It is within this framework that we seek to understand how social support networks arise and are able to facilitate day-to-day life.

Most immediate to the developing person are *microsystems*. They are the joint product of physical settings and behavioral interactions in which individuals experience and create day-to-day reality. Microsystems are the places people inhabit, the people who are there with them, and the things they do together. At first, most children experience only one, quite small microsystem—the home— involving interaction with one person at a time in relatively simple activities such as feeding, bathing, and cuddling. As the child develops, complexity normally increases—the child does more, with more people, in more places. By adulthood the individual participates in many microsystems and can have a large role in directing them. As we shall see, however, the significance of these settings depends on their subjective meaning to the developing person.

We know that the management of "survival needs" (such as eating and eliminating) is a critical issue in the developing child's microsystem. Play, and later work, also figure prominently in the microsystem from the early months of life. Playing, working, and loving—what Freud deemed the essence of normal human existence—are the principal classes of activities that characterize the individual's microsystem. However, the extent to which these activities take place, their quality, and their level of complexity are variables. Developmental risk derives from a microsystem characterized by a narrowly restricted range and level of activities; impoverished experience in playing, working, and loving; or stunted reciprocity in which genuine *interaction* is lacking and either participant seeks to avoid or be impervious to the other. Such neglect and rejection are developmentally dangerous (Rohner, 1975; Polansky, 1976; Rohner & Nielson, 1978; Garbarino, 1980a). In contrast, enduring, reciprocal, multifaceted relationships that emphasize playing, working, and loving provide environmental opportunities for a person.

One very important aspect of a microsystem is social density. We can consider the existence of relationships that go beyond simple dyads (two people). Where the individual can observe and learn from being exposed to other dyads (such as his mother and father), development is enhanced. This is also true where the person can observe differences in his own dyadic experience because a third party is present. As long as increased numbers in a microsystem mean more enduring reciprocal relationships, larger and more complex microsystems, as a function of age, mean enhanced development. Social riches are measured by enduring, reciprocal, multifaceted relationships that emphasize playing, working, and loving. A rich person participates in multiple and diverse microsystems; a rich environment offers participation in such settings. As development proceeds the person needs more and can profit from more microsystems. But the individual needs connected microsystems, what Bronfenbrenner calls mesosystems.

Mesosystems are the relationships *between* contexts (microsystems) in which the developing person experiences reality. Important mesosystems for children include relationships among home, peer group, school, church, and neighborhood. For adults we can add work and government. The number of links, the value consensus, and the diversity among microsystems indicate the richness of a person's mesosystems. In this sense, a socially dense ecology is a positive influence because the richness of mesosystems derives from the size (number) and quality (depth) of connections. One obvious implication is to consider how well professional human services function as mesosystems with home, neighborhood, and peer group, that is, with social support systems that exist "naturally."

The school–home mesosystem, for example, is of great developmental significance to the child. In general, we would expect enhanced development when this mesosystem is "characterized by more frequent interaction between parents and school personnel, a greater number of persons known in common by members of the two settings, and more frequent communications between home and school, more information in each setting about the other" (Bronfenbrenner, 1979, p. 218).

The same number of microsystems can account for significantly different numbers of mesosystems. At one extreme we might have a person involved in four microsystems (e.g., home, school, neighborhood, and church), but no mesosystems. The same number of microsystems could be associated with at least six mesosystems, however, if all the possible microsystem pairs were related behaviorally and psychologically. The latter environment is more socially dense, and probably more supportive of overall development because these mesosystems *tend* to function as social support networks. However, we must add the proviso "that such interconnections not undermine the motivation and capacity of these persons who deal directly with the . . . [person] . . . to act on his behalf. In the case of the school, this qualification gives negative weight to actions by school personnel that degrade parents or to parental demands that undermine the professional morale or effectiveness of the teacher" (Bronfenbrenner, 1979, p. 218). Those familiar with contemporary schooling know that both situations often are problems. In contemporary communities, the quality of school–home mesosystems is variable. It seems here as elsewhere that Aristotle's golden mean prevails: in all things moderation.

Thus, with mesosystems, high social density is generally good. It can be a problem, however, when those in significant roles are crowded out, e.g., the parents from the school or a client's kin from the service agency. In general, the stronger, more positive, and more diverse the links between settings, the more powerful and beneficial the resulting mesosystem will be as an influence on the individual's development. A rich range of mesosystems is a developmental opportunity; a poor set of mesosystems produces impaired development, particularly when the mesosystems involve home and school for children, and home and work for adults. Events in systems in which the individual does not participate but in which things happen that have a direct impact on people with whom he or she does interact often determine the quality of a person's mesosystems. Bronfenbrenner calls these settings "exosystems."

Exosystems are situations that affect a person's development but in which the developing person does not play a direct role. Exosystems have power over one's life even though one does not participate in them. For children they include the workplaces of parents (since most children do not have direct contact with them), and those centers of power, such as school boards and planning commissions, that make decisions affecting the child's day-to-day life. For adults they include these same political agencies plus centers of economic influence and the child's peer group and school. These exosystems enhance development when they make life easier for the significant people in one's life and undermine development when they make life harder for those people. Exosystem opportunity lies in situations where forces are at work to support one's support network. When people "have friends in high places" the opportunities for development increase. The political initiative taken by the powerful Kennedy family on behalf of retarded children is an example. More typically, however, institutions (offices and structures) in the exosystem are generally of greater importance. Thus, the relevance of exosystems to our concern with social support networks lies mainly in how they affect micro- and mesosystems.

For example, one very important exosystem for children and parents is the planning board. This group can play a significant role in determining how well the authorities incorporate interests of children into decisions about land use. Given that a physical environment attractive to children may be unattractive by adult standards, a planning board sensitive to the needs of both groups is vital (Michelson & Roberts, 1979). For example, children may thrive on both empty lots, which they fill with games, and on the integration of commercial with residential properties, which many adults see as economically disadvantageous. As Barker has noted, "planning has, over the years, stressed the separation of uses. I think that many planners, particularly those working in the city, realize the fallacy of that policy, and that diversity is, in fact, a strength rather than a weakness" (1979, p. 118).

Meso- and exosystems are embedded in the broad ideological and institutional patterns of a particular culture or subculture, and show how the ecological pieces fit together. Meso- and exosystem patterns constitute the *macrosystem*—the "blueprints" for a culture's ecology of human development. These blueprints reflect a people's shared assumptions about "how things should be done," such as who and how much one should help. A macrosystem encompasses the norms about how development proceeds and the appropriate nature and structure of micro-, meso-, and exosystems. Conventional cultural and ethnic labels (e.g., Latin, Italian, Indian) suggest unique clusters of ideological and behavioral patterns. Beyond these labels, however, we need to define operationally and examine ideologies and behaviors and their implications for development. In terms of their consequences for human functioning, we need to know, for example, how different cultures respond to economic crises that diminish the ability of some people to pay for services, how the nature of friendship and neighboring differs among ethnic groups, how cultures define and respond to dependency, and how different political ideologies allocate authority between public and private agencies (Berger & Neuhaus, 1977; Rotenberg, 1977; Warren & Warren, 1977; Kahn & Kamerman, 1979).

Environmental opportunity in a macrosystem lies in an ideology and a set of institutions that support and encourage healthy social relations. For example, a society's assumption that families stricken by economic or medical tragedy have a right to public support represents macrosystem opportunity. A strong political base of support for child services is another manifestation of macrosystem opportunity. A third is a commitment to gearing the construction and maintenance of residential environments to meet people's social needs rather than exclusively to the economic needs of corporations.

What is environmental risk in a macrosystem? It is an ideology or cultural alignment that threatens to impoverish people's microsystems and mesosystems, and set exosystems against them. It can be a national economic policy that tolerates or even increases the chances of economic dislocations and poverty for families. It can be institutionalized support for high levels of geographic mobility that disrupt neighborhoods and social networks. It can be a pattern of demands and reinforcements that tolerates or even aggravates conflicts between the roles of worker and parent. It can be patterns of racist, sexist, or other values that demean people, thereby undermining the psychological security of their children and threatening each child's self-esteem. In general, macrosystem risk is any social pattern or social event that diminishes the ability and willingness to people to act cooperatively and supportively in social networks. Macrosystem risk is a social event or a pattern that disrupts and impedes the caring community.

As noted before, the microsystem is the immediate setting in which the person develops. Microsystems evolve and develop much as the individual does, through forces from within and from without. The setting "school" is very different in June than it was in September for the same children (who are themselves, of course, not the same). The setting of the family as experienced by the firstborn child is different from that experienced by subsequent children. We must remember that the microsystem has a life of its own; it also develops.

It is also important to remember that Bronfenbrenner's definition speaks of the microsystem as a pattern *experienced* by the developing person. The cognitive maps we carry around in our heads are the reality we live by and act upon. One might consider who said it better: Shakespeare in *Hamlet* (II, ii, 249–250): "for there is nothing good or bad/but thinking makes it so . . .," or sociologist W. I. Thomas: "If men define situations as real, they are real in their consequences." The individual constructs the microsystems as much as he or she is shaped by them. Thus, in our efforts to understand helping we must start not with our professional perspective, but with the perspective of the general population. Whom do they see as helpers? To whom do they go for assistance? How do they define the sources of support and guidance in the social environment?

WHO HELPS?

Who helps? Certainly professionals play a significant role. No one can deny that for some problems, some of the time, the expertise and neutrality (but not necessarily impersonality) of the professional helper are necessary and even are welcomed (Unger & Powell, 1980). The available evidence suggests a critical role for the helping professional (Lindenthal, Thomas, & Myers, 1971; Leutz, 1976; Garbarino, Stocking, & Associates, 1980).

People are much more likely to perceive professional help as relevant and to seek it when servere personal impairment or stress is present (Lindenthal, Thomas, & Myers, 1971). Indeed, workers who have sought to improve the integration of professionals into social support networks acknowledge that the professional stands at the end of a multistage process whereby people in need ultimately find themselves *or their problem* referred to a professional if earlier (lay) helpers do not succeed (Collins & Pancoast, 1976; Leutz, 1976; Unger & Powell, 1980). What is more, the professional often has a crucial function in facilitating both informal social support networks (such as groups of friends, neighbors, kin or co-workers) and social support groups (such as Alcoholics Anonymous, Foster Parents Association, and Parents Without Partners, which bring together people "in the same boat" to provide both emotional and instrumental assistance in coping with specific problems or challenges).

Informal social support networks function on their own, and although the professional can often work through and with them, efforts to organize or professionalize them may be socially lethal (Garbarino, Stocking, & Associates, 1980). Social support groups, on the other hand, often *need* professional encouragement (Gartner & Riessman, 1975).

The experience of the Parents Anonymous self-help groups shows this with particular clarity (Lieber & Baker, 1977). Such groups will not succeed on the basis of professional interest and activity alone, but they often cannot make a go of it without professional assistance and facilitation.

The same body of evidence that tells us that the professional role is vital also tells us that it is limited. The professional (and the client) suffers when the helper fails to recognize the limits of the professional role and to acknowledge the importance of the friends, relatives, neighbors, and others for whom social helping is not the primary mission. As people concerned about the quality of living in our society, we must understand the limitations of our role and how to complement and augment it by collaborating with informal helping networks. The mechanics of this process are the topic of Chapter 2, where "how to" will be dealt with. This chapter considers only the "why for."

We must begin by reorienting our perspective because our training and culture impose some conceptual baggage that stands in our way. One of my favorite metaphors is the saying, "If the only tool you have is a hammer, then you tend to treat every problem as if it were a nail." The dominant perspective in human services has been a dyadic one, even though there is a subsidiary tradition of environmental helping. Our principal tool is one-to-one intervention, professional-to-client. Some professionals have gone so far as to treat whole families as their clients, as revealed by the increase in family therapy across the country. However, few professionals have really reoriented their basic thinking about helping. They have not incorporated the various social tools potentially available to them. They continue to see most, if not all, of their clients and their problems as nails for which the hammer of direct dyadic interaction is the appropriate tool. This is built into our ideas about human processes, and an elaborate institutional and ideological structure supports and depends upon it. It is therefore our "paradigm," as Thomas Kuhn (1970) uses the term.

The hammer–nail metaphor is powerful because it highlights how our investment in professional roles and practices may blind us to other tools and resources for improving the quality of human life. The first step is to consider briefly the tools potentially available in the existing and potential social realities. Our paradigm, our conception of the problem–solution systems, needs shaking up.

A GLOSSARY OF HELPING

Most of us have heard and appreciated the classic tale of the nine blind men who were asked to describe an elephant while touching only one of its parts (trunk, tail, leg, ear, tusk, etc.). The result, of course, was nine different conclusions about the nature and identity of the object. One man decided he was touching a snake (tail), while another decided he was faced with a tree trunk (leg). None "saw" an elephant; each relied on too limited a source of data and thus each was too narrow in his conclusion. We face much the same problem in seeing the broad picture, the nature of the beast, as it were, in describing helping and social support as generic terms. We need to review and categorize the various forms of helping so that we may see social support for what it is *in context*. We must examine the human ecology of helping to see how each system relates to the others and fits into the total social picture. When we do this we see a growing multitude of terms, all of which refer to helping and social support in one way or another.

These various terms and definitions reflect the rich diversity of professional orientations in the field, including social workers, community psychologists, psychiatrists, clergy, clinical psychologists, nurses, and sociologists, among others. They also reflect the different frameworks within which these people work. For example, some orientations emphasize self-help whereas others focus on social healing. The former is an activity that depends primarily on the individual, whereas the latter necessarily involves *interpersonal* activity. Some perspectives focus on formal groups while others rely on informal sets of relationships. Some highlight empowering the client, while others see the professional's problem-solving expertise as paramount.

Some of the common terms in this corpus of helping concepts are listed in Table 1-1. Some of these terms have a relatively longer history than others and are well established in practice, theory, and research, e.g., self-help groups (Gartner & Riessman, 1977). Others are new, and have a brief track record, e.g., neighborhood network consultant (Collins & Pancoast, 1976, among others).

Table 1-1. Terminology for concepts of help

Natural caregiving
Self-help
Neighborhood network consultant
Support group
Social network
Formal and informal support system
Helping network
Natural helper
Lay helper
Central figure
Natural helping network
Social support network
Mutual aid

Whatever their history, these terms refer to help that has been either "discovered" or "invented," employing the distinction Pfohl (1977) used in discussing social definitions of child abuse. Like abuse and neglect, "help" can be a social creation or a social discovery. It can arise from the efforts of professionals to create a service or from the recreational, vocational, religious, or political activities of lay people. We can start with the assumption that most formal help is created. Governments and private philanthropies initiate formal human services. Thus, the state, the church, or the private foundation creates child welfare agencies, old age homes, counseling centers, and schools to meet basic human needs that would otherwise go unmet. The history of human services is primarily the story of how and why existing institutions created the apparatus to provide programs of this sort.

Informal helping tends to be much less deliberate—certainly from the formal institution's point of view—and much more likely to represent imperceptible social evolution. Thus, the task for the professional is typically to discover what exists already: people in social networks, community figures serving as gatekeepers and auxiliary counselors, neighborhood institutions that amass a great deal of social capital and grow into a helper role naturally, or regular but informal meetings of people who share basic needs and exchange mutual help. Once discovered, informal help can become part of the service arsenal of the professional. Chapter 2 will identify exactly where informal helping fits into the overall constellation of human services, and the remaining chapters will explore the payoffs and potential for incorporating these strategies in selected fields of practice.

The proliferation of academic and clinical work concerned with social support in its forms requires that we reach for some systematic way to consider help that is discovered (i.e., exists "naturally" to be found) in contrast to that which is created (and creatable). Furthermore, we need to examine the relationships between discovered and created help, in practice and in

Table 1-2. A framework for classifying help

	Personal	Social
Resources	Competence (communication skills, empathy, ego strength)	Support system (nurturance and feedback)
Processes	Self-help + empowerment	Natural helping network + support group (informal) (formal)

principle. As we shall see in later chapters, we need to understand how these relationships vary from area to area in the human services, e.g., from schools to drug abuse to the elderly.

Whether or not we can discover or create help depends partly on our view of the social landscape. The assumptions we bring to the topic can significantly influence what we can and will find. This book seeks to provide a map of the social landscape to help professionals locate helping resources. We can consider the framework presented in Table 1-2 as a way of summarizing and reducing the diversity.

Table 1-2 focuses on the key distinction between personally and socially oriented forms of helping. Within those categories, it identifies the resources that each approach seeks to enhance and the processes by which these resources are marshalled. "Personal" refers to help that comes primarily from within the individual. Most conventional human service approaches seek to help by increasing the individual's personal resources, although there is a growing trend toward including social resources in the treatment goals. Thus, for example, a counselor may seek to build up communication skills, an educator knowledge, a nurse physical well-being, a psychologist stress management skills, a development specialist job training, and a political activist power. All of these personal approaches seek to arm the individual against stress and threat, be it from within (e.g., alcoholism) or without (e.g., poverty). Some seek to involve the client in more supportive social relationships. Given the individualistic nature of our culture, it is not surprising that the overriding assumption is that the individual must ultimately sink or swim alone. Whether the focus of a professional service is remediation (e.g., rectifying deficient empathy in abusive parents) or enhancement (e.g., improving the sense of self-actualization in a functioning old person), all are primarily concerned with the individual's own psychological resources and generally seek to "immunize" the at-risk client against the pathogens in the social environment. And all, therefore, stand in distinction to more fully socially-oriented approaches that focus on support systems, on collective resources.

On the "social" side, we have a concern for the web of interpersonal relationships that tie the individual together with others and in so doing provide a reliable system of helping. Here the emphasis is on the nurturance and feedback people give to and receive from each other. Rather than look-ing to the individual, those working within this framework look to the col-lective—to the social network, to the extended family, to the group. In one of its limited forms, this approach may consist of complementing individual therapy with efforts to prepare family members to accept and encourage the "new" individual (Heller, 1979). Proponents of this approach see that social resources can compensate for individual inadequacies and provide buoyancy so that individuals need not sink even if they do not know how to swim. What is more, those who emphasize social resources argue that no one can master the heaviest seas of life alone and that even those with normally adequate levels of personal resources may need to be thrown a lifeline or even a life raft in time of extraordinary stress. There is some professional recognition of this perspective in network therapy (Speck & Attneave, 1973), which convenes a meeting of a client's friends to deal with his problem.

Before proceeding, I should briefly elaborate on what I mean by "per-sonal" resources. Personal resources are an individual's own characteris-tics—characteristics that make for competence. Much has been made of intelligence as adaptability, the ability to respond effectively to the changing environment. Although much maligned in some circles, intelligence is a useful concept for understanding human functioning. Similarly, the psycho-dynamic concept of ego is valuable. The individual's ability to deal with the problem of negotiating the best solution for meeting inner needs within the constraints of external realities is crucial. But both intelligence and ego are insufficient to ensure a personal foundation for success in the world. The broader term competence does a better job of it, arising as it does from efforts to conceptualize the individual's innate motive to master the environ-ment (White, 1959). McClelland defines competence as "successful perfor-mance in specific social contexts" (1973, p. 10). This context-specific ap-proach is essential for understanding what comes later in our discussion. Our ecological perspective tells us that there is no such thing as context-free development (Garbarino & Gilliam, 1980). All development represents a transaction between organism and environmental system. Only at the most general level can we accurately speak of general abilities. The more specific the situation, the clearer the need to specify the components of competence.

While arguing that competence is situationally defined, McClelland cites four characteristics that are generally relevant to success in most social con-texts: communication skills, patience, moderate goal setting, and ego strength. Communication skills are important because transactions require the flow of information (in the broad sense) back and forth between the parties. Being proficient in sending and receiving messages is crucial, as observations of individuals in a new and different cultural context demon-strate. Patience is a second general "skill" that bodes well for success in the social environment. Inability to cope with delays and inefficiency in social settings leaves one vulnerable in many ways. Likewise, those who characteristically set their goals too low or too high set themselves up for failure. Ego strength refers to a general reservoir of positive motivation toward dealing with the world. One threat to competence involves environmental circumstances that either punish or ignore attempts to comprehend and work with the social environment. Thus, the competent person is likely to be someone who will not easily be "turned off" by circumstances. These four abilities together provide the tools one needs to do well in most settings in which one is asked to function.

Each of these characteristics implies a mixture of learning (experience) and innate capacity (temperament). Each must be translated into specific behaviors for each context or class of contexts (such as school, family, or work). Individuals bring their track record of competence, or incompetence, to each new situation (such as the transition to parenthood), and their experiences have a cumulative effect. This track record of competence or incompetence is one important aspect of the differences among individuals and between groups, and it is an important determinant of the level of social resources available from a group to its members.

One of the pioneers in the professional study and uses of social support, Gerald Caplan, has recently explored the concept of mastery in his efforts to understand how to protect people against the deleterious aspects of stress and help them convert stress into growth-inducing challenge. He defines mastery as:

> behavior by the individual that (1) results in reducing to tolerable limits physiological and psychological manifestations of emotional arousal during and shortly after the stressful event and also (2) mobilizes the individual's internal and external resources and develops new capabilities in him that lead to his changing his environment or his relation to it, so that he reduces the threat or finds alternate sources of satisfaction for what is lost (1981, p. 413).

Mastery represents the joint product of personal and social resources. The help available to an individual consists of what he or she brings to the situation and what he or she can call upon in the social environment, his or her competence and social resources. Our goal as professionals, of course, is to strive for a state in which everyone copes successfully with every stress and converts these stresses into growth-inducing challenges. With this as a goal, we must inevitably recognize that we can go only so far in cultivating personal resources through direct professional intervention. The harsh fiscal realities of the 1980's have brought home the point that research on social support systems was already establishing: to achieve the greatest possible level of mastery in our communities we must attend to, facilitate, enhance, and collaborate with social support networks based on naturally occurring or possible interpersonal relationships. This will advance our progress toward the mastery society envisioned by Caplan and others.

SOCIAL SUPPORT AND THE MASTERY OF STRESS

In an essay on "Space: An Ecological Variable in Social Work Practice," Germain concludes that: "Where the environment is supportive, creative adaptation and growth occur. Where the environment is nonprotective or depriving, stress is created and growth and adaptive functioning may be impeded" (1978, p. 522). This emphasis on support, adaptation, and stress is consonant with our emerging understanding of how human development proceeds as an interaction of the personal and the social (Bronfenbrenner, 1979). Emphasis on the environment is consistent with the efforts to measure and improve the quality of life for individuals and families that are notable in the social indicators movement (Brim, 1975) and the family impact analysis movement (Johnson, 1978). Such efforts reflect a growing appreciation for how the quality of community life affects families (Bronfenbrenner, Garbarino, and Moen, 1983) and how people's very sense of existential meaningfulness depends on the social richness of their interpersonal relationships (Campbell, 1975).

North American professionals typically see the solution to social problems in terms of dyads, when we move beyond the individual at all. How does the public differ from professionals on this score? The picture is mixed. On the one hand, it seems that many people recognize just how dependent they are on *social* support. Campbell (1975) reports, for example, that the best predictor of how meaningful and satisfying people rate their day-to-day existence is how they rate the quality and scope of their enduring interpersonal relationships. What is more, many people seem to sense that the best way to deal with trouble is to get together. As Pilisuk and Parks note: "The existence and application of adequate descriptions of the structure of support groups are necessary . . . if social policy is to reflect the knowledge which natural helpers intuitively grasp when they provide care and folk wisdom to a needy friend, or when people with a common life crisis band together to share their concerns and to extend and receive nurturance" (1980, p. 175). We have some evidence (Leichter & Mitchell, 1975; Campbell, 1975; Garbarino, 1977) that many professional helpers work from the assumption that mental health often requires curing pathogenic social ties and that interpersonal liberation is an avenue to mental health. Whether the problem be child abuse, alcoholism, teenage pregnancy, or violence in schools, we "naturally" adopt a dyadic model for dealing with the phenomenon. Victim–perpetrator, pusher–user, teacher–student: our understanding of the problem is always shaped by the notion that behavior is best understood as the interaction of individuals. This book asks us to look further, to the social networks of people.

We typically seek cures in individual rehabilitation and therapy, but we can learn to seek out collective routes to improving the human condition. Our individualistic orientation has not served very well in dealing with many of our most pressing social issues, whatever its benefits in other ways (e.g., fostering creativity). A price is paid for privacy (Garbarino, 1977). Many of the most successful treatment and rehabilitation programs incorporate a collective orientation. For example, self-help groups in which individuals become part of a collective entity have gained favor. Parents Anonymous is such a self-help group in which the collective function is quite strong (Lieber & Baker, 1977), while Alcoholics Anonymous is another. Other chapters in this book describe many others.

In some respects, then, we are moving haltingly and sometimes even unconsciously from a purely individualistic approach to one that incorporates the notion of artificially created groups as the unit and vehicle for rehabilitation and therapy. The challenge before us is to make this advance more widespread and more systematic without buying into some of the traditional costs of collectively oriented approaches, e.g., evoking shame and feelings of intrusiveness.

The operative aspect of the social resources we seek to tap is the support system, and that concept is used in the spirit of Caplan's benchmark formulation as:

> continuing social aggregates that provide individuals with opportunities for feedback about themselves and for validations for their expectations about others, which may offset deficiencies in these communications within the larger community context. . . . People have a variety of specific needs that demand satisfaction through enduring interpersonal relationships, such as for love and affection, for intimacy that provides the freedom to express feelings easily and unself-consciously, for validation of personal identity and worth, for satisfaction of nurturance and dependency, for help with tasks, and for support in handling emotion and controlling impulses:
>
> They tell him [the individual] what is expected of him and guide him in what to do. They watch what he does and they judge his performance. (1974, pp. 4–6).

The research on support systems, particularly on informal support systems and their positive effects, is growing rapidly. This research demonstrates that social support, from kin, friends, neighbors, and volunteer layhelpers is vitally important. A few examples, beginning with the animal world and working onward to man, follow.

> —Lab animals exposed to shock do not show symptoms of stress when they are with members of their own species, but they do when exposed alone (Cassel, 1974).
> —Gorillas develop patterns of child abuse and neglect when left to rear their babies in isolation but do not do so when they remain in the company of their group (Rock, 1978; Nadler, 1979).
> —Studies of both lower animals and humans show higher rates of illness and death among those who have experienced disruptions of social relationships (Cassel, 1976 a, b).

—Inmates in concentration camps coped better when they had a family member or at least someone preceived as a fellow (Eitinger, 1964).

—Blood samples from workers at stressful work sites show fewer biochemical indications of stress when the workplace is an interpersonally supportive setting (French, 1973).

—Women with medically at-risk pregnancies suffer only one-third the complications at birth if they are well-connected socially, with more friends and relatives in frequent contact (Nuckolls, Cassel, & Kaplan, 1972).

—Women with active husband-coaches in prepared childbirth have shorter and more successful labors (Garbarino, 1980b).

—Men experiencing life changes (such as unemployment) report greater psychological well-being if they have the support of wives and friends (Cobb, 1976; French, Rodgers, & Cobb, 1974; Gore, 1978; Wilcox, 1979).

—A study of people who had been abused as children showed that those who had strong and active social networks were much less likely to repeat the abusive pattern in their own childrearing than those without such a support system (Hunter & Kilstrom, 1979).

—Family is not enough: a recent national survey on domestic violence reports that when family comprise the *only* social contacts, stress produces greater violence than when family is augmented by social relationships beyond kin (Straus, 1980).

—Evaluation research shows that, on the average, self-help or mutual-help support groups can be as effective or even more effective than casework or individual therapy approaches in dealing with child maltreatment. In terms of cost-effectiveness, they are the clear winners (Cohn, 1979).

—Surveys and studies repeatedly show that people first go to friends, relatives, neighbors, and lay helpers such as beauticians and bartenders for information and help (Cowen *et al.*, 1978; Gottlieb, 1980).

All this is not designed to show that the professional helper is irrelevant or superfluous. Far from it. These studies carry the message that professional helpers can and should play a very important role, but it is a different role from that for which most professionals have been trained.

As research, case studies, and personal experience suggest, one threat to social richness is an imbalance of needs versus resources. When people feel that their own security is threatened by the neediness of others, they tend to become ambivalent, if not hostile, about "neighborly exchanges" of goods and services (Stack, 1974). We found this in our studies in the high-risk neighborhoods (Garbarino & Sherman, 1980): many mothers felt that they could not share because they were too vulnerable to being exploited. This feeling stands in contrast to being "free from drain" (Collins & Pancoast, 1976), and thus able to serve as a central neighbor and form the basis for a natural helping network (Pancoast, 1980). One role for professionals is to help people become "free from drain" so that they can serve as central neighbors. Another is to enhance competence to decrease the need for social support. Either strategy will be a good investment, but we believe that the former has the added benefit of linking professional services to needy families through powerful intermediaries (Gourash, 1978).

This emphasis on building up the network and decreasing personal need

Table 1-3. Building social vs. personal resources

Social support	Personal competence
Client investment (the helped become helpers)	Client flow (the helped move out of the system)
Central figure as intermediary	Helper–client dyad
Interdependence	Independence
Professional as consultant	Professional as clinician
Empowering	Serving

Source: Danish, personal communication.

reflects a large set of issues, which are identified in Table 1-3 (Danish, personal communication). We shall develop these themes in the remaining chapters of the book. Here, our task is to note these differences and move on to consider further the role of socioeconomic factors in shaping the need for and availability of social resources.

The density, diversity, and size of one's social network are prime aspects of one's social resources (Cochran & Brassard, 1979; Polister & Pattison, 1980). Clearly, there are individual and group differences in both personal and social resources. Some individuals are more competent for a variety of reasons. The professional's access to the social network of families is likely to be through one or more individuals who are free from drain. Their special competence can extend beyond mastering their own lives to becoming a social resource, a central figure who rises to an important position in the informal support system by dint of personal characteristics and social position. "Central figures in networks that are mutually supportive attain their centrality by playing key helping roles and by matching resources to need. Calling these people 'natural helpers' emphasizes the personal attributes they bring to relationships in their networks" (Pancoast, in Garbarino, Stocking, & Associates, 1980, p. 114). These individuals are the primary resource for professionals seeking to work with and through informal social support systems; they can provide the core around which to build informal support systems and the vehicle for bridging formal and informal systems. Like individuals, some groups are more competent because of their traditions or privileged positions in the social order. The social environment is defined in significant measure by its access to socioeconomic resources. One need not be a Marxist to recognize that, as ever, the principal threat to individual and family life is socioeconomic impoverishment ("to deprive of strength, richness or fertility by depleting or draining of something essential," according to Webster). The National Academy of Sciences reached this conclusion in its report, *Toward a National Policy for Children and Families* (1976). A Carnegie Foundation report (*All Our Children*) echoes this theme (Keniston, 1977). Research linking social indicators to family survey data makes the same point (Kogan, Smith, & Jenkins, 1977), as did Sophie Tucker when she uttered her classic "I've been rich and I've been poor and rich is better." Economic deprivation pushes individuals and families below the point where basic physical needs are met and primarily interpersonal factors predominate. Economic inadequacy—very much a social rather than simply a financial concept—jeopardizes relationships.

Economic deprivation is the principal deleterious influence, of course, but it is the social impoverishment it produces that concerns us most. Social impoverishment denudes life of supportive relationships and "protective behaviors" (Emlen, 1977). It stands in contrast to social enrichment, in which the individual is enmeshed in an elaborate web of caring that can compensate for individual failings (Campbell, 1975). Jane Howard describes this social enrichment when she says of her strong family: "But we are numerous enough and connected enough not to let anyone's worst prevail for long. For any given poison, our pooled resources can come up with an antidote" (1978, p. 60). Social support networks provide the antidote and are of great importance in promoting healthy relations in the first place.

We would be negligent, however, if we did not explore limitations to the social support network as a helping resource. These limitations are of three varieties: those that are inherent, those that may be present as a function of the characteristics of the members, and those that derive from the social context (including the social policy context) in which social support networks operate. In short, for all our belief in social support networks as a "prescription for the human services," we need to add a cautionary note lest we leave a simplistic and overgeneralized conclusion.

INHERENT LIMITATIONS

Because social support networks depend on mutual exchanges, they require that everyone have *something* of value to give in return for what he or she receives. As Gottlieb and Todd report: "People solve personal problems, accomplish tasks, develop social competencies and address collective issues through an ongoing exchange of resources with members of their personal community. This exchange of resources, whether tangible goods like information or money or intangible resources like emotional nurturance, can be viewed broadly as social support" (1979, p. 183). This means that when people are heavily in debt to their network and cannot master resources to exchange (even emotional ones), they may cut themselves off from future transactions or be cut off. Supportive behavior can be extinguished when not reinforced. Consequently, a professional may need to pump in resources to restart the process for a bankrupt member of such a network. This is particularly true of child protective service workers (Garbarino, Stocking, & Associates, 1980).

CHARACTERISTICS OF MEMBERS

The central dilemma of social intervention is that "those who have the most gain the most," or "the rich get richer and the poor get poorer." The socially isolated are often most in need of help from social support networks but are least accessible and amenable to them unless someone (often a professional) takes the initiative to lead them into participation. Such isolation tends to be associated with deficits in social skills that are part of a vicious cycle in which the isolated become more incompetent and thus more isolated. The professional can play a vital role in overcoming this process and integrating the individual or family into the desperately needed social support networks.

SOCIAL CONTEXT

The social context can facilitate or impede social support networks. When public policy opposes or thwarts private helping (e.g., from neighborhood, church, and kin) it can create a climate inimical to the smooth and potent functioning of social support networks (Berger and Neuhaus, 1977). Government action can have this effect, for example, through military assignment policies that break up peer groups of soldiers, tax policies that discourage child care by kin and friends, and zoning policies that aid commercial exploitation of neighborhoods. Just as the functioning of individuals depends on a supportive environment, so do social networks depend on a supportive environment.

CONCLUSION

If we can learn anything from this chapter, it is that any professional helper should be concerned with finding ways to complement rather than ignore or compete with informal social support networks. The power and appropriateness of a social network approach may vary from service issue to service issue, but it is almost always greater than we have typically acknowledged in the day-to-day practice of human services. As Unger and Powell conclude in their excellent review of the role of social networks in supporting families under stress:

> . . . an understanding of the use of social networks in coping with stress should include the interactive process of the family member in need of aid (i.e., cultural values, view of costs) in relation to social networks (i.e., availability and frequency of contacts, reciprocal relations) and the situation involved (i.e., type of crisis, aid needed). Thus, the key question is not whether social net-

works provide support, but when and under what conditions are social networks a means of support? (1980, p. 571).

How do we respond? I believe that the key to this puzzle lies in the
paradox upon which many religions are built: only by losing ourselves can
we find ourselves. We must lose ourselves in the social landscape, blend in
with the human terrain, become part of the natural ecology of human social
life. At present, far too much of what we call human service systems projects above the natural social horizon or is out of harmony with the social
scene it seeks to aid.

In the next chapter we take up the general, practical issues of integrating
professional practice with social support networks. Having discussed the
"why for," we can turn to the "how to."

CHAPTER 2
Mutual Helping in Human Service Practice

James K. Whittaker

The purpose of this chapter is to illustrate how and where social support networks fit into an overall framework of human service practice. This effort must be seen as a statement of work in progress, since at present there is no clear and universally accepted definition for either set of terms. In fact, "human services," as "social support," means many things to many people. Following the working definition offered in Chapter 1, I take *social support network* to mean "a set of interconnected relationships among a group of people that provides enduring patterns of nurturance (in any or all forms) and provides contingent reinforcement for efforts to cope with life on a day-to-day basis." Such support may occur naturally, as in an extended helping network of family and friends, or be contrived, as in widow-to-widow helping programs (Silverman and Associates, 1974; Stack, 1974; Silverman, 1980). Social support networks may enhance, complement, or serve as alternatives to interpersonal helping services offered by professionals: social workers, clinical and community psychologists, nurses, physicians, teachers, and so on.

By "human services," I follow Kahn's definition of that term as "the American equivalent of 'social services' as used elsewhere in the world, covering six systems: income transfers, education, health, housing, employment [and] 'personal social services' " (1979, p. 23). Within this broad human services framework, we will touch on education and health, though our major focus will be directed to what Kahn would identify as "personal social services":

> These personal, or general, social services are programs that protect or restore family life, help individuals cope with external or internalized problems, enhance development, and facilitate access through information, guidance, advocacy, and concrete help of several kinds (1979, p. 19).

Such services encompass a field with changing boundaries and include freestanding programs (such as child welfare, or family services), as well as programs that are located within other institutions (e.g., social and psychological services offered in schools, medical settings, public housing, and industry) (Kahn, 1979). Many of the sectors of human services examined in the later chapters will be associated predominantly with a particular profession—e.g., child welfare with social work, health with medicine, and schools with teaching. Other human services, however, are more newly emergent and cross-disciplinary in nature, e.g., delinquency services, services to the elderly, and youth services. Some services, such as those designed to reach the chemically dependent, are new enough as to have no clear permanent home under the broad human services umbrella.

Whether deeply rooted or newly emergent, virtually all sectors of human services are directing more resources toward providing primary social support and adding this new "secret weapon" to their armory of professional helping services. That this is so is a given. *Why* it is so reflects the curious and often contradictory set of values and assumptions that underlie our collective national efforts to aid those whose "private troubles" have become "public concerns (Mills, 1959).

For Sam Brown, former head of the federal volunteer service bureau (ACTION), "self-help" with all the connotations of material and social support that it conjures is, simply, an old idea whose time has come (Brown, 1981). Brown represents a new breed of activist disdaining both liberal and conservative responses to the poor—his enthusiasm for self-help efforts is not at the expense of larger social service programs. He quotes Vernon Jordan's observation that "a man can't pull himself up by the bootstraps if he doesn't have any boots" and acknowledges that the larger social service programs are the boots for many people. What appeals to Brown and to many others is that self-help deals with human concerns in specific and practical ways:

> Self-help involves poor people in the fundamental decisions that affect their lives. They participate as leaders, workers, builders, voters and shareholders—activities that are not offered to a client at the end of a welfare line. Self-help shifts people from a totally passive dependency on government aid to active use of community, private and government resources . . . [and] reaffirms in people their self-respect and confidence. (Brown, 1981, p. 16)

Almost immediately following this accolade, the author cautions against overenthusiasm for self-help measures. ("It makes no sense to call for self-reliance for a five-year-old who should be in a Head Start program.") This point is well taken by the members of the American Public Welfare Association in whose journal he writes.

Berger and Neuhaus (1977) extend the argument for the benefits of individual participation in self-help and mutual-aid efforts to the very structures of society itself. They argue that if self-help and local empowerment schemes are essential to a healthy citizenry, it is equally true that full and active participation of certain social institutions in carrying out the mandate of social policies is essential to a healthy society. From this initial proposition, Berger and Neuhaus derive two broad programmatic recommendations:

> 1. Public policy should protect and foster "mediating structures" [the family, the church, the neighborhood, voluntary associations, and so on] and
> 2. Whenever possible, public policy should utilize mediating structures for the realization of social purposes. (1977, p. 6)

Mediating structures are seen as the agencies in society that generate and maintain values; without them, values would derive solely from the megastructure of the state—a hallmark of totalitarianism. The role of government is twofold: to "cease and desist from damaging mediating structures," and, at the same time, to use these structures to accomplish the ends of social policy through what the authors term empowerment. Apart from recognizing the inevitable conflict in these minimalist and maximalist positions, Berger and Neuhaus offer few specifics on how the public and private service sectors will work together, with the exception of the fact that there will be more limited roles for both professionals and paraprofessionals in their service design:

> Professional standards are of course important in some areas. But they must be viewed with skepticism when expertise claims jurisdiction, as it were, over the way people run their lives . . . [similarly] much of the paraprofessional development is in fact empire building by professional and union monopolists who would incorporate lower status occupations into their hierarchy. (1977, pp. 36–37)

Such statements serve to reinforce the perception of some in the human services that greater reliance on mediating structures and informal helping will lead, inevitably, to a demise of the professional role and a reduction of the quality of service. Two recent volumes by Gottlieb (1981) and Froland et al. (1981), both of whom are leading contributors to the literature on social support networks, take the position that professional and informal helping *are* necessary and complementary elements in an overall service network. Their insightful analysis of the barriers to such relationships, as well as the earlier critical review by Lenrow (1978), will be summarized in a later section of this chapter. Furthermore, arguments for informal and voluntary helping are not inextricably yoked to the kind of residual model of social welfare implicit in the Berger and Neuhaus perspective. The late Richard M. Titmuss of the London School of Economics, an advocate of "universalist services" delivered outside the market on the basis of need, also saw the value to society of altruism, as in his comparative study of blood donorship, *The Gift Relationship* (1971). Although he would have vehemently opposed the "re-privatization" of social services, as argued by Berger and Neuhaus, Titmuss nonetheless saw the broadly integrative function of voluntary giving within the welfare state:

> The grant, or the gift or unilateral transfer—whether it takes the form of cash, time, energy, satisfaction, blood, or even life itself—is the distinguishing mark of the social (in policy and administration) just as exchange or bilateral transfer is the mark of economic (Titmuss, 1968, p. 22).

Social policy in the compassionate society ought not to be concerned simply with relieving individual needs but with furthering a sense of common citizenship. The social growth engendered by such a model goes "to the very texture of the relationship between human beings" and illustrates what "a compassionate society can achieve when a philosophy of social justice and public accountability is translated into a hundred and one detailed acts of imagination and tolerance" (Titmuss, 1974, p. 50; Reisman, 1977, p. 69). Such a vision recognizes, at least implicitly, the value to both helper and helped in a system of care-giving that blends at the highest and lowest levels those broad programmatic responses which flow from a sense of public responsibility and those deeply personal acts of helping which spring from a sense of individual altrusim. Similarly, the Wolfenden Committee report on *The Future of Voluntary Organizations* in Britain envisions a strong role for informal helping in a service mix heavily dominated by the public sector: "We place a high value on this [the informal] system of care both because of its intrinsic value and because its replacement by a more institutionalized form of caring would be intolerably costly (1978, p. 182).

Alfred Kahn, perhaps social welfare's foremost scholar on the subject of social services, proposes a "neighborhood information center" as the all-purpose entry point to the total human service system. One of the essential features of such a center would be to provide social support. It could also serve to help people with common problems to organize on their own (Kahn, 1979). It is worth noting that Kahn is also an advocate of the institutional model of social welfare that views social services as "public social utilities," and he envisions a major role for social workers and other professionals in providing services. In short, it is erroneous to equate advocacy for social support networks and informal helping with either a residual view of social welfare or an antiprofessional attitude. A few investigators are now offering suggestions for reaching this marriage of formal and informal helping. Burke and Weir (1981) advance a number of reasons for blending the two. Among them is the reduction of alienation and reluctance of citizens to use public services for preventive purposes. Pilisuk, Chandler, and D'Onofrio (1979) similarly suggest that combining the resources of the professional and lay helper can have the salutary effect of "reweaving the social fabric." Among others who envision the benefits of partnership between human service professionals and informal helpers are Gottlieb and Schroter (1978), Caplan (1974) and Caplan and Killilea (1976), Turkat (1980), Unger and Powell (1980), and Sarason and Lorentz (1979). What is now needed in human services is a new conceptual framework that allows us to use simultaneously the contributions of both formal and informal helping. The remainder of this chapter will concern itself with three things: (1) some problems and issues in human service practice that seem to suggest the desirability of a combined approach to helping, (2) a beginning framework for integrating what I would term "social treatment" (professional interpersonal helping) and social support, and (3) a brief review of some of the barriers and incentives to combining formal and informal helping efforts.

SOME PROBLEMS AND ISSUES IN CURRENT HUMAN SERVICE PRACTICE

GROWING AWARENESS OF THE IMPORTANCE OF AN ECOLOGICAL PERSPECTIVE

In the initial chapter of this book, Garbarino makes the case for a broad perspective on the interrelationship between the individual and the various environmental systems. These systems impinge upon the individual, and, in turn, the individual reshapes the systems. Following the taxonomy of Bronfenbrenner, he elaborates the ever-widening "concentric circles" of environment that surround the individual: the microsystem, the mesosystem, the exosystem, the macrosystem, and so on. Taken as a whole, this view of the relationship of the individual to these various environments has come to be called an "ecological" perspective. Maluccio notes that the emphasis of this ecological approach is on the interface between people and their impinging environments (Maluccio and Sinanoglu, 1981, p. 24). Practice within such an ecological framework is directed toward "improving the transactions between people and environments in order to enhance adaptive capacities *and* improve environments for all who function within them" (Germain, 1979, p. 8). Such a perspective has long been part of thinking in the human services, but under different names. For example, Mary Richmond, the pioneer theorist of social casework, recognized the importance of "social diagnosis" of individual problems based on data from such collateral sources as schools, neighborhoods, fraternal orders, and employers (1917, pp. 232–251). Richmond also saw the importance of community customs and mores as powerful intervening variables in shaping attitudes toward agency-based helping (1917, p. 384). In the epigraph of her classic *Social Diagnosis*, Richmond quotes a leading physician of her day, James Jackson Putnam, on the importance of a broad environmental perspective in understanding human problems:

One of the most striking facts with regard to the conscious life of any human being is that it is interwoven with the lives of others. It is in each man's social relations that his mental history is mainly written *and it is in his social relationship likewise that the causes of the disorders that threaten his happiness and his effectiveness and the means for securing his recovery are to be mainly sought* [emphasis added]. (Putnam quoted in Richmond, 1917, p. 4)

From such a perspective Richmond's definition of "social treatment" emerges as "those processes which develop personality through adjustment consciously effected, individual by individual, between men and their social environment" (1922, p. 98). For Richmond, as for so many other pioneers in the emerging field of the human services, understanding the social context was seen as a necessary antecedent to effective interpersonal helping. Such conviction prompted Dr. Richard Clark Cabot, a Harvard-trained physician, to found the first social service department in a general hospital (Massachusetts General Hospital, 1905) to provide a more comprehensive understanding of the environmental factors involved in the diagnosis and treatment of physical illness. Social workers participated not only in direct clinical work, but in teaching students from the Harvard Medical School about the social aspects of illness (Cannon, 1913; Cabot, 1915, p. 220; Richmond, 1917, p. 36). Much has been written about social work's shift to a psychiatric phase in the 1920's, emphasizing individual adjustment, psychoanalytically oriented casework, and psychopathology (Jarrett, 1918; Briar and Miller, 1971). The social welfare historian Clarke Chambers quotes a social work pioneer from the period on the effect of the "new psychology" on casework practice: "To a very large extent they [caseworkers] have substituted the concept of personal inadequacy and individual maladjustment for the theory of the responsibility of the environment" (Chambers, 1967, p. 95). Recent studies have cast doubt, however, on the actual extent of this "psychiatric deluge" as evidenced in a sample of social agency case records from the period (Alexander, 1972). Moreover, the leading casework theoreticians from the 1930's to the 1960's all recognized the importance of environmental helping and the view of client as person-in-situation (Hamilton, 1951; Perlman, 1957; Hollis, 1972). Probably closer to the mark is the observation of Grinnell and his colleagues that although social workers have recognized the importance of environment, it is only recently that they have begun to conceptualize, codify, and articulate the knowledge, roles, and skills necessary for effective environmental modification (1981, p. 152). Of late, the social work literature has contained a number of important contributions to our understanding of environmental helping. Pincus and Minahan (1973) skillfully transpose the systems change concepts of Lippitt, Watson, and Westley (1957) from the level of community to the individual, the family, and the small group. Their expanded view of the context of social work practice gives us a new perspective on the "client system" and the "action system." Hartman's (1978) concept of the family "eco-map" provides a useful set of questions for assessing families *in situ*. Grinnell offers a conceptual framework as well as practical suggestions for implementing environmental interventions (Grinnell and Kyte, 1974 and 1975; Grinnell, Kyte, and Bostwick, 1981). Carel Germain has made a substantial contribution to our understanding of environmental helping through her development of the "life-model" of social work practice with its emphasis on meeting environmental problems and needs and a perspective that encompasses lifespan development (Germain, 1979; Germain and Gitterman, 1980). As Maluccio suggests, the focus of helping in the life-model of practice is on identifying, supporting, and mobilizing the natural resources of clients. The unit of attention is always the client system within its ecological context (Maluccio and Sinanoglu, 1981, p. 25). Such a perspective elevates environmental helping to its proper place as a full-fledged therapeutic tool, rather than simply an ancillary support to more conventional forms of interpersonal helping.

In psychology and psychiatry, the work of such scholars as Erikson (1950), and Roger Barker (Barker and Wright, 1954; Barker and Gump, 1964) has added greatly to our understanding of the influence of social context on development and behavior over the life course. The landmark contributions of Gerald Caplan and his colleagues at the Harvard Laboratory for Community Psychiatry help define in practical terms what an ecological perspective means in multidisciplinary mental health practice. Caplan's work on support systems and mutual aid extends the dimensions of professional helping from the therapy room to the broader and infinitely more complex environments wherein clients reside (Caplan, 1974; Caplan and Killilea, 1976). The contributions of Nicholas Hobbs represent a singularly significant achievement in that he gave form and substance, through *Project RE-ED*, to an ecological model for helping emotionally disturbed children and their families (Hobbs, 1966). This model project foreshadowed by nearly a decade the attempts at community-based helping for troubled youth in the 1970's. Another pioneer, Wolf Wolfensberger, whose contribution of the "normalization" perspective greatly altered the field of developmental disabilities, extends the ecological perspective by offering both a logic and a means for normalizing services by extending them to the less restrictive environment of the broader community (Wolfensberger, 1972, 1980). Finally, Rogers-Warren and Warren (1977) offer a tentative model for blending the insights gained from a broad ecological perspective with the technologies of applied behavioral analysis and modification. One of their concerns is that particularistic, targeted behavioral change strategies may be ineffective and that they may have unanticipated effects if the client's broader environment is not taken into account. Such concern appears to be borne out in the ground-breaking research of Wahler and his colleagues whose work with "insular" mothers suggests that demonstrably successful behav-

ioral parent training programs may not be effective and may even be counterproductive with socially isolated families whose only contacts are with
formal social agencies (such as welfare or the courts) and a few close relatives. Such parenting programs need to be augmented by behavioral strategies for increasing positive social contacts and providing social support if
they are to be successful (Wahler, Afton, & Fox, 1979; Wahler, Leske, &
Rogers, 1979; Wahler, 1980b).

In summary, Bronfenbrenner's conceptual model of "the ecology of human development" summarized by Garbarino in Chapter 1 greatly expands
our vision of what an ecological perspective really *means* both in terms of
developmental research and service provision (Bronfenbrenner, 1979).
Drawing heavily on the earlier and seminal work of Kurt Lewin (Lewin,
1948, 1951), Bronfenbrenner offers an exquisite and bold set of sketches for
extending the ecological perspective from the realm of theory to the crucible
of present-day human services: it is our task for the foreseeable future to
render these sketches of the helping environment into detailed blueprints
and working drawings.

The two paramount implications of the ecological perspective in human
service practice are summarized in an excellent review by Holahan and his
colleagues:

> On the one hand, the *environmental* emphasis of the ecological view supports
> environmentally oriented interventions directed toward strengthening or estab-
> lishing methods of social support. On the other hand, the *transactional* emphasis
> of the ecological perspective fosters individually oriented interventions directed
> toward promoting personal competencies for dealing with institutional or envi-
> ronmental blocks to achieving personal objectives. (Holahan *et al.*, 1979, p. 6)

This statement captures the essence of what an ecological perspective is all
about in human service practice: building more supportive, helpful, and
nurturing environments for clients through environmental helping *and* increasing their competence in dealing with the environment by teaching basic
life skills. Such skills teaching may occur in a variety of formats including
client education (parent training), self-help (Alcoholics Anonymous), and
formalized treatment (structural family therapy). Thus, the ecological perspective contains at its heart a broadly *inclusive* view of effective human
service practice, a view which:

1. Recognizes the complementarity of person-in-environment, and seeks to
strengthen each component.
2. Accepts the fact that an exclusive focus on *either* the individual *or* his or
her immediate environment will generally not produce effective helping.
3. Acknowledges that interpersonal help may take many forms, as long as
its goal is to teach skills for effectively coping with the environment.
4. Views social support not simply as a desirable concomitant to professional
help but as an inextricable component of an overall helping strategy.

5. Recognizes the distinct and salutary features of *both* professional and lay helping efforts in an overall framework for services.

The ecological perspective, then, more than simply supplying a useful metaphor for human service practice, actually forces us to shift fully half of our attention from interpersonal to environmental helping *and,* as we shall see, affects the role of the professional in fundamental and visible ways. Such a perspective provides, finally, a logic and an imperative for examining the contributions of social support networks in various sectors of human service practice. As such, its desirability and centrality constitute a bedrock assumption of this volume.

SOME FUNDAMENTAL QUESTIONING OF THE PURPOSE, AUSPICE, AND LIMITS OF HUMAN SERVICES

Perhaps no single phrase as succinctly captures the current disagreement over the mission and scope of human service practice as the title of social historian Roy Lubove's book, *The Professional Altruist* (1965). Does our conception of human services flow from an institutional view of social welfare wherein the state takes major responsibility for social provision through the delivery of professional services? Or does it flow from a much more restrictive view of social welfare, which limits help—largely provided through private charity—only to those clearly incapable of functioning on their own? Such questions are raised increasingly by policy analysts, historians, and critics of the "welfare state" who see, in the progressive reforms of the early 20th century and the expansion of government social programs from the 1930's through the 1960's, a record of marginal achievement at best.

Even among advocates of an expanded role for the government in social reform and social services there appears, with increasing frequency, a skepticism about the results of their efforts. A recent review of a book by former H.E.W. Secretary Joseph Califano, advisor to several Democratic presidents, reflects this doubt:

> Califano ended his tenure at HEW with what sounds almost like a Reaganesque manifesto of despair over the efficacy of Rooseveltian government. "I felt the frustration, sometimes anger, of failure: in welfare reform, national health, and the difficulty of erasing racial discrimination. . . . Intricate federal regulations . . . in turn encourage even lengthier and more specific rules as state, local, and private institutions struggle to comply. . . . People trying to help each other feel suffocated, frustrated . . . as their freedom to act on matters they face each day is increasingly circumscribed." (Frady, 1981, p. 18)

A similar, though sharper and less equivocal view of government-sponsored social services is offered by Ira Glasser in an essay entitled "Prisoners of Benevolence." Glasser challenges what he assumes to be the singular liberal criticism of public social services: namely, that they are too few and inadequately funded:

> This undifferentiated view of social service . . . tended to blind liberals to certain unanticipated consequences of their good works. Because their motives were benevolent, their ends good, and their purpose caring, *they assumed the posture of parents* towards the recipients of their largesse. They failed utterly to resist the impulse toward paternalism, which in another context Bernard Bailyn called "the endlessly propulsive tendency" of power to expand itself and establish dominion over people's lives. (Glasser, 1978, p. 107)

Recent works by social historians, in particular David Rothman, elaborate this view of the state as parent and advance the notion that social control is frequently a concomitant of, if not always an unstated objective of, an expanding role for the public sector in the delivery of human services (Rothman, 1971, 1980). Even those less critical of progressive intent express puzzlement over what went wrong with social interventions. Consider the reflections offered 50 years later by Robert Maynard Hutchins, who was active in the 1920's in juvenile justice reform:

> When I graduated from law school some fifty years ago, the aspiring liberals among us thought we knew what was the trouble with the law. It was too narrow and too formalistic . . . we hailed those developments which emphasized the differences in "fact situations," which required the interposition of the social sciences, and which sought to temper the wind to the shorn lamb by the exercise of discretion.
>
> In those far-off days the word *bureaucracy* was never heard; perhaps it had not been invented. The liberal hope was in the agents and agencies of government.
>
> The juvenile court, then only 25 years old, reflected the responsibility of the state as *parens patriae*, which could rescue children from the law, and from those agents of government whom we did not trust, like policemen, prosecutors, judges in criminal courts, and wardens of jails and penitentiaries. It could even rescue children from their parents. To us the juvenile court, with which few of us had any experience, looked like the fulfillment of our dreams. It had come into existence through the efforts of persons whose ideals we shared. It was packed with discretion from stem to stern. It relied on social workers. It aimed at "saving the child," not punishing him. If it had not existed, we would have tried to invent it. . . . *How wrong we were.* (1976, pp. VII–VIII)

Hutchins's candor reflects the optimism of the early progressive reforms that, given the humanitarian quality of their program, it was eminently proper to grant vast authority to the state and, by extension, considerable "discretion" to its rapidly growing cadre of professionals. In fact, says David

Rothman, "the most distinguishing characteristic of Progressivism was its fundamental trust in the power of the state to do good" (1980, p. 60). Whether we agree or disagree with Rothman's historical generalizations, there does appear to be a consensus emerging from both within and without the human services that suggests the following:

1. Large government-sponsored social programs should seek to support, not supplant, informal helping efforts.

2. Increasing professionalization alone is not the key to improving quality of human services; rather, the key lies in the ability creatively to combine professional and lay helping resources in an overall service strategy.

3. There are (and many would argue should be) limits to the role of the public sector in service provision. A healthy and vital human service requires options for clients and a strong and central role for voluntary associations and lay helping.

4. Reciprocity, mutuality and informality—all characteristics of informal helping—are also those qualities often cited as lacking in human service bureaucracies as well as in professional helping.

Whatever the validity of these assertions, there remains a compelling argument for factoring informal helping into our human service planning. Perhaps, as Gilbert Steiner suggests with respect to the futility of family policy, the time is simply wrong for a greatly expanded government role in social programming: "Whatever the validity of the discovery and of the family policy prescription, the timing is wrong. Family policy implies intervention . . . [yet] the national swing is to nonintervention, deregulation, fiscal restraint, reliance on market forces" (1981, p. 205). A more positive rationale is offered by Abels and Abels, who argue that social work's purposes are contextually determined and that now the context is calling clearly for a major professional effort directed *toward strengthening mutual and reciprocal relationships:* "Addressing this task contributes to the improvement of social arrangements and attends to social work's historical participatory commitment by effectively moving away from the role of expert in treatment or method. The development of nonhierarchial community competence is crucial for the maintenance of this country's democratic character" (1980, p. 32).

Thus, from a deeply rooted conviction about the centrality of the professional helping role in achieving social purposes, the argument of Abels and Abels ends on a note strikingly similar to that of the previously cited conservative scholars Berger and Neuhaus in their call for citizen participation and local empowerment of mediating structures as the key to a healthy society. In short, sufficient questions are raised from all points of the political spectrum about the purpose, scope, and effects of the human service enterprise—particularly in its large, public, bureaucratic manifestation—to warrant placing the issue of informal helping and social support high on the action agenda for the coming decade.

A GROWING CONSENSUS ON THE NEED FOR A COMPETENCY ORIENTATION TO PRACTICE

A final theme in human services that suggests the desirability of social support strategies is the steady move away from a pathology model of practice and toward a competence model. Maluccio's (1981) review of competency perspectives in human services suggests the desirability of the *ecological competence* formulation as a framework for informing practice. Following the conceptualization offered by Sundberg, Snowden, and Reynolds (1978), such a perspective takes into account all relevant personal dimensions—skills, qualities, expectations—as well as environmental stimuli and situational expectations. Competence-oriented practice, then, focuses on the strengths that people have within themselves and the resources in their environments that they use to cope with their problems. Maluccio suggests three major components of ecological competence as capacities and skills, motivational aspects, and environmental qualities:

> *Capacities and Skills.* This dimension includes capacities of the person in diverse spheres such as cognition, perception, intelligence, language and physical health. It also encompasses a person's qualities in such areas as flexibility, tolerance for diversity, initiative or self direction, reality testing, judgement, and tolerance for anxiety. In addition, it refers to specific proficiencies in such areas as athletics, interpersonal skills . . . and emotional skills . . .
> *Motivational Aspects.* This category comprises the person's interests, hopes, aspirations—in short, the set of drives or energies variously described as "effectance" or "competance motivation" (White, 1959), "intrinsic motivation" (Deci, 1975), "the search for meaning" (Maddi, 1970), or "self actualization" (Maslow, 1954). . . . [These refer] to the human being's motivation to deal with the environment, to seek stimulation, to cope with challenges, to accomplish, to master, to feel competent, and self-determining.
> *Environmental Qualities.* A major component in our definition of competence consists of significant environmental qualities impinging on a person's functioning at any given point. Examples include environmental resources and supports such as social networks, environmental demands, institutional pressures and supports.
> Effective behavior requires a "good fit" between personal abilities and environmental demands and supports. (1981, pp. 7–8)

Growing interest in such competency perspectives in human services probably stems from a number of factors, including dissatisfaction with pathology-oriented, symptom–disease models of interpersonal helping; recognition of the person-in-situation as the proper focus for intervention, rather than strategies that focus on the person alone; and, finally, increasing recognition of both the limits and demands of day-to-day practice. To take this last factor first, limits of funding and the press of client demand are forcing many service settings to focus on short-term, task-centered models of practice that emphasize teaching basic skills of coping and survival. Some examples in the later chapters of this volume include teaching skills for independent city living to the newly deinstitutionalized adult schizophrenic, health promotion and "wellness" to the frail elderly, skills in managing sexuality for school-age parents, survival skills for adolescent delinquents leaving a state training school; and communication and negotiation skills for behavior-disordered adolescents and for multiproblem families. The rapid and recent development of skills training approaches (Danish, D'Augelli, & Hauer, 1980) and "task-centered" approaches to practice (Reid and Epstein, 1972, 1977) has in large measure been stimulated by the pressing problems of clients who find their way into the human service system, as well as by the diminishing probability that more traditional, elaborate, and expensive modes of treatment could be made available—even if they were deemed desirable. Moreover, there is increasing skepticism in the human service field about the utility of the psychopathology model as a framework for practice. It is interesting to note, for example, how much the forward thinking of such trailblazers as Nicholas Hobbs has become incorporated into mainstream attitude, say, in child mental health. Formulating a philosophy for his famous project RE-ED in the early 1960's, Hobbs identified several "biases":

> *A learning bias.* The task of reeducation is to help the child learn new and more effective ways of construing himself and his world and to learn habits that lead to more effective functioning. We assume that the child is not diseased but that he has acquired bad habits.
> *A social system's bias.* We are trying to move beyond concepts of individual adjustment, beyond concern for family-child relationships . . . to a program of intervention that constantly assesses and tries to change . . . the child . . . and all of the special people of importance or potential importance in his world.
> *A bias away from "dynamic psychology".* With no clear advantage to be gained from the use of therapeutic strategy (psychoanalytically oriented psychotherapy) that calls for a high level of psychological sophistication, we have chosen the simpler course: We are impressed enough by the complexity of the simplest seeming solution to helping the disturbed child.
> *An adiagnostic bias.* The formal psychiatric diagnosis is of little value. . . . We have not been able to specify different treatment procedures for different diagnoses. (Hobbs, 1964, pp. 3–6)

The previously cited trend toward the normalization of services, with its emphasis on community integration and services offered in the least restrictive environment, has likewise provided a policy perspective in mental health, youth services, developmental disabilities, and many other service sectors that is quite compatible with a competence orientation to practice (Wolfensberger, 1972; Flynn and Nitsch, 1980).

A third factor in the growing acceptance of competency-oriented models of practice is the belief that assessment and intervention need to be directed equally to the person *and* the situation: "competence is most effectively achieved when intervention is directed toward an ecological unit, consisting of a person and his immediate social environment, rather than toward the person alone" (Gladwin, 1967, p. 37). This is, in short, the action extension of the ecological perspective detailed in Chapter 1 and earlier in this chapter. Maluccio identifies a number of features of competence-oriented practice, many of which underscore the importance of the ecological perspective in assessment and intervention (1981, p. 11):

1. A humanistic perspective
2. Redefinition of human problems in transactional terms
3. Reformulation of assessment as competence clarification
4. Redefinition of client and practitioner roles, with clients viewed primarily as resources and worker as enabling agents
5. Redefinition of the client worker relationship
6. Focus on life processes and life experiences
7. Emphasis on using the environment
8. Regular use of client feedback

The significance of Maluccio's conceptual model of competency-oriented practice for our present topic, social support networks, is, essentially, that the one will lead us to the other—that is, as models of practice develop that emphasize direct teaching of coping and mastery skills, the crucialness of social support will become increasingly evident. As the previously cited work by Wahler (Wahler, Leske, and Rogers, 1979; Wahler, 1980 a, b) in teaching parent skills suggests, demonstrably effective models of skills training will not work—and may even be counterproductive—in the absence of social support. We can expect to see these two strategies, social skills training and social support networks, increasingly "packaged" as complementary and mutually reinforcing interventions. Similarly, the notion of seeing the ecological unit—person-in-situation—as the focus for intervention will stimulate the development of assessment tools and intervention techniques for identifying and using social support networks where they naturally exist and contriving them where they do not. In short, to the extent that the human services adopt a competency- and skills-oriented approach to practice, they will also increasingly emphasize social support networks as a critical component of an overall helping strategy.

To summarize our discussion of problems and issues: I have suggested that three issues are paramount in uderstanding the present state of the human services. The first issue concerns an awareness of the importance of an ecological person-in-situation perspective in understanding and intervening in human problems. The second reflects a growing doubt about the purpose, limits, and auspices of service strategies in general, and the third concerns a growing consensus on the need for a competency- and skills-oriented approach to practice in all areas of the human services. Careful analysis of these issues and an attempt to resolve some of the problems they pose will lead us inexorably in the direction of social support networks. Put more simply: *A good deal of what ails the human services at present will be greatly improved by an infusion of ordinary lay people—friends, neighbors, kinfolk, and volunteers—doing what they do best: providing support, criticism, encouragement, and hope to people in distress.* Such a prescription cannot be seen and should not be offered as a panacea. If, as Bronfenbrenner (1976) suggests from the old Russian proverb, "you can't pay someone to do those things a mother does for nothing," it is equally true that there are some things best left to a competent, skillful, and rigorously trained professional helper. Partnership is not only a desirable but a necessary condition for effective, efficient, and truly humane services. The guideposts to establishing that partnership will be emphasized in the next section.

SOCIAL TREATMENT AND SOCIAL SUPPORT: TOWARD A BEGINNING INTEGRATION

SETTING THE STAGE FOR THINKING ABOUT FORMAL AND INFORMAL HELPING

As noted earlier, a focus on environmental modification and a concern for the linkages between formal and informal helping are traditions in the human services. This is true in spite of the fact that the development and elaboration of these concepts suffered until recently at the expense of more person-centered, intrapsychic models of intervention. Recent reviews by such prominent investigators as Froland *et al.* (1981) and Gottlieb (1981) strongly suggest (as did the earlier reviews by Collins and Pancoast [1976] and Caplan and Killilea [1976]) that interest in various uses of social support has long been part of the most creative and informed thinking in the human service field. In addition to the work of such pioneers as Mary Richmond (1917), attention is frequently directed to the contribution of Coit (1892) in involving neighborhood representatives in the work of the settlements, Kropotkin (1914) on the functions of mutual aid in a civilized society, and Abraham Low (1950) on the values of self-help in treating mental illness. The group work tradition with its emphasis on promoting citizen participation and mutual helping provides many illustrations of an early attempt to blend formal and informal helping. For example, by the early 1950's the Department of Neighborhood Clubs of the Boston Children's Services Association was experimenting with a community-based group work strategy that enlisted the aid of neighborhood peers in the treatment of a single referred child (Bernstein, 1965). Such groups used naturally occurring or contrived networks of social support as the loci for clinical behavioral change strategies. It is also interesting to note that within this same group work tradition, theoreticians like Robert Vinter were writing in the late 1950's about the need to pay attention to "extra-group means of influence"—the web of potentially useful links that exist between the formed group and the other social systems in which the individual member participates (Vinter, 1967). Perhaps it was because the group worker's methods of intervention often took him beyond the agency boundaries, to the street corner, public school, or community center, that the interest in informal helping and systems linking was so early in evidence. As a final example, the commitment to neighborhood-based group work strategies for combatting delinquency, as in Mobilization For Youth, an outgrowth of the earlier "grey areas" project in New York City in the early 1960's, resulted in the development of many novel approaches to linking formal and informal helping.

More recently, Gottlieb (1981) has provided a rich and detailed review of the theoretical and empirical antecedents of the present interest in social support in community mental health, which holds considerable importance for the human services as a whole. Gottlieb cites, among others, the following antecedents to the present interest in informal helping in community mental health: (1) early ecological investigations of social environment and health (e.g., Faris and Dunham, 1939; Dunham, 1959; Leighton, 1959; French and Kahn, 1962; Hinkle, 1974) and (2) use of lay resources in mental health (e.g., Dunham, 1959; Gurin, Veroff, and Feld, 1960; Kelly, 1966). Gottlieb links these investigations with the later work of John Cassel (1974) on the potential effects of such environmental conditions as crowding, inadequate housing, and deteriorating neighborhoods on physical and mental health and with Gerald Caplan's now familiar work on support systems. Gottlieb, in particular, focuses Caplan's scheme for classifying types of support systems and detailing activities that community mental health workers could pursue both to initiate and to stimulate the development of supportive attachments in local catchment areas (1981, pp. 22–25). Gottlieb offers the following rationale for why the fruits of such earlier endeavors found favor in the later works of Cassel (1974) and Caplan (1964; 1974):

> Caplan's and Cassel's ideas about the role of social support in health protection were favorably received . . . because they dovetailed with recent formulations about the epidemiology of mental disorder, and because they suggested an agenda for research on stress and coping that could best be accomplished via the sort of naturalistic and "ecologically valid" methods of inquiry to which a growing number of applied social scientists had become committed. (1981, p. 27)

What precisely do the reviews by Gottlieb (1981) and Froland et al. (1981), and others by Unger and Powell (1980), Politser (1980), Gottlieb and Hall (1980), and Trimble (1980), suggest to the human service practitioner who wants to incorporate informal helping strategies with professional practice, say, in a mental health center, child and family service agency, hospital, school, or nursing home?

First, such reviews illustrate (as do the later chapters) that social support can occur in a variety of forms. For example, social support occurs in networks of family, friends, and neighbors, or in specially created support groups. Moreover, such social support networks may be linked to professional helping by a variety of organizational forms and agency strategies. Froland and his colleagues in their study of helping networks and human services identify five distinct program strategies for linking formal and informal helping that range from use of personal networks, through mutual aid groups and community empowerment. (These program strategies will be examined more closely later in this chapter.) What is so useful about Froland's research is that it provides both a typology of various approaches to linking formal and informal helping efforts and offers at least a tentative analysis of the costs and consequences of adopting any particular strategy. Such research is all the more valuable since the focus of attention is on "whole cloth" agency programs actually operating in a number of culturally diverse communities. Although careful to point out the exploratory nature of their work, the investigators conclude that their findings clearly point "to the potential benefits of adopting strategies for interweaving formal and informal sources of care" (Froland *et al.*, 1981, p. 107). At the very least, studies such as Froland's quickly dispel the mistaken concreteness that comes with equating social support with any particular form of informal helping— e.g., "natural helping network" or any particular organizational arrangement.

Second, virtually all reviews of the potential linkages between formal and informal helping in the human services point to fundamental shifts in the role of the professional helper if a successful integrated strategy is to be adopted. For example, some reviews go to great lengths to illustrate the differences between "orthodox" therapy and various forms of self-help groups in such key variables as relationships, confidentiality and self-disclosure, and goals and strategies of helping (Caplan & Killilea, 1976, pp. 64–66; Lieberman & Borman, 1979, pp. 136–149). As an illustration, Riessman posits the differences between professional and aprofessional dimensions of helping which is presented and compared in Table 2-1.

Other investigators stress the increased emphasis on new professional roles such as "human services coordinator" (Curtis, 1973), "liason specialist" (Docecki, 1977), "network consultant" (Collins and Pancoast, 1976), or the expansion and redefinition of old roles. For example, Turkat (1980) describes a "case manager" role in the Georgia Mental Health system that, in addition to the more common functions of assessment, planning, monitoring, and advocacy, includes responsibility for actually bringing together the client, the formal service providers, and the "folk support system" in a social network assembly (1980). Such developments suggest in their simplest implication that professional providers must be prepared to assume a variety of roles in aiding clients. Many of these roles have to do, essentially, with working through existing sources of social support and *on behalf of*

Table 2-1. Professional and aprofessional dimensions of helping compared

Professional	Aprofessional
Emphasis on knowledge and insight, underlying principles, theory, structure	Emphasis on feeling, affect; concrete, practical.
Systematic	Experience, common sense, and intuition are central; folk knowledge
"Objective": use of distance and perspective, self-awareness, control of transference	Closeness and self-involvement; subjective
Empathy, controlled warmth	Identification
Standardized performance	Extemporaneous, spontaneous (expressions of own personality)
Outsider orientation	Insider orientation; indigenous
Praxis	Practice
Careful, limited use of time; systematic evaluation; curing	Slow, time no issue; informal; direct accountability; caring

Source: From Riessman, 1976a, p. 45.

clients, rather than in direct, face-to-face interventions. Such conclusions are neither new nor profound, but they do suggest that traditional professional roles may carry within them a set of attitudes, proscriptions, and behaviors that may be counterproductive to the task of forging links with social support networks. Some of these potential barriers of professional roles will be explored more fully later in this chapter. Again, at the very least, practitioners approaching this whole area of social support must be prepared for the fact that what needs to be done may not be immediately self-evident and may produce dissonance with cherished notions of what "ought" to be done in linking formal and informal helping efforts.

A third point derived from these reviews is that social support networks serve a variety of functions rather than a single purpose and, in relation to professionally delivered human services, they may enhance, augment, or actually serve as a locus for interventions that range from prevention through remediation. Typically, such functions include the provision of emotional and moral support, physical care and nurturance, information and advice, and tangible aid, i.e., food, money, clothing, and shelter. Caplan suggests that social support systems usually consist of three elements: "The significant others help the individual mobilize his psychological resources and master his emotional burdens; they share his tasks and they provide him with extra supplies of money, materials, tools, skills, and cognitive guidance" (1974, p. 6). These elements are similar to the set of relational functions proposed earlier by Weiss (1969): intimacy, social integration, nurturing behavior, reassurance, and assistance. Most recently, Froland (1979, p. 19) has identified several functions for social support systems that have particular relevance for human service practice. They include help to the client in *defining problems* (networks as mediators of cultural norms regarding deviance), *seeking help* (networks as lay referral systems), *mediating illness* (networks as sources of social support and buffers to stress), and *enhancing professional intervention* (networks as supports before, during, and after professional intervention). In relation to formal professional helping efforts, social support networks may be used in a wide variety of ways. For example, Trimble (1980), in his recent review of network interventions, identifies at least seven distinct modalities in which professional and informal helping are blended in a unified effort. They range between full-scale "family network assemblies" (Speck and Attneave, 1973; Rueveni, 1979), where the total network is the focal point for clinical intervention and professional consultation, to "natural helping networks" described by Collins and Pancoast (1976).

"SOCIAL TREATMENT": A CONCEPTUAL SCHEMA FOR HELPING PRACTICE

The foregoing discussion suggests several considerations in designing a framework for human service practice that includes formal and informal helping. First, it appears evident that some sort of conceptual scheme is necessary to aid practitioners in the task of incorporating informal helping strategies into their repertoire of professional behaviors. I suggest that this is so primarily because the very nature of informal helping is so markedly different from professional practice in its form, substance, and style. These differences pose a learning task that is substantially different from, say, learning a new practice method such as structural family therapy, or teaching parenting skills—where the content may be unfamiliar, but the "container" (i.e., the notion of a *method* of professional practice) is thoroughly familiar. In asking human service professionals to consider informal helping, we are charting a voyage into unfamiliar waters. Before learning the specific skills involved in engaging, supporting, and aiding social support networks, we shall require some conceptual overview of the territory we are about to enter in order to identify some old and familiar landmarks (professional roles, tasks, and functions) in relation to the new surroundings. Such a framework must be ecologically oriented, i.e., it must make the person-in-situation the primary unit of attention and it must view environmental modification as an integral component of the helping process.

Moreover, given the many and varied forms that social support can take, it seems desirable to construct a framework that incorporates social support as an *integral* part of practice rather than separating it out as a distinct strategy or method of intervention. It is also desirable to think of social support in relation to the *multiple* roles that human service practitioners perform rather than confine it within one or another specific role configuration, e.g., "network consultant." Finally, such a framework should be broadly eclectic in its theory base since the "cutting edge" models of formal–informal collaboration reflect a wide array of theoretical underpinnings and practice methods from psychodynamic to behavioral.

I have elsewhere defined *social treatment* as "an approach to interpersonal helping that uses direct and indirect strategies of intervention to aid individuals, families and small groups in improving social functioning and coping with social problems" (Whittaker, 1974, p. 49). A process view of social treatment is illustrated in Fig. 2–1. In fact, as others have noted, social treatment is a concept deeply rooted in the tradition of social work (Siporin, 1970). For Mary Richmond, social treatment represented the complement to social diagnosis: a blending of direct and indirect interventions resulting in "adjustment . . . [between] men and their social environments" (1922, p. 98). For Richmond and other pioneers, casework help, or "friendly visiting," could and often did include: material aid (cash relief, a load of coal, a basket of food), advice giving, and indirect intervention (e.g., advocacy with a school system, employer, or landlord), as well as information and referral. Working on behalf of the client often included such mundane tasks as advising on which type of fuel burned best over a long winter, counseling on the danger of buying on the installment plan, or on what foods constituted the best bargain on a limited budget. Combining such direct and indirect measures came easily to this first generation of social practitioners, not yet shaped by the role prescriptions of the later psychological phase of casework (Jarrett, 1918). In a similar way, these early workers saw no conflict between "social treatment" and "social reform"—Mary Richmond spoke of the "interdependence of individual and mass betterment" (1917, p. 365). Although they lacked the taxonomy and the language of, say, Bronfenbrenner's (1979) ecological framework, they would have been fully in accord with its practice implications: from the "micro" to the "macro." Moreover, if there were no clear-cut directions for what to do with the information, there was at least recognition of the fact that informal systems often played a powerful role in shaping client behavior. Mary Richmond, for example, draws on Synge's classic study of the Aran islanders (1907/1979) in making a point about the powerful nature of kin systems, and she even records an early network intervention in the field of probation (1917, p. 185). Finally, similar environmental themes are found also in the historical roots of present-day community psychology and social psychiatry (Healy, 1915; Duhl, 1963; Caplan, 1980).

Social treatment, then, as the term is used here, does not mean any particular method of helping, or synthesis and integration of diverse practice methods. It reflects, instead, a point of view about practice. In short, it provides a useful framework for thinking about human service practice, which focuses our attention on several things (Whittaker, 1974, pp. 49–61):

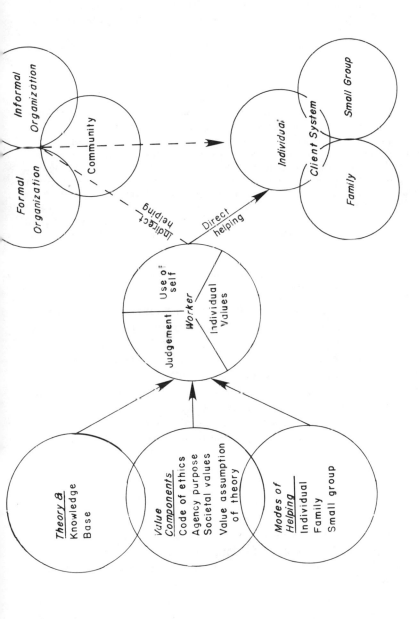

Fig. 2-1. Social treatment: a process view. (From Whittaker, 1974, p. 52; reprinted with permission of the publisher.)

1. *Social functioning and social problems.* The social problem as related by the client is the starting point for practice. Problems are seen as the result of the complex interplay between individual and environment; goals have to do with improvement of social functioning.

2. *Direct and indirect intervention.* Social treatment assumes that not all helping occurs in a direct face-to-face encounter between client and worker, but consists as well of a whole range of activities undertaken on a client's behalf.

3. *Interpersonal helping.* Social treatment is concerned with helping individuals, families, and small groups. In Bronfenbrenner's (1979) scheme, this suggests a framework that stops just short of the macro, or societal, level of intervention, simply because such large-scale interventions are not the primary focus of most practitioners and also because broad-scale, societal interventions require a level of analysis beyond the scope of this book. It is important to note, however, that this limit of focus is an arbitrary one and that the systems framework offered by Garbarino in Chapter 1 clearly points to the potential for broad-scale societal interventions designed, say, to enhance or to create social support for individuals or families.

4. *An eclectic view of practice methods.* Helping strategies are derived from many different theoretical and empirical bodies of knowledge and range from preventive to remedial. I suggest that the case for eclecticism needs to be made strongly in a field in which a current practice method (e.g., social casework, psychotherapy, client advocacy) all too often becomes mistakenly identified with professional role and mission.

To conclude, the social treatment paradigm is offered as a useful framework for thinking about human service practice, although it is clearly not the only such framework available. Recent conceptual contributions by Pincus and Minahan (1973) on "generalist practice," Germain and Gitterman (1980) on the "life model of practice," and Maluccio (1981) on the "competence" model of practice, whatever their differences of scope and language, all flow from an ecological perspective, all stress improvement of social functioning, and all see a broad range of environmental assessment and modification strategies as central to the helping process. I strongly suggest that unless one begins with just such an overarching view of what human service practice is all about, there is a very real risk of seeing the topic at hand—social support networks—as merely ancillary, or adjunctive to more familiar forms of professional helping, such as psychotherapy, counseling, and casework.

Professional Helping Roles. Within this broad framework for practice are a number of different professional helping roles, and it is within each of these that one begins to see the enormous potential for combining formal and informal strategies of helping. Four such clusters of roles: *treatment agent, teacher–counselor, broker of services/resources,* and *advocate* have already been described (Whittaker, 1974, pp. 56–60). I would now add a fifth: *network/system consultant.*

Treatment agent. This first role subsumes all professional activities directed toward helping clients to cope with a biopsychosocial problem through direct, face-to-face, therapeutic intervention. Treatment may focus on an individual, family, or small group, as in individual psychotherapy, conjoint family treatment, or group therapy. Goals of therapy range from changing attitudes and specific behaviors to aiding clients (patients) in developing insight. Duration and focus of treatment may be short-term, task-oriented, or long-term and open-ended. Some examples of human service professionals acting in the role of treatment agent would be:

—A psychoanalytically trained psychotherapist working with an adult neurotic patient
—A behavioral therapist working on a program of desensitization with a school-phobic child
—A clinical social worker coordinating a therapeutic milieu for psychotic adolescents in residential treatment
—A family therapist conducting family network therapy with a network assembly of family, friends, and associates of a patient in a mental health center
—A play therapist working with an individual child in a therapeutic preschool

Teacher–Counselor. In this role cluster, the professional provides advice and information, teaches a specific set of skills or behaviors, or helps a client prepare for a specific social role, e.g., parent, employee, or cancer patient. The distinctions between this role and that of treatment agent are not always well defined, although, in general, the professional in this role acts in a more directive, focused, and often didactic manner. The growth of professional activities subsumed under this role suggests, perhaps, a move toward more direct teaching of skills for practitioners with all age groups and populations. Examples include:

—Teaching exercise, nutrition, and activity skills to the elderly in a community center-based wellness program
—Teaching "street strategies" for survival to a group of suburban runaway youth in an inner city
—Teaching stress management and child management skills to young parents on a military base
—Counseling displaced homemakers on self-assessment, confidence building, and career planning
—Counseling a group of school-age children on how to make friends
—Teaching semi-independent living skills to a group of newly deinstitutionalized young retarded adults

Broker of services/resources. Here the professional acts less in direct intervention with his or her client and more on behalf of clients by brokering needed services and resources. Major activities might include assessing needs, locating resources, and monitoring cases. In effect, the worker becomes a kind of case manager who initiates, orchestrates, and coordinates needed services, assessing their impact, and planning for termination. In certain fields of practice like child welfare and developmental disabilities, the case manager role has become the dominant one for human service professionals, particularly in the large public service agencies. Some examples are:

—Providing case management services in a local child welfare office to a foster care caseload
—Directing citizens to needed services or resources in a neighborhood information center
—Locating home help and transportation services for a family with a developmentally disabled child
—Identifying additional resources for frail homebound elderly in a chore services program
—Coordinating drug treatment and employment counseling services for a caseload of probationers

Advocate. The professional acting as an advocate serves as an intermediary or ombudsman for his or her client by championing such things as civil rights or the right to needed services, as well as by helping the client to negotiate the often complex rules and regulations of the service bureaucracy. Advocacy activities may be undertaken on behalf of an individual client, a family, or a group of clients with common interests or problems. The advocate role may be institutionalized within the service bureaucracy—as in the position of ombudsman—though, more commonly, it is seen as complementary to the professional's other major roles. In some human service professions, notably social work, the professional code of ethics speaks directly and unequivocally of the professional's responsibility to be an advocate for his or her client. Some examples of the advocacy role in practice are:

—Attending an I.E.P. conference as an advocate for parents of a child in special education
—Serving as a "guardian ad litem" for a child involved in a neglect proceeding in juvenile court
—Advocating for a neighborhood group desiring better street lighting and more police patrols
—Helping a client obtain redress for sexual harassment in her place of work
—Lobbying officials for better mental health services for disturbed residents in the county jail

Network/system consultant. In this last role cluster, perhaps most obviously related to our present topic, the professional person works through a preexisting or contrived support system to aid an individual client or a group of clients. The reasons for such consultation may be prevention, case finding, service integration, reinforcement for other professional services, or a host of other purposes. In practice, this role cluster subsumes a number of different professional activities including direct consultation, providing liaison services, and creating and maintaining networks. Recent interest in social support as a helping strategy has stimulated the development of many variations to this role from such seminal contributors as Gerald Caplan (1974) and Collins and Pancoast (1976). Examples include:

—Serving as liaison specialist between public school, mental health system, and family in a community-based program for disturbed children

—Teaching basic crisis intervention and marital counseling skills to community gatekeepers: beauticians, barbers, doctors, policemen, school crossing guards, and bartenders

—Consulting with an informal network of day-care neighbors to improve preventive and protective services for children

—Enlisting elderly citizens in a foster grandparent program for mentally retarded children

—Recruiting and training peer counselors for high school students with academic, social, and emotional problems

All five role clusters share a common knowledge base (e.g., social role theory and an environmental systems perspective) and, in addition, each has special knowledge requirements of its own. For example, the teacher–counselor role in its relation to various forms of skills teaching requires knowledge of applied behavior analysis, training needs assessment and evaluation, and group dynamics. Particular manifestations of the treatment agent role (e.g., psychotherapist) require specific knowledge in psychodynamic psychology and psychopathology. The advocate role requires specific knowledge in the area of organization and community change. With respect to social support, each role cluster contains within it specific professional activities, methods, and strategies that combine formal and informal helping in a variety of ways. Specific examples are found in the later chapters; by way of illustration only a few examples are given here. There are, for example, a number of network-based interventions that utilize the role of treatment agent. Trimble (1980) identifies several clinical network applications: "full-scale family network assemblies" (Speck and Attneave, 1973; Rueveni, 1979, 1980; Attneave, 1980); "network sessions" (Garrison, 1976; Hansell, Wodarczyk, & Handlon-Lathrop, 1970; Garrison, 1976); "generalist problem solving" (Curtis, 1973, 1974, 1976); "ecological system intervention" (Auerswald, 1971); "community network therapy" (Gatti and Colman, 1976); "network construction" (Cohen and Sokolovsky, 1978; Hammer, Makiesky-Barrow, and Gutwirth, 1978; Turkat, 1980). Trimble's review of these various practice approaches makes the very important point that specific network interventions do not cluster neatly under one or another of the professional roles, but may involve several. For example, a specific application of community network therapy may well require the professional to act as network consultant and advocate as well as therapist. The rich and growing body of empirical and clinical work on social networks and schizophrenia suggests a variety of roles for professional helpers (*Schizophrenia Bulletin*, 1978, 1981). Pilisuk, Chandler, and D'Onofrio (1979) identify seven different forms of social support facilitation that fall generally under one or another of the roles discussed above. For example, their "family system therapy," "family network therapy," and "community network therapy" fall primarily under the role of treatment agent, whereas "system consultation," "supportive consultation with natural helpers" and "patient group education" appear to fall under network/system consultant and teacher–counselor roles. Within the role of professional as network/system consultant, Turkat (1980) identifies a number of specific functions having to do with devising and coordinating social support networks; he also addresses the role of the professional as case advocate within an overall network intervention. Silverman (1980) also identifies the consultation function as an important professional contribution to self-help groups, and Lieberman and Borman (1979) discuss the important contribution professionals can make in initiating, supporting, and consulting to self-help groups. Pilisuk and Minkler (1980) describe a self-help group for the elderly that uses professionals to teach such skills as yoga, meditation, and biofeedback. Similarly, many self-help groups for parents of developmentally disabled children regularly use professionals to teach specific parenting skills or provide an update on the latest etiological research concerning their child's disorder. In the area of service brokerage, Curtis (1973) describes a creative approach to enlisting citizens in locating resources, identifying problems, and planning programs in a mental health center.

Implicit in the foregoing is that viewing informal helping from the perspective of the professional role is a useful exercise for several reasons. First, as professionals we need to begin thinking about informal helping in a more systematic and discriminating way. Creating or utilizing a social support network, for example, will not always require a full-scale network assembly. Less dramatic forms of consultation or facilitation may be sufficient to help, say, a troubled adult return home from a psychiatric hospitalization. Just as the research of Froland and his colleagues (1981) helps us to identify the strengths and limitations of various organizational strategies for using helping networks, a similar analysis of role-specific activities will help us to identify key practice and research issues. For example, what precisely are the knowledge and skill components involved in the following network interventions: conducting a therapy session with a full-scale network assembly; teaching stress management skills in a widow-to-widow mutual aid group; consulting to an informal group of day care mothers? The groundbreaking work of such investigators as Attneave (1980), Silverman (1974, 1980) and Collins and Pancoast (1976) has begun to answer those specific questions. The fruits of their developmental research must be related to the existing body of knowledge, skills, and helping technologies that underpin each of the previously described professional roles to ascertain what can be transferred and used from that considerable corpus of empirically based practice research and reservoir of practice wisdom. In short, as interested practitioners and agencies, we need a framework for organizing the often bewildering array of data presently being generated on network-based intervention. As practitioners, we need to construct simple matrixes to organize the knowledge we are developing within our own agencies: for example, on interventions with naturally occurring versus contrived networks. Interventions where the network provides the focus and locus for professional activ-

Table 2-2. Forms of network intervention: Some hypothetical examples

Form	Focus for professional intervention	Support to professional intervention
Naturally occurring	Conducting therapy sessions with an extended family network	Enlisting neighborhood peers in aiding reentry of deinstitutionalized, developmentally disabled adolescent
Contrived	Teaching stress management skills to a team of volunteers in a hospice unit	Recruiting parent aides to enhance a treatment program for neglectful parents

ity can, likewise, be plotted against interventions where the network provides support to a separate professional intervention. Such a matrix is illustrated in Table 2-2. Eventually, the cluster of activities in each cell of the matrix will suggest specific knowledge and skill considerations, as well as help us to frame key questions for practice research. Moreover, as the previously cited work of Wahler (1980 a, b) suggests, we need to begin thinking about *compatible* and *complementary* helping strategies—such as social skills training and social support facilitation—across a range of client populations. Such service packages may well require the same professional to act in a very different role capacity with the same client or family at different points in the intervention. A framework for analyzing the multiple

Table 2-3. Social treatment and social support: A framework for integration: Definitions

Social treatment	An approach to interpersonal helping that uses direct and indirect strategies of intervention to aid individuals, families, and small groups in improving social functioning and coping with social problems
Social support network	A set of interconnected relationships among a group of people that provides enduring patterns of nurturance, in any or all forms, and provides contingent reinforcement for coping with life on a day-to-day basis
Loci of intervention	
Microsystem	The product of physical settings and behavioral interactions in which individuals experience day-to-day reality, e.g., family, school, church, peer group, neighborhood
Mesosystem	The links between microsystems, e.g., home and school, day care center and neighborhood, church, and family
Exosystem	Settings that have power over one's life, yet in which one does not participate; e.g., the workplace of parents, a spouse's friendship network, a local school board
Macrosystem	The broader sociocultural system that provides the "blueprints" for society; more typically the locus for large-scale social planning, not typically the locus for social treatment

Table 2-4. Social treatment and social support: A framework for integration: Helping strategies and examples of their application in major professional roles

Strategies of helping	Major professional roles				
	Treatment agent	Teacher/ counselor	Broker of services and resources	Advocate	Network/systems consultant
Professional strategies Type 1 Professional helping without connection to social support network; isolated intervention	Psychotherapy with an adult depressive Play therapy with a disturbed child	Marital couple counseling in a family service agency	Determining benefit eligibility for a developmentally disabled client	Providing individual case advocacy for a single elderly client with the welfare department	Providing clinical case consultation to mental health professionals
Blended strategies Type 2 Social support network as focus and locus for direct, face-to-face, professional intervention	Family network therapy Community network therapy	Teaching cognitive-behavioral skills to an existing women's support group	Locating summer camp facilities for a network of neighborhood day care providers	Appearing as an advocate with a tenants' coalition before the public housing authority	Consulting to an informal network of day care providers on prevention of child abuse and neglect

Blended strategies					
Type 3 Social support network as supplement, complement, enhancement, to professional helping	Creating a support group for parents of children in a residential treatment center	Stimulating formation of a support group for single parents who have completed a parenting skills class	Providing story telling hours as an adjunct to resource information meetings for the elderly at a "little city hall"	Planning group "socials" as a reinforcement to an advocacy strategy with tenants in a public housing project	Providing peer support groups for lay volunteers enrolled in a training program to work with retarded citizens
Type 4 Social support network as primary method of help; professional helping ancillary—supportive	Periodic treatment sessions with an individual member of a community self-help group	Providing alcohol education to an existing support group for spouses of alcoholics	Securing mops and detergent for a self-initiating group of neighborhood "home helps" to the elderly	Reinforcing the school safety concerns of a local block organization of parents by testifying before the school board	Making local mental health officials aware of the existence of informal helping networks among local "street people"
Informal strategies					
Type 5 Social support networks as the sole method of helping; no professional involvement	Informal helping through "natural neighbors," indigenous self-help groups, "natural helping networks," mutual aid groups, fraternal associations, folk healing				

Table 2-5. Social treatment and social support: A framework for integration: Representative examples of knowledge and skills foundations for professional practice

	Treatment agent	Teacher/counselor	Broker of services and resources	Advocate	Network/systems consultant
Generic	Ecological understanding of human behavior and social environment; competence perspective; assessment skills: intrapersonal, interpersonal, environmental; communications skills; individual, family, and group dynamics; cultural awareness; practice evaluation skills				
Role-specific	Differential diagnosis, classification, and treatment Clinical practice theory/skill, e.g., "psychodynamic," "behavioral"	Learning needs assessment Group counseling Curriculum design, implementation, and evaluation for "skills" teaching, e.g., social, cognitive	Coordination, collaboration skills Information and referral Needs assessment Resource location and allocation	Negotiation and conflict resolution skills Knowledge of organizational and community change processes Lobbying skills	Consultation skills Skills in identifying, supporting, and creating helping networks Organizational analysis

roles of professionals helps us to anticipate where and when such role shifts occur. Finally, continuing to review periodically the principal activities, roles, and tasks we are called on to perform as individual practitioners and as agencies may be helpful in orienting us to new and untapped sources of knowledge and technology. For example, a family social agency moving from an individual casework strategy to a skills training/support group strategy may require a very different focus of training and consultation than its clinically oriented practitioners are used to. This might entail a move away from didactic sessions on personal dynamics and individual case consultation, in favor of group sessions on designing formats for social skills teaching. Facilitating and consulting to support groups would be an additional tactic.

In summary, I suggest that we need a broad ecological framework for understanding human service practice. Such a framework, following the ecological–systems perspective introduced by Garbarino in Chapter 1, will compel us to do several things: (1) view the client *and* the situation—the "ecological unit"—as the proper focus for assessment and intervention, (2) see the teaching of environmental coping skills as the primary purpose of helping, and (3) place environmental modification and the provision of concrete services on an equal plane with direct, face-to-face intervention with clients.

Moreover, I suggest that it is useful to think about social support as an integral and pervasive component of such a practice framework, rather than isolating it as a single strategy or method of helping. Similarly, it is desirable to think of social support and informal helping in relation to the multiple roles that human service practitioners perform, rather than confining it within any single helping role. I identify five such roles: treatment agent, teacher–counselor, broker of services and resources, advocate, and systems/network consultant. Such a differential role analysis of social support facilitation will complement the kind of organizational and programmatic analysis of informal helping undertaken by Froland and his colleagues, which resulted in the identification of five distinct program strategies: personal network, volunteer linking, mutual aid networks, neighborhood helpers, and community empowerment. It will also help us to identify the multiple professional roles involved in packages of complementary interventions (such as direct treatment, skills teaching, and network consultation), as well as orient us to existing bodies of knowledge and technology to help with implementation. I suggest that the social treatment formulation, a way of thinking about practice deeply rooted in the social service tradition, provides a useful framework for integrating concepts of formal and informal helping as illustrated in Tables 2-3, 2-4, and 2-5.

It is obvious from the table that considerable overlap may occur between individual cells in the matrix. Examples of each combination is presented to illustrate that it is at least theoretically possible to blend formal and informal helping across a wide range of interventions. In fact, many of the specific illustrations correspond to actual practice examples in the topical chapters to follow. The work of filling in such a matrix—of altering roles and adding new ones—will occupy practitioners for some years to come. Considerable work has already been accomplished in many different fields of practice as evidenced in the later chapters in this volume. It is also worth noting that each individual cell, as well as each role cluster, may be regarded as having a knowledge and skill component of its own. Moreover, it is useful to think about distinctive *person-centered, family-centered, group-centered,* and *neighborhood-centered* interventions across each of the five major roles. Further developmental research is needed in each of these categories of intervention so that they may be eventually integrated with the research of Froland *et al.* (1981) and of others on program strategies that combine formal and informal helping.

BARRIERS AND INCENTIVES TO INTEGRATING SOCIAL TREATMENT AND SOCIAL SUPPORT: SOME FINAL THOUGHTS

This final section, identifies some of the potential hurdles involved in achieving the kind of integrated approach to helping described above. Specific examples of practical issues in combining professional and informal helping in various fields of practice, such as mental health, services to the elderly, and youth services, will follow. At issue here is the more basic question of whether or not there are any *inherent* contradictions between professional and lay helping that render their coming together unlikely. Peter Lenrow (1978) in an insightful and stimulating review on the subject argues NO. Lenrow identifies a number of dilemmas confronting professionals, having to do with a whole range of concerns including "client self-determination," "informed consent," "personal values," "the role of judgement," and so on. Lenrow argues rather convincingly that there is nothing unique in these dilemmas for the professional helper. The dilemmas of the helping relationship, to the extent that they are problematic, are part of *every* helping relationship, professional or lay: "the major dilemmas experienced by professional helpers are built into social life *apart from the specifics of professional roles*" (1978, p. 287). Lenrow goes on to acknowledge that there are certain structural sources of discontinuity between professional and "folk" helping roles that can constitute a considerable barrier to both effective helping *and* partnership with informal support systems. These discontinuities have to do, essentially, with the manner in which professional services are delivered. Lenrow provides the following illustration:

Bureaucratic organization. Such things as centralization of authority, division of labor according to function, specialized roles . . . hierarchical relations . . . may take the form of regulations restricting the professional's choices of whom to help, how to go about it, within what time period, in what surroundings. . . . When a professional's work is imbedded in a bureaucratic structure, his role may be incompatible with helping in the sense that many of his actions are not intended to help and that the clients do not perceive the professional's actions as intended to help them. (1978, p. 279)

Lenrow identifies other structural sources of discontinuity as "economic self interest" (i.e., when fees for service arrangements conflict with the ideals of professional role), "technology supremacy" (the narrow technical focus of professional roles during and after training), "defensive self aggrandizement" (the hierarchical structure of professional, paraprofessional, and nonprofessional roles), "ethnocentrism" ("the institutional definition of services that perpetuates beliefs of the dominant group in society about the lives of relatively powerless groups," e.g., *blaming the victims*) (1978, pp. 279–281). Although the problems created by such structural discontinuities may be real and severe for many clients in the present human services, Lenrow's remedy flies in the face of much conventional wisdom. Rather than deprofessionalizing the system through a diminished professional presence, he argues for a *more* professional system, i.e., one more faithful to the classical values that define the professional role: impartiality, rationality, empirical knowledge, and ethics committed to the dignity of the individual and to public welfare (1978, p. 268). The distinction between these two remedies is crucial. Lenrow's proposal suggests, in sharp contrast to the defined and diminished role for professionals envisioned by Berger and Neuhaus, a strong and determined attempt to bring to human social problems those values which lie at the very core of the professional role. What needs changing, according to Lenrow, are the structures and hierarchies through which those core values are rendered less potent in actual practice. This is, essentially, an optimistic view. It focuses more attention on the marriage of informal and formal helping and ways to overcome obstacles to it. It does not begin with the presumption that the marriage ceremony will never take place.

Froland's research identified three modal types of professional–lay relationships among 30 social agencies that constituted the study sample: coordinative, collegial, and directive (Froland *et al.*, 1981, p. 62). The *coordinative* relationship is characterized by a relatively high degree of independent action by lay helpers: deciding what to work on, taking responsibility for tasks and activities, and operating with, at most, minimal supervision from agency staff. An example is offered from one program in which professional staff organized task forces of neighbors to provide services to elderly people living in an inner-city neighborhood. These teams undertook the major responsibility for proving help, and staff coordinated the separate activities of individual teams to ensure that a full range of services was available. The *collegial* relationship is characterized more by interdependence between individual staff members and individual lay helpers. In an example taken from the area of aging, a professional staff person working with an individual client may, with the client's permission, identify and encourage the participation of a family member, friend, or relative in the helping process. In the *directive* relationship, the professional recruits, monitors, and supervises the lay helper on a range of limited, staff-determined tasks. The example in this case is taken from the field of disability, where staff might identify a lay helper who is especially knowledgable or skillful in some aspect of independent living, e.g., using public transportation, and use that person to train their severely disabled client in that particular skill (1981, pp. 61–64).

Froland and his colleagues conclude that each of these relationships offers a more autonomous role for the informal helpers than is generally found in volunteer opportunities in the human services. Whatever the validity of that assertion (and no hard data are given to support it) I think that these investigators are fundamentally correct in their observation that *control* (or lack thereof) is a key variable in the kind of relationship forged between professionals and lay helpers. Such relationships, whatever their nuances and structural differences, have to begin with what Lenrow and Burch term the professional resolve to "take interdependence seriously" (1981, p. 246). Such resolve applies to professional–client as well as to professional–lay helper relationships. This means, essentially, that the professional approaches both groups with the assumption that he or she *needs* their active collaboration and contributions if effective services are to be delivered. Such conviction is evident to me in the five program strategies for linking formal and informal helping identified in the Froland research. In Froland's *personal networks strategy*, professional staff consult, support, and assist the informal helping efforts of family, friends, and neighbors known to a client. The *volunteer linking strategy* involves matching lay helpers and clients where existing sources of social support are limited. The *mutual aid strategy*, also the object of such investigators as Silverman (1980) and Lieberman and Borman (1979), involves bringing together individuals with common problems, interests, and backgrounds for the purpose of sharing resources and reducing social isolation. The *neighborhood helping strategy* involves consulting with the "natural neighbors" identified earlier by Collins and Pancoast (1976, p. 131)—i.e., those already performing key helping roles informally—to support those patterns of help and, possibly, avoid the need for formal, professional services. The final strategy, *community empowerment*, involves "the development of ties among informal opinion leaders within a community to plan improvements in services and to identify existing resources for meeting needs" (Froland *et al.*, 1981, pp. 64–65). Table 2-6 gives the investigators' summary of these program strategies and their relationship to the three patterns of formal–informal partnership. The significance of this exploratory study, it seems to me, is that it allows us to focus our attention

Table 2-6. A typology of program strategies

Strategies	Objectives	Informal helping networks	Relationship
Personal network	Consult with client's significant others: supporting existing efforts Convene network of providers and family, friends and others to resolve problems Expand client's range of social ties	Family members, friends, neighbors, service providers	Primarily collegial
Volunteer linking	Provide lay therapists for counseling Establish companionate relationships Recruit and link volunteer advocates to client	Citizen volunteers People with skills, interests relevant to client's needs People with similar experience	Primarily directive
Mutual aid networks	Establish peer support groups Consult with existing groups and support activities	Local church associates Clients with similar problems People with shared concerns	More collegial with existing network Either directive or coordinative for created networks
Neighborhood helpers	Establish consultative arrangement with neighbor to monitor problems Convene neighbors to promote local helping	Neighbors Clerks, managers in local businesses Religious leaders	More collegial but may be coordinative
Community empowerment	Establish local task forces for meeting community needs Provide for community forums to have input into local policies	Opinion leaders in local business, religious institutions Members of local voluntary associations Neighborhood leaders	Primarily coordinative

Source: Reprinted from Froland *et al.*, 1981, with permission of the publisher.

on the barriers and role considerations in blending formal and informal helping in a particular agency program. For example, the sort of relationship envisioned in the "neighborhood helpers" and "community empowerment" strategies involves a set of behaviors most closely associated with the professional roles that I have identified as "network/systems consultant," "advocate" and "broker of services and resources," respectively. This immediately orients us to a considerable body of knowledge—some of it derived from empirical research, some of it from practice wisdom—that will help us to identify the requisite skills and organizational factors that make for successful role performance. If such a typology does not immediately answer all of our specific questions, it at least limits the field of inquiry for the interested practitioner or agency and provides the framework within which those specific questions will ultimately be resolved.

What are the implications of the social network approach for human service practitioners? First, it is by no means self-evident that there is an inherent contradiction between professional and lay helping: the problems or discontinuities flow more from the structural arrangements through which services are often delivered and from the narrowness that often results from particularistic forms of professional training. These are remediable problems. Structural impediments, such as stifling bureaucratic procedures, can be altered. Professional training and education can be broadened to include a more complete view of the person-in-situation, with a greatly expanded view of potential helping resources. Moreover, as Froland's research illustrates, there are already working models of professional–lay collaboration in a wide range of human service areas. The chapters that follow are replete with other examples. As professionals we need to begin with a statement of conviction: not simply that a collaborative relationship with informal helpers is desirable, but that it is *essential* and *attainable*. Mitchell and Hurley (1981) call for a "demystification" of paraprofessional and informal helping roles. Such an exercise in demystification could be profitably extended to professional roles as well. These authors introduce a level of specificity into the discussion of barriers—e.g., specifying the outcomes and processes of informal helping transactions—that moves us considerably ahead of a "laundry-list" analysis of how professional and lay helpers differ. We need to move to an analysis of the barriers to collaboration attendant to specific program strategies, modal helping relationships, and professional roles. This need raises some immediate questions of interest for practice research. What professional roles are most conducive to collaboration with existing helping networks? Are there structural factors that can mitigate the barriers to collaboration and partnership attendant to certain professional roles? For example, the charge of fostering undue dependency in clients has long been a concern of clinicians. Yet it is that very kind of dependency relationship and the familiarity that goes with it that characterizes much informal helping: the difference, for example, between the lay helper's "closeness," "self-involvement" and "identification" and the professional's "self-awareness," "control of transference" and "empathy" (Riessman, 1976a). However, in certain innovative treatment programs, such as home-based, crisis services to multiproblem families, the limits on time (often imposed by the funding agency) and the pressures to focus on specific and immediate problems (such as prevention of premature out-of-home placement for a troubled child) serve to reduce the therapist's concerns about fostering dependency. As one therapist told me: "We don't worry a lot about dependency in working with these families . . . we know we'll be gone after the initial contract period is up . . . we'll talk to *anyone* (mother, father, child, grandparent, friend) to get the process started and we'll talk anywhere" (Booth, 1981).

It is at least a reasonable hunch that the structural features of such treatment programs—their time limits, their focus on immediate problems, the fact they are carried out on the client's home turf—have a good deal to do with reducing the barriers between therapists and clients and between therapists and potential informal helpers in the client's life web. Reid and Epstein's Task Centered Casework (1972, 1977) provides an excellent example of a paradigm for treatment intervention with many structural features that make it a desirable therapeutic complement to social support strategies.

In identifying barriers to collaboration specific to role, program strategy, and type of helping relationship, one key tool available to practitioners is the use of consumer evaluation. What Montrose Wolf (1976) calls the "social validity" of our programs has to do, essentially, with how they are perceived, experienced, and valued by our various "consumer" groups: clients, informal helpers, referring agents, neighbors, and so on. Some successful programs, like the "Teaching Family model" for adolescents, make extensive use of such simple, straightforward consumer evaluations and use the results systematically to alter staff training and program procedures (Willner *et al.*, 1977). Such formats would seem to offer much to the social agency desirous of linking formal and informal helping strategies. Beyond this issue, Mitchell and Hurley (1981), in their review of the paraprofessional literature, identify several areas of inquiry that yield the following questions of interest:

> Are particular *types* of support more helpful than others in dealing with particular types of difficulties?
> Are some *sources* of help more potent than others?
> Does support have its salutary effects primarily in buffering stress or does it serve more general health promotive functions?
> Do coping styles influence one's ability to use support that is offered? (1981, pp. 286–287)

The answers to such basic questions will come from many different lines of research activity: the kind of exploratory studies of "whole cloth" models of formal and informal helping undertaken by Collins and Pancoast (1976) and by Froland and his colleagues (1981), the practice experiments in network interventions of clinicians like Attneave (1980), Caplan (1974), and Gottlieb (1981), as well as the kind of applications from more basic network research suggested by Wellman (1981). For example, using network analysis techniques, Cohen and Sokolovsky (1981) recently completed a study of skid row residents that dispelled the notion that such people are completely isolated, incapable of intimacy, and unable to enlist peer support in response to deteriorating health. Their research, in addition, contains many potentially fruitful implications for both the locus and focus of agency-based network interventions.

In the meantime, the overriding implication for practitioners appears to be flexibility: in problem definition, role behaviors, program structures, and procedures. Such flexibility should come not so much from a lack of conviction as from a desire to achieve true interdependence between formal and informal helping efforts. In professional education and training programs, for example, much more attention must be paid to "painting-in the scenery:" exploring the ecological perspective outlined in this and the initial chapter. Unless practitioners begin with this expanded view of the environment—as both a source of the problem *and* a source of remedy—they will continue to turn to individualistic, intrapsychic models as guides to assessment and intervention. Similarly, the often neglected skills of advocacy tactics, consultation, collaboration, and environmental assessment deserve to be put on an equal footing with direct-practice clinical/education skills as a necessary component of the professional repertoire. Much of the actual work of forging the links between professional and lay helping will involve these indirect practice skills in a major way. We need to begin in our service agencies by identifying potential sources of social support for clients and assessing, through consumer evaluations, *their* view of our formal services. Such evaluations need to become a part of the boiler plate of agency service evaluation.

Finally, all of us in the human services need to acknowledge that we are in the very early stages of the development of a new social technology. This technology, when it reaches maturity, will allow us to combine the very best elements of formal and informal helping in specific ways to meet the needs of people in distress. It is worth noting here that such an exercise will require us to look at new sources of data, many of which, like "folk helping" and "self-help" strategies, will appear, at first, as foreign objects to the untrained professional eye. Perhaps it is well to conclude with the observation that pragmatism has always been at the heart of good practice and good research in the human services. I use pragmatism here, not in the pejorative sense in which it is all too frequently used, but in the sense intended by the philosopher Santayana when he called it "impassioned empiricism." We shall need many such impassioned empiricists in the human services if we are to execute the kind of practice demonstration- and mission-oriented research required ultimately to answer the question of how best to link the private and public worlds of helping. Perhaps the best and the only thing to cling tenaciously to in the human services is our statement of mission. Here, I draw again on Jane Addams's simple but eloquent rendering of that purpose as: "the raising of life to its highest value" (1910). Beyond that, let the data take us where they will.

PART II
Services for Mental Health, Health Care, and the Elderly

CHAPTER 3
Social Support Networks in Mental Health

Anthony D'Augelli

One may easily conceive the young girl's loneliness and misery, deprived so cruelly of her mother, abandoned by her aunt and uncle (as it must have seemed), and treated indifferently by her father. Fortunately she was in the care of sensible and devoted attendants, particularly her governess. By the age of twelve or thirteen, Anna could speak three languages besides her native Ukrainian, was familiar with good literature, and demonstrated a considerable degree of talent in music. She enjoyed dancing, and was able to attend ballet classes at the lycée. This had the advantage of giving her an opportunity to form friendships, and she became, by her own account, quite sociable and popular. Altogether, then, she survived the loss of her mother better than many, or perhaps most, children would have done.

D. M. Thomas, *The White Hotel*, Viking, 1981, p. 94

It can be said with little equivocation that the existence of social support is the sine qua non of mental health. Social connections are the vehicle by which individuals grow and develop. Human development may be seen as the process by which the physical connection of one to another at birth is replaced by the symbolic connections of socialization. Life is the management of social networks over time, the interplay between independence, interdependence, and dependence, and the balance between self and other. It is therefore not surprising that themes of loneliness and conflict in relationships with others are ubiquitous elements of psychosocial distress. Since creativity also correlates with distance from others, it would appear that deviation from the normative experience of social life presents both dysfunctions and challenges. How one relates to the world of social relationships and how one's social networks operate to provide support, caring, and challenge are the two essential components of mental health. The social network can be a powerful indicator of mental health, far superior to the ordinary personologically oriented models so common to discussions of coping and adaptation.

Social networks have become the new mental health discovery. Although the concept existed in various forms for years, it was not until Gerald Caplan's (1974) series of lectures that the term "support systems" gained much attention. The convergence of several traditions, for example, those of community ecology, social milieus, and social systems, as Froland (1978) has noted, provided a broader context for the concept of social support. Caplan's earlier (1964) concept, psychosocial resources, did not capture the imagination as forcefully: it did not suggest a set of structural characteristics, a morphology, that could allow an examination of a person's milieu in an objective way. Social support soon became a commodity provided by a network, that is, a set of others whose relationship to the receiver could be mathematically portrayed. The extension of the network broke disciplinary boundaries conceptually, and work in social integration done by anthropologists and sociologists became important. With this came conceptual confusions to be expected when diverse disciplines explore a newly identified social phenomenon: there were different definitions, different analytic tools, different data sets, and different conclusions. The symbolic power of social networks soon obscured the very real questions that needed to be asked about the role of social support networks in mental health. While scholars asked increasingly complex questions (e.g., Heller, 1979; Mitchell & Trickett, 1980), mental health delivery systems started to gear up to incorporate the new discovery. At least initially, traditional therapy groups for hospitalized patients were relabeled "social support" groups.

As the concept of social networks was becoming the new solution to mental illness, not to mention unhappiness and isolation, the institutional system of mental health services was completing a transition to "community services," a change in which social networks have a critical role. But, like most discoveries in mental health, the once startling insight has given way to a more reflective stance. This chapter, designed not as a complete review of the literature on social support networks and mental health, which several others have already done (see Froland et al., 1981; Gottlieb, 1981), will analyze the proposition that social support networks are required for mental health and that optimal development can be usefully seen as the successful resolution of issues posed by social networks. Caplan wrote:

> Most people develop and maintain a sense of well-being by involving themselves in a range of relationships in their lives that in toto satisfy their specific needs, such as: marriage, parenthood, other forms of loving and intimate ties, friendships, relationships with colleagues at work, membership in religious congregations and in social, cultural, political, and recreational associations and acquaintanceships with neighbors, shopkeepers, and providers of services; intermittent relationships of help-seeking from professional caregivers such as doctors, nurses, lawyers, and social workers; and continuing dependence for education and guidance on teachers, clergymen, intellectuals, and community leaders, and [people] of authority and influence (1974, p. 5).

This array of connections shapes and reinforces a person's sense of competence and mastery, a position presented forcefully in Caplan's (1981) most recent work. The personal sense of security due to the mastery gained from social connectedness provides the reserve from which the stresses of life events can be managed and from which opportunities for change can be directed. The life event of divorce became manageable for the "Mrs. Franklin" of Strong's case study because of the strength, perspective, and example provided by her own mother. Not all social connections would have helped her:

> Although she especially needed closeness (emotional support), she could have gotten that from a few others besides her mother. However, of those who were close to her, only her mother had something extra to offer which directly addressed Mrs. Franklin's concerns about coping. That is, her mother had lost her own husband, but still had managed to raise children and later remarried. . . . Mrs. Franklin has available a model—someone who had managed to survive that experience (1978, p. 462).

SUPPORT NETWORKS AND PSYCHOPATHOLOGY

In 1967 Hamburg and Adams asked a seemingly simple but surprisingly difficult question: "Why doesn't everyone break down?" They note the personally threatening and stressful common experiences that many encounter: separation from parents in childhood, displacement by siblings, childhood experiences of rejection, illness and injuries in childhood, illness and death of parents, severe illnesses and injuries of the adult years, the initial transition from home to school, puberty, later school transitions (e.g., from grade to high school), competitive graduate education, marriage, pregnancy, menopause, necessity for periodic moves to a new environment, retirement, rapid technological and social change, and wars and threats of wars. How one confronts these life occurrences involves a mixture of active coping and equally active rejection: the former is the marshalling of personal and social resources; the latter is the avoidance of aspects of events for self-protective purposes. The distressing components of life events, those aspects over which the person has little control, are rejected by using classical defense mechanisms such as denial, rationalization, intellectualization, and so on. In their clinical work with patients with severe injuries, Hamburg and Adams wondered about the active coping process, those aspects of behavior that involve maintaining a sense of personal worth, retaining significant contacts with others, and increasing the likelihood that a personally valued resolution will occur. Essential to the process of active coping was a social network:

In the studies of severely burned patients and of patients with severe polio-myelitis, we observed that they made efforts toward the testing of key figures in their personal environment in order to determine whether they would still be regarded with positive feelings in spite of their damaged conditions, whether they could still win affection and respect in ways that had proved effective in the past, and whether new patterns of interaction would be required (Hamburg & Adams, 1967, p. 279).

In general, then, the initial question is neither facetious nor rhetorical: the mediators of life events must be known in order to understand the remark-able stamina most people have when facing those events. That most people do not seek professional mental health or other human services is not com-pletely explained by the stigma often associated with seeking such help. Rather, the minimal use of formalized help is more parsimoniously ex-plained: people do not break down because they routinely receive help from their social networks. Alice Schiff, an elderly woman whose move to a new apartment complex for older adults was chronicled in *The New York Times* (August 13, 1981), had a plan to deal with her transition from her former home of 16 years: "I hope eventually to find one or two persons with whom I can be a little closer." It is unlikely that Ms. Schiff will join the ranks of the psychiatrically impaired elderly.

It is hardly insightful, however, to point out the protective character of contact with others. More specific understanding of the mental health func-tions of social networks is much more difficult. A clear description of how social networks operate to promote mental health and prevent debilitating distress has proved elusive. Similarly, the means by which social networks create distress or exacerbate it are equally unknown. Further, this more pessimistic view of social networks runs counter to the current spirit of the times, which often assumes the untarnished (and unrealistic) benevolence of social networks. To understand the mental health functions of social net-works is to examine processes at multiple levels of analysis. Conceptually, the social network can be considered as a personal, family, or community resource. Is a social network a sociocultural, familial, or personal phenom-enon? When we discuss social networks, do we really mean community attachment, marital and family contentment, or personal social competence? The analytic issues are complex, and the ideological issues involved are not trivial. As noted by Hammer:

> Support may be one function of a set of social connections. As such, it may prove misleading if we are not alert to the complementary impact of restraint, opposition, demandingness, mere presence, range of access, and whatever-else-may-matter, within these sets of social connections. To focus on "support" rather than on demands, restrictions, or social facilitation reflects a pathology-oriented approach that assumes the need for help in coping with problems to be of primary importance. (1981, p. 47)

The practical matters of mental health service delivery are far from being trivial in the understanding of social networks. Garrison and Podell vividly formulate the issue:

> To our knowledge there are no guidelines for the assessment of the quality of support other than those for more usual clinical judgments. How does one, for example, assess the significance of the support provided to a chronic schizophrenic with no family and few, if any friends, by a nonintimate tie with a helpful neighbor? How does one weigh the support as against the exploitation involved in a relationship between a young schizophrenic prostitute and her pimp when it was he who made it possible for her to become independent of her mother who first introduced her to prostitution? (1981, p. 105)

Moving beyond the current situation in which social networks have taken on a mythical character—similar in some ways to the myths of psychotherapy described by Kiesler (1966)—is essential for the development of a realistic perspective on social networks and mental health.

MACROSYSTEMS AND MICROSYSTEMS

The broad sociohistorical backdrop and the individual's social behavior represent the extremes of the analytic continuum of social networks. The questions of whether certain epochs encouraged social integration and in what forms this occurred are historical in nature. Borchert's (1980) analysis of the back alleys of Washington, D.C. during the 1800's and how families and neighborhoods were organized for mutual support and help is the latest in a rich tradition. The impact of the Industrial Revolution, the world wars, the Great Depression, the Cold War era, the 1960's, and other periods on the nature of social networks is difficult to study but presents a template against which to consider current social networks and their impact on mental health. The influence of historical change is the subject of social demography; for example, current trends in divorce and remarriage are de facto evidence of structural changes in many social networks. However, more often such issues are discussed at the community or neighborhood level. It is intriguing to wonder about the impact of the Depression on the formation, evaluation, and dissolution of a person's social network, but current researchers have more typically inquired about a person's community rather than his or her place in history.

The community as proximal environment, the community as neighborhood, the community as interface of macroenvironment and microenvironment, the community as refuge from the winds of change are the parameters of what Wellman and Leighton call the "community question." They point out that "definitions of community tend to include three ingredients—networks of interpersonal ties (outside the household) which provide sociability and support to members, residence in a community locality, and solidarity sentiments and activities" (1979, p. 365). Community psychology, for instance, has focused on (1) the consequences for mental health of services provided by nonprofessionals and indigenous workers, (2) the impact of social environments on mental health, and, finally, (3) the circumstances that lead to the development of a psychological sense of community (Sarason, 1974). The result has been a piecemeal literature concerned with the linkages between each of these issues and mental health. But the community too is part of a larger structured network:

> The local community is viewed as a complex system of friendship and kinship networks and formal and informal associational ties rooted in family life and ongoing socialization processes. At the same time it is fashioned by the large scale institutions of mass society. Indeed, it is a generic structure of mass society, whose focus, content, and *effectiveness* vary widely and whose defects and disarticulations reflect the social problems of the contemporary period (Kasarda & Janowitz, 1974, p. 329).

Just as individuals have a coping repertoire that is stable and cross-situational in nature, neighborhoods, communities, and societies have stable characteristics that influence the mental health challenges produced by change. Mass unemployment, reflecting the economic lability and misdirection of a nation, will obviously affect not only the particular individuals who are unemployed. Even a neighborhood with strong ties, a set of sturdy voluntary associations, and a stable and secure family life, will be influenced by events on a societal level. Some communities can adapt and change; others respond less constructively to social change. The quality of the linkages within a helping community, to some degree a correlate of the quantity of linkages (i.e., high-quality linkages are, by chance, more likely if there is a range of options), is the critical determinant of success or failure:

> One man who was asked to resign from the insurance company where he had worked for 22 years did not even wait to reach home to tell his wife. "I felt betrayed," he said. "I questioned my own ability and initially felt it had to be my fault. So I phoned her and said, 'I'm sorry, but I must share the burden of this with you immediately.' " The wife, who is employed herself, recalled that phone conversation: "I was more upset for him than for the situation. I didn't stop to think that his pay would be cut off, my first thought was to give him moral support" (Brozan, 1981).

Clearly, the impact of changes in the macrosystem filters through the more immediate social network. The argument among social theorists about the level of analysis of network impact takes the form of traditional structuralist versus functionalist: is it the *existence* or the *character* of social aggregates that matters? Wellman and Leighton (1979) note that "neighborhood" and "community" are often used interchangeably. Such usage, they write, assumes a "spatial determinism"; it assumes that proximity has power. Moreover, it ignores major ties that people have outside their communities, especially at work, and it ignores the fact that the presence of many local relationships does not necessarily create discrete neighborhoods. In a similar manner, the disastrous effects presumed of a technological society, especially the replacement of primary groups (kinship ties, neighbors, and friends) by bureaucratic proxies, has yielded to empirical evidence that the functions of the primary group are not replaceable (Litwak & Szelenyi, 1969). Recovering from a fear of the impact of bureaucracy and technocratic dominance, social scientists (especially sociologists) have asserted that extended kin relations can survive. Currently, obituaries for the family are no longer commonplace (Spanier, 1981). The primacy of affectivity, of the need for closeness, of the security afforded by some close ties, may, of course, be ephemeral. Events could occur in the macrosystem that could overwhelm social networks. Uprootings caused by social upheaval, famine, and war deplete social reserves by severing the ties that bind. Coehlo, Yuan, and Ahmed (1980) describe the consequences of rapid uprooting, and they are devastating: a difficulty in communicating, verbally and nonverbally; a loss of sensory contact with a familiar physical environment; the need to learn new behavior patterns; and the loss of opportunities for intimate and informal interactions based on close friendships. Not all families, neighborhoods, or communities can cope with social disruption, and the most vulnerable (the poor, children, and the elderly) invariably suffer most and complain the least. A full-employment economy is a macroenvironmental mental health intervention (Keniston, 1977) not because of its concrete results, but because it removes stress from the networks that people symbolically and literally inhabit. The connection between levels of networks is well described by Catalano:

> After measuring the relationship between ecological variables and health problems, several obvious interventions may emerge. It may be that the most effective way to reduce stress-related illnesses, for example, is to stabilize the local economy, thereby reducing economic stress and normalizing the age structure. Another intervention might involve educational programs designed to increase the ability to cope with life cycle and economic stress (1979, p. 135).

Certainly a macrosystem event would change the nature of social networks, but it is probably naive to assume that providing a job (or even a "career") by itself will prevent unhappiness. Distal social structures, whether neighborhoods, communities, or environments, have mental health consequences (Monahan & Vaux, 1980), but the consistent closest mediators are invari-

ably social and interpersonal. Such mediators are exemplified by the dysfunctions of communication in a schizophrenogenic family, the power struggle of a "psychosomatic family" (Minuchin, Rossman, & Baker, 1978), the
neglect and abuse of the young and the old, the loneliness of the distraught
and battered spouse, the isolation of those undergoing marital disruption,
and the brittle fragility of the recently widowed (Insel, 1980). As Insel notes,
demographic, economic, geographical, and cultural conditions affect human
development throughout the life span through one's closest proximal affectional ties. The family is both primary support network and microcosm.

The social conditions of local communities and neighborhoods set the
stage for the functioning of social networks, and these networks in turn
influence family functioning (Powell, 1979). How parents rear their children
is the usual focal point of such discussions, since local attitudes can shape
disciplinary practices, local schools can extend and institutionalize such
norms, and the inadequacies of local resources can strain families and lead
to abuse and neglect. To take a material resource as an example, the lack of
quality day care for young children limits the options of a family in which two
salaries are seen as a necessity. Regardless of whether low-paying work
is conducive to a spouse's sense of personal mastery, the availability of such
work serves to decompress the family system. (The quality dimension must
be preserved here, too, for if a working parent perceives child-care arrangements to be detrimental to the child yet believes that no real alternative is
possible, the resultant guilt may offset any financial relief.) But to focus
exclusively on the child in understanding how social conditions influence
families for mental health is to dwell only on that aspect of family life for
which our society traditionally feels any responsibility. Social networks are
the vehicle by which adult friendships develop, adolescents achieve a sense
of autonomy, young adults consider career alternatives, aging adults learn
to talk to their middle-aged children, and these children learn how to act
when their "old-old" parents become helpless.

Communities must be helping networks across the life span, contrary to
the ordinary expectation that equates adulthood with the lack of interdependence. Indeed, perhaps the best kept secret of our culture, a secret that
runs counter to the American way (Sampson, 1977), is that interdependence
is the spring of life. Societal structures that promote independence ultimately produce alienation and anomie, although they may simultaneously
produce the illusion of wealth and happiness. Wellman and Leighton (1979)
decry the "community lost" argument: the contention that there are no
local solidarities or interdependences in our centralized, bureaucratic society. Nor is the "community saved" argument supported. The supposition
that there are no shades of variability between and within communities, and
that all communities (and, by analogy for my purpose, families) provide
support and sociability is equally misleading. Rather, the "community–family liberated" view seems on the mark: admittedly modern society involves

weakened local communities and changes in the structure of family life (i.e., there are more two-paycheck families, more divorce and remarriage, people living longer, and so on); however, the primary social network of community and family life, the social embeddedness that is inescapable, is still essential to human development. As Wellman and Leighton (1979) note, the networks of modern individuals are different from earlier networks because technological and structural change has "liberated" communities from neighborhoods and dispersed network ties. They characterize these networks as follows:

1. Urbanites are limited members of several social networks, including the neighborhood.

2. These networks vary in the breadth of strands of relationships between network members.

3. The ties within networks vary in intensity.

4. The ties are organized into a series of networks with few connections between them.

5. The networks are sparsely knit, though parts, especially those based on kinship, are more densely knit.

6. The networks are loosely bounded, ramifying structures that branch out to link with added people and resources.

7. There is little structural basis for solidarity activities and sentiments in the overall networks, although some solidarity clusters of ties are present.

8. Some network ties can be mobilized for general or specific purposes and for routine or emergency matters.

This "network-liberated" perspective does not seek to ignore the very real changes that will have an effect on mental health. The litany presented by a current reading of social demographics by Camara, Baker, and Dayton (1980)—the increases in the number of separations and divorces among the young, younger remarriages, the greater proportion of children affected by marital disruptions, the number of single-parent households, especially those headed by women—typically produces cries for increased human services. This is too simple a solution and is misdirected. Rather, the assumption should be made that, without interference by "do-gooders," most people will form ties to accomplish their goals and that people will seek out networks for coping. This does not imply, however, that human service agencies have no role, as will be detailed later.

DEFINITIONAL CONCERNS: STRUCTURE AND FUNCTION

In a study of the social networks of Laotian peasants who came to be labeled *baa* (crazy or insane) by other villagers, Westermeyer and Pattison (1981) gathered data about social contacts from a variety of informants. The *baa* person was not a source of the data, and reports were solicited about repeated transactions, not just those that were deemed significant by the informant. The results are not radically different from other studies of social networks of distressed persons: the *baa* have small networks composed mostly of family and kin; their instrumental exchanges with their networks are asymmetrical (the *baa* give little); and a decline in the network is a prelude to increasingly erratic behavior. But the clarity of the method is unique in its demonstration of a concern for both the structure of the *baa's* network (average size of seven members; most had only one "plexus group," or a group in which members know each other) as well as its functioning (some *baa* have extensive networks of peasants who are returning obligations incurred much earlier). Few empirical studies consider both structural qualities of networks and the specific nature of "important," "meaningful," or "helpful" ties. As Hammer remarks, this distinction between social network and social support has important implications: "The difference between social networks and support systems is not a mere terminological distinction, since it leads to different formulations of the research problems, with different choices of the kinds of measures to be used, different perspectives on the role of basic social research, and a different potential for theoretical analysis" (1981, p. 45). Hammer's argument that an excessive concern with close relationships when the reality may be that weak or distant connections matter (at least under some circumstances) is a minority opinion, on the basis of the typical ways in which the social network construct is made operational. In her view, *social connections* are more researchable, and the tightly knit network that is the common image may exist only in the self-reports of the focal persons. Yet ignoring primary relationships is equally, if not more, myopic. If access to others is the definition of social network, what of access to a demeaning and rejecting spouse? An exclusive focus on the beneficial aspects of social networks is not required to maintain a phenomenological and qualitative definition. Many close relationships are full of conflict.

Thus it seems heuristic and realistic to examine both structural and functional characteristics of social networks. The variability of definitions of social networks is well demonstrated in Mitchell and Trickett's review (1980, p. 46), and they also provide a reasonable listing of network characteristics. The *structural characteristics* are size or range, density, and degree of connection; *the characteristics of component linkages* are intensity, durability, multidimensionality (or multiplexity), directedness or reciprocity, relationship density, dispersion, frequency of contact, and homogeneity; the *normative contexts* are those of primary kin, secondary kin or extended family, friend, neighbor, or work acquaintance; and the *functions* served include emotional support, task-oriented assistance, maintenance of a social identity, and access to new and diverse social contacts and information. The final component, the *nature of the exchange process*, can be categorized using Burns's (1973) typology: mutually exploitative, mutually considerate, mutually benevolent, mutually hostile, or considerate-benevolent (see also Ridley & Avery, 1979). The mental health consequences are most directly seen in the exchange and its quality. During the Normandy invasion in World War II, for example, the wartime context clearly influenced both the structure and the function of linkages, yet the quality of the exchange was paramount for coping: "Soldiers, particularly those who had been through combat, concealed little from each other or from themselves. The understanding and uncritical gaze with which a group of soldiers would watch a man weep revealed a mutual insight into their despair and their common strength. There was little that they did not already know about each other—why suddenly become coy?" (Wagner, 1946, p. 346).

ETIOLOGY: SOCIAL NETWORK AS CAUSE

Reviewers of the studies on attempts to prevent psychopathology are in agreement that highly specific socioenvironmental causes of dysfunction have yet to be identified (Kessler & Albec, 1975). On the other hand, the intuitive appeal of the proposition remains, substantiated by decades of clinical insights. Although longitudinal data that would demonstrate causality do not exist, it seems certain that some children who are born into families undergoing multiple stressful life events, in which interactional styles are continually inconsistent and conflictual, in which few meaningful connections with neighbors exist, and in which the family's integration into the normative structure of the community is poor, are at risk for developing dysfunctional behavioral patterns. That *some* children survive and excel, that *some* families cope, and that *some* communities adapt, given the same conditions is the paradox that challenges the understanding of how social life affects mental health. Deficiencies in both the structure and the functioning of social networks lay the foundation for distress since they contribute to behavioral patterns that are likely to come to the attention of others. (Definitions of mental illness are ultimately social in that some other must evaluate an event as indicative.) In addition, such deficiencies may shape the person's ability to use others, both formal and informal helpers, to deal with life events. A person growing up in a schizophrenogenic context, for example, not only will acquire a deviant set of behavioral patterns, but the most salient characteristic of these patterns is that they impede direct communication and thereby compound the problem in a substantial way. Thus, although the immutability implied in traditional psychodynamic formulations deserves its current disfavor because it is overstated, the power of one's social context over the life span cannot be denied. Furthermore, the psychological impact of loss or the fear of losing significant others in early life may be the mediator of future mental health consequences, just as the presence of a significant other appears to mediate mental health at the other end of the life course. That individuals are highly dependent, both at birth and near death, may well be the situational commonality that explains the emotional power of social networks at these times.

How can one explain the finding of one study that 6% of a group of third- to sixth-graders had no classroom friends and that an additional 12% had only one friend (Asher, Oden, & Gottman, 1977)? To view social networks as etiological agents demands a consideration of how such outcomes could have evolved, an assumption that these deficiencies (assuming they are) are not random. Consider this definition of social skill: "Social skill is the ability to interact with others in a given social context in specific ways that are socially acceptable or valued and at the same time personally beneficial, mutually beneficial, or beneficial primarily to others" (Combs & Slaby, 1977). A model of mental distress that is conceptually rooted in interactional excesses and deficits and that considers impairment as an interactional event (Pattison, 1977b) is more likely to trace antecedents to social network characteristics than a model that is basically intrapsychic. Of course, this is a false distinction theoretically, but it helps to explain the relative lack of emphasis on social networks in considering precursors (versus correlates) of distress. Yet it remains true, in Pattison, Llamas, and Hurd's works, that "the psychosocial network . . . is a fundamental social matrix that can be either health-promoting or pathology-promoting, depending upon its composition and nature" (1979, p. 63).

In their discussion of whether life events cause illness, Dohrenwend and Dohrenwend (1978) describe four factors that can mediate the effects of life events: previous experience with the life event, social bonds, anticipation of the noxious stimulus, and control of the noxious stimulus. Each of these factors has a qualitative dimension such that enhanced coping or depleted coping would result. An understanding of the qualitative dimensions would enable a clearer portrait of continuities and discontinuities in successful coping over the life span. At what point in life does "learned helplessness" become so embedded that it is a durable pattern? When does demoralization (Frank, 1978) become a stable trait? There can be little doubt that such coping responses are modeled by significant others who are most likely members of networks for whom there are few substitutes. It seems equally likely that change in the patterning of social networks in early development from an exclusive reliance on family to extended reliance on neighborhood and school contexts (in which greater diversity of coping repertoires are displayed) can account for the variability even within families of reactions to problematic family circumstances.

The transition to school from family provides a rare opportunity to view children's acquired coping and, particularly, children's ability to form and use social bonds—the effective way to resolve this life transition. How attachment to a social network outside the family occurs is de facto evidence of the social skillfulness shaped and modeled in the family. There is a distinctly adult-oriented slant to writings on social networks. Gourash (1978) writes of the four functions of social networks—buffering the experience of stress, providing support and services, referring others to formal services, and transmitting values and norms about help-seeking (I would add help-giving)—with little recognition of their importance for children. This is ironic since it is during childhood that the mental health-promotive functions of social networks are so critical. Children's social networks are also, apparently, less visible, possibly because young children do not provide articulated reports. Children experience more acutely the three kinds of potentially stressful events described by Lieberman and Glidewell (1978): nonnormative events (illness, a close friend leaving), normative events (transition to school, interaction with various child care-givers), and more persistent problems embedded in roles or role strains (being the only child of a poor, separated mother unable to find work). No longer can the mental health consequences for children of different social networks be ignored.

When social networks are understood in terms of both their emotional and socialization functions, the negative consequences of networks become crystallized. Caplan writes:

> Disorders in marital and parent–child relationships whereby an individual is not perceived as a person in his own right whose idiosyncratic needs are worthy of assessment and satisfaction but serves as a displacement object or scapegoat for vicariously satisfying the needs of other family members are commonplace in our clinical practice. Likewise, disorders of family communication such as double binds and mystification are a usual finding in our clinical cases. We often think of these distortions of relationship and communication as directly pathogenic, but our present thesis raises the possibility of conceptualizing them also as defects in the family support system that have failed to protect the individuals from the effects of inadequate feedback in the outside world. (1974, pp. 9–10)

Croog's (1970) review corroborates Caplan's point in its finding that many negative circumstances of adulthood can be easily traced back to stressful family situations or family structures. Structural qualities of the family network have long been suspect as having consequences for mental health. As Croog has noted:

> Particular positions within the family structure have been identified as likely to involve individuals in networks of interaction or with role dilemmas sufficiently stressful to lead to deviance or illness behavior. For example, the possibility of being the first-born in the family has been hypothesized as involving special vulnerabilities, some of which derive from the fact that parents are still in the process of learning their own roles in child-rearing. (1970, p. 43)

Other vulnerabilities that Croog neglects to mention may be more powerful—for example, the intense emotionality invested in the firstborn because the parents have no other love objects, which in turn may place emotional demands on the child to reciprocate in ways that are gratifying to the parents (e.g., achievement). If social support is a prime, if not *the* prime, determinant of well-being over the life span, the early development of one's social "convoys" (Kahn & Antonucci, 1980) may predict mental health with some consistency, especially if there are serious deficits in one's family network:

> Neurotic conflict between parents, parental rejection of children, inconsistent punishment, and coldness and hostility in family relationships are among the many factors that have been commonly cited as sources of difficulties in families, and these have been identified as being among the roots of specific types of mental disorders, marital conflicts and dissolutions, aggressive and withdrawn behavior, as well as delinquency, criminality, drug addiction, and other forms of deviant behavior (Croog, 1970, p. 44).

It should come as little surprise that a recent study of discharged schizophrenic patients found that the best prediction of relapse in the nine months after discharge was the level in the patients' key relatives of expressed emotion (high levels of intrusiveness, distress, blaming) (Vaughn & Leff, 1981). Although there are no data to document that these families are demonstrating the identical pathology-producing patterns that years earlier may have shaped a schizophrenic, the power of the social network of the family to affect mental health seems clear. Brown and Harris's (1978) brilliant work on the social origins of depression in women found that the loss of mothers before age 11 was one of four major risk factors; it was the only factor that was not a current, circumstantial one.

In their review of social support over the life span, Kahn and Antonucci suggest that support be defined as "interpersonal transactions that include one or more of the following key elements: positive affect, affirmation, and aid" (1980, p. 267). It is a small conceptual leap to equate support with attachment, a term with much power in describing the development of children and their parents. It is perhaps more important to consider the family network as an ecosystem in which parents shape the social behavior of their children and vice versa. The personal resources of the parents, the characteristics of the child, and the sources of stress and support for the family unit jointly determine competence in both adults and children (Belsky, Robins, & Gamble, 1982). To equate parental competence, for example, with "parenting that is *sensitively* attuned to children's capabilities and to the develpmental tasks they face," as Belsky and his colleagues do (1982, p. 6), is tautological. Yet it is likely that the nature of early bonding and attachment is a crucial link in understanding the ontogeny of psychosocial distress. Bretherton (1980) discusses the concept of attachment in early development, and she suggests clues as to the types of early disruptions that later result in the inability either to provide or receive social support through networks. Echoing Miller, Galanter, and Pribram (1960), she emphasizes the development of synchronized, reciprocal behavior patterns that provide security for the growing child. The bond, the linkage in this dyadic network, is an "underlying reciprocal organization," of five sets of skills in both partners: perceptual skills; locomotor skills; cognitive ability, especially for spatial representation; interpersonal skills; and symbolic skills, especially those involving increased decentering. Parental sensitivity, of course, is central to this view, but its effect on the child's development is best viewed in interpersonal outcomes for both:

> Mothers who either cannot read their infants' signals appropriately, or who choose to ignore infant signals during the first three months of life, tend, at the end of the first year, to have less harmonious (or well meshed) relationships. The quality of the relationship or bond is thus dependent on both partners' ability and willingness to interface their behavior, to construct many well-adapted, shared interactive plans (Bretherton, 1980, p. 190).

Cannot the consistent finding that schizophrenics' social exchanges are non-reciprocal (Pattison, Llamas, & Hurd, 1979) be considered a possible long-term consequence of a learning history in which intimate social networks operated in consistently erratic (discordant) ways? To return to Bretherton:

> The quality of the dyad's interactions is based on the degree of mutuality in the "shared programs." Sometimes mutual adaptation or interfacing of behavior plans is permanently hampered by either partner's inability or unwillingness to read the partner's signals. There are a number of reasons why this might happen: one partner's signals may be weak or deviant; alternatively, the partner may be deliberately or unwittingly "dyslexic" (1980, p. 189).

It is beyond the scope of this discussion to review the plethora of circumstances in early development—environment, familial, dyadic, or personological—that presage social disability. The outcome is clear, however:

> The process of social development includes critical skills in social network construction. Thus, if a person learns how to create and participate in effective social networks, he (she) will be at less risk of developing psychopathologic symptoms than if he (she) does not participate in such a network. The person who fails to acquire such skills because he (she) has grown up in a dysfunctional social network not only will be adversely affected by the network itself, but will also be unable to effectively build supportive social networks in the future (Pattison, Llamas, & Hurd, 1979, p. 67).

For example, in addition to the correlates of social acceptance such as immutables like a child's name, age, and sex, and situational characteristics such as high population mobility and size of social groups, Asher, Oden, and Gottman (1977) detail the social skills needed for a child to develop that most crucial network, friendship. The skills include responding positively to others, communicating accurately, being competent in some valued activity, and having the ability to initiate a relationship. In a similar, though broader way, Combs and Slaby (1977) define social competence as the possession of skills encouraging both cooperation and sharing, thus including both instrumental and expressive components. Negotiating interpersonal events in constructive ways, that is, using self-expression with simultaneous respect for the other person, is not explicitly taught, but rather is learned in the family context. That this skill is not consistently acquired has very real disadvantages in a child's often fragile social world:

> Children are faced early with situations that call for assertive behavior, yet they typically receive very little guidance in learning appropriate responses. For example, few children know how to respond with verbal assertiveness when another child attacks, intrudes, or takes objects. Most react in ways that often have negative consequences for both themselves and for the aggressor—by fussing, running away, submitting, retaliating physically or verbally, or seeking an adult's assistance (Combs & Slaby, 1977, p. 192).

Unless intervention occurs to improve social skills, peer rejection and isolation will result, accelerating a process of social deviance. The data are consistent that popular children are more adept in interpersonal reinforcement and reciprocity (see, for example, Hartup, Glazer, & Charlesworth, 1967; Gottman, Gonso, & Rasmussen, 1975). Other data on handicapped children's arrival in classrooms under mainstreaming are more provocative: the mere social presence of "normals" does not ensure facile interactions among all the children (Gresham, 1981). The social incompetence acquired by handicapped children in their early years provides a social handicap that interferes with the development of friendships and attachments. Structure does not ensure function in social networks.

A summary of the etiological role of social networks in mental health can be inferred from the propositions of Weinraub, Brooks, and Lewis (1977):

> 1. People are by nature social animals and from birth enter into social networks.
> 2. The social network at birth is ordinarily made up of a variety of social objects, including female and male adult caregivers, siblings, other relatives, and friends.
> 3. The social network involves social objects, functions, and situations.
> 4. The social network of an individual is embedded in and varies as a function of a larger social environment.
> 5. The person's social behavior and the composition of the social network change as a function of developmental status.

6. The person has a repertoire of behaviors that are enacted within the social network in ways that are relevant to the object, function, and situation of the specific interaction.

7. The person acquires knowledge through interaction with members of the social network.

8. The structural aspects of the social network consist at least of interactions and relationships that are arranged in hierarchical order. Interactions and relationships may not directly correspond.

It is worth noting that these propositions are not necessarily age-specific and thus also apply to adolescents, adults, and the elderly. The unique character of early experience as it relates to emotional development in a social context, however, is powerful. The "social capital" acquired can facilitate, though not ensure, successful coping throughout life, both because life events (most of which are social in nature or have social consequences) can be more securely confronted and because access to social resources has not been truncated by handicaps stemming from troubled early social experiences.

SOCIAL NETWORK CORRELATES OF MENTAL HEALTH

That current social network characteristics have mental health correlates and consequences has intuitive truth for clinicians. Beels states: "We were aware that the patient had a better chance of being maintained without relapse if the web of relationships connecting family, fellow workers, and clinic were characterized by the right positive tone, the right amount of open space and flexibility, and a good understanding among its key members. We also knew that when a relapse occurred, it often followed some disruption in the patient's social network" (1978, p. 512). A person's social network can define a life event as a stressor or a nonstressor, can enhance or diminish the person's idiosyncratic perception of an event, can offer normative expectations and ways to process stress, and can interfere with or augment coping (Pattison et al., 1979). Concurrent events in the social network can cause, mediate, trigger, moderate, or buffer stress (Hammer, 1981). Except for distress caused directly by members of a social network or caused by radical changes in the character of the network (especially loss), the availability of *social support* is indicative of better adjustment. The quality of the support is paramount, and support that is unconflicted enables coping (Sandler & Barrera, 1980). That many people with persistent problems have limited access to unconflicted support has prompted Pattison and his colleagues (1979) to distinguish three kinds of social networks: the normal, the "neurotic type," and the "psychotic type." His portraits of these distinct networks are as follows:

Normal: 22–25 persons, with 5–6 in each of four subgroups (family, relatives, friends-neighbors, and social or work associates); person has frequent contact and the experience is emotionally positive; network members provide each other with instrumental assistance and relationships are symmetrically reciprocal (viz., Bretherton, 1980). Network provides consistent norms and expectations, resources for stress management, emotional support, little conflict, a sense of distance and respect, and access to larger networks.

Neurotic: About 15 people in network, higher reliance on nuclear family ties, frequent negative and weak emotional interaction, many seen infrequently or not at all. The interconnectedness of network members is not uniform. This network is impoverished and isolating. Interactions are characterized by avoidance of contact and ambivalent connections. Asymmetry is common and easy reciprocity is not normative. There is no reliable set of social norms and expectations to guide or provide feedback. Stress is catalyzed into anxiety and symptomatology

Psychotic: About 10 to 12 network members, almost all interacting with each other. Relationships are negative or ambivalent and asymmetric. The person is trapped by a "collusive closed system" with few outside linkages. High degrees of stress are not buffered, leading to the production of dysfunctional instrumental acts. (Pattison *et al.*, 1979, pp. 65–66; see also Pattison *et al.*, 1975)

In another report, Pattison and Pattison (1981) describe the "intimate psychosocial network" of schizophrenics. Such networks are generally characterized by the inclusion of people with whom there is no long-term relationship and the exclusion of socially salient others, by emotional ambivalence, and by emotional confusion and captivity. Froland *et al.* (1979) compared four groups: a group of ward patients in a state hospital, a group from that hospital's day treatment program, a set of outpatients, and a "normal" sample from the community. Their description of the first three groups is similar to Pattison's. The networks of all three clinical groups were smaller in size than those of the community sample; had fewer ties with kin; fewer differing sources of friendships; fewer long-term friends; less interaction with family, friends, and relatives; fewer friends who knew family members; and greater degrees of instability. The authors portrayed the poor adjustment of these people in network terms as a "disaffection for family and experience of instability in relationships, and inability to obtain help or assistance without engendering feelings of burden in the network" (pp. 42–43). Tolsdorf (1976), in an interview study comparing hospitalized psychiatric and medical patients, found parallel distinctions. The networks of psychiatric patients involved fewer people but served more interpersonal functions, and the exchanges were again nonreciprocal. Those members of the network who were functioning best were in a more dominant position in the psychiatric networks. Furthermore, all the psychiatric participants reported strong negative feelings about their networks, which predated their symptoms and often were dated to early childhood, corroborating the point made earlier about the persistence of early network deficits. Patients actively strove to prevent their networks from helping by not divulging sufficient information to enable others to be helpful. When advice was offered, it was not followed. Finally, the networks of psychiatric patients could not be mobilized to handle life events: "The psychiatric subjects experienced some significant life stress with which they attempted to cope using individual mobilization. When this strategy failed, they chose not to mobilize their networks, relying instead on their own resources, which had already been shown to be inadequate. This resulted in more failure, higher anxiety, a drop in performance and self-esteem, followed eventually by a psychotic episode" (Tolsdorf, 1976, p. 415). Certainly, these networks were not perceived as dependable or reliable, characteristics that would encourage help-seeking (Lieberman, 1982). Even if access were possible, it is unclear whether the networks of seriously distressed people could routinely be expected to provide the effective feedback and coping resources needed to handle stress. The restricted range of contacts, the relative instability of the network, and the lowered interconnectedness within it are structural correlates of the lack of psychological support of these networks. Similar results have been well summarized by Hammer, Makiesky-Barrow, and Gutwirth (1978), who propose a theory of schizophrenia based on inadequate acquisition of expected behavioral patterns due to lack of consistent, socializing feedback from networks. Finally, the unusual study of mental illness in rural Laos discussed above (Westermeyer & Pattison, 1981) yielded consistent evidence of the distinctive quality of the networks of 35 *baa* Laotians.

The mental health correlates of social networks are most forcefully seen in studies of the impact of life events on individuals. Holmes and Rahe's (1967) work served to quantify an intuitively clear relationship between the amount of change particular life circumstances require of an individual and the subsequent mental and physical stress. The general sequence of events is outlined by Rabkin and Struening (1976):

Social
stressors   Mediating   Onset of
of life   →   factors   →   Stress →   illness
events

These general formulations have been subject to considerable critical scrutiny, and the low significant correlations between the occurrence of life events and subsequent dysfunction have stimulated more sophisticated frameworks (e.g., Hultsch & Plemons, 1979). Cassel (1974) argues against the utility of views that environmental stressors will have specific etiological power and that this power will follow a doselike gradient. There is little uniformity to the impact of distinct events because the meaning of the events is so highly idiosyncratic (Streiner *et al.*, 1981) and because much variability is introduced in the above equation by "mediating factors." Yet there are certain givens:

1. Life events are ubiquitous: In a study of 2300 Chicagoans, 85% of the interviewees reported at least one important life event over a 4- to 5-year period (Lieberman & Mullan, 1978).

2. Life events involving serious disruptions in social networks can be debilitating (Brown & Birley, 1968; Dohrenwend & Egri, 1981).

3. Life events are more problematic if one is unaccustomed to them; i.e., familiar events require less disruption in behavioral routines (Eaton, 1978). Overall undersirability of events is more predictive of outcome than frequency of occurrence (Gersten et al., 1977).

4. Perhaps the most powerful set of mediators independent of the individual's prior response to similar occurrences is the availability of social support (Cobb, 1976; Dean & Lin, 1977).

The data about the social network correlates of most people's current mental health are clear and consistent. For each of the events listed below, there is evidence of the mediating role of social support. (Although most of the research testifies to the buffering role of networks, it seems equally likely that relevant inquiry would produce ample evidence that conflicted, uneven, or destructive "social support" would be similarly powerful.)

1. *Parenthood* (Abernathy, 1973): structurally tighter networks provide both emotional support and physical help, but they also furnish consistent interpretations of infant behavior and thereby prevent conflicts. Social network contact and sense of parental competence are correlated.

2. *Early childhood* (Sandler, 1980): the presence of two parents and older siblings is associated with less maladjustment.

3. *Unemployment* (Gore, 1978): social support can ease the transition to unemployment and prevent increases in illness.

4. *Adolescence* (Burke & Weir, 1978): the more satisfactory the informal help provided to youth by their parents, the more positive is adolescents' view of life in general; they experience less stress and report fewer symptoms and fewer negative affective states.

5. *Middle age* (Menaghen, 1978): among help-seekers with concerns about their own children (adolescent and adult), less distress is associated with greater use of family members as helping resources.

6. *Divorce* (Colletta, 1979): parents with support were found to be less likely to resort to spanking their children.

7. *Marriage* (Burke & Weir, 1977): the more stress in a marriage, the more pronounced is the positive effect of help received from spouses. Greater satisfaction with marital help is correlated with greater self-disclosure, greater trust and reliance, a larger repertoire of potentially supportive behaviors, and a more active use of these behaviors.

8. *Pregnancy* (Nuckolls, Cassel & Kaplan, 1972): more women with high "psychosocial assets" (i.e., social support networks) ended their pregnancies with normal (versus complicated) births than those with deficient resources.

9. *Life-threatening illness* (myocardial infarctions: Finlayson, 1976): wives whose husbands had favorable outcomes acknowledged help from a wider network.

10. *Unexpected injuries* (road accidents: Porritt, 1979): providing a caring and empathic network is associated with better recovery, better work adjustment, and greater life enjoyment.

11. *Aging* (Lowenthal & Haven, 1968): the presence of one important other in a diminishing social network is crucial to positive adaptation.

12. *Bereavement* (Walker, MacBride, & Vachon, 1977): the availability to a widow or widower of a social network of others who have successfully weath-

ered this loss provides both strength and a model for mastery when personal resources are close to depletion.

It seems safe to summarize these findings by saying that responsive, caring networks, which are usually tightly knit, are essential for emotional support and for connections through the network to broader social resources (whether informal or formal help, material aid, or other resources). It must be remembered that in the case of most life events the social network is not a detached set of uninterested bystanders. Indeed, the likelihood that events have meanings for both the person and important others makes them stressful: "It is not so much the event itself but the effect the event has on the role-functioning of individuals in day to day living that is the major source of distress in human lives" (Lieberman & Mullan, 1978, p. 516). The meaning of an event for a person-in-a-network is exceedingly complex, but it is no accident that concerns related to loss of loved ones are the thematic commonalities in many events and their meaningfulness. Brown and Harris provide a poignant example: "One of the patients developed a severe depression a few weeks after the birth of her first child. Several weeks earlier her father had died. His death was in no way part of the context of the birth. . . . But, for the woman, his death appeared to have been an ever-present part of the significance of having her first child; she could not help thinking of how she had looked forward to him seeing his first grandchild and now he could not see it" (1978, p. 110).

The meaning of events, the quality of one's support network, the nature of one's social skills and resources—all of these factors interact to individualize life circumstances. A lack of social skills, vulnerability, and isolation from supportive others pose severe threats to people's ability to cope. Indeed, it may be possible to reinterpret the various hypotheses relating social class to psychopathology by replacing social class with social network characteristics, a line of reasoning followed by Hammer and co-workers (1978). The greater prevalence of severe psychopathology among the poor, in this view, is a reflection of the more severe life events experienced, the uncertain social resources available to the person and his or her support network (which, for example, cannot purchase services or material goods that could mitigate stress), and the fact that the only available exogenous sources of help are institutional systems run by middle-class professionals.

Stressful life events have been most consistently linked to schizophrenic episodes and to depression. Brown and his colleagues (Brown & Birley, 1968; Brown & Harris, 1978) have argued that in schizophrenia events are *triggers*, whereas in depression events are *formative* because they create dysfunction in previously well-functioning individuals. In the 1968 study, Brown and Birley examined the rate of stressful life events during the four 3-week periods before the onset of the schizophrenic episode. They argue that for schizophrenia, in particular, emotional arousal itself is debilitating, so they

include both positive and negative events. They also considered all events
that might be associated with the presence of schizophrenia. They found
that 95% of the independent events (those which the patient's condition
could not have elicited) were clearly out of the person's control. Nearly one-
half (46%) of the patients had at least one stressful independent event in
the 3-week period immediately before onset of the disorder. A large percentage of the events occurring near onset were unexpected. In addition,
many of the homes of these people were troubled by chronic tension of a
low level, so that the events occurred against a backdrop of routine vulnerability. Dohrenwend and Egri's (1981) analysis is complementary to Brown's.
They too discern unanticipated events outside the person's control as causes
of breakdown, especially those events that strip one of social support. They
extend the point by noting that our cultural reaction to schizophrenia (i.e.,
fear and lack of support) increases the stress of life events. In addition, they
wonder how any life event cannot be perceived as threatening in the family
of a schizophrenic: "We believe that a person who has first-degree relatives
diagnosed as schizophrenic and/or as suffering from possibly related disorders is likely to experience stressful events as a direct result of his or her
family situation—events that are more clearly outside his or her control than
such ordinary events as changes in job and residence" (p. 19). In their view,
the social network of the schizophrenic is chronically troubled, and life events
can easily lead to demoralization and symptomatology.

Brown's later study (Brown & Harris, 1978) shows how clinical depression develops as a result of everyday events. Brown and Harris compared
three groups of women: those with clearly diagnosed clinical depression,
those with some symptoms (borderline cases), and those with minor or no
symptoms (normals). They found that at least one-half of the depressed
women had a recent life event of etiological importance. Most important
were events with a "marked long-term threat," i.e., events that focused on
the person herself or jointly with another, or in which the person played a
causal or critical role. The common features of precipitative events are loss
and disappointment. The events involved six kinds of loss or disappoint-
ments: separation or the threat of it, an unpleasant revelation about someone else, a life-threatening illness to someone else, a major material loss or
disappointment (or threat of either), an enforced change in residence (or
threat of it), and a group of crises involving loss (for example, being considered useless in a former job). It is important to see these events as resulting in discontinuities in assumed plans, as disruptions in the synchrony
of self and others, as changes in role identities and relationships. Self-esteem, locus of control, and the sense of affective and instrumental mastery
are the phenomenological consistencies that can be shattered by life events.
Although it is true that lower-class individuals may, almost by definition,
have fewer sources of strength in crisis, it is misleading to consider social
class per se as causative. Problems in social integration and social embed-

dedness in communities, neighborhoods, and families are easily overshadowed by the social class construct. The less educated and the poor are more exposed to hardships and, at the same time, less likely to have the means to fend off the resulting stresses. Not only are life problems distributed unequally among social groups, but it is apparent that the ability to deal with problems is similarly unequal (Pearlin & Schooler, 1978, p. 17). The social origins of depression, Brown and Harris (1978) conclude, are not socioeconomic. They use as evidence data on the incidence of depression on an isolated island in the Outer Hebrides. In that setting, more important in predicting depression was whether or not a particular woman was brought up on the island, whether she lived in a crofting or fishing family, and how regular her church attendance was. Simply put, society provides protective social networks, but those of the poor are unfortunately less able to provide the help needed to successfully weather difficult life events. The four major risk factors discovered by Brown and Harris (1978)—lack of a full or part-time job, lack of a close relationship with one's spouse, having three or more children in the household under the age of 14, and the loss of one's mother before the age of 11—are generally more likely to occur among poor women. But it is probably the occurrence of these events, not their social class context, that is the sufficient cause of breakdown. Loss and tension are the essential precursors and correlates of dyfunctions in mental health, and no doubt they are caused and manifested in different ways in diverse social and cultural groups.

A concise summary of the mental health correlates of social support networks can be provided by a brief review of Garrison's (1978) provocative analysis of the support systems of Puerto Rican women in New York City. She conducted an extensive study of the naturally occurring support networks for five groups of women: three groups of neighborhood residents, a group of outpatient schizophrenics, and a group of inpatient schizophrenics. All were first-generation migrants and 90% were born in Puerto Rico. She found seven kinds of social networks. Brief definitions follow:

1. *Rotarian network:* consists of 15 to 25 important people and up to 200 acquaintances. Husband is most common support figure, although 34% of these women have used a spirtualist helper.

2. *Good friend network:* same as the first, except one friend in neighborhood is confided in more than anyone else. This network is typical of women without spouses, for whom the confidant is a psychological substitute.

3. *Sectarian network:* church-connected network.

4. *Grouping network:* social and emotional supports are found in group activities, not dyadic interpersonal relationships.

5. *Cultic network:* primary source of aid and support is from spiritist cult participation.

6. *One friend pattern:* network consists solely of one other person.

7. *Null pattern:* network involves intense parent–child dependency in which adult is closely bonded to older generation. No nonkin relationships exist and kin networks are truncated, involving one or two family members.

Her data show that the continuum from the ideal/normal Rotarian type to the null pattern is associated with increased incidence and severity of emotional disturbance. The schizophrenic women are withdrawn and isolated, and their few interpersonal contacts are shallow or highly dependent. Garrison's study demonstrates the richness of an analysis that combines social network and social class views of psychopathology, suggesting that in a pluralistic society there are subcultural variations on the social network theme. She also notes that the well-intentioned strategies of mental health professionals to treat mental illness by routinely attempting to rekindle family ties betrays an ethnocentrism that will most likely be self-defeating. This caution is an apt one with which to begin a discussion of the uses of social networks in treatment of mental distress.

SOCIAL NETWORK INTERVENTIONS

The use of social networks to improve mental health is based on a simple proposition that relates to the foregoing discussion: "If certain types of networks can be unambiguously shown to have positive psychological effects, this should serve to give greatly increased impetus to attempts to aid the psychologically distressed persons by helping them to restructure their social networks" (Brim, 1974, p. 328). The inherent truth in this idea must be contrasted to the long history of reluctance in mental health services to embrace a network view of either psychopathology or behavior change. It is naive to assume, for example, that current interest in social support networks has resulted from disenchantment with the medical model of psychopathology which, in its psychological variant, assumes that the person has acquired a deficit and that a relationship with a professional other in a one-to-one context will be curative. The paradox of helping is that despite the long tradition of viewing social contexts as causative (especially, of course, the family), relatively few have argued the need for methods of psychotherapy that involve network members. Indeed, traditional psychoanalytic therapy explicitly strives to exclude the actual significant other while encouraging the analysand to convert the therapist into a symbolic surrogate so that transference and its analysis will occur. Although it is easy to rail against the preempting of significant others in such views, it is more realistic to understand that the social networks of distressed people have been so unambiguously indicted in their etiological role that separation became required. Most prominent early theorists conceptualized therapeutic endeavors as "prosthetic networks," to use Beels's (1978) term. The assumption that change within the interpersonal therapeutic context would generalize to other interpersonal contexts was not always explicit (though Sullivan [1953] is a worthy exception), but the exclusion of a person's social networks from active involvement served to thwart short-term and long-term outcomes.

The rejection implied by an intimate relationship between one's spouse and a significant other (therapist) is a predictable by-product of this model of intervention, one seldom detailed in professional circles. Thus, although social networks have been viewed as central to change, most models of helping have implicitly relegated them to backdrop status. Therapeutic processes can be seen as "the purchase of a network," to alter Schofield's (1964) idea. Interest in social networks has not been spurred by the limitations of these exchanges, but rather by the need for a humane social policy to guide the deinstitutionalization of those whose networks had, in more liberal days, been provided by public largesse.

Although most interventions that are provided for mental health problems are interpersonal, there has been a consistent trend toward increased active involvement with social networks. Pattison (1977a) details the history of this movement from involvement of parents in the 1920's to group psychotherapy in the 1930's, to family therapy in the 1940's and 1950's, to the more recent work with multiple families and even extended families. This trend is also reflected in changes in institutional settings over time: the mental hospital as refuge yielded to mental hospital as milieu, which evolved into a community mental health center (CMHC). The CMHC started as a community vehicle for traditional services, but also, at least for awhile, took into consideration the social context of the community and its institutions and how this context might affect psychosocial problems. Just as individual psychotherapists do not feel sanctioned to confront social networks, CMHCs were never able to deal consistently with broad socioenvironmental circumstances. The inability of our mental health systems to design circumstances that would remove symptomatology can be seen as the consequence of the mistaken belief that artificial social networks can be instrumental in producing lasting change in everyday life. The illusion that people can be saved from pernicious social involvements without replacing those involvements with more positive ones (and *technology* for designing a social network that provides affective and instrumental aid may be in principle unlikely) has led to recognition of the powerlessness of mental institutions and skepticism of the preventive functions of CMHCs. Bassuk and Gerson (1978) conclude on a note of resignation: "One must accept the fact that psychiatry is not now able to cure some forms of severe emotional disability, and that psychiatry alone cannot assume the broad responsibilities of a society to care for its helpless fellows" (p. 153). The exclusive focus of our mental health programs on the person without an accompanying emphasis on his or her social network has led to this impasse and simultaneously suggests the solution.

Deinstitutionalization provided both a natural experiment on the strength of mental patients' social networks and a challenge to consider how to create social support. The problems that arose from a policy that essentially dumped patients in local communities with neither support nor aftercare exemplify the inhumane nature of our attitudes toward the chronically mentally ill.

The plight of people whom society had earlier deemed worth isolating—many of whom spent years in total institutions acquiring patterns of dependency that no psychotropic drug could so consistently produce, and most of whose relationships with their networks were strained and distant at best—must be considered one of the major tragedies of our times. The resident population of our mental institutions has been reduced by two-thirds in a 20-year period (Bassuk & Gerson, 1978), and reintegration of the 1.5 million chronic patients living outside institutions (Platman, 1982) has often taken the form of tragedy: "Many of them drift to substandard and inner-city housing that is overcrowded, unsafe, dirty, and isolated. Often they come together to form a new kind of ghetto subpopulation, a captive market for unscrupulous landlords. Their appearance and their sometimes bizarre behavior may disturb the neighborhood and they are usually shunned and frequently feared" (Bassuk & Gerson, 1978, p. 50). It is accurate, though demeaning, to say that these individuals are the victims of a "systems transition" (Turner & TenHoor, 1978). The prototypical "system" in which many chronic patients end their transition is the single-room-occupancy (SRO) hotel in the inner-city. In a series of studies, Cohen and Sokolovksy (Sokolovsky et al., 1978; Cohen & Sokolovsky, 1978) demonstrate that networks develop even within these seemingly alienating environments. Several distinct social groups emerged in a New York City hotel: "matrifocal quasi-families" in which a dominant Black woman feeds, protects, and cares for 6 to 11 tenants; drinking-socialization cliques revolving around central males; three-to-five person food-sharing groups; card players; and two-to-four person female social cliques. Certain residents quickly become stigmatized, their odd behavior earning the labels "vegetables" or "lunatics," and thereby reinforcing their social isolation. The residents of the hotel were categorized as schizophrenics with moderate to severe chronic symptoms, schizophrenics with miminal symptoms, and people with no psychopathology. Schizophrenics were found to have smaller networks, although not even the worst schizophrenic was totally isolated. The schizophrenics with or without residual symptoms who had small, nonmultiplex networks with low degrees of connectedness had higher rates of rehospitalization than those with extensive networks. No density differences were found, but the schizophrenics with minimal symptoms were predictably able to form more instrumental linkages. For those who formed few, if any, links outside the hotel, the lack of linkages within the hotel may have been the most influential factor in readmission. Since 9 of the 10 severely troubled schizophrenics and 8 of the 19 mildly troubled schizophrenics were readmitted (Cohen & Sokolovsky, 1978), the SRO cannot be considered a necessarily better attempt at constructing social networks for mental health than the mental hospital. The availability of social support as buffer does not ensure that active access is possible, certainly not for someone who is deemed a "vegetable."

Active efforts to develop community helping networks for formerly chronic patients can change the course of events. Rehospitalization is an adaptive response to demoralization, because there is every reasonable expectation that some caring and meeting of material needs will be provided. Artificial networks such as the lodges that Fairweather (1979) pioneered and the mobilization of family and community resources are alternatives, since it is unrealistic to assume that every ex-patient will live independently. The SRO hotel is a social organization poorly designed for the problem.

> At the present, it appears that the typical situation is of a man or woman aged 30 living with one or both parents aged 60 or more years. The individual has to cope with the after-effects of his/her illness, the possibility of relapse, continuous medication, and difficulties in picking up the threads of a normal life again. The parents have to cope with a grown-up son or daughter who is socially isolated or dependent on their care, but often demanding of time and energy, and unpredictable from day to day regarding behavior or mood. (Platman, 1982, p. 294)

Families whose chronic problems were partially responsible for the onset of the illness are, of course, easily overwhelmed and need help from neighbors and local agencies. The "myth of rehabilitation" (Turner & TenHoor, 1978) and the "myth of reintegration" must be replaced with a realistic attempt at network building that recognizes that this will be difficult because the patient may not be the most ingratiating help-seeker nor will his or her family exhibit the kind of genteel assertiveness that yields results from human service providers. Community support systems are not the pseudonetworks of earlier mental hospitals but are networks of "caring and responsible people committed to assisting a vulnerable population to meet their needs and develop their potentials without being unnecessarily isolated or excluded from the community" (Turner & TenHoor, 1978, p. 329). An outstanding example of how this network can be developed has been recently provided by Edmundson and colleagues (1982). Their Community Network Development Project (CNDP) operates through peers to mobilize support and resources for ex-patients. Critical to the CNDP's operation is an intermediary, an advocate for each client, someone whose responsibility is to involve the patient's network in his or her adjustment to community life.

Other specific applications of social network ideas to treatment exist. *Network therapy* (Speck & Attneave, 1973 Rueveni, 1979) mobilizes the entire set of social connections of a distressed family, enacting tribal meetings in which mutual responsibility for help is facilitated. Rueveni's (1979) report exemplifies the process: a couple who sought help for marital problems soon began focusing on their tensions with their adolescent son in front of a "network assembly" of 35 family members, relatives, friends, and neighbors. In his view, the only way to discourage the intergenerational transmission of madness is to intervene at the network level, shaping open and direct expression of conflict and eliciting support, solidarity, and reassurance in the face of life events. Pattison *et al.* (1975) describe a model for *psychosocial systems therapy*, which works against the cultural norm that excludes the extended kinship system from continuing involvement in each other's lives. Both approaches assume that networks can be expected to be helpful when given responsibility for others. Interpersonal models for psychotherapy have been proposed (e.g., Carson, 1969; Benjamin, 1977), but these will not be reviewed here, nor will the efforts to teach social skills (skills needed to develop and maintain social contact and relationships) be discussed, since they are reviewed in detail elsewhere (e.g., Asher, Oden, & Gottman, 1977; Trower, Bryant, & Argyle, 1978; Gresham, 1981).

SUPPORT NETWORKS AND THE MAINTENANCE OF MENTAL HEALTH

HELP-SEEKING IN COMMUNITIES

Dohrenwend and Dohrenwend (1981) recently summarized the conventional wisdom about the prevalence of mental disorders in our communities. Anywhere from 16 to 25% of the population might be viewed as having mental disorders, and an additional 13% or more suffer from severe psychosomatic distress for which no diagnostic label can be provided. The statistics represent those who, at a given observation, demonstrated characteristics associated with distress. These data most likely underestimate those who during any particular life event could be said to be seriously stressed. Since we know that life events are unavoidable and that many are difficult, we need to explain why more people do not become clinical cases. Clearly, individuals maintain their own mental health with little help from the rank of mental health professionals. Most people prevent psychopathology in their own lives, intentionally or unwittingly, by tapping naturally occurring helping networks or by gravitating toward the informal, aprofessional help of self-help groups and community caregivers, thus providing themselves with "lay treatment" (Gottlieb, 1976). When subjects were asked by Froland (1978) to whom they would turn in a series of hypothetical problem situations, there were distinct differences among a group of community residents and three groups of psychiatric patients: the patients placed much more emphasis on professionals, whereas those in the community strongly relied on their families. Whether this represents a professional colonization of family functioning or an accurate appraisal of sources of help is unknown, of course. But we do know that access to formal help is mediated by natural networks: "Few help-seekers take a socially independent approach to making their decisions about service utilization. Most people, instead, talk to their friends and to other community contacts they have, using these people's past experience and accumulated knowledge to help them sift through the agencies and sort out the best match for themselves" (Gottlieb, 1981, p. 80).

Much evidence has accumulated on informal help-seeking. In a short report entitled "Upon Whom Do You Depend?," Morosan and Pearson (1981) ask four questions:

1. Who are the people upon whom you depend?
2. What type of support do you receive from them?
3. What sort of interpersonal support do you find yourself lacking?
4. How could you go about remedying those support deficiencies? (p. 5)

Partial answers were provided over 20 years ago by Gurin, Veroff, and Feld (1960). One-quarter of their sample of 2,460 adults reported a problem for which professional help would have been useful, though only one-seventh actually sought help. Of the latter group, 28% consulted traditional sources of professional help, 42% consulted clergy, and 29% consulted physicians. Of those who reported turning to a nonprofessional person for help with worries, most (56%) named their spouses. Friends were the most common source of help for "unhappiness." J. R. Ewalt presented this comment in his staff review of the data:

> What do they do about day-to-day worries, or their periods of unhappiness that are not seen as requiring professional assistance? Many do nothing, or forget about it, essentially passive reactions that permit the situation to run its own course. Those who try to cope with their troubles on their own often turn to their spouses, other members of their families, or friends. Another sizeable group prays. Sixteen percent pray as a means of handling their daily worries and even more—a third—pray when faced with a critical unhappy period in their lives. (In Gurin, Veroff, and Feld, 1960, p. xxiii)

One of the authors of that report has recently updated the results (Veroff, 1981), she found that 14% of the men and 26% of the women in her sample admitted to fearing a "nervous breakdown." Large proportions (34% of the men, 48% of the women) agreed that they sometimes felt that problems were too hard to handle. When asked about social supports, only 9% of the men and 5% of the women reported talking to no one about problems. Although women were twice as likely as men to talk to friends often or very often, 85% of the men and 93% of the women had some, if intermittent, help. Several other studies have documented the way most mental health problems are handled within natural networks (Leighton, 1959; Gottlieb, 1976; Fischer et al., 1977; Srole et al., 1977; Warren, 1981; Young, Plantz, & Giles, 1982). Indeed, in a recent study of social support during divorce, Chiriboga, Coho, and Roberts (1979) found a much greater percentage of respondents considering friends rather than counselors as "most helpful."

There is apparently some consistancy in patterns of help-seeking, with men seeking help less often, with older adults seeking less help, and with Blacks seeking less help (Gourash, 1978). Brown (1978) found that those who do not seek any informal help fall into two categories, the *self-reliant* (who have strong networks and considerable resources) and the *reluctant nonseekers* (whose networks are unsupportive and unreliable, and who have reservations about access to them). The nature of the life event is important in understanding the help-seeking process. Most evidence shows that physical illness sooner or later leads to professional help-seeking. For marital problems, the help of one's spouse seems important whereas for psychological problems, friends are more helpful (Lieberman, 1982). During different phases of widowhood different social resources are helpful (Lieberman, 1982). Superiors at work have been shown to be resources for some but not all kinds of problems, (Burke & Weir, 1975), with the more personal problems being more difficult to discuss. All but 4% of a sample of 663 parents who lost a child said they turned to others for help, and most turned to multiple sources (Lieberman, 1982). Interestingly enough, dissatisfaction was most frequently reported with contacts with professional helpers. Norms of help-seeking follow the life span, with early life and old age being the most socially acceptable times to enact a help-seeking role. As Lowenthal and Robinson put it: "In our culture, only in old age does it become acceptable to seek help for rather vague or minor symptoms of psychological or physical fragility" (1976, p. 452). Surprisingly, in one study, only 55% of those who received help from spouses, relatives, or friends believed they had a right to expect such help, as compared to the 73% of those receiving professional help for whom the help was the essence of the exchange (Schreiber & Glidewell, 1978). Finally, there is some question about whether access to informal help matters, and in one study the outcomes did not differ for those who consulted their informal helping network and those who did not (Lieberman & Mullan, 1978).

This final generalization, of course, must be challenged since it runs counter to most suppositions about helping networks. Fortunately, Lieberman himself provides the appropriate qualifer: "We believe the major source of unexamined information that could critically affect our findings is the lack of specificity about kind of help given, for how long, with what quality, and based on what level of relationship" (1982, p. 16). Lowenthal and Haven (1968) showed that women who have been widows for 7 years and who have confidantes have higher morale than married women with no psychosocial intimacy in their lives. Closeness of helping networks, intimacy, and attachment are all qualitative dimensions of informal help that must not be considered of secondary importance. Consider the following turn of events taken from Hagestad, Smyer, and Stierman's study of middle-age divorce:

> Among the respondents who had parents living at the time of the marital disruption, nearly one-half of the men and three-fourths of the women said that

they discussed marital problems with their parents. When they did *not* talk to the parents, it was typically that they expected disapproval or lack of understanding from the parent. One woman said, "I am afraid to say it, but at fifty I am still afraid of what my mother thinks—she intimidates me. I was divorced almost a year before I told her—until she finally asked me. I hope my children don't feel that way about me." (1982, pp. 16–17)

Burke and Weir's research (1981) demonstrates consistent superiority of "process" helping, that is, helping that focuses on the person's *emotional circumstances and is appropriately responsive and caring.** When asked what kind of help they would prefer, people reported that directive behaviors were less valued, contrary to a usual equation of help with action. These results were corroborated by Young, Plantz, and Giles (1982) in a study of help-seeking in rural communities. Croog, Lipson, and Levine (1972) found that support was highly valued by men and women recovering from myocardial infarctions. The evidence is consistent in every study in which qualitative questions were asked. The nature of the presumed or actual response of a helper to a request for help, which in circumstances not involving illness is often equated with failure and lowered self-esteem, must be a critical factor. Although for material and physical needs the mere availability of networks is perhaps more important than their nature, it is the very essence of mental health that demands a *responsive other*. Furthermore, the exchange of helping resources between network members is not of a quid pro quo nature. Rather, as Schreiber and Glidewell (1978) note, the helpful interactions are those that are mutually enabling. Lowenthal and Robinson (1976) describe the regret in middle age of men who meet their needs for intimacy solely through marriage and who find their friendships to be shallow and impersonal. Such friendships may operate as buffers under certain stressful circumstances, but their limitations across the life span are obvious. How people in one's social network react to the vulnerabilities produced by life events determines whether one is able to cope successfully (even if this is via self-reliance) or whether one withdraws and becomes increasingly isolated. In describing the needs of the elderly, Gelfand and Gelfand (1982) argue that weak ties are important for a sense of control and independence, but that strong ties (those produced by high-quality exchanges) are essential for "emotional growth" and for the completion of the "life review." Guttman writes in a similar vein:

---

*This raises the question of what is help. Is help that is supportive and caring more helpful than help that is directive or even judgmental? The ideological history of the helping professions has not provided a distinct answer. Social influence is undoubtedly at the heart of any kind of help. Unfortunately, without objective assessment of the quality of help (which may ultimately be provided only by empirical data on outcome), qualitative concerns about helping networks will be unevenly addressed. The perceived transient experience of the help by the helpee can hardly provide an unbiased assessment.

Despite the availability of formal supports—i.e., government and church—it is mainly the family and ethnic friends in the neighborhood to whom elderly people turn in case of need, and their life satisfaction is closely connected with family relations. For almost one-third of the respondents, having a good family life is an important source of happiness. It is not astounding, therefore, that one-half of the sample did not prepare financially for an illness requiring long-term care, indicating that in case of such a crisis they will turn to their families for help. (1982, p. 25)

A helpful social network is not a "community of limited liability" in which individuals feel little personal responsibility for the mental health of others. Helping networks, rather, provide those interpersonal commodities Weiss (1974) described: attachment, social integration, opportunities for nurturance, reassurance of worth, a sense of reliable alliance, and guidance. Thus, not all informal linkages are helpful, just as not all professional helpers, self-help groups, or mutual support groups are helpful.

FORMS OF HELPING NETWORKS

That most people encountering life events turn to informal before formal help suggests that such natural helping takes many different forms. Informal help can be offered in group meetings in community facilities or in the privacy of one's home, with a friend, spouse, or relative. The continuum is one of self-consciousness: To what degree do the interactants call what they are doing "helping?" Libertoff recounts the following:

As long as people around these parts can remember, the old country lady, uneducated and coarse in appearance and speech, has been viewed as a natural helper, someone to turn to for advice, counsel, food, healing, occasionally money, or just a long, personal chat in front of her constantly burning wood-stove. Like many folks native to this region, she is a person who chooses her words carefully but when she speaks, people listen.

On a cool but sunny spring day, somewhere near the end of mud season and the sudden rush of spring, the old lady and I stopped to chat. During the course of our conversation, I began telling her of my interest in the way rural folks seem to help one another, particularly those who are obviously in need of assistance. She smiled knowingly when I told her that she was part of this natural helping network and laughed when I marveled over how the system seemed to operate without the assistance of professional human service workers. (1980, p. 5)

Contrast this helping network with the equally aprofessional, but more structured and formal help supplied by one of the half-million self-help groups providing mutual aid (Jeger, Slotnick, & Schure, 1982). Indeed, there is a need to distinguish among the variety of community networks providing informal help, because their structure, function, "entrance requirements," and natural histories differ. Politser and Pattison (1980) found five community group types with differing degrees of structure: self-interest groups, self-help groups, social communion groups, civic development groups, and recreational groups. If one views mental health as a broad mixture of community involvement and personal development, it is clear that these groups are implicitly mental health networks. Yet the existence of these groups does not ensure the transaction of quality help, as was noted above. To contrast Libertoff's accessible community helper with the help provided by a group of fellow cancer patients (see Kleiman, Mantell, & Alexander, 1976) and to emphasize the structured nature of the latter group is to once again assume that contact is intrinsically helpful. Indeed, arrogance is hardly confined to professional helping. Kleiman, Mantell, and Alexander complain of the lack of sensitivity of some volunteers in Can-Cervice (a mutual support group for cancer patients) and their intransigence:

> Most volunteers assumed that their experiences with cancer had endowed them with intuitive insights into the emotional problems of fellow cancer patients. As one remarked, "A feeling came over me in my first visit that whatever I said would be instinctively right." This sense of omiscience led volunteers to resist the American Cancer Society staff's control of the training and credentialing of the volunteers. "Who amongst you can judge us?" was the leitmotif of early discussions over the suitability of individual volunteers. (1976, p. 407)

Although it may be that the more devastating life events are such that the presence of another person is life-protecting, this should not obscure the consistent conclusion that psychological closeness is a requirement for helping. Physical proximity is correlated with intimacy, no doubt, but it is not a sufficient condition. Froland et al. (1981) detail six kinds of informal helping: from family and friends, neighbors, natural helpers (whose lives are centrally oriented to helping others), role-related helpers (community gatekeepers or those located in a central community location), people with similar problems (self-help, mutual aid groups), and volunteers (informal helper in a formal organization). Froland and his colleagues also distinguish *embedded* networks, in which ongoing helping is facilitated by other reasons for prolonged contact, from *created* networks, which are the "prosthetic networks" that are artificially developed. The nature of the helping exchanges most likely differs in these two kinds of networks. Little choice but to help may occur in the embedded network of adult children caring for their older parents (Lieberman, 1978), the family coping with a handicapped child, or the spouse trying to help his or her mate weather displacement from a job. Helping in such networks is less an option than a duty (Schreiber & Glidewell, 1978), and it involves a long-term commitment and sense of responsibility.

That so much focus in mental health services has been on created networks (see Gartner & Riessman, 1977, for example) most likely reflects both skepticism about the actual helpfulness of embedded networks and the frustration of knowing that these networks may be inaccessible to professionals "doing good." Created networks are often like professional services in that they generally have articulated models of help, clear roles for help-giving and help-receiving, and, often, hierarchical relationships among members. Compared to embedded networks, created networks are more vulnerable prey to the peril of professional ownership. Natural helpers, on the other hand, do not see themselves as competing with formal services.

Paradoxically, agencies attempting to help socially disabled people (e.g., chronic patients and handicapped children) become integrated into the mainstream need to employ formal networks to encourage the development of embedded networks. For long-term social integration, a consistent caring network is required, one that is not purely a result of temporary agency interest. Certainly embedded networks evolve among people living together over time, even in SRO hotels:

> We have observed that the attitudes and behaviors of several of the most important nonschizophrenic leaders indicate that a tacit chasm exists between themselves and the other tenants. These persons envision themselves as pseudo-staff. In many ways they are: One man of 63, with a BA degree in philosophy, conducts classes in his room for six tenants who wish to earn a high school equivalency diploma; a 40-year-old black woman not only heads the largest quasi-family but also runs the hotel's lunch program and weekly bingo games. (Sokolovsky et al., 1978, p. 10)

But too often the emphasis is on agencies fulfilling such critical functions, a strategy that is appropriate for short-term material needs, but in the long run, will most likely be self-defeating. Informal community helpers who have skills in maintaining helping networks are more likely to be successful. Nearly one-half of Guttman's (1982) sample of ethnic elderly reported social isolation to be a prominent problem. Can a human service agency create a network without careful analysis of the networks in which Estonians, Poles, Lithuanians, Latvians, and Hungarians are naturally embedded? Does not the lack of consistent relationships between mental health agencies and the religious networks of 62% of our population (Pargament, 1982) reveal a misunderstanding of how embedded networks promote mental health? That current estimates find from 50 to 85% of our population involved in voluntary associations (Wagner & Chapman, 1978) provides direction for the enrichment of networks for helping. Unfortunately, as Schreiber and Glidewell lament: "Help, however, has become specialized and professionalized. . . . Our research implies that, in 1975, at least half the adults in the Chicago area believed they had no rights to receive help from family and friends and that family and friends had no duty to supply help" (1978, p. 450).

"NETWORK LIBERATED" PERSPECTIVE

It would be unfortunate for human service agencies to consider the development of helping networks as the newest of an endless series of service system designs to meet the often documented need for help. This kind of "service" is radically different from the usual innovation because it permanently "subcontracts" help to natural environments. At various levels, the interests and abilities of people to care for themselves and their significant others must be developed and reinforced. There is no question that these networks will never replace the artificial networks of professional and institutional helping. Social isolation of a long-standing nature will make access to naturally occurring informal help difficult at best. For those with social network deficiencies, active efforts at creating networks are essential. This no doubt is a difficult task since it involves teaching social skills as well as arranging responsive social resources. We can no longer assume that we can mainstream those among us who have chronic problems of ambivalent (for whatever reason) attachments to others. We must realize that such people will experience life stress with acute sensitivity because they are not routinely buffered nor are they able to ask for help from intimates, who do not exist.

Others, indeed most of us, who are embedded in important networks must be able to seek support from others and value it. The stigmas attached to help-seeking must be decreased. The current recognition that routinely occurring life events may be stressful to anyone can be the spur to a willingness to be vulnerable. In a parallel fashion, attempts can be made to enrich natural helping without interfering with its spontaneity. Communicating to communities that it is appropriate (if not obligatory) to be concerned with one another, to families that they do indeed have the power to promote mental health; and to individuals that it is important to talk to friends and neighbors about difficult problems can strengthen helping networks, whereas campaigns to promote local mental health services can inadvertently demean the power of networks. Berger and Neuhaus (1977) have called for the enrichment of "mediating structures" to bridge the gap between the private and public lives of people. They suggest that these structures (the family, religious organizations, and voluntary associations) be strengthened and bolstered in our pluralistic society. This is the key to developing networks for mental health. Self-help and mutual support groups can also be added to their list of mediating structures. The very interdependence of these bonds provides their strength: "In informal support systems which may include kith and kin, mutual help associations, and self-help groups, acting in one's own interest is less likely to result in purely self-serving action, since the intimacy of the relationships such systems require are bound to promote a concern for how one's actions affect the well-being of others as well as oneself (Lewis, 1982, pp. 5–6).

CONCLUSION

The perspective that coping is an individual's responsibility has evolved mostly from clinical contexts where dysfunctional individuals are diagnosed and treated. The facts have been overlooked that people have learned how to cope in social networks, that inadequacies in social networks are partially responsible for dysfunction, and that networks must be involved for long-term community adaptation (Pearlin & Schooler, 1978). Not only does a clinical bias lead to the individualistic view of coping, but our cultural ethos of individualism expects self-sufficiency and resourcefulness, not interdependence. We may well have become a "community of limited liability" in which helping others to cope has become the function of a cadre of professional service providers. The social network model offers an escape from this collective egocentrism, providing a framework to help the isolated and to enrich the development of those embedded in social networks. Professionals will need to avoid interfering with social networks and instead should strive to strengthen and expand them. Empirical research can be instrumental in this task by describing the operations of naturally occurring helping processes and by determining the linkages between specific helping events and mental health consequences. Human service agencies can use the results of such research in collaborating with informal helpers to strengthen and enrich the caring provided and to supply the kinds of professional help unavailable in helping networks. An active collaboration between human service agency staff and informal helpers will help to avoid the view that promoting mental health in communities is merely a technological problem. As Ivan Illich put it: "Crisis understood as a call for acceleration not only puts more power under the control of the driver, while squeezing the passengers more tightly into their seat belts; it also justifies the depredation of space, time, and resources for the sake of motorized wheels, and it does so to the detriment of people who want to use their feet" (1977, p. 4).

ACKNOWLEDGMENT

I would like to thank the following helpful members of my social network for their useful comments on an earlier draft of this chapter: Robert Burgess, Steven Danish, Judith Frankel D'Augelli, Laurie Garduque, Ted Huston, Mick Smyer, Graham Spanier, and Carol Lawton Vernon.

CHAPTER 4
Social Support Networks in Health Care and Health Promotion

Betty J. Blythe

People need people in ways that health care professionals have only begun to examine. As our accelerated spending on the treatment of disease and disability fails to yield proportionately striking results (U.S. Department of Health, Education, and Welfare, 1979b), we are beginning to look beyond traditional health care activities for solutions. A host of studies suggests that social contacts play a role in determining whether people become ill (Berkman & Syme, 1979; Heller, 1979; Pilisuk & Froland, 1978). Facilitating the development of these contacts into social support networks has potentially preventive and rehabilitative functions.

Unfortunately, little has been written about the use of social support networks by human service professionals in health care settings. This chapter provides an overview of the evidence about the relationship between health and social support. It describes efforts to build formal social support networks for promoting health and methods of tapping clients' informal networks. Potential barriers to applying social support networks in health settings are identified. A discussion of future research, clinical, and educational issues concludes the chapter.

THE RELATIONSHIP BETWEEN HEALTH AND SOCIAL SUPPORT

Despite the fact that an empirical relationship exists between health and social support, the exact nature of the relationship is unclear. A review of the research suggests that social support reduces the risk of physical disorder, aids the recovery process, and provides a buffer against traumatic or stressful experiences.

REDUCING THE RISK OF ILL HEALTH

Numerous studies document the association between social support and reduced risk of physical disorders. For instance, married people have fewer illnesses across most classes of health problems and live longer than their single counterparts (Kraus & Lilienfeld, 1959). Additional convincing evidence comes from a cross-cultural study of coronary heart disease among Japanese men living in Japan, Hawaii, and California (Marmot & Syme, 1976). Although the highest rate of heart disease occurred among the Japanese men living in California, these men were less likely to experience elevated blood pressure or coronary disturbance when they maintained a traditional Japanese lifestyle that included strong family ties. This effect was independent of such common coronary risk factors as smoking, improper diet, and obesity. Other research indicates that the ties may not have to be familial to be effective. As an example, membership in a closely knit religious group is associated with reduced incidence of cancer and heart disease (Phillips, 1975). Similarly, Miller and Ingham (1976) found that adult men and women who had a confidant and friends in the neighborhood or at work reported lower levels of such physical symptoms as backache, headache, palpitations, dizziness, and breathlessness than those without such friends. Data from a longitudinal study of residents of Alameda County, California suggest that individuals with any one of four types of social relationships (marriage, contacts with close friends and relatives, church membership, and formal and informal associations) have lower mortality rates than people without such ties (Berkman & Syme, 1979). This correlation was found to be independent of socioeconomic status and health practices. On the other hand, at least one study proposes that the socioeconomic status of social network members may be important in determining preventive health behaviors. This survey of 383 adults suggests that individuals in networks characterized by high socioeconomic status and frequent interaction with neighbors, friends, and other nonfamily are more likely to use seat belts, to exercise, to maintain good nutrition, and to obtain regular medical examinations, dental care, and immunizations (Langlie, 1977).

AIDING THE RECOVERY PROCESS

Another area of research indicates that social support may be an important variable in the recovery process for people already suffering from physical ailments. Field experiments reveal that treating people with myocardial infarction (heart attack) at home may carry less risk than treating them in intensive care in hospitals (Mather, 1974). If treatment occurs in a hospital, emotional support from physicians can be a positive influence on the course of heart disease (Chambers & Reiser, 1953). Special supportive care from anesthetists may lead patients to require less pain medication and be discharged earlier than those without such care (Egbert *et al.*, 1964). These studies have clear implications for human service professionals working in hospitals.

The role of social support in the recovery process indicates that supportive ties can increase the likelihood that sick people will take care of themselves. Two reviews provide overwhelming evidence that social support variables are positively related to staying in treatment (Baekeland & Lundwall, 1975) and to complying with prescribed medical regimens (Haynes & Sackett, 1976). Gottlieb (1976) cites data supporting the notion of a "lay referral network" to explain the tendency for social ties to be an important factor in determining whether people experiencing symptomatic distress seek treatment. In this model, members of the lay referral network are consulted about health problems and appropriate treatments. Whether such referrals support or hinder the use of professional medical services depends on the values of the network.

PROVIDING A BUFFER AGAINST STRESS

Several authors hypothesize that social ties provide a buffer against traumatic or stressful experiences, thereby preventing stress-induced illnesses or other untoward physical consequences (Cobb, 1976; Eisenberg, 1979; Pilisuk & Froland, 1978). Partial support for the buffering theory comes from studies indicating that the loss of social and emotional relationships is associated with physical disorders. Death rates from coronary heart disease, for instance, are higher for divorced, widowed, or never-married people than for those who are currently married (Weiss, 1973). Likewise, loss of an important emotional relationship, change of residence or school, marital problems, and parental separation (for a child) are all related to cancer (Sklar & Anisman, 1981). Even more persuasive are studies of the relationship between social support and the incidence of health problems. Women who scored high in life change (e.g., shifts in daily routine, marital status, or economic resources) before and during a pregnancy and who had high levels of social support resources had only one-third as many complications during pregnancy as women with high life change scores and few social support resources (Nuckolls, Cassel, & Kaplan, 1972). Equally persuasive is Caplan's (1971) report that NASA administrators, engineers, and scientists were less likely to experience work-related stress and physiological strains if they had high levels of supportive interpersonal work relationships.

These empirical findings have obvious implications for health care professionals. Certainly, social support networks can be engaged to foster prevention of health problems. Such networks can promote remediation by helping sick people adjust to health problems, by preventing further deterioration of their health, and by improving their compliance with medical prescriptions. Human service workers must recognize that, aside from using medical and hospital services for immediate care and supervision, sick people are more likely to turn to family, friends, and neighbors for aid than to agencies and professionals (Croog, Lipson, & Levine, 1972). Whether or not social services have adequate financial resources, we will do well to acknowledge and enhance the potential of our clients' social support networks.

MODEL PROJECTS USING SOCIAL SUPPORT NETWORKS

Social support networks promote healthy behavior by providing material goods or services, emotional support, or referral and information about other resources (Unger & Powell, 1980). The projects outlined in this section all provide one or more of these forms of support. Formal networks, such as self-help groups, tend to develop when informal sources of support have broken down (MacElveen, 1978). Although most of the projects described here involve formal social support networks, informal networks are also discussed.

HOSPITAL VISITS

Individuals adjusting to new health conditions often find it helpful to talk to people with similar conditions. Thus, hospital wards that group patients suffering from the same disorder foster the development of informal support networks. In a more purposeful way, members of formal networks visit hospital patients who are experiencing the initial adjustment to a new physical condition. Such visitors offer emotional support, answer questions, and provide models of effective coping. They may facilitate patient–staff communication or connect the patient with an ongoing support network.

Reach-to-Recovery, conducted by the American Cancer Society, is a visitation program for women who have had mastectomies. Because current mastectomy procedures usually require that the mastectomy be performed during the same operation in which the diagnosis is made, the patient may have had little opportunity to talk about what the surgery means to her or what it involves. Moreover, many women find it easier to share questions and concerns with a visitor who has experienced a mastectomy than with a health professional who has not. The visitor may also play an important role but her contact is limited. Further, the visitors rarely meet in groups despite the program's formal network structure. There is little ongoing supportive contact among volunteer visitors or among visitors and visitees. Nor are all patients visited, because the visit by a Reach-to-Recovery volunteer must be requested by the attending physician. Finally, all volunteers are selected and supervised by the American Cancer Society and must take its pamphlets and prosthetic equipment to the visit.

Following a less structured approach, general hospitals sometimes arrange for newly disabled patients suffering from a variety of handicapping conditions to be visited by successful "veterans" on a case-by-case basis. Usually the visits are arranged when a patient is especially anxious or depressed. Guggenheim and O'Hara (1976) describe two such cases. The first, a 53-year-old housewife whose left leg was amputated and whose right leg was in danger of being lost, was visited by a 36-year-old man, an accountant, who had lost both legs and was confined to a wheelchair. In the presence of a nurse, both patients described their accidents, and the accountant related his stages of adjustment. He demonstrated his mobility in and out of the wheelchair and explained how he coped with embarrassing situations. The nurse asked questions that the patient seemed hesitant to ask. Later, the patient said she would not have believed it was possible to be so well-adjusted to the handicap and that the visit helped her to persevere. In the second case, an older man, a factory worker recovering from paralysis caused by Guillain-Barré syndrome and temporarily mute, was visited by a young tradesman and former Guillain-Barré patient who led an active life. The tradesman recounted how lonely and frustrating his earlier inability to talk had been and discussed how he communicated with others during the recovery period. After the visit, the factory worker became less depressed and began to take a more active role in his rehabilitation. He maintained a friendship with the tradesman and later offered to serve as a visitor himself. Guggenheim and O'Hara suggest that the professional's role is that of catalyst who sets up the visit and perhaps is present to facilitate discussion.

The International Association of Laryngectomees, also sponsored by the American Cancer Society, coordinates a hospital visitation program, and provides educational pamphlets and a newsletter. The visitor, likely to be more convincing and comforting than a human service worker, provides the patient with a positive model. Meeting a laryngectomee who uses esophageal speech helps patients begin their own rehabilitation plan. Other models of coping appear in the bimonthly newsletter, which prints letters from members and features a column about active, successful laryngectomees.

A third visitation program is operated by Mended Hearts, an organization founded in 1951 by four patients recovering from heart surgery in a Boston hospital. The organization grew rapidly to 88 chapters with approximately 10,000 members (Bond et al., 1979), an expansion due in part to a national board and an increase in the number of heart surgeries performed each year. Members keep in contact through formal, monthly business meetings and monthly newsletters organized by local chapters. Mended Hearts is a good model for other formal social support networks, and has been accepted by medical personnel.

Mended Hearts volunteers receive 8 to 10 hours of training, including lectures and role plays, and must pass a knowledge test to become an accredited visitor. Patients are visited in the hospital before and after surgery. The guidelines for visitors, reprinted in Bond et al. (1979), emphasize the need for respecting medical staff. They advise visitors to limit discussion on one's own surgery and to be enthusiastic about hospital care. Visitors answer questions and provide family members with information about restaurants, lodging, and other necessities.

Individual chapters approach hospitals and closely coordinate the Mended Hearts Program with hospital staff. Some hospitals permit visitors to see all heart patients, while others grant permission on an individual basis with the consent of the social services department or the physician in charge. One of the principal functions of the Mended Hearts visitors is to facilitate patient–staff communication. They frequently give staff members feedback about the fears and needs of patients. Unlike many self-help groups, and perhaps a key to the organization's success, Mended Hearts visitors speak favorably of medical and other professional staff members. In fact, part of the visitor's task is to endorse the hospital staff. In turn, hospital staff tend to be supportive of Mended Hearts, thereby giving legitimacy to the organization. Although the visitors gain much satisfaction from their duties (Bond et al., 1979), their impact on visitees, as compared to unvisited heart surgery patients, has yet to be assessed.

SUPPORT GROUPS FOR INDIVIDUALS WITH SIMILAR HEALTH PROBLEMS

Social support networks may develop among individuals with similar health problems. Usually formal in structure and featuring regular meetings to exchange information and emotional support, these networks function without the stigma or dependency often implicit in social services delivered by agencies. Such networks help members learn to live with disabling conditions. Professionals may be instrumental in establishing and maintaining the network, may be consultants to the network, or may not be involved at all.

Sometimes the major functions of the network are to provide material support and information. The Kidney Transplant/Dialysis Association, a national organization with over 1,200 members, provides funds for kidney patients with financial problems, publishes a free manual and a bimonthly newsletter, and sends children on dialysis to a summer camp, which provides appropriate medical care. Because it lacks a program for helping kidney patients establish contact with each other, however, the networking effect of this organization is somewhat limited. Further, although many support networks use newsletters to provide information and emotional support of an impersonal nature, the effectiveness of the approach is uncertain and should be empirically tested.

Another example of a network serving people with similar health problems is the Epilepsy Foundation of America. Because of the stigma of epilepsy (Schneider & Conrad, 1980), the major effort of this national group is toward educating the community about the condition. Mutual support groups by several local chapters are offered to epileptics and their parents. Information and referral services and advocacy for individuals discriminated against because of epilepsy are also available. As with other organizations that lack a visitation program and rely heavily on printed materials, the number of people that the Epilepsy Foundation reaches depends on the strength of its outreach effort and on the assertiveness of others in seeking its services.

Social support groups need not be national organizations with several chapters. Riessman (1976b) describes a support group for individuals with scleroderma, a form of arthritis, at a New York medical center. Scleroderma can cause a range of problems including eating and digesting difficulties and gnarled hands. Although the hospital staff initiated this group, members soon began to plan and conduct the meetings themselves. At the first session, members discussed their symptoms and experiences in living with the disability. The focus quickly turned to methods of coping, as members described ways of dealing with family and friends, beneficial exercises, and self-care skills. Several members disclosed their solutions to such common problems as tying shoes, buttoning shirts, cooking meals, and driving cars. Although this ongoing group meets at the clinic, medical staff are invited to attend these meetings as consultants and to respond to specific requests. Information, as well as motivation and courage are benefits that members derive from the group.

One investigation attempted to evaluate the outcomes of a social support group. In an experimental study of methods for improving adherence to anti-hypertensive regimens, Caplan and his colleagues (1976) compared three treatment conditions: a social support group, a lecture group, and a no-treatment control group. The social support group met six times in 2-hour weekly classes conducted by a nurse. Group members received the same factual information as those in the lecture group. After a pilot test, the investigators altered their original plan of pairing patients so that they could provide each other with support and encouragement outside the group and after its termination because the pilot test showed that patients preferred bringing a spouse or friend to the group to serve as a "buddy." Because of schedule conflicts and lack of a supportive friend, however, some patients in the social support group did not have a buddy. The agenda for the social support group included a number of exercises, such as patient-centered problem solving, and described therapist behaviors, such as reinforcing patients' contributions to the group sessions, to further infuse social support into the sessions (see Caplan *et al.*, 1976, for detailed session agenda). Findings show that patients in the social support and in the lecture treatment conditions scored higher than control patients on measures of adherence to regimens. Control patients, in addition, felt less able to manage their blood pressure and rated information from their physicians as inadequate. Interestingly, the measured levels of social support were about equal in the social support and lecture group. This finding, the investigators argue, means that the study actually compared two supportive treatments to a no-treatment control condition. In other words, the lecture environment, even though it was not designed to be highly personal, may have been much more supportive than conventional staff–patient interactions in clinical settings. But whatever the condition, the spouse and the physician were reported as the two most important sources of support. In spite of the somewhat ambiguous findings, the idea of generating social support in a group is an important one for practitioners and suggests an area for further study.

Informal social support networks also exist for people with similar health problems. For example, Kleiman (1980) describes a network of five women with cancer in the Oakland area. In addition to supportive group meetings, the women are "on call" to one another as needed. Thus, when one woman required emergency surgery, the others hurried to the hospital to be with her. Studying informal networks like this one may help us to learn how to improve formal networks. This network may reflect what some of the other formal networks were like in their developmental stages. Learning the variables that determine whether or not people join informal networks and maintain their membership may suggest ways for formal networks to solve their membership problems. It may also be useful to assess structural differences between formal and informal networks. Do informal networks offer supports that formal networks do not? Do the guidelines and regulations of formal networks prevent or inhibit certain kinds of supportive interactions?

SUPPORTING FAMILY MEMBERS

Informal and formal social support networks can also help families of ill or handicapped people learn ways to cope with the disability. Emotional support is as valuable to many families as practical advice and information.

Some networks involve the disabled person and the family. Make Today Count exemplifies a large formal support network of this type. Founded in 1974 by a cancer patient, the organization now has 270 chapters, 70 of which are sponsored by the American Cancer Society. Because membership

is extended to all individuals with "life-threatening" illnesses and their families, members may have dissimilar health problems but similar life circumstances and experiences. This large pool of potential members has allowed
the network to grow rapidly. Members meet bimonthly for 2 hours in their
local chapters; discussion, led by coordinators trained by Make Today Count,
include such topics as diet, exercise, stress management, community services, and coping skills. The following brief exchange reveals how a cancer
patient, Lee, gets some advice about talking to her husband from another
member, Robert, whose wife has a terminal illness.

> "I'm concerned about my husband," Lee says toward the end of the meeting.
> "He tries to be brave and cheerful for both of us. But I'm not sure how he
> really feels. I wish I were."
> "Have you asked him" asks Rosemary, a "Make Today Count" coordinator.
> "No, not really."
> "Well, let me tell you how my wife did just that for me," says Robert, a regular
> volunteer. "One night when she felt up to the effort, she insisted that we go
> out for dinner. Over coffee, she asked me how I felt. Eventually, I told her,
> not without some tears, that I was scared to death of losing her." ("Make
> Today Count Chapter . . .," 1981, p. 8)

Family members who join may continue to attend Make Today Count sessions even after the death of the ill person because of the emotional benefits
of belonging to the network.

Another network that provides support focuses on Alzheimer's disease,
an incurable form of mental impairment in old age. This disability often
takes a heavy toll on the afflicted person's family. Early symptoms of the
disorder are memory loss, disorientation, and reduced attention to personal
hygiene. During later stages, speech, movement, and the senses may be
impaired, and 24-hour nursing care becomes necessary (Burnside, 1979).
This incomplete list of symptoms suggests the enormous difficulties faced
by family members of Alzheimer's disease patients. Family members most
severely affected are usually spouses, but may include siblings and children,
especially if the spouse is too old to care for the patient or decides to obtain
a divorce. Lazarus and his colleagues (1981) report that a support group for
"caregiving" relatives increased participants' ability to communicate with
the afflicted family member and helped the family to feel that they had
more control over their lives.

Several local support networks have developed to help family members
cope with the medical, emotional, social, legal, and financial implications of
the disease. For example, the Alzheimer's Support Information Service Team
(A.S.I.S.T.) of Bellevue, Washington, sponsors several family support groups
that meet regularly to share problems and solutions and help members cope
with loneliness, frustration, and emotional strains. The group emphasizes

the need for family members to maintain a support system, social activities, regular exercise, and at least one confidante. The group offers peer counseling and support by telephone. Finally, A.S.I.S.T. is establishing a legal, financial, and psychiatric referral network to address the multiple problems that often accompany Alzheimer's disease.

Formal and informal networks often are composed of parents of ill children. These parents, occupied with their children's needs, frequently have no one to listen to their own fears, anxieties, and feelings. Candlelighters, an example of one such network, is a loosely structured national organization of parents whose children have had or currently have cancer. Its Washington, D.C. office coordinates local groups and lobbies the federal government for cancer research and cancer control activities. Along with its advocacy function, Candlelighters provides crisis lines and buddy systems to give parents emergency and ongoing emotional support. Monthly small group meetings help parents develop bonds and learn ways to cope with emotional and other stresses produced by their child's illness.

When disabling conditions cannot be remedied, support networks may aid family members, particularly parents, to adjust. Families may have to help children complete rehabilitation programs, learn to use special equipment, or adjust to their disability. Two such conditions, amenable to surgery but rarely corrected totally, are cleft palate and cleft lip. In addition to funding research, the American Cleft Palate Association sponsors local groups that provide emotional support and information to families with cleft palate and cleft lip youngsters. For example, a local chapter in Massachusetts sponsors a newborn program in which new parents are matched with experienced parents of cleft palate children. The experienced parents offer concern and practical help in monthly group meetings and thus ease the new parents' adjustment.

Networks in this category might also work with families and other individuals to build a social support system for the afflicted person. A unique Australian program works with parents, health professionals, teachers, and employers to overcome barriers to hemophiliac adolescents becoming personally and financially self-sufficient (Bellamy, 1977). Therapeutic groups for parents, along with outreach and education to specific teachers and community members, help to assemble a variety of supports for the hemophiliac.

Further illustrating possibilities for helping families, Kaplan and Mearig (1977) describe how a community support system was fashioned for a family in which three sons have muscular dystrophy. In this instance, an informal support network has provided emotional support and a range of material goods and services. First, a project was initiated to fulfill the family's housing requirements. Through a local architect, a service club supplied materials and labor for two bedrooms, a specially equipped bathroom, and a wheelchair ramp. Beyond the convenience and comfort of the addition, this project helped the family feel less isolated and more emotionally supported despite the hopelessness of their sons' disease. In addition, the family was aided by two student organizations at the local university. One group provided a live-in student to take the boys to school and to perform other tasks; in return, the student received free room and board. Both student groups raised money for a van that accommodated wheelchairs. Money was also provided for a vacation for the parents. During the parents' vacation, the students cared for the sons and built a sewing room and dining nook. Students also helped the parents deal with bureaucratic hassles when they became too tired or frustrated to be their own advocates. The relationship between the student groups and the family entailed reciprocal helping: the students received assistance in problem-solving from the parents, the experience of contributing to the welfare of others, friendship, and opportunities to learn. The family often invited students and community helpers to its celebrations. This extended, informal network, coordinated by a retired pediatrician and a psychologist, expanded the family's ability to cope with their sons' problems and provided psychological and material rewards for their helpers. The outcome far exceeded that of most professional services.

TEACHING NEW HEALTH BEHAVIORS AND SKILLS

Social support networks can be instrumental in helping people learn new skills and behaviors. Usually, the goals are changing unhealthy habits or promoting healthy lifestyles. The well-documented influence of peers on people of all ages underlies the important role of informal networks in developing healthy and unhealthy habits (McAlister, Perry, & Maccoby, 1979; Radelet, 1981). Nevertheless, although people may decide to join or to avoid social networks on the basis of health practices among group members, such network influences are not always obvious or consciously manipulated.

Childbirth and parenting are life experiences during which people often need to learn new skills. As extended families become less common and because people move more frequently away from their families of origin and their enduring social networks, new parents find themselves relying on health professionals, classes, and self-help books. Yet these resources are inadequate when at 4:00 A.M. and a baby has been crying inexplicably for hours. Understandably, parents are reluctant to call the pediatrician with minor questions about daily infant care (Mason, Jensen, & Ryzewicz, 1979). Moreover, couples are frequently unprepared for changes in marital relationships, social activities, and role expectations that accompany the arrival of a new child. As a result, they may feel isolated, confused, and unable to relax and enjoy their baby.

Formal and informal support networks for parents have developed to fill this gap (McGuire & Gottlieb, 1979; Wandersman, Wandersman & Kahn,

1980). Several groups help couples prepare for childbirth. Lamaze groups, for example, teach expectant fathers and mothers how to participate in and support each other during childbirth. Childbirth groups often meet again after the babies are born and many couples continue their friendship after formal sessions have ended, as they experience parenting together. Some local, informal networks help parents choose the kind of delivery that they will have, as doctors are frequently unable or unwilling to discuss alternative birthing facilities. These networks are valuable resources for couples searching for information about childbirth methods.

La Leche League International has been described as the "largest health network in the world" (Kleiman, 1980, p. 107). Since 1956, La Leche volunteers have provided information and support to women who want to breastfeed their babies. The group helps mothers overcome social obstacles to breastfeeding on the job, among friends, and elsewhere. Besides books, pamphlets, and a 20-page bimonthly newsletter, La Leche holds monthly meetings, usually in members' homes. For some women, League meetings provide the only situation in which their decision to breastfeed is fully supported. The most important source of support, however, is the 24-hour telephone service where volunteers answer members' questions about breastfeeding and provide encouragement.

The book by Mason, Jensen, and Ryzewicz (1979) is based on their experiences in developing a social support network for new parents. It can serve as a model for those trying to develop a formal social support network. The book describes how to screen and train volunteers, recruit and maintain membership, determine leadership, and handle legal issues. Another valuable resource provided by McGuire and Gottlieb (1979) suggests a framework for evaluating social support groups for new parents. The authors propose possible indicators of outcome and have designed and assembled measures for assessing outcome.

As fathers become increasingly involved in child care, human service workers should be aware that new mothers and fathers have distinct, albeit sometimes overlapping, needs for social support. Cronenwett and Kunst-Wilson (1981) suggest that any support network for new fathers provide emotional support, resource people who can contribute assistance and relief, information concerning coping with new personal and environmental problems, and sources of objective criteria for evaluating one's own performance. Wives, simultaneously adjusting to their new maternal roles, are unable to assume many of these supportive functions. In fact, spouses may be inappropriate sources of support—the expectant mother may not be the best person with whom the expectant father can share his problems with her pregnancy.

Exemplary of social support programs initiated by professionals and aimed at helping people learn new health habits is the Wallingford Wellness Project in Seattle, Washington (Mettler & Fallcreek, 1981). This health promotion effort uses a support network to teach people of all ages nutrition, physical fitness, stress management, assertiveness, and environmental awareness skills. Participants learn skills for improving or maintaining their own health and for advocating for a healthier environment. They meet in groups and are urged to bring their own support network to the 3-hour sessions—spouses, other family members, and friends of all ages are welcome. Group exercises maximize mutual helping among participants (Fallcreek & Mettler, 1981). Participatory leadership is practiced, and group members assume such tasks as determining agenda, preparing handouts, and making presentations. During the second half of each session, the group may take a lakeshore walk or tour a recycling center. These activities are usually determined by participants and encourage further network development. Finally, members practice new health behaviors together, outside of the sessions. Of course, participants vary considerably in ability. In order to overcome the difficulty in bringing participants together, group facilitators try to determine the contribution that each person can make to the group. For example, one person might know a lot about jogging whereas another may share with the group cooking expertise.

An innovative approach to using support networks to promote good health behaviors among older people uses peer tutors. One such program at the Turner Geriatric Clinic in Ann Arbor, Michigan, trains aged peer counselors to organize monthly health education workshops. The counselors also offer individual counseling and facilitate support groups in the community as well as in retirement and nursing homes.

Professionals often use social support principles when conducting groups designed to help members lose weight, quit smoking, reduce stress, and change other health behaviors (Blythe, 1981). Several interventive techniques foster an atmosphere of mutual helping. Having group members contract with each other to perform certain behaviors is one such technique. As an example, a member of a weight control group contracts to avoid desserts while his or her partner agrees to take four 20-minute walks during the coming week. After dyads complete contract negotiations, group members read their contracts aloud to the entire group to produce an additional element of public commitment. Buddy systems are also helpful. Participants choose one or more buddies with whom they exchange telephone numbers and schedule weekly phone calls to share progress reports; buddies are available during crises and after the formal sessions end. Group problem solving is another technique that helps build a supportive network in a behavioral-change group. In this case, participants describe situations that are difficult to handle—eliminating cigarettes after the evening meal, for example. Other group members share how they handled this problem or a similar one and generate new ideas to fit the particular participant's style. When they turn to others for consultation on difficult problems, participants discover that many problems have more than one solution. Less structured social support principles may also operate implicitly in behavioral-change groups. Clearly, a participant receives emotional support from a buddy's phone call, from group efforts to solve his or her problems, and from group recognition and praise for accomplishments. Simply knowing that others are experiencing similar struggles can render tremendous support and encouragement. Group members are also likely to be more willing, empathetic, and knowledgeable listeners than are other peers. Finally, the contribution of modeling should be recognized and fully exploited. Seeing others learn new behaviors and overcome old, deeply entrenched habits helps people realize that change is possible. As one member of a stress-reduction group put it, "Just knowing how much pressure Bill is under and watching him find time for these groups and for practicing relaxation exercises makes it easier for me to keep trying."

GUIDELINES FOR PRACTITIONERS

A range of social support networks exists that can help human service practitioners provide comprehensive health services to clients. Although social support networks have been in existence for a long time, many professionals lack experience in working with these less formal systems. Practitioners can identify, reinforce, initiate, consult, collaborate with, and refer to social support networks. A summary of guidelines for practitioners follows.

SUMMONING EXISTING INFORMAL NETWORKS

Most people prefer familiar faces and surroundings, especially when they are ill. Practitioners should bear in mind the potential resources within the client's family, friendships, and neighborhood. Some practitioners and agencies routinely ask about all of a client's existing and potential relationships during the intake interview and then maintain a record of the client's use of the network and the alterations in the composition of the network during the course of the service (Froland et al., 1981). Besides looking for potential resources, practitioners should be alert for gaps in the client's network. This is an especially important consideration in health care settings, given the evidence linking social isolation and health problems. Inquiring about recent friendship losses, especially among older people, and scanning for indicators of depression, loneliness, boredom, and grieving—are trademarks of thorough intake interviewing.

MacElveen (1978) stresses the importance of determining the client's "network style," a concept which refers to how the client typically meets needs for goods, services, information, and emotional support. Some people depend on themselves; others are interdependent with relatives and friends. MacElveen identified four network styles in a study of home dialysis patients. Criteria for determining network style are frequency of face-to-face visiting, of exchanging goods, services, and emotional support, and of sharing significant family occasions, holidays, and vacations. *Kinship* network style is characterized by frequent contacts with relatives for exchanging goods, services, information, and problem-solving assistance; socialization; and celebrating holidays. *Friendship* network style is similar to kinship network style in amount and type of contact but occurs with friends and neighbors. *Associate* network style involves regular contact with people sharing common interests such as work or recreational pastimes. Members of this type of network tend to give each other approval and recognition but less concrete help; they have fewer overall contacts than have individuals with kinship or friendship network styles. Finally, *restricted* network style refers to limited sharing and reciprocity with a small number of people.

The client's network style, as well as his or her particular needs and the resources available in the network, should be evaluated when the practitioner considers using the client's informal network. Then, if this approach seems feasible, the practitioner may need to help the client strengthen current relationships, renew former relationships, or develop new relationships in order to mobilize resources. During a crisis such as sudden or serious illness, some clients may be willing to make changes in their network style; they may become less restrictive, include new reference groups, or agree to increase the size of their network to include more people. In any event, the client, not the practitioner, decides what works best.

Besides recognizing a client's right of self-determination, human service workers must recognize that relatives and friends do not automatically qualify as natural helpers or social support–bearing resources. Practitioners should verify that members of the support network are capable of delivering the tangible or intangible support that is required. For example, a spouse or sibling may be physically unable to provide the necessary care for a handicapped person. Especially in cases of severe illness or disability, friends and relatives may have strong emotional reactions that leave them unable or unwilling to help. The possibility of past interpersonal strains is another reason for screening potential helpers.

Finally, agency managers and clinicians should note that mobilizing a client's network is time-consuming work. Network members typically are not reimbursed for helping the client, but the practitioner spends considerable time with each helper, providing support, education, feedback, and reinforcement. Practitioners must exercise patience, too, since natural helpers may be unable or unwilling to respond as promptly as professional services. Additional agency services are often required to supplement the resources in the client's network. In addition, if the client has a severe or long-term illness, natural helpers in the network may be unable to sustain their contributions. Agencies and hospitals sometimes have respite programs that allow helpers some time off from caring for ill family members.

PREPARING CLIENTS TO USE NETWORKS

In order to tap informal or formal networks for help of any sort, whether transportation, financial assistance, or companionship, clients must be able to express their needs to others and to accept offers of help. They also need good communication skills so that they can promote positive relationships with helpers and express appreciation.

All too often, those most in need of supportive networks are those least able to make effective contacts with network members (Caplan, 1979). For example, new members of Mended Hearts are usually patients who were themselves visited in the hospital. A survey of 779 heart patients suggests that people who join Mended Hearts tend to be "joiners," already belonging to several other organizations (Bond & Daiter, 1979). Perhaps social support networks largely help individuals who would help themselves anyway or those who have sufficient interpersonal skills to seek out supportive networks and similar forms of reinforcement. Conversely, it is possible that people who have the greatest need for the resources offered by a supportive network are those least able to approach the network or those most likely to undermine the efforts of its members. Although practitioners may have to invest extra effort to help clients make and maintain initial contacts with informal or formal networks, the extra support and encouragement should be rewarded as the network becomes able to help the client.

Practitioners should assess their clients' verbal and nonverbal skills, perhaps by observing the client interacting with network members. Accompanying clients to formal support network meetings provides an opportunity to view performances and to help clients become acquainted with group members and procedures. When necessary, practitioners can use role-play practice to teach clients more effective ways of communicating with others. An example from the author's practice shows how observation, feedback, and guided practice of target skills helped a young man with lung cancer benefit from a cancer support group. The client, Dennis, had alienated other group members by trying to dominate meetings, talking at length about his experiences, and failing to respond to the contributions of others. After audiotaping a session, the author replayed the tape to show Dennis how he was alienating other group members. During training sessions, I modeled and Dennis practiced ways of empathizing, listening, and paraphrasing. Although after these sessions, he was still a frequent contributor, Dennis received more support and reinforcement from others in the group as he learned to respond to their comments and to be a better listener.

Support groups may want to devote one or more sessions to communication skills. The Wallingford Wellness Project, for example, begins each series by teaching new members to listen, to give and receive feedback, and to express their opinions and feelings without offending others (Mettler & Fallcreek, 1981). Group leaders find that this preparation facilitates later group interactions and helps build supportive relationships.

SUPPORTING HELPERS IN INFORMAL AND FORMAL NETWORKS

Helpers in both informal and formal social support networks need reinforcement beyond the sense of personal satisfaction derived from helping others. Human service workers' own training and experience allow them to recognize and understand the delayed gratification and frustration that helpers may encounter. In short, helpers need reassurance that they are indeed helping clients and they need a chance to discuss problems they encounter.

The level of support given to a client by family, friends, and other network members appears to be related to the level of support helpers receive (DiMatteo & Hays, 1981). Not only must practitioners provide support, but clients (who sometimes need reminding) also must express their appreciation and offer understanding and encouragement to helpers. Such exchanges help families restore some of the equilibrium disturbed by the disability and ensure some rewards for helpers.

Nonetheless, burnout is common among natural helpers, friends, and relatives, especially when health problems are serious and the issues confronting clients are intense. Silverman (1980) suggests that helpers can be expected to continue in their roles for roughly 2 years, "particularly if the problem being dealt with is one, such as bereavement, that arises in the normal family life cycle" (p. 117). Even when helpers are working with routine problems, burnout may occur. Mason and her colleagues (1979) report a high rate of turnover among mothers on call to answer new mothers' questions about infant care.

Helpers are also lost to professionalization. Frequently they become interested in learning more about their work and secure advanced training. They soon become professional helpers, with the added advantage of having experienced first-hand the client's perspective. Sometimes new professional services emerge from helper's roles (Silverman, 1976). For example, services provided by members of a formal support network for ostomy patients led to a new profession, ostomy therapy.

Professionals need to be sensitive to helpers' burnout or their desire for more training and responsibility. Professionals should further be able to recognize when a helper is too frustrated, is overextended, or no longer shares the same interests as other members of the network. In fact, turnover of membership in networks can be a positive signal of new life, vitality, and direction for the network. Recruiting new members is an inherent part of work with social support networks.

SUPPORTING FORMAL NETWORKS

Agencies and individual practitioners can support formal networks through a variety of channels. In return, agencies receive additional resources to offer clients, and their clients are more likely to enjoy immediate attention from the network.

One of the most valuable resources an agency can supply is space. Often networks simply cannot afford to rent space unless they are large organizations. Hospitals and agencies, however, often have waiting rooms or lounges that can be used for group meetings, especially during evening hours. Access to typewriters, telephones, and office space is difficult, but not impossible, for agencies to arrange.

Referrals are another valuable contribution that agencies can make insofar as they expand the impact of formal networks. In actual practice, referrals go in both directions (Leutz, 1976). Thus, agencies and networks should periodically exchange information about services, eligibility requirements, fees, and other elements of accurate referrals (Gottlieb & Schroter, 1978). With careful communication, a formal support network and a human service agency can screen clients to ensure appropriate referrals, thereby enhancing their working relationship.

Agencies may even choose to sponsor the network. Sponsorship lends legitimacy to the network and increases referrals from the sponsor and from other sources. To some formal support networks, sponsorship may be crucial. As an example, each Mended Hearts chapter devotes sizable effort to obtaining hospital entry, a prerequisite for its visitation program. Mended Hearts visitors need cooperation from hospital staff to learn what patients are scheduled for heart surgery and when surgeries will occur. Some hospitals set aside a room for use by Mended Hearts visitors. Others grant blanket permission to visit all cardiac patients (Bond *et al.*, 1979).

Another way in which agencies and practitioners benefit support networks is by offering consultation (Baker, 1977). Of course, consultation helps network members only if it is invited and if it speaks directly to their request. For example, the scleroderma group mentioned above asked a nutritionist to speak at a group meeting. When the nutritionist began to give a general lecture on nutrition, group members politely but firmly asked her to respond to some of their specific concerns, such as high-potassium foods (Riessman, 1976b). In other words, professional consultation must respect the unique goals of the network and the cultural diversity and personal experiences of its members. Thoughtfully planned and delivered consultation increases helpers' knowledge of human behavior and extends the range of supports offered by the network.

Finally, practitioners may contribute to formal support networks by serving on advisory boards (Silverman, 1980). Such advisory boards help the network maintain ties with various professional organizations. Particularly in the health field, professionals are likely to have specialized expertise not otherwise available to members of a self-help group. Nonetheless, professionals should take care to offer their expertise only upon request. Since natural helpers may do things differently from professionals, practitioners serving as advisory board members must remain sensitive to the unique goals and services provided by the network. At the same time, they must examine their own ethical and legal responsibility for clients' health and general well-being, whether their professional role be that of advisory board member, consultant, sponsor, or referral source.

LAUNCHING FORMAL SOCIAL SUPPORT NETWORKS

Professionals who develop formal social support networks among present and past clients, or people in the community with similar problems, or both, usually aim to create adjuncts to agency services. Besides maximizing staff resources, this strategy helps individuals take greater responsibility for their welfare. Moreover, such a supportive network offers members a measure of empathy, understanding, and encouragement not available in most relationships with professionals.

Successfully launching a network requires that professionals thoroughly understand the nature of the health problem that unites network members. Clients' special needs must also be considered; sick individuals are often isolated because their mobility is hampered. Similarly, family members caring for incapacitated relatives may have difficulty getting away, even for 1 or 2 hours. Hence, network developers frequently must look for creative ways to bring network members to group meetings. Next, they must identify active helpers who can assume key roles in the emerging network. One useful resource in this area is supplied by Budman (1975), who offers guidelines for developing a social support network under professional auspices and then moving it outside the agency structure. He suggests initially bringing together clients or significant others for participation in a psychoeducational group. The professional's role in the group sessions is that of facilitator, enhancing group cohesion, encouraging discussion of personal experiences and of problems related to the disability, and fostering the exchange of various forms of social support. After formal group sessions within the agency end, the members may have formed a network that will continue to meet and can determine its own goals. When the network is functioning, professionals can move into the role of consultant, being mindful of previously stated admonitions to respect the group's autonomy. On the basis of her experiences organizing and developing a mutual help group for widows, Silverman (1980) provides another resource with detailed instructions for professionals embarking on this task.

APPLYING SOCIAL SUPPORT PRINCIPLES TO CLINICAL WORK

In some situations, human service workers are unable to organize or work with informal and formal social support networks. Nevertheless, they can use some of the same principles to increase the effectiveness of their routine work with clients. For example, the importance of unstructured or semi-structured social periods in group sessions should not be overlooked. This informal time allows members to get acquainted and to express anxieties, problems, and advice in a comfortable, nonthreatening atmosphere. At the same time, members begin to develop support networks that can function outside the group. Human service workers also may want to suggest that clients bring a friend or relative to group sessions. This associate helps timid clients feel less alone in a group of new faces. Furthermore, some continuity is established between what the client experiences and learns in the group and what occurs in his or her daily life.

In both individual and group work, practitioners themselves are a potential source of social support for clients. This contact will increase compliance with medical regimens (Caplan, 1979). Moreover, clients begin to view the health clinic staff as part of their social support network when staff members provide recognition, praise, encouragement, emotional comfort, and thoughtful answers to their questions.

That a client has at least one person to confide in is the final important consideration in all clinical work with individuals. Practitioners on hospital wards should encourage friendships among patients. Family members should be enlisted to monitor and support a client's adherence to the treatment regimen. At the same time, however, practitioners should consider potential unsolicited and harmful aspects of the client's social support network. Problems arise when network members interfere with compliance for any reason. Such interference may stem from lack of faith in the health care system, personal demands on the client's time or energy, or well-intentioned but misguided sympathy with the client's complaints. Moreover, members of the client's network may support such unhealthy habits as improper diet, smoking, or excessive drinking. Even though practitioners are unable to involve their clients' informal support networks, they should bear in mind the possible ill effects of such networks.

BARRIERS TO IMPLEMENTING AND USING SOCIAL SUPPORT NETWORKS IN HEALTH CARE SETTINGS

Ethical and legal concerns may suggest that relying on social support networks to provide client services is unwise, particularly in relationship to matters of health where mistakes can have grave and long-term implications. Natural helpers may be ill-equipped to respond to the needs or crises of clients who are seriously ill and to their families. Professionals may find that the legal risk of referring clients to support networks is too great. Natural helpers and their sponsoring organizations also must be concerned about legal risks. They can take steps to limit their liability with the help of legal counsel (Mason, Jensen, & Ryzewicz, 1979).

Another potential barrier to the use of social support networks is the status differential between helpers and practitioners. Helpers may feel somewhat in awe of professionals, particularly medical staff who have extensive, specialized education. Helpers may hesitate to act, fearing that practitioners are judging their work. Some helpers may feel inadequately prepared to help the client when they compare themselves to a professional who has advanced training and broad experience. On the other hand, professionals may undervalue helpers. Possessing a fair amount of education and experience, practitioners are likely to regard these qualifications as requisites for effective work with clients. Sometimes agency supervisors or administrators fear that clients will not be properly treated by helpers or that the agency will be at risk.

Just as some helpers are in awe of professionals, others have little respect or positive regard for practitioners. This can also form a barrier. People who are dissatisfied with conventional health care practices cite, with some accuracy, the fragmentation of the health care system, the impersonal treatment given by some practitioners in bureaucratic settings, and the failure to recognize that clients should have a voice in developing their own treatment plans. Although this frustration has spawned several self-help groups and formal support networks concerned with health problems, the members' distrust of health professionals and their contempt for mainstream health care often prevents collaboration. At the same time, an important element of collaboration, referrals, will be hindered.

Agency structure presents yet another kind of barrier to social support networks. The research of Froland *et al.* (1981) suggests that agencies that emphasize bureaucratic procedures and formal authority in service delivery may be less likely to enter into collaborative arrangements with informal or formal networks. "Chain of command" and methods of providing service are often obscure in social support networks. Hospitals frequently prefer and follow bureaucratic practices. Human service workers in such settings may find that they must move slowly; adapting the relationship with the network to meet agency standards may be a solution.

FUTURE ISSUES FOR SOCIAL SUPPORT NETWORKS IN HEALTH CARE AND HEALTH PROMOTION

Although they have existed for years, informal and formal social support networks have yet to be fully recognized and used by professionals. This section outlines basic research, clinical tools, and educational issues that remain to be addressed.

BASIC RESEARCH

The association between stressful life events and the onset, prevalence, and incidence of a wide range of physical disorders is well documented. Several authorities have posited that social support buffers the individual against stressful life events and subsequent illness (Dean & Lin, 1977; Heller, 1979). Gore (1978) argues that perceived social support may be more important than actual social support. Some studies suggest that loss of support, such as the death of a spouse or divorce, is a significant contributor to health problems (Heller, 1979). Basic research is needed to identify the mechanisms through which social support prevents or meliorates physical disorders.

Efforts should also be directed toward identifying variables relating to person, relationship, setting, and network that enhance good health and positive health behaviors. Such findings could specify points of intervention for practitioners and suggest further clinical research. The effects of demographic variables on perceptions of social support need to be examined (DiMatteo & Hays, 1981). For example, to what extent do ethnicity and social class determine whether or not a person is comfortable with support in the form of physical contact?

Few experimental studies of the efficacy of social support treatments have been conducted. By following standard rules of random sampling and using control groups and adequate sample size, research that aims to specify social support treatment methods will engender an improved definition of social support. Carefully defined outcomes should include measures of physical health and emotional well-being. Previous work by McGuire and Gottlieb (1979), Caplan et al. (1976), and others provide a basis for these research efforts.

CLINICAL TOOLS

Tools for quickly assessing the extent of clients' social support and their network style are needed. Because of the crisis nature of many health disorders and because of the multiple demands imposed on practitioners, rapid-assessment instruments are preferable (Levitt & Reid, 1981). Perhaps lengthy instruments developed for research purposes could be adapted to clinical settings (Luborsky, Todd, & Katcher, 1973; Caplan *et al.*, 1976). Certainly, prevention programs could use such tools to screen for individuals at risk; professionals working with sick clients could use the instruments to identify potential sources of support and to assess the likelihood that clients will take advantage of support networks.

Directories of formal support networks need to be developed to facilitate self-referrals and referrals by professionals. Surprisingly, agencies frequently are not aware of the resources available from support networks. Because they are less structured, support networks often change phone numbers and addresses, chapters open and close, and services are added or subtracted. Computerized information systems would be an ideal vehicle for organizing current and accurate information.

Although the literature points to the relationship between social isolation and increased health problems, little is known about how to reduce isolation. Working toward preventive measures, clinical researchers might begin to test methods of reducing isolation by helping individuals join informal networks. Teaching communication and other social skills may be a good starting point. Allied research might consider how to involve the hard-to-reach clients in formal support groups (Borman & Lieberman, 1979). Innovative outreach efforts, including sophisticated media techniques and enlisting the collaboration of other health care professionals, offer avenues for further exploration.

EDUCATION

Undergraduate and graduate programs in social and medical sciences need to include curricula related to the nature and function of social support networks. New and experienced professionals alike should be exposed to what is known about assessing social supports, identifying natural helpers, helping clients gain access to networks, evaluating the role of the health care professional, and establishing informal and formal networks. Training programs and in-services should also consider ethical and legal issues. Health planners and administrators, along with clinicians, need to be informed about social networks and ways to work with them.

In conclusion, informal and formal social support networks represent promising new approaches to providing services in health promotion and prevention. Given their history of concern for the client's social environment (Butterfield & Werking, 1981), human service practitioners are uniquely suited to design, conduct, and evaluate applications of support networks to myriad health problems. These efforts will increase clients' abilities to prevent physical disorders and to cope with illness.

ADDRESSES OF FORMAL SOCIAL SUPPORT NETWORKS

The following are addresses of the national offices of formal social support networks mentioned in this chapter. Most organizations have pamphlets, bibliographies, and newsletters available at little or no charge. Several have affiliate offices that can give more specific information about local networks and resources. The reader is reminded that these addresses may have changed since this chapter was written. If this is the case, public library reference desks, local health departments, and directory assistance operators can often provide current information.

Alzheimer's Support Information Service Team, A.S.I.S.T
1197–112th Avenue N.E.
Bellevue, Washington 98004

American Cleft Palate Association
331 Salk Hall
University of Pittsburgh
Pittsburgh, Pennsylvania 15621

Candlelighters Foundation
2025 I Street N.W.
Washington, D.C. 20006

Epilepsy Foundation of America
4351 Garden City Drive
Landover, Maryland 20785

International Association of Laryngectomees
219 E. 42nd Street
New York, New York 10017

Kidney Transplant and Dialysis Association
c/o Brigham and Women's Hospital
984 Washington Street
Dorchester, Massachusetts 02124

Laleche League International
9616 Minneapolis Avenue
Franklin Park, Illinois 60131

Lamaze
P.O. Box 20048
Minneapolis, Minnesota 55420

The Mended Hearts, Inc.
721 Huntington Avenue
Boston, Massachusetts 02115

Reach-to-Recovery
c/o The American Cancer Society
19 W 56th Street
New York, New York 10019

ACKNOWLEDGMENTS

The author thanks Molly K. Mettler, M.S.W., and M. Cecelia Runkle, A.C.S.W., M.P.H., for their critical review of this chapter. Ms. Mettler is Project Coordinator, Health Promotion with the Elderly Project. Ms. Runkle has worked as a medical social worker in hospital settings and is currently a doctoral student in Social Welfare at the University of California at Berkeley.

CHAPTER 5

Social Support Networks in Services to the Elderly

Nancy Hooyman

Helen is 84 years old and lives alone on $285 that she receives each month from Social Security. She has large medical bills from her husband's final illness. His pension stopped when he died. Although she is determined to remain in her small home, arthritis makes it hard for her to get around and to maintain it. Because of the crime rate in her neighborhood, it is difficult for her to go out at night. Her children live 1,000 miles away and, although they call frequently, she does not have as much interaction with them as she would like. She says that she wants to become involved in her community center but does not know whom to contact. Despite her worries about health and income, she remains optimistic and outgoing.

Helen's problems are typical of the kinds of situations facing many elderly people today. Although some formal services exist to solve Helen's problems, an informal system of family, friends, and neighbors could better address many of her needs. Numerous studies have confirmed the helping function of informal networks in the lives of older people. The elderly, like other age groups, turn first to an informal system for help before requesting formal services. In fact, even the most frail and apparently isolated and vulnerable elderly generally have some informal support networks. The presence or absence of such networks is a crucial predictor of an older person's well-being and autonomy. However, knowledge of how to develop effective interventions to create or strengthen informal supports for older people is recent and limited. In a time of scarce economic resources, it becomes imperative to formulate strategies to mobilize informal support systems for older people.

Informal personal networks are defined as a series of linkages along which information, emotional reassurances, and services flow to and from a person and his or her exchange relationships. These services may be economic, social, or emotional. What distinguishes informal social networks from traditional social service delivery systems is that within the former, exchanges are not formalized. Instead, informal networks rely on people caring about each other and on their natural helping tendencies. In addition to furnishing emotional support, informal networks provide goods and services necessary for daily functioning and special services during times of crises or exceptional stress.

This chapter reviews the existing knowledge about social supports for older people, identifies situations encountered in professional practice that are amenable to network interventions, describes programs designed to create or strengthen informal supports, and points to directions for research and practice. Demographic and social-psychological characteristics of the elderly are first reviewed, thereby highlighting the need for network interventions as one way to address the multiple health and social problems facing older people.

DEMOGRAPHIC AND SOCIAL TRENDS

The single most important demographic fact about the elderly is that because of medical advances, more people are living to face the challenges of old age. Nearly 25 million Americans (13.9 million women, 9.6 million men) or 11.2% of the population are over 65, an increase from 20 million or 9.8% of a decade ago. A man reaching 65 today has an average life expectancy of 13.9 years; a woman, 18.3 years. Approximately 59% of the population over 65 are women, and this group constitutes the fastest growing segment of the U.S. population. The proportion of the population aged 65 and over varies by race and ethnic origins: 8% are Blacks, 4% are those of Spanish origin, and approximately 6% are Asian Americans (Lowy, 1979). By the year 2020, largely because of the effect of the baby boom, individuals over 65 years of age will constitute approximately 32 million, or more than 15% of the population.

Moreover, the population of the very old will be increasing more rapidly in the years ahead. Presently, most older Americans are younger than 75. By the year 2000, nearly two out of three older Americans will be over the age of 75 (Lowy, 1979). This growth in the numbers of vulnerable or frail elderly, who generally have at least one chronic condition and may require multiple health and social supports, is particularly significant for human service practitioners.

A major consequence of an aging population is an increased demand for health care and social services. The population over 65 accounted for 25% of the federal budget (including Social Security), or $112 billion, in fiscal 1978. Despite the growth of health care services and medical technology, "we haven't, in some cases, been adding a lot of life to people's years" (Butler, 1979). Our culture, emphasizing youth and productivity, tends to view older people and the rapid increase in their numbers as a problem.

Yet aging itself is not the problem; that so many people are living longer is a success story. The problem is many of the conditions—poverty, chronic disease, mental illness, substandard housing, social isolation—facing older people.

Numerous myths and stereotypes surround the aging process. The older person is generally portrayed as passive, asexual, sick, and ineffective. The Western biological model of aging has tended to equate aging with disease. Most research has been conducted on the sick elderly; consequently, decline has been viewed as the key concept of late life. Contrary to these myths, most older people are mobile, are in contact with family, friends, or neighbors, and live in the community. Although 85% of the elderly have one or more chronic conditions, 81% are physically capable of getting around on their own without assistance. Approximately 8% of the elderly are homebound. Only 5% of the elderly are in institutions, although approximately 25% face institutionalization for some period of time before their death. Those with severe chronic conditions who attempt to remain in their homes have 80% of their home health care provided by their families. Less than 10% suffer dementia to some degree (Lowy, 1979).

It is important that human service practitioners take account of the tremendous diversity within the population over 65. Often, practitioners categorize older people and thus fail to recognize the different rates of the aging processes, both within and between individuals. In developing support network interventions, differences by gender, socioeconomic status, age (e.g., the young-old of 55–65 or the old-old of over 80 years), race, geographic location, and degree of physical and mental impairment must be considered.

The aging process does, however, bring some normal and intrinsic losses and stresses, such as declines in physical and mental capacities and losses of family members and friends. Other losses are superimposed by society, such as the loss of status, work, and income. Most older people are able to adjust to these losses, even though they may experience the common emotional reactions of grief, guilt, loneliness, or anxiety. For many elderly, however, these stresses and losses may result in physical and mental problems.

Such losses may have especially negative effects for older women, for minority elderly, and for the frail or "old-old" elderly. Older women like Helen, described at the beginning of this chapter, are more likely to be poor, to live alone, to be socially isolated, and to have chronic health problems than older men. Some older widows have difficulty forming friendships outside a couple's network. Even more so than older men, older women are likely to be culturally denigrated, especially by the mass media, and to incorporate the negative cultural view of themselves. Depression, alcoholism, drug misuse, and perhaps dementia are more common among older women than older men (Lowy, 1979).

The minority elderly face a position of triple jeopardy—that of being old, poor, and minority. They are more likely to live in poverty and to have more chronic health conditions than white elderly; the resultant role losses suggest that minority elderly would be particularly vulnerable to mental and physical problems. In addition, minority elderly undoubtedly face more barriers to utilizing formalized services. For example, Butler and Lewis (1977) describe how racial prejudice and discrimination affect both the quality and amount of mental health care available to minority elderly. For minority elderly, underinstitutionalization or inappropriate institutionalization, not over-institutionalization, tends to be a problem (Schafft, 1979). Minority elderly may be more likely to have and use extensive social networks than white elderly; in some cases, however, reliance on informal supports may result from a lack of formal sources and thus be by necessity rather than by choice (Schafft, 1979).

The population over age 75, or the frail elderly, presents a major challenge to human service practitioners to develop appropriate support systems. Although the frail elderly are more likely to be institutionalized, a large percentage attempt to remain in the community, often cared for by children or other relatives who are in their 60s and among the "young-old." Their needs are complex and long-term, often requiring multiple health and social services. The emotional aspects of their chronic illnesses may be as debilitating as their actual physical impairments. The frail or vulnerable elderly are the hardest to reach with appropriate services.

THEORETICAL PERSPECTIVES ON SOCIAL NETWORKS IN OLD AGE

A problem common to the majority of older people is a decline in their number of roles, their amount of interaction, and the variety of their social contacts (Lowenthal & Robinson, 1976). In fact, there has been controversy about the social-psychological impact of declining involvement in various social networks. This controversy is reflected in the ongoing debate in the gerontological literature among proponents of the various theories of aging (Havighurst & Albrecht, 1953; Cumming & Henry, 1961). Each of these theories takes a different view of the importance of an older person's involvement in social networks for his or her well-being. Various theories of aging—disengagement, activity, subcultural, developmental, and exchange—have influenced the design of social and health services and the formulation of specific interventions. Practitioners need to recognize the influence these different theories have on their expectations of the elderly's appropriate role and behavior. Whether one believes that aging is a withdrawal from active participation, that activity is essential to successful aging, that how one ages depends on lifelong habits of coping, or that environmental supports are necessary to compensate for diminished exchange resources, the theory in each case clearly affects the way in which providers perceive and interact with an older person and the kinds of interventions they are likely to use.

Disengagement theory, the most controversial, has had perhaps the most negative effects of segregating service systems for the elderly (Cumming & Henry, 1961). Reflecting the common-sense observation that older people are more subject to ill health and the probability of death than their younger counterparts, disengagement theorists asserted that a process of mutual withdrawal normally occurs in order to ensure both an optimum level of personal gratification and an uninterrupted continuation of the social system. For example, older people move out of social roles in order to make room for younger people, to maintain a balance between their own reduced energies and demands, and to conserve their emotional resources in order to prepare for death. The development of separate services, especially for the elderly who are chronically ill, reflects the assumption that disengagement is universal, inevitable, and functional for both the older person and society.

Activity theory presumes that people continue to adhere to middle-aged standards and expectations as they age and that activities must take place to offset the losses of old age, preserve morale, and sustain self-concepts. People are assumed to remain socially and psychologically fit by keeping active (Havighurst & Albrecht, 1953; Maddox, 1970). Practitioners who adhere to activity theory advocate that services and activities should be developed for older people, such as golden age club activities, senior centers, and other leisure pursuits. Activity theory, however, has received only limited empirical support and has been criticized as an oversimplification of the issues involved.

In contrast to the activity theory assumption that people continue to adhere to middle-aged standards and expectations as they age, the subcultural perspective asserts the development of a distinctive aged subculture (Rose, 1965). A strong relationship exists between peer group participation rates and the adjustment process of the elderly (Rosow, 1967; Hochschild, 1973). Individual involvement in an aged subculture depends on the solidarity of the age group itself, plus the nature and extent of contacts retained with the total society through families, the media, employment, or the older person's own resistance to aging. The development of an aged subculture is assumed to provide the basis for political and social action by the elderly.

The developmental perspective on aging conceives of personality as continually evolving, with adjustments at each successive stage reflecting earlier coping strategies as well as the matrix of current environmental factors (Birren, 1964; Havighurst, 1968). Most developmental psychologists also see a gradual turning inward over the life course, with older people being less attentive to external events and networks, and more attuned to their own inner states. Such turning inward could be a barrier to planned interventions to develop or strengthen the elderly's social networks.

Exchange theory provides an especially useful perspective on the elderly's social networks (Martin, 1971; Dowd, 1975, 1980). Similar to activity or disengagement theory, exchange theory predicts decreasing participation with age in major social institutions. The basis of this prediction, however, is different from that of the other theoretical approaches. According to exchange theory, differential possession of and access to the resources necessary for equitable social exchange strongly influences the elderly person's participation in all social institutions. Dowd identified five types of exchange resources: personal characteristics, material possessions, relational characteristics, authority, and generalized reinforcers. The elderly are systematically deprived of valued social resources and of access to acquiring new resources because of societal conditions, not through any responsibility of their own. For example, a mandatory retirement policy deprives older workers of material resources, relational and personal characteristic resources (e.g., the opportunity to develop friendships among co-workers), and resources based on authority. According to Blau (1973), compliance is the only commodity older people have for bargaining in the marketplace in order to win acceptance and support from others. In addition to commanding fewer resources, older people do not receive full compensation for their contributions. As occupants of a socially less-valued status, they are rewarded in interactions at a lower "exchange rate."

If the elderly do indeed lack valued resources, then appropriate interventions would center on ways to increase their resources. Accordingly, strategies to strengthen their informal support systems would be one way to increase both their relational and personal characteristic resources.

THE ROLE OF INFORMAL SOCIAL SUPPORTS

Although social networks and exchange resources generally decline in older age, most older people have some types of informal social supports to which they can turn for help (Rosow, 1967; Lopata, 1973; Shanas, 1979). Even among apparently isolated older people in a study in New York City, over two-thirds had intimates and interacted extensively with other neighbors. Those without informal supports tended to be of low socioeconomic status, in poor health, unmarried, and of lower intelligence (Cantor, 1975; Lowenthal & Robinson, 1976).

As noted throughout this book, the value of network building to promote mental and physical well-being for other age groups has been well documented (Attneave, 1969; Caplan, 1974; Collins & Pancoast, 1976). Caplan (1974), for example, found that the outcome of an individual's response during difficult times was influenced not only by the degree of stress and the individual's ego strength, but also by the quality of emotional support provided by his or her natural network. Cassel (1976a,b) determined that the absence of social supports increases one's susceptibility to disease.

Accordingly, social networks appear to buffer or mitigate the stresses of aging. Two studies have been particularly important to the field of aging: Berghorn and Schafer's (1979) finding that social supports reduced the impact of declining functional capacities on feelings of effective living, and Raphael's (1977) conclusion that many of the adverse effects associated with bereavement, such as susceptibility to physical and mental health breakdowns, were absent for individuals who maintained close supportive relationships. Stephens et al. (1978) found that as informal social support increases, planned engagement (orientation to the future), zestful engagement, child-centered participation, and leisure activity increase; accordingly, older people with extensive supports tend to have fewer psychosomatic complaints and are less likely to be depressed or alienated. Among older people not tied into informal supports, use of formal services tends to be higher (Kammeyer & Bolton, 1968), instances of personally reported well-being tends to decline (Tannebaum, 1975), the burdens of adjusting to widowhood tend to multiply (Lopata, 1973), and finally, the likelihood of institutionalization tends to increase (O'Brien & Whitelaw, 1973). In sum, social supports for older people appear to be related to high morale, less loneliness and worry, feelings of usefulness, a sense of individual respect within the community and a zest for life.

Friends and family are the most important informal supports for the elderly. Friends may be better suited to perform certain tasks and to provide emotional support than family, neighbors, or professionals. Older people who belong to friendship cliques consider themselves less old and have a more positive self-concept than those who are not part of a group (Blau, 1961). Having a confidante is related to high morale and less likelihood of depression, even when other role losses and disrupted ties exist (Lowenthal & Haven, 1968; Kaplan, Fleischer, & Regnier, 1979). Friendship and neighboring appear to be related to less loneliness and worry, to feelings of usefulness, and to a sense of individual respect within the community, and they may be a better resource than family ties for avoiding isolation in old age (Arling, 1976). In fact, elderly widows generally prefer help from confidants, because relatives may reinforce their loss of identity as "wife" (Rosen, 1973). The resilience of some older women may be rooted in their abilities to make friendships and invest them with intimacy (Hess, 1969). The quality or type of interaction with friends, not the quantity, appears to be most important for the saliency of the networks (Lemon, Bengston, & Peterson, 1972).

Contrary to the myth of alienation between older people and their families, the family is a primary support system for older people. Fifty percent of all in-home services are provided by the family; the rate increases to 80%

for the severely impaired (Comptroller General, 1977). Even when the family is not geographically accessible, the emotional bonds tend to be strong, creating "intimacy at a distance." The immediate family tend to be the elderly's major support during illness, whereas the extended family serves to tie them to the community (Shanas, 1979). The family is not only a source of direct assistance but also an advocate and information resource on the rights and entitlements of its aged members. Kin are often the major factor determining where an older person lives; people without family ties, primarily the widowed and the very old who have outlived their other family members, are most likely to be prematurely or inappropriately institutionalized (Maddox, 1970; Brody, Poulshock, & Maschiochhi, 1978).

Although the family's role is critical and the preferred source of support, a number of social and demographic trends may reduce the family's ability to provide such informal supports. These trends include fewer children in marriages, high divorce rates, increasing numbers of old-old who outlive their children, increased mobility of children, economic stresses, and the growing percentage of middle-aged women entering the labor force and thus facing multiple demands from their aged relatives, their children, and their employers. For some older people, these trends may result in a lack of family members or "responsible others" to whom they can turn in crisis (Kulys & Tobin, 1980). For families who do provide daily care, the burden can often be great, resulting in emotional and financial stress for the family caregivers and, in some cases, neglect and abuse of the older family member. When family ties are lacking or strained, the task for service providers is to strengthen or develop other forms of informal support that can perform family-like functions or to identify community supports that can relieve the burdens on families.

Whether older people turn to family, friends, or neighbors for support appears to be related to the type of tasks with which they need help and perhaps to their age. Although older people state that they prefer the assistance of family, especially for concrete help, over that of nonkin, in practice they may turn to friends or neighbors more or as much as they turn to family for help. In fact, close friends may come to be viewed as family (Gore, 1978). Neighbors may be even more valuable than family or friends in times of illness or emergency; their proximity and daily interactions enable them to respond quickly. Older people may resist becoming dependent on kin in an effort to maintain some equality of exchange with their children. At earlier stages in the aging process, the strongest potential for aid and for meeting an older person's socialization needs may rest with peers. As older people become more physically frail, they face more pressure to call on younger kin who will have a long-term commitment to them (Dono et al., 1979; Furstenberg, 1980); this creates a situation of dependency and inequality of exchange, especially when an older person's expressive contributions may become less valued as their instrumental needs strain the network beyond repair (Wentowski, 1980). Reciprocity of exchange is essential in maintaining positive interactions with both kin and nonkin.

PRACTICE PROBLEMS POTENTIALLY AMENABLE TO SOCIAL SUPPORT NETWORKS

Typically, three types of responses emerge among older people who face increased losses and dependency with old age. These patterns of response are: (1) remaining in one's own home, (2) moving in with family members, and (3) entering a nursing home. For each of these responses, carefully planned and implemented network intervention could ease the elderly's adjustment to loss and dependency. Reviewing these responses also serves to highlight what has been documented about the impact of social supports on the elderly.

REMAINING IN ONE'S OWN HOME

As noted above, most older people are in home settings; most are not living alone. Clearly, most older people prefer to remain in a home situation; only 1–7% prefer a nursing home as their dwelling (Dobrof & Litwak, 1979). The feasibility of remaining at home, however, declines with age, primarily because of increasing losses and the relatively limited community-based formal support systems, such as chore, home health, and homemaker services, to offset such losses and dependencies.

A decision facing the young-old, often the newly retired, is the type of living environment to choose, particularly whether to live in an age-segregated setting such as a retirement community or a senior high-rise building. Contrary to the steretype of the golden years in Sun City, most older people do not move to planned age-segregated communities. Many elderly, however, live in age-segregated environments out of necessity, such as low-income senior high-rises, because younger families have fled the inner-city or because of the aging of long-term residents in suburban areas. Although the findings are mixed on the benefits of living with age peers, most studies have found that an age-segregated environment tends to lead to more peer group interaction and satisfaction with one's environment. Hochschild (1973), for example, discovered strong helping and informational networks among the elderly women in a San Francisco high-rise. In a planned, middle-class retirement community, Longino and Lipman (1981) found that neighborhood interaction could compensate for reduced familial support. Age homogeneity clearly plays a strong role in friendship and interaction patterns, in part because of shared problems (e.g., health and reduced income) and life transitions, reduced cross-generational ties with children and work associates, and the parity of exchange possible between those sharing a problematic situation. It may be that age, as a basis for friendship, is most pronounced at those stages where the individual's ties to other networks are loosened (Hess, 1972).

A decision about remaining in one's home often becomes critical at the stage of widowhood, especially for women who have been dependent on the social, financial, and emotional support that had been provided by their husband. Many of the widows in Lopata's Chicago study (1973) were limited in the number of people they could turn to for support, in the activities in which they engaged, and in their use of formal resources. Well-meaning friends and relatives may prevail upon the widow to give up her home, either to move in with them or to enter a nursing home.

Yet for most older men and women, remaining in their own home is the most desirable option. Most older people prefer "intimacy at a distance" from their children—being close to and able to interact with their children, but remaining independent. The challenge facing family members and practitioners is how to support this choice, especially in a time of declining community-based alternatives (e.g., chore and home health services) to institutionalization. Family members who try to support their elderly relatives' desire for independence and thus, help them to remain in their home face financial burdens and the physical strains of keeping up two households (e.g., home maintenance, cleaning, shopping, and checkup calls). Although the formal organization may assume the tasks of housework and personal care, the family generally has major responsibility for the more idiosyncratic tasks, such as preparing meals, shopping for groceries, and traveling to the doctor (Cantor, 1980). In fact, in one study, women aged 60 or over spent an average of 22.7 hours a week providing care to an older relative in a separate household (Brody, 1980).

Many family members may be unaware of or may not qualify for formal support services; they may even adhere to the norm that they should be able to provide such help on their own. Practitioners thus need to develop informal support both for the family caregivers as well as for the older people who attempt to remain in their own home.

Supports should also be extended to neighbors and friends for older people who lack family ties (e.g., the never-married, the childless, or the frail widow) and for those whose relationships with family are strained, either by geographical distance or a history of negative interactions. In such cases, friends or neighbors can perform family-like functions, acting as a surrogate family or "fictive kin" (Sussman, 1976) by providing daily check-ins, by helping with routine tasks, and by giving emotional support.

MOVING IN WITH FAMILY MEMBERS

Although both children and parents generally prefer to maintain separate households, many families will have an older person move in with them before resorting to institutionalization. For every person who is in a nursing home, there are two people residing at home who are in need of the same level of care (Comptroller General, 1977). In practice, the daughter or daughter-in-law assumes most of the daily responsibility for care and faces the greatest strain of juggling responsibilities to aging relatives, children, spouse, and work. Although men may provide financial assistance to an older relative, they are less likely to share the daily care and emotional support and are, in turn, less likely to experience caregiving as stressful (Robinson & Thurnher, 1979; Shanas, 1979; Smith, 1979). For middle-aged women, the stress can become especially great as they become aware of their own aging and vulnerability and must, as well, deal with demands from grown children, many of whom remain at home. In many homes, the empty nest is being refilled by the frail elderly, especially as the number of four-generation families increases (Brody, 1980). Family members responsible for 24-hour care face numerous burdens: financial, emotional, and instrumental or those that are associated with the daily routine tasks of caregiving. In fact, households in which an older couple live with others are disproportionately low-income households, where the caregiver confronts also other competing economic demands (Myllyluoma & Soldo, 1980).

Research on familial caregiving has shown that the emotional strain of feeling alone and not having time for oneself or immediate family is greater than the demands of providing finances or daily physical care. Caregivers make considerable personal sacrifices (e.g., giving up their time for themselves, their socializing with friends, their privacy, and their vacations) and must restrict their lives to the essentials (Cantor, 1980). They often make numerous changes in their daily routines and income, and often experience increased interpersonal conflict with other family members (Lebowitz, 1978). Although families may not mention financial stress as the major strain, Brody (1980) found that 55% of families also experienced financial stress.

Such sacrifice is usually more tolerable to a spouse than to children; dissatisfaction and conflict with care is more likely when a child is the caregiver than a spouse, in part because of the inequality of exchange in the parent–child caregiving relationship (Horowitz & Shindelman 1980; Myllyluoma & Soldo, 1980). As noted in the discussion of exchange theory, the exchange of resources between adult children and an aging parent is often unequal, especially when the instrumental demands of daily care strain the relationship beyond repair, making emotional exchanges difficult. When the distribution of power and resources shifts, the adult child may be unable to cope with the dependency needs of an aged relative, who is culturally defined as roleless and noncontributing. An additional burden in caring for an elderly parent is that one generally cannot look forward to increasing independence and consequently reduced daily physical demands.

Few adult children have effective role models to help them resolve these multiple responsibilities. In contrast to the wide range of materials published and support groups available for parents regarding the child-rearing responsibilities, few guidelines exist regarding the responsibilities to aging parents. Most adult children know little about how to provide care for a dependent relative, where to locate resources, or how to handle their own mixed feelings toward their aged parents.

Accordingly, family members may feel negatively toward their aging relatives and to themselves. Feelings of anger, resentment, hopelessness, and guilt may culminate in instances of abuse and neglect of older relatives. In fact, recent research on familial elderly abuse and neglect suggests that the strains of providing care can negatively affect both the caregivers and the older person. Some families recognize their limitations and do ask for help. For example, in a New York City demonstration project, when families were asked what they needed, over 85% chose homemaker services and social supports, not financial incentives (Horowitz, 1980). Even though families did not initially recognize emotional support as a need, when they experienced it within a group, they found this supportive component to be the most helpful part of the program (Zimmer, Gross-Andrew, & Frankfather, 1977). Yet families often do not turn for help and support, if at all, until the stages of crisis and burnout. In fact, it may be that the more one needs support, the less likely one is to have the personal resources to reach out and obtain it (Garbarino and Stocking 1980).

The level of stress of caregiving is related not only to the extent of the older person's disability and amount of care needed, but also to whether the caregiver receives help and support from others. The burdens of caregiving are often intensified by the lack of effective support for family members who feel alone and who do not know how to develop support networks. Thus, the most vulnerable caregivers are those who do not have a support network (Zimmer, Gross-Andrew, & Frankfather, 1977; Cantor, 1980; Horowitz and Shindelman, 1980). In fact, families providing home care to older widowed female relatives may be the most prone to disruption, in part because many of these households are headed by women working out of economic necessity and with minimal support from family and friends (Myllyluoma & Soldo, 1980). A major practice issue, therefore, is how to develop social supports for family caregivers in order to reduce the burden of caregiving. Services are often provided to older people as if they were living totally alone, without any family network. The research on family caregiving clearly points to the importance of strengthening the resources and social supports available to families as a means to improve the quality of care for the elderly. An appropriate intervention thus appears to be the strengthening of family support systems, or, where none exists, the development of alternative supportive networks.

The Problem/Solution Inventory given in Table 5-1 illustrates a checklist of social supports that practitioners could develop and use with family members in helping them postpone problems faced by elderly relatives attempting to remain in the community (either in their own home or with

Table 5-1. Problem/solution inventory

Problem	Possible community resources
Difficulty arranging transportation to employment, volunteer site, senior center, medical appointment, etc.	Carpools: with neighbors, families of other older people, fellow volunteers or workers City provisions for older people: reduced bus fares, taxi cab scrip, "Trans-Aide" Volunteer services: Red Cross, Salvation Army, church organizations for emergency or occasional transportation
Living alone and fearing accidental injury or illness without access to assistance	Telephone check-up services: through local hospitals, or friends, neighbors, or relatives Postal alert: register with local senior center; sticker on mail box alerts letter carrier to check for accumulation of mail Newspaper delivery: parents of the delivery boy or girl can be given an emergency phone number if newpapers accumulate Neighbors: can check pattern of lights on/off
Needs assistance with personal care such as bathing and dressing	Private pay for hourly services: home aides from private agencies listed in phone book Visiting Nurse Association: services will include aide services when nurses are utilized Medicaid/Medicare: provisions for home aides are limited to strict eligibility requirements but such care is provided in certain situations Student help: posting notices on bulletin boards at nursing schools can yield inexpensive helpers Home sharing: sharing the home with another person who is willing to provide this kind of assistance in exchange for room and board
Needs occasional nursing care and/or physical therapy	Visiting nurse: services provided through Medicare or Medicaid or sliding scale fees, must be ordered by a physician Home health services: private providers listed in phone book; also nonprofit providers, Medicare and Medicaid reimbursement for authorized services Veteran's Administration Hospital Home Care: for veterans over 60 years old for specific situations
Difficulty cooking meals, shopping for food, and arranging nutritious diet	Home-delivered meals: "Meals on Wheels" delivers frozen meals once a week, sliding fees Nutrition sites: meals served at Senior Centers, churches, schools, and other sites Cooperatives: arrangements with neighbors to exchange a service for meals, food shopping, etc.

continued

Table 5-1. Problem/solution inventory (*continued*)

Problem	Possible community resources
Not enough contact with other people; insufficient activity or stimulation; loneliness and boredom	Senior centers: provide social opportunities, classes, volunteer opportunities, outings Church-sponsored clubs: social activities, volunteer opportunities, outings Support groups: for widows, stroke victims, and general support Adult day care: provides social interaction, classes, discussion groups, outings, exercise
Difficulty doing housework	Homemaker services: for those meeting income eligibility criteria Service exchanges: with neighbors and friends, i.e., babysitting exchanged for housework help Home helpers: hired through agencies or through employment listings at senior centers, schools, etc. Home sharing: renting out a room or portion of the home, reduced rent for help with housework
Forgetful about financial affairs; eyesight too poor for balancing checkbook and reading necessary information	Power of attorney: given to friend or relative for handling financial matters Joint checking account: with friend or relative for ease in paying bills Volunteer assistance: available from the Red Cross, Salvation Army, church groups, senior centers, and other organizations
Needs assistance with will, landlord–tenant concerns, property tax exemptions, guardianship, etc.	Senior citizens' legal services Lawyer referral service: offered by the county bar association City/county aging programs: hot lines for information and assistance in phone book

relatives). In general, practitioners should work with the family to help them identify community resources and natural helpers (for example, neighbors with whom services may be exchanged and relatives outside the immediate family who might be willing to provide occasional assistance). Family members should be encouraged to utilize these resources rather than strain themselves to the point where they can see institutional placement of the older person as the only option for their relief. Practitioners need to be advocates for family members, following up on referrals to community agencies to ensure that needed training, equipment, and services have been successfully acquired.

ENTERING A NURSING HOME

The availability of kin is an important factor in postponing, if not preventing, institutionalization, since almost half of the institutionalized elderly, primarily widowed and never-married women, have no close relatives (Monk, 1979). For most families, placing an older relative in a nursing home is viewed as a last resort. Research has continually shown that the critical factor influencing adult children's decision to institutionalize aged kin is the perception of the caregiving role as too burdensome rather than the actual health status of the aged person (Kraus, 1976; Brody, Poulshock, & Maschiochhi, 1978.)

Clearly, the family's perception of its ability to perform the caregiving role is greatly influenced by the existing support options it sees available. Here the problem is twofold. First, families view long-term care as synonomous with institutional care; this limited perspective prevents them from seeing the available range of care and thus adequately using community-based supports, such as respite services and adult day care. Second, the family tends to have a limited and narrow definition of the caregiver role as meaning only the direct provision of goods and services to the aged. Sussman, however, argues that an equally important role for the family is that of mediator between the human service bureaucracy and aged kin (1976).

When presented with a hypothetical situation of a woman needing care, only 8% of a sample of "responsible family members" believed that the woman should be placed in a nursing home, and nearly 50% preferred that the woman stay in her own home and that someone be hired to stay with her (Adams, Caston, & Danis, 1979). In general, families state that they prefer community-based alternatives over institutionalization. Yet in a 1977 study of the decision to institutionalize an older relative, most families did not use alternatives to institutional care and did not thoroughly investigate nursing homes. Fifty-one percent of the families did not even visit the home their relative was placed in prior to placement and 75% chose the home simply because a bed was available. Because most families do not explore the range of institutional options, such as congregate care facilities, day care, and retirement residences, the timing and manner of presenting information to families about alternatives to institutionalization is extremely important (York & Calsyn, 1977). Such information may need to be presented early in the caretaking cycle, before the point when families, feeling defeated, frustrated, or exhausted, see institutionalization as the only option.

One of the negative effects of institutionalization is on the informal social support system. The older person is removed from existing social networks as well as from that which is familiar and routine. No matter what the extenuating circumstances, the older person who has children interprets the move to an institution as rejection (Dobrof & Litwak, 1979). Removed from the private home, a large percentage of older people die within the year after admission to an institution. At the same time, adult children state that this time is often the saddest in their lives and report feeling totally frustrated by the event (Cath, 1972).

After institutionalization, the family support system may also be weakened, perhaps because of the family's guilt and sadness or because they do not know how to relate to their older relative in an institutional setting. Yet the family's involvement is critical to the care of the older person. In fact, there appears to be a relationship between the family's visiting and the quality of care received. In some families, however, institutionalization can result in a strengthening of family ties or renewed closeness between parent and child. As the institution meets the technical needs of elderly parents, the family can be freer to perform the nontechnical functions of its natural role as a primary group (Smith & Bengston, 1979).

The way in which the nursing home staff approaches families and the existence of family support and educational activities in the nursing home undoubtedly has an impact on the relationship between the family and its aged member. Therefore, a practical issue is how to maintain family ties after institutionalization or, where family ties do not exist, how to make use of friends or other residents as surrogate relatives for the institutionalized older person.

Each of the three responses to dependency—remaining in one's home, living with adult children, and institutionalization—point to the need to develop and strengthen support systems to benefit both the elderly and their family members. In the next section, projects that have intervened in these support systems to build networks will be discussed. Table 5-2 presents the types of interventions that can be used to achieve objectives related to these typical responses to dependency. It reviews what interventions serve to support older people remaining in their own homes, what interventions provide support to family caregivers, and what can be done to strengthen the informal supports of institutionalized elderly.

EXISTING PROJECTS TO STRENGTHEN OR CREATE SOCIAL SUPPORTS OF THE ELDERLY

Older people and their families may not use available community resources as they confront these issues surrounding home care and institutionalization for a number of reasons. These reasons include lack of information about the availability of services, service inaccessibility, the bureaucratic red tape within the service delivery system, impersonalization of services, and service fragmentation. In response to these barriers to the use of services, a number of programs around the country have begun to strengthen or build social networks as an intervention to reach and benefit older people and their families. These interventions can be categorized as personal network

Table 5-2. Types of interventions

Objectives of network intervention	Personal network building	Volunteer linking	Mutual help	Neighborhood and community empowerment
To support older people to remain in own home	Gatekeeper Project Postal alert Newspaper delivery Telephone checkups Church assurance and friendship contacts Neighborhood Care Program	Outreach Project Chore services Skills banks, service exchange Peer counseling	Benton, Ill. Model Shared housing Support groups for widows, stroke victims, etc.	Neighborhood family Tenderloin Project Activist groups (Older Women's League, Gray Panthers)
To support family caregivers	Church companionship programs (respite) Family education and support projects	Church volunteer opportunities Neighborhood respite care	Family support and education groups	
To strengthen informal supports of institutionalized elderly	Grandchildren's groups; school/grandparent programs Resident groups (orientation groups, welcoming committees) Family activities	Friendly visitor, companion programs Peer counseling	Resident councils, family support groups	Lobbying and advocacy groups Nursing home coalitions

149

building, volunteer linking, mutual aid networks, and neighborhood and community empowerment (Froland *et al.*, 1979). Each type can be used either in a community or an institutional setting, i.e., to enable the older person to remain in the community or to strengthen the networks of institutionalized elderly.

PERSONAL NETWORK BUILDING

Personal network building seeks to strengthen the existing ties among the network of an individual in need, often by making use of natural helpers. Natural helpers are individuals, e.g., friends, neighbors, relatives, to whom people turn in difficult times because of their concern, interest, and innate understanding. Not paid for their services, natural helpers are characterized by the equality and mutual exchange they bring to the act of helping. In work with older people, a number of natural helping resources must be considered: their primary group helpers or other family members and close friends; informal caregivers, such as neighbors; people with similar problems, often peers; and community gatekeepers, such as postal workers, grocery clerks, public utilities workers, apartment house managers, and local merchants. These helpers can provide the following kinds of social support: (1) emotionally sustaining help, such as contact with a trusted party during stressful periods; (2) problem-solving, such as providing new information or direct assistance; (3) indirect forms of assistance, such as simple availability and listening; and (4) advocacy. Older people and/or their families may be more likely to turn to these natural networks for information and skills because these networks are more accessible and more likely to be trusted than the formal service delivery system.

Admittedly, natural helpers may not exist in every network, and some individuals are not involved in supportive networks. Nevertheless, networks and central figures have been found in a variety of social settings, and few elderly are totally socially isolated (Wagner & Gleeson, 1980). Informal supports may have been rejected by an older person, but they may not necessarily be nonfunctional. Even if neighbors do not have daily contact with an older person who rejects their helping efforts, they may nevertheless know or suspect what is going on with him or her. Therefore, an approach based on identifying and strengthening natural networks seems warranted. Professional intervention would thus focus on expanding or mobilizing the skills and resources of the part of the social network that the older person does not already view as a source of support. Where helping networks do not exist, a preventive approach would be to create them as a means of outreach, detection, and service delivery.

In the Community. A natural helping system that is not used enough and that could provide information and support to the elderly consists of gatekeepers: role-related helpers, employed by businesses and community organizations, who provide informal services. These are people in visible "crossroads" positions who have access to valuable resources and regularly interact with the elderly. They include postal carriers, cab drivers, local merchants, receptionists in doctors' offices, beauticians, bank tellers, bus drivers, pharmacists, and ministers. Because of their visible positions, they are likely to be turned to for help, to know and keep an eye on others' actions, and to offer emotional support, practical aid, and information. Such gatekeepers have been found to provide companionship, advice, physical assistance, financial aid, transportation, and health care (Robinson & Regnier, 1980).

Because these informal caregivers already serve a valuable information and referral function, their front-line contributions could be strengthened by providing them with more information and skills training. For example, Southern California Rapid Transit bus drivers were trained to recognize the sensory and motor losses of aging (Robinson & Regnier, 1980). A gatekeeper project in Philadelphia provided training in crisis intervention as well as consultation and support to individual gatekeepers (Collins & Pancoast, 1976). In an effort to reach isolated elderly, the Community Mental Health Center in Spokane, Washington trains fuel oil dealers, meter readers, fire staff, taxi drivers, and postal carriers to watch for situations and symptoms which indicate need among the frail elderly for services. In fact, one of five of the Center's referrals comes from these gatekeepers (Information and Assistance Program, Elderly Services, 1980). Training programs specifically dealing with signs of mental and physical illnesses, available services, and reporting procedures could be implemented in communities and neighborhoods. As it is now, gatekeepers may suspect problems but not know what to do.

A proposed effort to strengthen natural helpers is a "Neighborhood Care" program to include respite care, neighborhood aides, and neighborhood elder sitting pools. A neighborhood block home for the elderly, similar to block houses for children, could be identified as a place where elderly people could turn for assistance. Neighborhood aides would routinely canvass the neighborhood, report problems, visit homebound elderly, and provide a link to community services. In sum, they would informally watch over the neighborhood and meet the needs of their elderly neighbors as they arise (O'Brien & Whitelaw, 1978)

Churches may also serve to strengthen and build personal networks, in some cases becoming a surrogate family. A Chicago study found that churches fulfill roles similar to those of the family, providing concrete help and psychological assurance in times of need. Services are provided on the basis of individual factors and close personal ties, rather than by more universal characteristics common to most formal social service agencies. The church is a flexible, semiformal neighborhood support, in which most services are informally designed by and for the lay congregants (Steinitz, 1980).

Natural helpers may also be called on to provide support and respite to families who are caring for aged relatives. Family caregivers need information, support, training in caretaking skills, links to services and to other caregivers, and occasional relief from their nearly constant responsibilities. All of these needs can be met by interventions that focus on strengthening natural helping networks.

Demonstration programs throughout the country have attempted to strengthen family networks by providing education, emotional support, help with instrumental tasks, and respite for families. In the Natural Support Program, sponsored by the Community Service Society in New York City, the family, not the service providers, defines the service need and thus acts as a "case manager." The program offers respite care, counseling to the caregiver, assistance in systems negotiation, linking with other types of helpers and groups for education, skills training, and emotional support of the caregivers. For 64% of the participants, the program's major benefit has been the support and mutual aid provided by the small informal discussion groups (Mellor & Getzel, 1980). A similar type of program, the Family/Friends Support Project of the Ebenezer Society in Minneapolis provides monetary reimbursement for some daily help, emergency backup for care, training on how to give care, and aid from a mutual support group (Gray et al., 1980). Both of these projects have the effect of expanding the caregivers' network and strengthening family ties by reducing some of the burdens on caregivers.

Within Institutional Settings. Nursing homes often work to strengthen the natural helping efforts of both family members and peers. Grandchildren are generally effective natural helpers, serving as a link between parent and grandparent; through nursing home–sponsored grandchildren's groups, grandchildren can act as supports and advocates for their grandparents. Special family activities, such as holiday celebrations, grandparent's day, refreshment hours on Sunday afternoons, and church services open to family members can also serve to build networks.

Because most nursing home residents lack families, practitioners must create "surrogate families" to strengthen or build networks. If residents lack family ties, school children may "adopt" them as grandparents. Some nursing homes have day care on the premises for staff children, allowing the children to interact regularly with the residents and thus be a means of network building.

Another source of network building within institutions is from the residents themselves. At the point of admission, orientation groups or resident welcoming committees are a means to help the new arrivals to adjust to role changes and to integrate them into the informal support systems of the nursing home (Pilisuk & Minkler, 1980; Wells & MacDonald, 1981).

VOLUNTEER LINKING

In the Community. Volunteer linking seeks to develop a new or enhanced support system for the individual through the use of volunteers. For example, through Oregon's Northwest Salem Community Association (NESCA), volunteers from local churches develop family-like networks for chronically mentally ill older people (*Networks for Helping*, 1978). Peer counseling and support systems, such as that at the Turner Geriatric Clinic in Ann Arbor, Michigan, have enlisted older volunteers to provide mental health services, including health education about topics such as memory problems, stress, and nutrition. Peers provide individual counseling, organize small support groups, and supply referral and information services in a health care clinic, a senior nutrition site, a nursing home, and a community hospital in a rural area. At the Nebraska Center for Aging, trained peer counselors facilitate assertiveness and problem solving in their clients (Select Committee on Aging, 1979). A review of peer counselor and outreach programs concluded that such efforts provide group support and expand opportunities for specific leadership roles (Campbell & Chenoweth, 1980).

A variety of outreach programs have used elderly volunteers to go into homes to assess problems visually (Toseland, Decker, & Bliesner, 1979), and to provide light housekeeping, shopping, meal preparation, and transportation (Select Committee on Aging, 1979). Senior centers often keep files on all volunteers in neighborhoods known to help their elderly neighbors and use this information to locate someone to provide help when needed. These block workers serve as a liaison between the senior center and more isolated elderly (Chapman, 1980). In San Antonio, elderly volunteers in a Hispanic neighborhood organized into task forces to provide friendly visiting, home repair, and help in dealing with agencies (Chapman, 1980). In Iowa's Project-Be-My-Guest, women from local churches reached out to friends, neighbors, and relatives and accompanied them to the agencies to explain available services and to increase their awareness of programs (Select Committee on Aging, 1979).

The Senior Block Information Service in San Francisco uses volunteers to develop leadership and self-help capacities among the elderly in a low-income neighborhood. By delivering a monthly newsletter, elderly volunteers are regularly in contact with frail residents, linking them to necessary resources and strengthening their problem-solving behavior. The distribution of a newsletter by volunteers is a means of creating and maintaining social networks on a block basis (Ruffini & Todd, 1979).

Within Institutional Settings. Within institutions, volunteers are asked primarily to substitute for family ties. Various organizations, such as the Red Cross, sponsor friendly visitor or companion programs of volunteers who regularly visit an older person. In some nursing homes, the residents expand their social networks through their own volunteer efforts, acting as confidantes and peer counselors to one another or participating in intergenerational programs for school children.

Volunteer efforts with older people appear to be most successful when tasks are time-limited and easily managed, when psychic rewards are immediate, and when participants have a wide choice of the degree of their involvement.

MUTUAL HELP GROUPS

A third approach aims to create or promote the supportive capacities within mutual help groups. Engaging in joint problem solving, such groups emphasize "watching out for each other." They also stress reciprocity in their exchange of resources. Mutual help efforts may occur spontaneously as "neighbor helps neighbor" or may be planned and facilitated by an outside professional. In their study of a public housing project in Milwaukee, Jonas and Wellin (1980) identified spontaneous patterns of interdependency with well-articulated norms of reciprocity. These patterns varied with gender and with degrees of prior acquaintance and intimacy.

In the Community. The Benton, Illinois, Mutual Help model, sponsored by an outside organization, assumed that money cannot buy community spirit or the willingness of neighbors to help each other (Ehrlich, 1979). Building on natural neighborhood ties, the Benton model drew on research showing that older people are more likely to bring problems to significant others who are neighborhood-bound than to formal agencies. In fact, the slogan for the Benton model was "Make Neighborhood a Cause." The Benton program was staffed by professionals familiar with consultation techniques and neighborhood workers well acquainted with local networks and cultural patterns. Participants themselves were the direct service providers of transportation, housekeeping, shopping, meal preparation, and so on. They organized key exchanges, neighborhood house watches, and transportation networks. Data gathered on the Benton model indicate that participants experienced the development of friendship and helping relationships, and reinforcement of social roles with a community orientation; they stated that the program's major benefit was that it reduced loneliness and increased psychological supports (Ehrlich, 1979).

Other examples of mutual help models serving older people are the Widow-to-Widow Program, stroke clubs, and Alzheimer support groups, which bring people together on the basis of a shared problem rather than their geographic location. As group participants engage in common problem solving, their own problem-solving capacity increases and they tend to rely less on formal services. Such groups also expand participants' social networks and thus reintegrate them into the community and provide new role models, reference groups, and opportunities to develop new skills and roles.

Another approach building upon mutual exchange and reciprocity is that of shared housing programs. Cross-generational households or the "affiliative family" bring together younger families who need low-cost housing with older people who have housing space but who need companionship and help with home maintenance (Clavan & Vatter, 1972; Sussman, 1976). In other situations, self-sufficient older people may share housing with less physically or mentally capable older people, exchanging helping services for a low-cost living situation (Sussman, 1976).

Mutual help groups can also provide education and support to family caregivers. One model is the multigenerational group, such as the group "As Parents Grow Older," developed through Child and Family Services in Ann Arbor, Michigan (Silverman, Kahn, & Anderson, 1977). Focusing on content, feelings, and interaction, these groups provide information about aging and community resources as well as mutual problem solving and support. Participants in "As Parents Grow Older" frequently cited the following positive outcomes: increased ability both to communicate with their older relative and to cope with the situation, and recognition of their own needs and their responsibility to themselves in setting realistic limits (Silverman, 1979).

Such mutual help programs could be offered through neighborhood centers, senior centers, family agencies, mental health centers, and religious institutions with relatively small expenditures of funds. Silverman's model of support groups cost, i.e., approximately $1,200 to replicate twice the first year, and $600 the second year. About $500 to $600 is needed for seed money for such groups. Volunteers from original groups could be trained to start and to facilitate new groups. The framework for providing such support to families may already exist in most communities; for example, most family service agencies probably offer either groups or training sessions. Support groups for caregivers of patients with particular chronic illness (such as Alzheimer's disease or stroke) are becoming more common, but support efforts have not been developed within a wide variety of settings (e.g., day centers, hospitals, or senior centers); nor have such group efforts been regarded specifically as a network intervention both to detect and prevent various problems confronting the elderly and their families.

Within Institutional Settings. Mutual help groups within nursing homes have been developed for both family members and residents. Family members and nursing home staff need to work as partners, with the staff assuming primary responsibility for routine or technical tasks and the family responsible for nonroutine or idiosyncratic tasks (Dobrof & Litwak, 1979). One way to achieve this partnership is for families to become more involved in the care of their institutionalized members. Families generally need to be informed about both the nursing home and the physical and psychological changes experienced by their older members. Many nursing homes are developing family groups as a means of providing both education and a sup portive context in which family members are free to express their concerns, ask questions, and deal with their feelings. Most families indicate an interest in attending such groups and appear to benefit from the exchange of information and support among others sharing similar concerns (York & Calsyn, 1977).

A variety of task groups can serve mutual help functions for residents. Such groups also provide opportunities for self-governance and the development of decision-making and leadership skills. Groups in nursing homes that emphasize reciprocity among participants have improved communication and social skills and promoted a sense of comradeship, role, and identity within the setting (Saul & Saul, 1974; Steritz & Blank, 1978).

NEIGHBORHOOD AND COMMUNITY EMPOWERMENT

In Community Settings. A neighborhood and community empowerment approach is an attempt to strengthen existing self-help in a given locality, often through the efforts of a formal agency to enhance a community's capacity to solve problems. An example of a mental health outreach program that empowered an inner-city community is the Neighborhood Family in Miami, Florida. This model assumes that older people living in the community can work together as a family to alter their stressful personal and environmental conditions. The organizational model was initiated by a staff gerontologist at the Jackson Memorial Hospital, Community Mental Health Services. Rather than establish a clinical outpatient program, the project's one staff person started with older people in a target area, who defined the problem services and activities and requested psychiatric assistance for approximately 15% of their cohort. Neighbors were able to identify physical and emotional changes, quickly pinpoint people needing service, and use peer pressure to encourage individuals to seek help. The staff person chose to work without other professional assistance in order to reinforce the necessity for every member's participation in decision-making roles. When additional staff were later added to the consumer-based and community-administered body, they functioned as members of the family, not apart from it as "staff." The decision-makers were the elderly participants who functioned as peers, and who in turn benefited emotionally from the family-like interaction (Ross, 1978).

The Tenderloin Project in San Francisco was initially geared directly toward building social networks. It provided health services and information primarily as a vehicle to help the network-building process. For example, public health nurses used free blood-pressure checkups in a hotel lobby as an initial basis for contact and remained in the lobby to answer questions as a means to establish rapport with residents. In the process, the nurses determined shared interests between people and linked them to larger groupings. Positive signs of network development were increased talking among local residents, greater concern with their neighbors' welfare, group parties, and residents' acting together around issues of common interest (Pilisuk & Minkler, 1980).

Within Institutional Settings. Decision-making structures that can influence the administration of nursing homes, such as resident councils, are a way to empower the community of nursing home residents. In part because of the activities of senior groups outside of nursing homes, such as the Gray Panthers, residents are becoming more involved in planning and carrying out programs rather than having programs presented to them by staff. In some cases, resident councils have joined together citywide to form a lobbying and advocacy group.

BARRIERS TO IMPLEMENTATION

Unfortunately, a number of barriers exist to implementing social support networks with the elderly or their families. They include federal regulations limiting reliance on family providers, norms of professionalism, and ageist assumptions that older people lack resources for exchange.

Present social policy has frequently forced families to choose between total responsibility and no responsibility for care of the elderly. Neither supplemental services such as chore services nor direct family supports such as counseling or respite are readily available to the elderly with caregiving families.

The Supplemental Security Income (SSI) program, for example, discourages families from relying on themselves. In computing the provision of room and board, the SSI recipient's benefit is reduced by one-third if the aged person resides with relatives. This reduction can be avoided only if the potential recipient can establish that he or she received no aid or paid an equivalent share of all household expenses. Thus the burden of proof is on the recipient. Other examples can be found in the provision of in-home supportive services to Medicaid and SSI recipients. In order to minimize such barriers, Sussman (1976) has proposed policy alternatives of funneling money and resources into the family system directly to support families in providing more personalized care for their aged members. Such benefits are intended to facilitate the care of the older person within the informal network, not to force filial responsibility. Recommended benefits include a direct monthly allotment of funds, flexible work schedules for employees to provide care, a tax write-off for family caregivers, and property tax waivers with a formula proportional to the dwelling place used by family members (Sussman, 1976).

Another barrier is a traditional model of service delivery that emphasizes professionalism and an expert–nonexpert dichotomy. Some professionals, viewing lay people as lacking sufficient expertise to intervene, may resist efforts to strengthen natural helping networks. Norms of confidentiality may be upheld without necessarily being in the older clients' best interests. In times of diminished professional resources, it may be necessary to modify rules of confidentiality by involving neighbors, friends, and volunteers in order to minimize the problems experienced by clients. In making decisions about confidentiality, professionals need to assess whether rules of confidentiality are benefiting the client or the professional and/or bureaucracies.

A network approach should not be viewed as an abdication of government or professional responsibility. A partnership is needed between professionals and natural helpers drawing upon each group's strengths and resources. Recognizing the unique role that natural helpers can play, professionals must be prepared to provide them with necessary resources and backup so that they are not hurt by their involvement. Policies are needed that support natural helpers and self-help efforts without weakening public responsibility.

A third barrier, more subtle and pervasive, is the societal and cultural ageism which assumes that older people lack resources for self-help and for mutual exchange. Such an assumption may be held even by professionals trained to work with older people, who think primarily in terms of the cost-effectiveness of delivering formal services rather than how to maximize the potential of older people. In our youth-oriented culture, the rich resources gained from life experience are often discounted. Well-meaning professionals and family members may infantilize older people, assuming that they need to be helped rather than seeing them as effective helpers.

INCENTIVES TO IMPLEMENTING SOCIAL SUPPORT NETWORKS WITH THE ELDERLY

Although younger generations may not recognize the exchange resources possessed by most older people, the elderly themselves tend to draw on peer supports of friends and neighbors more than on formal agencies (Cantor, 1975; Kahana & Felton, 1977; Jonas & Wellin, 1980). Reliance on informal helping systems appears to be consistent with the value systems of most older people. Self-sufficiency, self-determination, and responsibility are valued by many of the current cohort of elderly and and so would make efforts to strengthen natural helping networks easier.

What is perhaps most important is that participation in an informal support system also allows one to be a helper. Even a frail or ill older person may offer emotional support, availability, or unfocused talking and thus remain involved in reciprocal exchanges. For example, in a Milwaukee high-rise, a woman with a heart ailment seldom left the building, but she collected mail for other neighbors confined to their apartments. Another woman, who walked with a cane, rode the elevator regularly with a man more disabled than she to make sure that he got to his apartment safely (Jonas & Wellin, 1980). Even apparently isolated single room occupants (SROs) rely on informal supports. Accordingly, the most effective way to reach SROs is through informal gatekeepers, such as hotel and apartment managers, waitresses, and grocery clerks (Lally et al., 1979).

WORKING WITH THE SOCIAL SUPPORT NETWORKS OF THE ELDERLY

This review of the importance of informal supports suggests that professional time may need to be reallocated away from direct, after-the-fact restorative services and toward activities that strengthen natural support systems. Developing a partnership between professionals and informal caregivers should be an important goal. An appropriate professional role is to provide the natural support system with information, consultation, skills training, and support. Professionals can link isolated people with natural helpers, facilitate referrals to formal services through natural helpers, or act as advocates for natural helpers. Such collaborative consultation requires flexibility and creativity on the part of the professional and a thorough knowledge of existing community resources (Collins & Pancoast, 1976). Interventions must be carefully planned in order not to weaken or replace natural supports. Accordingly, interventions must be sensitive to the natural helper's value system and to cultural differences in helping styles and techniques.

As noted above, the balance between giving and taking in relationships may shift with age, with instrumental ties growing at the expense of expressive ones. Because of numerous losses, the elderly's networks are likely to be thinner than those of someone younger. Any network interventions must take into account both what is gone and what is vulnerable and must attempt to maintain a balance between instrumental and expressive linkages. Formal supports may be necessary to prevent instrumental needs from straining the network beyond its limits. For example, in the Benton Mutual Help model, none of the group members was willing to provide an insulin injection for a 75-year-old diabetic woman. The family had to hire someone to give their mother the injection. Yet the neighbors were willing to visit with this woman and to help her with shopping and household chores (Ehrlich, 1979). Thus staff must be sensitive to the role that a mutual help program is filling for group members and must have enough contact with the elderly neighbors and friends to be knowledgeable of their individual needs and preferences. In attempting to attain a balance between formal and informal services, staff must also consider the level of skill and technology required to perform a task, the limits on the energy of the informal providers, and the length of time for which assistance is likely to be needed. In the Benton model, for example, neighbors were often unwilling to obligate themselves to a permanent helping arrangement.

In order for professionals to work effectively with natural helpers, changes in the formal service delivery system are needed that will obviously require the expenditure of public dollars. Providers need to develop skills in identifying and interviewing natural leaders, in assessing needs, and in building collaborative relationships with informal leaders. Working with informal helpers often does not fit neatly into a formal organization, especially in terms of accountability requirements. It is easier to report that 30 elderly are receiving homemaker services than that 30 elderly have family, friends, and neighbors who provide the same service. It is also difficult to report the prevention of problems—for example, the person who has not had to be institutionalized because the informal system was mobilized (Chapman, 1980).

FUTURE DIRECTIONS

RESEARCH ISSUES

The issues of research, practice, and education are interrelated and revolve around ways in which an effective partnership can be achieved between formal and informal support systems.

A major area for research is the interaction between formal and informal systems of social support. As the relationship between the formal and informal systems changes, what are the consequences for both the informal support network and for the older client? In a time of declining resources for the formal system, policy makers are increasingly calling upon the informal networks of family, friends, neighbors, and volunteers to fill in the gaps. As housekeeping services have been cut, for example, private agencies, often church-based, are forming networks of volunteers to help the elderly with housekeeping tasks. In such a situation, volunteers are expected to make a commitment to deliver a routine service over a long period of time. This may be contrary to the informal systems' ability to respond to idiosyncratic tasks and may strain the informal network. The informal system is thus being asked to perform some tasks better suited to the formal system.

As practitioners and policy makers increasingly require the informal system to assume additional responsibilities, research is needed to assess the impact of these requests on the informal system. Current demands for the informal system to take up the slack may be unrealistic. For example, research is being conducted to determine how the elderly are coping with cuts in chore services; but information is needed about how the increased involvement of families may be affecting parent–child relationships, total family dynamics, and therefore the quality of care. Recent research on the stress of family caregiving and resultant familial abuse suggests that there are limits to relatives' abilities to provide care. Clearly, a partnership between the informal and formal support systems is necessary. In a 1980 study of caregivers, although 82% of the dependent elderly felt that their families were doing all they could for them, 62% indicated that if they did not get additional help from an agency, they could not continue to live independently in the community (Lewis et al., 1980).

As noted earlier, the elderly prefer help from the informal system whenever possible; likewise, the informal system can perform certain nonroutine tasks better than the formal system. Yet more research is needed on whether there are negative consequences for the older person who relies on an informal network. For example, how does interaction with the informal network help or block recognition of problems and the appropriate delivery of needed remedies? In some cases, reliance on the informal system may deter an older person from seeking the appropriate help from the formal system. This may be especially likely in ethnic communities, where tightly knit networks and suspicion of bureaucracies can keep members from seeking out necessary services.

Anecdotal accounts suggest that the informal support system is "working" and filling the gaps created by cuts in formal services. A thin line exists, however, between formal and informal systems cooperating in a partnership; the informal system maybe expected to perform routine, demanding, or long-term tasks for which it is not prepared. As Garbarino and Smyer (1980) note, the challenge is to find ways to support communities and families as mediating structures, not to demand that they be the sole structure providing care for the impaired elderly.

PRACTICE AND POLICY ISSUES

As noted above, research and demonstration projects are needed to assess the impact of various interventions on the informal support system. Policy makers are increasingly calling for various types of family support programs such as subsidies and tax benefits. However, little is known about the potential impact of the various family support strategies, in terms of their effect on either family behavior or cost savings. Generally, it is the lack of congruence between the elderly's needs and the family's resources that leads to institutionalization and the transfer of the caretaking reponsibility to the state. Therefore, effective intervention measures must be aimed at creating congruence by increasing family resources or by decreasing the elderly's needs. Direct family support services such as education programs, counseling, and respite care are intended to increase family resources. In contrast, client-directed services such as chore, homemaker, and nutrition programs are aimed at diminishing the needs of the aged to a level the family is able to meet. The effects of both types of family support programs need to be assessed. Direct supports to families also allow professional helpers or researchers to assess the impact of early intervention.

An issue facing very ill older people, many of whom are institutionalized and without effective family supports, is how to maintain a balance between giving and taking relationships and between instrumental and expressive ties. The low resource level of most nursing home residents may force them to concentrate on the cementing of their instrumental ties with staff rather than with peers, thus creating the paucity of friendships characteristic of many nursing homes (Schmidt, 1980). Accordingly, if only physical care is provided, the demands for that care increase as lonely people substitute it for more natural sources of companionship. Practitioners need to be sensitive to such dynamics, developing interventions that allow the frail older person to engage in reciprocal exchanges. Strategies that help an ill older person to maximize his or her own inner resources are one way to try to balance the exchange. For example, nursing home residents can get involved in an "Adopt-a-Grandchild" group or in developing oral histories as ways to maintain a giving relationship.

A practical issue on the community level is how to use businesses and community organizations more effectively to reach the apparently isolated elderly. A first step is to identify what kinds of help are already being given by existing retail and service organizations. Strategies then must be developed to expand existing services, to convince businesses that it is in their self-interest to provide services to older people, and to train employees to be more effective in meeting the elderly's needs. In Seattle, for example, a corporation is funding a series of seminars between business and senior organizations to identify needs, strategies, and specific ways to work together.

EDUCATION AND TRAINING ISSUES

The two targets for education are the informal support system itself and the professionals who work within that informal system. Most families, neighbors, and friends probably do have limited skills and information for providing care to an older person.

In our society, cultural guidelines or specific norms for behavior are lacking in the area of intergenerational relationships. The media, popular press, and a variety of handbooks all advise young parents about what to expect in caring for children; such information is generally absent for adult caregivers of the elderly. Most families have no opportunity to "rehearse" the role of caregiver. They may hold unrealistic expectations for themselves and for the older person which serve to increase the stresses they experience. The informal support system needs information about the aging process, knowledge of formal community resources, and more awareness of its own values and resources. Increased efforts could be made to reach such caregivers through public service ads. Providing the informal support system with more information is one way of directly supporting its efforts.

Health care professionals also need more information about the continuum of community options, which they can then share with the informal networks in a timely and appropriate manner. A major issue facing professionals is how to accommodate their professional identities, norms, and values to helpers who do not have a professional perspective. As noted above, in many cases, this may mean modifying their professionalism and recognizing the particular strengths of the informal system.

In many ways, the distinction between informal and formal is arbitrary and can be blurred in practice. The informal role may become more formalized (e.g., volunteers being reimbursed) or the formal role become more informal (e.g., home health aides who become very close to their patients and put in extra hours to visit them and help out). A challenge for professionals is not to destroy the informal system through their interventions. For example, people in a small Oregon town had been providing transportation aid to each other for years. When they were incorporated into a formal program that reimbursed them for expenses, their spontaneous helping disappeared. After the formal program lost its funding, it took considerable effort to rekindle natural helping (Chapman, 1980). Practitioners must be sensitive to this delicate balance and must build upon the informal system without damaging it.

CONCLUSION

The multiple losses faced by many older people heighten their need for deliberate social work interventions to strengthen and build networks of friends, neighbors, families, and volunteers. Any network interventions must include the older person's family, not just the older person alone, since the family remains the primary source of support for the elderly.

Most older people first respond to their increasing losses and dependencies by trying to remain independently in their own homes; friends, neighbors, and family members often try to support this independence, forming telephone reassurance systems and daily checkup procedures as well as helping with household chores and personal health care. When this option is no longer manageable for the older person or the informal network, the elderly and their families are faced with the difficult choices of moving in with adult children or institutionalization.

At each of these decision points, practitioners need to mobilize existing community resources, either to support the older person directly or to support the familial caregivers and thus benefit the elderly. Strategies of personal network building, volunteer linking, mutual help, and community empowerment are appropriate at each stage in deciding how to use care service options. In a time of reduced formal services, it is imperative that social workers develop skills to work effectively with the informal support systems at each stage.

PART III
Child and Family Services

CHAPTER 6
Social Support Networks in Child Welfare

James K. Whittaker

What the best and wisest parent wants for his own child, that must the community want for all of its children.

Lathrop, 1919*

THE CHANGING LANDSCAPE OF CHILD WELFARE

We are, as a nation, a long way from realizing Dewey's dictum for "all children." Even in the more circumscribed world of the dependent child, we struggle to provide what Dewey's contemporaries called for in child welfare service provision: "the right thing, for the right child, at the right time." Despite the state's shortcomings as "parens patriae," it has, through its public child welfare services, made great gains since the issue of child dependence was raised from a "private trouble" to a public concern in the first White House Conference on Children in 1909. Then, a central issue was whether or not children made dependent on the state by reason of parental death, desertion, poverty, or incapacity should be served in a family foster home or an institution. Resoundingly, the conference spoke in favor of the family arrangement: "The home is the highest and finest product of civilization, children should not be deprived of it for reasons of poverty alone" (*Proceedings of the [White House] Conference on the Care of Dependent Children*, 1909). As Kadushin points out, this one objective of reducing the number of purely dependent children in institutional settings was realized: "In 1933, 47.2 per cent of the dependent, neglected and emotionally disturbed children needing substitute care were living in foster family homes and 52.8 per cent were placed in institutions. In 1972, 80 per

---

*This is quoted from Julia C. Lathrop, First Chief of the U.S. Children's Bureau, quoting John Dewey in her Presidential address to the National Conference on Social Welfare (1919)

cent of children in substitute care were in foster families or group homes and only 20 per cent in institutions" (1980, p. 321). In time, this foster care solution to the problem of child dependence would create problems of its own by placing large numbers of children adrift in a world of temporary placements with no clear plan for a permanent living arrangement. Moreover, the fundamental emphasis on placement as a remedy, often in lieu of family supportive services designed to prevent unnecessary out-of-home care, would itself create problems only recently the concern of several national investigations (Children's Defense Fund, 1978; *Who Knows? Who Cares? Forgotten Children in Foster Care*, 1979). Recently passed federal legislation, the *Adoption Assistance and Child Welfare Act of 1980*, reaffirms preference for family-centered services and, most importantly, specifies in legislation the state's obligation to provide services that "prevent the unnecessary separation of children from their families by identifying family problems, assisting families in resolving their problems, and preventing breakup of the family where the prevention of child removal is desirable and possible (P.L. 96–272, 1980, p. 519).

Such language takes the field of child welfare closer to what its leaders have always seen as its central mission, the support and protection of children *and* families:

> The basic purpose of child welfare programs is the strengthening of family life. (Costin, 1979)
>
> Child welfare . . . is concerned with the antecedents, concomitants and consequences of a particular social milieu: the parent child relationship network. (Kadushin, 1980, p. 28)

Although such basic and encompassing definitions would probably have a high face validity among child welfare workers, many would agree with Kermit Wiltse that child welfare services, i.e., "the specific structure of statutes, programs, agencies and paraphernalia of service delivery . . . tend only to reach the 'social minimum' level" (1981, p. 3). Clearly, it is useful to differentiate between the broad and highest aims of child welfare and their particular representation in services at any given time for children statutorily defined as dependent, neglected, or otherwise at risk.

Such children, in a recent national study, number nearly 2 million and receive nearly a billion dollars worth of public child welfare services annually (Shyne & Schroeder, 1978). Most of these children are of school age, more than two-thirds are living with either one or both parents or with relatives, and nearly 30% are in foster family and residential care. Although some come from disadvantaged families, only two in five come from AFDC families. The most frequently provided services to this group include protective services (33%); health-related services (26%); foster family care (25%); counseling only (19%) and day care (16%) (Shyne & Schroeder, 1978).

The boundaries of what constitutes child welfare service vary widely from state to state, as do reliable and up-to-date figures on numbers of children and families in the system. (Recent congressional hearings on child welfare prompted the comment that we have a better count of benches in our national park system than of children in the foster care system.) Traditionally, child welfare services have included such things as foster family care, group and institutional care, protective services (for child abuse and neglect), in-home services, adoptions and related services to unmarried parents, day care, homemaker services, and counseling services. Typically, these roughly fall under the heading proposed by Kadushin (1980) of services that *support*, *supplement*, or *substitute* for family functions. In fact, much of what is covered in the separate chapters on divorced and stepfamilies, day care, youth services, delinquency, and schools in this volume might fall under the general auspice of child welfare in some states and jurisdictions.

The purpose of this chapter is to examine several prominent and historically meaningful areas of child welfare service—foster family care and adoption, group homes and residential treatment, protective services, and in-home family-centered services—to ascertain the potential use of social support networks in achieving their various service missions. Since our review will be for that purpose, the reader desirous of a more detailed survey of child welfare is directed to the following publications: Kadushin (1980), *Children's Bureau* (1978), Costin (1979), and Laird and Hartman (in press).

SOME CURRENT CONCERNS FOR CHILD WELFARE

Even a cursory analysis of the traditional child welfare services cited above reveals several deep and crosscutting concerns that touch not only the core of much that is presently wrong with child welfare, but also suggest to us the efficacy of social support networks as a partial remedy. Four concerns seem most important.

First, there is an abiding and growing concern in the field about the lack of *permanency* for many children presently in the child welfare service system. The central finding of Maas and Engler's classic study (1959)—that large numbers of children were cast adrift in the foster care system with no clear case plan for a permanent living arrangement—has been reiterated in numerous research inquiries and study commissions since that time: *Children Without Homes* (1978), *Who Knows? Who Cares? Forgotten Children In Foster Care* (1979), Fanshel (1976), Fanshel and Shinn (1978), Jenkins and Norman (1972), Bernstein, Snider, and Meezan (1975), and Gruber (1978). What might have begun as a short-term placement for a child experiencing a family crisis all too often became a long-term and unplanned consignment to the limbo of foster care. Counter to this trend of foster-care drift is what Wiltse describes as the "compelling idea [of] permanency" (1981). the conviction that all children need and deserve a permanent living arrangement with loving and caring adults and that the intent of every case plan should be to provide for such. The key is, of course, *intent* since no case plan, however well conceived, can guarantee permanency. Permanency as a concept has achieved a high degree of acceptance not only among child welfare professionals, but among ordinary citizens as well. It is indeed a compelling idea that can unite disparate publics and, as is evidenced from P.L. 96–272, it is an idea that can be transported from the realm of values and philosophy to the arena of political action. There is now a growing concern about overcoming the barriers to permanency and establishing what has come to be known as family-based services across all categories of child welfare services. Perhaps the greatest legacy of the various permanent planning efforts in foster care over the last several years and of the recently passed Adoption Assistance and Child Welfare Act has been to emphasize refocusing on the family along with the child as the proper unit of attention in child welfare services. Model projects in foster care around the country provide evidence that effective solutions exist to overcome the barriers to permanent planning for children in foster care. Such things as case review systems, specialized legal training, family-centered assessment, time-limited intervention, and parent contracts all constitute a part of the total answer for providing permanency for the dependent child (Emlen et al., 1977; Lahti et al., 1978; Stein, Gambrill, & Wiltse, 1978).

A second and related concern might be called *the challenge of working with parents as partners.* Building family-based services in foster care, adoptions, residential care, in-home services, and protective services requires the involvement of parents as full partners in the helping process. The recent volume by Maluccio and Sinanoglu (1981), *The Challenge of Partnership*, documents ways in which parents and professionals are working together in foster care and residential services. Sweeping changes in adoptions practice, including the development of adoptive and biological parent advocacy groups, are serving to create new partnerships in that arena. Organizations like the North American Conference on Adoptable Children (NACAC) and special projects like the Child Welfare League of America's North American Center on Adoptions and the regional adoption resource centers sponsored by the U. S. Children's Bureau have served to forge new links between adoptive parents' groups and professional adoption agencies. Such organizations have been involved in a variety of activities including social support groups, case finding, home studies, and advocacy. In protective services, groups like Parents Anonymous have brought formerly abusing and neglectful parents to the fore as helpers to others. The key implication of this increasing trend toward partnership with parents is that the field of child welfare practice will quite literally never be the same again. The service equation must now be extended to include not only professionals, but also parents as monitors, advocates, co-helpers, and teachers. Such a shift poses a challenge to traditional professional notions on the limits of parent involvement, as well as an opportunity to create a new form of service based on the notion of partnership and shared responsibility.

A third concern has to do with the *ecological validity* of child welfare services and, in particular, the *cultural relevance* of such services for ethnic minority children and families. Bronfenbrenner, speaking in the context of research on human development, defines ecological validity as "The extent to which the environment experienced by the subjects in scientific investigation has the properties it is supposed to or assumed to have by the investigator" (1979, p. 29). If we substitute "clients in a service program" for "subjects in a scientific investigation" and "child welfare worker" for "investigator," we come closer to the meaning intended in the present context. Simply stated: Do our child welfare services fit the various racial and ethnic groups to which they are targeted and the various physical-sociocultural environments wherein the recipients reside? To many who have studied the question, the answer is, resoundingly, no. Billingsley and Giovannoni in their socio-historical analysis of service delivery to black children and families offer the following: "The system of child welfare services in this country is failing black children. . . . That failure is a manifest result of racism" (1972, p. 3).

Chestang examines this assertion and documents the concern of a number of minority and majority scholars that a central theme in understanding the institutional racism of the child welfare system has to do with recognizing "misrepresentations," "misunderstandings," and "distortions" of black family life and the relationship between these misconceptions and the inadequacy of child welfare services (1978, p. 174). For example, he states that a core concern of many black child welfare experts is the removal of black and other minority group children from their homes for neglect or abuse when the basic cause of the family's problems is, essentially, economic. Chestang concludes: "The double jeopardy of racism and poverty, then, is the fundamental problem confronting minority groups, and any meaningful efforts to solve the problem [of child welfare] must address these factors" (1978, p. 180). Such concerns are, of course, not unique to black clients of child welfare services. The recently completed investigation by the National Commission on Children in Need of Parents concluded that special sensitivity is needed to ensure that cultural differences are respected and that assumptions and limitations of the dominant culture are not imposed in ways that put minority children at an even greater disadvantage (*Who Knows? Who Cares?*, 1979, p. 25). Further, specific recommendations point to the need to re-examine service alternatives previously considered substandard: "Child welfare agencies should evaluate how well minority children in informal placements are doing and help these families to meet the requirements necessary to continue caring for the child where the environment is basically beneficial" (1979, p. 25).

The recently passed *Indian Child Welfare Act of 1978* affirms that there is "no resource more vital to the continued existence and integrity of the Indian Tribe than their children" and acknowledges that "an alarmingly high percentage of Indian families are broken up by the removal, often unwarranted, of their children . . . by non-tribal public and private agencies" (1979). Again, a large part of the problem appears to be the failure of the cultural majority to understand the culturally specific childrearing factors and family patterns of the particular minority group for whom they are providing services (Children's Bureau, 1977; Ishisaka, 1978). When minority families are viewed in the context of their own culture and traditions (in Bronfenbrenner's terms, studied in "ecologically valid" ways) the implications for child welfare services are often considerable. For example, as Cochran and Brassard (1979) note in their recent review of child development and personal social networks, the work of investigators like Stack (1974) and Hill (1972) points to the central role that such personal networks play as a primary source of adoptive child care arrangements in the black community. The implications of even a moderate payoff from more active promotion and support for such naturally occurring resources are profound, when estimates of the number of black children in the pool of children awaiting adoption exceed 40% (Chestang, 1978, p. 174). Stokes and Greenstone (1981) offer practical suggestions for working through the black extended family and building on the informal child-caring practices identified by Hill (1977), Jones (1975), and others. Ishisaka (1978), in his study of Indian families whose children were in foster care, makes the useful distinction between reasons that are "norm violative" (physical abuse, neglect) and "non-norm violative" (family or economic problems) for entry into foster care. He found, as did Giovannoni and Billingsley (1970) in an earlier study of neglectful mothers, that environmental and situational stress and lack of resources were much in evidence among families in the child welfare system. Thus, the delivery of ecologically valid and culturally relevant child welfare services will require both a finely tuned and discriminating assessment of reasons for entry into the system, as well as a broad-ranging search for culturally indigenous helping patterns that may be supported and enhanced through professional helping.

A fourth issue confronting child welfare reflects the growing concern that *models of professional education and staff training are somehow not keeping pace with the demands of current practice.* Wiltse suggests a number of reasons for this apparent lack of fit including: lack of student financial aid and child welfare visibility in public sector social servies; declassification of many child welfare positions; lack of preparation in doing *in situ* assessments of "functioning parenting structures;" lack of a social systems perspective, and lack of clear specializations in child welfare (1981). Wiltse and others suggest that in some ways professional education, to the extent that it focuses on study, diagnosis, and treatment from an individual perspective, may actually serve as a barrier to effective practice in an arena where understanding the total family system's function/dysfunction and assessing and mobilizing environmental supports are keys to successful intervention. In large measure, the answers to the problem of education and training for effective child welfare practice already exist. David Fanshel, whose own extensive research on foster care represents a landmark in child welfare, observes the following of the state of the art:

> What makes the [practice] formulations so useful is that they have been tried in the field. . . . The work of Reid in task-centered casework in Chicago, Gambrill and Stein in behaviorally oriented work with parents in Alameda County, and Pike's work in the Oregon Permanency Project, provide real life experiences as examples for work that seeks to involve parents as active partners in service efforts designed to restore children to their families (In Maluccio & Sinanoglu, 1981, p. X).

Much of the work of developing curriculum and training materials in child welfare will involve first, culling the key practice strategies from such model demonstration projects and second, anchoring them in a framework like that broadly outlined in the first two chapters of this book. Such a foundation would surely include the elaboration of the ecological perspective on child and family development; the identification of a competence orientation as opposed to a psychopathology orientation to family work; skill in ecological child and family assessment as well as in short-term, task-focused approaches to family work; and effective case monitoring and management. The National and Regional Child Welfare Training Centers and other projects seeded by the U. S. Children's Bureau have already made impressive inroads on this task. What appears to emerge from virtually all sectors of the child welfare field is the finding that effective practice models will not be constituted of singular strategies such as parenting skills training, provision of concrete resources, social support groups, or task-focused family work, but rather will be made up of *packages* of such services carefully delivered and tracked in an overall system of case management and case review. The implications of this notion of service package are, as we shall see, critical to social support networks.

SOCIAL SUPPORT NETWORKS AND CHILD WELFARE: AN IDEA WHOSE TIME HAS COME

What central themes emerge from this brief overview of child welfare and what implications do they have for practitioners? Three interwoven sets of ideas seem to us to be central:

1. The idea of the family as the ideal developmental context for the child.
2. The notion of child welfare services as family-supportive and family-strengthening.
3. The primary focus on meeting the basic developmental needs of the child, as opposed to identifying and treating child–family pathology.

In general terms, these three ideas argue for the kind of ecological perspective and competence orientation discussed in the initial chapter of this book. We need to include in our child welfare case plans and service programs the key environmental factors that support, enhance, or constrain the development of children and the well-being of their families. Specifically, we believe that there is more than a little evidence that greater use of social support networks in child welfare, in partnership with professional services, will not only bring us closer to the goal of a more family-supportive, competence-focused practice, but may actually help to solve some short-range concerns as well. Such concerns have to do with (1) enhancing the effectiveness of our present services, (2) increasing their potential for normalization, and (3) making better use of existing child welfare resources. In short, although social support networks are not a panacea for what ails child welfare, social support, properly understood and used conjointly with professional help, has the potential to become one of those compelling ideas that can bring us closer to providing ecologically valid, family-supportive, and competence-focused child welfare services. What is our rationale for focusing on social support as an important concept for child welfare?

ENHANCING SERVICE EFFECTIVENESS

There is a growing corpus of research in child, youth, and family services which suggests that "success," however defined, at the point of discharge or termination of services is not necessarily a good predictor of the child's ultimate adjustment to the community. A more powerful predictor appears to be the presence or absence of a social support network which can continue, enhance, and build on gains made during the course of formal services. From residential child care, we have a growing number of studies that identify the supports available to the child in the postdischarge environment as being the key factor in determining readjustment to family, neighborhood, school, and community. Allerhand, Weber, and Haug, in a follow-up study of 50 boys discharged from Bellefaire, a large residential treatment center in the midwest, found that the clinical improvement of the child at the point of discharge was a useful predictor of community adjustment only at the extremes of the sample range, i.e., for those youngsters so resilient that they could withstand the most impoverished posttreatment environment and for those youngsters so troubled that even the most supportive community environment was not sufficient to ensure successful adaptation. For over two-thirds of the sample, the key to predicting successful postdischarge adaptation lay in the quality of supportive family, neighborhood, and school arrangements available in the community. The investigators conclude:

> Perhaps the most striking finding of the study is that none of the measurements of within Bellefaire performance at discharge, either in casework or in cottage and school roles, were useful in themselves in predicting post-discharge adaptability and adaptation. Only when the situation to which the child returned was taken into account were performances at Bellefaire related to post-discharge adequacies. In a stressful community situation, strengths nurtured within the institution tended to break down, whereas in a supportive situation, these strengths tended to be reinforced. (1966, p. 140)

Similar conclusions were reached in a follow-up study of 75 children discharged from Children's Village, a residential treatment center in Connecticut (Taylor & Alpert, 1973). This study focused on continuity and support in the postdischarge environment in relation to preadmission and postdischarge adaptation. The specific hypotheses of the study were: (1) The greater the degree of *continuity* in the postdischarge environment, the greater the degree of the child's adaptation to the environment. (2) The greater the degree of *support* in the postdischarge environment, the greater the degree of the child's adaptation to the environment. (3) The greater the degree of *preadmission adaptation*, the greater the degree of postdischarge adaptation. (4) The greater the degree of *adaptation* gained in the institution, the greater the degree of postdischarge adaption (Taylor and Alpert, 1973).

"Adaptation" was measured by client responses to a Community Adaptation Schedule, which attempted to measure social adaptation in such areas as peer relationships, work relations, recreation patterns, and relationships with the opposite sex, as well as by professional ratings. The most conclusive result of the study is that family support emerges as the most important single factor in determining postdischarge adaptation, thus supporting the second hypothesis. Partial support was found for the first hypothesis, in that when children had *both* continuity and support, they were more likely to have a positive postdischarge adaptation. The third hypothesis was not supported: preadmission characteristics were not, in themselves, sufficient to predict postdischarge outcomes. The investigators comment that:

> Whether or not a family was intact at time of admission did not matter in terms of how the youngster adapted in the post-discharge environment. However . . . stability within the family provided a positive relationship with outcome. . . . This is interpreted to mean that when the child is clear regarding what is happening with his parents he has a better chance of working through his feelings regarding the separation (Taylor & Alpert, 1973, pp. 36–37).

As in the earlier Bellefaire study, the investigators found a lack of association between improvement while in residential treatment and postdischarge functioning: "social and behavioral adaptation is in large part a function of environmental situation and is *not* transferred from one dissimilar situation to another" (Taylor & Alpert, 1973, pp. 45–56). Related results are reported by Nelson, Singer, and Johnson (1978). These investigators found that children leaving residential treatment who were part of some supportive network maintained 71% of the goals they obtained in treatment, whereas those without adequate support showed only a 50% maintenance rate. Cavior, Schmidt, and Karacki (1972) reported similar results in a follow-up study of delinquent youth discharged from a federal youth center. They found that what happens to the youth after release depends as much on the kind of support and assistance he or she receives in the community as on the service he or she receives at the youth center.

Other sectors of child welfare service provide at least partial evidence that social supports are an important resource for families. Metcalf's (1980) study of single-parent families confirms the correlation between positive social network and measures of self-image for both mothers and children, as well as measures of positive family interaction. The work of Wahler (1980a) on parent training with insular families demonstrates the inadequacy of such single-focus training approaches—unless the family's wider network of social contact also becomes a focal point for intervention. Studying foster care, Fanshel (1975; 1976) found that the continued involvement of biological parents, through visitation, is a powerful predictor of the child's eventual return to the family of origin: "Like the frequent monitoring of body temperature information, the visitation of children should be carefully scrutinized as the best indicator we have concerning the long term fate of children in care" (Fanshel, 1975, p. 513).

Collins and Pancoast (1976) describe an informal network of "day care neighbors" as a potential strategy for overcoming abuse and neglect. Garbarino, Stocking, and associates (1980) outline a number of potentially useful ways in which naturally occurring and contrived social support networks can be used in conjunction with professional services to overcome social isolation and to support families and protect children from abuse and neglect. In sum, the evidence continues to mount that effective child welfare services in the future must include more than treatment technologies and case monitoring. They will need to take into account the links between professionally delivered services and contrived or naturally occurring sources of social support in the client's social network. The case for such emphasis on social support does not, at present, rest entirely on hard evidence: much experimentation and evaluation remains to be done. As Gottlieb (1980) observes, however, it is difficult to ignore the hard data accumulating from a series of studies in fields such as health care, which contrast the health of people who are enmeshed in an informal support network with the health of those who are socially isolated. Such studies strongly suggest that social support networks are indeed an important resource for the field of child welfare.

ENHANCING CHILD DEVELOPMENT

Even if the use of social support networks were not as effective as it appears to be, a sufficient case for introducing social support networks in child welfare can be made on developmental grounds alone. Their increased use in conjunction with professional services can make the service setting— residential center, day care center, foster home, or child's own home—a more developmentally sound environment. Cochran and Brassard identify three ways in which the personal social networks of parents can influence the development of the child:

> 1. The parents' social network can come to bear upon the child indirectly through the kinds of influences network members have upon the parents themselves as developing individuals.
> 2. Network members may also have indirect but enduring impact upon the child by linking the parent to the outside world in such a way as to open up new life possibilities.
> 3. Network members [may] engage in activities and exchanges with parents which make that role easier or more dificult to fulfill, and which limit the child rearing repertoire of parents to a greater or lesser degree. (1979, p. 602)

The authors suggest that such network influences can offer parents support by providing emotional and material assistance, childrearing controls (on the parent), and a wide range of role models. Among other recent studies, they cite the work of Hetherington, Cox, and Cox (1976), which indicates that the more support from friends, neighbors, and kin is available to divorced families, the more effective is the mother in interactions with her preschool child. This study (Hetherington, Cox, & Cox, 1978a, b) yields the same general conclusions as the previously cited work of Metcalf on single-parent mothers and of others discussed in Chapter 8: "Our expectation was that a positive social network will enhance a parent's self image and a parent's perception of family interaction which in turn will increase a child's perception of family interaction and self image . . . [we found that] . . . these measures are statistically linked in just such a logical association" (Metcalf, 1980, p. 20). In addition to such network influences mediated through the parents, Cochran and Brassard suggest a variety of ways in which the personal social network of the parents can directly influence the developing child by providing: "(1) cognitive and social stimulation, (2) direct support [e.g., through informal child care], (3) observational models for the child, and (4) opportunities for active participation in the network" (1979, pp. 604–605):

The answer to the question of how personal networks influence child development can be summarized as follows: network influence is both direct and indirect. It includes the sanctioning of parental behavior and the provision of material and emotional support for both parent and child. Network members also serve as models for parent and child, they stimulate the child directly and they involve the child more generally in network activities. These processes interact with the developmental age of the child to stimulate the basic trust, empathy and mastery of the reciprocal exchange skills essential to network building. (1979, pp. 606–607)

The authors suggest a range of developmental outcomes that are affected by such network influences—independence behavior, perceptions of social role, conceptions of childrearing, self-concept formation, perceptual differentiation, task completion, representational thinking, and cognitive receptivity—and propose a number of research enquiries to validate empirically their model of network influences on child development (1979, p. 614).

Child welfare practitioners need not await such studies before including social support networks as part of their service strategies. The evidence of positive effects on the developing child is sufficiently strong at present to justify some service experiments. Moreover, the children in the care of the child welfare system—in foster families, group homes, and temporary shelters—cannot arrest their development until the final results are in. In the meantime, Bronfenbrenner's proposition, "that the developmental potential of a child rearing setting is increased as a function of the number of supportive links between that setting and other contexts involving the child or persons responsible for his or her care" (1979, p. 844), needs to be tested in the crucible of day-to-day practice. For many children currently in the child welfare system, those "other contexts" are the foster family homes, group homes, and institutions where they temporarily reside. One of our present tasks involves building links between such settings through shared communication and activities with the child's family of origin, such that the "other context" is viewed by the parent as a help and support, not as a substitute or as a sign of irreversible failure. In short, we are a long way from resolving conclusively the issue of effectiveness with the children and families now in the child welfare system. It is an issue that will no doubt occupy us for the rest of our professional lifetimes. In the meantime, we do know some things about creating developmentally sound, humane, and caring environments for children. Such knowledge compels us to make the enhancement of naturally occurring or contrived social support networks of parents a first-order task for building family-based child welfare services.

An additional two reasons, *service normalization* and *service efficiency*, provide a rationale for initiating a major focus on social support networks. The first of these, service normalization, involves what is essentially a value argument: namely, that the move toward offering service in the least restrictive environment that has begun in the fields of mental retardation and special education can and should be extended to the full range of child welfare services. Flynn and Nitsch advance the concept of normalization beyond simple physical integration: "Normalization means sharing a normal rhythm of the day, with privacy, activities and social responsibilities; a normal rhythm of the week, with a home to live in, a school or work to go to, and leisure time with a modicum of social interaction" (1980, pp. 32–33).

Such definitions begin to offer further specificity to the work of Wolfensberger, cited in Chapter 2, which defines normalization as "the utilization of means which are as culturally normative as possible, in order to establish and/or maintain personal behaviors and characteristics which are as culturally normative as possible" (1972, p. 28). For children and families of color, this means that foster and adoptive placement, when it is necessary, should be within race whenever possible and should follow the culturally approved pattern of informal child care arrangements within the minority community. In residential care, the studies cited earlier in this chapter offer tantalizing, if inconclusive, evidence of the importance of the child's perception of continuity with his or her biological family before, during, and after placement and later during community adjustment. In cases of child abuse and neglect, the use of neighborhood lay helpers and formerly abusive parents (through groups like Parents Anonymous) has shown effectiveness and promise in reaching the hard-to-reach family in more culturally acceptable ways, i.e., through informal helping. Thus, we suggest that increased use of social support networks will move us closer to our goal of normalization for child welfare services. The involvement of family, friends, neighbors, community gatekeepers, and other informal helpers will increase the probability that our child welfare services will occur in more nearly normal settings in more nearly normal ways.

A final reason for introducing social support networks into our equation for child welfare services has to do with the need for a more efficient use of resources. We need to use the existing systems in new and creative ways in order to deliver what traditionally have been viewed as child welfare services. This is especially true in the immediate future where the goal for many of our child welfare agencies (and the families they serve) is purely and simply survival. Draconian budget cuts in child and family services, the continuing shortage of professionally trained child welfare staff, and the limits posed by energy shortages and by inflation all argue for the elevation of informal helping strategies to a first-order priority in child welfare.

We argue for a partnership in child welfare, not, as some do, for the elimination of a professional presence. Our public concerns, as reflected in alarming statistics on child abuse and neglect and foster-care drift, will not go away simply by making them private troubles once again. We suggest that, in an era of diminishing fiscal resources, we look more closely to our human resources—through the creation and use of social support networks—to develop new and effective ways of reaching and aiding the dependent, neglected, abused, or otherwise needy child. We recognize and agree with the implicit support for such an approach in the recently completed report of the Massachusetts Governor's Advisory Committee on Children and the Family: "Government can best act to strengthen families first by reviewing existing policies to assess their impact on family life, and second *by enabling families to sustain or restructure their own environments on behalf of their children and of themselves*" [emphasis added] (1980, p. 11). Such "enabling," we believe, means something particular in child welfare: it means adopting a state of mind that views strengthening the family and identifying social support networks as the primary goals and providing direct professional help as the secondary goal in service provision.

APPLICATION OF SOCIAL SUPPORT NETWORKS IN CHILD WELFARE

As mentioned earlier, the chapters in this volume on youth services, schools, delinquency prevention, divorced and stepfamilies, and early childhood services each contain numerous illustrations of social support networks in the service of children and families. Such illustrations show the potential for using a network approach in the traditional child welfare services: foster care and adoptions, residential care, preventive services, and in-home services. Equally promising is the fact that within each of these more traditional services, grass-roots innovations have occurred over the last few years which combine formal and informal helping in new and creative ways.

In *foster family care*, the research of David Fanshel suggests the importance of "parental visiting" as "the best indicator we have concerning the long-term fate of children in care" (1975). Such findings have served, along with other factors, to stimulate interest in working with biological parents of children in foster care. As part of its overall commitment to permanency planning, the U. S. Children's Bureau recently funded several projects of national significance to examine the quality of supports available to biological parents of children in foster care. Maluccio and Sinanoglu (1981) and Sinanoglu and Maluccio (1981) document a number of such efforts to understand and deal with the problem of involving biological parents. These efforts include: (1) developing parent organizations, (2) using foster parents as counselors and supports to biological parents, and (3) using task-centered, goal-oriented, and time-limited interventions to help parents regain custody of their children. Other efforts to reach biological parents include using foster parents as role models for biological parents (Davies & Bland, 1978), "joint parenting" (Galaway, 1976, 1978), 5-day-a-week foster care (Loewe & Hanrahan, 1975) involving natural parents in placement decision-making (Simmons, Gumpert, & Rothman, 1973), and parent–child joint placement (Nayman & Witkin, 1978). Parents in Crisis offers peer support for parents of children in substitute care in Victoria, British Columbia, through parent groups, social activities, and a monthly newsletter (*Natural Parent Newsletter*, 1980). What such efforts appear to have in common are various forms of partnership between child welfare workers, foster parents, and biological parents, and a firm conviction that temporary separation from the family of origin need not destroy involvement or continuity. Drawing from her own extensive research on the impact of placement on parents as well as from the work of others on attachment, Jenkins (1981; Jenkins & Norman, 1972, 1975) makes the critical points that physical separation of parent and child is not a *sufficient* condition for deprivation (it depends on the circumstances of the separation) and that bonding between parent and child need not be broken by temporary placement in foster care. Jenkins recognizes the ambivalent feelings many parents exhibit at placement ("sad at separation, happy for care") and suggests that in dealing with these feelings, workers help to separate the affect that is directly focused on the parent–child relationship from that which is directed toward other family members, the foster care agency, and so on (1981, pp. 46–47). We can summarize these findings by saying that the corpus of research and practice demonstrations in foster care strongly suggests the wisdom of continued involvement of biological parents. This continued involvement can be achieved through visitation, shared care, and a host of other arrangements; with it, continuing social support is necessary for coping with the sequelae of separation and preparing for reunification. Moreover, as Pecora suggests, professional attitudes toward the foster care system and toward parents can have a great deal to do with facilitating reunification:

> Social worker attitudes toward the foster care system (if negative) and toward maternal/family adequacy (if positive) are associated with increased likelihood of a child's returning home (Jenkins and Norman, 1975). A negative worker attitude toward the foster care system . . . [may be] beneficial in that it . . . [can] result in more use of informal procedures and increased service to children and their families (1980, p.1).

Such informal procedures may be an indirect indicator of the potential for involving informal helping efforts (shared care, foster parents as counselors, natural parent support groups, and so on) as part of the service package.

In the related area of *adoptions*, the virtual revolution in practice over the last 15 years has brought informal helping in many and varied forms to the forefront of service delivery. Informal social support groups have emerged for virtually all participants in the adoption scene. They include groups of adult adoptees seeking their biological identity, families awaiting placement, and families who have adopted children with special needs. Moreover, recently passed child welfare legislation (P.L. 96-272), the growing concern about protection of cultural and racial heritage in adoption, and the initiation of many new information–service networks around the "special needs" child have all spurred the development of informal helping efforts to meet the needs of children and families. For example, the Child Welfare League of America's North American Center on Adoptions engages in policy-related and advocacy activities on behalf of adoptive parent groups, as does the North American Council on Adoptable Children. Over the last several years, the U. S. Children's Bureau has created Adoption Resource Centers in each of the ten federal regions—all of which have strong ties to adoptive parent groups. Kadushin (1980, pp. 505–507 and 533–539) describes a number of support groups for families involved in transracial adoption, as well as for families involved in international adoptions. The concern we noted above about culturally relevant child welfare has spurred efforts to identify special resources within minority communities to meet the needs of children for adoptive placements. Hill (1972) stresses the extended kinship system and social network existing within many black communities as special resources for child welfare. Walker (1981) describes cultural and ethnic issues involved in working with black families in the child welfare system. Stokes and Greenstone (1981) describe an innovative group program in Chicago to help black grandparents and older parents cope with rearing young children. Such support groups may be an important aid to substitute child care arrangements in many black communities, where:

> Grandparents . . . participate actively in child rearing . . . and [may] provide extensive daytime or afterschool care for youngsters. In more extreme yet common situations, children are absorbed into the extended family by "informal adoption" (Hill, 1977; Jones, 1975; Martin and Martin, 1978). To place a child in either foster care or adoption outside of the family violates the values of many black families to such an extent that it occurs only when there is no other alternative. (Stokes and Greenstone, 1981, p. 692)

In fact, as Cole points out, the number of adoptions by relatives is increasing for all groups—by 20% from 1968 through 1973—and may reflect the increase in divorces, remarriages, and subsequent adoptions of a new spouse's children (1978, p. 134). Such trends may signal the need for similar support groups for the older spouse suddenly thrust into the role of parenting young children. As such relative adoptions and other "open" adoptions (Baran, Pannor, & Sorosky, 1976) increase, the need for social support networks and network-based professional interventions will increase as well. Presently, such efforts occur through social support and advocacy groups like the Adoptees Liberty Movement Association (ALMA), the various support groups for adoptive parents, the special efforts to identify and support placement resources within minority communities, and the use of innovative methods in professional adoption practice (Churchill *et al.*, 1979). The methods that use adoptive parents and foster parents as co-helpers constitute, in their totality, a series of natural experiments on how formal and informal helpers can work effectively together in adoptions practice.

In the area of *preventive services* designed to protect children from abuse and neglect, much interest has been shown in using social support networks as both a preventive and rehabilitative tool in working with at-risk families. Commenting on his own extensive research on the ecology of child abuse as well as the work of others, Garbarino offers the following observation:

> From the ecological perspective, a critical need of parents . . . is for the nurturance and feedback that come from day-to-day interpersonal relationships. . . . What transforms individual risk into abuse? [This same] perspective argues that it is the social context in which families live . . . the social and economic deprivation in the environment of families (In Garbarino, Stocking, and Associates, 1980, pp. 6–7).

He cites the work of other investigators who have repeatedly demonstrated that social isolation is a correlate of child maltreatment (Bryant *et al.*, 1963; Elmer, 1967; Bakan, 1971; Lauer, Ten Broeck, & Grossman, 1974; Smith, Hanson, & Noble, 1974; Helfer & Kempe, 1976). Garbarino suggests that:

> Parents who maltreat children prefer to solve problems on their own. They have few relationships outside the home, and they are likely to discourage outside involvement on the part of their children. They tend to be transient, at least in urban areas . . . and to have a lifelong history of avoiding activities that would bring them into contact with other adults. This does not necessarily mean that social isolation *causes* child maltreatment. But social isolation is an indicator of lifelong pattern of estrangement. (In Garbarino, Stocking, and Associates, 1980, p. 8)

Whether such isolation is a cause, effect, or correlate of abuse and neglect remains unresolved (Polansky *et al.*, 1981, pp. 86–96). There does seem to be growing consensus in the field of protective services about fostering social support for abusing and neglectful families. Such support may take many forms. Parents Anonymous is representative of a self-help group for parents that has enjoyed widespread acceptance among both parents and professionals over the last several years (Behavior Associates, 1977; Lieber & Baker, 1977). If nothing else, Parents Anonymous offers great hope to those who seek to expand the concept of parent support groups to child welfare—this, in spite of the fact that its identified population consists of those whom society has judged most culpable of failing to provide adequate care for their children. Other examples include neighborhood-based family support interventions (Tietjen, 1980; Warren, 1980) such as open pre-schools and a broadly gauged program of parent education that includes family supports. Gottlieb (1980, p. 50) provides insight into the affiliative skills needed to participate in such networks, calling to mind the link between social skills training and social support networks identified in Chapter 2. Along the same lines, Collins (1980) and Pancoast (1980) offer specific practice suggestions for enlisting neighbors in preventive services. Bertsche and his colleagues at the University of Montana have developed a special workbook for child welfare workers to help them identify informal helping resources for their clients (Bertsche, Clark, & Iversen, 1981). What precise balance will be found with respect to clinical treatment and social support approaches in working with abusing and neglecting families remains to be seen. Polansky offers the following observation from his extensive research on neglectful parents:

> [They] were isolated from helping networks . . . [though] the isolation was more general than it first appeared, extending to both formal and informal participation with others. . . . [This] lack of social involvement was visible already in adolescence, prior to their becoming parents. The data led, in other words, from a fact about their ecology to observations on character structure. . . . If anxieties and hostilities limit contacts with others, if personality limitations leave one with little to give to others, then . . . one lacks the supports other people can take for granted. One is left with a "spiral of causation" as they say in general systems theory, leading downward. So the ecological and personalistic approaches must be seen as complementary rather than mutually exclusive. (In Polansky *et al.*, 1981, pp. 95–96)

Without discounting personalistic variables, Garbarino and Gilliam acknowledge the need for a broader kind of transforming experiment which would reduce the negative aspects of privacy without paying too high a price in the freedom and integrity of the individual. "We need," they conclude, "a more positive concept of dependency" (1980, p. 48). Whatever particular form social support strategies may take, it is clear that they should play a key role in our overall armamentarium of preventive services. In a way, this is both a logical and beneficial consequence of elevating child abuse and neglect from a private trouble to a public concern.

Another area of child welfare service that has witnessed an interest in social support is *residential care* and *in-home services*. Residential child care is, in fact, a composite of many different types of out-of-home placement: residential treatment centers, group homes, child care institutions, shelter care, receiving homes, respite care facilities, diagnostic centers, half-way houses, and so on. For a variety of cultural, philosophical, and theoretical reasons, residential child care services have suffered from a dual isolation:

first, from the other services in the child and family service continuum and, second, from the parents of the children in care (Wolins, 1974; Whittaker, 1979; Small & Whittaker, 1979; Kadushin, 1980, pp. 583–631; Rothman, 1980, pp. 205–231). The fruits of such isolation have been an alarming amount of institutional abuse and neglect and, as detailed earlier, a less-than-impressive record of helping troubled children readjust to their families, neighborhoods, schools, and communities (Wooden, 1976; Children's Defense Fund, 1978; National Center on Child Abuse and Neglect, 1978). Such concerns, along with the chronic problem of funding what surely is the most expensive child welfare service, have prompted professionals in the field to experiment with innovative ways of more closely linking the residential child care setting to its ecological context. Hobbs's Project RE-ED (1966), cited in chapter 2, was a bold attempt to link the specialized residential setting to the child's family, school, and community in as normalized an environment as possible (Whittaker, 1979, pp. 71–79). One of the roles emerging from this creative residential experiment, the "liaison specialist," offers a model of system linking applicable to other areas of human services as well (Dokecki, 1977; Hobbs, 1982). The Teaching Family Model (formerly Achievement Place) offers a family-based group home model for behavior-disordered youth with a strong focus on teaching skills for normal community living. This program, through its continuing care project, developed specific skill packages to help youths overcome the problem of community readjustment (Watson et al., 1980). Finkelstein (1981) describes a family-centered residential setting for children, and Carbino (1981) offers advice on setting up an organization for parents of children in substitute care. Programs like the Children's Center in San Antonio (Children's Defense Fund, 1978, pp. 157–159) and the Family Advocacy Center in Maine (*Family Advocacy Council*, 1979) have developed family-based residential programs with strong attention to involving parents as partners. Like many state associations of voluntary children's services, the California Association of Services for Children (*C.S.C.*, 1982) has among its member agencies a number that are experimenting with various forms of family involvement including intensive in-home services and residential services within the same agency auspice. Whittaker (1981) has proposed social support groups for parents as part of an overall structure for maintaining family links when a child is placed in residence.

In the area of home-based services, Maybanks and Bryce (1979) and Bryce and Lloyd (1981) document a number of innovative service programs around the country that combine formal and informal helping to prevent unnecessary out-of-home placement. Some in-home programs like Homebuilders of Tacoma, Washington (Kinney et al., 1977) and In Home Family Support Services of Des Moines, Iowa (Stephens, 1979) function as part of a larger multiservice agency; others operate as free-standing programs. All are committed to reaching out to families on their own turf and helping them resolve problems within the communities, neighborhoods, and cultural contexts they inhabit. Bryce and Lloyd articulate this philosophy:

> The first and greatest resource investment is made in the care and treatment of children in their own homes before more radical measures are taken.
>
> The service setting is primarily the home but includes problem-solving efforts in the family's ecological system (i.e., where the family interfaces with community systems).
>
> There is maximum utilization of family resources, extended family and community. (1981, p. 7)

It is but a small leap from such a philosophy to many of the service innovations described in the home-based literature that combine formal and informal efforts in creative ways. Perhaps it is, as Horejsi suggests in his reexamination of the St. Paul Family Centered Project of the 1950's, like "exploring an old gold mine:" to *rediscover* what effective practice with families in their own environment is all about (Bryce & Lloyd, 1981, pp. 12–23). Some innovations involving professional treatment and social support include: (1) home support for families with disturbed children, (2) using the extended family as a focus for service, (3) using caretakers as an alternative to placement, and (4) using "lay therapists" to work with suspected abusing families (Bryce & Lloyd, 1981). The home-based services movement is presently serving as a catalyst in the child welfare field to create programs and strategies that combine the best elements of competent professional service with indigenous social support.

SOME PRACTICAL SUGGESTIONS FOR INCORPORATING SOCIAL SUPPORT NETWORKS IN CHILD WELFARE

We have argued in this chapter and earlier in the book that social support networks have an important role in making traditional child welfare services more effective, developmentally sound, and culturally relevant. A few simple suggestions are now in order to guide our efforts:

1. *Social support networks offer no panacea for child welfare and should not be seen as a substitute for professionally delivered services.* We have stressed throughout this volume the notion of *partnership* as a key to success in incorporating social support and social treatment. Many of the children and families in the present child welfare system have special needs requiring sophisticated clinical treatment—family therapy, for example—that go well

beyond their other considerable needs for social support and, often, tangible aid.

2. *One barrier to even considering joining formal and informal helping in child welfare resides in our own concrete thinking:* "All of this sounds like the volunteer effort we tried a few years ago and couldn't get off the ground." or, "Our kids and families have no informal helping networks."

Each child welfare practitioner and agency carries a particular history of efforts in this area: a failed volunteer program; firm convictions about what would and would not work with *our* families, and so on. These blinders often constrain us from thinking of the creative use of new resources to accomplish our goals. Such barriers must be set aside, but since they are real in their consequences, the attitudes and fears accompanying them must be dealt with in a supportive professional environment which encourages risk-taking behavior.

3. *When one thinks about social support and child welfare, it doesn't necessarily follow that total program upheaval must occur before some of these ideas can be tested.* We need to lay out a realistic time frame for our practice experiments—and start small: for example, using social support strategies as an adjunct to family therapy, rather than launching a program of clinical intervention with full-scale network assemblies. Such an approach is less threatening and can be unifying in a child welfare agency where social support strategies may be compatible and reinforcing to much of traditional practice.

4. *In thinking about social supports and child welfare, we need to caution against purchasing "whole cloth" models: we'll probably need to construct our own.* Presently there simply is not a range of well-developed models for how to incorporate social support networks into foster care, residential services, adoptions, and all the other child welfare services. Remembering what was said earlier about the need for ecological validity, i.e., the "fitness" of services for the environments in which they will be delivered, this is not altogether a bad thing. We have no grand experiment to answer the question of how best to help the children and families presently in the child welfare system. Instead, we expect that the fruits of hundreds of smaller experiments will each provide a piece of the overall answer.

CHAPTER 7
Social Support Networks in Day Care and Early Child Development

Florence Long

It is becoming increasingly common for young children to spend part of each week in the care of someone other than their parents. Statistics from the Bureau of the Census (Simons, 1981) show that in 1975, 47% of all 3- to 13-year-olds spent part of each day away from their parents. Concern over this trend is widespread because many believe that parents are the most appropriate caregivers for their young children. Parents cannot always stay home. Fortunately, a growing body of literature asserts that good-quality day care does not have harmful effects on children or their parents. Child care professionals and day care experts continue to express concern that center-based day care alone cannot meet the needs of children and families, however.

This chapter explores patterns of child care that currently exist in the United States. Much of the child care system is already based on informal support networks that have been given little attention in discussions of day care. These informal networks can enhance the quality and expand the availability of day care to all who seek it. The title of this chapter emphasizes the linkages between day care environments and the development of young children. Although institutionalized day care has received a great deal of attention from people concerned with child development, informal child care networks have been relatively ignored. Child care professionals are beginning to recognize that formal and informal child care services can collaborate to meet the instrumental and psychological needs of families.

Institutionalized child care (day care centers, nursery schools, and pre-schools) traditionally has served three purposes: (1) to provide custodial care for children whose parents are unavailable during the day, (2) to provide opportunities for education and socialization, and (3) to reduce risk due to socioeconomic disadvantage. Formal day care to the children of working mothers became necessary in urban areas during the 1800's because many single mothers and young widows were cut off from family,

189

neighbors, church congregations, and other traditional sources of informal child care support. Preschools, on the other hand, evolved from what we know as nursery schools, as programs providing educational and socialization experiences for preschoolers. These programs are usually open a half-day, and 3- to 5-year-olds are eligible. Day care centers are frequently still perceived as merely custodial, even though the activities in a good quality day care center are often indistinguishable from those in a preschool. As more and more children require care outside the home for part or all of each day, these two types of programs have come to serve children with similar backgrounds and needs.

As the statistics presented later in this chapter will show, these formal child care services account for only a portion of the child care which families use. Although institutionalized child care is more visible, informal child care arrangements made privately between parents and providers may be more common. The chapter examines the use of different types of child care and the options available to families seeking care. It then looks at some of the issues in child care delivery from the perspectives of the parents and the providers. The discussion focuses on the functions of formal and informal child care networks in supporting families, and how the needs of child care providers and families can be integrated. Programs that offer child care to meet a broad range of needs are also described. Finally, some of the current problems encountered in attempting to develop informal child care support networks will be examined. Some suggestions for applying support networks will be proposed and future directions explored. The term "day care" as it is used generically throughout this chapter refers to any setting (in or outside their own homes) where children are cared for by someone other than their parents for part of the day.

CHILD CARE OPTIONS

As mothers of young children have entered the work force in increasing numbers, the concern for children in institutionalized day care, and for those cared for at home, has also grown. In the past three decades the percentage of mothers in the work force has grown from 18.6 to 56.7% (Simons, 1981). In 1980, 43% of preschool children and 57% of school-aged children had working mothers. According to the 1980 census figures, there are 19,940,000 children under 6 years old. This means that there could be as many as 8 million young children cared for by someone other than their mothers for part of the time. Another 17 million school-aged children of working mothers potentially need after-school care.

Proponents of increased formal child care services look at these figures and point out that there are only 1.6 million licensed spaces in preschools and day care programs to meet the needs of these children (Berk & Berson,

1981). Obviously someone is caring for many children outside of day care centers. When we examine the alternatives for child care, we have to question whether creating more formal child care services will meet the needs of working parents and their children.

Figures from the National Child Care Consumer Study (Rodes & Moore, 1975) showed that in 28.5% of the "working" families—single-parent families in which the parent worked or two-parent families in which both parents worked—parents still arranged to share care of their children under 14 years old in their own home. Table 7-1 summarizes the figures by employment status of parents and age of the child. Working parents are often most satisfied that they are fulfilling their childrearing responsibilities when they care for their children themselves, but arranging two work schedules around child care needs can create a great deal of stress for parents. Research has shown that in dual-worker families there are fewer opportunities to spend time together as a family; when the parents are together they are often tired from their work and housekeeping responsibilities. Women especially feel drained by their dual roles, since they continue to perform most routine housekeeping tasks (Blehar, 1979).

Another 24.8% of working households (Table 7-1) had someone else come into the home to care for the children. This person could have been either a relative or a nonrelative. It is difficult to document the quality and quantity of in-home care by nonparents because this kind of care is transient and informal. It is also difficult to enter homes because of the family's right to privacy. In-home care has the advantages of being convenient for children and parents, less disruptive for young children, and relatively inexpensive. Who is available however to come into a home to provide care, especially on a full-time basis? If not a relative, the most frequent choice is a teenaged girl, or an older woman. Since these arrangements often are not long-lasting, parents have to periodically locate a new caregiver.

When parents do not arrange for child care in their own homes, they often choose another person's home rather than center-based care. More than one-half the parents who place their children in the home of another (16.4% of all families) use the home of a relative, whereas 11.8% use the home of a nonrelative. Arrangements with relatives often allow flexibility and convenience for the parent as well as security for the child. Care by relatives are usually nonpaying arrangements (Moore, 1980), and may also ensure that the alternative caregiver shares the parent's values (Steinberg & Green, 1979; Moore, 1980). On the other hand, relying on a relative may create resentments between family members, especially because of the exchange of services without pay.

Care of children in the home of a nonrelative is known as family day care. Family day care is largely unregulated and undocumented. Perhaps as few as 10% of all family day care homes are licensed or registered (Michigan State Department of Social Services, 1977). Family day care shares many of

Table 7-1. Child care use by age of child and employment status of parent

Main method of care	Percentage of households with children under 6		Percentage of households with children 6 through 13, only		Working families	All families
	With single parent employed and both parents employed	With single parent not employed; with 2 parents: 1 employed or both unemployed	With single parent employed and both parents employed	With single parent not employed; with 2 parents: 1 employed or both unemployed		
In own home						
By relative	13.0	17.6	12.8	10.5	12.9	13.5
By nonrelative	15.6	17.4	8.3	7.8	11.9	12.3
In other home						
Of relative	18.1	20.5	14.5	12.7	16.3	16.4
Of nonrelative	21.6	5.5	14.4	5.9	18.0	11.8
Nursery schools	9.9	4.4	0.4	—	5.2	3.7
Group centers (incl. Head Start)	10.1	2.8	4.2	2.9	7.2	5.0
Used no extramural method	11.7	31.8	45.4	60.2	28.5	37.3
Total household Percentage	100.0	100.0	100.0	100.0	100.0	100.0
Number (in thousands)	4,544	9,229	4,734	5,885	9,278	24,392

Source: Adapted from Costin *et al.* (1977, p. 6), based on the National Childcare Consumer Study.

the advantages of care in the child's own home: convenience, individualized care for the child, relatively low cost, and nonseparation of siblings. Family day care has the disadvantages of other forms of in-home care, however: it is transient, sometimes undependable, and of varying quality. It is an option though that, if developed, could meet many of the needs of parents and children. Impetus to develop family day care comes from both the clients and the providers. The latter group is presently seeking ways to upgrade their professional role to ensure the quality of day care as well as to increase the respect they receive.

Only 8.7% of all parents surveyed by the National Childcare Consumer study chose to put their children in day care centers. Parents choose centers for several reasons. Because centers can be identified and regulated more carefully than informal care arrangements, their quality may be more uniform. They are preferred for 3- to 5-year-olds because of their educational program (Romero & Thomas, 1975). There is little evidence that good quality center-based care is harmful to children (Belsky & Steinberg, 1978; Kilmer, 1979). However, parents may opt against center care for other reasons. It is generally more expensive unless public funding is available (Woolsey, 1977). Centers may not be conveniently located, especially in rural areas, and often cannot meet the needs of sick children or parents who work odd shifts.

Full-time day care, because it traditionally has been oriented to custodial care of children, has developed greater flexibility than preschools or nursery schools in terms of hours available and ages of the children accepted. Preschools often cannot adapt to the needs of working parents' for care of all their children through the day. For lack of a better option, some parents have to shuttle their children daily between preschool and babysitter or some other combination of settings. Romero and Thomas (1975), in a survey of users of day care centers, found that 83% of the families used another type of care in addition to the day care center. Often day care for infants is not provided in the same center as care for preschoolers, so that parents with several children have to scatter them among centers or seek in-home care. At least a million school-aged children have no adult supervision for several hours each day after school.

FACTORS INFLUENCING DAY CARE CHOICE

Several factors influence parents' choice of child care. The option parents select, however, may be determined more by availability than desirability. For instance, age of the child limits the type of care parents can select. Only 39,849 children under 2 years of age and 81,974 2-year-olds attended day care centers in 1977 (Simons, 1981). This represents, as a rough estimate, 4% of all children under 3 years, yet approximately one-third of children under 3 have mothers who work. Many infants and toddlers are cared for in other settings, either in family day care or in their own homes. The reason for this may be that the demand for center-based day care greatly exceeds availability, or it may be that parents prefer care in a home environment, with a small number of children and one consistent caregiver, to center-based care for infants. On the other hand, about 20% of the 3- to 5-year-olds of working mothers were enrolled in day care centers in 1977.

The cost of child care is another factor that parents must consider in selecting child care arrangements. Center-based day care is currently funded both privately and publicly; public support for child care is almost always restricted to low-income parents. Thus, low- and high-income parents can afford center-based care, whereas families in the middle range may not be able to. (Estimates vary widely, but it costs roughly $2,000–$3,000 per year to keep one preschooler in full-time center-based care.) Family day care or an in-home sitter is usually a less expensive option for middle-income families and larger families (Kamerman & Kahn, 1976; Moore, 1980).

Although other factors may influence day care choice, they have not been documented. Convenience and location of care are suggested, as are such family characteristics as family size or structure. None of these factors has a clear relationship to the type of care that families use, and different surveys have produced contradictory findings. In one study that asked parents what they looked for in selecting a day care center, the following was found: characteristics of the staff, the educational program, and the child's opportunities for social development were more important to them than cost, facilities, or special services offered (Romero & Thomas, 1975).

SATISFACTION WITH CHILD CARE

Parents seem to express satisfaction with different types of care for different reasons (Prescott, 1972; Romero & Thomas, 1975; Steinberg & Green, 1979; Moore, 1980). Parents who employ an in-home sitter cite greater control over their child's care but less satisfaction with specific childrearing techniques the sitter uses. Parents with children in family day care feel that it meets their children's needs for emotional attachment and discipline as well as being convenient and flexible for themselves. Parents who choose center-based care mention the educational program and the assurance that the care is of good quality because the center is licensed. Thus parents may select center- or home-based care for different reasons. However, they do not always have a choice. Demand for center-based care may exceed availability in a particular community. Parents may not know how to locate a family day care provider near their home. They may prefer a type of care that they cannot afford. Thus, matching families with available options is a necessary priority in expanding child care services.

Despite the fact that parents express satisfaction with their current arrangement, whatever type it is, several surveys have found that most parents prefer home-based options (Strand et al., 1970; Feldman & Feldman, 1973; Auerbach, 1975). That many parents prefer in-home care, even if they themselves do not use it, suggests that we need to develop such options. Organizations such as the National Family Day Care Advisory Panel are working toward this goal by building community awareness about family day care. Another option that receives less attention is building informal child care supports: babysitting cooperatives, neighborhood play groups, and so on. Many of these informal child care arrangements could be reinforced through policy incentives—for instance, tax breaks for informal child care provided by extended family members, or supports for employers who want to sponsor child care for their employees. These issues will be discussed in more depth below. Here I wish to point out that these informal supports have been overshadowed by the emphasis on formal day care services, in spite of the fact that they may facilitate the home-based care that many families prefer.

WHO ARE THE PROVIDERS?

The people who provide child care are, not surprisingly, mostly women, but beyond this fact it is difficult to draw generalizations. They may be women with advanced degrees looking for a way to help children while their own children are home, or older women whose children have grown. Some have training in education, psychology, or social work, while others have minimal educational backgrounds relevant to child care. Increasing numbers of men are entering the child care professions, although their percentage is still small.

A primary factor influencing the quality of child care is the caregiver (Clarke-Stewart, 1977). In most states little training is required to become a child care worker in a center-based program, and virtually none is required of family day care providers. The requirements for training vary from state to state. Head teachers in center programs are usually required to have some college training in child development, and some form of certification, such as in early childhood education or child care. Aides often need only to meet age and literacy requirements (Almy, 1980). States also vary in the amount of in-service training that is required or available to child care workers. Although specific training in child care has not been found to relate significantly to all aspects of the quality of care provided, many parents still prefer to leave their children in the care of individuals who have training or degrees in the field (Peters & Kostelnik, 1981).

Caregivers' wages in centers are notoriously low (minimum wage is not unusual and benefits are virtually nonexistent). Family day care has long had the reputation of being the only employment option for a low-income single mother, or as means of obtaining pocket money for a woman who otherwise would not work. Since many people assume that "anyone can take care of children," child care workers have not received the respect they deserve for their important role. Efforts to upgrade the training and the image of child care workers are under way. The role of support networks in fulfilling this goal is examined in the following sections.

ISSUES IN THE PROVISION OF CHILD CARE

THE PARENT'S POINT OF VIEW

Simply locating adequate and affordable child care is often a difficult task for parents. This is especially true for families with particular needs. Families with infants find limited center-based care available, so they often have to turn to family day care or in-home care. Center-based infant care is expensive because of the necessarily high staff–child ratios that centers are required to maintain. Families with school-aged children also find few after-school care centers, leaving many grade-school children to fend for themselves each afternoon. Rural families may have to travel great distances to find either center or family day care. Parents who work odd shifts may not find a 24-hour center or someone willing to care for their children. Families with moderate incomes may struggle to purchase services equal to those provided to low-income families.

Powell and Eisenstadt (in press) studied the resources and strategies that parents in Detroit employed in locating child care services. They found that parents rely on informal sources of information (relatives, friends, neighbors, and co-workers) more than formal means (social service agencies, publications, and institutions). However, parents differed on the resources available to them and their use of these resources. Parents clustered into several groups, predominantly those who tended to have close reciprocal exchange relationships with friends versus those who had friendships with frequent contact but low levels of reciprocal exchange of goods and services (called associative friendships). Parents consulted associative friends after reciprocal friends, but associative friends were usually more effective in locating care. Parents who had fewer friendships of the associative type were more likely to rely on the formal services in locating child care. Parents also frequently approached relatives first, both for information about child care services and to ask if the relative would be able to provide care. The research by Powell and Eisenstadt demonstrated that people depended first on their informal network to locate child care, and they turned to formal services only if that network was limited or unable to help.

After families locate child care, other issues arise. The increasing cost of providing child care is one of the major concerns of parents and caregivers alike. The largest budgetary item for any child care program is staff salaries. Creative people can reduce equipment costs greatly by scavenging materials for activities from many sources or by recruiting parents or volunteers to build and repair equipment. Housing costs are minimal in family day care (in fact, income tax advantages are possible) and many day care centers obtain low-cost space by sharing old school buildings, church space not used during the week, or other community resources. But cutting corners on staff salaries is not possible. Child care workers are generally poorly paid. The National Day Care Study (Ruopp, 1979) found that in 1977, 68% of caregivers earned less than $3.00 per hour, and only 7% made over $5.00 per hour. Most caregivers (92%) did not reach the level of $10,000 annually, which was the Department of Labor's low-income budget for a family of four in 1977. Because parents need inexpensive child care, they cannot be the ones to support increased salary demands of child care personnel.

It must be borne in mind that a large number of parents (45% of those using child care, according to Woolsey, 1977) do not incur costs for child care because they make nonpaying arrangements with relatives and friends. To document the cost of child care, we must examine these informal relationships. Reciprocal exchanges among friends and relatives provide a source of child care that is little understood but more prevalent than the literature on formal day care would suggest.

The regulations imposed on child care programs have, at times, been blamed for rising costs; strict structural codes, staff–child ratios, and educational requirements for caregivers all contribute to the price of care. Most people are concerned that children be housed safely. However, in some states the same building regulations are applied to family day care homes that are applicable to public schools and institutions, greatly increasing the costs for a private provider who wants to meet regulations in making her home safe for children (Costin et al., 1977). At least 13 states are currently considering revisions of their family day care regulations, including applying health and safety controls appropriate to homes rather than institutions (Garduque & Long, in preparation).

The closeness and convenience of available day care sites may depend on the population density and demographic characteristics of the area where a family lives. Child care options may be abundant in neighborhoods where many families with young children live, or in professional communities where two-career families can purchase care. They may be less common in communities of predominantly older families and in rural areas (Genovese, 1980; Powell & Eisenstadt, in press). The success that Collins and her colleagues had in locating an informal day care support system in Portland, Oregon (see the section on Programs, below) was not duplicated by Powell and Eisenstadt in Detroit, perhaps because of the characteristics of the neighborhoods in which they worked.

Convenience of the child care setting includes its hours of operation as well as its location. Half-day programs may not benefit parents who work full time. Parents who work odd shifts or holidays also have difficulties locating care at all the times they need it. The community may not offer options that meet all the day care needs of its members: it may face a shortage of family day care homes or of center spaces.

Some parents have been offered what appears to be an ideal care arrangement in terms of convenience: care on the work site. Yet not all parents have taken advantage of this kind of care, and some employers are now disillusioned that their attempt to provide a social service was unsuccessful. Employers have offered center-based care when they did not have the employee base to support it, or when their employees preferred other care options. What is convenient care for one parent may not appeal to another.

Issues of cost and convenience may be addressed by the family's social support network. In informal arrangements between friends and relatives, parents rarely pay a large fee (Woolsey, 1977; Moore, 1980). These arrangements could be facilitated through babysitting cooperatives, neighborhood resource and referral agencies, or by locating and supporting day care neighbors. (See the section on Programs for some examples.) Looking beyond informal support systems, we see that formal child care agents can also become incorporated into the support network of the family. What are some of the functions that a child care support network can fulfill for children and their families?

For parents, child care within or outside the home can simply facilitate their ability to work and earn a living. The Pennsylvania Day Care Study (Elliott, 1972) demonstrated that families with their children in day care had higher incomes than a comparison group on day care waiting lists. The same study (Myers, 1972) found enhanced marital satisfaction among the mothers who placed their children in day care.

Unger and Powell (1980) suggest three functions of support networks: instrumental support (material goods and services), emotional support, and information and referral to fill needs. Table 7-2 illustrates how child care serves these three functions. Child care is obviously instrumental support for families. It can also provide emotional support by reassuring parents of their parenting skills and by promoting positive parent–child relationships. Parent–parent relationships can be fostered within a child care program through social and learning activities that may develop into continuing social contacts between families. Finally, day care can incorporate comprehensive services (e.g., physical and mental health, nutrition, and social services) or referrals to families for needed services. It can provide information through newsletters, parent groups, and informal communication on parent education, consumer skills, child development, and other relevant topics.

By increasing the connectedness between parents and the supportive groups in their environment, we ultimately serve children. The educational

Table 7-2. Three functions of support networks in child care

Function	Examples of support to families	Examples of support to child care workers
Instrumental support	Provision of child care Payments of child care fees Health care Nutritional supplements	Toys, equipment Loans for equipment, home repairs
Emotional support	Parenting skills to promote positive parent–child relations Stress relief	Stress relief Shared problem-solving
Information and referral	Child care location services Connections to other social services Child care information	Child care placement services Child care information Business management information

intervention programs of the 1960's and 1970's showed this: children whose parents were involved in the intervention programs often gained more intellectually from the programs and maintained those gains better than children whose parents were not involved (Bronfenbrenner, 1974). As an extreme negative example, abusive parents are often isolated from the common informal supports that most parents have (Garbarino & Sherman, 1980a). Providing child care for abused children can draw abusive parents into contact with others who can provide emotional and instrumental support, reducing the likelihood that they will continue to abuse their children.

Day care can also support young children directly. In the past two decades a picture of "developmental day care" has formed that integrates care, supervision, an educational program, health care, nutrition, mental health services, and family social work (Kamerman & Kahn, 1976). These services are all thought necessary for healthy child development. Few programs have integrated all of them; the costs are too great to be supported in the current fiscal climate. But day care programs can facilitate access to other needed services through collaboration, links to other agencies, and referral. Training to make staff aware of children's basic needs for health, diet, and education may be more practical than bringing other agents in to provide these services.

These factors could be considered the "instrumental supports" of childhood, but what about emotional support? Critics of day care are concerned with its effect on the parent–child relationship. Although the data are mixed, studies seem to indicate that children in day care maintain positive emotional attachments with their mothers. Day care may also enhance father–child relationships. Men with working wives tend to share child care responsibilities when the child is at home (Blehar, 1979). Such children approach their fathers as well as their mothers for attention and play (Field, 1978).

Children also form attachment relationships with their caregivers that do not interfere with their ties to their parents (Fox, 1977; Ragozin, 1980). Rutter (1979) has suggested that when the home environment lacks emotional support for children, alternate adults may fill this role. This idea is difficult to test; Rutter provides anecdotal examples from the extended family and schools. Focusing on the importance of the mother–child relationship has blinded us to the importance of other adults, siblings, and peers in the child's environment. We have also ignored the role that peers play in developing the child's social and intellectual skills. Michael Lewis and his colleagues (Weinraub, Brooks, & Lewis, 1977; Lewis & Schaeffer, 1981) have suggested that children develop social networks among their peers that operate independently of adult–child relationships. They have demonstrated this with abused children. In observations of peer interaction, abused children were indistinguishable from nonabused children in the quality of their play. Thus, children with disturbed parental relationships were still able to interact normally with peers. We need to examine the supplementary role that peers may fill for the child who lacks positive adult relationships. Day care, by providing social contacts, may provide emotional support not available to children at home.

THE PRACTIONERS' POINT OF VIEW

The "quality of care" is an elusive term. To some people the crucial element is warm and affectionate caregiving and individual attention. To others, quality care emphasizes cognitive stimulation and opportunities to learn preacademic skills. Others may associate quality with the discipline and values that children acquire in the setting. All of these features are difficult to mandate. Instead, regulations have focused on the tangible aspects of child care: the physical setting, staff–child ratio, and qualifications of the staff.

Few people would question the need to safeguard young children from accidents and illness, so the physical requirements for day care are not often challenged. But regulation of staff–child ratios and staff qualifications has become controversial. In 1968 a government panel set out standards (the Federal Interagency Day Care Requirements) for the operation of child care centers that included small staff–child ratios and small group sizes. In 1974 Title XX of the Social Security Act required that centers receiving Title XX funds meet these standards before receiving funding. Because in many areas of the country the federal requirements were more stringent than the state requirements already in force, meeting federal standards in order to receive funding would have incurred considerable costs (either through increasing staff or reducing enrollment) for many centers. The resultant outcry led federal officials to delay implementing the requirements until states could come into compliance. It is currently unlikely that these regulations will ever be enforced because of changes in federal funding for child care.

The issues involved in regulation become even more complex when we consider family day care. Whereas it seems well accepted that centers should be approved through a licensing procedure (although the standards imposed are subject to debate), people often are upset by the notion that someone's home needs a license or approval. Many parents feel that they are qualified to recognize a care setting of good quality; others want the state to decide what an adequate setting is. Family day care is difficult and costly to monitor: the turnover of providers is high; homes are numerous and widely scattered. Caregivers often prefer to remain unidentified for a number of reasons. They may not want to declare the income they receive from child care. They may think that their homes cannot meet the regulations and may perceive inspection as an unwarranted intrusion into their privacy.

When family day care is the issue, the legal base for inspecting private homes is questionable. There is a fine line between family day care as a neighborly act and family day care as a business. Why regulate informal support between neighbors? How can we safeguard young children without interfering with informal, neighborly arrangements? Some also argue that regulations discourage diversity and innovation in forms. Because of these difficulties with regulating day care homes, many states are considering reducing requirements to minimum acceptable standards. Regulation can also be educational and supportive, rather than punitive, by offering access to expert consultants, connections between providers, and resources such as books and equipment.

The qualifications of child care workers continue to concern those attempting to regulate child care. The National Day Care Study data suggested that providers who are more qualified are not necessarily better providers, but there are some indications that child care workers with course work or experience in early childhood education spend more time engaged with children. In addition, parents prefer preschool teachers who have had formal training (Peters & Kostelnik, 1981). Hiring teachers who are better qualified has not been found to raise the cost of care significantly (Ruopp, 1979); however, this may be because the current salaries available to child care workers are not commensurate with the qualifications of many staff members.

Another issue related to the training of caregivers is the respect they receive as professionals. We find ambivalence in attitudes toward child care workers: on the one hand, many people acknowledge that they are second only to parents in rearing and socializing young children and are therefore very important. On the other hand, many feel that anyone (or any *female*) can care for children. In addition, many of the custodial tasks involved in child care are not glamorous. There is not much glory in changing diapers or cleaning up spilled milk. Caregivers who work in programs with an educational focus recognize that even these custodial tasks can be learning experiences for young children. Child care workers seek recognition of the important job they do, and thus, they are forming associations and support groups. By gathering together, they can share information on procedures, techniques, and community resources; educate themselves on issues in the field; become resources for each other in solving problems; or provide emotional support. They can obtain and share material resources by trading toys or substituting for each other. They can also organize group benefits, such as group insurance for family day care providers, or advocate for changes in the state regulations regarding child care. These instrumental supports can facilitate quality care at reduced cost: sharing toys and equipment eliminates the need for each provider to invest individually in these items. Sharing information and linking providers to needed services enhances the quality of care they can offer. Networks of child care workers also provide valuable emotional support. Emotional support for human service workers is very important in maintaining work satisfaction and involvement in the job (Daley, 1979). Child care workers are susceptible to worker burnout as are other human service professionals. Full-time day care employees are especially susceptible when it is difficult to schedule work breaks or staffing time because of the constant demands made by children. Family day care providers frequently complain of burnout. In addition, they suffer from isolation because caring for several young children limits their opportunities to spend time outside their own homes. In the section on Programs we shall examine some possibilities for overcoming these difficulties in day care provision by building support systems for families and child care workers.

The amount of communication that occurs between parent and caregiver seems to be more important to caregivers than to parents. Caregivers often find that events at home affect the way the child acts in the day care setting. Knowing about these events, the caregiver can make adjustments to the child's behavior. Child care workers are also growing increasingly aware of the importance of incorporating the values of the child's home into the day care environment in order to build the child's self-concept. Caregivers feel that it is important to share with parents the events of the child's day; such sharing gives parents a sense of participation in day care activities. With very young children it is especially important that parents not miss out on the new milestones of growth that their children may achieve each day. Yet systematic attempts to involve parents in day care are often frustrated; caregivers lament that parents do not share with them either the events of the child's day with the caregiver or family circumstances that may influence the child's behavior. When communication between parents and caregivers is high, both groups perceive that parents have an impact on the care the child receives (Romero & Thomas, 1975).

Powell (1981) investigated parents' and teachers' perceptions of communication and found differences between the two groups in what topics they thought were important to discuss. Although both groups thought it was appropriate to discuss the child's activities during the day, parents were less likely than caregivers to desire discussions of family activities or problems. Interestingly, parents perceived caregivers as sources of information about child development and childrearing, but neither group thought it appropriate to discuss the *parent's* view on childrearing practies. On the whole, parents were more satisfied than caregivers with the quality and quantity of their exchanges. Powell also found that the frequency and diversity of communication about the child increased when friendships developed between staff members and parents.

This section has presented some of the issues in child care delivery from the perspectives of the parents and the providers. Some of the needs of families that can be met through formal and informal child care supports have been highlighted. The next section will describe several programs that incorporate these supports.

PROGRAMS

The programs described below were selected to illustrate ways in which formal helping services can work with informal networks to promote child care options. In several cases formal supports facilitate or extend already existing child care networks, providing parents with options and enhancing the ability of caregivers to provide good-quality care. In each case we shall examine the types of support offered by the program.

DAY CARE NEIGHBORS

When Collins and Watson (1976) set out to build up child care services in Portland, Oregon, they found a network of natural helpers that was already linking people in need of child care with providers. These natural helpers were people in the community who had contact with a broad enough range of individuals to know who might be able to provide care. The natural helpers served as matchmakers between families and providers. Knowing both the client and the potential providers, they sensitively sought matches that were best suited to the needs of both families and caregivers. Collins and Watson were able to strengthen these natural helpers and, through them, the informal child care structure of the community, by consulting on difficult problems and encouraging the helpers to continue their supportive roles. The formal child care services in the community were enhanced by fostering the informal child care network. Through the day care neighbors, people who could provide care were encouraged to do so, families who needed care were connected with providers whom they might not otherwise locate, and providers were given emotional and instrumental support that encouraged them to continue providing care.

The natural helpers were also the type of people others turned to when they needed help or assistance on topics other than child care. Because others sought their advice on personal problems, the day care neighbors were able to connect their network members with formal social services through the assistance of the social worker. Sometimes encouraging the natural helper to step into a difficult situation was all that was required. At other times the social worker advised the helper to refer her friend to social services. The action ultimately was in the hands of the natural helper. People who ordinarily would not have sought social services were reached in this way.

This model of child care has much appeal: it relies on the resources available in the community, matches families with their desired type of care, requires low investment from formal services, and is unobtrusive. But the research conducted by Powell and Eisenstadt (in press) showed that it may not be a realistic alternative in every community. One of the major findings of their research was that there did not appear to be an informal structure of child care referral within the community they studied (Detroit). That is, there was no particular core of people who were helpful in locating child care. This finding contrasts sharply with the work of Collins and her colleagues. In areas lacking a child care network, tactics to create support systems must be implemented first.

EMPLOYER-SPONSORED CHILD CARE

A form of child care that is receiving increasing attention and support is care provided on the parent's work site or in some way supported by the employer. Work-site centers have been instituted in several large corporations across the country, with limited success. Some businesses have been disappointed to find that parents do not take advantage of the service; others have been upset to find that child care is not a money-making proposition. Michael Romaine, the director of the day care center operated by Zale Corporation in Dallas, reports that their center loses $2,500 each month in spite of a moderate fee paid by parents ("Corporate Day Care," 1981). Such losses are absorbed by a large company and may be compensated by reduced absenteeism, worker satisfaction, and lowered employee turnover (factors few companies have yet documented). However, smaller companies would have difficulty accepting such losses.

Employer-sponsored child care had a surge of popularity in the early 1970's but many employers were discouraged by the results. For some it was a losing financial proposition either because they had not recognized the costs involved or because the parents in their employ did not subscribe. Parents were often hesitant to disrupt their current child care arrangement until they were sure that the work-site center would operate successfully. This experience is common for day care programs: they are underenrolled for several months until their reputation spreads. Initial forays into employer-sponsored child care emphasized work-site centers without exploring other options that could be less costly to employers and more satisfactory to the diverse desires of parents. Some centers were unsuccessful because parents preferred other forms of care. Current efforts in this area are aimed at exploring multiple methods of meeting employees' child care needs.

When an on-site center is not feasible, other options exist for the employers. The work-site center can be opened to families outside the corporation. Some employers have given their employees vouchers for purchasing care in the community, established information and referral services within the company, or contracted with a community center or family day care network to provide care for their employees. In Sunnyvale, California, several small companies have joined together to form a child care information consortium.

Employer involvement in child care can be important to families for several reasons. Where child care is difficult to obtain, an information source within the company facilitates the search process. Some parents feel more comfortable having their children near enough to check in on them during breaks from work. Subsidized child care, at least to the employees on the lower end of the income scale, relieves the financial stress that child care fees can cause. Finally, in some companies, child care is only one part of a network of activities (e.g., outings, picnics, and holiday celebrations) that encourage families to get to know other families working at the same site.

Employer-sponsored child care also benefits the employer. Work satisfaction on the part of the mother has been correlated with satisfaction with the child care arrangement (Harrell, 1973; Blehar, 1979), and satisfaction with work may reduce employee turnover. A direct example of this is found in the health care field, where nurses are in great demand. Nurses perpetually have difficulty finding child care because they often must work nights and weekends. In San Mateo County, California, the county Child Care Coordinating Council (4-Cs) has contracted with several hospitals to facilitate child care for the hospital staffs. The 4-Cs staff interviews employees seeking child care and surveys the community for the setting that meets their needs. It is up to the employee to make an agreement with the child care provider. The 4-Cs staff serve as matchmakers, leaving parents free to choose the type of care they prefer.

The program has drawn women into the work force who had been forced by child care needs to stay home. It appears to benefit employees beyond facilitating child care during their working hours: night-shift employees have been able to locate daytime care during the hours they need to sleep, and employees have been encouraged to form a babysitting co-op to give them additional free time for recreation or errands ("Child Care Referrals for Hospital Workers," 1981). This program, similar in concept to the program developed by Collins and Watson, employs a professional to connect the informal networks of the community with families seeking care. In the process, employers benefit with a small investment.

COMPREHENSIVE CHILD CARE

Compensatory education programs for low-income children during the 1960s brought with them the notion of *comprehensive* child care services. Comprehensive child care grew with the idea that in order to benefit children, child care must be more than merely custodial. Children from low-income homes, especially, needed experiences to stimulate their intellectual growth, to ensure physical health and good nutrition, and to provide positive emotional experiences. In addition, their families usually needed social services. Head Start was created to work toward this goal of comprehensive developmental child care. Head Start began as a center-based intervention program, but different variations have been added to serve the needs of different families and communities (O'Keefe, 1979). In spite of its focus on children, Head Start from its inception has sought to strengthen families. Parents take an active role in designing educational goals for their children and in shaping the policies of the program.

Two programs stemming from Head Start were especially effective in meeting the needs of families (O'Keefe, 1979). Home Start delivered educational and social services to families in their own homes. The home visitor assessed family needs and arranged services to meet these needs. For instance, he or she might drive family members to the dentist if the family had no car, or arrange for the family to receive food stamps. Parents in Home Start learned how to conduct educational activities at home. A home visit often had the advantage over center care of drawing all the children in the family into the educational program. Because of the benefits to both families and educators that resulted from home visits (information exchange, enhanced parent participation, carry-over of the child's gains from center to home), some Head Start programs currently combine center-based and home-based intervention for all their children.

The Parent–Child Centers were established to provide a wide range of social services to low-income families with at least one child under 3 years of age, including health care, job skills, child development education, referrals to other agencies, and funds for family emergencies. One evaluation found that parents used the Parent–Child Centers to meet their own needs as well as those of the child: they heavily used such services offered by the Centers as job training and health care. Parent involvement was greatest when the program focused on issues of concern to parents, and mothers perceived the Center as a place to go when they were lonely (O'Keefe, 1979). These findings demonstrate that parents also have needs that a child-centered program can meet when it takes a comprehensive approach to services. In fact, parent involvement with their children could be encouraged by meeting the parent's own perceived needs first.

One of the major goals of Head Start has been to strengthen children by strengthening families. The evaluations of Head Start suggest that the program has benefited families who would not otherwise have received a wide range of needed services. Although long-term effects of Head Start are only now being published, it appears that the program has enhanced the educational performance of participating children. In addition, parents report more knowledge of children, more control and satisfaction in their own lives, better job skills, and reduced family crises after they became involved in Head Start (O'Keefe, 1979). Unfortunately, changes in federal support for early education have placed the future of these programs in question.

The alternative service models developed through Head Start were virtually unheard of 15 years ago; now they are accepted practice in early childhood intervention. Child service professionals have come to recognize that, in the long run, drawing families into a network of emotionally and instrumentally supportive services will benefit children.

Another view of the meaning of "comprehensive developmental" child care is represented in the Parent–Child Development Program (PCDP) at the Acoma Indian Reservation in New Mexico (Galinsky & Hooks, 1977). Recognizing that their community already had strong foundations in child-rearing, the designers sought a program that would support existing patterns. The community built two centers from scratch. In addition, a network of family day care homes was established especially for the care of infants and toddlers. Parents who wished to care for their own children at home but who desired education for themselves and their children received home visits, as well as opportunities to attend educational programs, especially for parents.

Recently the PCDP has joined forces with the local Acoma Head Start program. By coordinating PCDP and Head Start services, a number of families who would not otherwise be reached are receiving services. Handicapped children who normally receive home visits come into one of the three day care centers once each week for therapy and for cultural experiences with other children. Infants and toddlers who normally would not receive educational intervention can be prepared for their Head Start experience in PCDP home visits. The home visitors also act as role models for the parents. PCDP sponsors "family learning nights," inviting parents to the centers to learn what their children do during the day and why these activities are important to child development. PCDP coordinates its activities with those of the local school system in order to integrate children successfully into kindergarten.

Some educational and health screening is offered to PCDP families through Head Start and through the Indian Health Service. A goal of the PCDP is the improvement of the program's screening, diagnosis, and programming capability through the development of the skills of its own staff. For instance, family day care providers may be trained to administer developmental screening tests to identify children who need special educational programs.

RESOURCE AND REFERRAL

Not all solutions to finding child care revolve around day care homes and centers. Many creative ideas are being developed that offer support to parents and caregivers. One example is the Child Care Resource Center/Southside in Minneapolis (Galinsky & Hooks, 1977). The Resource Center began as a child care political action group for the community members (the Southside Child Care Committee), and gradually expanded to include several other independent child care supports: a lending library, a computerized child care Resource and Referral Center, and an advocacy agency for local child care workers. The Resource Center holds workshops for parents and providers and has a library of child development, child care, and children's books. It is a drop-in care center for neighborhood children, houses an adolescent parent's group, and is home for parent-run play groups. One of the primary functions of the Resource Center is to link parents with child care by providing referrals to centers and day care homes suited to the parent's and child's needs.

Two functions of the Child Care Resource Center reemphasize the role that formal service agencies can play in strengthening informal child care supports. The first is its Infant Care Incentive Program. Through a Community Development Block Grant, the Center has been able to pay family day care providers $5.00 per week in addition to the fees they receive from parents for infant care. Subscribing providers participate in an infant care training and support program. Family day care providers and parents seeking child care are often located through an annual door-to-door campaign to familiarize the community with the program.

The Child Care Workers Alliance is another function of the Resource Center that can enchance informal networks, in this case focusing on providers. The Alliance gathers information and raises community consciousness about the working conditions of child care professionals in order to increase county subsidies for home-based care and to improve working conditions in centers. The Alliance gives child care workers who provide different types of care—preschool teachers, family day care providers, latchkey (after school) teachers—a forum for sharing their common concerns.

This cluster of projects is interesting for several reasons. The projects were begun by individuals who recognized a need in their community and set out to fill it. They have been funded by a patchwork of small contributions and matching grants, demonstrating that it *is* possible to run a program on almost nothing. They have remained flexible and open to the needs of the community and have expanded to meet these needs. The projects are autonomous but have learned to share resources and cooperate in order to reduce expenses and maximize services.

SUPPORT FOR PROVIDERS

The Child Care Resource Center benefits both families seeking care and providers of that care. We have yet to examine in detail the needs of day care providers that can be met through social support networks. Two types of needs were met in the Child Care Resource Center program: information on child care and financial support met instrumental needs of providers as well as parents, and the Child Care Workers Alliance provided emotional support.

Professional organizations of child care workers can work to upgrade the image of caregivers in the community and can arrange educational programs for caregivers, providing support to caregivers in meeting regulations. They can bring providers together to share ideas, equipment, and emotional support and can offer other resources such as referrals to link parents and providers. Many counties have child care councils that serve some of these purposes. Agencies can work to bring caregivers into a network of services and supports. As several programs have illustrated, the agency can serve as a referral organization linking parents to providers who have space for additional children. It can provide centralized resources and consultants on how to improve the quality of care. The organization can also lobby for legislative support and regulations that benefit both the providers and the families they serve.

The services offered by the Child Development Council of Centre County, Pennsylvania, are typical of these agencies. Field supervisors make regular visits to day care homes to consult on issues of concern to the providers. They assist providers in meeting regulations and make available equipment such as infant furniture. A monthly newsletter gives providers opportunities to hear what their colleagues are doing. Training workshops inform caregivers on child development, health, and nutrition. Simply by meeting other providers, these child care professionals develop their own informal support networks. They can call on each other for substitution on sick days or team up for a special trip. Hearing that others share their difficulties, they gain emotional support and share solutions.

PREVENTING PROBLEMS FOR LATCHKEY CHILDREN

Some programs offer seemingly simple preventive solutions to potentially serious problems. A newspaper clipping in the Dayton, Ohio, *Daily News* ("Denver Apartment Block Pioneers 1-Parent Style," 1979) illustrates one form of support to a highly stressed group. The Warren United Methodist Church owns a building whose apartments are rented at subsidized rates to single parents. There is a day care center in the building; a full-time staff helps the residents obtain needed social services. Besides relieving the living problems that many single parents face, the community provides healthy role models for children. One parent said, "It makes a difference to [the children] to know that, despite what they read or see on TV, a whole lot of families are living in one-parent families. . . . They learn you're not 'weird' because you don't have a father or you don't have a mother."

Such an arrangement, where a small community looks out for all its members, can be especially beneficial for latchkey children, children who spend part of the day on their own because their parents work. Some neighbors naturally take on responsibility for the children in the neighborhood because they are at home and enjoy having children around (Genovese, 1980). Unfortunately, these natural helpers are not to be found in every neighborhood.

To provide a resource for children who may not have such a helper in their neighborhoods, a voluntary organization in a central Pennsylvania community recently instituted a hot line for latchkey children. Children can call when they have problems and cannot reach their parents. Because the program began very recently, its impact cannot be assessed. Calls during the first months of operation indicate that the children's main concerns are loneliness and boredom, although several crises (including a sexual assault) have been dealt with.

SUMMARY

Table 7-2 summarizes contributions that support networks can make to child care. All the programs reviewed provide a common commodity—information. This emphasizes yet again one of the basic needs in child care today: increased information about resources available to parents, children, and caregivers. Formal child care services can perhaps serve the most people most effectively and cost-efficiently by establishing resource and referral centers that link providers and families. These programs also meet the instrumental needs of families and providers. Increasing day care placements is an obvious outcome of all of these programs except the latchkey phone line.

The emotional support offered by each of these programs is difficult to document. The emotional needs of family day care providers have been met by developing connections between individual providers, drawing them out of isolation. For parents, having satisfactory child care alleviates the stress they may feel about working (Harrell, 1973). Support in parenting builds their self-confidence and enhances their relationships with their children.

The emotional support children receive directly from child care is largely unexplored. We assume that good-quality child care arrangements provide children with a positive socioemotional setting for growth. But the specific emotional supports children receive from day care as distinguished from home care by their own parents are not well understood.

BARRIERS TO THE DEVELOPMENT OF CHILD CARE SUPPORT NETWORKS

In the past, many barriers have hindered the functioning of social support networks in child care, but as more families demand child care alternatives, the barriers are falling. We can examine these barriers from the point of view of either child care workers or parents.

For the child care worker, especially for those offering care in their own homes, one of the greatest barriers has been the physical and social isolation of the providers. A woman taking care of several young children in her own home has difficulty locating others who can support her role. This is exactly why support systems are so important to the child care worker. Without them, the job can be stressful and indeed harmful (or at least not beneficial) to the children involved. Workers in center-based settings have the advantage of more contacts with others. However, full-day staff are often cut off from opportunities to discuss policy and individual cases with other staff. Similarly, they are cut off from opportunities for in-service training and exploring resources in their community, which their work schedules preclude.

Isolation of caregivers can contribute to competition for clients and unwillingness to share resources that are beneficial to all. A day care network benefits providers by matching them with clients; the demand for child care is great enough currently that individuals providing good-quality care will most likely be able to attract clients without competition. Cooperative efforts that draw caregivers out of isolation will enhance the quality of care that centers and individuals can provide.

Agencies referring parents to child care sources often are hesitant to make evaluations of these sources, although parents would like to have them. An information and referral agency may not have the staff resources to visit and evaluate all the care providers in its area, or it may not consider evaluations to be part of its job. Yet many parents ask about the quality of the care provided, or they assume that the referral implies that the agency oversees the quality of the providers. A referral, however, often does not represent an endorsement, and some centralized child care agencies have chosen to stop making referrals rather than to risk referring a parent to a poor-quality setting.

These barriers can be overcome if quality control is viewed supportively instead of punitively. In several states, voluntary registration has replaced mandatory licensing of family day care homes. In these states, parents must take a more active role in monitoring the quality of the care their children receive. In some states, registration entitles the provider to such support services as toy lending libraries, consultation on home improvements, group insurance, and information newsletters. These efforts can bring caregivers together to learn and to support each other's needs, thereby enhancing the quality of the care they give. Child care workers in centers encounter few vehicles for support except in professional organizations.

From the parent's point of view, barriers to developing support systems in child care stem from our ambivalence about the responsibility of parents to care for their children. Every parent has the right to choose the type of child care he or she prefers, whether it be by the parent, a relative in the home, or some type of out-of-home care. Parents have turned to relatives and close friends first to find care, so extensive networks of day care helpers have not developed. Parents have found providers by happenstance rather than design, or their economic situation has determined the type of care they selected. With increased community awareness of the options that exist, these haphazard connections can be strengthened. As increasing numbers of parents seek information, more people will have information to share. The information flow will also facilitate connections between parents and providers.

Several good reasons exist for incorporating formal with informal support systems of child care. One is to assist the delivery of comprehensive social services. The argument for comprehensive services based in the day care center or preschool program grew from the notion that all families with young children need certain kinds of services: health and dental care, nutrition information, and parent education. Some but not all parents also need the services of social workers, to whom they can be referred through links between the day care setting and other agencies.

Formal social services, however, are a less important form of support to most families than the support fostered by enhancing personal relationships between family members and others in the community. Powell (1980) found that parents who participated actively in the programs associated with a day care center were less likely to have a broad range of close reciprocal relationships than those who did not participate. However, the number of friends a person had outside the program correlated positively with the number of friendships made within the program. Parents seemed to use the program to supplement their support network but not to substitute for one. It also appeared that parents either sought formal advice from the staff about services, or they developed informal supportive relationships with other parents instead of with staff. These findings were substantiated by the study on locating child care by Powell and Eisenstadt (in press), in which parents with close reciprocal relationships tended to rely more on formal agencies to find child care, but parents with many associative (nonreciprocal) friendships turned to their friends. It seems important to develop both types of support in order to meet the needs of two different types of parents. But we must reach out more to isolated families to draw them into formal networks. More research is needed in order to describe the childrearing supports available (or lacking) to parents who do not get involved in the life of the day care center.

Informal support systems in child care have traditionally arisen because they provide care in a context that is convenient, consistent with the parent's values, and relatively inexpensive. Many friends and relatives make informal arrangements on an exchange basis. These arrangements are harder to find for regular care today because relatives live farther apart and more women work, reducing the pool of available caregivers. People are forced to turn to strangers, and business arrangements, including fees, result. To reduce the cost of child care we need to foster informal supports (e.g., an after-school sitting cooperative in which different neighbors take the children one day each week). We also need to examine forces outside the day care–family system that can relieve the difficulties inherent in child care arrangements (e.g., work schedules adjusted to parents' needs, flextime, and part-time jobs).

IDENTIFYING AND STRENGTHENING CHILD CARE SUPPORT NETWORKS

Several projects were reviewed above that are already putting social support networks to work to serve the day care needs of families. Most of these programs are organized under the auspices of formal agencies. There are, in addition, some more informal ways that support networks can work in child care.

First, we can foster child care arrangements among friends and associates. Powell and Eisenstadt's research showed that parents did not always turn to neighbors for help in locating or providing child care. This may be because in many communities people now spend more time outside their homes, in work and other activities. People outside their own neighborhoods become contacts for information and resources. These individuals may share the same lifestyles and activities of the parents, making it likely that they too have needed child care. Such people could form a core of individuals who could swap care arrangements, go together to form a cooperative, or together seek work-based or community-based arrangements that meet their demands. Public child care agencies can assist in organizing these programs.

Genovese (1980) points out that finding support systems within the neighborhood may be a function of the age of the neighborhood. In a newly opened townhouse development with many young families, an active support system formed among the women. It extended beyond child care to group purchases of bulk foods, transportation, and swapping services such as hairstyling. In an older neighborhood, residents may not have so much in common and thus may turn to acquaintances outside the neighborhood for support.

Much informal child care is not recognized as such. A house in the neighborhood where all the children gravitate after school is a relief to the working mother who knows that the neighbor will keep an eye on her child. Friends trade mornings of babysitting 2 days each week to have time for shopping and errands. A father who works a late shift takes his neighbor's children along with his to the day care center; the neighbor picks them up. All of these arrangements of convenience ease the stress of coordinating multiple family responsibilities.

Another important use of support networks in child care would be to tie into other services benefiting families. The exemplar of this is the attempt of Collins (1980) and of Pancoast (1980) to work through community helpers to prevent the need for intervention or, when necessary, to locate the services that families needed to stay together. Centralized family service units could collaborate with informal systems by providing information, referrals, and resources on a broad range of issues, in much the same way as the Child Care Resource Center/Southside in Minneapolis does for providers. On a smaller scale, consulting could be offered to individuals providing child care informally in their own homes on issues of interest to people dealing with young children. One vehicle for doing this might be a telephone "dial-a-tape" system like those that are becoming popular throughout the country for medical information. People could call in to request tapes on topics like what to do on rainy days, toilet training, nutrition for children, or how to recognize the symptoms of childhood illnesses. These tapes could refer to agencies in the community that have more detailed information or services.

One of the most important applications of social support networks to the field of child care is the development of support networks for child care providers. This is especially important for home based child care workers. The benefits of these networks have been emphasized throughout this chapter: enhanced quality of care through increased information and resources, and social support for the role as well as decreased isolation of the providers.

Developing support systems for child care will make the process of finding child care less difficult than it has been in the past. Many parents point out the difficulties of locating care for their children; those who have found care often express concern over the quality of the arrangement. Building supports will increase the options available to parents as well as make the options easier to identify.

FUTURE GOALS FOR DAY CARE

One of the apparent major conflicts in the field of child care is that the options available to parents contrast to the type of care they prefer. Parents seem to prefer relatives as caregivers; many also prefer in-home care. However, not all relatives want to care for their grandchildren, nieces, or nephews. And thus, economic incentives to relatives who do wish to provide care might facilitate arrangements between family members. We need to document which people want to provide care, where they desire the care, and whether these spaces exist. We also need to know whether parents are generally satisfied with their current child care arrangements, or what they would prefer to change about them. Pluralism of alternatives is currently lacking in child care, and we cannot develop these alternatives without a sense of what methods families prefer.

Another issue that requires further examination is the quality of care. Researchers have attempted to define this concept during the last decade on the basis of outcomes for children, but they have failed to take into account the parent's perception of the determinants of quality. Many parents place their children into situations daily that they perceive as adequate (or their only option), yet these situations make professionals uncomfortable. Parents and professionals need to reach a consensus on what determines a reasonable level of quality of care. Without this consensus, parent and child care professionals cannot collaborate to extend good-quality care to young children.

Child care workers share a growing concern over the definition of their role as professionals. Center-based and home-based workers need support and resources to enhance their capabilities and to enrich the lives of the children they serve. Child care workers deserve our respect and recognition. However, most parents cannot afford to pay anyone the professional wage that accompanies that recognition. We need to seek avenues of informal support that will reduce costs while giving child care workers a decent living. More swapping arrangements for irregular care may be one way to achieve this, so that parents do not have to spend money to get a few hours of relief from caring for their children. On the other hand, locating individuals who enjoy caring for children and referring parents to them will improve salaries by bringing more children into the homes and centers of people interested in caring for them. However, these strategies alone will not markedly reduce the financial stresses; support from other systems such as employer-sponsors and community organizations must also be sought.

The ultimate goal of improving child care is to enhance the environments in which young children spend their time. For years, day care was viewed as depriving children of necessary experiences. Despite the prevalent view that time away from parents must be harmful to young children, few recent studies have documented adverse effects to children who spend time in the care of someone outside their immediate families (Belsky & Steinberg, 1978). In fact, a secure child care setting offers children other adults and children with whom they can develop supportive relationships, as well as opportunities to learn cognitive and social skills and to expand their experiences in diverse living settings. By creating a variety of options for families seeking child care, we increase their opportunities to find settings satisfactory to them and beneficial to their children.

An emergent role for parents today is to coordinate their children's activities (Keniston, 1977). A generation ago, parents were the primary source of their children's socialization and early education experiences. Today more adults enter the lives of some children—preschool teachers, sports coaches, and dancing instructors, for example—while parents leave home more frequently to pursue careers. Thus parents have become coordinators of their children's care, being less directly involved and more frequently selecting those with whom the children will have contact. In order to select wisely they need information, options, and support: in short, a social network that is broad, deep, and enduring.

ACKNOWLEDGMENT

I would like to thank Laurie Garduque, Donald Peters, Douglas Powell, and Patricia Rowan for their thoughtful comments on an earlier version of this chapter. Margaret Boyer of the Child Care Resource Center/Southside, Minneapolis, and Arthur Cruz of the Parent-Child Development Program/Head Start, Pueblo of Acoma, New Mexico, provided information about their programs.

CHAPTER 8
Social Support Networks for Divorced and Stepfamilies

Rhonda Richardson and Carol Pfeiffenberger

The traditional nuclear family, consisting of a mother, father, and their biological offspring, has long been considered the ideal family situation. Yet, with recent upswings in the number of divorces and subsequent remarriages, alternative family forms are emerging that defy the typical conceptualizations of the nuclear unit. The focus of this chapter will be on two of the family systems that come about after voluntary marital dissolution: single-parent households and step- or reconstituted families. The discussion will center on the life issues faced by adults and children who constitute such units and the relationships of these people with each other and with people outside of the immediate family boundaries.

No professional can approach a topic such as this one without personal biases that affect how the subject matter is selected and, most importantly, interpreted. There is a tendency to plunge into the theoretical and substantive issues of a topic without first defining the authors' rather influential underlying perspectives. Therefore, it is imperative that we take some time to describe our perspective on the functioning of single-parent and reconstituted families and the advantages of using informal support networks in working with them. Quite simply, we have adopted a process- and life-span–oriented, *nonpathological* approach to the study of families in transition.

PROCESS AND LIFE SPAN ORIENTATION

Critical life events such as divorce and remarriage are a much discussed topic in human development literature (e.g., Hultsch & Plemons, 1979). One aspect of understanding such events is defining them either as markers or as processes. Events viewed as markers are discrete transition points occurring at one moment in time (Neugarten & Hagestad, 1976). On the other

219

hand, events defined as processes have "histories of their own from the time they are anticipated through their occurrences until their aftermaths have been determined and assessed" (Danish, Smyer, & Nowak, 1980, p. 4). The latter notion is the one we see as most applicable to the two events of divorce and remarriage.

A couple's divorce entails more than the legal proceedings and court settlement. It is preceded by a decision to separate and by the actual separation itself, and it is followed by the state of being single and, in most cases, remarriage. Each of these periods is accompanied by its own set of issues and experiences. As an illustration, Brown (1976) identified four stages of the divorce experience, namely, decision-making during the preseparation phase; the physical separation stage; the restructuring stage before legal divorce, which entails emotional, legal, parent–child, economic, and social adjustments; and a final restructuring phase in which the individuals establish a workable, autonomous existence for themselves. Similarly, Bohannon (1970) identified what he terms the "stations" of divorce: (1) the emotional divorce, which focuses on the preseparation period; (2) the legal divorce; (3) the economic divorce, which deals with financial settlement between the couple; (4) the co-parental divorce involving not only custody decisions but also single parenting and visitation; (5) the community divorce based on changes in relationships with friends and others outside the family during and after the divorce; and (6) the psychic divorce during which the individual strives to achieve a sense of autonomy (see Salts, 1979).

Carrying such a process-oriented analysis even further, Ransom, Schlesinger, and Derdeyn (1979) proposed that three developmental stages be used to conceptualize the remarriage process for the marital dyad: recovering from a loss and entering a new relationship, understanding and planning the new relationship, and actually entering the new marriage. Using a perspective based on the family life cycle, McGoldrick and Carter (1980) expanded this basic schema to incorporate issues involved not only in recoupling but also in *family* reconstitution. The developmental issues identified included restructuring family boundaries to allow for inclusion of the new spouse and stepparent, sharing memories and histories to enhance stepfamily integration, and making room for relationships of all children with biological (noncustodial) parents, grandparents, and other extended family members.

The last concern is one that must be dealt with throughout the entire family life cycle, suggesting that adjustment with regard to family dissolution and reconstitution is never truly completed. Rather, it represents a continuing process extending across the entire life span. This is especially true when children are involved. For example, a seemingly obvious yet often overlooked fact is that one can indeed be an ex-spouse or an ex-in-law but never an ex-parent. Biological ties to one's offspring are irrevocable. As one's children pass through their life courses, this very permanence of parenthood requires occasional reuniting of ex-spouses and ex-in-laws, or the coming together of current spouses with ex-partners, biological parents with stepparents, for the celebrations of such milestones as graduations, marriages, and births. Each of these periodic events can be a potentially stressful as well as joyous occasion. During such times, individual, familial, and extrafamilial resources may continue to serve a supportive function for the family members.

Thus, in attempting to understand the experience of divorce and remarriage, we cannot look solely at two isolated events as though they occurred in a vacuum. They represent a process whose phases pose unique concerns throughout the individual life courses of the family members involved. It is this process and life span orientation that leads us to refer to our population as families in transition. Along with this emphasis on the continuous nature of the experience of divorce and remarriage, it is important to note that adapting to lifestyles such as being single or a member of a stepfamily does not necessarily entail crisis and debilitating stress. That is, we can adopt a nonpathological approach to our discussion of social support networks for families in transition.

NONPATHOLOGICAL PERSPECTIVE

There is a plethora of literature dealing with the adjustment of both adults and children to the process of divorce and remarriage (see Bloom, Asher, & White, 1978; Longfellow, 1979; Pais & White, 1979; Price-Bonham & Balswick, 1980; Wallerstein & Kelly, 1980). In general, available evidence points to the times of separation, divorce, postdivorce, and family reconstitution as being stressful periods for those involved.

No one discounts the fact that divorce is a difficult transition for all involved. Nor is the task of combining two family units into one cohesive system an enviable one. Most adults and children who are involved in family dissolution and reconstitution must grapple with certain immediate financial, emotional, and social issues. However, as we shall point out later, the perspective taken by most investigators has been unjustifiably one-sided and pathogenic. Rather than recognizing that divorce and remarriage can entail benefits as well as costs, researchers have viewed the single-parent family and the stepfamily as purely dysfunctional units.

A more realistic approach, one that recognizes that the inevitable occurrence of long-term deleterious effects of divorce and remarriage, has yet to be convincingly documented. Numerous demographic and psychological variables shape the individual's experience. How an individual meets the challenges and opportunities of his or her unique situation depends on both personal coping mechanisms and the social resources available. It is the thesis of this chapter that human service professionals can play a major role in strengthening the latter and, thereby, in minimizing negative and maximizing positive responses to family dissolution and reconstitution across the life span.

Along with the above issues specifically concerning families in transition, some items related to social support networks also help to define our perspective. As stated in Chapter 1, a social support network can be thought of as "a set of interconnected relationships among a group of people that provides enduring patterns of nurturance (in any or all forms) and provides contingent reinforcement for efforts to cope with life on a day-to-day basis." From this broad definition, we can move further to the identification of two types of social support networks: formal and informal. Formal networks are those that originate within the context of professional helping services. Examples would include therapy groups for single parents, crisis intervention for individuals in the process of divorce, and counseling programs for troubled stepfamilies. Informal social support networks, on the other hand, are those potential resources that exist outside the established helping services. It is this type of help that people usually seek first when dealing with problems (Gottlieb, 1976). It is also this course of help that social service professionals should be recognizing and capitalizing upon as a way to enhance the well-being of the population at large and specific subgroups such as families of divorce and remarriage.

With *informal* networks of social support, yet a further delineation is possible and will be used throughout this chapter. This is the dichotomy between organized and unorganized support networks. The former category consists primarily of community organizations such as Boy Scouts, Girl Scouts, PTA, and Parents Without Partners. These groups typically have established guidelines, leaders, and regular meeting times. For parents and children of divorce and remarriage, participation in such organizations may provide a valuable source of support outside of the formal helping services system. In contrast to this type of informal support system is the unorganized type. Included in this category are family members, friends, neighbors, and community gatekeepers such as beauticians, bartenders, cab drivers, teachers, attorneys, and clergy. Contact with these sources of support may be random or regular, repeated or unitary.

This type of informal, naturally occurring network will be the primary focus of this chapter. Such systems serve several functions for members of families in transition. Before considering our specific population, however, it is important to understand in general what types of support are typically sought and under what circumstances such aid is solicited.

In a recent review of the role played by social support networks for families under stress, Unger and Powell (1980) identified three basic types of aid: instrumental, emotional, and referral and information. Instrumental support includes the sharing of material goods and services. Emotional support refers to conveying a sense of belongingness and acceptance to network members. Referral and information consists of the social support network's ability to influence interactions with formal helping systems (e.g., schools) and to identify other sources of aid. As we shall discuss later, this last type of support is an integral part of a powerful linking mechanism between the professional helper and the informal helping network.

Thus, social networks can fulfill a variety of purposes. However, not every individual in a social support network is required to answer every need that arises during stressful times. As shown by Litwak and Szelenyi (1969), for example, family members call upon certain segments of their support networks for different services. Friends or peer groups serve best in helping individuals handle major transitions in their lifestyles. The kinship network, characterized by permanency of its membership, provides more long-term commitment than any other group. In contrast, neighbors are called upon most often for aid in emergency, on-the-spot situations.

In addition to such differences in the timing of their usage, components of a social support network vary in the extent to which they are relied upon. Some may serve multiple roles whereas others serve only a unitary one. With regard to families in transition, for example, the family of origin (i.e., one's own parents) provides several kinds of resources—instrumental as well as emotional support—whereas a given friend or organization tends to be used for one distinct type of support (McLanahan, Wedemeyer, & Adelberg, 1981). We would expect one-sided relationships to exist also between family members and community gatekeepers. As we shall see, these issues of timing and content of social support contacts for families of divorce and remarriage will have implications for helping professionals' involvement.

To summarize the perspective that is the basis of this chapter, we view divorce and remarriage as a process encompassing the entire life span and providing opportunities for growth and adaptation as well as possible problems. Parents and children of family dissolution and reconstitution, in dealing with the transitions they face, may find many sources of support outside of the formal human services system. Recognizing and fostering the effectiveness of these informal social support networks has potential benefits for both helping professionals and family members. This approach builds on an ecological perspective of human development that is the foundation of this volume. Having thus outlined the key elements of our viewpoint, we can turn to our discussion of social support networks for families of divorce and remarriage.

We shall begin by identifying population parameters that highlight the prevalence of family dissolution and reconstitution. Next, we shall discuss the particular issues confronting transitional families and the types of programs that are being used to help them cope. We shall move then to a consideration of barriers and incentives to implementing social support networks for parents and children of divorce and remarriage. Finally, we shall discuss the need to develop informal social supports for dealing with family dissolution and reconstitution and how their development can be facilitated.

Our goal is to provide human service professionals with the information they need to adopt and implement an ecological perspective on divorce and remarriage.

POPULATION PARAMETERS

Recent census data reveal the now widely publicized fact that a significant proportion of adults and children in the United States are, in some way, involved in the process of marital dissolution, single parenting, remarriage, and family reconstitution.

For the past several decades, the annual divorce rate has been rising consistently and is currently at 5.3 per 1,000 in the population. In fact, roughly 1,182,000 couples were granted divorces in 1980 alone (National Center for Health Statistics, 1981a). This increase in the rate of marital dissolution has been accompanied by an upswing in the number of children involved. In 1979, over 1.1 million children under 18 years of age experienced the divorce of their parents. This figure has more than doubled in the past 16 years and has more than tripled in the past 22 years (National Center for Health Statistics, 1981b). Indeed, the proportion of children in the total population whose parents underwent a divorce reached a record high of 18.9 per 1,000 in 1979 (National Center for Health Statistics, 1981b).

As a result of the above trends, the 1970's saw a dramatic increase in the proportion of single-parent families. Although the number of two-parent families decreased by about 4% within the past decade, the prevalence of single-parent households increased significantly. As of 1979, approximately 19% of all families with children under 18 residing at home were single-parent units. Of these, 5,288,000 or roughly 90% were female-headed. Some 38% were the result of divorces (U. S. Bureau of the Census, 1980).

As our earlier discussion of divorce and remarriage as a process would suggest, not all individuals choose to be single as a permanent lifestyle. Indeed, the majority eventually remarry and tend to do so at a relatively high rate. About three-fourths of the women and five-sixths of the men who divorce eventually remarry by middle age (45–54) (Glick, 1980). Given the significant number of children involved in divorce, remarriage for adults often entails the formation of a new family; however, the number of stepfamilies in the United States today can only be estimated. According to Glick (1980), in 1978, in the United States, approximately 10.2% (6.5 million) of all children under 18 were residing with a biological parent and a stepparent. By 1990, Glick (1979) projects, this number may exceed 7 million, or 11% of all children. Even these estimates are conservative, since they do not include children living with a natural father and stepmother. Children in this situation may account for up to 10% of all stepchildren (Glick, 1980).

In summary, then, current statistics show the rapid rise in the number of alternate family lifestyles. Although the two-parent primary intact family is still the most prevalent form, a significant proportion of the population is opting out of unhappy first and even subsequent marriages and seeking alternatives. Single-parent families are the fastest-growing form, and most of them are headed by women. Yet as the high remarriage rate indicates, divorced men and women are not forsaking marriage as a potentially viable institution. Stepfamilies are also growing in number, the highest percentage involving a biological mother and a stepfather. Who are these people? What characteristics best define these nonnuclear family members?

Price-Bonham and Balswick (1980) provide an excellent review of variables identified within the past decade that are associated with divorce and remarriage. Table 8-1 describes the relationship between such factors and the likelihood of divorce and remarriage. Age, race, income, education, religion, employment status of women, the number of children, marital and family history, and premarital pregnancy have all been found to be related to the likelihood of divorce, remarriage, or both. A caveat must be issued here, however. The correlations noted above are meant to provide a very broad, global summary of the factors identified most often in the literature. The purpose in citing them is *not* to promote a stereotypical image of a single parent or a remarried individual. Most assuredly, all single parents and all remarried individuals are not alike. Rather, the very dynamic, unique nature of individuals as well as the interaction of numerous factors and the impact of various contexts cannot be underestimated. Thus, social service providers are urged to use such correlates as reference points, bearing in mind that each case is unique.

We have detailed the prevalence of the forms of the nonnuclear family and the general characteristics that identify the individuals involved. We now turn to the issues most commonly faced by families of divorce and remarriage as the individuals, marital couple, and parent–child dyad strive to succeed as family systems. We shall then consider current and potential uses of social support networks for facilitating adjustment to family dissolution and reconstitution.

ISSUES CONFRONTING TRANSITIONAL FAMILIES

Alerted by increases in divorce and remarriage, social scientists have begun to concentrate their research efforts on understanding the individuals involved in the divorce process. This, however, is a fairly new area of investigation. The literature on families in transition is relatively sparse and fraught with methodological problems. These limitations include inadequate sample sizes, frequent use of nonrandom sampling procedures, heavy reliance on cross-sectional analyses, overuse of retrospective data, a ten-

Table 8-1. Demographic factors as they relate to the likelihood of divorce and remarriage

	Divorce	Remarriage
Age	Inverse relationship between age at first marriage and likelihood to divorce	Negative relationship between age at divorce and likelihood to remarry
Race	Higher rate of marital dissolution for blacks than for whites Interracial marriages less stable than intraracial ones	Likelihood to remarry greater for white than for black women
Income	Inverse relationship between income and marital dissolution	Possible inverse relationship between women's economic resources and likelihood to remarry
Education	Conflicting evidence: in general, education is inversely related to likelihood to divorce. Relationship may disappear if age at marriage, race, religion are taken into account.	Likelihood to remarry greater for individuals with high school education than for those with one or more years of college
Employment status of women	Positive relationship between wife's income and marital dissolution	—
Religion	Catholics have lower rate of divorce than do Protestants. Jews have the lowest rate of all; Catholics may have higher rates of separation Mixed marriages more prone to divorce than religiously homogeneous marriages	—
Presence/number of children	Positive relationship between the number of children involved and the likelihood to divorce	Conflicting evidence: presence of children *may* enhance, hinder, or not affect a woman's opportunity to remarry, depending on the age at which she entered the remarriage market (Koo & Suchindran, 1980)
Marital history	Those who marry three or more times are more likely to divorce than those married one or two times	Divorced women more likely to remarry than widowed women (Spanier & Glick, 1980)
Family history	Individuals who grew up in homes broken by divorce are more likely to get divorced themselves than those whose parents did not divorce	—
Premarital pregnancy	*Strong* relationship to marital dissolution. Those who were pregnant prior to marriage are more likely to divorce than those who were not pregnant	—

Adapted from Price-Bonham & Balswick, 1980.

dency to infer cause and effect from correlational data, and the adoption of a general pathogenic approach to the study of families of divorce and re-marriage.

Despite these limitations, the investigations discussed below help us to identify some salient issues confronting divorced people, single-parents, and stepfamily members. They also lay some preliminary groundwork for un-derstanding the costs and benefits of the divorce and remarriage experience.

Lauren is a single parent who has been divorced for a year and a half. While visiting her sister, she recounts her experiences since the separation:

> I guess it was roughest in the beginning, right after we separated. I remem-ber only a big empty feeling inside and I wondered if it would ever go away. Even after the *divorce*, problems kept cropping up. Money was a major con-cern. I had to return to work and good day care for my four-year-old son was expensive and hard to find. If I wasn't worrying about supporting me and the kids, I was feeling sorry for myself.
>
> I don't know what I would have done without my parents. They really came through with money, advice, and were always there for me and the kids. Their support got me through the hard times and helped me see that, gee, I was still a really worthwhile person.
>
> In the beginning things were rough with the kids. I found it hard to com-municate with them. I was so concerned about myself, I couldn't put as much energy into them as I should have. My disciplining was so erratic. One minute I'd blow up and just come down hard. The next minute, a perhaps more serious incident wouldn't even phase me!
>
> I caught my four-year-old crying in bed one night. I kept asking him what was wrong. He finally told me that he just *knew* that he was the one who made his daddy and I fight so much. I *never* knew that he felt that way.
>
> My teenage son turned out to be a real help to me. He understood things a little better about why the marriage ended, I mean. I know it was rough on him when we had to move to another part of town so I could be closer to work. He had to change schools and at first it was rough making new friends. Now, though, he spends more time with them than he does with me.
>
> Don't get me wrong. Things haven't only gone bad! As time went on, my life got smoothed out. In fact, I'm beginning to feel really good about myself again. I mean, I've proven that I can fend for myself. I'm a good parent, now. My kids and I are closer than we've ever been and I look forward to tomorrow. Things are looking up!

Research has shown that Lauren is not alone in her experiences as a divorced adult. Adjustments concerning one's personal well-being as well as one's parental role must be made as the individual passes through the di-vorce process.

Separation has been clearly defined as the most stressful period (Pearlin & Johnson, 1977; White & Bloom, 1981). Such stress could result from financial strain, interpersonal tensions, drastic changes in habits, or the loss of a highly significant other (Weiss, 1975; Salts, 1979).

As the case of Lauren also demonstrates, many challenges continue to confront the divorced adult throughout the postdivorce period as well. Difficulties with finances (Albrecht, 1980; see Schlesinger, 1978), deficits or declines in social relations (Gasser & Taylor, 1976; Albrecht, 1980; Smith, 1980), and a lack of familial and community support (see Schlesinger, 1978; Smith, 1980) are the three most commonly cited issues facing both men and women. These factors have been found to be significantly correlated with postdivorce adjustment. That is, the fewer the economic problems (Spanier & Casto, 1979), the greater the amount of social participation (Raschke, 1977; Spanier & Casto, 1979), and the more family and peer support received (Hunt & Hunt, 1977; Spanier & Casto, 1979; Berman & Turk, 1981), the better the adjustment. In addition, most divorced women continue or return to work. Such labor force participation has also been found to be positively related to adjustment to divorce (Raschke, 1977).

Gender differences have been noted, however. Women tend to experience more financial difficulties (Brandwein, Brown, & Fox, 1974) and a more limited social life (Raschke, 1977) than their male counterparts, especially when children are involved. Thus, women tend to be at a greater risk for poor postdivorce adjustment.

Single parenting brings with it a unique set of individual and family issues. Stress often occurs with the increase of child care responsibilities (Brandwein, Brown, & Fox, 1974) as well as the imposed limitations on social activities and finances. Custody arrangements may also affect adjustment, especially for noncustodial fathers who visit the children infrequently (e.g., Hetherington, Cox, & Cox, 1978a; Keshet & Rosenthal, 1978; Schlesinger, 1978). Adequate and affordable day care, and obtaining information about basic child care and development (e.g., see Keshet & Rosenthal, 1978; Schlesinger, 1978) are also common concerns, especially for single fathers. Parent–child relations tend to become strained, at least temporarily, and are marked by a general decline in parental competence (Hetherington, Cox, & Cox, 1978b; Wallerstein & Kelly, 1980; Weingarten, 1980). For example, Hetherington, Cox, and Cox found that divorced parents "made fewer maturity demands, communicated less well, and showed marked inconsistencies in discipline and control of their children in comparison to married parents" (1978a, p. 163), and that sons were more affected than daughters.

The problems associated with single parenthood often go unnoticed by the society as a whole. Indeed, researchers have speculated about one broad cultural value that may exacerbate the stress experienced by divorced people. This value is the general tendency to view divorce as a social stigma (Hancock, 1980) and to idealize the nuclear family to such an extent that any deviation from the nuclear unit is considered inferior. As Potter stated, "most formerly married persons whom I have interviewed responded that they feel like second-class citizens. This is especially true of those who have been divorced or who are unwed parents. They claim that society has put them in a classification which denies them the status and sense of belonging they would like to enjoy" (1979, p. 319). As a result of this social stigma, there is a definite lack of role clarity for the single parent. For example, no societal guidelines exist for how to coordinate one's life when child care, financial, and household management responsibilities suddenly rest solely on one individual. This is especially true for single fathers (Mendes, 1976a, b).

ADJUSTMENT BY ADULTS AND CHILDREN

Despite the stress associated with divorce and single parenthood, significant financial, social, and emotional strains do not appear to be long-lasting. Clinical reports and interview data indicate that after the initial stresses of adjusting to the lifestyle are overcome, divorced adults experience an increase in well-being (Spanier & Furstenberg, 1981) as well as more confidence, satisfaction, and pride about themselves as individuals and as parents (Orthner, Brown, & Ferguson, 1976; Boston Women's Health Book Collective, 1978; Keshet & Rosenthal, 1978). After approximately 1 year following the divorce, there appears to be a gradual improvement in parenting and parent–child relationships (Hetherington, Cox, & Cox, 1978a; Wallerstein & Kelly, 1980). Benefits of single-parenting begin to emerge. Parents are drawn closer to their children and single-parent fathers seize the opportunity to display previously socially unacceptable nurturant behavior (Orthner, Brown, & Ferguson, 1976).

Thus, adult adjustment to divorce involves many challenges, ranging from handling financial problems to adapting to new roles within society and the family. However, any adverse effects appear to be temporary in nature. Individuals gradually come to feel more positive about themselves and gain some sense of equilibrium in terms of the personal, social, and parental life. Nonetheless, during the initial periods of the divorce process, a single parent's personal struggle can affect the child's adjustment. A parent's unstable financial situation can adversely influence child care both in terms of the basic provisions available and the very quality of parent–child interactions. In addition, families are likely to move after a divorce. Consequently, children change schools and switch neighborhoods. Both changes imply the need to construct a new peer group. Such mobility is often accompanied by a high degree of social isolation (Pearlin & Johnson, 1977).

There is no doubt, then, that such social and emotional upheavals can produce stress for all family members. What is the effect of such stress on the children? To say the least, evidence about children's adjustment to divorce is contradictory. Children from one-parent families exhibit a relative deficit in cognitive capacities (e.g., Shinn, 1978) and manifest more behavioral problems (Hetherington, Cox, & Cox, 1978b) than do children from intact families. Yet, there appears to be a general absence of significant long-range effects. Summarizing the literature on boys in father-absent families, for example, Herzog and Sudia (1971) concluded that there is no consistent evidence that living in a single-parent home is detrimental to the child's overall development. Similarly, Raschke and Raschke (1979) found no significant differences in the self-concepts of children from primary nuclear, single-parent, and stepfamilies. Kulka and Weingarten (1979), after studying the long-term effect on children of the separation of the primary family, concluded that children of divorce and subsequent remarriage learn to cope as successfully with life as do their counterparts who live in primary intact homes. Furthermore, living in a one-parent home may foster early maturity for adolescents as the child gains independence, self-esteem, and a sense of competence (Weiss, 1979).

Thus, there is a wide range of responses among children to the divorce process. As Hetherington (1979) points out, how an individual child copes with divorce is affected by a number of factors. The two most frequently discussed factors are gender and the developmental stage of the child. In short, boys seem to be harder hit than girls in terms of both social and emotional development (Hetherington, Cox, & Cox, 1978a). Boys exhibit more behavioral problems at home and at school, being less compliant and more aggressive (Hetherington, Cox, & Cox, 1978a). These gender differences, however, tend to lessen over time and, on the whole, are more evident in younger children (Wallerstein & Kelly, 1980; Kurdek *et al.*, in press). Reasons for this difference are unclear. However, it has been suggested that boys may be more affected because they are more often exposed to stress, frustration, and aggression and also have fewer supports available to them than do girls (Hetherington, 1979).

Qualitative differences in youngsters' response to divorce may also be attributed to the child's developmental stage at the time of the divorce (Wallerstein & Kelly, 1980). Children of divorce may be most fragile in the preschool period. At this stage, a child is not cognitively ready to interpret realistically the reasons behind his or her parents' divorce. Facts tend to be distorted and children tend to blame themselves for disrupting the marriage. Such problems as bed wetting, depressed play, and disturbances in eating patterns and behavior may occur. In contrast, a deep sense of loss and abandonment is experienced by the school-age child. Youngsters in this age group often withdraw, do more poorly in school, and obsess over why the divorce had to occur in the first place. Adolescents, at a stage in cognitive development in which they can appropriately assess the situation, are the least vulnerable. After experiencing anger and pain, most adolescents can understand why the parents separated and can resolve interpersonal conflicts. They do, however, have a tendency to disengage, seeking support from systems external to the family—i.e., the peer group and the school system.

Thus, just as with adults, the changes incurred by marital dissolution cause initial stresses for children. How each child is affected by such transitions depends in part on his or her developmental stage and gender. Furthermore, evidence for long-term deleterious effects on a child's intellectual and cognitive development is far from convincing. Available literature indicates that children from single-parent households do not differ significantly in their development from youngsters in intact families. Indeed, they may actually benefit from the experience.

About 3 years after divorcing Susan, Gordon married Kristen, a divorced mother with custody of her two children. Gordon's son lived with Susan. Here, Gordon and Kristen tell of the early phases of stepfamily life:

Gordon: Wow! Everything at once. I never thought I'd have a rough time. First I have to say that I'm happier now than I've been. Kristen and I have a solid marriage. But I must admit I've had my problems as far as George (Kristen's former husband), and the kids were concerned. I often saw everybody in the house picking sides and I was the odd man out. The kids didn't have any idea as to where their loyalties should be. And they were even more confused by the unspoken but constant rivalry for attention that I was experiencing with George. I also didn't know how to act as a stepparent, believe it or not. When one of the kids stayed out one hour past curfew, I tried to discipline him in the same way I discipline my own son but I felt uneasy doing it and, worst of all, ineffective. It's still hard going out with them and having to introduce them as my stepchildren. I don't like the term and I'm not sure how people will react.

Kristen: I really looked forward to Gordon and I having a life together. I guess I didn't anticipate all the possible problems. I hated seeing the kids so confused about whom they should listen to and where they really belonged—that is, with their dad or me. I felt uneasy around Gordon's son for the entire first summer he spent with us. I wanted, and finally expected, everything to be fine—immediately. I mean, I was his dad's wife, I loved him, too, or did I? The love and harmony didn't come until much later. Even now, conflicts arise but we resolve them eventually and they're over with.

Gordon has been great. You know, he says he's uncertain about his parenting abilities, but he gets so involved. Much more so than George ever did. I mean, he helps with almost all household tasks, and does a lot to relieve more of the responsibilities with the kids.

I know we've complained a lot. But we know now, through experience, what we didn't know then at the beginning. That is, all families have problems. We just take the ones that come our way one step at a time.

As seen with Gordon and Kristen's family, adjustment to stepfamily life involves a different set of challenges for each member. This point is revealed in the current literature on remarriage and family reconstitution.

The most salient issues for stepfathers are discipline (Stern, 1978; Bohannon, 1979) and finances (Duberman, 1975; Messinger, 1976). Other issues include joining an already functioning group, guilt about abandoning previous family members, and inadequate societal norms governing sexuality within the stepfamily (Fast & Cain, 1966; Visher & Visher, 1979). Stepchildren often struggle with divided loyalties, possible guilt carried over from parents' divorce, and the question of where they belong (Visher & Visher, 1979).

Another problem discussed in the literature is the difficulty that the child and his or her family have in recognizing and accepting the inevitable presence of two intermingling family units (Messinger, 1976; Messinger, Walker, & Freeman, 1978). Stepfamily members may have a difficult time clearly delineating family boundaries (Colvin, Hicks, & Greenwood, 1981). For example, a former spouse, although physically absent, often remains psychologically present, causing disequilibrium and stress. Visher and Visher (1979) cite three major aspects of the reconstituted family that may account for some of the stress experienced by stepparents and stepchildren. They consist of the existence of interpersonal bonds predating the couple's relationship that may result in jealousy, rivalries, and guilt among all family members; incomplete mourning; and the presence of the other natural parents as a determinant of the stepparent's role. Additional problems include lack of awareness of and insensitivity to the needs of all concerned, as well as insufficient community and familial support systems.

Just as with single parenthood, a source of stress during the process of family reconstitution is society's failure to recognize and accept the stepfamily as a structurally and functionally unique, viable family form. This prime example of cultural lag results in insufficiently defined roles for stepparents and children (Messinger, 1976). Stepmothers, for example, must compete with the image of their wicked counterpart portrayed in such children's classics as Cinderella and Hansel and Gretel. In addition, the idealization of the nuclear family places added pressures on stepfamily members to experience instant love for one another and instant adjustment. Thus, appropriate socialization for stepparenthood is nonexistent (Kompara, 1980). However, it is not only the stepparent role that is unclearly defined. Children, too, grappling with divided loyalties, possible guilt or anger, not to mention confused parents, suddenly become stepchildren with several adults willing to "parent" them.

Despite this abundance of issues involved in family reconstitution, evidence concerning the adjustment of individuals within the stepfamily, although sketchy, is fairly encouraging. The effects of remarriage and the reconstitution process on the sociopsychological development of youngsters and adults and the individuals' adjustment to marital and parental roles will be summarized below.

There is conflicting evidence on the perceived well-being of the remarried adults themselves. White (1979) found several interactions between sex and marital status and effects on global happiness. Remarried men, White reports, viewed themselves as being significantly more happy than their counterparts in first marriages. Remarried women, on the other hand, were less happy than women in their first marriages. In a study using data from a national survey, Weingarten (1980) compared remarried and first-married individuals on measures of well-being and family role adjustment and found no significant difference between the groups for measures reflecting present-oriented adjustment (i.e., self-acceptance, self-esteem, and personal efficacy).

Studies centering on the qualitative aspects of remarriage are also relatively scarce but generally depict remarital life as a happy state. Remarried and first-married individuals do not differ significantly in reported marital happiness (Glenn & Weaver, 1977; Weingarten, 1980). In fact, satisfaction with second and subsequent marriages may even be greater than with first marriages (Albrecht, 1979). Weingarten hastens to add, however, that the two marriage experiences are not identical. For example, although they report themselves happier, remarried people are more likely to feel inadequate in their marital roles. They do, however, perceive themselves as being more involved in housework and childcare activities than do their first married peers. In fact, among the primary caretakers, the remarried respondents in Weingarten's (1980) study were more likely to report that their spouses "often help." Therefore, stepparents were viewed as being cooperative in the childrearing role.

There has been little discussion of the adjustment to the parental role within the stepfamily. In general, remarried individuals are more likely to feel inadequate in their family role performance (Bohannon, 1979; Weingarten, 1980) and more often report difficulties in maintaining and fulfilling emotional and physical contact with children (Weingarten, 1980). Weingarten (1980) found no differences between first-married and remarried respondents in their reports of how children changed their personal lives, of their feelings that parenthood fulfills values, and of their feelings that children restrict personal endeavors.

And what of children's adaptation to stepfamily life? Several investigations have noted adverse effects of family reconstitution on children's mental health (Langner & Michael, 1963; Rosenberg, 1965; Perkins & Kahan, 1979) and social behavior (Touliatos & Lindholm, 1980). A recent study of intrafamilial stress in stepfamilies (Colvin, Hicks, & Greenwood, 1981) found that adolescents living in families with a stepfather or stepmother report poorer family relations than their peers living in families with their natural parents. In general, however, most available investigations report an absence of deleterious effects of living in a stepfamily. For example, studying the effects of stepfathers on the psychosocial development of late-adolescent boys, Oshman and Manosevitz (1976) found that the presence of a stepfather helps to mitigate the possible harmful outcomes stemming from the absence of the father. Wilson et al. (1975), using data from two national surveys, reported that children, regardless of family type, undergo very diverse social and sociopsychological experiences. There were no significant differences between children in intact and stepfamilies. Using adolescents as the target population, other studies report essentially the same results. Bohannon (1979) administered questionnaires to children from both intact and stepfamilies. The latter perceived themselves to be just as happy and well-adjusted as their nuclear-family counterparts.

Several factors have been found to be associated with the adaptation of both adults and children to stepfamily life, age and gender being the most frequently documented variables. The age of the adults has been found to be associated with several areas of stepfamily functioning, and a more positive picture has emerged for younger people. For example, family integration is perceived to be higher by younger than by older remarried couples (Duberman, 1975). In addition, stepmothers who are under 40 more often have excellent relationships with their spouses' children than do women who are over 40. Similarly, younger stepfathers perceive better stepsibling relationships than do older stepfathers.

The age of the child is also an important factor. Touliatos and Lindholm (1980) note an interesting interaction with grade in school for items dealing with conduct problems and social delinquency. In stepmother families, the frequency of these behavioral disorders is positively related to grade. For primary intact families, however, although there is a similar increase in the early school years, the incidence of behavioral problems levels off in later grades. Duberman (1975) found that more stepmothers with younger stepchildren (under 13 years old) reported having excellent parent–child relationships than did their counterparts with stepchildren older than 13.

Along with the developmental stage of the parent and child, we must also consider gender as a factor that may affect adjustment to the stepparenting role. For instance, Bowerman and Irish's clinical investigation (1962) suggests that stepmothers with adolescent children have a much more difficult role than do stepfathers or stepmothers with younger children. Weingarten (1980) noted that remarried men were somewhat less invested in parenting than were the women of either marital status and first-married men. In addition, Touliatos and Lindholm (1980) report that boys in stepmother families were seen as having more conduct problems and were rated lower on the inadequacy—immaturity continuum (e.g., short attention span, passivity) than their female counterparts.

Remarried adults and their families, then, face a variety of personal and interpersonal challenges following family reconstitution. As with adjustment to divorce, adaptation to stepfamily life can involve an initial period of stress. Most people are not permanently adversely affected by the adjustment process however; they eventually discover how to make stepfamily life a fulfilling experience. Indeed, the benefits of remarriage often go unreported. Johnson (1980) lists several positive aspects, including relief from constant childcare, the acquisition of stepsiblings and other new relatives for the children, and the opportunity for parents to be happy and satisfied and thus be able to give more to their children. One perfect example of a positive view of stepfamily life comes from Gordon Bawker in *Stepparents Forum,* a newsletter containing current research findings as well as personal accounts dealing with remarriage and stepfamilies: "Stepparents are . . . prepared to take chances. . . . They may indicate a . . . readiness to experiment, to work . . . at relationships, to dispense with old ideas and ancient stigmas. In a sense, parents have taken a *step.* Perhaps that's what we should take the term to mean" (1975, p. 3).

STRATEGIES FOR HELPING FAMILIES IN TRANSITION

In response to the concerns facing members of divorced and blended families, human service professionals have adopted many different helping strategies. For review here, a representative sample has been selected from the programs that have been described in professional journals. The most common type of intervention is targeted at the people most directly involved: the divorced adults. Recognizing that many of the problems and conflicts faced by divorcing couples stem from the nature of the legal system, which pits husband and wife against one another, divorce mediation has been developed in some regions as an alternative to the adversarial system (Coogler, Weber, & McKenry, 1979). According to this technique, clients seeking a divorce make their own decisions under the guidance of an impartial mediator who has training in the human services. During 10 hours of mediation time, only practical matters related to the divorce are discussed; emotional issues are not dealt with. When agreement is reached on the salient concerns, an attorney is called in to complete the necessary legal steps. Such an approach provides a unique opportunity for professionals to deal with divorcing couples in a nonclinical human service context, and it benefits both couples and attorneys by reducing the stress that is normally associated with divorce proceedings.

Another chance for social workers to link up with the legal system is exemplified by the Marital Counseling Service, a court-related agency in Detroit (Brown & Manela, 1977). Couples who have come through the court for divorce proceedings are provided with counseling, skills training, and referral as needed in order to foster postdivorce adjustment for them and their children. This type of program does not build on the concept of social support networks, and therefore may be less beneficial than other intervention techniques. As mentioned above, one of the problems frequently facing newly divorced individuals is loneliness and a sense of isolation.

In light of this, many group services have been developed. Most of these group programs, although called by different names, have the same general goals. These goals include helping divorced people to regain autonomy and develop a self-identity, to work through their grief reactions, to discharge their emotions, to understand the dynamics of their former marital relationship, to cope with reality demands such as employment and child care, and to become part of a social support network composed of others who have shared the same experience. Clearly, this last goal capitalizes on the notion of support systems, and such programs fall into the category of formal support networks discussed above. Some of these groups are designed to help individuals through the crisis of divorce (Hassall & Madar, 1980), whereas others are implemented after the crisis-oriented phase to facilitate growth (Kessler, 1976; Morris & Prescott, 1976; Beatrice, 1979). These programs are offered through social service agencies and consist of anywhere from 5 to 15 weekly 2-hour meetings. A human service professional serves as group facilitator, although a loose structure is suggested. Along with specific goal-directed problem-solving, group members have the chance to share feelings and concerns informally. Evaluations of these programs suggest that the group technique is an effective way to provide divorced people with needed support and companionship and to foster divorce-related growth.

Whereas the programs reviewed so far have evolved around the needs of divorced individuals, others have been designed to answer the needs of single parents. Parenting Alone Successfully (PALS) (Leavitt et al., 1979) addresses unique single-parent difficulties in addition to teaching general child management techniques. In addition to weekly group training, the parents participating in this program attend weekly individualized consultation sessions to discuss their specific single-parent problems. One of the strong points of PALS is its creators' recognition of the special need of single parents for a support group. In order that accomplishments (e.g., teaching the children new skills) do not go unrecognized, that decisions are not made without input from others, and that feelings of being the only one with certain problems do not arise, a buddy system is included in the program. Each parent is matched with another parent, and these pairs are encouraged to assist one another throughout the program by discussing problems, providing encouragement and recognition, and developing strategies to change their children's behavior. The incorporation of this element into an otherwise standard single-parent training program is an excellent example of how human service professionals can and should facilitate the establishment of social support networks for families of divorce and remarriage.

Practitioners have also attempted to deal with the needs of children of divorce. Some of these efforts consist merely of clinical divorce-specific counseling, such as the Children of Divorce Project, which has been located since 1971 at the Community Mental Health Center of Marin County, California (Wallerstein & Kelly, 1977). This program involves both parents and children in the intervention: it teaches the custodial parent methods to deal with child behavior problems and to provide support to preschool children, while offering children an opportunity to discuss their concerns. It also recognizes and facilitates the on-going relationship between the noncus-todial parent (usually the father) and the child. Although noteworthy in this last respect, this particular program does little to link family members to social support networks.

In contrast is a program, also called Children of Divorce, that was spe-cifically designed to provide support for children encountering the dissolu-tion of an existing family (Guerney & Jordan, 1979). This community-based and community-sponsored education–support group was created to help children develop realistic appraisals of their own situations in relation to life during and after divorce; to help children acquire the knowledge and skill necessary for problem-solving in specific situations that arise from the di-vorce experience; and to help children feel good about themselves. During the six 1-hour sessions, participants have opportunities to discuss their feel-ings, to view films relevant to the topic of divorce, and to play games that elicit opinions. The children are also given materials to read outside of the weekly sessions. Evaluation of this support-group experience has been pos-itive; children have found that the group helps them talk about and under-stand their parents' divorce. Given the effectiveness of this type of program, human service professionals should be encouraged to establish more of these formal support networks in their attempts to answer the needs of families in transition.

Just as most of the research dealing with families in transition focuses on divorce and single-parenthood, so do the majority of intervention programs. Perhaps there is an implicit assumption on the part of human service work-ers that remarriage is the panacea for problems faced by divorced families. We hope that our review of the issues related to family reconstitution has dispelled this notion among readers of this chapter. Given the special con-cerns of stepfamilies, intervention with this group should be deemed worth-while. The dearth of programs is surprising and unfortunate.

In response to the lack of professional help for families preparing for or participating in remarriage, Messinger, Walker, and Freeman (1978) orga-nized a series of small discussion groups for such individuals. The weekly meetings provided remarried couples with an opportunity to share questions and concerns, clarify their feelings, and acquire information and techniques for dealing with the stepfamily situation. Upon completion of the program all of the couples reported that the new knowledge and the social support they had gained made the experience an invaluable one. A few groups even continued to meet on their own and introduced activities for their children and stepchildren. Clearly, this type of program should be implemented more often for families in transition. Not only can it help the stepfamily members work through their process of social change, but it also has the potential to contribute to a greater understanding of remarriage in the larger society (Messinger, Walker, & Freeman, 1978). The work of Messinger and her colleagues serves as a good model for how human service professionals can foster the development of social support networks for families facing divorce or remarriage.

Until now, we have reviewed only intervention efforts that evolved from within the helping services. As such, those few support systems that we have discussed fall into the category of formal social supports outlined above. It is important to recognize, however, that informal sources of support also exist for families in transition. Among them are groups that have been developed and sustained without the guidance of professional human service workers. For example, probably the best-known organization of single parents is Parents Without Partners (PWP). This self-help group, which has nearly 1,000 chapters and approximately 150,000 members, provides stimulating new growth and social patterns as well as socially acceptable substitutes for some of the amenities of married life, and is thereby able to neutralize the solitude of divorce (Parks, 1977). The group does not include specific education, goal-directed counseling, or prescriptive therapy as part of its practices, but concentrates instead on using social activities, rap groups, and informal conversation to provide both custodial and noncustodial parents with the companionship, moral support, and advice of others who are similarly situated. Very little has been done to evaluate the effects of PWP on parents and children, although subjective reports by participants have indicated that the organization is a valuable means of forming new emotional attachments and reducing the sense of isolation that often accompanies divorce (Weiss, 1973).

A similar result has been achieved by small-scale local groups such as one in Eureka, California, which was established by and for single fathers as an outlet for sharing the worries, problems, and satisfactions associated with raising children in a motherless home (Thompson, 1981). Unfortunately, most social service workers do not endow such self-help groups with the esteem to which they are entitled. Perhaps if they would recognize the value of positive, supportive social contacts for people after divorce or remarriage, professionals would begin efforts to link the public to informal social support networks. There are undoubtedly numerous other informal support systems either already addressing or with the potential to address the needs of families in transition. Church groups, PTA chapters, Boy Scout, and Girl Scout troops are all potentially valuable outlets for family members involved in divorce or remarriage, as are school teachers, attorneys, pediatricians, bartenders, hairdressers, and cab drivers. Clearly, such sources of social support can and should be made accessible and responsive to individuals confronted with family dissolution and reconstitution. Human service professionals can play a major part in facilitating support from these sources. As we move in this direction, there are several barriers and also incentives to recognize. These will be considered next after which we shall present some practical suggestions as to how social service workers can contribute to the development of more extensive social support networks for families in transition.

BARRIERS AND INCENTIVES TO USING SOCIAL SUPPORT NETWORKS

Perhaps one of the strongest barriers to the implementation by professionals of social support networks is that these workers are not convinced of the importance of such informal sources of help. In addition, those human service workers who do recognize the value of social support systems may be reluctant to encourage their use. One reason for this could be the myth of "professionalism" according to which only trained mental health professionals are competent to help people deal with problems (Broskowski & Baker, 1974). Another may be that with present funding limitations, the survival of agencies is increasingly dependent on fee-paying clients. Consequently, human service professionals, in order to keep people in the system and to ensure their own employment, would not want to encourage the public to look for help among their families and friends, and may in fact actively discourage it. Professionals may feel threatened by the prospect of having untrained "intruders" taking over their functions.

Furthermore, by training people such as community gatekeepers for nonprofessional helping roles, mental health professionals may feel that they are then accountable for the outcome of their efforts. That is, they may fear being held responsible in instances where a trained informal helper makes a mistake. Also, professionals who consider working with informal network members may see it as conflicting with licensure laws. They would be, in essence, encouraging and teaching nonprofessional helpers in the community to practice psychology without a license. Finally, a general resistance to change may present a barrier. After all, standard clinical techniques have been helpful to many divorced individuals (Mowatt, 1972; Baideme, Hill, & Serritella, 1978; Dreyfus, 1979). With a satisfactory approach already available, why take on the task of adopting new ideas?

All of the above issues suggest that one of our first tasks is to sell the perspective to professionals. We need to convince them of the usefulness and necessity of the social support network approach to helping families in transition. Even this will not clear the way for success, however. Along with the lack of belief, we also must be aware of a lack of education among human service workers. As we shall discuss further, fostering the effectiveness of informal social support systems requires indirect activities such as consultation, training, and education. Unfortunately, the training and education of most professionals ignores such skills and concentrates instead on the tools needed for individual and small group counseling.

Even if we can meet the challenge of convincing and training professionals to link families of divorce and remarriage to informal social support networks, there are other barriers that must be confronted. Measuring the size and density of an individual's network is a complex task. In the matter of size, for instance, people may not name the same people as being important from one day to the next, and cultural differences may influence how many people one considers to be important in the first place (Politser, 1980). For example, if a single mother has just made it through an extremely hectic week during which the day care center was closed and she had to rely on her neighbor to watch her preschool child, she is likely to perceive that neighbor as being a very important member of her social network. If, on the other hand, the day care center is open the following week, she may report that it, rather than her neighbor, is the most notable part of her support system.

Related to this issue of size is the density of a network. Politser (1980) has defined density as the total number of relationships that exist between people divided by the total number of possible relationships. This means that the more people in an individual's social network, the less dense it is, since there is less chance that the network members know each other. So, for example, we may have two different stepmothers, one of whom has frequent contact with a minister, her children's teachers, her neighbors, her co-workers, and her parents and in-laws. The other may live in a small town where she has had the same neighbors for years and where her parents live just down the street. Clearly, the first stepmother has a larger social network, but its members probably do not know one another. The second woman, however, has a smaller and more closely knit network. Because density is positively related to the effectiveness of the network, the latter woman is better off (Unger & Powell, 1980). If we are going to foster the effectiveness of people's social support systems we must be able to determine how extensive they are. Furthermore, we need to be able to identify the members of the network.

Several distinct characteristics of our specific target population can make this identification process a difficult task. Married couples tend to have mutual friends and acquaintances. In-laws enter into one's social network. Yet, a separation, divorce, and subsequent remarriage tend to disrupt these established friendship patterns. Adults must undergo a confusing process of redefining their now tenuous relationships. The divorced and remarried population is also a highly mobile one. For example, a career-oriented single mother often faces job changes and a major geographic move after being divorced. Or, a woman planning to remarry may choose to accommodate her lifestyle to that of her new husband. This decision may involve a career change as well as a residential change. In either case, children are uprooted; they change schools, adjust to new neighborhoods, and, at least for a period of time, must establish new peer groups. Often, such changes in residence result in less frequent contact with extended kin, especially those of the noncustodial parent; and additional stepkin may be incorporated into the children's networks. Therefore, for both adults and children, support networks may be in a temporary state of flux with members moving in and out.

These barriers are not insurmountable, however. The timing of the intervention is an important factor to consider. That is, these problems are most likely to occur if the client is in the early stages of adjustment to divorce or remarriage. After an individual begins to settle into a new lifestyle and adjust to a new job and residence, his or her network becomes more stable and predictable. Also, not all networks are ill-defined during this early period. Friendship and in-law kinship networks are the ones most subject to change, whereas those based on obligation and family loyalty are more long-lasting (McLanahan, Wedemeyer, & Adelberg, 1981). Knowing this, professionals can gear their intervention efforts to the more durable network structures.

Along with issues of size, density, and identification, another factor to consider is the timing of the network contact. Because family dissolution and reconstitution is a continuous process, the issues that family members are dealing with vary between individuals and across time. One divorced man may be trying to cope with living without his children, while another may be facing the concern of telling his parents that he is going to remarry. Or, a mother's major problem at one point may be dealing with employment, child care, and household maintenance as a single parent, whereas 10 years later she is remarried and more concerned about seeing her ex-husband at her daughter's wedding. To be truly beneficial, members of social networks for families in transition should be able to deal with individuals throughout the entire process. This obviously requires a lot of training.

This discussion of barriers to implementing social support systems for families in transition is not intended to imply that the situation is hopeless or that we would be better off investing our time and energy in other activities. Rather, one should keep such hindrances in mind but concentrate on the incentives. Perhaps the greatest of these is the fact that natural helpers are so very accessible. An individual does not have to pay a fee or schedule an appointment to talk to family or friends. Usually they are available any time of day, any day of the week. If in the course of daily routine a family member is compelled to share a problem or satisfaction with someone who will listen, bartenders, cab drivers, and beauticians are there. Teachers provide the encouragement and attention that children of divorce may feel that they cannot get from their busy mothers. Everyone seeking a divorce comes into contact with an attorney. In most towns, Parents Without Partners chapters are located nearby and open to new members. In short, these sources of social support are always available. Thus, families in transition are assured of network contacts. If professionals will see to it that these contacts are beneficial, then families of divorce and remarriage will be assured of help.

If this is not incentive enough to pursue the development of social support systems for families in transition, we can also add the fact that adopting such a cause will aid in the dismissal of the pathogenic view of family dissolution and reconstitution that currently seems to prevail. If community people begin listening to the thoughts of family members, they will discover the positive aspects of the divorce and remarriage experience. They will see their relatives, friends, customers, students, and the like learning from and adapting to their changing family lives. As a result, these network members may begin to respond more positively to families in transition. This in turn will aid the family members in feeling more positive about themselves, giving them a better outlook on their situations, and providing yet further evidence to their informal helpers that divorce and remarriage are not completely debilitating experiences. In addition, if social networks can begin to respond to the needs of changing families, members of these families can be less dependent on the help of professionals in dealing with divorce and remarriage. Family dissolution and reconstitution will be perceived less and less as circumstances requiring "treatment."

Despite such incentives for focusing on informal networks as a resource for families in transition, very few efforts have been made to study social support correlates of adjustment to divorce and remarriage. What little research is available suggests that contact with members of the extended family may be beneficial. In fact, after a divorce, relatives become a more important source of social support than they were before (Albrecht, 1980). This is particularly true for single mothers who may seek help with child care, finances, job problems, and household chores (McLanahan, Wedemeyer, & Adelberg, 1981). Most likely, a woman's contact will be with her own kin rather than with her ex-spouse's kin (Anspach, 1976). Divorced fathers, in contrast, rarely depend on their extended kin for help with child care arrangements, relying instead on friends or even their ex-wives for help and advice (Keshet & Rosenthal, 1978). Mendes (1976) has suggested that the lack of help from family members could be a function of geographic distance, a reluctance to ask for assistance, or both.

The support that divorced individuals receive from extended kin is beneficial in decreasing mood disturbance and heightening life satisfaction (Berman & Turk, 1981). In addition, it has implications for childrearing. Hetherington, Cox, and Cox (1978a) found that, during the first two years after divorce, a mother's contact with relatives and close friends enhances her effectiveness in dealing with her children. Exploring this issue further, Colletta (1979) has concluded that satisfaction with the support received is a better predictor of childrearing practices than is support per se. More satisfied mothers are less authoritarian and more responsive to their children's needs than are those who are less content with the social support they have available. The mechanism accounting for this is most likely the fact that effective resources take some of the load and accompanying stress off the single mother. Consequently, she is able to be more relaxed and thereby to deal more effectively with her children (Christensen & McDonald, 1976).

Clearly, supportive social networks benefit children as well as adults involved in divorce and remarriage. This benefit accrues not only through improved parental behavior, but also more directly. In particular, negative effects of divorce are greatly mitigated when positive relationships with both parents are maintained. The child's relationship with the noncustodial parent (usually the father) is as important as the continuing relationship with the custodial parent (Hess & Camara, 1979). In addition, friends, siblings, classmates, teachers, grandparents, cousins, neighbors, and parents of good friends are possible sources of help for children (Kurdek, 1981). Interestingly, however, help-seeking among children of divorce appears to be a generalized trait, in that children who turn to parents for assistance are also likely to turn to friends and teachers (Wallerstein & Kelly, 1980). Overall, the situation is one of feast or famine concerning social supports for children in single-parent families.

Adults, too, may find nonfamilial resources beneficial. As mentioned above, for example, Parents Without Partners fulfills many single parents' needs for social activity and friendship. Similarly, parents facing remarriage have found self help groups valuable in working through their concerns and becoming comfortable with the stepfamily situation (Messinger, Walker, & Freeman, 1978). Messinger's is the only documented evidence of social networks facilitating adjustment to family reconstitution. Clearly we have much to learn about the role of support systems in aiding single-parents and stepfamily members. In spite of our limited knowledge, however, we can use what we know about divorce and remarriage to suggest potential uses of informal support networks for our population.

SOURCES AND FUNCTIONS OF SOCIAL SUPPORT FOR FAMILIES IN TRANSITION

Social networks have a variety of possible functions. Foremost is that of providing needed support, be it informational, emotional, or congratulatory, for members of families in transition. Many different people have the potential to be very helpful to families involved in divorce and remarriage. Most obvious are members of the extended family. A woman may rely on her parents, her sisters and brothers, cousins, aunts and uncles, and sometimes even former in-laws to provide financial aid, babysitting services, advice, emotional support, or opportunities for socializing. Friends and neighbors are also readily available.

In addition, there is a large group of people sometimes referred to as community gatekeepers who may be important outlets to families in transition. Teachers can help children of divorce and remarriage understand the family situation and can provide emotional support. They can include lessons and materials in their curricula that will increase youngsters' awareness of what it is like to be a member of a single-parent family or a stepfamily. They can consult with divorced or remarried parents about a child's problem behavior. Ricci (1979) has pointed out that school policies and procedures are not conducive to helping families in transition. In the case of a single-parent family, for instance, the noncustodial parent is not allowed access to his or her child's records, is not included in parent–teacher conferences, and does not receive report cards and parent notices. Textbooks rarely portray single-parent or stepfamilies. Classroom activities such as asking first-graders to draw their family can be extremely confusing for a child who has both a stepfather and a natural father. Clearly, together with direct help by teachers, there are many indirect ways in which schools can serve as important sources of support for families in transition.

Divorce attorneys can work with their clients to make the divorce experience less stressful by avoiding an antagonistic stance toward the ex-spouse, by giving advice about financial settlements, and by being empathetic. They can also encourage divorcing couples to plan for their children's needs (Woody, 1978). Clergy are another potential source of advice and support, as are cab drivers, bartenders, and beauticians. They can be particularly helpful in acknowledging family members' accomplishments and successes as they learn about and adapt to their new single or stepfamily lifestyles. There has also been some suggestion that pediatricians can play an important role for families in transition. They can consult with a noncustodial father regarding his continuing importance to his children; they can hear and support a single mother, discussing, for example, age-appropriate roles for her child; they can help a child to understand that his or her parents' divorce is final, and they can enlist a relative or friends of the child to take an interest in him or her (Derdeyn, 1977). Scout troops may provide children from families in transition with an important opportunity to socialize with peers and to engage in activities and hobbies that a single parent might not have time to contribute to. They may also be a good outlet for discussing concerns about one's family life with an objective listener. Similarly, for the parents in our families, PTA meetings can be a place to discuss children's behavior problems with other single or stepparents, or merely to meet other adults. Parents Without Partners provides informational and emotional support for divorced parents.

Aside from this direct support as an end in itself, there is another more indirect way in which social support networks can benefit families in transition. This is by serving as a referral source that links the public to professional helping services. Community gatekeepers are especially important in this regard. As bartenders, hairdressers, and cabdrivers listen to customers expressing concerns related to divorce or remarriage, they can suggest the names of local counseling centers, support groups, family therapists, and the like.

The social support networks that we have been discussing may also be a valuable resource for human service professionals. For example, by making referrals, they might actually send more fee-paying clients into the professional helping system, thereby enabling service providers to reach a greater segment of the population. Given the fact that this situation may perpetuate the pathogenic view of family dissolution and reconstitution, it may not really be advantageous. That is, we might prefer to keep people out of the clinical establishments. However, in light of current funding situations, professional helpers would certainly see increased use of their services as an advantage. Thus, although it may ultimately have an undesirable effect, the potential referral function of social support networks may be a powerful way to get professionals interested in the idea of fostering networks.

Finally, members of the support networks of families in transition can serve as a source of information for professionals who are conducting needs assessments for this population. For example, a social service planner could interview local ministers, bartenders, cabdrivers, hairdressers, and attorneys about what specific concerns they hear from their divorced and remarried constituents. They can then use this information to create programs to answer these concerns.

FUTURE DIRECTIONS FOR PRACTICE AND RESEARCH

Clearly, the potential functions and natural, informal support networks for families in transition are many. But how can we realize this potential? One step is to establish a link between human service professionals and the informal helping networks of families in transition. To facilitate this, several tasks must be accomplished.

As Danish and D'Augelli (1980) contend, many, if not all, intrapersonal and interpersonal dilemmas are due to a lack of knowledge, lack of skills, and/or inability to assess the risks involved in a situation. The first two components of this model are particularly relevant to our discussion. If professionals will disseminate to the general public more knowledge of the challenges and opportunities facing families of divorce and remarriage, social network members may be able to function more adequately when called upon for help. Likewise, their supportive capabilities can be enhanced through helping skills training. If professionals are to increase the knowledge and skills of social support providers, several research and training issues require immediate attention.

Most important, the ever-recurring theme in literature dealing with family dissolution and reconstitution must be reiterated: more research is needed.

There is a serious deficit of methodologically sound, nonpathogenically oriented, longitudinal investigations into the adjustment of adults and children to divorce and remarriage. A greater comprehension of what the adjustment process entails can only enrich the professional's understanding of his or her clients' strengths and needs.

Most specifically, we need to reach a deeper understanding of the roles performed by the social support networks of divorced and stepfamilies. Within the past decades, several studies have informed us of some global, general facts about the frequency and purposes of the contact that divorced and remarried adults have with the consanguineous and in-law kin (e.g., Spicer & Hampe, 1975; Weiss, 1975; Anspach, 1976; Furstenberg & Spanier, 1980), friends, and social organizations (Keshet & Rosenthal, 1978; Albrecht, 1978, 1980; Smith, 1980; Berman & Turk, 1981), and how such contact relates to adjustment (Spanier & Hanson, 1978; Spanier & Casto, 1979). As discussed previously, studies concerning the children in single-parent and reconstituted families and their support networks are sparse and inconclusive in their findings. The only well-documented result is that the individuals to whom the child turns for support vary according to his or her developmental stage (e.g., Wallerstein & Kelly, 1975).

These investigations have provided valuable measures of the quantitative aspects of social support systems. In general, however, such studies have touched only tangentially or have by-passed completely the qualitative nature of such helping interactions. Various aspects of the social support rendered during the adjustment periods can be explored by tapping the perspectives of adults as well as children and of the recipients as well as the providers. Questions that could be addressed include: When supoort is given, what is the quality of such support? How willing are both parties to render or to solicit such support? Is the aid given constant over an extended period of time or is it short-lived? What factors are involved in the process of establishing new support networks and of adapting old networks to accommodate one's new lifestyle?

Research directed toward these broad questions will serve to increase the professional's understanding of the dynamics of these informal helping relationships. With a more complete knowledge of what each relationship entails, the professional can better assess the assets and barriers that can facilitate or hinder the use of such networks. Additional information about the process of developing and rearranging social ties will also help to pinpoint optimal times for intervening and will assist in identifying significant others for clients at different stages of the divorce and remarriage process.

In addition to these research efforts, there are several training needs that must be addressed if a link between professional service providers and informal helping networks is to be established. Dissemination of information about family dissolution and reconstitution to human service providers as well as to their clients, their significant others, and the public as a whole is essential and can occur through various channels. Researchers have a responsibility to publish their findings in scientific journals, making valuable information available to the professional population. They should also be encouraged, however, to distribute knowledge to the lay sector. This can be accomplished through such media as television, magazines, Sunday supplements, radio spots, and pamphlets. Professionals must learn how to report facts about the problems and rewards that face families of divorce and remarriage in a manner that is both accurate and conducive to public consumption. A recent content analysis of popular magazines found that too often information on this topic that is given to the general public consists only of personal accounts and journalistic impressions and fails to reflect what is really known about divorce and remarriage (Richardson, 1981).

Human service workers also need to undertake direct intervention with informal support systems. To fulfill their potential role as referral sources, for example, members of helping networks need information about what kinds of professional services for families in transition are available in the community. Finally, in order to enhance their abilities to provide emotional support to families of divorce and remarriage, network members should be educated in the use of basic helping skills. Human service workers can assume a pivotal role in training community members to be more effective at listening and responding to the concerns of families in transition. A cost-effective way of doing this is to make a training program self-sufficient.

An example of such an effort is the Community Helpers Project (D'Augelli & Vallance, 1981). In this program, which was instituted in two rural communities in central Pennsylvania, people who are "natural helpers" in the community were identified and recruited through the use of the media. The goal was to build upon and respect the natural talent of these helpers, enhancing their natural helping function by teaching them skills to use in dealing better with common problems brought to them by friends, acquaintances, and family. In order to spread the impact of the training, a local network of trainers was developed. Thus, within the two communities, 32 trainers were trained by professional staff. These indigenous trainers then worked in pairs to offer the same program in basic helping skills to their local helpers. The Community Helpers Project appears to be a valuable step in capitalizing on the helping talents of natural caregivers, thereby strengthening neighborhood-based support systems. It is the type of approach that human service professionals can adopt in facilitating the development of informal support networks for families of divorce and remarriage.

In summary, it can be seen that not enough is being done to facilitate the development of social support systems for minimizing the problems and optimizing the positive opportunities associated with the divorce and remarriage process. The numerous potential functions of various members of informal helping networks should be recognized, and research and training activities should be pursued to foster their growth. By undertaking such a task, human service professionals can play a major role in helping individuals to deal with family dissolution and reconstitution across the life span.

PART IV
Services
to Adolescents

CHAPTER 9
|Social Support Networks and the |Schools

Elliott Asp and James Garbarino

"Education is too important to leave to the professionals."

WE HAVE MET THE CLIENTS AND THEY ARE US

Education in the United States is truly a public concern. Unlike the other issues discussed in this volume, which only indirectly affect most Americans (although that effect may be great), the schools have a direct influence on almost all of us. The public views education as important and wants our schools to be safe, humane places where children are taught the skills needed for successful living. The amount and intensity of public debate that ensues whenever the schools are discussed reflects the strength of this desire. Regardless of the setting or the participants, whether it be in the *Ladies Home Journal* or *The New York Times,* a school board meeting or teachers' lounge, construction site or the dinner table, the halls of Congress or a neighborhood bar, Americans everywhere seem to have an opinion on the needs and problems of the schools, and most are eager to express it.

This high level of public interest is due to the schools' unique position in the field of human services. What sets the schools apart? The first distinguishing characteristic is our almost universal experience with the institution. For the most part, we have all been a client of the schools. In fact, most of us have been in the system for 12 years or longer. Therefore, we all have some idea of how schools operate. We know what goes on there and many of us have some notion of what *should* be going on instead.

Because of this experience with the institution, we have some understanding of the nature of its particular problems. We know what the professionals are trying to do and the methods they use. Thus, unlike many of the problems dealt with by other human service agencies, school-related difficulties are not viewed as technical dilemmas understandable only by experts. Most of us can propose a solution for academic failure, but few have any idea of how to deal with drug abuse or depression. Solutions in the latter two cases take on a magical, almost mystical quality. We treat drug abuse by sending the patient through a "black box" device, known as a drug treatment center. He goes in addicted and comes out cured (we hope), but we have little idea of what happens in between. We do not know what is inside the black box. This is not to trivialize school problems or in any way demean the technical expertise of those who try to deal with them, but rather to point out how familiar we are with this institution. In fact, it is our opinion that in the case of the schools, familiarity breeds concern rather than contempt.

A second feature of the school that sets it apart from other human service institutions is the width and breadth of the problems that become its concern. In 1974, the passage of the mainstreaming act (P.L. 94-142), made mandatory the placement of the full range of handicapped children in regular schools wherever possible; the schools must now deal with all children and, furthermore, are supposed to be universally successful. Because of this mandate, the schools, in one way or another, have to grapple with almost every conceivable social problem as well as their own unique set of difficulties. This makes the school (whether public or private) a truly public institution, one in which our society is heavily invested both psychologically and economically. Whether it be as service providers or receivers (school personnel or students), indirect participants (parents or school board members), or interested observers (residents of communities and taxpayers), we all have some direct contact with the schools, and many of us are involved in several capacities.

Family and school are the two great socializers in our culture. We depend on schools to turn out well-adjusted, productive individuals who will contribute to the quality of life in this society. If the school fails, we all fail. Thus, when we speak of clients in terms of the schools, we are literally referring to all of us.

What does this mean as far as employment of social support networks in the schools? It marks the schools as a prime candidate for the use of social support networks for two reasons. First, because of the large client population, there is a strong possibility that many overlapping, interlocking networks already exist, networks that may have great power in overcoming problems. Second, because of unifying common goals regarding the institution (education is valued and desired; we all want good schools) and our familiarity with it, there is a great willingness on the part of the "client population" to become involved.

The schools are fertile ground for developing and using social support networks and, indeed, there is a long tradition of cooperation between professional and lay helpers within the institution. However, as will be seen, the role of informal support systems is a highly restricted one and could certainly be expanded. Our purpose is to examine the current use of social support networks in the schools and to consider programs that seek to broaden the role of such networks. Before discussing solutions, the problems should first be identified. For that we turn to our client population and a closer look at the characteristics of this group that are related to problems in the schools, problems that we believe are particularly amenable to control through the use of social support systems.

THE CLIENT POPULATION

Our client population is a large one. In order to better understand the problems facing the schools, this group will be divided into two parts: those who "live in the school" and those who do not. Finally, we shall take a look at the school itself.

INSIDE THE SCHOOLS

There are three subgroups of our client population that spend a great deal of their waking hours inside the schools: students, teachers, and administrators.

The Students. What do we know about today's students? We do know that all (or almost all) elementary and secondary students are children. But is the converse true? Are all children students? The answer seems obvious. Compulsory attendance laws demand this, but a look at the data belies popular belief.

According to 1970 U.S. census data, nearly 2 million youngsters (4.2% of the total) between ages 7 and 17 were not attending school in the 3 months prior to enumeration. This figure included 10.2% of the 16- to 17-year-olds. By 1977, the figure for 16- and 17-year-olds had increased to over 11%. Even though these figures seem high, they appear to be quite conservative compared with other sources. For example, in 1974, a report by the Children's Defense Fund (CDF), *Children Out of School in America*, found the Census Bureau's figures to be less than accurate. First, the census figures are very conservative estimates. *The Children's Defense Fund* has identified a number of sources of undernumeration in the census reports. They include the fact that minority children, who are particularly likely to be out of school, are underrepresented in the census; that census procedures tend to miss children from very large families (more than seven people), who tend to be out of school; and that the census questionnaire is structured to include in its estimate children who are considered to be attending school despite erratic attendance. Second, the rates of nonattendance are not distributed uniformly across regions and social classes. That is, the rates for nonattendance are higher in some states than others and higher for children from low-income families. It seems that the CDF figures for children out of school were generally much higher than those reported by the Census Bureau (Garbarino and Asp, 1981).

The CDF report itself further illustrates the problem: "In the 30 areas we surveyed we found 5.4 percent of all children six to 17 years old out of school for at least 45 days, one quarter of the school year 19.6 percent of the 16 and 17 year olds we found were out of school" (CDF, 1974).

These figures are disturbing, but the reasons for nonattendance are even more so. If asked to explain this phenomenon, our first guess would probably be that most of these children are not in school because they chose to leave or were expelled for some violation of school rules. However, this is not the case. The CDF study revealed that the major source of nonattendance was exclusion by the school. Heading the list of reasons for exclusion was not suspension or expulsion, but rather the inability of students and their families to meet school demands for fees, meal charges, books, and other supplies.

The second source of exclusion, according to the CDF, was problems presented by the student to the operation or value base of the school. Examples range from mental or physical handicaps to adolescent pregnancy. Many schools refused to accept students with even marginal handicaps, despite public and governmental pressure to do so. It seems that the schools are engaged in a labeling process in which they decide who fits and who does not. Interestingly enough, the suspension of students for problem behavior was found to rank only third as a reason for exclusion from school.

This breakdown tells only part of the story, however. According to the National Center for Educational Statistics (NCES, 1980), the retention rates of schools have stabilized over the last decade. Seventy-five percent of all students who started fifth grade in 1968 graduated from high school with their class, and 47% went on to college. This means that 25% of those starting school do not finish with their class. Twenty percent never complete high school. This last figure is alarming in a social and historical period in which the lack of a high school diploma essentially excludes one from full participation in society. Even more alarming is that of this 20%, lower SES groups and members of racial minorities are highly overrepresented (Garbarino and Asp, 1981).

Even those students who remain in school are having problems, however. We see evidence that many students who finish high school are not leaving with the basic skills needed to succeed in today's economy; those aspiring to higher education are finding themselves ill-prepared to function in a college environment. For example, the scores of American youth on the Scholastic Aptitude Test (SAT) declined from 1963 (when they raached their height after nearly two decades of increase) through the 1970's (NCES, 1980). Many colleges have had to institute remedial or developmental programs in basic skills (especially writing). As an illustration, the Pennsylvania State University reports that one-third of all entering students are lacking in basic skills (Garbarino and Asp, 1981). Edward Hollander, New Jersey Chancellor of Higher Education, reported that 80% of the students in New Jersey's colleges have had some form of remedial instruction; one-half of the incoming freshmen will need some form of special tutoring to keep from failing (NCES, 1980).

Beyond the academic area, we see a decline in the standards of conduct in our students. Maintaining order has become a problem in schools, where rebellion and flouting of rules is the most common form of worker rebellion (Garbarino and Asp, 1981). For example, 28% of all schools experience at least one act of vandalism per month, at an average cost of $81 per incident (Garbarino and Asp, 1981). Many schools now must employ security guards: approximately 25,000 guards were employed in 1976, as compared with 5,000 in 1966 (Ban & Ciminillo, 1977). The U.S. Department of Health, Education, and Welfare reported that 50% of all assaults on 12- to 15-year-olds occur in schools and that 33% of all junior high students in urban schools report being afraid to enter three or more areas in their schools (Baker & Rubel, 1980).

Student alienation is also a significant problem. Many students feel disaffected by school; they are not part of it. In a New York State survey, 60% of the students responding indicated that they did not enjoy school and 28% reported viewing school as a negative experience (NYS Commission . . . , 1972). A number of researchers report an increased sense of alienation and a growing trend toward social isolationism among students (Heath, 1970; Bronfenbrenner, 1975; Mackey, 1978; Garbarino and Asp, 1981).

Clearly, many of the students who pass through our school system do not receive all they could, should, or need to from the experience. However, our purpose here is not to indict the schools. The reasons for many of the trends cited above are extremely complex and involve many factors outside of the classroom. As Christopher Hurn states: "What we see as failure is not necessarily failure in any objective sense (there is little evidence, for example, that schools are any less successful now than they were in the past in transmitting basic skills to students), but failure relative to our heightened expectations for what schools can do" (1978, p. 14). We are not saying that schools are the problem, rather that schools have problems, many of which they may have inherited from the society in which they are embedded. The problems are serious and may have far-reaching consequences for students and society, and these problems deserve our attention.

In summary, we see that today's students are beset by a number of difficulties. Many are not in school and those who are not may not get much from being there. The skills usually associated with high school graduation are of course, a necessary condition for successful integration into today's society; it appears that a number of young people are doomed to failure because they are not getting these skills. This situation is especially relevant to our discussion because social support networks can be effective in providing alternative solutions to the problems of academic failure and student alienation.

The Teachers. Although we could delve into the demographic characteristics of teachers, this seems secondary to our main purpose. For our purpose, it seems far more important to examine affective changes among teachers.

How does it feel to be a teacher? Unfortunately, for many the answer is "not good." Teachers seem to be tiring of teaching. Although teaching is a career with a traditionally high turnover rate (Lortie, 1975), today's teachers seem to be leaving the profession in greater numbers for different reasons. A nationwide survey of teachers conducted in both 1965 and 1971 reported that in 1965, 70% saw teaching as getting better, while only 34% felt that way in 1971 (National Educational Association, 1979b). Twenty-six percent of those responding in 1965 were no longer teaching in 1971. By 1979, the situation had worsened. The National Education Association (1979a) reported that one-third of those currently teaching would *not* choose education as a career if they could go back to college and start over. When New York City laid off 9,000 teachers in 1978, only 2,900 returned when asked (Reed, 1980). The NEA has also noted that only 6 of 10 teachers planned to stay in teaching until retirement, and the number of teachers with 20 years or more experience has dropped by 50% in the past 15 years. "We can ask for no clearer indication that teachers are frustrated with teaching and want out" (NEA, 1979b).

Why are teachers leaving the profession? Some investigators cite high levels of stress as the problem, and judging from some of the student behavior we have already described, it seems apparent that teaching is fast becoming a highly stressful (if it was not already) and sometimes physically risky job. However, we think that the causes go deeper than a particular set of stresses. Teaching has always been an emotionally draining job, and it is not likely to change in that respect. What seems to be at the root of this problem is the teacher's sense of isolation. Teachers are not afraid of emotional strain, but they tire quickly of feeling alone. Teaching is a lonely job (Lortie, 1975).

The factors contributing to the isolation of teachers are many, but a few illustrations will serve to make our point. First, the organization of the schools physically isolates teachers from each other (Lortie, 1975). Teachers spend most of their day in a room with 25 to 30 children and have few opportunities for contact with other adults. Second, the training and socialization of teachers does little to encourage collegial interaction (Lortie, 1975). Teacher training programs do not emphasize a common technical culture, and most teachers assemble their particular educational philosophy and teaching style from a hodgepoge of past experience rather than their college preparation (Lortie, 1975). Also, their introduction to the job is in a "sink or swim" vein. First-year teachers are literally thrown to the wolves with no extra help or supervision. They are called upon to do the same job as those who have been teaching for years. They are trained in the same way. There is no emphasis on group process in teacher education; such programs almost always set up aspiring teachers to work alone, and that is what happens. According to the NEA (Lortie, 1975) only 12% of all teachers teach in teams. In middle schools, where teaming is a basic philosophical tenent, only 15–20% are involved in that practice (Brooks and Edwards, 1978). In the same way, the system for evaluation and career advancement (including decisions about pay and tenure) supports autonomy rather than mutual cooperation and collegial interaction (Lortie, 1975). Teachers are trained and socialized to act independently in that they are enmeshed fully in the brand of individualism characteristically American as was discussed in Chapter 1.

In light of this, it comes as no surprise that teachers feel isolated, that they have no one with whom to share their problems. In a study of 150 teachers, Erlandson and Pastor (1981) reported that teachers saw their greatest need or want as the desire for close collegial relationships. Professional journals and magazines echo this theme. The reason that many teachers suffer "burnout" is their emotional isolation. The lack of an occupational support system plagues the profession:

> People in other lines of work also have occasion to doubt their personal efficacy and the value of the services they offer. But in fields where people perceive their knowledge (and their ignorance) as jointly shared, the individual burden is reduced. A person can take comfort from his compliance with normal expectations within the occupation; he can feel that he did everything possible within "the state of the art." (Physicians so argue when they are charged with malpractice.) Thus the individual can cope with unpleasant outcomes by sharing the weight of his failure and guilt; his inadequacy is part of the larger inadequacy of the field. Teachers derive little consolation from this source; an individualistic conception of practice exacerbates the burden of failure. (Lortie, 1975, p. 81)

This is a serious problem. The monetary and status rewards in teaching are low enough, but emotional exhaustion is asking too much. We are losing too many good teachers to other professions, and reducing the isolation and loneliness in the job could help stem this tide. As we shall see, social support networks could play a vital role in achieving that goal.

The Administrators. The demographic characteristics of school administrators have undergone significant changes in the past 20 years (McCleary & Thompson, 1979). There has been a large increase in the number of high school principals who are 40 to 55 years of age and a substantial decrease of those over 55. The number of younger principals has also decreased, and the average age at assuming one's first principalship has increased to over

35 (McCleary & Thompson, 1979). Today's high school principals are more highly educated than in the early 1960's; 85% have done work beyond the master's degree (including holding specialist or doctoral degrees) compared with 56% of the principals in 1960. However, as a group, they remain basically male and white; 7% are female, and 4% list their ethnic origin as nonwhite (McCleary & Thompson, 1979).

The story is much the same for elementary principals. The average elementary principal is 46 years old, has a master's degree, is white, and is a man (NEA, 1979a). In contrast to the trends in many professions, the 1970's saw a decrease in the proportion of elementary school administrators who were women, from 22% in 1968 to 18% in 1978 (NEA, 1979a). Also, less than 10% of today's elementary principals are from minority groups (NEA, 1979a).

This same pattern holds true for middle school administrators as well. Middle school principals are predominantly men (94%), between 40 and 50 years of age, and hold a master's or a higher degree (Brooks & Edwards, 1978). Thus, we see that across the range of precollegiate education, administrators are a fairly uniform group whose age range is becoming increasingly restricted.

Why is this the case? Certainly some of the uniformity is due to societal discrimination (especially with regard to women and ethnic groups), but the restriction in age range particularly seems to reflect some changes in the role of the administrator (McCleary & Thompson, 1979). The nature of the principal's job and its complexity have undergone definite changes over the past 30 years (Kellams, 1979). Although the principal was at one time the instructional leader of his school, that is no longer true in most cases. The principal of today is a social-organizational engineer, a manager (Sarason, 1971; Kellams, 1979; Poppenhagen, Mingus, & Rogers, 1979). In fact, in large schools, and most of our schools are large (NCES, 1980), the principal's job closely resembles that of managers in institutions outside of education (Poppenhagen, Mingus, & Rogers, 1979).

Along with this change in the nature of the job itself, we have also seen that being a principal has become an increasingly complex and time-consuming task (McCleary & Thompson, 1979; Poppenhagen, Mingus, & Rogers, 1979; Brown & Carlton, 1980). A 1977 survey of 1,200 Oregon school administrators found that complying with increasing complex regulations was the single most difficult part of the job (Brown & Carlton, 1980). A report issued by the National Association of Secondary School Principals (McCleary & Thompson, 1979), which was the result of a massive study of the high school principalship, showed that most high school principals saw their job as becoming increasingly complex and hard to deal with: "The new problems that parents, school boards and Federal and state governments have piled on the principal's shoulders are staggering—student violence, teacher militancy, complex regulations, changing educational standards" (Seligmann, 1978, p. 76). As a Denver principal states, "The teachers think you should control every one of the 1,800 kids. Parents expect you to make the halls safe and their kids normal in every way. When a teacher isn't dynamic, productive, and well prepared, the board of education orders the principal to make him into a great teacher" (Seligmann, 1978, p. 76).

Principals work an average of 56 hours per week, 3 evenings per week, 50 weeks a year for an average annual income of $20,000 to $28,000 (Seligmann, 1978; McCleary & Thompson, 1979). And, as the burden becomes heavier and more complex, they are finding they must carry it alone (Seligmann, 1978; Poppenhagen, Mingus, & Rogers, 1979). Although student body sizes have nearly doubled in the past 15 years, the administrative staff in most schools has remained about the same (Seligmann, 1978; Garbarino, 1980b). As a University of Utah researcher put it, "Most schools have more assistant football coaches than assistant principals" (Seligmann, 1978, p. 76). In sum, principals are working long hours, performing tasks that are more managerial than instructional, and are having to deal with the complexities of today's educational systems on their own.

How do principals feel about that? Mostly, they feel isolated. Even more than teachers, principals feel that they have no one to talk to about their job (Herlihy & Herlihy, 1980). A survey of principals (Herlihy & Herlihy, 1980) revealed that when asked with whom they share problems, most principals responded "no one." There are very few opportunities to "safely" discuss the rigors of the job. This means that as the job becomes more and more demanding, the principal is becoming more and more isolated.

What are they doing about it? Unfortunately, they are quitting. This shows up in the decrease in the number of older principals. The complexity of the job is reflected in the increased educational level of most principals and the later age at assumption of first principalship. It simply takes more time to accumulate the credentials and experience required for the job. Even though 82% of high school principals recently reported that the principalship offers a chance to fulfill "one's unique capabilities," most effective principals are not planning to stay (Herlihy & Herlihy, 1980). As the resignation rate is rising, more and more administrators report that the source or critical factor is loneliness (Herlihy & Herlihy, 1980). Principals are spending less time with people and more time with paper. The principal is increasingly isolated and overworked, struggling with an increasingly difficult job that is becoming less satisfying. As is the case with teachers, social support networks can do much to alleviate the principals' isolation.

CLIENTS OUTSIDE THE SCHOOL—THE COMMUNITIES

There have been many changes in our communities over the past 20 years, and a few are of particular interest here. The first is the dramatic increase in the number of single-parent families in America. It is estimated that nearly half of today's children will spend at least a year living with only one parent (Norton, 1971). An overwhelming percentage of these children will spend that time living with their mothers. Despite some changes in the father's role in the parenting process in our society at large, only 10% of the children in single-parent families live with their fathers, and that figure has remained constant since 1960. In fact, only 1% of all children live only with their fathers (Norton, 1979).

A second change in the makeup of our communities that concerns us here is the entrance of many mothers into the work force. The increase is due both to more children being in single-parent households and to the proportion of mothers in two-parent households who work outside the home. A large number of single-parent mothers work (60%), but that figure has risen only slightly over the past ten years. It is the "traditional" mother who is going to work in ever-increasing numbers. An interesting sidelight is that this development has created a growing number of latchkey children—children who come home to an empty house after school and take care of themselves for several hours or more (Garbarino, 1981). Nineteen percent of children who live only with their mother fall into this category, whereas only 12% of children from two-parent homes are latchkey kids (Norton, 1979). At any rate, more children are growing up in homes where the adults (or adult) are working.

The mobility of today's family is also important. The lyrics from a popular song, "Doesn't anybody stay in one place anymore?" summarize the situation. We are a transient society. The average child is much more likely to attend a number of different schools than his or her counterpart of the 1950's.

Two other changes in the characteristics of communities have greatly affected the schools. One is the reduction in the size of the family (Norton, 1980). Americans are getting married at later ages and delaying having children—if they decide to do either (Norton, 1980). Second, being single, or married and childless is becoming an acceptable lifestyle for adults. People are choosing to live that way for extended periods of time; it is no longer appropriate only for those in their early 20's to do so.

One final point is that the population is also growing older. For the first time in our history, the number of Americans 55 or older will be greater than our school population (Hubbell, 1979). By 1990, one out of every five Americans will be at least 55.

What do these trends mean for the schools? Generally, they mean that the links between community and school have been drastically reduced. In single-parent families, there are just not as many available adults; consequently, there is less opportunity for the parent to attempt contact with the school. If the parent is working, the time left for school activities is even

Table 9-1. Change over 10 years in percentage of U.S. adults with children in school

Year	Public school parents (%)	Private/parochial school parents (%)	No children in school (%)
1969	44	7	50
1978	28	5	68

further reduced. When both parents in an intact family are working, the same situation holds.

Smaller family size, the acceptability (even glorification) of the single or childless lifestyle, and the increasing age of the population all add up to a reduction in the number of "public school parents." Only a minority of the adults in the United States of the 1980's are "public school parents" (Hubbell, 1979). This change is reflected in the composition of the national probability sample over 10 years of the Gallup poll "Public's Attitude Towards the Public Schools," as shown in Table 9-1. The figures are clear: fewer people have children in schools. This is an important development because people with children in school feel much better informed about the schools than those who do not have children there. It seems that most public school parents feel well informed about the schools in their community, whereas only one-fourth of adults with no school-age children share this opinion. Forty percent of nonparents feel that they know very little about the public schools (Hubbell, 1979). These differences between parents and nonparents are shown in Table 9-2, which summarizes 74 opinion polls regarding public attitudes toward the schools.

How do public school parents find out about the schools? They are informed through the experience and reports of their children (Hubbell, 1979). The major sources of information about the schools for parents and nonparents are contrasted below (Hubbell, 1979).

Public school parents list these major sources of information about the

Table 9-2. Summary of 74 opinion polls on the public's attitude toward the schools

Attitude	All respondents (%)	Public school parents (%)	No school-age children (%)
Feel well informed	42	54	25
Somewhat informed	29	31	30
Not too informed	25	14	40
Can't say	4	1	5

public schools: their children, newspapers, teachers and other school employees, what other people say, and school district publications.

Adults with no school-age children rely on these sources of information about public schools: newspapers, what other people say, children, school district publications, and teachers and other school employees.

Nonparents not only know less about the schools (or at least feel that way), but also their information comes from mostly nonschool sources, sources which almost always emphasize sensational, usually negative, aspects of the school (Hubbell, 1979). Parents and nonparents not only have different sources, they also get different stories.

It is no surprise, then, that parents of public school children feel better about the schools than adults who do not have children in school. An example from the 1981 Gallup poll of the "Public's Attitude Toward the Public Schools" illustrates our point. The sample was asked to respond to the following question: "Students are often given the grades A, B, C, D, and FAIL to denote the quality of their work. Suppose the public schools themselves, in this community, were graded in the same way. What grade would you give the public schools here—A, B, C, D, or FAIL?" Their answers are listed in Table 9-3.

It seems as if our revised adage, "familiarity breeds concern (or caring)," holds true. Those who have some direct link to the schools feel better about them; they see the institution in a more positive light. This tendency is also apparent in the higher rating given local schools than the schools as a whole in the same Gallup poll. Unfortunately, two out of three adults have no personal contact with the public schools. Our communities are isolated from their schools—and it shows. Contact seems to be the key to positive relations. If we can no longer depend on child-to-parent-to-school relationships, then other ways must be found to link home and school. We believe that social support networks can be useful in this situation. However, before we take a look at how social support systems can be employed for this and other school problems, we should examine one final aspect of our client population: the school itself.

Table 9-3. The public's ratings of the public schools

By parents with:	Rating of the public schools					
	A (%)	B (%)	C (%)	D (%)	Fail (%)	Don't know (%)
Children in public schools	11	35	34	10	6	4
Children in nonpublic schools	6	19	37	18	12	8
No children in school	8	23	34	13	8	14

Source: From Gallup, 1981.

THE SCHOOLS

For today's children, school will most likely be remembered as a shining concrete and steel edifice, housing thousands of students who arrived there each day in a fleet of buses. This image of school reflects the major changes in the size and number of schools and school systems over the past 30 years. Schools have gotten bigger; the small school now seems a thing of the past.

This demographic change is very relevant to our discussion because it symbolizes and, at the same time, is at the root of many of the problems we have previously identified. Although it is beyond the scope of this chapter to present a comprehensive analysis of the consequences of increasing school size (for that we refer the reader to Garbarino and Asp, 1981), it is important to outline the basic data in order to understand the effect this change has had on our client population.

According to the NCES (1980), the past 30 years have seen a substantial decrease in the number of school systems with a concurrent increase in the number of students served by those systems. For example, in 1945 there were 101,382 school districts in the United States, and by 1977 there were only 16,211 (NCES, 1980). On the other hand, in 1945, United States school systems had an enrollment of 23.3 million pupils, and by 1977 the figure had risen to 43.7 million. We can see therefore, that the average enrollment per school system rose from 230 students per district in 1945 to 2,700 students per district in 1977.

How did this affect school size? The number of high schools in America has remained much the same since 1930, whereas the number of students in them has nearly tripled (Garbarino, 1980b). Simple division tells us that schools have increased in size. In New York State, for example, by 1970, 85% of students were attending schools with enrollments of 700 or more (Garbarino, 1973).

What effect does school size have, if any? Before answering that question, it should first be noted that school size seems to be a dichotomous rather than a continuous variable. It seems that a threshold applies to school size and that when the school population exceeds the threshold figure, increases in size no longer have appreciable effects (Garbarino, 1980b). The threshold between "large" and "small" appears to be on the order of 500 students for grades 9–12 (Garbarino, 1980b). Therefore, most of our schools are large schools. In fact, many communities have no small schools. For example, even as early as 1961, the enrollment in Chicago's high schools ranged from 620 to 4,085, with an average enrollment of 2,841. Large school size, then, is an environmental factor affecting most of our client population.

Several investigators have examined the effects of school size. A common theme arises from their efforts: small schools encourage participation, while large schools encourage passivity (Barker & Gump, 1964; Garbarino, 1980b).

Students from small schools reported satisfactions that clustered around the development of responsibility, competence, challenge, and a sense of identity. Students from large schools emphasized vicarious enjoyment, being part of a large crowd, and generally experiencing what the investigators termed a "herd feeling."

Even though large schools provide more opportunities for participation, the increased number of students more than compensates for this advantage, resulting in net reduction of opportunities for student involvement. Barker and Gump (1964) found in their study of Kansas schools that although a large school might have 20 times as many students as a nearby small school, it would provide only five times as many extracurricular activities.

The effects of school size seem to be particularly strong for marginal students (those who have academic difficulty, lower IQ, and come from lower socioeconomic backgrounds). In the large schools such students are not included: they are considered superfluous and they report specific incidents of exclusion. In the small schools, similarly marginal students are genuinely needed to maintain activities and functions. They report specific instances of being included, rather than excluded because of their marginal competence and social desirability. Not surprisingly, marginal students in small schools were found to be more active (four times more active than their large-school counterparts) and to display a stronger sense of responsibility for, and toward, the school and its activities than their counterparts in large schools (Willems, 1967).

The large school breeds passivity and irresponsibility as adaptations by students (and staff) to an unresponsive environment. Leaders and teachers in small schools are not "nicer" than the leaders and staff in the large schools. Rather, the characteristics of the situation make the marginal students needed in the small school and superfluous in the large school (Garbarino, 1980b).

Why does school size have this effect? Small schools encourage overlapping roles and relationships, a system of networks, which builds a base for positive interaction between young people and adults (Garbarino & Bronfenbrenner, 1976). Large schools seem to promote impersonal conditions, whereas small schools encourage personalized conditions. "Large schools emphasize what one is, rather than who" (Garbarino, 1980b).

This situation affects teachers and administrators as well as students (Coleman et al., 1974). Teachers in large schools see the system as inflexible and unresponsive. They become isolated from the administration and each other. They feel the need to organize and be organized. In the same vein, administrators become managers and not educators. As we have seen, the increase in school size has not been met with an increase in administrative staff. As schools get larger, principals become increasingly isolated and alone. Overall, it seems that when schools become large, there is less interaction between the school as an institution and the individuals who "live there," as well as less interaction among those individuals themselves.

This trend appears to apply to the interaction between schools and communities as well. As we have observed, the number of connections is decreasing between school and community; the increasing size of schools exacerbates this problem. When schools have thousands of students and a staff numbering in the hundreds, it becomes difficult for parents as well as other community members to feel a part of, or close to, the institution. This becomes especially critical when the usual connections between school and community have been reduced or severed completely, as is the case when a large number of the population do not have children in school or are in some way alienated from the institution. Parents from lower SES groups are prime examples. They often feel at odds with the school when they try to discuss their children's problems (or in some way be educationally involved) with white middle-class school officials who use technical jargon and have little empathy with or understanding of those who come from lower-class backgrounds (deLone, 1979). The situation is compounded by the fact that the largest schools are in the largest metropolitan areas, which also have large populations of lower SES groups.

We see a common theme regarding school size cutting across the client population: *isolation*. Large schools paradoxically encourage the isolation of the various parts of the school's ecology from each other. These parts are not united in pursuing their professed common goal, namely, quality education. In a broader sense, this theme serves to focus our entire discussion of the client group. We observed this trend emerging time after time as we examined the various subgroups that are affected by problems in the school. Students are isolated from teachers and the schools. Students, teachers, and administrators operate in separate realities with little contact between or among them. Communities are becoming less connected with the schools; the institution they share has become so large that it no longer unites these groups in a common effort. In fact, it may work against unification.

Although we acknowledge that the use of social support networks cannot solve all these problems, it can be an effective tool in reducing the isolation and alienation so evident in our client population. In a time of diminishing resources when many feel that the schools already have enough money to do the job (Gallup, 1981), the role of such networks may become even more important. How can we employ social support systems in dealing with problems in the schools? A review and evaluation of existing programs and suggestions for the future is our next topic.

SOCIAL SUPPORT NETWORKS IN THE SCHOOLS: EXISTING AND NEEDED PROGRAMS

As a preface to our review of current programs, we should advise the reader that the number and variety of programs that employ social support networks in dealing with problems in the schools is great indeed; the potential for using them is even greater. However, many of these programs are similar in structure and function, and we do not need to recount the many permutations of any one type of program. Our purpose here is to provide a general idea of the ways in which social support networks are currently being used in the schools (and how they are not), and how effective this resource is in dealing with particular problems. We shall examine some subgroups of our client population for whom the use of social support systems is limited and make some suggestions for increasing their usefulness. However, we shall not outline how to organize and develop particular programs for specific problems. For that we refer the reader to our list of sources at the end of the chapter.

There are many themes that cut across the use of social support systems in education (such as solving particular problems like academic failure or community–school alienation) which could serve as a focus for our review. However, in line with our purpose of presenting a general overview, our discussion will examine the use of social support networks in terms of who is involved in the network itself. We shall first look at networks among peers and then turn to school–community interconnections.

PEER NETWORKS

Networks among peers can do much to promote positive outcomes in schools. The natural connections between people who have shared experiences and common goals, rewards, and stresses can be marshalled in the cause of mutual support. Our discussion will focus on the use of peer networks in dealing with school problems in four subgroups of our client population: students, teachers, administrators, and parents.

Students. The use of student networks as solutions for school-related problems has received a good deal of attention in recent years; many such programs are currently in operation. Although a variety of names and particular organizational schemes are associated with the use of student networks, most fall into one of two categories: peer tutoring and peer counseling. These programs are basically very similar in organizational structure, differing mostly in the problems addressed. As the names imply, peer-tutoring programs deal primarily with academic problems whereas peer-counseling programs are oriented more toward interpersonal or emotional difficulties. Both involve the use of students acting as "caregivers" to other students. Essentially, counselors or tutors are recruited, trained, and then assigned. In some schools, a highly selective scheme is used in deciding who will be a tutor or a counselor, typical criteria being academic achievement, personality, and personal reputation. Although such programs may exist within individual classrooms, most operate at the school level and are organized by a counselor or administrator. These programs may involve children of the same age or mixed ages; in particular, older students often tutor younger ones. In the case of cross-age tutoring, the training may be more elaborate and include instruction to the helpers about specific techniques for dealing with young children. These tutors usually work closely with the child's classroom teacher as well, in order to coordinate their efforts (Hetherington & Parke, 1979). It is important to emphasize here that peer network programs are *not* designed as replacements or substitutes for the professional–child relationship, but rather as a means of enhancing the work of teachers and other school personnel. The programs are not particularly complex; we refer the reader to the appendix for details of their operation. Here we shall focus on their effectiveness.

Do these programs work? Since most of the research has been done on peer-tutoring programs, we shall review them first. Despite a body of research that is plagued with a host of methodological difficulties, it is generally concluded that such programs do indeed work. As Devin-Sheehan, Feldman, and Allen make clear in their comprehensive review of the literature:

> Perhaps the most remarkable feature about the field studies just discussed is the variety of participants, goals, and procedures that they employed. Tutors were elementary school students, junior high and high school students, and adults: participants were sometimes paid but more often not; there were both underachievers and high achievers. Tutees were in one case high school students, but more typically were grade school students. Goals ranged from the structured and programmed tutoring project's concern with tutees' reading achievement to the inner-city projects' emphasis on social and academic achievement—both for the high school tutors and for their elementary or high school tutees. We can conclude from the evidence presented above that several different kinds of tutoring programs can effectively improve academic performance of tutees and, in some cases, that of tutors as well. (1976, p. 363)

A very interesting finding from studies of the effectiveness of these programs (other than that they seem to work) is that in many cases the benefits to the tutor are as great or greater than to the tutee (Cloward, 1967; Allen & Feldman, 1974; Hetherington & Parke, 1979). For example, Cloward (1967) reported that in a tutorial program designed to increase reading achievement, although the tutees showed a significant gain of 6.2 months in reading level over a 5-month period (compared to 3.2 for the nontutored group), the tutors themselves showed an average improvement of 19 months over a 7-month span! Morgan and Toy (1970) report similar results from a study of cross-age tutoring in a rural setting. They found that both tutors and tutees made significant gains on measures of reading, spelling, and arithmetic skills after being involved in the program, but that the tutors made by far the greatest gains. Morgan and Toy's results are especially important because of the wide age range of the participants and the method of selecting the tutors, as well as the broad number of subject areas involved. The tutors were volunteers from grades 8 to 12, while the tutees were identified by teachers as needing help and ranged from second- to fifth-graders. The benefits for the tutor seem to cut across grades and subject areas.

Furthermore, it seems that being a tutor can be a beneficial experience for those students who are likely candidates to receive peer tutoring or counseling (Devin-Sheehan, Feldman, & Allen, 1976). The experience of tutoring has been shown to lead to progress in both the cognitive and affective realms for low-achieving students. A number of studies report that low-achievers in reading make significant gains in reading achievement after having tutored younger children. For example, it was found that sixth-grade low-achievers made significant gains in reading after only 2 months of tutoring low-achieving second-graders in reading (Klentschy, 1971). Marascuilo, Levin, and James (1969) found that ninth-grade remedial readers showed significant gains in reading comprehension after their (paid) tutoring of a seventh-grade low-achiever in reading. In another study, Robertson (1971) found that although fifth-graders who were poor readers did not improve in reading achievement as a result of tutoring, they did show more positive attitudes toward teachers, reading, and themselves. Allen and Feldman (1974) went on to show that it is the act of tutoring itself that is behind the positive changes. They compared two groups of fifth-graders, one that tutored third-graders in a particular subject and another that studied the same material alone. At the end of the experiment, the tutors showed significantly better grasp of the material than those who studied alone, even though initially those in the alone group were the better performers. It was the tutoring, not just the extra studying, that resulted in increased academic achievement.

It seems as if peer tutoring programs have a bidirectional effect, with the helpers deriving as much gain as those who are helped. Thus, clients and caregiver become one in the same, an interesting and unintended consequence of this and probably many other helping networks.

Peer-tutoring programs are not particularly new and do not necessarily involve only small groups of students within a single school. For instance, New York City's High School Homework Helpers Program was developed in 1963. Ten years later, the program employed 1,000 tutors (mostly high school students) who worked with 6,000 clients (Devin-Sheehan, Feldman, & Allen, 1976). Youth Tutoring Youth (YTY), which developed under the auspices of the National Commission on Youth, Inc., is another massive program that operated in a number of cities (e.g., Chicago, Atlanta, and Washington, D.C.) and was initiated in the 1960's. Both of these programs have been the object of methodologically sound studies that report academic success for tutors and tutees alike (Devin-Sheehan, Feldman, & Allen, 1976).

One side benefit of peer-tutoring programs that we noted only briefly earlier deserves note here. That is, besides the academic gains received, participants in these types of programs seem to grow in affective areas as well. Many studies report heightened self-esteem, increased interest in and more positive attitudes toward school, and better classroom behavior (Hetherington & Parke, 1979). Thus, this type of networking might be effective for a number of problems above and beyond academic failure for, as the reader well knows, problems in school are rarely isolated events. Self-concept, home environment, academic failure, and antisocial behavior, for example, are highly related issues; so would certainly expect that a program that results in positive outcomes in one of these areas might also have a similar effect on related problems.

There are many factors that may influence the outcome of peer-teaching programs, such as personal characteristics of the tutor and tutee (e.g., race, sex, SES, and age), general tutor effectiveness, and characteristics of the tutoring situation (e.g., length of sessions, sessions per week, number of tutees per tutor, amount of tutor training). However, research gives us little conclusive evidence about the effect of any of these factors. We refer the reader to the list of research resources at the end of the chapter.

In summary, we can expect that peer-tutoring programs can be effective in dealing with academic failure as well as other related problems. We have seen that both tutors and tutees can benefit from their involvement and that marginal students can be effective tutors as well as being helped when they are objects of such programs. In short, peer tutoring can enhance and reinforce positive connections among students, between students and school personnel, and between students and the school itself.

It seems appropriate here to comment on the nature of peer-tutoring programs as they are currently operating. Until now, we have discussed formal programs that are highly organized, and are developed and run by adults. Although these programs, as we have seen, can be effective in dealing with some problems, the number of students they can involve is limited. What we also need is to encourage truly informal helping networks, that is, kids helping each other within classrooms and throughout school. This is not a new idea; it happens thousands of times in schools everyday. What is missing, however, is formal encouragement of this phenomenon by the institution itself. At this point, the academic evaluation procedures used in most schools discourage informal collective action. Students are evaluated for the most part on an individualistic, competitive basis that in a sense requires failure; if some are to do well in such a system, then others must fail. Thus, there are no common goals regarding academics. There is no encouragement of support for the learning of all; rather, each must succeed or fail on his own. There are other ways of doing things. We need to expand and modify our notion of school and what it can and should provide for students.

For example, classes can be "graded" on the basis of their collective success in mastering basic skills and in promoting the involvement of those who are natural candidates for alienation. Interpersonal competition would be eliminated as a motivator for academic achievement, to be replaced by intrapersonal competition with interpersonal support. Students would be encouraged to help each other learn, rather than to compete against each other for grades. Nonmastery would mean that a student would have to keep trying (maybe with extra help) until he achieved mastery, but it would not brand him as a failure. And certainly no student would ever be passed along without first having mastered the skills needed for success at the next educational level. Interscholastic contests in academic competence would join interscholastic athletics. Intramural academics, like their parallel in intramural athletics, would be designed to develop universal fitness and provide an opportunity for personal challenge and testing.

What about peer-counseling programs? Since these programs closely resemble peer tutoring, we need only make a few additional comments here. As we mentioned earlier, these programs unlike peer tutoring, are designed to deal specifically with affective concerns. Sussman provides a definition: "[Peer group counseling] is a process in which trained and supervised students offer listening, support, and alternatives and other verbal and nonverbal interaction, but little or no advice to students who refer themselves (1973, p. 5).

Although this is the standard mode of operation, there are also peer counseling programs acting more as encounter groups, with participants serving as both clients and counselors. However, as with peer tutoring, generally all participants seem to gain from the counseling experience regardless of the approach used (Heifeisen, 1973; Samuels & Samuels, 1975).

Type of program aside, what these programs are trying to do is to marshall the force of the peer group to act in a positive, supporting direction. We are all aware of the effectiveness of peer-counseling groups with adults. Alcoholic Anonymous and Weight Watchers are good examples, as are the effective use of peers in treating adolescent drug addicts (Samuels & Samuels, 1975). But will such techniques work in schools? The answer appears to be yes.

Successful peer-counseling programs have been reported in a number of schools across the nation (Samuels & Samuels, 1975). As Alwine states in his discussion of one such program in a Blandesburg, Maryland, high school:

> Since during adolescence the peer group becomes the "significant other" of whom approval is sought, there were, ideally, sensitive and empathetic peers with whom adolescents could relate, many daily emotional crises and disruptive situations could be avoided or interdicted. Student–student help is not a new phenomenon, yet a formal training program followed by intensive skill training may be. . . . What has happened in our school in terms of relationships and communication is exciting. The contribution of a positive peer model to the

school environment can only be a positive force and another alternative to reaching understanding among a school population, as well as reaching toward a more positive mental health. (1974, p. 463).

Other investigators also report positive outcomes from peer-counseling programs in helping youngsters deal with social and emotional problems (Coleman, 1959; McDill, Myers, & Rigsby, 1966; Wolff, 1969; Kern & Kirby, 1971; Mosher & Sprinthall, 1971; Etkin & Snyder, 1972; Sussman, 1973); as Samuels and Samuels point out, peer counseling can be as beneficial for the counselor as for the client: "Peer counseling is also a meaningful experience for the student-counselor. Students directly involved in a peer counseling program not only provide invaluable services to other students, the school, and community, but are able to find new alternatives for themselves" (1975, p. 105).

Peer-counseling programs can help students and schools deal with a number of perplexing problems ranging from academic failure to family breakups or vandalism and school crime. Students are often more willing to listen to another student than to adults; many of today's students face problems that are new territory for most adults (Maultsby, Knipping, & Carpenter, 1974). Margaret Mead argued that it is unrealistic to expect adults to understand the emotional stresses of growing up in today's world.

Peer counseling can make use of the influence youngsters naturally have on each other. It effects changes in both behavior and attitude and may be more effective than costly programs using professional adult helpers. When schools fail to utilize this naturally occurring resource, they are ignoring a potentially powerful positive influence in the lives of their students and are running the risk of allowing this support system to operate in a negative way. "When peer influence is channeled for positive change, commitment to change is enhanced by helping students discover affiliation with other students who wish to make similar changes" (Brown, 1965, p. 816.)

> The peer-group counseling concept has great potential to promote individual and human development. It reaches the student as a person, encourages self-expression, and gives students an opportunity to provide significant help to others. In adolescence, young people listen to and are influenced by other young people. Expanded availability of this type of interaction provides maximum opportunity for personal growth. Peer-group counseling is one method of stimulating this growth in a positive direction (Sussman, 1973, p. 112).

Teachers. For networks among teachers, there is little research to report. Informal networks do exist among teachers and they provide a great deal of support for some. However, they are inconsistent and uncoordinated efforts at best and, as we have already seen, most teachers feel alone in their jobs. The only peer networks that exist for teachers on a formal basis are the two major professional organizations (The National Education Association and The American Federation of Teachers), but they provide support mostly in the area of salary and other labor–management contractual concerns (e.g., job security and nonsalary benefits). They are of little help in overcoming the loneliness and isolation that lead many teachers to leave the profession. Thus, there is not much in the way of existing programs to evaluate or discuss. For that reason we shall focus on the issue of what can be rather than what is.

We have discussed the loneliness that many teachers feel and the reasons for it. As a final summary and a focus for our discussion of what can be, Goodlad and Klein's statement seems especially appropriate: "It would appear that teachers are very much alone in their work. It is not just a matter of being alone with children . . . it is a feeling of not being supported by someone who knows their work, is sympathetic to it, wants to help, and does" (1974, p. 94).

When they do reach out, teachers turn to other teachers most often when they need assistance (Sarason, 1971; Lortie, 1975; Rogus & Martin, 1979). Although this does occur spontaneously in some schools, we know from our review of the client population that several factors act to hinder this process (such as the organizational pattern of the school, the training of teachers, and the pattern of socialization into the profession). Of course, teachers can be encouraged to try to overcome the barriers that separate and isolate them. However, two organizational changes would contribute greatly to the development of social support systems among teachers. One is for administrators and other supervisory personnel actively to encourage teachers to depend on each other for both emotional and professional support. The second is for colleges and universities to make appropriate alterations in their teacher preparation programs, in an effort to promote group activity and cooperation. The results of these changes would contrast with the present situation which, for the most part, leads to the development of autonomy and isolation.

What can administratiors do to foster the growth of social support networks among their teachers? Grossnickle (1978, p. 136) suggests that they can:

    1. Encourage teachers to diversify their interests. Administrators may do this by helping to organize jogging and exercise groups, for example. Short segments of institute days could be devoted to interests and hobbies of faculty.

    2. Provide for attendance at professional conferences.

    3. Encourage inter- and intraschool teacher visitation.

    4. Expand opportunities for adult contact and a feeling of teamwork and esprit d'corps.

    5. Develop employees assistance programs that attempt to help faculty members who are experiencing personal problems that may interfere with their work.

    6. Sponsor events, retreats, and attitude-adjustment opportunities.

    7. Provide for faculty meetings in small groups whenever possible to encourage mutual exchange of ideas.

The ideas cited above are action-oriented. Rogus and Martin provide some suggestions for developing teacher support systems that are more philosophical in nature:

> Encourage the staff to team on an informal basis. Emphasize the potential benefits for *teachers* rather than for students.
>
> Reinforce teachers for the identification of problems encountered in the classroom setting. Often historically, classroom effectiveness has been equated with the absence of problems. Teachers have consequently learned to deny their difficulties to others. Principal example is an excellent way to legitimate problem identification by teachers.
>
> Work with staff toward developing two attitudes essential to working effectively with each other: (1) "if there is a problem, I caused it;" and (2) "each person with whom we work is doing the best he/she is able." The first attitude, if internalized, makes each staff member a part of any problem's solution rather than its creation. It creates a helping set and commits each to helping others to grow. The second is closely related to the first, and if internalized, it minimizes nonproductive judgments. The two attitudes in combination make much defensive and "lonesome" behavior unnecessary. Again principal example in daily interactions with staff constitutes a powerful model from which teachers might learn. (1979, pp. 86–87)

From these lists, it becomes obvious that administrators must analyze their own school and particular situation when deciding the best way or ways to encourage the growth of teacher support networks. It is not the means, but the ends that are important here. The universal imperative is that administrators must become aware of the need for such support systems and take active steps to encourage their development (Reed, 1980; Ricken, 1980; Erlandson & Pastor, 1981).

Our second proposal for increasing the number and use of teacher support systems concerned the training of teachers. We share the opinion of others that teacher training does little to encourage collective action on the part of teachers. In fact, it probably hinders it (Lortie, 1975). What can be done? Generally, prospective teachers need practice in cooperative interaction (Lortie, 1975). They need to see teaching as a collective activity undertaken by professionals with a common goal. Professionals who can frequently work together *should* depend on each other for help. This can be done in a number of ways. For example, teachers-in-training could be required to team with each other, plan lessons in groups of three of four, visit each other's classrooms, have frequent and regular sessions where mutual and individual problems are discussed, and so on. Again, the ideal program does not exist. What is ideal depends on the situation, but the experience of a colleague might serve as a general example.

Our friend was assigned to student-teach at a junior high school, along with six other prospective teachers, as part of a 1-year teacher certification program at a large university. The department to which they were assigned contained only four members. Thus, from the beginning, the opportunity for individual experiences was greatly reduced because of the large ratio of "students" (i.e., interns) to teachers. The students were assigned to the junior high for three-quarters of the school year (late August until mid-March). This situation is already unique in two respects: (1) the large intern-to-teacher ratio (it is usually one to one), and (2) the length of time spent in the school (most student teaching experiences range from 10 weeks to a semester). The instructional assistants (as they were called) were active in the classroom almost from the time they entered the building. They were led through a series of increasingly more involved activities beginning with acting as aides or tutors. Sometimes they started as observers and slowly progressed to the point where they would teach two to three classes per week without the presence of the cooperating teacher. This progression occurred over several months. At the same time, the students were encouraged to involve themselves in special projects and extracurricular activities as well. The group put on plays, sponsored clubs, served as intramural supervisors, and in some instances served as assistant coaches. However, because of the large number of interns, almost all activity was done in groups of two or more. There were just not enough activities for each intern to act individually. By accident rather than design, the student teachers were involved daily in group activity and mutual cooperation.

The instructional assistants observed each other often, and informal sessions of criticism and suggestions became an everyday occurrence. By the time they were actually ready to student-teach, a pattern of cooperative activity had been established. Thus, even though they worked independently in separate classrooms, the mutual support continued. They contnued to observe each other and to provide suggestions and criticism, and they occasionally met in large groups to discuss individual problems and propose solutions. Students shared concerns and worries, asked each other for help, freely admitted problems, accepted advice, and generally learned from each other. As time went on, the cooperating faculty also came to participate in the informal and formal sessions, adding comments and soliciting and accepting advice themselves. As the reader may imagine, this type of teaching experience stands in vivid contrast to the type of isolation most teachers face.

These student teachers had come to see teaching as a cooperative, dependent activity, rather than as an autonomous, independent endeavor. This was accomplished by moving the prospective teacher slowly into a position of full responsibility and by continuously stressing cooperation and mutual support, both of which serve to prevent teacher isolation (e.g., Lortie, 1975). A change of emphasis in teacher education of this type requires no huge reallocation of funds or massive changes in curricular organization, but rather a change in mind set by those in charge. It seems that peer network systems will never provide the support they might until we change our notion of what teaching is or can be.

Administrators. In considering the entire client population, it appears that in many ways administrators are worse off than teachers. They have less job security (no tenure), a less active and powerful professional organization, and virtually no peers in the workplace to talk with about the day-to-day stresses of their job. According to Bird (1977), the key to administrative survival is having someone to lean on. However, that someone must be a person in a comparable position. A spouse does not really understand the administrator's position because he or she is not in the school. The teachers are not available because many times the administrator's problems concern them, making discussion inappropriate if not unethical, and upper-level administrators might interpret such discussions as a sign of incompetence or "weakness" on the part of the principal. In some schools, assistant principals and the principal may find that they can establish some sort of support network, but these associations usually fall prey to the difficulties inherent in supervisor–employee relationships (Bird, 1977). If principals are to establish a support network, the responsibility for its development belongs primarily to two parties: the principals themselves and the school district administrative staff. The fact that such systems are needed is well known. Principals are not leaving education because the job is too tough, but rather because they are tired of carrying the load alone. They are tired of not having anyone to listen or understand them. Therefore, it is vitally important that district officials encourage collegial interaction among their administrators. Many of the steps we suggested as being helpful for the development of teacher support systems are also appropriate here. Also, administrators themselves need to seek out and develop friendships within the profession that can form the basis for a mutual support group composed of trusted individuals (Bird, 1977; Brown & Carlton, 1980; Herlihy & Herlihy, 1980). Institutions that offer training for potential administrators need to be aware of this as well and provide experience in developing and maintaining cooperative relationships among administrators in much the same vein as we suggested for teacher training. As we stressed with teachers, how these relationships are established is not important; the fact of their establishment is. In an era of declining resources and fast-paced social change, the administrator's job can only get tougher, and the chances of extra help grow increasingly small. The development of mutual support groups may be the key to keeping good administrators in the profession.

Parents. "The Parents Movement" is the title of a section in a recent volume on citizen involvement in the schools. As it suggests, there is a growing sentiment in the country that parents should take on a more active role in their children's education (Rioux, 1980). Parental participation in the educational process can take several forms, most of which are a continuation or expansion of the traditional role of parents in education (serving on advisory boards, helping in classrooms, participating in fund raising projects, helping their children with their homework, and so on). We shall consider many of these forms in a later section. Here we want to examine a different relationship of parents to schools: the growing inclination on the part of parents to form their own organizations apart from the schools.

In the past, parent-initiated groups were usually of three types: the single-issue or crisis group (like ones organized to deal with busing or to oppose sex education), a school-affiliated group (such as the PTA), or non-crisis special interest groups (such as parents of retarded or minority children) (NSPRA, 1977). However, currently, new action-oriented parent organizations are developing in many communities. These groups are concerned with more than single events or issues—they came into being in order to give parents a greater influence in the decision-making process in the schools.

Why do parents need their own organization? Why don't traditional groups such as the PTA meet their needs? First, groups that contain only parents tend to be organized with the needs and wants of *only* parents in mind. They are not concerned with the particular problems of other groups, such as teachers or administrators (at least not directly), and therefore can avoid some conflict-of-interest problems that are inherent in groups like the PTA. In fact, most parent groups are formed under the premise that parents have a unique relationship with the schools. Key aspects of this relationship have been summarized by the National Committee for Citizens in Education (Rioux, 1980):

> For one thing, parents don't work for the school district; they are in a unique position to question school policies. Teachers, of course, aren't so free to oppose policies set by those who renew their contracts.
>
> Second, parents have a financial stake in the education of their children, but they traditionally have been denied a voice in how their tax money is used in the education process. The decisions are made at various levels of the school bureaucracy; teachers generally abide by those decisions (they don't want to lose their jobs); and parents all too often are completely left out of the policy-making picture.
>
> Third, parents generally know what they want for their children. They have a better feel for what their children need and what they can and can't do. (p. 234)

Along the same lines, parents are realizing that they have legal rights in regard to their child's education (Brandt, 1979; Rioux, 1980). Some of these include access to student's records and the right to free, appropriate education for handicapped students (Rioux, 1980).

What do these parent-only groups do? A few examples should suffice to illustrate their activities (Rioux, 1980):

1. Some parent groups have succeeded in establishing special resource centers within schools, where parents can obtain information and develop skills for reinforcing student learning at home.

2. The Montclair, New Jersey, Concerned Citizens Association challenged a

state-approved segregation plan on the grounds that parents were excluded from participating in its development. By so doing they gained much greater input into the monitoring and administration of the plan as it was implemented in their schools.

3. Parents in Dallas organized and recruited other parents into a "Better Reading through Parents Program," which involved classes for parents that helped them develop skills that they could use to increase their child's reading ability.

4. The Citizens School Committees of Chicago played a major role in getting legislation passed that called for parent involvement in the selection of school principals.

It seems that parents do have specific needs and interests that traditional parent–teacher groups may not serve. In increasing numbers they are "discarding the old 'leave it to the pros' attitude and are coming together to declare and press for their full rights under the law" (Rioux, 1980, p. 2). They are employing the natural links among them to build political power. Social networks become the basis for mutual support and the sharing of information, which results in greater influence in the schools.

Parents networks can organize and operate in many ways (for specific "how to" information, we again refer the reader to our list of sources), but once families in neighborhoods become introduced to each other (a natural consequence of parents uniting in a peer support group), a number of benefits above and beyond a more powerful and informed presence in the schools may be realized. When families are introduced to each other we see the "informal helping patterns which are described in the literature as so characteristic of natural helping networks, begin to unfold" (Cochran & Woolener, 1980, p. 12). For example, a program in Syracuse, New York, called Family Matters encouraged parents to become part of neighborhood clusters that participated in a number of group activities. Cochran and Woolener relate three vignettes which they believe are typical of the outcomes of the Syracuse project.

First, in one of our racially mixed neighborhoods a Black and a white family were introduced to each other through the program. The white parents felt positive toward and had good connections in the nearby elementary school; the Black parents and children were very negative toward the same school. In this instance, via the connections of their new friends, the same Black parents were able to find a way to make the school work for them. At the same time, the teenagers in the Black family have begun to do baby-sitting for the neighboring Family Matters child.

In the second case, in a different neighborhood, two families became friends through the program. When one couple decided to separate, each partner was able to receive emotional support from the same sex counterpart in the other couple.

The third example involves a couple who had been advised by the nursery school teacher not to enroll the Family Matters child in kindergarten at the prescribed time, but to wait a year. Eager to have the child start school, but anxious to do the "right thing," the parents shared their concerns in the neighborhood cluster to which they belonged. The other parents in the cluster supported the idea of kindergarten enrollment, pointing out that the social experiences would be positive and that the worst consequence would only be the need to repeat the year of kindergarten. The parents went ahead with confidence and a commitment to work with the school in order that the experience be a positive one for the child. (1981, p. 12)

As these examples make clear, parent networks can be a positive force in dealing with issues that go beyond schools. They can help provide that sense of community which is so lacking in our "client population." Formed to grapple with educational concerns, parent groups can branch out and become involved in more general issues as well. In fact, according to the Institute for Responsive Education (IRE) the most successful parent groups are those whose activities are not restricted solely to the educational arena (NSPRA, 1977). We can see that parent support groups are a valuable and needed outgrowth of existing social networks because they can empower parents, enabling them to deal effectively with the schools in meeting their unique needs. The parent groups also provide a way of building neighborhood networks where their influence can go beyond the schools to make differences in the quality of life within a community.

THE SCHOOLS AND THE COMMUNITY: DRAWING THEM TOGETHER

As we pointed out at the beginning of our discussion, the schools affect all of us and therefore we all have a stake in what goes on there. Schools and communities are naturally linked along social, legal, and emotional lines. However, as we have pointed out, some of these connections have eroded in recent years. We want to show how we might reestablish or strengthen those links. Our analysis will examine the role of the community in the school and that of the school in the community, focusing on how social support networks might pull the two together.

There are three general ways in which citizens can be involved in their schools: as helpers, as resource people, and as partners. As we shall see, the school can also serve in some of these capacities within the community.

Probably the oldest and most widespread use of citizens in the schools is in the helper role (Della-Dora, 1979). In this capacity, members of the community (especially parents) perform such duties as helping on field trips, raising funds for equipment or supplies, serving as classroom aids, assisting with extracurricular activities (such as dances or sporting events), and so forth. Generally, they perform unskilled labor under school direction (Della-Dora, 1979). Citizens take little personal initiative when they serve in this capacity, but rather act almost totally under the direction of the school. Although this type of activity is the traditional way in which the public has been involved in the schools, citizens can perform more technical tasks that are highly linked to the heart of the educational process.

Many times, use of citizens as resources in the schools happens on an informal basis, as when a teacher invites a person from the community who has a particular skill to come to school and share that expertise with his or her students. For example, someone in the community may be knowledgeable about wildlife of the area, have a special collection of some kind, work in an unusual occupation, or be able to act as a living history text (as in the case of some senior citizens). Besides these informal contacts between a single teacher and an individual in the community, a number of formal programs that encourage this type of school–community interaction are operating at the school, district, and national level. A report issued by the National School Public Relations Association (1977) lists several examples on the local level:

—"Motor Moms" in the Lisle, Ill., Community School District work with small groups of kindergarten children to develop motor skills through such activities as skipping, tossing a ball, and using a balance beam. Each "Mom" plans her own half-hour program using a handbook that explains the principles of the program and suggests activities.
—Volunteers in Public Schools (VIPS) screen all Houston kindergarteners each September—testing hearing, vision, social maturity and language development. The volunteers are trained in two large downtown Houston churches.
—"Picture Ladies" in the Peoria, Ill., Public Schools personalize art appreciation by bringing art prints into the classroom. Each "Picture Lady" selects one grade level and speaks to each class in that grade once a month.
—Guest speakers at Indian Hills High School in Oakland, N.J., have included ambulance drivers, police officers, and motor vehicle inspectors, who come to the school to speak to health classes. Planning board members, and real estate and insurance agents speak to social studies classes.
—Foreign-born parents have added a special dimension to foreign language classes.

Many states also support this type of citizen involvement. For example, Rhode Island has a statewide volunteer program known as VIRIS (Volunteers in Rhode Island's Schools), which helps school districts develop volunteer programs (Rioux, 1980). On the national level, the National School Volunteer Program, Inc., provides many services to those interested in starting and maintaining volunteer programs in their schools (Brandt, 1979). (See the list of suggested sources at the end of the chapter for more information about these and other parent groups.)

According to the NSPRA, "the use of school volunteers (citizens who agree to share their time and expertise for no monetary benefit) has expanded greatly in recent years and shows no sign of abating." In 1974, over 2 million citizens were involved as resources in the schools, putting in an average of 6 hours per week (NSPRA, 1977, p. 2). Some school districts employ thousands of volunteers; for example, Los Angeles has 20,000 citizens involved in its schools, while Miami used over 10,000 citizens as resource persons.

Are the programs helpful? Specific studies are scarce, but we do know that interest in what happens at school is valuable for increasing children's learning (Rioux, 1980). From our discussion of the sources of citizen information about the schools, we can conclude that increasing contact with the schools would decrease the reliance on sensational accounts from newspapers and other media as sources of information (which unfortunately, a majority in the United States now list as their prime resource for information about the schools). In light of this, it seems that programs that promote citizen involvement in the educational process would be helpful. Such programs draw the schools and the community together, providing more access to first-hand information about the schools and also increasing motivation on the part of the public (especially parents) to keep abreast of current practice and policies. Reports of negative consequences resulting from the use of citizens as resources in the school are rare indeed.

The use of volunteers as resources can be a two-way street. Many schools are now active sponsors of student-as-resource programs. Students can work in day care centers, provide companionship to senior citizens, help in nursing homes, tutor and counsel children and adults, serve as aides in centers for the blind, become involved in community action programs, and help to screen other students for learning disabilities. The list goes on and on.

Some schools give credit for volunteer work or even require it for graduation from high school (NSPRA, 1977). For example, students at Taft High School in the Bronx, New York, help protect senior citizens from harm by providing an escort service in dangerous neighborhoods. The students accompany elderly people to such places as the grocery store, the bank, and hot lunch programs. Students perform this service during school hours, and this work is recorded as part of their official school records. The high school Community Internship Timesharing Experience (CITE) program in Belmont, Massachusetts, is an example of the school offering community service opportunities to students as a class option; in essence, it is part of the curriculum (NSPRA, 1977). The students are assigned to a community service agency or business office for a grading period, putting in an average of 2 hours per day, 2–3 days a week. They can receive academic credit for their internship by submitting a proposal to the school's committee on independent study, which must approve it. The student must then keep a log, which is reviewed by a supervisor. The experience provides students with career-exploration opportunities as well as academic and emotional rewards. As a director of the program states: "The value of the volunteer experience is unrelated to course credit. Many students have more credits than they need to graduate. I feel it's much more important to have actual work experience on their records than any credit hours they would earn" (NSPRA, 1977, p. 29).

CITE students have explored such careers as physical therapist, motorcycle mechanic, dentist, landscape architect, travel agent, potter, florist, and lobbyist, as well as having worked in a variety of community service agencies and organizations. The Riverdale School, a private school in Fieldston, New York, places such a high value on this type of experience that it requires 60 hours of community service in order to qualify for a high school diploma (NSPRA, 1977).

What are the effects of such programs? Although formal studies are few (other than those already mentioned regarding peer tutoring or peer counseling), common sense and the experience of several national organizations that have sponsored such programs attest to their value. For example, the National Commission on Resources for Youth, which operates a clearinghouse of successful youth volunteer programs, lists a number of benefits that their experience has shown such programs to provide (NSPRA, 1977):

1. They fill genuine needs for adolescents and society.
2. They offer active learning in an age of spectatorship.
3. They offer challenge—providing youth a chance to do something that is difficult as well as meaningful.
4. They promote maturity and responsibility.
5. They give adolescents a taste of the options available in the real world.
6. They involve working partnerships between youth and adults.
7. They offer a community experience—a sense of belonging to an extended family, and the exhilaration that comes from being associated with others in significant activities.

Clearly such programs could do much to improve school–community relations by repairing and reinforcing the natural links that already exist between the two. Allowing and encouraging student involvement in the community under the auspices of the school can be a very positive force in reducing the isolation of community from school.

A special case of citizen-as-resource in the school should also be noted here, and that is using members of the community as consultants to the school. We are referring to the use of the specialized, professional knowledge of some citizens by either individual teachers, schools, or districts as a whole, as well as the participation of parents and other citizens on various advisory boards and committees.

In the capacity of consultants, citizens could contribute their special skills to the school so that it does not have to pay for these services. For example, a landscape architect might help a group of students and teachers plan an environmental project for improving school grounds. In another instance, a labor union official and a personnel manager from a local company might help a high school curriculum committee plan a unit or class on labor relations (Della-Dora, 1979). In some areas, local businesses provide inservice training to teachers in the working of the American economic system and one-on-one seminars on the role of business in the economy (NSPRA, 1977).

Probably the most useful service that business could provide to schools, especially in light of the school's increasing size and complexity, is to help school officials manage the institution more effectively: "Such assistance is not limited to large school districts with multimillion dollar budgets. In fact, this kind of expertise is present to some degree in every community and could be used to advantage in most school districts." (NSPRA, 1977, p. 33). For example, management advisory teams have been used in communities such as Elyria, Ohio (enrollment 13,000), St. Louis, Missouri (enrollment 82,000), and Dallas, Texas (enrollment 177,000 and growing), and at the state level as well (Washington).

Such programs can have positive benefits for both parties (a consequence we have observed in other programs involving social networks). This is clear in the following description of the outcomes of a joint project between the Dallas Chamber of Commerce and the Dallas Public Schools.

> In addition to benefits of efficiency, and project led to "a general increase in public confidence in school operations," said the Chamber, because the new partnership showed taxpayers "that the schools are genuinely interested in efficiency and economy." Businesspeople who participated said they "gained as much as they put in," the Chamber added. "Being able to observe first-hand has given them a new interest in educational affairs in the city." Several of the consultants went on to speak to civic groups about the new alliance between business and the schools. (NSPRA, 1977, p. 36)

What about the other role for citizens as consultants, namely, as members of advisory boards? Although the information supplied by citizen advisory boards is not as technically oriented as that provided by the particular specialists discussed above, participation of citizens in this capacity is still highly valued. Many state and federal programs require a citizens advisory council of some sort before they will award appropriate funds (Hobson, 1979; Steinberg, 1979; Rioux, 1980). For example, Title I of the Elementary and Secondary Education Act of 1965 requires that every school and school distrct applying for Title I funds have an existing Parent Advisory Council (PAC) before receiving funds. Head Start also specifies that parents be involved as "consultants" to local programs as a requirement for funding on the state level. Alaska, Maryland, and North Carolina have passed or are considering legislation that calls for the formation of citizen advisory councils. Several cities, such as Denver and Boston, are under court-ordered mandates to involve citizen committees in the desegregation process.

A 1977 study conducted by the IRE indicated that there were 1,200,000 citizens serving on government-mandated councils (Steinberg, 1979). A vast majority of these participants (900,000) were involved in Title I PACs. About

200,000 were serving in Head Start, Follow Through, and other federal programs, and about 75,000 were active in state and local projects. These figures point out some problems wth current use of citizen advisory councils. First, most participants are involved in programs initiated at the federal level, and certainly federal regulation is no guarantee that citizen advisors will have any real decision-making power (Rioux, 1980). As an IRE study indicates, "Most of these programs [those that require some type of parent/citizen advisory committee at the local] level stress membership requirements and committee composition. They are often detailed and prescriptive on membership, and very vague and general in regard to functions and conditions of operation" (Davies, 1978, p. 30). The story at the state and local level is much the same: "School councils are not now, by and large, effective vehicles for citizens to affect education policies and decisions. But they are an unrealized potential to become mechanisms for producing power sharing and partnership between citizens and educators" (Davies, 1977, p. 6). "Policy makers who intended that the councils provide a means to develop participatory democracy at the grassroots level were reported to be disappointed with the results. Parents and citizens who served on the councils "were even more frustrated" (Steinberg, 1979, p. 50).

A major problem with federal and state regulations supporting citizens as participants in the educational process is the very fact that they are state and federal regulations. That is, there is very little involvement of citizens or administrators at the local level in initiating such programs, and few resources are available for administering or monitoring progress in the involvement of citizens in local councils (Steinberg, 1979). While the federal and state regulations we have mentioned were directing much of the activity in local school districts, the role of citizens under these laws was relegated to the local level. Citizens had little input into state and federal policy even though more and more of the decisions about resources and programs were being made at those levels (Steinberg, 1979). In some ways, the situation takes on a "Catch-22" flavor; the more the federal and state governments tried to require the involvement of citizens in the schools, the less power citizens actually gained.

Even those citizen advisory groups that operate at the level of the school building appear to afford citizen advisors little clout (Steinberg, 1979). These groups tend to be dominated by the professionals (mostly administrators) who seem to want to minimize citizen involvement in those areas traditionally considered subject to management prerogative (Davies, 1977). Local school boards also have little use for advisory councils and tend to see them as threats to their own power (Steinberg, 1979). In fact, board members rarely communicate with these councils, relying mostly on administrators for information about council activities (Davies, 1977).

We need to put the situation in perspective. Studies before 1970 indicated that most school systems were closed to the input of citizen groups into school policy. It appears that while federal, state, and local action since that time may have legitimated the role of such groups in the educational process, the potential of citizens as advisors (at least in this sense) has not been realized (Steinberg, 1979). It is clear that there is much work to be done in this area. Citizen advisory boards can play a major role in the schools. From decisions regarding curricular content to the design of special programs, the citizen-as-advisor can be a valuable resource. This is especially true because this type of citizen participation creates a role fo nonparents, giving them an opportunity to obtain first-hand information about the school and a true sense of ownership of and responsibility for it. Again we see unintended positive outcomes as natural consequences of involving citizens in this way. Schools get valuable information about the community's views and a fresh look at their concerns while increasing public knowledge and (more than likely) public support of the school.

We now turn to our final category of school–community linkage: citizens as partners in the educational process. In this type of involvement, community members actually play a direct role in the relationship between teacher and student. In some cases, as we shall see, this even involves citizens as teachers in their own right. Because of the nature of this discussion we shall be referring mostly to parents, although there are certainly ways that nonparents and schools can also be partners.

As with many of the programs mentioned previously, the organization of parents-as-partners programs can take a number of forms. We see two general patterns. One involves the attempt to help children by increasing the resources of the family. Such programs give parents remedial training in language and math as well as nutrition and parenting information. Although family resource programs are an outgrowth of the natural links between school and home, they are more involved in general schemes of community development and, as such, will not be discussed here. They have been much studied and have generated great controversy over their general effectiveness and the duration of their effects. For more information about these efforts (for example Head Start and Follow Through) we refer the reader to our list of sources at the end of the chapter.

The other prototype for parents-as-partners programs involves encouraging parents to become actively involved in the educational process and to perform specific tasks, functioning as tutors, as sponsors of academic activity, or as teachers in their own right. Smith (1968), for example, developed a program where parents were asked to listen to the child read, to read themselves in the child's presence, to show interest by looking at the child's homework, to provide a no-television time for study, and so forth. Parents were not asked to help with the child's homework and were told that the teacher would be checking on whether the child did the work, not on how well it was done. Similar programs in which parents agreed to perform certain nonacademic tasks are on-going in Dallas and Chicago (Granowsky, Middleton, & Mumford, 1979; Walberg, Bole, and Waxman, 1980).

Jesse Jackson's "PUSH for Excellence Program" is an example of the encouragement of this type of parent involvement at the national level (Rioux, 1980). Jackson's system (as does other similar projects) requires parents and teachers to sign "contracts" outlining their own particular set of responsibilities in the education of the child. Figure 9-1 shows each party's agreement.

The Home Study Institute (HSI) of Trinity College in Washington, D.C., takes parent involvement one step further, advocating an even larger role for parents in their child's education: "Parents are able to play a far more active role (than in programs like PUSH), building on and going beyond the school to enhance their children's interests and achievement. Clearly, additional involvement strategies need to be developed within a programmatic structure" (Rich, Van Dien, & Mattox, 1979, p. 33). HSI and others have done just that.

The Home Study Institute begins with a nondeficit model of the family. This is in direct contrast to many home–school programs (e.g., the massive efforts of the 1960's and early 1970's such as Head Start) which adopted a

PARENTS' CONTRACT

WHEREAS __ __   _____ ____

attends _ _____ School in the

_____ _____ School District, and

WHEREAS, I understand that my child will spend the most important years of his or her life in school, and

WHEREAS, I want to help the _____ Public Schools give my child the best possible education,

THEREFORE, I promise, agree, and pledge myself:
1. To see that my child gets to school on time.
2. To see that my child goes to school every day.
3. To meet with and speak to my child's teacher as many times as possible.
4. To reply to all letters, messages, notes or telephone calls from the schools.
5. To make sure that my child has some quiet time for homework each evening with the TV turned off. This time will be agreed upon between myself and my child.
6. To speak with my child every day about what was done at school.
7. To urge my child to respect himself or herself and to respect the rights and property of others.
8. To urge my child to be sensitive to the feelings of other people—both children and adults.
9. To speak to my child in a positive manner about school.

Parent _____

Dated: _____ _____   Parent _____

EDUCATORS' CONTRACT

WHEREAS _____

attends _____ school in the

_____ School District and

WHEREAS, we understand your child will spend the most important years of his or her life in schools and,

WHEREAS, we want to give your child the best possible education,

THEREFORE, we promise, agree and pledge:

1. To see that your child is protected while in school from physical or psychological harm.
2. To see that your child receives a full day of instruction for each day in attendance.
3. To meet with and speak to you as parents as many times as possible.
4. To reply to all letters, messages, notes or telephone calls from you and to occasionally write you about something positive in connection with your child's performance.
5. To give your child more special attention each day.
6. To recognize that we are models for your child; therefore, we will respect ourselves and the rights of children and parents including your right to see school records and your child's right to a fair hearing prior to any disciplinary action.
7. To be sensitive to the unique feelings and needs of your child.
8. To indicate by our positive behavior that your child has strengths and can achieve.

Teacher _____
(Special)

Dated: _____   Teacher _____

Fig. 9-1. Sample contracts for parents (A) and teachers (B), clarifying the responsibility and commitment of each to a child's education.

deficit approach; that is, their assumption was that because of lack of resources in the family (deficits in language, quality of home experience, neighborhood quality, and so on) the child was doomed to fail in school and eventually in life. The HSI nondeficit model is based on the following assumptions (Rich, Van Dien, & Mattox, 1979, p. 32):

1. All children have had meaningful experiences. However, the disadvantaged child's experiences have been different and fewer in number in contributing to preparation for success in school.

2. Home environments, no matter how poor, are a citadel of care and concern for children.

3. All parents intrinsically possess the abilities to help their children succeed in school.

4. Family concern can be readily translated into practical support for children and for schools. Professionals need only to provide the materials and support to enable parents to become both more active and more skilled participants in their child's education.

5. Schools should start with what the family has instead of worry about what it doesn't have.

6. Schools, no matter how understaffed or underequipped, have the capability of reaching out and affecting parent involvement by using easy, inexpensive materials, without waiting for what probably will not come: organizational change or massive government funding.

Hoping to promote a "mutually reinforcing home–school system," this non-deficit approach attempts to assist families to: (1) Use strategies at home to supplement the school's work. The HSI parent involvement model is built on the basic premise of separate but complementary roles for parent and teacher. (2) Understand that accountability for a child's education can be shared between school and home. Parents are helped in their role as key people in the student's learning process. (Rich, Van Dien, & Mattox, 1979, p. 33).

In attempting to accomplish these aims, HSI has developed one strategy (among others) that they call "Home Learning Recipes." It consists of "specific, no-cost activities for learning at home" (Rich, Van Dien, & Mattox, 1979). Recipes are usually one-page outlines that encourage the use of home and community resources in addition to stressing the development of basic skills. These activities are not duplicates of school efforts, but rather are intended to enhance and reinforce classroom learning. A number of different cities have used the HSI's program in various home–school intervention projects.

We have seen that parents can take an active role in the education of their children through "non-academic or academic" means. But does it do any good? Do the programs work? The answer seems to be a strong yes, at least as far as we know. The program in Chicago mentioned earlier, for example, resulted in a significant and substantial increase in children's reading scores (Walberg, Bole, & Waxman, 1980). A number of investigators report similar results (Smith, 1968; Sprigle & Van de Reit, 1969; Mize, 1977; Gordon, 1979a,b; Rich, Van Dien, & Mattox, 1979; Rioux, 1980). Results from studies of the HSI's "home recipe program" and other similar projects also report academic gains as well (Gordon, 1979; Rich, Van Dien, & Mattox, 1979). Interestingly enough, just as before, there are positive unintended consequences of these programs that go beyond the academic realm. For example, Stearns (1973) describes the effects of parent-as-tutor/teacher programs as increasing the child's motivation and the parent's self-esteem along with developing the child's academic capability. In programs operating within a nondeficit framework Rich and her colleagues (1979) look for results such as increased motivational skills of parents to work with their child, increased parenting skills and understanding of the school's role, and increased interaction between parent and child.

Another significant outcome of this type of parent involvement is that remedial programs become much cheaper. A cost effectiveness study conducted in Benton, Michigan (Rich, Van Dien, & Mattox, 1979), where a "home recipe" approach had been employed, showed that gains per pupil were achieved at $4.83 per child in the "recipe" program, while special class instructional costs (putting the child in some sort of remedial class) ran $563 per child per year. Walberg and his colleagues (1980) also see the parent-as-tutor approach as being much cheaper and potentially as effective as the remedial class approach.

However, there seem to be two problems with the research in this area. First, we know little about the use of these programs beyond the first years of elementary school, because only preschool programs have been extensively studied (Gordon, 1979). Second, we do not know if the gains achieved are long lasting, or if they fade as soon as the program ends (Gordon, 1979a,b; Walberg, Bole, & Waxman, 1980). Although such programs can easily become self-sustaining because of the highly positive academic and affective outcomes for all parties involved, this alone does not demonstrate permanency.

We mentioned at the beginning of our discussion of this topic that parents are not the only citizens who can become partners with the schools and be directly involved in the educational process. Certainly, other citizens could become tutors or teachers in the same way as parents. But citizens (including parents) can also be directly involved in the curriculum development process; not just as advisors, but actually helping to develop courses and plans of study (Della-Dora, 1979). In California, for example, the legislature has mandated (The Ryan Act) that any school district receiving state funds for curriculum and/or staff development must have a School Site Council and that half of its members must be parents (Della-Dora, 1979). Colleges and universities in California that offer a teacher credential program must describe how it will involve parents (and other community people) in planning for, carrying out, and evaluating these programs (Della-Dora, 1979). Many are calling for more of this type of citizen involvement in the actual formation of the materials to be studied in the schools, although use of citizens in this capacity is certainly not widespread (Brandt, 1979).

It is clear that citizens can be an effective force as partners with the schools. Such interaction can build academic skill in children, self-esteem in parents, and positive feelings in the community. As Rich and her colleagues point out:

> The involvement of parents in the education of their own children means building a program as it should be built, from the bottom up, rather than from the top down. It creates a foundation of support and commitment for other kinds of involvement efforts (such as changes in the school and community). It may also obviate the need for many other kinds of public relations efforts as families begin to understand what is really involved in the education of children. (1979, p. 30)

NETWORKING AND THE SCHOOLS—BARRIERS AND INCENTIVES: WHERE DO WE GO FROM HERE?

In our review of existing programs, a number of issues related to the encouragement or restriction of naturally occurring support systems that could both enhance the lives of those involved in schools and reinforce the educational process itself have been alluded to and discussed. A brief summary of these barriers and incentives to social support networks will serve to conclude our discussion and focus our attention on ways in which we can promote the use of social support networks in the schools.

BARRIERS

Although there are many barriers to the greater use of "natural helpers" in educational settings, two common themes emerge. First, despite our universal experience in the public schools and the supposedly high value we place on citizen control of education, the American love of experts still shines through. As almost any teacher will affirm, most Americans want the schools to "just do their job" and not bother them with requests for help or offers of opportunities for participation. One need only attend parent functions at most schools to see how hard it is to get the community to take an active part in the education of their children. Most people want the schools to handle their problems quietly, and with a high degree of success, even though we as citizens and parents may have created many of the difficulties. As we have seen, typical examples of citizen involvement in the schools are attending a high school football game or serving as a "room mother" who prepares cookies for an elementary school class. There is certainly nothing wrong with that kind of participation, but we can do much more. However, citizen apathy or a vague "leave it to the expert" notion on the part of parents is not totally responsible.

Schools themselves do much to exclude parents and other citizens. Our educational institutions give community members very little real power in making decisions (except for school boards, and one could challenge their independence from the influence of district officials). Maybe citizens are not involved in schools because they want something real to do in the schools. They want to know that their actions make a difference (Brandt, 1979), and they know that currently that is not the case. If schools want citizen input, then they need to give up some of their own power and trust more in the people who support them; yet, we have seen that in many instances they will not. Our discussion of citizen advisory boards is a prime example. As we have observed, most of these boards have been so dominated by the professionals that their decisions have been merely rubber-stamp approvals of current district or school policy.

Many of the compensatory education programs of the 1960's founded on a family deficit model gave parents much the same message. By assuming that parents cannot really help their children without some kind of massive intervention to make up for their (the parents') shortcomings, we were telling families that we did not want their input and, furthermore, that they were incapable of giving any. This message is not reserved just for low-income families, but is given to many citizens who wish to be involved in the schools (Della-Dora, 1979).

A more useful approach may be to give citizens the opportunity for action along with the knowledge that they can make differences in their communities and in the education of their children. Those of low socioeconomic status need to know that the schools understand their problems and will be responsive to their needs. To be helpful, the schools must listen and then respond. Currently, however, the schools do most of the talking and thus are more foe than friend (deLone, 1979). It seems that while our "leave it to the experts" notion may be an explanation for citizen apathy, it is not the cause. Although lack of citizen participation and the withholding of power by the schools go hand-in-hand, one appears to cause the other, and we suspect the schools.

The second major theme regarding barriers to the further use of helping networks in the school is confusion about the role of the school in our society. We have seen that teachers, students, administrators, and communities seem isolated from each other and many times act in opposing directions, even though they are supposedly working toward the same ends. Much of this results from what appears to be a conflict between the actions of the school system and its stated objectives. That is, we want all of our young people to get the "basic skills" needed for success in our society, but the schools are organized and operated as a sorting mechanism. We seem intent on catching students who have not acquired the prerequisites for success in our society and punishing them, rather than insisting on the mastery of those skills. We have a common goal, a *collective* end, but we are trying to get there through *individualistic* means. As long as students are encouraged to compete with their peers, rather than help them, and teachers and administrators are asked to succeed or fail in isolation, we shall, in one sense, be defeating ourselves. The high regard for individual autonomous action, which the organization and evaluatory schemes of the school engender in both students and faculty, is the antithesis of the kind of collective activity we have been discussing—activity, which, as we have seen, could be so beneficial in reaching our common goal. The individualistic nature of the school in general, and the competitive process of student evaluation, in particular, separate students from one another and parents from schools. The only real support system students have for academic success is their family. It is students and parents versus the school. With the credentials inflation present in today's society, success or failure in that contest is psychologically, socially, and economically important.

It is no wonder, then, that the inability of our educational system to provide the basics to 20% or more of its clients (as well as problems in school experienced by many "successful students") results in a rash of finger-pointing and blaming rather than serving as a cause for reexamining and rededicating our efforts. Parents blame teachers and administrators; teachers and administrators blame students, parents, and communities; these groups feel the need to look out for their own interests, and professional organizations or special interest lobbies result. Some of this is helpful because it creates a dialogue that airs differing views within the context of public debate. However, this seems to have gone too far.

Certainly, with the vast number of people who have a stake in the schools, we are rarely if ever going to reach total agreement on a particular issue or set of issues, but at this point we seem more set on satisfying our own needs than on guaranteeing universal success to our students. There may be a fine line between encouraging opposing points of view and squabbling among ourselves, but we must resolve this problem. Much of the support we could lend to each other is negated when we become so afraid of losing our personal rights that we feel we have to close ourselves off from others. Our schools are *not* cooperative institutions as far as students are concerned, at least in terms of the development of academic skills (Garbarino and Asp, 1981). The natural connections among and between us could help change that if we can somehow allow them to grow and take advantage of their existence.

On a more positive note, several incentives to the use of networks have emerged in the course of our discussion. As we pointed out many times, Americans profess a high regard for education and see the need for it. Also, we are willing to become involved in the schools and believe that they are relatively worthwhile institutions. Several items from recent Gallup polls (1980, 1981) point this out. When asked if they were willing to become involved in a more direct way in their local schools, 90% of those citizens responding (from a national probability sample) answered yes. Also, respondents valued the schools as an institution over others such as Congress, state government, organized labor, and big business. Along the same line, a large percentage of respondents wanted more contact with the schools and thought that school–community relations could be improved. They put forth the following as means to that end (Gallup, 1981):

1. *Better communication.* The local community cannot be expected to take a keen interest in the schools if people know little about them. The media should carry much more school news, especially news about the achievement of students and the schools, the means being taken to deal with school problems, and new developments in education. Media research has shown that there is far greater interest in schools and in education than most journalists think. At the

same time, the schools should not rely solely on the major media. Newsletters are important to convey information that the media cannot be expected to report.

2. *More conferences.* Many of those included in the survey recommend that more conferences about the progress and problems of students be held with parents—both father and mother. Special monthly parent meetings and workshops are also suggested as a way to bring teachers, administrators, and parents together. Survey respondents also recommend courses for parents and special lectures. PTA meetings, some suggest, could be more useful to parents if school problems and educational developments were given more attention.

3. *Invite volunteers.* Some respondents suggest that, if more members of the community could serve in a volunteer capacity in the classrooms and elsewhere in the school, they would further better community understanding of the problems faced by the schools. In addition, their involvement in school operations would increase their own interest in educational improvement at the local level.

4. *Plan special occasions.* Interest in the schools and in education could be improved, some suggest, by inviting members of the community—both those who have children in the schools and those who do not—to attend meetings, lectures, and social events in the school buildings.

The public's suggestions are similar to those we have made. Clearly, Americans want to be involved in their schools.

Other incentives for using social support systems to enhance the work of the schools include the factors of low-cost and local control. In an era of retrenchment, of declining resources, the low-cost option of helping each other to educate our children becomes even more appealing. We have already seen some figures indicating how remediation might be accomplished at a much lower cost through use of social support systems. Also, when so much of what we do in schools is regulated by federal and state agencies, the idea of improving education without the need for federal and state aid and their concomitant regulation is good news to many.

Finally, the structures for social support are already in place. Students naturally turn to each other for help, as do teachers and parents (and as administrators would like to). Why not let them do so and provide incentives to ensure such action? Communities and schools are mutually dependent systems. Why not encourage that dependency and exploit this relationship for the good of all? Some programs, as we have seen, have already done so, but much could still be done.

WHERE DO WE GO FROM HERE?

Operating from the assumption that social support systems are a valuable and underused (if not ignored) resource for education, there are several steps we can take to encourage their development and utilization. First, we can encourage research on their effectiveness, research that examines more than relatively easily measured outcomes, such as gains on achievement tests.

For example, we need information about enhancing the quality of professional life for administrators and teachers and how that might affect academic outcomes. We also need to study what results from more citizen input in the organization and operation of the school. In this instance, we need to examine the effects on both parties involved. Research in other areas could be beneficial as well—for instance, the role of social support networks in helping schools deal with social issues such as desegregation, teenage drug abuse, adolescent sexuality, and declining enrollment. In short, we need to know more about the usefulness of this resource and where it can be the most helpful.

Second, we need to expand our ideas of how schools might be of service to communities. The "community school" movement is a good example. Proponents of this modification of the role of schools want them to be open almost 24 hours a day, providing a variety of services above and beyond the education of children (Gordon, 1979a,b). The school would open its doors to students of all ages and also provide facilities for community recreation (Markun, 1973). Thus, the school may house K–12 programs during the day and adult education or craft programs at night. The Mott Foundation has done much to encourage the development of this idea in the United States. The concept of community education centers goes even further. As Clincy states:

> The notions of joint occupancy and multiple use of space grow naturally into the idea of creating not just schools but public facilities that serve a wide variety of community purposes—adult education, day care, services for the elderly, employment centers, recreation for old and young, vocational training, social casework services, legal aid, and places for people to simply get together and enjoy themselves.
> The need for a new school may, in many cases, be the catalyst for the creation of such broadly based community centers, but the aim is to create a new institution that is far more useful to more people than the conventional school. (1973, p. 27)

This leads to our third and final point. Schools need to join the ranks of human services. We need networks between community groups (such as those attempting to revitalize neighborhoods and those trying to help schools) and professionals who are working within the community (e.g., teachers and social workers). For too long schools have been excluded from membership in the human service field. Even our federal government sets schools apart from human assistance agencies. Schools and other social service providers need to depend on and support each other. For example, the schools can do much to aid in the prevention and identification of child abuse, and social workers and family counselors can provide teachers with valuable information regarding the out-of-school factors affecting student performance.

Promoting informal contacts among these professionals will greatly enhance the likelihood that they will call on each other for help. Community groups can unite to support each other in the same way. Interestingly, the Institute for Responsive Education calls this process *networking* and has been studying how to promote the sharing of resources and information among various citizens interest groups (NSPRA, 1977).

Social support networks are a viable and valuable means of enhancing the work of the professionals in the schools. Many existing programs have been shown to be effective, and there is great potential for further use of this resource in education. Professional and lay people alike can do much to promote the utilization of these natural helping systems and thus help to stem the increasing tide of isolation of schools from their clients. We must realize that we may have made a mistake in isolating education from the rest of the world, and especially from the life of the immediate community that surrounds the school. Perhaps what children need is not just to learn to read, write, and figure, but also to grasp what the larger society is all about, to experience it as it really is, and to begin to understand how it operates and what their place in it might be. One commentator puts it:

> In order to do this, it is important to make "school" into a place where all sorts of things are happening, especially *adult* activities—shopping, recreation, offices, adult education centers, political activities, day care, social assistance agencies, and so on. Such activities not only broaden the education of children, but they also contribute to the community as a whole. In short, schools may become only one part of much larger community centers that share programs and facilities as time and common sense dictate. Perhaps the entire community can become the educational system. (Clincy, 1973, pp. 25–26)

SOURCES OF ADDITIONAL INFORMATION

PEER TUTORING

Allen, V. (Ed.). *Children as teachers*. New York: Academic Press, 1976.

Allen, V., & Feldman, R. Learning through tutoring: low-achieving children as tutors. *Journal of Experimental Education*, 1974, *42*, 1–5.

Cloward, R. Studies in tutoring. *The Journal of Experimental Education*, 1967, *36*, 14–25.

Devin-Sheehan, L., Feldman, R., & Allen, V. Research on children tutoring children: A critical review. *Review of Educational Research*, 1976, *46*, 355–385.

Granowsky, A., Middleton, F., & Mumford, J. Parents as partners in education. *The Reading Teacher*, 1979, *32*, 826–830.

Landrum, J., & Martin, M. When students teach others. *Educational Leadership*, 1970, *27*, 446–448.

Mainiero, J., Gillogly, B., Nease, O., Sherertz, D., & Wilkinson, P. *A cross-age teaching resource manual*. Ontario-Montclair, PA. School District, 1971. (Funded under Title III, Elementary and Secondary Education Act of 1965.)

Richardson, D., & Havilcek, L. High-school students as reading instructors. *Elementary School Journal*, 1975, *75*, 384–393.

Weinstein, G., Ungerleider, C., Preston, F., Osborn, C., & Bannister, L. *Youth tutoring youth*. New York: National Commission on Resources for Youth, Inc., 1970.

Wolf, A. *Tutoring is caring*. Altoona, PA: Aldine D. Wolf, 1976.

PEER COUNSELING

Frank, M., Ferdinand, B., & Bailey, W. Peer group counseling: A challenge to grow. *The School Counselor*, 1975, *22*, 267–272.

Kern, R., & Kirby, J. Utilizing peer helper influence in group counseling. *Elementary School Guidance and Counseling*, 1971, *6*, 70–75.

Mosher, R., & Sprinthall, N. Psychological education: A means to promote personal development during adolescence. *The Counseling Psychologist*, 1971, *2*, 3–92.

Robert, M. *Loneliness in the schools (What to do about it)*. Niles, IL: Argus Communications, 1974.

Samuels, M., & Samuels, D. *The complete handbook of peer counseling*. Miami, FL: Fiesta, 1975.

PARENT GROUPS

Brandt, R. (Ed.). *Partners: Parents and schools*. Alexandria, VA: Association for Supervision and Curriculum Development, 1979.

Davies, D. *Schools where parents make a difference*. Boston: Institute for Responsive Education, 1977.

National Committee for Citizens in Education. *Parents organizing to improve schools*. Columbia, MD: National Committee for Citizens in Education, 1976.

National School Public Relations Association. *Linking schools and the community*. Arlington, VA: National School Public Relations Association, 1977.

Rioux, W. *You can improve your child's school*. New York: Simon and Schuster, 1980.

TEACHER–ADMINISTRATOR PEER NETWORKS

Bird, D. The key word is survival. *NAASP Bulletin*, 1977, *62*, 12–15.

Brown, G., & Carlton, P. How to conquer stress when you can and cope with it when you can't. *National Elementary Principal*, 1980, *59*, 37–39.

Cichon, D., & Koff, R. Stress and teaching. *NASSP Bulletin*, 1980, *64*, 91–103.

Erlandson, D., & Pastor, M. Teacher motivation, job satisfaction, and alternatives—Directions for principals. *NASSP Bulletin*, 1981, *65*, 5–9.

Galloway, C., Seltzer, M., & Truman, W. Exchange and mutuality: Growth conditions for teacher development. *Theory into Practice*, *19*, 262–270.

Grossnickle, R. A life support system for teachers. *Clearing House*, 1978, *54*, 135–137.

Hendrikson, B. Teacher burnout: How to recognize it, what to do about it. *Learning*, 1980, *7*, 37–39.

Lortie, D. *Schoolteacher: A sociological study*. Chicago: University of Chicago Press, 1975.

Reed, S. What you can do to prevent teacher burnout. *National Elementary School Principal*, 1980, *59*, 67–70.

Ricken, R. Teacher burnout—A failure of the supervisory process. *NASSP Bulletin*, 1980, *64*, 21–24.

Rogus, J., & Martin, M. The principal and staff development: Countering the school culture. *NASSP Bulletin*, 1979, *63*, 81–87.

Sanders, D., & Schwab, M. A school context for teacher development. *Theory into Practice*, *19*, 271–277.

Young, B. Anxiety and stress—How they affect teachers teaching. *NASSP Bulletin*, 1978, *62*, 78–83.

PARENT AND CITIZEN INVOLVEMENT IN THE SCHOOLS

Ainsworth, E. Parent involvement in schools. A parent's view. *Thrust for Educational Leadership*, 1977, *6*, 6–8.

Brandt, R. (Ed.). *Partners: Parents and schools*. Alexandria, VA: Association for Supervision and Curriculum Development, 1979.

Carter, M. *School and community: Partners in problem solving*. Chicago: Center for New Schools, 1976.

Craft, M., Raynor, J., & Cohen, L. (Eds.). *Linking home and school*. London: Longmans, Green, 1967.

Davies, D. *Schools where parents make a difference*. Boston: Institute for Responsive Education, 1977.

Devault, M. *Parent involvement in your school*. Bulletin No. 9142, Madison, WI: Wisconsin State Department of Public Instruction, 1977.

Granowsky, A., Middleton, F., & Mumford, J. Parents as partners in education. *The Reading Teacher*, 1979, *32*, 826–830.

Hager, D. *Community involvement for classroom teachers*. Charlottesville, VA: Community Collaborators (P.O. Box 5429), 1977.

Home and School Institute. *Families learning together*. Washington, DC: Home and School Institute, 1979.

Litwak, E., & Meyer, H. *School, family and neighborhood: Theory and practice of school–community relations*. New York: Columbia University Press, 1974.

Miller, S. *Bringing learning home*. New York: Harper and Row, 1981.

National Education Association, *Parent–teacher cooperation*. Washington, DC: National Education Association, 1979.

National School Public Relations Association. *Linking schools and the community*. Arlington, VA: National School Public Relations Association, 1977.

Rioux, W. *You can improve your child's school*. New York: Simon and Schuster, 1980.

Sikula, R. A crucial issue, school–community relations: A systematic approach. *NASSP Bulletin*, 1980, *65*, 55–62.

Walberg, H., Bole, R., & Waxman, H. School-based family socialization and reading achievement in the inner city. *Psychology in the Schools*, 1980, *117*, 509–514.

Williams, B., & Dale, E. Volunteer programs give big payoffs. *Thrust for Educational Leadership*, 1980, *9*, 24–26.

ORGANIZATIONAL RESOURCES

Center for the Study of Parent Involvement
2544 Etna Street
Berkeley, California 94704

Institute for Responsive Education
704 Commonwealth Avenue
Boston, Masachusetts 02215

National Committee for Citizens in Education
Suite 410
Wild Lake Village Green
Columbia, Maryland 21044

National School Volunteer Program
300 N. Washington Street
Alexandria, Virginia 22314

Office of Citizen Participation
U.S. Department of Education
Washington, D.C. 20036

Operation PUSH-EXCEL Program
930 East 50th Street
Chicago, Illinois 60615

CHAPTER 10
Social Support Networks in Services for Adolescents and Their Families

Richard Barth

Adolescents and their families increasingly require mental health, juvenile justice, medical, and child welfare servies (Bernstein, Snider, & Meezan, 1975; President's Commission on Mental Health, 1978; Sarri, 1980). Unfortunately, formal services for troubled youth are scarce and plagued by inadequate funding, mistrust from youth, and uncertain outcomes (McCord, 1978). At the same time, adolescents and their families underestimate their own needs and under-enroll in available services (Burke & Weir, 1978). Social support networks offer a fresh resource for families and youth struggling with the conflicts of adolescence.

This chapter addresses the use of social support networks on behalf of adolescents and their families. The first section considers the stresses of adolescence as they influence the family and how peer and family social supports can ameliorate these stresses. Next the chapter details the uses of social supports in problems specific to this population: during family crises, with runaways, for gay and prostituting youth, on behalf of teenage parents, and with incest victims. The final section considers preventive and clinical uses of social support networks along with impediments to clinical application.

STRESSES AND AMELIORATIVE SOCIAL SUPPORTS

Adolescents and their families encounter myriad social and developmental stresses, often without full awareness of their influence. Preteen menarche, blended families, high school preprofessionalism, and limited employment account for but a few. Suicide, throwaways, sexual and physical abuse, and assault may result. The magnitude and range of conflict for this trouble-prone group is quite evident; few continue to regard adolescence as a romantic period of rebellion, search, and freedom, or a carefree hiatus between childhood and adulthood. Indeed, because adolescents are neither children nor adults, they do not receive the privileges and services given to their younger and older counterparts.

Families of adolescents may contribute to the irregular ways of their teenage offspring. Some parents enter a transitional stage of their own along with their children, and then both suffer restlessness and crisis (Stierlin, 1974; Levinson et al., 1978). Parents may even join youth "on the run." Since they are increasingly transient and tend to be employed full-time, parents have few opportunities to develop close relationships outside the family; at one time, such relationships might have absorbed family stress. Separation and divorce, once localized to the beginning years of marriage, increasingly claim partners with adolescent children. More than a million new children experience first-hand family dissolution each year (Bureau of the Census, 1980).

Family and personal transitions are occurring amid legal commotion. The partial deregulation of such "status" offenses as truancy, drinking, and running away blurs and weakens societal support for family units. Similarly, deinstitutionalization creates new problems even while solving old ones (Levine, 1977). The law can no longer contain adolescent–parent conflict with therapeutic rulings or mandated referrals for family treatment. Crisis and family-reunification centers in juvenile detention centers across the states have been closed or repopulated by youth charged with adult crimes.

Changes in sexuality also introduce complications for adolescents and families. Adolescents' earlier puberty and sexual activity is manifest in more and earlier pregnancies, higher rates of venereal disease, and an increased awareness of alternative sexual habits (Institute of Medicine, 1978; Gilchrist & Schinke, in press). More incidents of the sexual abuse of male and female adolescents by fathers, kin, and siblings have been reported (Garbarino, 1980a), possibly one consequence of the blended home with its potential for obscuring already weakened incest prohibitions. As adolescents more often identify themselves as gay, they confuse parents, siblings, peers, counselors, and often themselves (Malyon, 1981). Typifying the sexual conundrum, runaways may leave sexually abusive families only to be raped and enlisted in the growing corps of teenage prostitutes (Lloyd, 1976; Miller et al., 1980).

The remedies of adolescents and their families for their ills may be no better than the disease; family violence, alcohol abuse, and running away often arise from efforts to manage family conflict. Thus, adolescents are victims of one-third of all child batteries (Garbarino, Potter, & Carson, 1977) and probably an even greater percentage of sexual molestations. Drinking by one or both parties (parent or child) often sets the scene for sexual and physical assaults (Meiselman, 1978; Strauss et al., 1980). Parental alcohol use is also a powerful predictor of running away (Van Houten & Golembiewski, 1978). Subsequently, runaways themselves frequently try to manage the stress of nomadic life with alcohol; one in three engages in self-abusive drinking (Miller et al., 1980).

Just as strong families absorb the distress of their adolescents, social supports protect families from stress. Adequate social supports from peers—other families, neighbors, and friends—can defend families against conflicts that would otherwise result in the need for formal services. The following section reviews informal supports available to families and peers, along with limitations and possibilities for helping.

SOCIAL SUPPORTS FOR FAMILIES

Families, like individuals, use social supports to buffer stress (Stack, 1974; Sandler & Block, 1979; Albee, 1980; Gad & Johnson, 1980; Sandler, 1980). Even though cultural norms emphasize family self-sufficiency, insularity, and independence (Keniston, 1977), exchanges between family members and their environment are ongoing and profound (Caplan & Killilea, 1976; Powell, 1979). Parent and adolescent relationships, marital functioning, and child–school contacts all benefit from a surrounding network of others, both young and old (Burke & Weir, 1977, 1978, 1979; Cochran & Brassard, 1979). Conversely, families isolated from supports are vulnerable to medical and psychosocial difficulty (Garbarino, 1976; Andrews et al.,1978; Hotaling, Atwell, & Linsky, 1978).

Families support each other in naturally informal ways. They help one another prevent accumulations of intolerable stress, manage crises, and adapt to family decomposition (Froland & Pancoast, 1979). Often serving as lay consultants on the need for professional care, kin seem to provide the first line of defense (Rosenblatt & Mayer, 1972; Turner, Kimbrough, & Traynham, 1977; McAdoo, 1978). Kin may be "neighbors and friends who are close" (Stack, 1974, p. 38). Such extended social networks provide background support for caregiving efforts and directly affect children by providing cognitive and social stimulation, as well as opportunities to engage in significant social relations (Cochran & Brassard, 1979).

Gaining stamina and stability from outside resources, families pass the benefits on to youthful members (Caplan & Killilea, 1976). Broadly based support systems, composed of friends of all ages, work associates, neighbors, and retailers, provide the family with material and emotional aid, referents and models for behavior, sources of information, and breathers from stress (Powell, 1979). Networks supportive of families exchange goods and services ranging from informal adoption of children to needed furniture to car pools; emotional support is similarly traded. Some cultures demand strict adherence to the "reciprocity rule"; that is, people share generously because they know their efforts will be returned (Stack, 1974). Others share cautiously. However shared, social supports inoculate families emotionally and materially against stress and give them the strength needed to help their young people during transitional crisis.

Further social networks press families to adopt values and practices congruent with their own ecologies. Thus, families who accept their adolescent as merely independent may discover that others regard him or her as highly delinquent. Conversely, families using physically coercive child-management techniques may be censured by kindred families. Also families may recapitulate their own closeness or conflict within their multi-family support networks.

Enlisting Family Supports. *Webster's Dictionary* notwithstanding, peers are not just "same-aged individuals"; families also have peers. Too little is written or done, however, to help families act as resources for one another. Family-to-family supports can help transcend parent–youth polarization. For example, parents often observe the discrepancy between their child's behavior with them and his or her behavior with network members. How many parents have made comments to themselves (or even out loud) like this one? "My son is so grizzly with me, but he talks to Mrs. Green for an hour— and while fixing her door! He won't even start his chores at home without a fight. And, I know Mrs. Green's daughter bickers constantly at her mother, but treats me like an old friend. Hmm!" At these and other times, parents contemplate informal child swapping, probably a thousand times for each time it is attempted. But the potential of this and other less dramatic forms of family-to-family supports remains largely unexplored.

Family-to-family helping is unfortunately limited, since not only do adolescents have trouble getting along with their families, but their families also have trouble getting along with them. Parents are often as embarrassed about this conflict as their offspring, and this embarrassment frequently breeds isolation and leaves families without needed allies. Cut off from referents provided by social supports, such families may soon suffer from shifting norms. That is, as family conflict escalates, youths or parents (and usually both) adopt increasingly extreme behavior. Soon they forget reasoned and reasonable patterns of interaction, and screaming, hitting, room searches, stealing, and quasi-extortion become routine. Such families, and there are many, find room in their homes for almost any act short of lethal abuse and family breakup.

Family therapy recognizes the value of using allies and social supports in helping. Often practiced in juvenile halls and youth service bureaus, family therapy relies on the social supports of nonrelated significant others and multiple treatment personnel. As one example, the Mental Research Institute in Palo Alto, California, uses as many as five adjunct therapists to observe family sessions. They relay suggestions by phone to therapists or family members who join the family in the therapy room. Serving as social supports to the family and the therapist, these auxiliary professionals provide information, hope, breathers, and alternative perspectives.

Networking incorporates family and friends to an even greater extent (Rueveni, 1979). Although still a therapeutic rather than a natural helping process, networking respects the potential of the natural support system to effect change. Network therapists insist that families assemble a large and diverse network and that network meetings continue after professional workers withdraw. Networks tolerate the risks and short-term inefficiencies of tribal therapy to tap the irrational and incomparable commitment of friends and family. Whether they cite scriptures at ungodly moments, or "get high" before family meetings, network members are available and committed to family long after the social worker has become an administrator. Family and friends also provide assistance that professionals cannot or will not provide, such as a timely visit to Juvenile Hall, a restraining word after one too many Quaaludes, a second opinion on the merits of an older suitor, a partner for practicing an overdue confrontation with an adolescent daughter, or clarifications about birth control. By enlisting participants, by modeling problem solving and realistic goal setting, and by encouraging ongoing work, networkers tap the strengths of the extended family and friends.

Families can also come together under the auspices of self-help. For example, the common bond of living in an alcoholic home may be uniting. Alcoholic families (especially AA families) share an understanding of the periodic shame, crises, anger, and hopelessness of life in alcoholic homes. Adolescents in Alateen learn that they have the right and will have the need to get away from their own families at times. Thus, they may stay over with the Al-Anon sponsor of their Alateen chapter, or, on occasion, with their teenage sponsor. Yet staying over at another alcoholic home is not always a respite. In the best of circumstances, neighbors and friends who live in sober homes will also provide respite care.

SOCIAL SUPPORTS FOR YOUTH

Just as networks bring information to families, families bring it to youth. The family provides the adolescent with guidelines for judgment, with discipline or violations of the family code, and with rewards for compliance. Adolescents learn family values, traditions, and myths, and may gain explicit instruction about facts, strategies, and referrals that mediate stress (Turner, Kimbrough, & Traynham, 1977). Families also offer adolescents refuge from work or school, from economic strain, and from conflict arising within the broader network (Wahler, 1980a).

Social service providers increasingly recognize the value of family support for youth. Even as early emancipation from the family is made more possible with expressly designed social service programs, the unique contributions of the family deserve recognition. Economic and social constraints diminish youth's opportunities to attend vocational training or college, rent an apartment, join a union, or buy a car. On their own, adolescent parents, runaways, or minors court personal and economic bankruptcy. Intact families and supportive networks are a great boon to adolescent development.

Although the potential of natural support networks to enhance family cohesion is clear, its realization is uncertain. Whether extended families are romantic fictions or an endangered species, few will claim that they are currently vital—except perhaps for minority families in poverty (Hays & Mindel, 1973; Allen, 1979). Otherwise, families are often insulated by transience, mistrust, abridged leisure time, and embarrassing divorce and marital conflict. In fact, Howell argues that professional services may inadvertently contribute to the undoing of families' support for each other:

> The use of social support networks and mutual help groups . . . will be increased when families put faith in their own abilities to solve problems and recognize that while complex and scholarly procedures exist for helping, healing, and changing behavior, many ancient and folky bits of knowledge exist. The hopeless, helpless family is not our only alternative to a dependent reliance on professional services. We are not locked into the choice that experts have presented to use between isolated, secretive, scarce-resource "nuclear" families—deficient in the ability to care for individual family members and threatened by guilt-ridden failure at every turn—and an invasion of paternalistic strangers providing professional resources and services. (1975, p. 49)

Howell's critique is only one argument for enlisting volunteers, kin, neighbors, and naturally helping peers to help families stay intact and build the competencies of all members.

Peer-to-Peer Social Supports. Peers are as necessary to adolescent socialization as family (Hartup, 1979). Research and common knowledge agree that youth are very concerned with their peers (Thornburg, 1971). Peers have strong influence on one another, provide opportunities to observe skillful models, to try out new ways, to gain feedback on their performance (however indirect or coded), and to receive rewards for pursuing autonomy from families. As one observer notes, "the teenager measures his whole being by the reactions of his peers" (Wagner, 1971, p. 53). As an illustration, adolescents are more stimulated to violence by watching peers act violently than by watching adults (Hicks, 1965; Cohen, 1971). Peer influence is, of course, equally capable of shaping leadership, altruism, and commitment (Wispe, 1978).

Impediments to Peer Helping. Tapping the advantages of peer influence and social support for troubled youth is no small matter; on their own, adolescents have difficulty gaining access to the full benefits of social supports. Most adolescent peer helping focuses on material provisions: cigarettes, money, and food (Todd, 1979). Teens do not confide easily about personal and family problems, perhaps because showing that one knows everything, as opposed to showing uncertainty, is rewarded with social status. Youth with serious family problems may suffer even more isolation, since adolescents' preoccupation with independence and autonomy leaves little room for peer discussions of family concerns and ties. Being hip is being carefree. Thus, same-age relationships are frequently tightly knit but lonely (Al-Anon Family Groups, 1973; *D&SU We Love You*, 1980).

Reaching youth outside the mainstream is especially perplexing. In a study of helping in high school, Todd (1979) found that marginal youth are often alienated and at odds with school rules and authorities and, although routinely engaging in informal interaction with adults, rarely seek or accept aid from adults. In describing the difficulty of enlisting unconventional youth in mainstream relationships or networks, Todd captures some complexities of adult-to-adolescent helping:

> These boys do seem responsive to a strong expression of self-confidence, concern, patience and above all straightforwardness on the part of adults. In contrast, the teacher who is tolerant without expecting anything is taken advantage of, and the adult who makes demands arbitrarily is rebelled against, or, if possible, avoided. *Under these conditions, it is the rare adult who is effective, and trying is more often stigmatizing than it is encouraged and rewarded. . . .* Prerequisite to any valid change is the development among school adults of a spirit of receptive and respectful inquiry into the interests, orientations, and prejudices of tribe boys. Most of the people who counsel and teach (and do research!) are not prepared to make sense of a culture that is organized around events that seem to them insignificant. (1979, p. 185)

Even such established peer self-help groups as Alateen face knotty problems in helping adolescents support one another. Getting and keeping requisite Al-Anon sponsors is one difficulty for Alateen groups. Among the reasons Al-Anons gave for not sponsoring Alateen groups at a sponsor recruitment meeting were: "Might as well stay at home with my own kids," foul language, discipline problems, and confidentiality conflicts. Scrapes with the parents of participating teens are common, since sponsors who discipline Alateen group members risk the ire of the members' parents. Paradoxically, developing strong attachments between sponsors and teens also risks anger, jealousy, and censure. Alateen sponsors may end up as outsiders among their own peers, since other Al-Anon members may fear the disclosures of their adolescent children. Inadequate spot-relief to cover sponsor absences and teens' mistrust of Al-Anons who did not themselves grow up in an alcoholic situation also discourage sponsorship.

As difficult as finding adults willing and able to help teens build support networks is finding youth to participate in peer support programs—whether group therapy, hot lines, network therapy, or one-to-one counseling. Finding capable and willing leaders who are credible to their often less conventional peers is one challenge. One peer-to-peer high school program in the Seattle area used a school-wide vote to select natural helpers. Even though chosen by their peers, involvement in peer-to-peer training led to jealousy and resentment about the new clique of helpers. Although many helpers tried to stay anonymous but act more skillfully when helping situations arose, full anonymity was rarely possible. Travel to training retreats, participation in on-site training, and fellow helpers' indiscrete disclosures readily identified program members. Such side effects of participation in the natural helpers program may dampen students' excitement about their roles.

Even youth who are capable and eager to engage in peer-to-peer helping may find themselves discouraged because helping seems slow or impossible and the hoped-for appreciation from youthful helpees is not forthcoming. Finally, pressed for time by other employment and learning requirements, these volunteers too commonly fade away or quit (Fine, Knight-Webb, & Vernon, 1977). Other teens, even those screened by professionals, may be judgmental, easily panicked, timid, unknowingly sarcastic, homophobic, or prone to confusing their own issues with their clients' (Bauer, 1975). And, however qualified and willing, adolescent helpers finally age and leave.

Peer Training. With quality training, peer helpers can reach many contemporaries and offer high-quality support. Although the efficacy of peer helping is not well documented, two effective programs use well-trained peer leaders (Ross & McKay, 1976; Perry *et al.*, 1980). Less satisfying results in other programs have been attributed to insufficient training (Bauer, 1975; Fine, Knight-Webb, & Vernon, 1977).

Peer training often focuses on paraphrasing, direct communication, active listening, awareness of community resources, and referral (Golin & Safferston, 1971; Dellworth *et al.*, 1974; Gray & Tindall, 1978a). However, material on promoting social support networks might in part replace or supplement the empathy–communications approach to peer counselor training. Such a curriculum might include two new features: (1) methods for helping youth mobilize social support networks, and (2) stages of the networking process. Thus, peer helpers might first learn to assist helpers in identifying sources of emotional support, information, materials, and services, and survival skills. After this systematic resource identification, helpers might learn skills in problem solving and behavioral rehearsal for assisting peers in gaining help from their own networks.

In conjunction, teaching peer helpers the stages of the networking process might enhance skill and perseverance. In a simplification of Speck and Attneave's (1971) proposals, peer helpers might be informed that they are likely to encounter the following stages: (1) acquaintance with the person and problem, (2) action, (3) discouragement from setbacks and impasse, (4) overcoming new and persistent obstacles, and, one hopes, (5) relief and renewal with the passing of the immediate crisis. Predicting the discouragement stage may help youth—with their characteristic ideals and impatience—to avoid disillusionment and thus to forewarn other social support members about the difficulties of networking. To help them arrive at reasonable expectations, adolescents might also be informed that psychotherapists, educators, and caseworkers find even small behavior changes to be hard-won and significant. Such awareness will help preempt teen helpers' frustration when their efforts do not result in marked changes in situation or personality. Scaled-down expectations should increase self-rewards for predictably small helping accomplishments.

Clinicians will almost certainly have more difficulty promoting and maintaining peer-to-peer networks than they have with peer-to-adult or adult-to-adult networks. Hope, however, is justified. One strategy is to link troubled youth in therapy groups with less troubled peer participants. Exposure to each other's strengths and shortcomings can make the experience mutually valuable. Also, peer sponsorship benefits individual youth in various human service programs, its most promising use being to help youth venture into new and socially sanctioned lifestyles. Thus, gay youth can team up to come out of the closet and pregnant girls can reach out to other pregnant and parenting adolescents. Nonadmitting alcoholics, pimps, male prostitutes, and other self-styled youthful outcasts are less likely to welcome contact with reformed or conventional peers. The limits and possibilities of peer-to-peer aid will become clearer as clinical trials accumulate.

Even minor changes in educational curricula could encourage more widespread giving and receiving of peer aid. Schools continue to expose children and youth to prevention programming. Some districts mandate drug prevention classes; others welcome materials on preventing smoking, child abuse, marital dissolution, unwanted conceptions, and even prostitution. Fundamental to many of these programs is the teaching of decision making, problem solving, and communication skills (Gilchrist, Schinke, & Blythe, 1979). If each prevention curriculum emphasized the association between social support and well-being, mutual dependence might increase and problems decline. For example, teachers might encourage students to include others in their problem-solving processes. Students might learn to enlist peer help to pinpoint problems, brainstorm solutions, evaluate solutions and outcomes, and encourage second efforts. Class exercises and role plays might desensitize youth to the initial awkwardness of requesting help and show the superiority of collaborative over unilateral action.

SOCIAL SUPPORTS FOR FAMILY—ADOLESCENT PROBLEMS

Not only are they vital for preventing family dysfunction, but social supports can also be crucial to remediating adolescent problems. In addition to assisting adolescents with problems of criminality, education, and drug-taking (as discussed in related chapters), social supports help runaways, prostitutes, youth and parents in conflict, homosexuals, parents, and the sexually assaulted. The following section explores existing social support-based services for adolescents and their families (see Table 10-1), and proposes additional applications.

Table 10-1. Social support groups for families and adolescents

Social support group	Target group	Presenting problem	Mode of support	Setting	Professional role
Alateen (Al-Anon Family Group Headquarters; P.O. Box 182; Madison Square Garden; New York, NY 10159)	Youth in alcoholic homes	Participants need not have particular problems, although many suffer from psychological and interpersonal conflict	Regular weekly or semi-weekly meetings with adult sponsors; some peer sponsorship; occasional outings and "fun" activities	Often where AA meetings are held	No professional role. Adult Al-Anon sponsors do help recruit members and provide support. Adult leadership is minimized although disciplinary actions are often required
Daughters & Sons United (Institute of the Community as Extended Family; P.O. Box 952; San Jose, CA 95108)	Sexually abused youth	Sexual abuse of teens and preteens; often temporary family breakup	Groups; adult and peer sponsorship; newsletter	Mental health clinics, receiving homes, juvenile halls	Professionals guide the meetings, act as sponsors, and recruit volunteers
Gay Foster-Parents (Informal or via Youth Service Bureaus or County Extension Services)	Homeless gay youth	Youth need acceptance, positive role models, and to escape the vagaries of street life	Access to material resources; models of success; and a peer group	Homes of gay couples	Foster arrangements are often made informally, but can arise from agency initiative. Professionals may advocate for the licensing of gay homes and help recruit street youth

Federation of Parents and Friends of Lesbians and Gays (c/o Adele Starr; P.O. Box 24565; Los Angeles, CA 90024)	Parents troubled by having gay children	Family disruption, self-blame, anger, isolation	Supports for parents with discomfort because children are gay; assistance for youth in coming out to their parents; arranging for families to meet other gays; education for gay youth about homosexuality	Homes of parents, gay community centers, churches	Professional mental health workers and clergy participate as peers and often use their contacts to arrange for meeting space and guest speakers
Sisterhood of Black Single Parents (1360 Fulton Street; Room 423; Brooklyn, NY 11216)	Teenage parents	Participants need not have special problems, but are a high-risk group. Most need material and social support	Sponsorship by older black women; social events; childcare; models of success; money	Housing projects may facilitate initial contacts and cooperative childcare, but SBSPs could be operated in other urban, suburban, and rural settings	Black, single professionals—including lawyers, health professionals, and housing specialists—help the young parents to navigate through social and health systems
TOUGHLOVE (Community Service Foundation; P.O. Box 70; Sellersville, PA 18960)	Families in crisis	Potential runaways, family disruption	Group meetings; members help each other set limits and cope with community contacts	Public meeting halls and schools, but preferably not homes	Professionals developed the self-help manual, but chapters are designed to operate without professional help

FAMILY CRISIS

When parent–child conflict grows into parent–adolescent conflict, the change can be dramatic. Many youth use their increased opportunities, strength, and sexuality in ways their parents find difficult to accept or understand. Their actions may violate legal as well as familial constraints. Whatever the depth or breadth of discrepancies between adolescent and parental expectations for home life, families and adolescents often profit from informal assistance.

TOUGHLOVE. A new, promising, but unresearched self-help group for families depends heavily on between-family social support (York & York, 1980). When they were awakened by shotgun-toting police looking for their daughter, the founders of TOUGHLOVE, themselves professional counselors, reached out to other parents with law- or norm-violating children (Leo, 1981). The prescription they developed provides tight structure for the family and sets tough limits on adolescents. For TOUGHLOVE the key to maintaining this structure, or any consistent plan, is the support, caring, and concern from others who agree, i.e., the support group.

In keeping with this approach, TOUGHLOVE's self-help manual begins by underscoring the isolated struggles of parents with children in trouble. A crisis checklist helps parents feel less alone by asking them if they, too, think: "What's wrong with my kid?" "If I don't argue or yell it will get better," "I want to kill my kid," "God is punishing me," "I'm going to run away," "I'm sure nothing will work." The manual also lends community to distressed readers by identifying beliefs and actions shared by parents with disrupted family relationships, such as "I am crazy [or a monster or alone]," "I never should have had children," "My child is doomed," "My kid is crazy." Parents learn that they are not the only ones who make ineffectual efforts to resolve problems by pleading, listening, setting a good example, getting sick, screaming, threatening, locking their teenagers in their rooms, or protecting their child from natural, legal, and social consequences. The manual instructs parents to develop and maintain their own network:

> Call your best friend and say: I'm concerned about my teenager's behavior and I would like your help. Will you come to a meeting at my house? . . . Call another friend. . . . Call your relatives. So what if you have lied to them and covered up for your kid. You need help now, not fake opinions of your kid. . . . Call the parents of your teenager's friends. You cannot afford to be isolated. It does nothing for your crises. . . . Call other parents who have had difficulty with your kid. (York & York, 1980, pp. 41–42)

Once a group assembles, TOUGHLOVE guidelines help parents run the first meeting. The manual offers sample meeting agendas and foretells probable concerns, doubts, helpful approaches, activities, and responses of support group members. Again, membership in the support group is the cornerstone of this approach. Members help during prescheduled meetings and at times of crisis; they commonly accompany parents to court appointments and school conferences. To ameliorate the influences of anger and guilt and help maintain a firm bargaining position, support group members serve as intermediaries when runaways return or call home.

TOUGHLOVE does not disregard the difficulties of enlisting and working with a support group. Its manual predicts changes that parents will undergo in their relationship to their network. Thus, after the initial excitement, parents typically think that the dependence on the group is a bore and represents "babyish" behavior. They tire of other people's advice and problems. The manual helps parents anticipate their child's use of ridicule, threats, placations, and undermining to break the parent-to-group bond. Such evenhanded appraisals of the complexities of work with a supportive network are critical for preempting crises of confidence.

How capable are families of giving and receiving help from other families? As yet, no one knows. Nevertheless, this program suggests that cultural barriers traditionally isolating individuals and families can be moved—with family stress pushing from the rear, the promise of support pulling from the front, and reasoned instruction and example greasing the skids. That even two professional helpers learned what the support of their friends during crisis might do is itself a testimony to the possibilities of mutual family aid.

RUNAWAYS

Running away removes young people from intolerable situations—at least termporarily. Minors leave home under diverse circumstances—some leave home voluntarily, while others go on command. Some run to escape crisis, others to experience pleasure (Brennan, Huizinga, & Elliott, 1978). Many do not run far or stay away for long periods (Opinion Research Corporation, 1976), although more than ever runaways do not return to the long-term care of their families (Beyer, 1980). Whatever the causes, the outcomes for runaway youth and their families often include the ignominies of rape, disease, sexual slavery, violence, prostitution, and larceny.

Runaways, whether gay or straight, male of female, trade the certain intolerability or home for the uncertain promise of a new locale. Some tap networks of other runaways—Perhaps the most notorious example is that of Charles Manson whose "family" found him through the runaway grapevine. Certainly, many runaways carry with them the baggage of the poor peer-relations and a prospensity toward social estrangement (Adams, 1980). Hungry for membership in a caring network, unable to find one or to feel like they fit anywhere, runaways represent the essence of our culture's current ambivalence about attachment.

Few runaways seek contact with social service providers. As "aliens in their own land," runaways avoid people who are unappreciative and threatening to their independence (Miller et al., 1980). Even "throwaways," frequently blaming themselves for their status and harboring fears of future confrontations with parents, will shun formal services in order to avoid further rejection. This underserved cohort maintains its distance from standard adult service providers (Schipp & Vivian, 1982). The distance from professionals both necessitates and impedes the implementation of social support networks.

Social Supports for Runaways. Runaways, as different as they are similar, present special problems for social support networks. Runaway typologies, however, provide some logic for the application of social support networks (Brennan, 1980). Class 1 runaways are "not highly delinquent, and nonalienated" and differ from Class 2 runaways, who are "delinquent and alienated." Class 1 runaways fall into subtypes of young escapists from overcontrolling parents, middle-class loners, or partially emancipated, peer-oriented youth. Class 1 adolescents seem more amenable than Class 2 runaways to services that incorporate social support networking.

Families of Class 1 runaways differ little from those of nonrunaways (Nye, 1980). They can often profit from family therapy, school counseling, and social skills training (Adams, 1980). Social supports can complement such services in rebuilding runaways' attachments to their families, to the neighborhood–school community, or to both. For youths escaping overcontrolling parents, networking provides the family with information on reasonable norms, positive models of negotiation, and a boost to family morale (Rueveni, 1979).

Although they may be relatively open to networking, middle-class loners may be even more open to intense contacts with a single peer or adult. The strain at home may be eased by contact with peer-to-peer counselors (Gray & Tindall, 1978b), attachments at the work site (Steinberg et al., in press), and the instruction and incentives for building friendships provided by network members. Finally, the unrestrained, peer-directed youth may be ready for emancipation and not in need of "treatment." Nevertheless, these youth may need encouragement and skills in order to develop community-based supports that will help them through the initial adjustments of "not quite adult" life (Schenk & Schenk, 1978). A thorough network analysis, described below, may help runaways locate previously unrecognized social buffers of the stresses that precipitate running or follow emancipation.

PROSTITUTING AND GAY YOUTH

Runaway youth often find their own "social supports"—frequently older, street-wise, or settled adults drawn by adolescents' marketable sexuality.

The link between sexuality and runaways is familiar from newspapers and magazine articles and TV and from strips and bus depots in cities of all sizes. Runaways often assume one of three compromised sexual roles: male prostitutes, kept male homosexuals, and female prostitutes. Each role creates barriers as well as possibilities for social support networking.

At present, male adolescent prostitutes may outnumber their female counterparts. For many heterosexual male prostitutes, often the recipients and not the providers of fellatio, confusion about sexual identification is but one conflict. Still more punishing is the street hustler's constant fight with the police and the underlife of the street. Boy prostitutes are vulnerable to older, sometimes tougher customers—one 14-year-old was badly beaten when his customer found him sucking his thumb during sex (Lloyd, 1976).

These young men are dramatically alone. Few have pimps or stable mates or patrons. Boy prostitutes encounter violence and disease, and are oftimes arrested. They find social supports only temporarily in their "fellow chickens" and in friendly "chicken hawks." Doorways, rooftops, park benches, and beaches are considered home for many runaway–prostitutes. They have many opportunities for business, but few safe havens. *Where the Young Ones Are*, a guide to amusement parks, hamburger stands, beaches, and street corners across the United States where boys are available has reportedly sold 750,000 copies. There is no doubt that fee-for-service sex lures many boys and adult customers. Some boys find that a life in prostitution surpasses home life; others find that they have traded purgatories.

Female prostitutes and pimps are also young—as many as one of every two prostitutes is a teenager. "Popcorn" or "bubblegum" pimps, most of them living in the neighborhood with their "girls," are often adolescents themselves (Baizerman, Thompson, Stafford-White, 1979). These young hustlers, like their female protégés, are estranged from family, lack education, and have little access to conventional peers or work.

Young female runaways, like their male counterparts, seek money and the friendship, security, and affection that was unavailable at home (Bracey, 1979). Even local girls get involved. One route for these girls begins with boarding away with a lover/pimp who demands that they stay out all night and engage in other misdeeds that sever family ties. Meeting his friends and other women, the new runaway finds a new social network. She begins to show her love and support for her pimp with fee-for-service sex. For these young women, the difficulties of prostitution may barely intrude on their commitment to their new romance. In many instances, running away cuts family and friendship bonds and reduces personal and social constraints against prostitution. Her pimp's affection and social milieu temporarily quiets her dread of being alone.

Incipient and confirmed gay youth, often throwaways from rejecting families or seeking a gay peer group, struggle with similar concerns. In their search for income and sexual contact, these youth may appear indistinguishable from hetero-hustlers. The difference is their struggle to find a nonexploitative sexual relationship. Sometimes they find genuine caring, but more often the transaction is an exchange of services, such that "the older person gets the body in exchange for keeping it alive" (Morris Kight quoted in Lloyd, 1976, p. 206). The cost is high when the transaction and the unfulfilled promise of love is accompanies, as it so often is, by an empty wallet and an empty belly, a wearier and less marketable body, and no new skills for an alternative future.

Social Supports for Prostitutes. Too young to frequent lounges or bars, adolescent prostitutes work the street. Natural helpers must also know the street. Youth workers can get the word out when shelters or informal havens are available. Runaway houses like Minnesota's Bridge Runaway Project, Seattle's Shelter, New York's "Door," and San Francisco's Huckleberry House provide youth with the benefits of conventional support: medical assistance, vocational hope, and psychological rest. Further support may be offered through peer-helping opportunities. These may arise when ex-prostitutes work as shelter counselors. Because reciprocity strengthens networks, enlisting youthful prostitutes in helping other adolescents to avoid or escape prostitution can deepen their attachment to the straight life. Extra caution is warranted, however, before employing recent prostitutes as outreach workers, because it can cut the other way: youth may be susceptible to pressure to return to hustling. Nevertheless, enlisting young prostitutes in the social support networks of others, including the aged, disabled, or teenage parents, builds new networks and weakens old ones. Retreats to camp sites or private homes may foster cohesion and permit pondering of a life without fear of family or street abuse.

Natural helping solutions for male and female adolescent prostitutes and for gay youth are not obvious. Earnestly seeking companionship and community, these youth entangle themselves in abusive relationships. Although providing access to social supports that do not degrade or exploit them seems a promising alternative, these supports lack the appeals of sexuality and moneyed life. On the other hand, natural helping avoids the problems of the law enforcement approach, one which inadvertently strengthens the cohesion of abusive dyads. This approach to helping youth is both promising and perplexing.

Social Supports for Gay Youth. Social support solutions for homosexual adolescents rely on the network of gays and the family of origin.

> On his high-school-graduation day one young sixteen-year-old gay youth from a small Pennsylvania town was given a one-way ticket to New York City and put on the bus; his Baptist-minister father, in a familiarly Christian act, told him never to show his face there again, not even to *write* home. Three weeks later he stumbled into our offices, sick, starving and anguished. He'd slept in Central Park for several nights and then been discovered by a series of older men who fed him and had sex with him until he couldn't stand it any longer.

> Somehow someone in a gay bar sent him to us. We found him a job and a place
> to stay until he saved enough to rent his own apartment. Now he's thriving.
> (Lloyd, 1976, p. 208)

The potential for support in the gay community exists; in fact, there are more than 1,500 local gay groups in our larger and smaller metropolitan areas (Voeller, 1981). Whether organized or informal, these networks protect gay and straight adolescent runaways from exploitation. Social support networks could be especially helpful to very young gay runaways, because the gay community is often eager to counteract accusations by antigay groups that older homosexuals influence the sexual preferences of minors. Housing and service programs with joint gay and straight sponsors might show good faith and provide young gays needed support.

Another support for gay youth involves formal and informal adoption by homosexual couples and households. Such arrangements—which are increasing for social and economic reasons—provide temporary and enduring social networks for runaway gay youth. Hundreds of gay teenagers have now been placed with gay foster parents in Washington, D.C., Minneapolis, San Francisco, Los Angeles, Seattle, and New York. In addition to traditional referrals from human service personnel, placements in gay foster homes can originate from gay and straight customers, gay bartenders, peers, gay retailers and proprietors, police, local gay organizations, and more traditional service centers. Professionals will need to advocate for gay homes. Such advocacy recently helped repeal Washington State's assignment of the label "community-concern home" to gay homes and its requirement that youth undergo psychological testing before placement in gay homes.

Legal, social, and logistical constraints on licensing gay homes means the continuing reliance on less desirable alternatives. Clearly, the main hazard in formulating any informal solution is the lack of sanctions against exploitations. Even gay advocates are outspoken in identifying the vulnerability of gay youth to exploitation by gay adults. Yet, the older man who boards and beds a gay youth may provide the youth with a better alternative than either the street or a rejecting family. Casework support can ensure access to psychological parenting, self-accepting models, and positive nonsexual activities (Malyon, 1981). The case presented below serves as a good example

> Another young man didn't come to us until years later in his life, but he had a
> similar beginning. At fifteen he was beaten grievously by his father when his
> mother intercepted a love letter from another fifteen-year-old boy. His father
> threw him bodily out of the house and told him never to return. Al wandered
> from his Long Island town to Times Square, hustled his ass for three years, as
> much to find a little human warmth from another person as to earn survival
> dollars. One of these men discovered Al's remarkable musical talent and took

him in. He helped him apply to, and work through, Juilliard. Al now is a successful flute player with one of the country's major symphonies and spends his spare time helping gay waifs. (Lloyd, 1976, p. 209) Linking gay teens to informal networks will accelerate as people accept homosexuality as a healthy stratum in the individual, school, and community. Caring people of all sexual identifications can help young people appreciate their own sexual orientations and those of their peers. Gay teenage rap groups, however desirable, are not necessary to increase social support. Parents of gay youth also need support to overcome stigma and to continue to care for themselves and their children. The Federation of Parents and Friends of Lesbians and of Gays is one self-help group working toward that end. Support can also come from clergy, siblings, PTA groups, and friends as much as from homogeneous, problem-focused self-help groups.

PREGNANT AND PARENTING ADOLESCENTS

The demands of motherhood are legion and often yield depression, anxiety, and isolation in the best of situations (Brown, Bhrolchain, & Harris, 1975; Pearlin & Johnson, 1977). The one out of six mothers who are still children themselves find these demands intensified by strain from the maturational stresses caused by adolescence (Zelnik, Kim, & Kanter, 1979). Psychosocial difficulties may find expression in child maltreatment, running away, depression, and dissolution of the birth parents' relationship (Jurich & Jurich, 1975; Nettleton & Cline, 1975; Bolton, 1980).

That social support networks relieve the environmental stress and personal strain of mothers is well known (Brown, Bhrolchain & Harris, 1975; Nuttall, 1979; Epstein, 1980). Teenage parents may benefit even more than older new mothers from the knowledge, material supports, and emotional encouragement of kith and kin. Social supports lessen pre- and postpartum complications (Nuckolls, Cassel, & Kaplan, 1972); a supportive companion in the delivery room lowers mortality rates, medical costs, and even the chance of brain damage resulting from delivery (Sosa et al., 1980). Grow (1979) found an association between young mothers' use of community supports and their contentment as well as their babies' welfare at 18 months and at 3 years. Black mothers under 15 especially rely on informal supports for financial aid, babysitting, decision making, and material needs (Zitner & Miller, 1980). Almost all such mothers reported weekly contacts with neighbors. Cannon-Bonventre and Kahn findings are in agreement with the importance of social support. They provide an account of one adolescent mother's search for support:

> There was no one around to be friends with. I just wouldn't do anything but be with my mother all the time. Then, too, I stayed home a lot. I looked up women's clubs and groups in the phone book—like Catholic Mothers and the Mother's League. But, they all had meetings at night and that wasn't good for

me. I didn't know where to look for friends, and didn't have the time it took to think of some old friends to call. At the hospital I remembered that they had told me to go to the playground just before 12 or after 3 and there would be lots of mothers and their kids there. Well, one day I went to the playground and this girl talked to me. She told me to come visit her and I did. We got to be good friends, she's the girl who came over this morning and dropped her baby off. Before that the most people I ever saw, let alone talked to, were at the hospital clinic. Otherwise, there was really no one. (1979, p. 47)

Mothers without support may lack opportunities for contact, or the interpersonal skills for initiating or maintaining contact. Mothers who maltreat their offspring more than mothers who provide excellent care, may alienate, reject, and, in turn, be ignored by friends and family members (Egeland, Breitenbucher, & Rosenberg, 1980). Of course, social support is more than social contact, and adolescents are uniquely prone to conflict with peers and family. Mothers exposed to unsolicited and disruptive contacts are less successful as parents than mothers not so exposed (Wahler, Leske & Rogers, 1979). Adolescent parents interviewed in this author's study (Barth et al., 1981) report that they find the unsolicited advice of parents and relatives to be stress-inducing. Family support may have diminishing returns and may even become one more thing a young person can get too much of (Lee, 1979).

In some families adolescent parenthood is in keeping with family traditions and values, while in other families, it is shocking. In either case, the dependence–independence conflicts for youth and their families frequently make natural helping available, yet ironically inaccessible. Asking for help may leave the young person feeling relieved but dependent. Conversely, maintaining absolute control over the baby's care invites personal depletion and isolation. By not providing willing help, resenting families may pressure their pregnant and parenting offspring to adopt-out. Or, the baby's grandparents may encourage their daughters to adopt-in by usurping their confidence as parents and, in the guise of helping, assume control over the baby's upbringing. Similar, if more subtle, forces affect many families of young parents, making social supports elusive or costly.

The Sisterhood. Having a mentor, perhaps a family member, who helps "negotiate the system" help a young mother to cope well with the problems of parenthood. Sometimes such family members assume the role of social worker by making referrals and liaison contacts on behalf of the teenage parent (Cannon-Bonventre & Kahn, 1979). The importance of mentors was recognized by Daphne Busby, who directs the Sisterhood of Black Single Mothers in New York. Because of the family and social network support she received during the medically troubled infancy of her son, Busby fashioned an organization in which adolescent parents are paired with older single parents or "big sisters." Big sisters, aided by members from various professions, help their little sisters navigate health, education, employment, and legal and social service systems. They provide child care and a reprieve from the isolation of parenthood (McHenry, 1980). The Sisters use parties to help build cohesion and nonparent support; they encourage girls to stay with their families and ask families to become part of the network. Their emphasis on maintaining access to family social supports is heartily endorsed by research (Grow, 1979; Furstenberg & Crawford, 1981). The Sisterhood counsels girls with family conflicts. An example of one such dialog is as follows: "Before you go struggle with this system out here, you'd better struggle with the system you were built into—which is your family—because in the long run, that's going to be a better source for you" (Busby, 1980).

Child care problems plague most parents; teenage mothers are no exception. The Sisterhood network provides each little sister with a weekly child care stipend that is often passed on to the little sister's grandmother, mother, sibling, or aunt. This practice recognizes the important, but exhaustible, contributions of family social supports and the critical role of reciprocity in networking. Every member of the family feels the financial strain of the new baby—all appreciate its alleviation. Providing the adolescent parent with something to contribute to the family allows her to more readily ask for and receive needed supports.

The interest and support of the Ford Foundation in the Sisterhood has culminated in a one-half million dollar, six-site demonstration project and has helped establish similar projects in St. Louis and Chicago (Ford Foundation, 1979). The St. Louis project hires women living in a public housing project to serve as surrogate mothers and grandmothers to young families in two "share-care"drop-in centers. These staff members hold discussions on family life and help teenagers enroll in and attend school or obtain job training. Along with the Illinois Family Planning Council, and, for the first time, state and Federal Title XX funds, the Ford Foundation supports a similar surrogate mothers project in the Woodlawn area.

SEXUAL ABUSE

Child molestation and incest occur as often as 2,000 times each week (U.S. Department of Health, Education, and Welfare, 1979a). Although sexual abuse of boys is not as prevalent as that of girls, young boys are not spared from molestation (Finkelhor, 1979). Abusers are seldom strangers; they are commonly a parent, older relative, mother's boyfriend, or a sibling (Herjanic & Wilbois, 1978). Arguments currently in vogue on the propriety of some adult–child sexual contact should not distract clinicians from feeling shock over these many incidents.

The abusive sexual relationship, confused by love, threats, fear of family breakup, and deception, leaves the abuser and the abused isolated from social supports and unable to ask for help. As one molested teen writes, "I hate being molested. I don't think it is fun or funny, that's why I don't talk about it" (D & SU, 1980). Professionals in the area of sexual abuse generally agree that incidents precipitating abuse reports are most commonly part of a long series of sexual encounters previously protected by isolation and secrecy. This silence is the result of a collision between mores against public discussion of sexual and family matters and legal sanctions against adult–child sex.

Peer Support. Peers often play leading roles in the disclosure of sexual abuse and the treatment for abusing families. Pressures from peers often instigates confrontation with the abusing adults. Child–adult sex frequently comes to light when a child becomes a teenager and begins to share more extended time, information, and activities with peers. Boys may then hear perjorative comments about male-to-male sex and begin to resent sexual participation with adult men. Girls who never hear anyone talk about having sex with her father may wonder about their own situation. The desire for peer heterosexual relationships, may cause jealousy in fathers or abusing relatives, thus precipitating a confrontation. Some confrontations may end the sexual relationship without disrupting the family, while others have no immediate impact, and the molestation continues. In still others, the child is supported by peers which precipitates a family crisis and arrest of the abuser; shelter care or juvenile hall is often provided for the adolescent.

Daughters and Sons United (D & SU). Daughters and Sons United (Giarretto, Giarretto, & Sgroi, 1978) and Parents United provide social support for abused children and adolescents. The title of their umbrella agency—the Institute for the Community as Extended Family—captures the grand design of these programs: to enlist the community as an ally in preventing sexual abuse and in supporting changes in abusing families. A community of professional and nonprofessional helpers and abused and nonabused youth work together toward this goal.

> I go to Daughters and Sons United and I love the meetings. They make me feel like I'm not the only one that has this problem. I like to talk to the other kids and try to solve their problems even if mine don't get solved because I'm in the hall. I've been there for 63 days waiting for a foster home but I will get out sooner or later. (Debbie; *D & SU We Love You*, 1980, p. 20)

Community support for child abuse victims and child abusers is fostered through multiple activities. D & SU has boys' and girls' groups for preteen and adolescent victims and a group for young male offenders. As sponsors and as big sisters or big brothers, long-term members facilitate the entry of new members into D & SU and provide ongoing support. With permission of an abused child's parent, and initially in coordination with interns and Parents United members, peer sponsors call on potential new members within the first few days of the reported molestation. Sponsors may visit children who remain in the home or are in shelter care of juvenile detention halls. Sponsors accompany new members to their first group meeting and debrief them afterward. Usually chosen for their natural helping qualities, these sponsors provide attention without pressuring for immediate disclosure or engagement.

While attempting to strengthen youths' peer affiliations, D & SU works toward its overall treatment goal of family unification. One goal of its Child Sexual Abuse Treatment Program (CSATP) is an understanding of the family's sexual history that is compatible with an optimistic future (Giarretto, 1981). Developing normal relationships between victims and their fathers, once thought undesirable and impossible, is now viewed as the key to securing future mental health for both the father and daughter and for the family as a unit (Giarretto, 1981). Support for the family from Parents United and D & SU avoids polarizing mothers, children, and fathers. Instead, it promotes family reunification. An independent evaluation found marked improvements in the youth's personal well-being, peer contact, and relationships with family, especially with fathers (Kroth, 1979).

Valuable as they are, structured self-help groups are not prerequisites for service to youth and families with sexual abuse experiences. Therapists, probation officers, social workers, and community psychologists can enlist natural helpers on behalf of sexually abused adolescents. Every community has potential sponsors with sexual abuse backgrounds. Professionals can identity sexually abused victims and can learn of others through agency or regional meetings. Friends, whether molested or not, may be recruited as natural helpers for the sexually abused adolescent (Giarretto, 1978). Again, professionals can act as liaisons between isolated, abused adolescents and possible natural helpers.

Another way professionals can assist natural helpers or sponsors is by discussing sexual abuse with them. Since sexual abuse is difficult to discuss, hard to understand, and complex in etiology and implication, work with the abuser is exceedingly difficult. However, uncomfortable, discussions of sexual abuse demand the willingness to ask probing questions to identify the antecedents and consequences of the molestation. Sponsors may profit from rehearsal with a consultant or a similar group of natural helpers, or both.

Helpers or sponsors who were themselves previously involved in incestuous relationships will also need consultation. Painfully cognizant of their own experience, victims may be blind to that of others, and to alternative reactions to sexual abuse. The dangers of countertransference or overgeneralization from a single exposure are many; for example, helpers who were coerced into sex may not tolerate or comprehend descriptions of positive or reciprocal cross-age sexual exchanges that occurred with minimal or no threat. Sometimes people, previously abused as children, who work with wives of abusers experience conflict because mothers are often viewed as villainous silent betrayers of their abused children. Careful matching of helper and helpee is perhaps as critical as helper training.

PREVENTIVE AND CLINICAL USE OF SOCIAL SUPPORTS

The human service provider can use social supports to improve preventive and clinical service. Preventive networking uses central figures in existing networks to scan for potential problems and to take action unilaterally or after consultation. Alternatively, clinical networking begins with troubled families or youth and strategically connects them with natural helpers or social supports. Differentiating these practical uses of social supports is helpful, but the demarcation is as permeable as most other practice distinctions; the methods clearly overlap. Consequently, although preventive networking will be described first, much of the material to follow is also relevant to clinical networking.

PREVENTIVE NETWORKING

Like other human service practices, work with networks involves assessment, an agreement for mutual work, skills training, maintenance, and evaluation. The goal of the initial assessment is to identify central figures and natural helpers in the networks of troubled youth and their families (Pancoast, 1980). Pancoast indicates that people become central figures by playing key helping roles in mutually supportive networks and by matching resources to need. Pancoast uses "central figures" and "natural helpers" as interchangeable terms. Here, central figures are distinguished as people in key network roles. Natural helpers are people with attributes of use to members of their networks. The ideal partner for networking is both a central figure and a natural helper.

Central figures may occupy key roles in different kinds of networks. Much previous work focuses on central figures in geographic neighborhoods (Collins & Pancoast, 1976; Collins & Watson, 1976; Garbarino & Sherman, 1980b; Warren, 1980). However, other "communities of identity" (Howell, 1975) affect youth and families. Such support groups as the homosexual community, the union, the Chicano community, or others made up of runaways transcend geographic boundaries but maintain powerful potential for prosocial influence. Locales also have central figures. They are found at beaches, parks, strips, recreation halls, shopping malls, school parking lots, movie houses, fast-food hangouts, bars, and gas stations. In a matter of speaking, by their minds and their movements, adolescents bring their networks with them.

Identifying Central Figures and Natural Helpers. Central figures can be identified in several ways. Specifying the neighborhood, community of identity, or locale—hence, the "network"—is the first step. When feasible, practitioners can consult an expert on the network to yield nominees for central figures (Pancoast, 1980). This expert may, naturally, be a central figure. Such current helpers as coaches, nurses, dance teachers, typing instructors, hair stylists, secretaries, and park attendants, may all be central figures or know of them. Professional counterparts in nearby community service agencies may not know neighborhood central figures, but they may suggest central figures in nongeographical networks that extend into their communities. Human service workers from allied professions may also know people at network crossroads as would the police. Although it is time-consuming and the approach is hindered by the privacy of families and adolescent networks, just hanging out and keeping their ears and eyes open may lead practitioners to discover central figures. Finally, peer nominations are an efficient, if seldom practical, method for identifying central figures.

How to contact central figures is more complex than where to locate them. The goals of the initial contact are to confirm the individual's importance to the network, to assess attributes that might promote or limit natural helping, and to enlist the central figure in some mutually agreeable activity.

Confirming centrality may be uncomplicated, because the position of the central figure may have consensual validation from network members, network observers, the individual's observable access to network-sustaining resources, and the self-report of the central figure. Examples of such central figures might include a pimp, a great-grandmother of a parenting adolescent, or a religious youth-cult leader. Sometimes observing the actions of the person one hopes to be a central figure reduces uncertainty about centrality. Incoming phone calls, a full calendar, familiarity with network members, knowledge of allied helpers, and awareness of resources all show centrality.

Once the human service worker is sure of centrality, he or she can evaluate the potential and availability for helping. Several networkers offer guidance. Pancoast (1980) recommends people who are: stable and committed to long-term involvement in the network; accessible to the consultant and to people likely to fill in the salient problem population; empathic; experienced with the concerns of network members; well informed or the key to resources, or both; especially interested in others; and less likely to be affected by stress. Gatti and Colman (1976) expect natural networkers to be healthy, able, and self-confident.

Choosing natural helpers for work with families and youth may require a less selective approach. For example, few adolescents or family members are "never too busy to listen" (Pancoast, 1980, p. 16). Flawless helpers are not to be found, and, in theory, may be too dissimilar to helpees to provide valued advice (Lenrow, 1978). For example, helpees learn more from teachers who can articulate the process of the struggle for mastery than from those for whom there never was a real struggle (Meichenbaum, 1977). Thus, parents of troubled adolescents should not be overlooked as helpers. They have learned the ropes, if regrettably late. So, too, might adolescents with school problems or court contacts be suited for helping peers and younger youth.

Interestingly enough, human service providers may find that natural helpers are not whom they suspected. Recipients of peer nominations as natural helpers in one local peer-to-peer program surprised teachers and students alike. Differences in networks dictate different helper attributes. As Collins (1980) explains, helpers must fulfill their role for their constituents; they need not fulfill the expectations of professionals. Those who seek natural helpers for youth and their families should remember this truth.

Initiating the Agency–Helper Relationship. After identifying a natural helper, preferably one who is also a central figure, human service providers must initiate the consultation relationship. Whether they contact natural helpers informally while pounding the helping beat of know them from previous clinical proceedings, consultants have a strong base for initiating or renewing a working relationship. Because many human service providers are accustomed to responding to requests for consultation, they may at first find it awkward to recruit consultees. Thus, when initiating a collaborative relationship, consultants should follow the rules in commencing client or peer contact, especially: (1) anticipate the concerns of the natural helper, (2) identify the range of positive and negative outcomes from collaboration, (3) specify mutual obligations, (4) suggest periodic review of the contract, and (5) offer a routine structure for modifying the relationship.

The following transcript shows a consultant talking with Mrs. Pacheco, a natural helper and potential consultee. The consultant, Ms. Mamone, is a social worker from a youth services bureau; she determines centrality, confirms the helping qualities, and ascertains the willingness to collaborate.

Mrs. Pacheco: Hello, Ms. Mamone, I was surprised by your call.
Consultant: Well, I've thought of you several times recently and wanted to talk with you. I'm glad that you are open to my stopping by.
Mrs. Pacheco: Yes, after you told me that Linda hadn't broken any new laws I was relaxed enough to have you over. Sit down, please, while I answer the phone. [A few minutes later] My sister, Anita, is going through it with her son, Hector. He fights with her, and now she caught him sniffing paint. Worse, is Nancy, my niece.
Consultant: What's going on with Hector and Nancy?
Mrs. Pacheco: Nancy, she's young, but looks like she's getting wild like Linda did. I told Anita to come by later and bring Nancy. Linda will be home after her community service hours and can eat ice cream and watch TV with Nancy while Anita and I take a walk and

	talk about Hector. Linda knows about the guys Nancy runs with. She said they were rough.
Consultant:	And how's Hector?
Mrs. Pacheco:	Oh yea, Hector. He's not a bad kid, but doesn't do things with kids his age. He goes with a girl who's 20. He's only 16. So his father keeps him in. He thinks she's up to no good going out with a young boy. He's afraid Nancy will run around, too, if Hector does. He's strict like his own father was. It reminds me of how I was with Linda. I think he needs to get out of the house before there's an explosion and the roof comes off. I'm going to see if Mr. Pacheco can use him in his upholstery shop after school.

By this time, the social worker knows that Mrs. Pacheco is interested in helping others—kin, at least—and that she has learned from her experiences with her own daughter. The social worker does not know much more about Mrs. Pacheco's centrality, although in this case she was previously aware that Mrs. Pacheco had attended parenting classes given by the school psychologist. Mrs. Pacheco does, therefore, know other families. If the consultant were still unsure of Mrs. Pacheco's centrality, she might say, "I'm interested in this neighborhood, because too many kids from here are ending up at Juvenile Hall and Crisis House. I thought that you might know a lot of families and kids in this neighborhood. Is that true?" Further questioning should confirm initial hunches. In this case, no further probes are needed, and after some talk about the parenting classes, the social worker asks Mrs. Pacheco to work with her.

Consultant:	Mrs. Pacheco, I called to ask you to work with me to help out the families in this neighborhood. I know that lots of families are going through troubles like you had with Linda and like your sister is having. I see many families from this area at the Crisis House and Juvenile Hall. I know that you try to help families already. I'd like to help you to do that in any way I can. We would meet regularly if you are willing. Before I say more, is this at all an interesting idea to you?
Mrs. Pacheco:	I don't know. You mean, I would help you in your job? I don't know, I really don't have schooling or anything. I try to help, but it's not much. Tell me again what I'd do.
Consultant:	What you would do is almost exactly what you do now, except you and I would meet to talk over new things we could do to help families in your neighborhood. We would meet once a month by ourselves and once in two months with other community helpers like you. You would tell me what goes on and what you do to help in your neighborhood and I would try to answer questions you have about helping.
Mrs. Pacheco:	You don't mean that I'd tell you everything that's going wrong with families I know? That isn't how I do it. I sometimes gossip, but not too much.

Consultant:	No, you wouldn't tell me everything that goes on. Once in a while you might tell me about families you feel may benefit from parenting classes, or from a talk with social workers like myself. Mostly, though we would talk about problems you face in trying to help the families you know, and what kinds of aid and services are available to these families, and what kinds of programs—like parenting classes—might help. Together we will try to help families before they beat each other up, or the kids end up in gang fights or in the Youth Authority.
Mrs. Pacheco:	So I just do what I always do, but I talk about it to you sometimes. Do I pay you? Or do you pay me? Ha! This is all new to me!
Consultant:	That's right, you just keep doing what you've been doing. Sometimes I might suggest new things you might try. And, about the pay, you certainly don't pay me, and I won't pay you either. I will pay you back for gas to the meetings and if it's okay with you, will take you to lunch for some of your meetings, but that's all the agency can do. I hope our talks, meeting the other community helpers, and helping more families will make it worthwhile.
Mrs. Pacheco:	So far, I think I'd like to try it.
Consultant:	Before you sign on, though, I should warn you about a few things. First, this might make you feel uneasy sometimes. You might think you are supposed to do something for every family you hear has trouble. Or, people—especially teenagers—might think you are against them because you meet with a social worker who also works at Juvenile Hall. Or, people might start feeling that you have answers for everything. I think we can handle these problems by talking about them together and with the group, but you should know that some other community helpers like you have had similar problems. And one other thing. If you tell me about families where the kids get beat up or there is sex going on between an adult and child in the family, the law says that I will have to investigate or report them. This, of course, might help end a very bad situation. At the same time, this will put you in a tough spot if the abuse families are close friends or family or may want revenge. You will have to use your best judgment on reporting, and we will talk about this and about helping families before they need reporting.
Mrs. Pacheco:	Well, I still think I'd like to try it. It's true that other families call me anyway. Can I think about it and call you next week?
Consultant:	Yes, of course. Here's my card. I look forward to your call. Thanks for the coffee and for giving this idea a chance. I hope we get to work together, but I know that whatever happens you'll be helping people.

Conversations like these may occur with gay bartenders, hotel managers in SRO districts, arcade operators, residents of housing projects, school cafeteria workers, or any other potential helpers. Linkages between agencies and teens are hard to establish and sometimes short-lived. Even so, the benefits to both helpees and helper merit the investment. In order to get collaboration from natural helpers, innovation diffusion specialists (e.g., Aleshire & Strommen, 1978) suggest the importance of ascertaining and then demonstrating the "yield" of new efforts. Yields vary by groups and by individuals, but they include increased status, new skills, feelings of protectiveness or maturity, knowing that one is helping others to get by more smoothly than they were, or the novelty of attending staff meetings at the agency.

Consulting with natural helpers, whether adults or youths, requires delicacy. Supporting their judgment, protecting their nonprofessional role by not oversupervising, and listening to shallow analyses of clinical issues is at times taxing. Especially talkative helpers or groups can even make agency staff meetings seem refreshing by contrast.

Consultants can assist natural helpers to identify problems, recognize the cues of problem severity, and realize when they need professional support. Consultants and helpers alike struggle with the dilemmas of helping (Lenrow, 1978). Predicting such conflicts and facilitating helper-to-helper exchanges clarify the issues and make them more manageable.

Support for natural helpers is essential. Easy phone access to the agency or other helpers will reduce strain; specific feedback for at least a sample of helping efforts increases the feeling of importance for each effort. Providing small, tangible expressions of status and regard like wallet cards that identify community agencies is specially appreciated by youthful helpers. In addition to consultant's praise for helping, helpers benefit from specific instruction in noticing and praising small increments of their own and clients' progress. Consultants can also lend support to helpers' efforts by dispelling the myth that cure is the endpoint of helping.

CLINICAL NETWORKING

Natural helpers or social support providers can assist human service workers and clients to achieve their mutual goals. Adjunct help is valuable and needed, whatever the agency's resources. Connecting clients with informal helping does more than save clinicians' time: networking also provides clients with corrective experiences that clinicians usually cannot offer. After careful assessment of the clients' presenting problem and social support resources and needs, clinicians may mobilize natural helping on behalf of a single client, as the following illustration demonstrates.

As consultant to a foster home, Mr. Fallon, a social worker, meets one young resident. Eric is a 15-year-old boy—bright, lonely, gregarious, and effeminate. He frequents the nearby airport terminal looking for "tricks," skips school, and is prone to running away and stealing cars. The other foster children in his home scorn him because of his apparent gayness and his incomprehensible interests. Although his foster parents enjoy his wit and warmth they are confused by his sexuality, and live in fear that his propensity toward stealing cars and the possibility of having or causing an accident will cause trouble. The social worker concludes that Eric is often bored before his joy rides and airport "excursions."

After briefly chatting with Eric, his probation officer, and his foster parents, Mr. Fallon decides to help Eric make contact with a wider network. Mr. Fallon discusses his plan with Eric and then begins to explore his current support network. To do this, he can employ any or all of four social support assessment techniques: (1) a Community Supports Assessment; (2) a social network diagram; (3) the reconstructed week, and (4) a Youth Support Inventory. The Community Supports Assessment (Figure 10-1) that Eric completed during routing intake at the community mental health center offers some ideas about his network. A network diagram can supplement this form by helping Eric to draw a map of people he resides with, as well as local and remote kin, friends, neighbors, school associates, and caregivers. The role of network members is further established with questions like "Who can you talk to when you really don't know what to do about a problem?" Or, for teens who report no supportive relationships, a technique called "reconstructed week" may provide a broader sample of possible allies. By pinpointing specific events and personal contacts during the prior week, adolescents are often better able to recall both fleeting and substantial social contacts and thereby expand their network diagrams.

Community Support Systems Assessment

1. Ethnic/cultural background _ _____ _____

2. Social network members
   a. Household
   b. Work/school
   c. Kin
   d. Neighbors
   e. Groups
3. Religious attendance
   a. Where? _____ ____ ___ _____

   b. How often?   1   2   3   4   5   6   7
                    hardly   very
                    ever   often
4. Beliefs about the causes of problems _____

   _____

5. Use of other resources _____

   _____

6. Core support system (who you can count on, talk to) _____

_____

Fig. 10-1. Sample form for assessing community support systems. (Adapted from Garrison & Podell, 1981.)

Special care is needed to help youth identify the cost of accepting support from others. The Youth Support Inventory (Figure 10-2) is sensitive to the price of support. Youths can identify some costs easily, such as the loss of autonomy. They have extensive experience evaluating the implicit contingencies and contracts of family life, and they know the psychological tradeoffs well. Less obvious to them are the costs of nonfamily, resource-bearing relationships. Young people too often become victims and lose liberties unsuspectingly. Free places to crash, enlightenment from initiated peers, sexual contact, and even fee-for-service relationships may give the illusion of mutual aid. In a detailed and systematic fashion, mutual help facilitators can enumerate direct and indirect costs of resources acquired from formal, conventional, informal, and unconventional sources.

In the case described above, the social network diagram and Youth Support Inventory (YSI) helped locate a gay man, Albert, whom Eric had known from a prior stay at a runaway house. On the form, Eric indicated that Albert was a person who provided housing and was easy to talk with about troubles. Unlike other older people on Eric's YSI, Albert did not require compromises in return for his aid. Eric and Albert had unfortunately lost track of each other; Eric thought that Albert had left the runaway house and was working as a furniture wholesaler. The social worker's efforts to reach out piqued Albert's memory and interest. Although wearied by the constant flow of runaways, Albert did enjoy helping. Contact with Eric was established and visits and outings commenced. Eric began to spend weekends working or wandering at the showroom; Albert repaid him with home-cooked dinners and movies. Albert introduced Eric to his partner and shared with him a model of a loving, working, forward-looking, agreeably unconventional life.

Preventive and clinical use of social support networks requires some willingness to relinquish control and place faith in natural helpers. Although Mrs. Pacheco and Albert may employ guilt, sarcasm, or other clinical anathemas as part of their helping style, their accessibility and credibility will enable them to provide therapeutic experiences. Opportunities for corrective action and direct feedback seem to be the common elements of successful behavior change programs (Goldfried, 1980). Natural helpers readily and frequently provide youth and families with these experiences: with these and more.

Faith in natural helpers should not, of course, replace reasoned evaluation of service. Natural helpers can show the extent of services by providing the consultant with an overview of activities, perhaps via tape recordings (Collins, 1980). Simple self-reports of natural helpers' well-being, perceived effectiveness, and enjoyment of their role can inform consultants about stress, discouragement, or overload. Contact with allied agancies and referred con-

Youth Support Inventory

On this form you will fill in the grid to indicate the kind of support you can expect from people you know. First, write people's names down the left hand side. Then, put an X in the box across from each name and under each kind of support you could get. Then, *circle* each X that shows support you can't get without doing something you really don't want to do.

	SUPPORT	Share good times	Talk about troubles	Housing	Transportation	Money	New skills	Information
PEOPLE								
Friends								
1. _____		□	□	□	□	□	□	□
2. _____		□	□	□	□	□	□	□
3. _____		□	□	□	□	□	□	□
Family								
1. _____		□	□	□	□	□	□	□
2. _____		□	□	□	□	□	□	□
3. _____		□	□	□	□	□	□	□
Work or school contacts								
1. _____		□	□	□	□	□	□	□
2. _____		□	□	□	□	□	□	□
Relatives								
1. _____		□	□	□	□	□	□	□
2. _____		□	□	□	□	□	□	□
Other								
1. _____		□	□	□	□	□	□	□
2. _____		□	□	□	□	□	□	□

Fig. 10-2. Sample Youth Support Inventory.

sultees should illuminate natural helpers' respective successes in prevention and remediation. Consultants and helpers should also check for mutual satisfaction.

IMPEDIMENTS TO CLINICAL APPLICATIONS OF SOCIAL SUPPORTS

To increase the clinical use of social supports, professional training must change. As the opening pages of this volume show, professionals can use social supports in many ways. Unfortunately, human services training rarely reflects professionals' need to know about and share social support. Not only is course content on social support networks all but unavailable, but teaching methods and agency training procedures rarely promote mutual aid. As Haley poignantly observes, only "when mental health workers can learn to rely on each other will they model that reliance for clients" (1980, p. 123).

Training for mobilizing and using social supports should be as concrete as the ensuing benefits. After exposure to empirical justification for networking, professionals deserve opportunities to practice setting up and maintaining prevention and clinical arrangements. Role playing with peers is an appropriate beginning. Peer consultation teaches professionals to give and take with colleagues. Field practica offer students the opportunity to attend group and individual consultations with natural helpers. Students can practice assessing social supports by using assessment instruments in their neighborhoods or with fellow students in the same course or year of the program. Thus, assessing social networks, if not always enlisting them, becomes an expected rather than exceptional part of clinical practice.

Research can benefit training for networking. That social support has an ameliorative function needs little additional evidence. Unfortunately, knowledge about the active ingredients in social support and how it is delivered effectively is scanty. The area is admittedly too new for sophisticated experimental studies between programs with and without social networking components or between programs using competing delivery systems. Even descriptive studies showing what natural helpers actually do would help clinician consultants find natural helpers, engage them, and then avoid interferring with them. Such data are badly needed. Assessing the specifics of the need for social supports would also assist clinical work. Studying the timing and form of network use by families and youth who successfully bypass crises may lend clues for helping those who are less successful.

Perhaps the abstract quality of earlier writing about social support concepts is partly responsible for current deficits in research and training. Although anthropological, sociological, mathematical, and epidemiological findings have contributed to the current knowledge base and interest in networks, clinicians now need more practice-relevant descriptions of social networks and their use. Detailed models of the uses of social support will facilitate clinical efforts. Promising or successful uses will win agency, private-sector, and third-party interest, and in turn, influence policies to further the use and evaluation of support networking. In this way, the promise for clinical uses of social supports for adolescents and their families, however great or small, can be realized.

CHAPTER 11
Social Support Networks in Delinquency Prevention and Treatment

J. David Hawkins and Mark W. Fraser

This chapter explores the promise and possible uses of social support approaches for preventing and treating juvenile delinquency. We place special emphasis on delinquency prevention as opposed to treatment. Three general strategies are explored. They are the provision of social supports to families, the development of supportive relationships for youths themselves, and the strengthening of linkages among families and schools, the units which are responsible for the social development of young people. In the first part of the chapter the rationale for exploring social support approaches for preventing delinquency is developed.

A FOCUS ON SOCIAL SUPPORT AND DELINQUENCY PREVENTION

From 1970 to 1978 the violent crime rate in the United States (murder, rape, robbery, and aggravated assault) increased by 34%, and the property crime rate (burglary, larceny, and motor vehicle theft) increased by 28%. Public concern about crime as measured by fear of being victimized rose from 41% in 1973 to 45% in 1977 (Weis & Henney, 1980, p. 699). A significant proportion of crimes detected by law enforcement agencies are attributable to youths. Forty-six percent of property offenses and 21% of violent offenses in 1977 were committed by youths under 18 years of age. Eighteen percent of all arrests for property crimes in 1977 were of children under the age of 15 (Flanagan, Hindelang, & Gottfredson, 1980, p. 462).

From the passage of the first juvenile court statute in Illinois in 1899 to the signing of the Juvenile Justice and Delinquency Prevention Act of 1974, juvenile courts and juvenile correctional agencies had almost total responsibility for both the prevention and control of juvenile crime in the United States. Yet, historically, these institutions have engaged primarily in the control of juvenile offenders and presumed predelinquents and neglected the mandate to prevent juvenile offenses (Weis et al., 1979, p. 1–6). In 1974, in response to collective criticisms against juvenile justice systems, which showed scant evidence of their effectiveness (see Empey, 1978), a new juvenile justice philosophy was embodied in the Juvenile Justice and Delinquency Prevention Act. The new "dual functions" philosophy of juvenile justice separates formal legal control from prevention (Hawkins & Weis, 1980). Juvenile courts' responsibilities have been limited to the control of juvenile criminals. The task of preventing youth crime has been removed from the courts and returned to communities. The change reflects the belief that informal units of socialization such as families and schools are both more appropriate and more likely to succeed in preventing juvenile crime than are juvenile justice agencies. In some respects it is ironic that the primary responsibility for preventing youth crime has been returned to families, schools, and communities, since these social units appear to have failed to prevent increasing rates of juvenile criminal behavior in recent decades. Clearly, if the current emphasis on preventing juvenile crime is to be successful, more effective means must be found.

Research on the etiology of delinquency has revealed several important correlates and causes. It appears that when young people are not attached and committed to their families, schools, and communities, they are more likely to engage in delinquent behaviors (Hirschi, 1969; Hindelang, 1973). Moreover, young people who are not bonded socially to these units appear more likely to associate with delinquent peers (Hirschi, 1969; Hindelang, 1973). Involvement with delinquent peers is one of the strongest correlates of delinquent behavior (Weis et al., 1981). Thus, it would appear that effective delinquency prevention requires the use of approaches that lead to the development of bonds of attachment and commitment to family, school, and community, and that discourage involvement with delinquent peers. In this way, positive social networks will replace negative social networks.

The characteristics of social units that achieve the goals of attachment and commitment have been identified and described (Hawkins & Weis, 1980; Weis & Hawkins, 1982). Social bonds of attachment and commitment appear most likely to develop when families, schools, and communities consistently provide young people with the opportunities to be involved in meaningful ways, with the requisite skills to successfully carry out their responsibilities, and with consistent rewards for skillful involvement.

From this perspective, the apparent increase in youth crime reflects the partial failure of families and schools to provide certain youngsters with the involvements, skills, and rewards necessary to ensure that they develop a social bond to society that is capable of preventing delinquency. Society's response has been to provide direct services to juvenile offenders through the efforts of social workers, caseworkers, juvenile probation and parole officers, and, in extreme cases, juvenile institutions and training schools. Unfortunately, the direct provision of services to juvenile offenders has not proved very effective (see Empey, 1978, pp. 484–524, for a review). It is not difficult to suggest a reason for this. If the families, schools, and communities in which juvenile offenders have been socialized have not bonded these youngsters in a manner capable of preventing their delinquent behavior, it is unlikely that they will have the capacity to control subsequent delinquency unless these social units are themselves altered (Coates, Miller, & Ohlin, 1978).

The social network perspective suggests an alternative to the individual treatment of delinquent youngsters. Delinquency should be reduced by interventions that assist the people whom youngsters encounter in their daily lives to provide greater opportunities for involvement, skills for participation, and consistent rewards for pursuing positive and productive lines of action. Thus, developing and strengthening positive social supports for parents, teachers, and youngsters themselves may be a promising means to achieve the goal of preventing delinquency.

From a social development perspective, social support interventions can enhance social bonding in two important ways. First, social support interventions can enhance opportunities for young people to develop stronger bonds of attachment to adults and nondelinquent youths. Second, social support interventions can create, in youths' environments, enduring systems of reciprocal contingencies that reward both sustained interaction with conventional others and involvement in nondelinquent behaviors.

This chapter focuses largely on social support interventions that seek to prevent delinquency before young people become engaged in delinquent behavior. The focus on prevention is not meant to preclude attention to the rehabilitation of juvenile offenders. In fact, several interventions that have been used with delinquent youngsters will be discussed. The emphasis here on prevention comes from a recognition of the importance of developing effective prevention strategies if this country's dual functions philosophy of juvenile justice is to be successfully implemented. Effective crime prevention is fundamental, yet it remains an underdeveloped area of practice.

SOCIAL SUPPORT FOR FAMILIES

The family is the first socializing unit in the process of social development. For young children, parental support and attachment are important predictors of difficulty in school and the community. Family experiences appear to be linked both directly and indirectly to delinquency (Bahr, 1979). Children who have not developed strong bonds to family are more likely to get in trouble in school (Elliott & Voss, 1974) and in the community. Thus, the family appears to be an important arena for intervention to prevent delinquency.

Unfortunately, a number of prior delinquency prevention efforts that aimed at youths and their families have failed to demonstrate effectiveness when subjected to rigorous research (see Berleman, 1980, for a review). The social casework and counseling model of individual and family interventions tested in the Cambridge–Somerville Youth Study failed to prevent officially recorded delinquent offenses (Powers & Witmer, 1951; Berleman, 1980). The child guidance model tested by the New York City Youth Board, based on the Glueck Social Prediction Table (Glueck & Glueck, 1950), and the view that disorganized family life was the source of delinquent behavior, also failed to prevent officially recorded delinquency (Craig & Furst, 1965; Berleman, 1980). Similarly, Washington, D.C.'s Maximum Benefits Project, a social casework–oriented model based on the Glueck Prediction Table also failed to prevent delinquency (Tait & Hodges, 1962; Berleman, 1980). These prior family counseling and casework approaches to delinquency prevention apparently did not adequately address the variables that are important in the family's etiological role in delinquency. To some extent, this failure may be a consequence of the fundamental view of the family on which these interventions were based.

Historically, in the United States, the family has been viewed as a socially independent unit with full responsibility for its members. Only when the family has been shown to be incapable has the larger society assumed any responsibilities, and then only under prescribed conditions. Typically these situations have included the death of parents, child abuse or neglect, severe mental or physical disability, incorrigibility of children, and juvenile delinquency. In such circumstances, the state's response often has been to separate children considered to be in jeopardy from the rest of the family unit and in some cases to place them in institutions. The policies of separation and institutionalization suggest the assumption that families are either healthy and functioning well or are seriously flawed, failing, and in need of replacement. Even family counseling and casework interventions that have stopped far short of separation and institutionalization have typically assumed that families themselves are deficient or defective, an assumption which has provided the license for intervention.

In recent years, a radically different approach to families has received increasing attention. This approach focuses less on addressing presumed internal deficiencies in families and, instead, seeks to increase the support available from beyond the family to assist families in weathering difficulties and solving problems. The principal assumption underlying this approach is the recognition that the ability of parents to successfully raise their children depends in large part on the social context in which families live (Garbarino, Stocking, & Associates, 1980). The assumption is that families may be able to successfully negotiate difficulties that inhibit effective childrearing and to develop parent–child attachments *if* provided with adequate supportive assistance from the environment.

Child development research supports family-oriented delinquency prevention, which augments the ability of families to function within the community and remain together (Whittaker, 1980). Family-oriented approaches seek to increase parent–child attachment, increase the consistency of discipline in the home, expose the child to adult role models who are committed to conventional lines of action, and increase consistency across socializing situations (Hawkins & Weis, 1980). These factors are related to delinquency (McCord & McCord, 1958; Hirschi, 1969; Hawkins & Weis, 1980). The interventions reviewed below attempt to achieve these goals by strengthening the environmental supports for families' efforts to raise their children. They mobilize informal supports in addition to or in place of the formal efforts of helping professionals. Some approaches seek to teach family members to utilize the formal and informal helping resources available to them. Others seek to strengthen key network members in the family environment in their helping roles or to create new supportive network resources for families. Both types of approaches are reviewed below and their potential for preventing delinquency explored.

SUPPORTING PARENTS IN SOLVING PROBLEMS: SUPPLEMENTARY CLINICAL STRATEGIES

Counseling and educational interventions that focus on families have become widespread, but often these efforts have failed to serve targeted families because forces beyond the families prevented members from taking full advantage of the services. For example, in the course of his 3-year project, Gordon (1970, 1972, 1979b) reported that low-income parents were deterred from consistent participation in parent training classes by concerns about overriding concrete problems such as loss of a paycheck, unemployment, sickness, or lack of transportation. To enhance the effectiveness of parent training, Gordon used a social support approach. He enlisted home visitors who were parents themselves to provide concrete problem-solving services to participants facing such problems. Gordon (1970, 1972, 1979b) reported success with this approach. His report is consistent with the results of recent research by Wahler, Afton & Fox (1979) and Wahler, Leske and Rogers (1979), who compared the outcomes of middle- and low-income parents participating in child-care training. Wahler and his associates found that low-income parents from high-crime, deteriorated neighborhoods did not benefit from parent skills training. They seemed to be overwhelmed by urgent survival and security needs. Like Gordon, Wahler attempted to help reduce these difficulties.

Wahler developed the "Mand Review" technique based on his insularity hypothesis (Wahler, Leske & Rogers, 1979b), an extension of Patterson's coercion principle (Patterson & Reid, 1970; Patterson, Reid, Jones & Conger, 1975), which describes the parent–child relationship in troubled families as reciprocally manipulative or coercive. The child whines to elicit a particular response from the parent, and the parent reprimands to produce a particular response from the child. These commanding, demanding, and reprimanding relationships are called "mands" (Skinner, 1953) and, according to Wahler, lead to "the gradual dissolution of affectional interchanges between parent and child" (Wahler, Leske & Rogers, 1979:115). The erosion of attachment between parent and child increases the risk that the child will become involved in delinquent behavior (Hirschi, 1969).

Wahler suggested that similar manding patterns exist in some families' social environments. He argued that when coercive communication patterns are extended to extrafamilial interactions, social isolation or insularity may result; affectional ties to network resources gradually diminish. According to Wahler, parents living in disorganized and dangerous neighborhoods may have manding relationships with neighbors, the police, and social service agencies. Natural helping networks may dissipate in such environments. Networks may be impoverished in resources and thus limited in their capacity for helping families to solve problems. Families may become trapped in isolation conditions. Entrapped families may comply with treatment efforts and service programs in the context of the mand process, i.e., they may feel coerced rather than actively seeking to profit from services. Because they lack enduring sources of support for change and problem-solving, their participation in treatment may be superficial and the impact of treatment, if any, may quickly atrophy (Wahler, Afton & Fox, 1979).

The theoretical links that Wahler suggested between socioeconomic status and family isolation are not confirmed by ethnographic studies of low-income families. Several researchers have documented rich networks of support and exchange that facilitate survival among low-income urban blacks (Stack, 1974), native Americans (Guillemin, 1975), and AFDC recipients (Felt, 1971). Nevertheless, some families may experience the isolation that Wahler described because of antisocial behavior or other conduct disorders of adult members. Even those whose members are better integrated may find that their networks do not consistently support childrearing practices that focus on behavior management or positive development. In such cases, Wahler's (1980b) Mand Review process may be a social support strategy that can strengthen the effectiveness of clinical intervention.

In the Mand Review process, to reduce social isolation and increase the probability of successful clinical outcomes, therapists, parents, and specific members of the family's social network meet regularly to discuss or review recent conflicts that affect child management. All kinds of family issues are reviewed in detail, and the trainer points out "relationships among various recurring trap episodes" (Wahler, 1980b, p. 46). Through this process of involving social network members as supporters of family efforts at child-rearing, parents are able to gain support in breaking patterns of coercive relationships. This approach is reported to lead to positive behavioral changes in children (Wahler, 1980a).

CONVENING NETWORKS AND PARTIAL NETWORKS TO SOLVE PROBLEMS

A related approach to enhancing supports for families involves convening social network members in network assemblies. This approach seeks to broaden the range of people who support family members in socializing children and should also increase the consistency experienced by children in their social environments. Network assemblies have been used in solving family-related problems such as child abuse, mental illness, and drug addiction as reported by Callan, Garrison, and Zerger (1975), Curtis (1973), Speck and Attneave (1973), Levine and McDaid (1978), and Stephens (1979). In each of these efforts, paraprofessionals or professionals provide individualized problem-focused education or therapy. In addition, the members of clients' networks are recruited to supplement formal services by participating in problem-solving sessions. In some cases, neighbors are involved (Collins & Pancoast, 1976); in others, extended family participate (Callan, Garrison, & Zerger, 1975); in others, service providers are mobilized (Curtis, 1973; Levine & McDaid, 1978; Stephens, 1979); and in still others entire social networks are convened (Rueveni, 1979; Speck & Attneave, 1973). In comparison to the Mand Review process, the network assembly approach places less emphasis on cognitive understanding and more emphasis on concrete problem-solving. Discussion topics may include virtually any problem that affects the home environment, e.g., drug use by friends, health care practices, or parental unemployment. Sessions can focus on mobilizing resources to resolve immediate crises or on developing long-term plans of action. For example, Callan, Garrison, and Zerger (1975) used network sessions to involve the families of drug abusers in the reentry phase of treatment, when patients leaving residential programs were thought to be especially vulnerable to situational inducements and peer pressure to return to drug use. Caplan and Killilea (1976) reported the mobilization of the networks of the families of wounded and fallen soldiers in response to the crisis of the Yom Kippur War. Friends, neighbors, and relatives helped with shopping, chores, and child care while primary family members cared for the wounded or mourned the loved ones killed in action. In both cases, networks were mobilized to fulfill a natural supportive function.

The most ambitious intervention of this type is Speck and Attneave's (1973) family network assembly. In it, the primary therapist or "conductor," along with three to five co-conductors, assembles an entire family's network of neighbors, relatives, friends, work supervisors, and the like in two to four sessions designed to resolve a problem that has proved unresolvable by other means. The conductor guides the group through seven stages (tribalization, polarization, mobilization, depression, breakthrough, elation, and retribalization), which are rooted in the concept of tribe. A tribe, it is thought, has a sense of history and a sense of membership. In it lies a "healing energy," which the conductor attempts to release. The intervention bridges the gap between individual and interactional interventions. Unfortunately, to date, family network assemblies have been described in case studies only and have not been subjected to rigorous research on their effects.

Critics of the network assembly have argued that it is difficult to implement because it requires the congregation of too many people with busy schedules. This criticism has led to the partial network strategy. To deal with some of the problems of the assembly technique, Garrison (1976) and others have proposed an abbreviated approach, which appears to hold promise. The partial network session is a meeting of significant network members. Whereas Speck and Attneave reported assemblies of dozens of people, Garrison's strategy in working with institutionalized psychiatric patients involved the 10 to 12 people identified as keys to resources needed by the patient for community adjustment. Similarly, Curtis (1973, 1974) convened partial networks as a method of case management. In these examples, the network session supplemented professional services by organizing the client's support system. In these interventions, the emphasis on creating a sense of "tribe" was replaced by a focus on stepwise problem-solving. The conductor's task was to mobilize a team of network members by encouraging them to list problems and propose solutions. Evidence for the effectiveness of these approaches is largely subjective, but Curtis (1976) reported that brief partial network session treatment through a state mental health center was equally effective and one-fifth as expensive as traditional mental health services.

The potential applicability of the network assembly approach for delinquency prevention and treatment is apparent. When parents are having difficulties that keep them from effectively managing their children's behavior or when children have begun to be involved in misbehaviors in the community, network sessions can mobilize community members to provide support to family members and simultaneously to help in supervising behavior. For example, neighborhood shopkeepers alerted to a problem of truancy or shoplifting through participation in a network session may be involved as part of an informal network of social control, calling relevant school officials or parents if misbehavior is suspected or observed.

SOCIAL SUPPORT FOR YOUTHS IN THE COMMUNITY

Strengthening social supports for families should increase their ability to provide positive bonds of attachment in the home. Such attachments decrease the likelihood of delinquency. But delinquent behavior is also affected by the support and social influence experienced by youths outside the family. Schools and communities are contexts for social interactions among youths and between youths and adults. Such interactions shape the behaviors of youths toward or away from delinquency.

The relationship between delinquent friends and delinquent behavior has been documented in numerous studies of both officially recorded delinquency (Morris, 1965; Frease, 1972; Severy, 1973; Polk, Frease, & Richmond, 1974; Noblit, 1976) and self-reported delinquency (Short, 1957, 1960; Reiss & Rhodes, 1964; Gold, 1970; Frease, 1972; Hindelang, 1973; Hepburn, 1977). The influence of delinquent friends appears crucial in the etiology of delinquent behavior even when the effects of other variables are taken into account (Weis et al., 1981). Thus, an important task for delinquency prevention and control programs should be to assist youths to develop social bonds of attachment with nondelinquents outside the family.

Coates, Miller, and Ohlin (1978) identified the importance of interactions with nondelinquent others in the community in their study of state training schools in Massachusetts. They found that behavioral gains made in treatment programs eroded as youths returned to their communities: "It seems clear that most of the youths are in programs that, while more closely linked to local communities than the training schools of the past, are still not adequately interacting with the youths' network of family, peers, school officials, and vocational opportunities (1978, p. 176). In the Coates et al. (1978) study, youths who reported illegal acts after they were released from custody were influenced by "negative peer subcultures" that even community-based treatment programs were unable to penetrate. In contrast, youths who did not get into trouble seemed to develop an attachment to some adult in the community who was engaged in conventional activities and who subscribed to legal values and beliefs. These "successful" youths also appeared to have made new friends who were not involved in delinquent peer cultures. Their networks supported legal activities and mitigated delinquent peer influences. For the prevention of juvenile crime, the implications of the Massachusetts study and other research (see, e.g., Hirschi, 1969; Elliot and Voss, 1974; Akers et al., 1979) are clear. There is a need to attend to issues of social support in the community for youths themselves in preventing and treating delinquency.

How can systems of interaction be created that are more supportive of prosocial behavior and less supportive of delinquency in the community? Delinquency may be prevented by providing youths with opportunities to interact with conventional adults and youth, and by providing rewards for maintaining attachments to youths and adults who are not involved in delin-quent or criminal subcultures. A primary goal of a community-based youth support program is, therefore, to create opportunities for interactions that may lead to attachments to nondelinquent community members. A second goal should be to ensure that the new interactions provide positive rein-forcements if they are to countervail the influences of delinquent peers. There must be rewards for sustaining interactions with rewards for com-munity members if such interactions are to preclude delinquency. In short, youths' relationships with nondelinquent others should become stakes in conformity that are likely to be jeopardized by violating the law (Toby, 1957).

Two broad strategies have been used for achieving these goals. Some programs have sought to intervene with existing groups of delinquent youths to redirect them toward more conventional behaviors. Some efforts of this type have targeted naturally occurring youth gangs or groups through de-tached gang workers. Others have constituted groups of adjudicated delin-quents in institutions or in community settings to participate in Guided Group Interaction programs.

In contrast, a second general strategy has been to seek to replace delin-quent influences by creating new attachments to nondelinquents. Efforts of this type have included community development projects that increase op-portunities for adult and youth interaction; individually focused partnership projects that link a community adult with an individual youth; and Positive Peer Culture programs that seek to bring together diverse youths into artif-ically created groups, which work to influence members' behaviors in much the same way as do Guided Group Interaction programs. Each of these approaches is reviewed below. We begin with approaches designed to in-crease links to community adults and then turn to programs that seek to alter peer interactions and influences.

AUGMENTING COMMUNITY NETWORKS THROUGH COMMUNITY-LEVEL ADVOCACY

A number of programs have attempted to increase support for youth by increasing community interaction (see Wall *et al.*, 1981). In Playa Ponce, Puerto Rico, for example, Centro de Orientacion y Servicios organized a corps of 10 "advocates" to initiate community projects to bring youths and adults together on an equal footing.

In mediating a confrontation between youths and adults in Barrio Pal-mita, the advocates organized a community meeting from which emerged a youth–adult project to build a basketball court. Perhaps more important than the court itself was the fact that the project encouraged youths and adults to collaborate in a series of fund-raising activities (steel-drum band shows, a radio marathon, and a hot lunch service for nearby factory workers). A community structure was created that gave youths greater opportunity to interact with conventional adults. Evaluated in 1976, El Centro's program was associated with a reduction in court petitions in its catchment district (20 compared with 144 in the year before its start) and was perceived by Playa Ponce's policemen as an aid to preventing delinquency (Silberman, 1978).

This approach is a move away from counseling and educational interventions. It places youth workers in mediation and planning roles. The knowledge, skills, and attitudes that help workers assume such roles appear closely linked to community organizing. These skills were used in Clifford R. Shaw's and Henry McKay's classic Chicago Area Delinquency Prevention Projects (Sorentino, 1959). But unlike these projects, which attempted to alter the quality of community life more broadly, the approach discussed here seeks to create social structures that bring youths and adults together in responsible interaction. To accomplish this, youth workers need to respond to critical incidents in ways that quickly defuse anger and motivate youths and adults to find solutions to problems which benefit both. When this is done, youths' networks may be broadened to include adults who are supportive of nondelinquent behavior.

AUGMENTING COMMUNITY NETWORKS THROUGH INDIVIDUAL LINKAGES WITH ADULTS

A second approach to providing support to youths is to build specific linkages between individual volunteer community members and youths in trouble in school, with their families, or with the law. Though it does not attempt to reduce community-level conflict between youths and adults or to create neighborhood problem-solving structures, this approach attempts to provide opportunities for youths to build attachments to adults involved in conventional activities. Programs like Partners, in Denver, explicitly focus on one-to-one relationships between youth and adults (see Wall et al., 1981).

The Partners program aims to provide resources to youths who are likely to be involved in juvenile crime. "Junior partners" are referred to Partners through the juvenile justice system, but their participation is voluntary. Community adults or "senior partners" are recruited through television and radio talk-shows, public service spots, presentations by Partners staff to local businesses, and newspaper articles. Junior and senior partners are matched on the basis of interests and are required to spend at least 3 hours a week in a one-to-one activity. Although no specific type of activity has been required, Partners provides a broad range of discount-priced recreational opportunities and encourages partnership activities that develop youths' effectiveness in coping with problems of living. Currently, the program is emphasizing the role of the senior partner as a source of modeling and reinforcement for involvement in prosocial activities.

The program has been evaluated several times, and it appears to be associated with a reduced likelihood that youths who participate will get into trouble more serious than the behavior that led to their initial court referral. The opportunities to build attachments to adults who are committed to prosocial lines of action may reduce the influence of the delinquent peer group.

REORIENTING INDIGENOUS PEER GROUPS

Four approaches have focused explicitly on youths' interactions with other youths. The first, the detached gang worker approach, seeks to redirect members of existing delinquent street gangs toward more positive pursuits. The other approaches attempt to alter the composition of youths' social networks and to create greater support from new peers for nondelinquent behaviors.

The broadly focused community development efforts of the Chicago Area Project of Shaw and McKay were overshadowed after World War II by community-based delinquency prevention programs that focused more narrowly on delinquent gangs and their internal structures and interactions. By 1957, detached gang workers were being used in over 25 delinquency control projects in 12 cities (Miller, 1957) to intervene specifically with delinquent gangs. A variety of methods have been used by detached gang workers ranging from individual counseling with especially delinquent gang members to weekly club meetings and special group activities. Generally, detached gang workers have sought to transform existing gangs into more pro-social clubs. The goal has been to reform the social support system in which delinquent behavior is embedded rather than to replace the members of an existing network.

Unfortunately, research on the detached gang worker approach has not shown it effective in preventing or reducing delinquency (Miller, 1962; Klein, 1969). This approach appears to have several problems. First, detached gang workers frequently spend only small proportions of their time with gang members themselves. Klein (1969) found that only 37% of detached gang workers' time in Los Angeles was directed toward gang members. Further, the workers did not spend a great deal of their time actively trying to redirect and resocialize the gangs with which they worked. Rather, their behaviors appeared to focus largely on becoming friends with gang members and on providing the members with opportunities to engage in a range of activities. As documented in existing studies, detached gang workers apparently do not provide greater support for conventional, as opposed to delinquent, activities. Gang workers seem to have little effect on the values, attitudes, and behaviors of gang members (Spergel, 1966; Klein, 1969). In fact, some analysts of the approach have argued that detached gang workers serve to solidify gang structure and identity by their presence, facilitating recruitment to the group and gang cohesion. To date, efforts to reform naturally occurring delinquent social support systems in the community have not proved effective.

CREATING PEER SUPPORTS IN INSTITUTIONS: GUIDED GROUP INTERACTION

A more structured approach to changing attitudes, values, and behaviors of delinquent youths through the peer group is the Guided Group Interaction approach. Guided Group Interaction was one of the first intervention approaches to specifically and explicitly focus on peer supports in delinquency control. First implemented by Bixby and McCorkle with institutionalized delinquents in New Jersey shortly after World War II (Weis *et al.*, 1981), the approach has been used in both residential (McCorkle, 1952; McCorkle, Elias, & Bixby, 1958; Weeks, 1958) and nonresidential settings (Empey & Rabow, 1961; Empey & Erickson, 1972) across the country. Typically, Guided Group Interaction brings together a group of approximately 10 delinquents for daily meetings with an adult facilitator. The goal of the meetings is to create a new and compelling set of peer influences away from delinquency among the members of the group. In contrast to the efforts of detached gang workers, Guided Group Interaction uses a relatively structured approach. Members begin participation by "telling their story" of delinquent involvements and behaviors. These stories then become the basis for arriving at subsequent group decisions about the individual who will be the focus of each meeting. At each meeting, after a consensus is reached on the focus, the targeted individual is confronted by group members who question and discuss his behavior. They seek to eliminate any rationalizations for delinquency and to encourage him to adopt the group's interpretation of delinquent behavior and its causes. The hope is that, over time, groups will move from loosely structured aggregations whose members are reticent participants to cohesive bodies whose members share a common bond, a sense of responsibility for themselves and their peers, and a set of internalized anticriminal norms (see Weis *et al.*, 1981).

Evaluations of Guided Group Interaction programs have produced mixed results (see McCorkle, Elias, & Bixby, 1958; Weeks, 1958; Scarpitti and Stephenson, 1966; Empey and Lubeck, 1971; Stephenson and Scarpitti, 1974). Youths who completed Guided Group Interaction in institutions had

lower recidivism rates than delinquent youths released from more traditional reformatories, but youths in Guided Group Interaction programs fared
no better than similar youths placed on probation.

Although a number of explanations for these results are possible, perhaps
the most telling from the perspective of peer support is the finding that
Guided Group Interaction does not seem to change participants' self-concepts, attitudes toward conventional activities, or feelings of responsibility
in the predicted directions (Weeks, 1958). The artificially created groups of
delinquent youths do not appear to be successful at developing and promoting nondelinquent norms and attitudes that can be internalized and
maintained by their members. Two possible reasons for this failure are the
composition of the groups (delinquent youths and a facilitator) and the
lack of community follow-up to ensure integration of group members into
conventional support systems that could reinforce nondelinquent behavior.
These possible weaknesses have been addressed, at least partially, by Positive Peer Culture, a school-based approach to preventing delinquency which
has borrowed heavily from the methods of guided group interaction.

POSITIVE PEER CULTURE

Positive Peer Culture (Malcolm & Young, 1978) and similar school-based,
peer-oriented prevention programs such as peer dynamics (Sheda & Winger, 1978) and peer culture development (Boehm & Larsen, 1978) seek to
create heterogeneous groups of "natural leaders" who represent a number
of cliques or groups in a school. Rather than recruiting only delinquent
youths for group membership as in Guided Group Interaction, these approaches strive for a balance between youths who exhibit behavioral problems and academically successful, prosocial youths. The goal is to harness
"the natural power of the peer group . . . to provide an impetus for behavioral and attitudinal change" (Weis et al., 1981, p. 31). Youths identified as
influential leaders (whether positive or negative) by teachers and students
are recruited to participate in voluntary "leadership groups." Group meetings follow a series of steps: (1) members report on problems and issues not
previously discussed; (2) a focal problem or individual is selected by group
consensus; (3) the group discusses the problem and the individual, confronting rationalizations and denials of responsibility and offering suggestions for resolution; (4) an adult facilitator summarizes the meeting. It is
hoped that through repetition of this process, members will develop an influential network of peers who support "appropriate" behaviors and who
do not reinforce undesired behaviors. It is also hoped that by involving
student leaders from various groups, nondelinquent attitudes and behaviors
will be transmitted throughout the peer networks of the school.

Evaluations of this school-based approach to creating peer supports have reported improvements in participants' attitudes toward school (Malcolm & Young, 1978), increases in participants' feelings of individual responsibility (Peterson, Meriwether, & Buell, 1976), reductions in school absences and disciplinary referrals (Boehm & Larson, 1978), and decreases in participants' official and self-reported delinquency (Boehm & Larson, 1978). Unfortunately, the research designs used in these studies do not allow the elimination of alternative explanations for the findings. It cannot be asserted confidently that participation in these peer support programs caused the observed changes in participants.

Recent research on the Positive Peer Culture program in Omaha, Nebraska, by Weis *et al.* (1981) has revealed apparent decreases in self-reported delinquent behavior among participants when compared with a nonequivalent group of students from the general school population. Moreover, these improvements are most obvious in the behavior of "high-risk" students, suggesting the promise of this peer support strategy. It should be noted, however, that the approach has not been shown to have school-wide influence on peer norms and student behaviors. In addition, some programs seem to have had difficulty in recruiting balanced groups of leaders of both positive and negative cliques in schools. When offered on a voluntary basis, positive peer culture programs are generally more successful in recruiting academically successful and conventional youths than youths with behavior problems (Weis *et al.*, 1981).

ALTERING YOUTH'S PEER NETWORKS
IN THE COMMUNITY

The structured methods of Guided Group Interaction and Positive Peer Culture programs have sought to develop peer support for more conventional lines of action in juvenile institutions and public schools. A final approach to developing peer supports operates, as do detached gang workers, in communities. However, in this approach, the focus is not on reorienting existing gangs of delinquents but rather on developing sustaining relationships with nondelinquent youths in the community.

In 1966 in Manchester, England, a small group of social workers and community members who had been running a teen canteen in a low-income working-class area with a high delinquency rate inaugurated a detached street work project. Project Wincroft adopted an eclectic social support philosophy that focused on "the failure in social relationships, usually with the mother or father," and youths' needs to sustain affiliations with nondelinquent youths (Smith, Farrant, & Marchant, 1972, p. 29). This philosophy manifested itself in the project's networking approach. As in the Partners program, boys or small groups of boys were matched with adult community volunteers, and youth–adult pairs were offered a range of inexpensive recreational and vocational activities. But, in contrast to Partners, these activities also were provided selectively to members of boys' social networks. Project Wincroft staff and community volunteers offered the nondelinquent friends of experimental boys regular outings and vocational opportunities through the invitation of the experimental boys. This approach encouraged association by targeted youths with their more prosocial peers and rewarded both the experimental boys and their selected friends for sustained interaction.

At the end of a 2½-year period of service, Project Wincroft was judged modestly successful in preventing delinquency. At the start of the project, 46.3% of the boys in the experimental condition and 48.6% of the boys in the matched control condition had been convicted at least once in court. In July, 1968, 37% of the experimental and 54.4% of the control boys had had a subsequent court appearance. In addition, the controls had a significantly higher number of convictions and officially reported offenses, though control and experimental boys did not differ on measures of home life, employment, and social attitudes. In sum, this project seems to have touched upon a promising method of altering youths' peer supports in the community.

Given the importance of delinquent peers in the etiology of delinquency, delinquency prevention and control strategies that seek to increase social supports for nondelinquent behavior patterns seem warranted. The available research on prior efforts of this type suggests that approaches that try to link youths with more prosocial others, whether adults or peers, are more promising than efforts to redirect the activities, values, and behaviors of groups of already delinquent youths. It is particularly difficult to reorient existing delinquent groups such as street gangs away from delinquent activities. However, both preventive and treatment strategies that link youths with nondelinquent adult or age-contemporary role models hold promise for reducing delinquent behavior.

STRENGTHENING LINKS BETWEEN HOME AND SCHOOL

A final general approach to social support development that may help in preventing delinquency is the strengthening of linkages between the members of socializing institutions in the community. Perhaps the most important linkages are those between the family and school, since both are important in the etiology of delinquency and since there is evidence that relationships at home influence school success, attachment to school, and commitment to educational goals. All of these factors are related to delinquency. Two types of school–family programs have been developed to increase the consistency of support across home and school: home-based rewards for school behavior, and parent involvement in school management. Each is reviewed briefly below.

PROVIDING HOME SUPPORT FOR YOUTHS' SCHOOL BEHAVIORS

Home-based reward programs are well supported by research. Use of reinforcement and token economies has been shown to be effective in a variety of mainstream (Hall *et al.*, 1968), special (Koegel & Rincover, 1974), and institutional (Meichenbaum, Bowers, & Ross, 1968) educational settings. Just as behavioral therapists have sought to extend clinical contingencies into the home, educational researchers have attempted to extend classroom contingencies into the home. Toward this end, parents have been recruited and trained to provide special support in the form of social and physical rewards for appropriate classroom behavior. By setting up simple home–school note systems, parents, working cooperatively with teachers, have been able to decrease the problem behaviors of children in their own homes (Karraker, 1972; Lahey *et al.*, 1977) and in group home settings (Bailey, Wolf, & Phillips, 1970; Thoresen *et al.*, 1977). In the school setting, parent collaboration with the teacher has been used to increase homework completion rates; to improve math, spelling, and reading scores; and to reduce truancy and disruptive behavior (MacDonald, Gallimore, & MacDonald, 1970; Karraker, 1972; Patterson, 1974; Ayllon, Garber, & Pisor, 1975; Fairchild, 1976). For example, Ayllon, Garber, and Pisor (1975), implemented a token economy for a classroom of black third-graders who were achieving below grade level and who were reported to be highly disruptive. Following parent, teacher, and principal conferences, parents agreed to provide rewards if a child brought home a good behavior note and to administer some form of mild punishment if no note was brought home. Over a 24-day period, disruptive behavior was significantly reduced. Unfortunately, no untreated control or comparison group existed with which these results could be compared.

Promising results from more rigorous research are reported by Trovato and Bucher (1980), who used home-based reinforcement to augment a cross-age tutoring program. Second-, third-, and fourth-graders were randomly assigned to a regular classroom control condition, a cross-age tutoring condition, or a cross-age tutoring condition with a home–school reward system. Although the reading improvement scores of both tutoring conditions were significantly better than the control condition, the students whose parents were involved in providing home rewards also showed significant reading gains over the students who received only cross-age tutoring. Such studies support the contention that school behavior is linked to both the classroom and family contexts and that "school behavior can come under the control of home-based reinforcement contingencies" (Barth, 1979, p. 453). In summary, home-based reward programs have been shown effective in reducing disruptive behavior and increasing academic achievement (Atkeson & Forehand, 1978). Both variables are significant predictors of delinquency (Elliott & Voss, 1974). This approach is potentially important for delinquency prevention.

INVOLVING PARENTS

The link between parent involvement in schools and delinquency prevention is less clear empirically. In theory, parent involvement in schools should increase the consistency of expectations across the home and school settings and should, therefore, reduce the likelihood of delinquency. Involving parents as classroom or administrative aides, as educational resource persons, or as frequent school visitors has been reported in educational journals (Goodsen & Hess, 1975; Dougherty & Dyal, 1976; Granowsky, Middleton, & Mumford, 1979). "Open Door" policies encourage parents to visit their child's classroom without securing a visitor's pass or registering at the principal's office. Active involvement of parents in school management has also been reported as promising. School-site management projects in Salt Lake City have created school councils composed of parents, teachers, and community members. Those councils have been given substantial authority to make school decisions. Thomas (1979) has reported dramatic decreases in school vandalism after school councils were established. Clearly, the school setting has the potential for many types of parental involvement that could increase the consistency of support that youths receive for prosocial behavior. Unfortunately, there is, as yet, little controlled research to document the effects of such efforts on preventing delinquency.

IMPLEMENTATION ISSUES

VIOLATION OF PRIVACY

Whenever human service workers attempt to alter social relationships, confidential information becomes available to actors in related systems. The extension of official agencies, even with the best intention, into arenas heretofore considered solely private has potential for abuse. Clearly, youth support programs should be developed with consideration of confidentiality. It is difficult to imagine how social network assemblies, for example, can be used without revealing sensitive information to many people. On the other hand, community-level advocacy programs do not appear as vulnerable to abuses of confidentiality, though they are founded on many of the same ideas. Alternatively, home support of school behavior does appear to extend social control from the school to the family. Such extensions may be seen by many as undesirable and should be carefully evaluated.

The anonymity and isolation that sometimes characterize urban life and that may inhibit families from developing support for childrearing are, themselves, a type of protection from the scrutiny and interference of other community members. Those who have lived in rural areas or small towns know that the free flow of confidential information among nonprofessional community members can be used destructively as well as in support of positive development. In a very real sense, a fundamental issue in the creation, expansion, and use of supportive social networks is the risk implied in sharing confidential information beyond the client family and the professional social service worker or educator. The social support strategies suggested here may be vigorously resisted by many unless protective guarantees can be established.

RECRUITMENT AND ATTRITION

With the exception of the Mand Review and supplemental problem-solving techniques, all of the social support strategies discussed here require the active participation of significant others, and this leaves each strategy vulnerable to problems of recruitment and attrition. Partnership programs depend on their ability to recruit volunteers to work with youths, and the network assembly interventions need the active participation of family members, neighbors, workmates, and friends to be successful. Some programs can use experienced members to orient new members, but home-based rewards and parent involvement programs must be able to elicit consistently high levels of interest in order to achieve an effect. In these cases, the outcome of the intervention is directly related to the level of participation.

There appear to be no shortcuts in battling the problems of recruitment and attrition. Delinquency prevention workers must actively reach out to community volunteers and youths' network members by explaining the importance of participation. Hawkins (1979 p. 56) argues for an action-oriented staff approach: "Staff would provide a personal link . . . would recruit [participants], explain the program, and introduce [participants] in a shared social context." If such an approach is used, staff must be skilled in individual, family, and group techniques, and must be willing to assume nontraditional clinical roles in order to implement social support interventions fully.

CONCLUSION

The social environment is constantly changing, and these changes affect the ways youths, their families, peer groups, schools, and communities function. Recent changes probably have reduced the family's traditional effectiveness in crime prevention and have increased the likelihood that children will be induced to participate in criminal acts.

> The networks of family support systems are smaller, and, by the very nature of the urban environment, even when present, are less likely to affect young people. One does not often encounter an aunt, uncle, or cousin who can report to one's parents, as happens in smaller communities or in rural areas. In addition, more of the activities formerly confined to the family are now performed elsewhere, from pre-school through a longer and more extended school period where primary adult groups have minimal impact. (Lukoff, 1980)

This chapter has explored preventive approaches that account for environmental factors that contribute to delinquency. Social support development allows the professional helper to intervene in larger social systems to address these factors. We have briefly reviewed several social support interventions, citing empirical support and implementation issues, in the hope that the reader will be encouraged to experiment with this general strategy. Although social support development is only one strategy that should be included in a comprehensive approach to delinquency prevention (Hawkins and Weis, 1980), it is a strategy with great promise.

The social changes now occurring in our society can most effectively be addressed by institutional change. For that reason we have considered approaches which, if implemented, would alter relationships between families and the other social institutions that influence youths' behavior. The interventions seek to reduce the influence of delinquent peer groups and to enhance the networks of support that permit families, community members, and schools to fulfill their traditional functions. In so doing, they should reduce the likelihood of delinquency.

PART V
Services to the Chemically Dependent

CHAPTER 12
Social Support Networks in Treating Drug Abuse

J. David Hawkins and Mark W. Fraser

Drug use and misuse have become among the most compelling realities of contemporary existence.

Drug Abuse Council, 1980.

Drug abuse and its treatment have become costly social realities. In 1978 there were 240,000 treatment "slots" in the United States specifically designated for treating drug abuse (NIDA, 1978). Sixty percent of these were for heroin users. When the value of law enforcement, judicial review, corrections, lost labor, drug traffic control, unemployability, drug-related death, and absenteeism were considered, the tangible cost of heroin abuse alone was estimated to be $6.4 billion in 1975 (Rufener, Rachal, & Cruze, 1980). Of these costs, close to half (48%) were direct governmental expenditures. In 1978, the total Federal budget for drug treatment and prevention was $483.5 million, and the Federal law enforcement budget allocated to the control of drugs was $400.6 million (Drug Abuse Council, 1980).

This chapter reviews the empirical evidence on the role of social factors in the etiology and treatment of drug abuse. On the basis of data on the social networks of street drug abusers before and after treatment, the promise of social support development in treating drug abuse is explored, and specific models for developing social supports are presented. Finally, approaches that use social supports are discussed in terms of their implications for the roles of practitioners.

Historically, the treatment and control of drug abuse have been largely the responsibility of the medical and legal professions. Shifts in responsibility between these professions have accompanied periodic policy changes signaling the predominance of the legal or medical model of addiction as uncontrolled behavior or illness, respectively (see Lewis & Sessler, 1980). But

355

two decades of research on the etiology of drug abuse and over a decade of intensive effort to treat it have broadened our understanding of this phenomenon. As with other maladies as disparate as schizophrenia and heart disease, evidence has accumulated to suggest the importance of immediate social or interactional factors in both the etiology and the treatment of drug abuse. Thus, in the last decade, with the development of a national system of drug abuse treatment there has simultaneously been a growing resolve to address adequately the social factors in the rehabilitation of substance abusers. This emphasis has moved the problem squarely into the realm of social work practice. In the past decade, social workers have assumed major roles in the management and delivery of drug treatment services. Even those not directly involved in drug treatment agencies have been confronted with clients for whom substance abuse is a problem. This chapter explores the implications of our knowledge about the social aspects of addiction for social workers whose clients are engaged in substance-abusing behavior. It investigates possible ways in which practitioners can effectively address the social aspects of drug abuse by using and creating informal social supports.

Although the misuse of drugs and alcohol clearly transcends heroin addiction and the abuse of other "street drugs" (Drug Abuse Council, 1980, p. 4), this chapter is concerned primarily with street drug abuse. Street drug abuse is the misuse of psychoactive drugs that are not prescribed legitimately by a physician. It includes drug abuse that is supported by crimes such as drug dealing, burglary, pimping, and prostitution, as well as drug misuse supported by writing counterfeit prescriptions for drugs or by obtaining prescriptions from physicians who make a practice of prescribing drugs for nonmedical uses. Street drug abuse is somewhat distinct from the abuse of alcohol or the misuse of medically prescribed drugs in that it is generally associated with involvement in other illegal and socially unacceptable activities, which may come to constitute a deviant lifestyle for the user. Although there has been much speculation about the role of drugs in this lifestyle, whether as cause or result, the successful treatment of street drug addiction is obviously made more difficult by the fact that substance abuse is enmeshed in a particular kind of lifestyle. Because of this distinctive aspect of street drug abuse, this type of abuse will be our primary focus. We do not mean to imply that other types of drug and alcohol abuse are without any similarity to street drug abuse or that the social support approaches described in this chapter could not be applied successfully in the treatment of alcoholism or prescription drug abuse. Clearly, social support has been fundamental in the self-help approach of Alcoholics Anonymous (Katz & Bender, 1976). Yet, street drug abuse represents an extreme case. It warrants investigation if only to explore the limits of socially oriented interventions in the treatment of substance abuse.

THE SOCIAL BASES OF DRUG ABUSE: EMPIRICAL EVIDENCE AND THEORETICAL PERSPECTIVES

Historically, street drug addiction has been viewed as a problem associated with ethnic minority and with low socioeconomic and low-income statuses (Schur, 1962). Although there is evidence for ethnic differences in patterns of drug use and rates of admission into treatment for drug abuse (Curtis & Simpson, 1977; Sherman & Peterson, 1978), recent evidence does not confirm the stereotype of drug addiction as a phenomenon of the lower socioeconomic classes (Hawks, 1974; Curtis & Simpson, 1977; Jessor, Chase, & Donovan, 1980). Available evidence tends not to support the view that drug abuse is a direct response to macro- or structural-level social and economic variables (Hirschi, 1969; Hindelang, 1973), as suggested by opportunity or strain theorists (Cloward & Ohlin, 1960). Rather, drug abuse appears to be associated with interpersonal experiences in the immediate social environment. One's interactions with family, friends, and community members appear to be the social events that determine patterns of drug usage.

Relationships have been documented between drug use patterns and social norms and expectations (Cavan, 1966; MacAndrew & Edgerton, 1969; Mizruchi & Perrucci, 1970; Wilkinson, 1970; DeRios & Smith, 1976; DuToit, 1977; Harding & Zinberg, 1977), peer influence (Abelson, Cohen, & Schrayer, 1972; Ray, 1972; Tec, 1972a, b; Abelson et al., 1973; Kandel, 1973, 1974, 1980; Marlatt, Demming, & Reid, 1973; Tolone & Dermott, 1975; West, 1975; Dembo, Schmeidler, & Koval, 1976; Kandel et al., 1976; Sorosiak, Thomas, & Balet, 1976; Spevak & Pihl, 1976; Zinberg, Harding, & Winkeller, 1977; Apsler, 1979; Zinberg & Harding, 1979), parental drug use patterns and parental influence (Cevaline, 1968; Ray, 1972; Sebald, 1972; Smart & Fejer, 1972; Lawrence & Vellerman, 1974; Tec, 1974; West, 1975), and family relationships (Streit & Oliver, 1972; Streit, Halsted, & Pascale, 1974; Alexander & Dibb, 1975; Harbin & Maziar, 1975; Stanton et al., 1978; Stanton, 1979), to name but a few. Ethnographers have suggested that street drug abusers develop lifestyles that are organized around the procurement of illicit drugs (Preble & Casey, 1969). Their patterns of daily living are shaped by the associations that they must maintain in order to secure a consistent supply of drugs (Fiddle, 1976). Ethnographic studies have described a web of social relationships that provide little support for conventional behavior and have suggested that the most serious forms of drug abuse, particularly heroin abuse, are maintained and reinforced by the immediate social context in which they are embedded (Waldorf, 1973; Waldorf & Biernacki, 1981). Unfortunately, however, there is not a clear consensus about how social factors interact in the etiology of drug use and abuse, and about how they should be addressed in treating drug abuse. As the Drug Abuse Council succinctly puts it: "The underlying social dynamics and problems that lead to drug misuse are so exceedingly complex as to as yet elude totally satisfactory solutions" (1980, p. 5).

Efforts to adequately address the social factors in drug abuse require an empirically sound base of knowledge for intervention. Moreover, a framework for integrating and organizing knowledge about the social aspects of drug abuse is required if socially oriented interventions are to be more than haphazard. Social theory provides such a framework for knowledge, intergrating it into an explanatory paradigm that can provide blueprints for action. Thus, it is important to use theory as a framework for organizing our understanding of the social aspects of drug abuse.

There are numerous theories of deviance. However, two theories, social control and cultural deviance both have received support from empirical research on delinquency (Hirschi, 1969; Hindelang, 1973; Kornhauser, 1978; Akers *et al.*, 1979) and are particularly relevant in this regard (see Hawkins, 1979). The two theories describe different social dynamics in the initiation, maintenance, and return to deviance. Nevertheless, both theories are useful frameworks for thinking about treatment planning because both appear to explain partially the observed relationships while offering competing propositions about the social dynamics of drug abuse. We review them here because they imply different approaches to developing social supports in the treatment of drug abuse.

TWO SOCIAL THEORIES OF DEVIANCE

Social control theory postulates that deviance such as drug abuse occurs because people are inadequately socialized. Drug abuse is viewed as nonconformity to the shared cultural values in society. This nonconformity is possible because people do not develop a social bond of involvement, commitment, attachment, and belief that is capable of preventing deviance (Hirschi, 1969). "The theory asserts that youngsters who do not develop a bond to the conventional order because of incomplete socialization feel no moral obligation to conform" (Weis, 1977, p. 35). Control theory does not posit the existence of subcultures with deviant values within the larger society, and it does not recognize bonds to deviant social groups as a source of deviance. The theory also disregards the possible role of deviant friends and companions in the initiation and maintenance of deviance (Hindelang, 1973, p. 487). Control theory views drug abusers as poorly socialized individuals who are not successful in the larger society, who fail to develop commitments and attachments within that society, and who fail to adopt the beliefs of that society. When presented with the opportunity to engage in deviant behavior such as drug abuse, these people do so because they have no stake in conformity and no bond to society that would inhibit such behavior (Reiss, 1951; Nye, 1958; Hirschi, 1969; Nettler, 1974).

On the other hand, cultural deviance theorists assert that social bonds are present among delinquents and drug abusers, and that socialization takes place normally. Deviance occurs because behavioral norms within subgroups of society have such variation that the standards of some subcultures are inherently deviant when compared to those of the dominant social group (Sutherland, 1956). This theory does not assume individual causes of drug abuse and crime. Deviance, from this perspective, arises from conflicts between the values of subcultures and the values of more powerful cultures. The well-known case of criminal subcultures in India is described by Sutherland:

> Culture relating to criminal law is not uniform or homogeneous in any modern society. This lack of homogeneity is illustrated . . . in the criminal tribes of India. Two cultures are in sharp conflict there. One is the tribal culture which prescribes certain types of assault on persons outside the tribe, in some cases with religious compulsions. The other is the legal culture as stated by the Indian . . . governments. . . . Culture conflict . . . is the basic principle in the explanation of crime. (1956, p. 20)

Cultural deviance theorests contend that children learn deviant behaviors socially. Sutherland (1947) called this process "differential association," because he wished to emphasize the importance of role models. In 1966, Burgess and Akers reformulated Sutherland's hypotheses by incorporating in them the principles of social learning theory espoused by Skinner (1953, 1959), Bandura (Bandura & Walters, 1963; Bandura, 1969, 1977), and others. Today this perspective has several names: cultural deviance, differential association, and subcultural theory. In general, the result of Burgess and Akers's (1966) work was to clarify the social learning processes by which children in subcultures become delinquent. Behavior, it is argued, arises from exposure to others and subsequent imitation or modeling of others' actions. When imitation is followed by positive consequences, it is more likely to recur than when it is followed by the absence of consequences or negative consequences. Such differential reinforcement of imitated behavior affects cognition, as children eventually learn to value some behaviors over other behaviors. The more an activity is defined as potentially rewarding or good, the more likely children will engage in it. "Social definitions" of behaviors derive from consequences provided by peers, parents, and others who tend to reward behaviors that are consistent with prevailing values, norms, and attitudes (Akers et al., 1979). Through social learning, children are socialized into subcultures, and in the sense of control theory, are bonded to the values, behaviors, and institutions of the subculture.

The major distinction between control and cultural deviance theories is in the nature of this bond. In control theory, the presence of a bond, independent of its etiology, reduces the likelihood of deviance. In cultural deviance theory, the bond, social definitions, or values are normative in the subculture but illicit in society at large. Successful socialization and bonding to a deviant lifestyle lead to delinquency and drug abuse. For control theorists, inadequate socialization is a necessary and sufficient condition to produce drug abuse. But for subcultural theorists, poor socialization to society at large is necessary but not sufficient. Socialization or commitment to deviant values is required.

A fundamental issue distinguishing control theory from cultural deviance theory is the degree to which normality is presumed to characterize the social interactions of drug users (Hansell & Wiatrowski, 1980). Cultural deviance theories view users of street drugs as people with social networks that do not differ structurally or interactively from those of more conventional people. These people have become drug users because the values and beliefs of those with whom they interact are different from those of the dominant society. The processes of exchange and interaction are the same as those found in more conventional relationships. Only the content of interaction (what flows among members of the network) and the extent of deviance of members are different. Cultural deviance theory implies that the networks of users are composed of other users of drugs whose values favor drug use and who are not involved in conventional roles in work, school, or other organizations.

In contrast, social control theories view users of hard drugs as people whose social skills are limited as a result of inadequate socialization, and whose social networks are distinct from those of more conventional people in structure, interaction, and content. The social control theory implies that the relationships of drug users with members of their social network are unreciprocated, of shorter duration than those of more conventional people, less hierarchical and more shifting in status relationships, less cohesive, less intense, less dense, more single-stranded (less multiplex), and not characterized by mutual esteem or role modeling. Control theory implies that street drug users' social networks include both drug users and nonusers, and it seems to imply that their networks are smaller than the networks of more conventional people because the users have been poorly socialized in the skills necessary to develop and maintain social relationships. These contrasting views of the social networks of drug abusers are stated in Table 12-1 as a set of competing propositions consistent with each theory (see also Hansell & Wiatrowski, 1980). Note that only the third proposition is common to both social control and cultural deviance theories.

Cultural deviance theory implies that the rehabilitation of drug abusers should include disconnecting them from their old social networks so that they can be resocialized to new sets of values and become bonded to new networks whose members hold these values. To the extent that the theory is valid, we can expect that the establishment of new social networks will be made difficult by the strong influence exercised by the members of the

Table 12-1. Competing propositions of cultural deviance and control theories regarding the social networks of street drug abusers

Propositions consistent with cultural deviance theory	Propositions consistent with social control theory
1. Street drug abusers' social networks are of equivalent size to the social networks of conventional people.	1. Street drug abusers' social networks are smaller than the social networks of conventional people.
2. Street drug abusers' social networks are composed primarily of members who use drugs, who are favorable to drug use, and who are unsupportive of abstinence from drugs.	2. Street drug abusers' social networks are composed of drug users as well as a substantial proportion of nonusers.
3. Street drug abusers' social networks contain small proportions of people from work, school, and organizational settings.	3. Street drug abusers' social networks contain small proportions of people from work, school, and organizational settings.
4. A large proportion of the relationships of street drug abusers and their social network members are characterized by personal reciprocity.	4. A small proportion of the relationships of street drug abusers and their network members are characterized by personal reciprocity.
5. A large proportion of the relationships of street drug abusers and their network members are characterized by mutual admiration and esteem (value similarity and role modeling).	5. A small proportion of the relationships of street drug abusers and their network members are characterized by mutual admiration and esteem (value similarity and role modeling).
6. A large proportion of the relationships of street drug abusers and network members are "multiplex" relationships in which several activities and interests are shared.	6. A small proportion of the relationships of street drug abusers and network members are "multiplex" relationships in which several activities and interests are shared.
7. The social networks of street drug abusers are dense.	7. The social networks of street drug abusers are not dense.
8. The social networks of street drug abusers are hierarchical, with a larger proportion of members being perceived by the abusers as higher and lower in status rather than equal in status to themselves.	8. The social networks of street drug abusers are not hierarchical; most members are perceived by abusers as equal in status to themselves.
9. A large proportion of the relationships between street drug abusers and their network members are stable.	9. A small proportion of the relationships between street drug abusers and their network members are stable.

prior network. Dense networks exert a constant and consistent influence on their members (Bott, 1957). They may, in this case, provide social support for the maintenance of drug abuse. According to cultural deviance theory, a critical problem for addicts seeking to establish more socially productive lives is to extricate themselves from their previous networks.

Control theory asserts that drug abusers have not been truly bonded to their prior networks. It implies that new bonds of attachment must be developed, not so much as a replacement for old bonds, but rather to provide a stake in maintaining a more conventional style of living. Thus, according to control theory, the rehabilitation of drug abusers is likely to be difficult, but for reasons different from those implied by cultural deviance theory. The successful development of skills is required for true integration into a social network, as are opportunities to establish new networks supportive of conventional living patterns.

In the literature on drug abuse, strains can be found that are consistent with each theory. Some ethnographers have characterized street drug abusers in terms consistent with cultural deviance theory: "Their behavior is anything but an escape from life. They are actively engaged in meaningful activities and relationships seven days a week. The brief moments of euphoria after each administration of a small amount of heroin constitute a small fraction of their daily lives. The rest of the time they are aggressively pursuing a career that is exciting, challenging, adventurous, and rewarding" (Preble & Casey, 1969, p. 2). Research on the recovery from opiate addiction also has suggested a cultural deviance perspective. A number of studies have reported that extrication of the addict from the drug subculture is an important factor (Winick, 1964; Scharse, 1966; O'Donnell, 1969; Maddux & Desmond, 1979; Desmond & Maddux, 1980; Waldorf & Biernacki, 1981).

In contrast, therapeutic communities have generally characterized drug abusers in terms consistent with control theory, attributing addiction to inadequate socialization in which people fail to learn to express and exchange personal needs and feelings, become personally insulated from others (rather than bonded), and engage in manipulative, dehumanized relationships to obtain what they desire (see Hampden-Turner, 1977; Hawkins & Wacker, in press).

Waldorf and Biernacki (1981) in reporting the results of their study of natural recovery from opiate addiction, contrast situational addicts and street addicts. Situational addicts, such as the soldiers who became addicted to opiates in Vietnam (Robins, 1973), are not deeply embedded in a deviant subculture. They use opiates largely because there are few constraints or controls that inhibit that use. This view of addiction is consistent with control theory. In contrast, they describe street addicts as people who have become deeply involved in and committed to the subculture of street drug abuse. This view of addiction is consistent with cultural deviance theory. Waldorf and Biernacki's research suggests that the two theories may apply differently to different individuals engaged in the abuse of street drugs.

Although prior research has documented the importance of social factors in drug-abusing behavior, little evidence has been available to determine whether the propositions of social control or cultural deviance theory most accurately describe the social lives of street drug abusers. Thus, it has been difficult to decide with certainty what approaches to developing social supports would be most likely to succeed. However, research that we recently completed on the social networks of residential drug program clients before and after treatment has provided pertinent new information. The results of the study are briefly reviewed here to provide an empirical basis for our suggestions that follow on developing social supports in drug abuse treatment.

THE STUDY OF TREATED STREET DRUG ABUSERS

We studied 106 residents in four residential treatment centers in two cities. (See Hawkins & Fraser, 1981, for a complete report of results.) These people had long histories of selling and using heroin, other opiates, amphetamines, and other drugs. Many had engaged in criminal behavior including crimes against persons and crimes of profit. Most were males (67%); 65% were white, 20% were black, and the rest were of other ethnic minority backgrounds. Comparison with data from national studies indicated that the sample was similar in most respects to clients in drug treatment program nationally. Forty-nine of the respondents were followed up 1 month and again 3 months after treatment. Forty-one (83.7%) of the 49 were interviewed successfully at 1 month, and 43 (87.7%) were interviewed success fully at 3 months following treatment. We collected information on respondents' social networks, drug use, and other related variables before treatment and during the follow-up periods.

We found that approximately two-fifths (42.5%) of the members of our respondents' social networks prior to treatment used hard drugs two or more times per week, and 46.1% of all pretreatment network members were reported to have positive attitudes toward drugs. The pretreatment social networks of opiate abusers contained significantly more hard drug users and members supportive of the use of hard drugs than did the networks of respondents who abused other street drugs. Further, opiate abusers' networks contained fewer members from conventional settings such as work, school, and organizations, and significantly more illegal business contacts than did the networks of other users.

Much of the interactional data on respondents' pretreatment networks suggested that a subculture does exist in which drug abusers are embedded. Respondents reported seeing 66.3% of their network members daily or several times per week. They viewed 63.1% of their members as close friends, and enjoyed seeing 68.1% of them. Surprisingly, they reported remembering birthdays or sharing holidays with 41.2% of their pretreatment network members, an indication of considerable personal reciprocity in these networks; 50.1% of the relationships were characterized by several different kinds of activities, and 35.2% involved reciprocal lending of household items, clothes, tools, or money. The networks were stable, with 55.7% of the members known over 3 years, and only 8.1% known less than 4 months. Finally, they were hierarchical: respondents viewed themselves as higher in status than 21.7% of their network members, lower than 38.5%, and equal in status with 39.6% of their members. All these findings seem to support the cultural deviance view. Abusers' interactions with network members appear to be stable, hierarchical, enjoyable, friendly, and reciprocal, with exchanges focused on a range of activities including, but not limited to, drug use.

However, one finding stood in opposition to the trends reported above. Respondents reported that before treatment they wanted to "be the kind of person" that only 15.2% of their pretreatment network members were. Furthermore, they reported that they did *not* want to be like 43.1% of the members of their personal networks. Apparently, though they liked many of their network members before treatment, respondents did not hold them in high esteem and did not, according to their self-reports, view them as role models to be imitated. Importantly, correlations indicated that the desire to imitate pretreatment network members was negatively related to the proportion of network members who were street-crime and drug-dealing associates. In contrast, respondents who wanted to be like network members had networks with more members from work or school and other conventional domains. In opposition to cultural deviance theory, these results suggest that even when active in street life, addicts are not necessarily *committed* to deviant social definitions. They do *not* want to be like their network members who engage in the most deviant activities. Rather, they appear to emulate network members when their networks include those who subscribe to noncriminal values and lines of action.

When we followed up clients who had left residential treatment, we found that the return to the community involved constituting a new social network. Even though respondents' networks before treatment were relatively dense and stable as predicted by cultural deviance theory, neither those who used opiates nor those who did not in the first 3 months after treatment returned entirely to their pretreatment social networks.

During the first month following treatment, both groups of returning clients had significantly fewer members in their social networks who favored drug use (a decrease from 47.8% pretreatment to 7.8% in the first month following treatment for the nonusers of opiates, and a decrease from 58.9% to 18.9% for the opiate users). Correspondingly, after treatment both groups had significantly more network members who were opposed to drug use, and both groups had significantly fewer street drug and crime contacts during the third month after treatment than they had before treatment. It appears from these data that the new networks that clients develop following treatment include different types of people from those who were included before residential treatment. Residential treatment is a dislocation that is associated with short-term changes in social network composition. In some respects, these changes appear positive in terms of rehabilitation.

The pretreatment networks of those who used opiates and those who did not during the first 3 months after treatment were quite similar. However, in the first month following treatment, the networks of those who used opiates and those who did not became significantly dissimilar in several respects. Those who did not use opiates in the 3 months after treatment reported significantly fewer regular users of hard drugs (3.4%) in their networks than did those who returned to opiate use (20.2%). Similarly, although the proportion of network members who used no hard drugs increased for both groups from pretreatment to 1-month follow-up, this increase was significant only for those who did not use opiates, whose networks contained significantly more nonusers (70.1%) than those of the opiate users (44.5%). In addition, the proportion of network members influencing the nonusers toward drug use decreased significantly, from 26.0% before treatment to 2.6% during the first month following treatment. The proportion of network members influencing the opiate users to use drugs showed only a modest nonsignificant decline: one-fifth (20.4%) of the network still influenced the users toward drug use during the first month after treatment. Again, the networks of the two groups differed significantly at 1-month follow-up in this respect. In sum, although the social networks of both groups changed in membership from before treatment to 1-month follow-up, those who used opiates after treatment had networks that provided significantly greater support for the use of hard drugs than the networks of those who did not use opiates.

Surprisingly, by 3 months after treatment, the networks of the opiate users were reported to include a greater proportion of conventional members than they did at 1-month follow-up. The regular users of hard drugs in users' networks had decreased to 11.2% of the networks, and those who used no illegal drugs now made up 61.2% of the networks. Yet these networks continued to include a greater proportion of members who influenced the respondents to use hard drugs (16.2%) than did the networks of nonusers (3.0%). Interestingly, the size of the posttreatment networks of the users appeared to constrict (to a mean of 12.2 members), whereas those of the nonusers remained virtually unchanged in size from the 1-month follow-up (with a mean at 3 months of 17.3 members). This constriction may account, in part, for the decrease in the proportion of hard drug users in opiate users' networks.

As the opiate users' networks constricted, they became more restricted in membership and more dense. Household members made up nearly a third (31.4%) of the opiate users' networks at 3 months, and their networks were as dense as they were before treatment. Further, the proportion of members whom users emulated decreased to 13.5%.

Given the small sample and short follow-up period of our study, the results on changes in networks over time cannot be considered conclusive. However, the data clearly suggest that a return to opiate use following treatment is accompanied by involvement in a social network that includes significant social influences toward use. While major changes in social network composition seem to follow residential treatment, and while returning clients seem to establish more prosocial networks of interaction during their first months back in the community, opiate use appears more likely when returning clients do not establish networks that provide consistent affective support and when their networks do not include role models whom they deem worthy of imitation. Under these conditions, the networks of former clients may constrict to include few members from legitimate social contexts beyond the immediate household. This may be detrimental in two respects. Household members may feel pressured to meet all of the former addict's needs for support, a situation that may soon exhaust the resources of the household. At the same time, the network will offer few alternative sources of support and solace when interactions at home become frustrating (see Gove & Geerken, 1977). When positive, supportive resources become strained or exhausted, the chances of opiate use are likely to increase.

IMPLICATIONS OF THE EVIDENCE FOR DEVELOPING SUPPORTIVE NETWORKS

Our data confirmed several of the propositions contained in cultural deviance theory, especially with regard to opiate abusers' pretreatment social networks. These networks were especially supportive of illicit drug use. So long as recovering drug abusers remain embedded in such networks, they are likely to continue to experience strong pressures to return to opiate use. The study also suggested that such social pressures are related to a relatively rapid posttreatment return to opiate use among clients of therapeutic communities. We found that clients who return to opiate use in the first 3 months after treatment report significantly more people in their networks who influence them to use drugs.

Thus, our study provides empirical support for the suggestion that an important goal in treating street drug abusers should be to help them to alter the composition of their social networks in order to eliminate members who support drug use. Changing network composition in this way is likely to take an intentional effort (Waldorf & Biernacki, 1981) and should become an explicit goal in drug abuse treatment.

If former opiate abusers are to be expected to stop interacting with drug users and other street associates, they need to become connected with people involved in more socially acceptable rounds of activities (Waldorf & Biernacki, 1981). Among clients of therapeutic communities, opiate abusers in particular are isolated from people from the domains of work, school, organizations, groups, and clubs. Our study showed that, before treatment, they are simply not connected with many people who could replace the drug-abusing peers in their networks. However, our research also revealed important information about the relationships of street drug abusers with their pretreatment networks. Street drug abusers like the members of their social networks. They like spending time with them, and they establish relatively long-lasting relationships with them that include a broad range of shared activities. The social rehabilitation of street drug abusers is not simply a matter of filling a social void in drug abusers' lives. If relationships with more prosocial network members are to be established, they will have to offer a measure of social bonding and social support at least equal to that provided by pretreatment, drug-oriented networks.

The follow-up results from our study of therapeutic community clients suggest that this replacement of network members is possible. The composition of respondents' networks after treatment changed to include fewer drug users and fewer long-time acquaintances, and both those who returned to opiate use and those who did not developed some degree of attachment to their posttreatment networks. Both groups reported networks in which approximately three-fifths of the members were close or very close friends. Both groups liked seeing nearly 70% of their network members after treatment. Both groups shared their thoughts and feelings with over a third of their network members, and both groups said that they would trust nearly half of their social networks with personally damaging information at the 1-month follow-up. It would appear that new ties can be developed in the community to replace old bonds to drug users and criminal business associates.

However, the fact that new bonds are possible does not guarantee that they will be supportive of more constructive lives. The data from our study suggest that the key to ensuring that new relationships are more supportive of rehabilitated lives is helping clients to connect with new members whom they admire and respect, people whom they can view as positive role models (see also Waldorf, 1973). Only this element of esteem appears to be consistently lacking in the relationships of drug abusers with their pretreatment networks, and it is precisely this element of esteem that seems to be absent when networks are predominated by hard drug users and illegal business associates. New networks supportive of rehabilitation are likely to take the place of pretreatment attachments when clients become linked with more prosocial others whom they respect as role models *and* when those others are people whom the clients enjoy seeing and with whom they can feel close, share time and thoughts, and exchange help on a reciprocal basis (see also Vaillant, 1973).

In summary, the available evidence suggests that three conditions should be met if the social factors contributing to drug abuse are to be adequately addressed in the treatment of street drug abusers.

1. Support in the social network for drug abuse should be minimized or eliminated.

2. Clients should be linked to network members who are engaged in positive activities and who can provide the attachment and support formerly provided by a network supportive of drug use (Stanton, 1979; Wolf & Kerr, 1979; Waldorf & Biernacki, 1981).

3. Special care should be taken to ensure that the new network contains viable role models whom the former abuser holds in high esteem.

MODELS FOR SOCIAL SUPPORT DEVELOPMENT

In the past decade, a number of efforts to provide greater social support to street drug abusers as part of the process of rehabilitation have been reported. Stanton (1978) has had positive results in applying structural family therapy with methadone maintenance clients. Wolf and Kerr (1979) report promising preliminary results from the application of companionship therapy with methadone clients, though they have had difficulty recruiting community volunteers to serve as companions. A broad range of self-help groups (Ashery, 1979; Ishiyama, 1979), as well as alumni associations (Ch'ien, 1979), have been initiated to provide ongoing supports for former drug abusers in the community. Currently, Dr. David Nurco of the University of Maryland (Nurco & Makofsky, 1981) and Dr. William McAuliffe of Harvard University are seeking ways in which practitioners from the helping professions can facilitate the development of self-help groups for drug abusers. Recently, the National Supported Work Demonstration found that ex-addicts participating in employment training with explicitly designed peer support features committed fewer crimes and had better employment success than did a randomly assigned no-treatment control group (Manpower Demonstration Research Corporation, 1980).

Approaches to social support development that hold promise for embedding former drug abusers in networks that will support their rehabilitated lives are explored in the rest of this chapter (see also Hawkins, 1979).

CONSULTATION TO EXISTING NETWORK MEMBERS

We have found that the pretreatment networks of some drug abusers include members with the potential to provide social support for rehabilitation. Yet these members may not function effectively in this regard and may even contribute to drug relapse (Stanton et al., 1978). Consultation to potentially supportive network members should help such members become more effective as social supports. Stanton (1978; Stanton & Todd, 1978) has involved family members of methadone maintenance clients in short-term structural family therapy using incentive payments for family member attendance and demonstrated drug abstinence by the client. Although assignment procedures, small numbers, and retention problems limit the conclusiveness of results, Stanton found that clients in this treatment program had a larger proportion of days free from the use of heroin, opiates, and other illegal drugs in the first 6 months following the treatment than did clients assigned to other types of family treatment (viewing movies or participating in family therapy without incentive payments) and a nonequivalent comparison group of clients not offered family treatment services. These results suggest the potential of supportive services to family members coupled with an explicit system of reinforcement for family involvement in supporting the former abuser's abstinence from drugs. Two additional approaches with promise are collaborative consultation and network assemblies.

Collaborative Consultation. In the collaborative consultation model, the client identifies a person in his or her network who best knows how to meet identified concrete needs. This may be an employer, spouse, friend, co-worker, or neighbor. The client invites that person to a consultation session. The client, network person, and practitioner review the need to be addressed or skill to be developed. The client and network member, with the practitioner serving as a consultant, then outline a plan for meeting the need, which they subsequently implement in the community. This approach enables network members to function effectively as social supports by engaging them in tangible collaborative tasks with clients. Collaborative consultation introduces the network member to a helping professional who will remain available as a consultant. Collaborative consultation sessions can be repeated sequentially with network members as needed to build a strong network of social supports with consultation backup.

Network Assemblies. A more ambitious approach is the mobilization of a portion of a client's social network. Assemblies of network members invited by the client seek to develop concrete plans to ensure the successful integration of the ex-abuser into the larger community and to identify the specific social support roles network members will play in the process (see Speck & Attneave, 1973). According to Speck and Attneave, network assemblies progress through a clearly recognizable sequence of phases. Staff take facilitative roles during network assemblies to help ensure progress through this sequence. Responsibility for developing and implementing plans rests with the client and network members. Again, throughout the process, practitioners can offer an ongoing consultative relationship to network members who compose the support system for the former abuser in the community. Network assemblies have been used in reentry planning for drug-abusing clients leaving therapeutic communities (Callan, Garrison, & Zerger, 1975).

FORMING NEW SOCIAL SUPPORTS

The data from our study suggest that opiate abusers, in particular, need more assistance in developing support for rehabilitation than can be provided by their existing social networks. When the networks of abusers do not provide adequate social supports for rehabilitation, additional community resources must be mobilized. The goal is to develop attachments between the former abuser and new network members who can provide such supports. The new relationships should become broad, rather than limited to a specialized content. They will differ in this respect from relationships of self-help groups, which revolve around a particular shared experience such as drug addiction or alcoholism (see Caplan, 1974, Ashery, 1979). The goal of mobilizing community resources is to create new friendships in the full sense of the word. Several approaches seem workable.

Activities Model. The activities model (Hawkins, 1979) is most applicable for those former abusers who are neither attached to supportive networks nor engaged in prosocial activities, such as jobs, which make them feel useful, competent, and part of something important. It is a companionship model (Wolf & Kerr, 1979) with an important variation. In this model, former abusers and new companions who are volunteers from the community become involved in activities selected for their potential to provide the former abuser with a meaningful role. The key elements of the model are:

1. The client explores specified activities with a companion. The client is responsible for determining whether an activity is worth pursuing on the basis of the answers to four questions: Is this activity interesting to me? Is it worth putting effort into? Do I have something to contribute? Would my contribution be important? If activities cannot be found that meet these criteria, it is unlikely that the client will become committed to them, and it is equally unlikely that the client will have a basis for establishing new and meaningful relationships with other participants in the activity.

2. The approach builds attachments between companions and clients by providing them a common task of screening and visiting activity settings. They may enter contexts unfamiliar to both. Facing a new environment together should increase their sense of commonality and hence their attachment to each other.

3. The companion assists the client to make decisions about what activities will be important, useful, and worthwhile, and assists the client in making specific plans for involvement. The companion seeks to function as an ally and friend, rather than as a counselor.

4. Small group sessions with other client–companion pairs to prepare for exploration and participation in community activities provide self-help supports and encouragement for clients without relying exclusively on relationships among former drug abusers as the basis for forming new social networks.

5. Participation provides opportunities for clients to learn and practice decision making, planning, and assessment skills in real contexts with the assistance of companion role models who possess such skills.

The model is applicable to a broad range of activities, allowing flexibility to meet particular interests and needs of individual clients. Activities may include becoming crisis-line telephone volunteers, or participating in civic groups, neighborhood councils, or campaigns focusing on issues of interest to the former drug abuser such as redlining, community health promotion, or law enforcement practices. The model can also be applied to job searches. In some activities, it may not be appropriate for the companion to participate fully after initial assessment visits are completed and plans are made for the client's ongoing participation. However, the companion should remain involved with the client in assessing ongoing participation in the activity to ensure that the client's participation is simultaneously providing a sense of usefulness, competence, and belonging while introducing the client to other potential network members.

In the activities model, the helping professional provides an initial personal link between the client and the companion. Staff members recruit, train, and give regular consultation to companions to discuss progress, problems, and possible solutions. They also facilitate small-group planning and debriefing sessions with companion–client pairs.

In this model, the selection of community volunteers to serve as companions is critical. Those selected should have (1) an ability to listen empathetically, (2) willingness to respond promptly to need, and (3) demonstrated capacity to care about others as evidenced in informal interactions in their own networks (Collins & Pancoast, 1976, p. 68). Clearly, the personal characteristics of companion volunteers will determine, in large measure, the success or failure of the approach. It may be desirable to recruit companions through informal word-of-mouth networks, rather than through public announcements. This does not preclude the use of community groups such as businesses, clubs, and civic organizations, but rather suggests that the leadership of such groups be approached informally for nominations of possible participants from the membership. It may be particularly appropriate to approach groups such as labor unions, religious organizations, and community clubs whose members share the same socioeconomic, ethnic, and cultural backgrounds as the clients with whom the companions will be matched. Weinman and Kleiner have noted the benefits of "community enablers" who come from comparable backgrounds: "The enablers' advantage in working as social change agents lay in their sharing of common socioeconomic backgrounds with the patients, communicating with them in a down-to-earth manner, and spending long periods of time assisting them with daily living activities" (1978, p. 141). Companions who have experienced social, economic, and cultural pressures conducive to street drug abuse and who have managed to escape that lifestyle can provide strong, realistic role models for former drug abusers. Companion pairs so constituted may develop strong attachments by participating in shared new experiences offered through the activities model.

The activities model holds potential for generating community support and involvement as well. A wide range of community groups may be encouraged to sponsor such a program. The model can be implemented by civic or fraternal organizations, Chamber of Commerce chapters, other business groups, or religious organizations. The sponsoring organization will influence the types of activities included. A project sponsored by a Chamber of Commerce or business group might target jobs and establish a program in which straight companions and ex-abusers initially visit work sites to learn about the nature of jobs performed and ultimately work toward meaningful job placements for the ex-abusers.

Nurco and Makofsky (1981) have developed an approach similar to the activities model described above which relies on developing positive relationships among former abusers rather than on community companions to provide a network supportive of rehabilitation. Practitioners in their Social Research Unit have recruited ex-addicts to become involved in self-help groups initiated by the Unit. Staff members serve as facilitators, allowing the groups to develop their own foci and activities. To date the groups have concentrated on developing specific projects such as working in prisons with inmate self-help groups. The ex-addicts have chosen an activities approach rather than a focus on personal problems, emphasizing that "we don't want therapy" (Nurco & Makofsky, 1981, p. 147). Although results on outcomes have not been reported, the project's experience suggests that groups focused on specific activities rather than on counseling or personal confrontation may provide former drug abusers with a palatable mechanism for continuing involvement in a supportive network.

Skills Training and Recreational Companionship Models. Less ambitious approaches to establishing supportive new linkages with community members seek to provide supplemental services in treatment. One approach is to assist clients in developing specific rudimentary skills for community functioning. Some clients need assistance in learning to open checking and savings accounts, to shop so as to conserve resources and ensure good nutrition, to use public transportation, and the like. When natural network members cannot be identified to assist in these tasks through the collaborative consultation process mentioned earlier, community volunteers can accompany ex-abusers to the locales where these skills are used and help them learn and practice them.

This is an inexpensive and effective model for ensuring that rudimentary survival skills are developed (Weinman & Kleiner, 1978). The focus is on development of specific behavioral compentencies (Stein & Test, 1978, p. 49). Most importantly, the model again provides a vehicle for involving community members in the reintegration process. However, the model's utility as a bonding strategy for drug-abusing clients may be limited. Few drug abusers are likely to need prolonged assistance in developing rudimentary skills in shopping, handling money, and the like. Companionship relationships based on providing such skills may therefore be short-lived. Additionally, this approach may have limited potential for the development of true friendships between companions, ones which are both multistranded and based on mutual esteem.

Community volunteers can also assist ex-abusers in finding ways to use leisure time that are not related to drugs. The effective use of leisure time appears to be an important characteristic of former clients who do not return to drug use (Simpson et al., 1981). Recreational activities could be shared by the companion pairs discussed above after rudimentary skills are learned. Shared recreational activities may facilitate the development of more durable relationships that include a broader range of shared interests.

Home Placements. Community volunteer families can provide living arrangements for clients. These arrangements are appropriate for those who have no other adult with whom to live or for those whose available living partners are drug users or family members likely to create stress and contribute to drug relapse (Stanton et al., 1978).

A diversity of home environments, ranging from roommates of the same age to intact nuclear family units, can be developed. Matching the former drug abuser and a home environment can provide an arrangement more responsive to specific needs than is possible in half-way houses or other group-living situations.

Polak has summarized the strength of the home placement approach in community mental health:

> Carefully selected individuals without formal training take on responsibilities usually carried out by professional staff. The family sponsors tend to quite naturally treat clients in their home as guests. They orient themselves more to the strengths and positive features of the clients than to their pathology, and are much less likely than . . . professionals to view all client behavior in an illness framework. . . . We provide little in the way of formal training, focusing instead on encouraging sponsor families to utilize their already existing skills. . . . Sponsor families provide a clear model of healthy individual and family behavior which can be generalized to the client's [own life]. (Polak, 1978, p. 127)

There is evidence from the mental health field that the home placement approach can reduce the need for further formal treatment. Weinman and Kleiner (1978) found significantly greater recidivism (rehospitalization) when former mental patients lived independently (22%) than when they lived in the homes of community enablers (4%).

If experiences with home placements can be generalized to ex-abusers, they may offer ongoing primary social supports, reduce community members' prejudices toward ex-abusers, and in turn enhance the self-esteem of ex-abusers seeking to build new lives (Weinman & Kleiner, 1978, pp. 156–157). However, the home placement model involves risks. Both legitimate and unfounded prejudices regarding possible "rip-offs" and drug use in the home may limit the number of adequate home placements that can be found. Further, the model may have limited utility for ex-abusers. It is likely to be most appropriate for younger ex-abusers who have not yet established families of their own outside their parents' homes. Finally, well-trained staffs are required to screen volunteer families, to match ex-abusers with appropriate families, and to provide on-call consultation on a 24-hour basis. This model of supportive network development should be explored in small, carefully controlled demonstration projects.

Community Employment Models. Perhaps the most ambitious and promising approach to the establishment of new supportive networks is to combine interactive and structural strategies while focusing on employment. Work is central in defining roles and identities in this society. It can provide a sense of successful accomplishment, contribution, and participation, as well as tangible financial rewards. Thus, employment has great potential for providing a social bond that is a stake in conformity.

If work is to meet this goal, however, it must meet certain criteria. The work should be perceived as important; it should provide an opportunity to develop and exhibit competence; it should offer opportunities to contribute and be useful; it should provide a sense of participation and belonging (Polk & Kobrin, 1972), and it should provide opportunities to establish new networks. It is difficult to find jobs open to former drug abusers that include all these features. Nevertheless, the results of the National Supported Work Demonstration suggest that it is possible to create these conditions in employment for former drug abusers. The Demonstration established a range of work opportunities that provided close supervision, small work crews to facilitate peer support and attachment, graduated stress, and a wage structure tied to increasing productivity. Participants in the experimental program engaged in less criminal activity and had improved employment and earnings in their third year in the program, in comparison with a randomly assigned untreated control group. The benefits of the program appear to exceed the costs when savings due to reduced crime are considered (Manpower Demonstration Research Corporation, 1980). Thus, attention to social support development in employment-oriented programs for ex-abusers seems warranted.

Community Lodges. When former abusers need an ongoing supportive living and work environment in the community, community lodges may be an answer. Community lodges, pioneered by Fairweather and his associates, have demonstrated effectiveness as mental health aftercare programs. They have been shown to be less expensive and more effective in reducing recidivism than traditional community aftercare programs (Fairweather *et al.*, 1969). Lodges are independent, democratically run, residential units that arc also self-supporting cooperative business enterprises. (The lodges discussed by Fairweather and his colleagues developed financially successful janitorial and gardening services.) Staff serve only as consultants to the lodges after an initial set-up and transition period.

The community lodge model is similar to the business enterprises of Synanon and Delancey Street (Hampden-Turner, 1977), with an exception. The lodges do not depend on a model charismatic leader. Members are themselves responsible for decision making and for the success of their cooperatively owned, cooperatively run enterprise.

By providing employment opportunities and living arrangements with others seeking to establish new lives, community lodges can offer incentives and supports. Participants are responsible for all aspects of a business, including administration and management, contracting, purchasing, pricing, and production of marketable products or services. These tasks can provide inherent satisfactions for people with a wide range of interests and skills. Additionally, the success of the enterprise depends on the contribution of all members. As a result, structural arrangements (the reward system of the business) and interactional arrangements (peer pressure to do one's part) encourage a commitment to prosocial activity.

Though financially self-sufficient, lodges require community support and involvement. Sponsorship by a respected community organization such as a private corporation or group of business people (e.g., Rotary, Kiwanis, or Chamber of Commerce) may be especially helpful. The sponsoring group can groom the environment to minimize political problems likely to be encountered and to help secure initial funding. Group members can collaborate with founding lodge participants to identify a marketable product or service to be produced. They can provide needed assistance and consultation in establishing and maintaining the business. Skills in contracting, setting up books, purchasing, marketing, and a host of other tasks will be required in the new business. The expertise of community business people should be mobilized to help lodge members develop these skills. Similarly, labor unions may be enlisted to provide training and apprenticeship certification to lodge members, should the lodge engage in trades such as renovation of privately owned buildings. Again, these approaches can create attachments between former drug abusers and new network members, while providing commitment to and involvement in activities offering rewards for drug-free patterns of living.

ROLES FOR PRACTITIONERS

The successful recruitment and development of an ongoing supportive network cannot be accomplished by working one-on-one with a client in a counseling session. It is a task that simultaneously implies broadened roles for practitioners and suggests very real limits to what they can expect to achieve through formal treatment services. The general goals are not new to social work practitioners. Social group work has traditionally viewed the immediate social network as a potential medium, target, and agent of change (Cartwright, 1951). Cartwright recognized that groups could, through support and sanctions, influence their members and intentionally effect individual change if they so desired. Cressey (1955) adapted Cartwright's principles of group work in describing criteria for effective work with criminals:

1. If criminals are to be changed they must be assimilated into groups which emphasize values conducive to law-abiding behavior and, concurrently, alienated from groups emphasizing values conducive to criminality.

2. The more relevant the common purpose of the group to the reformation of or prevention of criminal activity, the greater will be its influence on criminal members' attitudes and values.

3. The more cohesive the group, the greater the member's readiness to influence others and the more relevant the problem of conformity to group norms.

4. Both reformed and those to be reformed must achieve status within the group by exhibition of "pro-reform" or anticriminal values and behavior patterns.

5. The most effective mechanism for exerting group pressure on members will be found in groups so organized that criminals are induced to join with noncriminals for the purpose of changing other criminals. Thus, the most effective means of producing conformity in Actor A is to include him or her in a group which actively seeks to change the behavior of Criminal B.

6. When an entire group is the target of change, strong pressure for change can be achieved by convincing the members of the need for change, thus making the group itself the source of pressure for change.

These principles for effective group work with criminals are quite similar to the three noted earlier that were generated from our study of street drug abusers. What we expect from the creation of supportive social networks is not much different from what those who have engaged in social group work with deviant populations have sought. What distinguishes the approaches suggested here is that, for the most part, they seek to utilize and create social support in the natural environment of the client rather than to use formally constituted therapy groups.

The mobilization or creation of an informal network that can provide, on a daily basis, the attachment and support necessary for the replacement of patterns of drug abuse requires that the right people be identified and recruited for the supportive network. Many will need training if they are to function effectively as supportive network members. Finally, network members themselves may need the support and assistance of a helping professional in working with former drug abusers. Thus, the role of the practitioner is likely to be largely one of facilitator and consultant rather than "treater." Social network members and community volunteers will themselves become the bonding nuclei of new networks supportive of rehabilitation. The shift in role to that of facilitator who recruits, orients, trains, and consults with natural network members and community volunteers is likely to be both important and difficult for practitioners.

Adopting the consultant role is important for two reasons. First, the development of informal systems of social support for the rehabilitation of substance abusers is very unlikely without intentional effort. Our research has shown that street drug abusers and opiate abusers in particular are not likely to have social networks that will, without assistance, produce the social support necessary for rehabilitation. Although Narcotics Anonymous (NA) groups have had limited success in establishing meetings in some cities, many street drug abusers cannot meet the demands of the NA philosophy or program (Nurco & Makofsky, 1981) and a number of groups have floundered and failed. Moreover, the stigma attached to street drug abuse and the very nature of the social networks of most street drug abusers continually augur against the unassisted creation and maintenance of self-help groups for this population. Finally, given the stigmatized status of street drug abusers, it is unlikely that community groups will voluntarily pursue social support development for them without encouragement from effective professional advocates.

The consultant role seems appropriate for a second reason. It allows the professional to act as a catalyst for the development of strong primary relationships between ex-abusers and conventional community members. The goal for the practitioner should be to broaden the consultative approach so that network members themselves become engaged as collaborators who participate with former drug abusers in planning, taking initiative for, and carrying out plans of action aimed at community reintegration. Practitioners should seek to provide consultation directly to network members. This collaborative consultation can increase the potential for creating strong primary attachments between ex-abusers and conventional others. Consulting with community volunteers and network members has been shown to be more effective than directly serving clients in aftercare programs for former mental patients (Weinman & Kleiner, 1978, p. 151).

Consultation to primary network members avoids the status inequality that typically exists between practitioner and client. Consultation facilitates the development of mutuality in primary relationships. Mutuality is a characteristic of supportive primary relationships whose members are of roughly equal status and whose members both give *and receive* help from one another (Patterson & Twente, 1972). The professional practitioner, because of the helping role, inevitably remains in a superordinate position vis-à-vis the client. However, the professional can accomplish through consultation to natural network members and lay volunteers what may never be accomplished through traditional casework: the development of a social network in which the former drug abuser is an active, positive contributer, sharing and exchanging support. Thus, through collaborative consultation, practitioners can assist former abusers to become attached and committed to a network supportive of a new way of life.

STRATEGIES AND PROSPECTS FOR COMMUNITY INVOLVEMENT

The approaches reviewed above have implied the active involvement of community members in creating supportive networks for ex-abusers. If involvement in school, work, and other organizational settings is to produce supportive links with members of these groups, these members will have to become actively involved with former drug abusers. Yet such involvement is in direct opposition to the dominant trend in social programs in the last century:

> Increased urbanization and industrialization in society have been accompanied by increased professionalism concentrated in formal agencies charged with responsibilities for solving social problems. . . . Furthermore, these agencies and their programs have tended to become "disengaged" from the community, or at best are peripheral to the mainstream of community life. They have not functioned as a central part of the life of the community (Pink and White, 1973, p. 29).

Rather than viewing drug abusers as community members who must somehow be effectively treated, resocialized, and reintegrated, community members have generally viewed them as stigmatized "outsiders" (King, 1969, pp. 218–219). These attitudes have been reflected in community resistance to the very presence of drug treatment programs in some neighborhoods (Lowinson & Langrod, 1975; Ruiz, Langrod, & Lowinson, 1975). Active community participation generally has been missing in drug abuse treatment. How can fraternal, civic, labor, and business groups, as well as individuals in the community be engaged in the task of rehabilitating street drug abusers? Only if they somehow come to accept the problem as their responsibility. If this is to happen, practitioners must take the initiative on yet another front. They must become entrepreneurs for community involvement and responsibility, approaching community groups and seeking to convince them of the need to participate in planning and developing programs. Professionals should not simply design and implement programs oriented toward supportive network development. Rather, the very process of program development should be one of collaborative consultation between professionals and members of community groups (Caplan & Grunebaum, 1967; Ruiz, Langrod, & Lowinson, 1975, pp. 153–154).

Community groups should be recruited to participate from the start in developing and appraising models. They should be asked to assess realistically the abilities of their own members to implement them. Ultimately, community organizations will need to provide the personnel to carry out the planned activities. Although this level of community participation will be difficult to achieve and more troublesome for staff of drug treatment programs than simply working with clients, it will be necessary if new approaches to the social integration of drug abusers are to be initiated under the present funding conditions. Additionally, such participation can create a feeling of ownership and responsibility among community members that will be important for the success of the approaches we describe here.

CONCLUSION

Patterns of social interaction are closely linked to the initiation, maintenance, and cessation of drug-abusing behavior. The available evidence suggests that street drug abuse is deeply embedded in social networks that support it, including those who engage in it. The evidence also suggests that the effective rehabilitation of street drug abusers requires separation from those network members who are supportive of drug abuse and the establishment of networks characterized by positive, affective ties and strong positive role models. Although these are likely to be difficult tasks, there is evidence that treated clients establish new social networks after treatment and that some existing network members can be successfully engaged in providing support. In this chapter, we have explored a range of approaches to the development of supportive networks for street drug abusers and have reviewed the implications of these approaches for the roles of practitioners who work with this population.

To implement these approaches, practitioners will need to develop skills in assessing the existing support in clients' social networks and in identifying where additional supportive members are needed. They will need to develop methods for effectively recruiting and actively involving those members of clients' networks who appear to hold the potential to provide support. This may be difficult if network members have given up on the client or if the client's addictive behavior maintains the equilibrium of an interactional system by focusing attention away from other problems. However, Stanton's success in using financial incentives to involve family members in structured family therapy with ex-addicts suggests that these obstacles may be overcome. Continued research and development is needed on this point. Similarly, practitioners will need to develop effective methods for recruiting community volunteers to be involved as positive role models in former abusers' networks. Again, the task promises to be difficult given the stigma attached to the problem. Nurco's limited success in constituting self-help groups of former addicts focused on specific advocacy activities provides an alternative model to the recruitment of "straight companions" but, to date, there is little evidence of the comparative strengths and weaknesses of these approaches. Finally, practitioners will need to work effectively with both natural network members and community volunteers to support their efforts to engage former abusers in ongoing supportive networks of reciprocal exchange and interaction.

Unfortunately, in the drug abuse treatment field, there is little hard empirical evidence to guide practitioners in developing the approaches, roles, and skills that appear to be needed. While the literature on collaborative consultation in community mental health provides a foundation for the exploration of new approaches in substance abuse treatment, creative and courageous thought and action will be required from practitioners who work with substance abuse problems. We hope that those who seek to advance this field will commit themselves to documenting rigorously their efforts and their results so that a basis of knowledge can be developed to guide the work of those who follow.

PART VI
Services to the Developmentally Disabled

CHAPTER 13
Social Support Networks in Developmental Disabilities

Robert F. Schilling and Steven Paul Schinke

Developmentally disabled populations depend more on enriched sources of support than other people. Being handicapped means having to cope with a world controlled by fully functioning people. Across the life span, developmentally disabled children and adults grow and prosper because of family, professionals, and institutional services. The survival of developmentally disabled persons requires special environments. For these reasons this chapter covers a spectrum of social networks from the most natural family supports to more artificial linkages developed and maintained by human service professionals.

First the target population is defined. We consider the diagnosing and labeling of developmentally disabled persons in light of past mistakes, professional limitations, and the continuing need to define disabilities in order to provide needed services. The need for social support by the developmentally disabled is viewed as a dual responsibility of informal helpers and professionals who support and enhance each other's efforts. We describe a variety of supportive networks and offer suggestions for improved and expanded use of networks. Human service professionals are asked to take responsibility for overcoming the many institutional, practical, and social barriers to increasing and strengthening supportive networks.

DEFINITIONS

Before we describe our target population, we should briefly reiterate the definition of social support network given in Chapter 1. It is "a set of interconnected relationships among a group of people that provides enduring patterns of nurturance . . . and provides contingent reinforcement for efforts to cope with life on a day-to-day basis." The essential elements of the social support network—the familiarity and close relationships of the people involved, its ongoing nature, the emphasis on the small tasks and inter-changes of daily life—are of particular importance to people who are developmentally disabled. The responsibility for their well-being falls first on their family and friends, despite wide acceptance of the idea of professional help. The care and nurturance of handicapped people is unquestionably long-term, even though many will achieve nearly independent lives. Furthermore, the problems of being handicapped are often basic problems of daily life: getting dressed, getting about, making oneself understood. With the social support network of the handicapped person established as unquestionably crucial to his or her quality of life, we now turn to an examination of just who we mean by "developmentally disabled people."

Terms for developmental disabilities have most frequently been applied to mental limitations and less often to neurologic, motoric, physical, and genetic problems (Sulzbacher, 1973). Only recently have impaired styles of learning, emotional control, sensory functioning, behavior management, and mobility been defined as developmental disabilities (Finkel, 1977).

Table 13-1, culled from the *Physicians' Current Procedural Terminology* (Finkel, 1977), *Diagnostic and Statistical Manual of Mental Disorders* (American Psychiatric Association, 1980), *Manual on Terminology and Classification in Mental Retardation* (Heber, 1961; Grossman, 1977), and *International Classification of Diseases* (Commission on Professional and Hospital Activities, 1978), hints at the range of disorders listed as developmental disabilities.

Although disabilities are classified by the locus of trauma, any developmental disability affects several systems. A mentally retarded child may be language-delayed, poorly coordinated, emotionally disturbed, learning impaired, and behaviorally troubled (Bennett, LaVeck, & Sells, 1978; Leconte, 1981). By the same token, individual disabilities have multiple sources. One disabling condition can be caused by genes, parents' age and blood type, mother's prenatal drinking, difficult labor and delivery, nutritional deficits, environmental hazards, viral diseases, high fever, violent accidents, and aging (Shipsey, 1977; Landesman-Dwyer & Emanuel, 1979). On the other hand, a single factor may explain many disabilities. For example, children whose mothers had prenatal rubella may have hearing, visual, or mental impairments (Chess, Korn, & Fernandez, 1971).

SCOPE

Public Law 91-517 defines a developmental disability as:

A disability attributable to mental retardation, cerebral palsy, epilepsy, or another neurological condition of an individual found by the Secretary to be closely related to mental retardation or to require treatment similar to that required for

Table 13-1. Common developmental disabilities grouped by locus of trauma

Behavioral	Genetic	Language
Arithmetical disorders	Down's syndrome	Aphasia
Attention deficit	Klinefelter's syndrome	Articulation disorder
Emotional disturbance	Sickle cell disease	Dyslalia
Hyperkinesis	Tay-Sachs disease	Elective mutism
Learning disability		Speech delay
Overactivity		
Metabolic	**Motoric**	**Multiple Traumas**
Diabetes mellitus	Benign congenital myopathy	Cleft lip
Phenylketonuria	Cerebral palsy	Dwarfism
Williams elfin facies syndrome	Congenital dislocation of joints	Infantile syndrome
	Coordination disorder	Mixed developmental disorder
	Head and neck underdevelopment	
	Gilles de la Tourette's syndrome	
Nutritional/Iatrogenic	**Neurologic**	**Sensory**
Difficult delivery	Incomplete CNS	Blindness
Fetal alcohol syndrome	Mental subnormality NOS	Deafness
Neonatal narcotic abstinence syndrome	Mild mental retardation (IQ from 50 to 70)	Mutism
Prolonged labor	Moderate mental retardation (IQ from 35 to 49)	
	Severe mental retardation (IQ from 20 to 34)	
	Profound mental retardation (IQ below 20)	
	Myoclonic jerks	
	Prader-Willi syndrome	
	Spina bifida	

mentally retarded individuals, which disability originates before such individual attains age eighteen, which has continued or can be expected to continue indefinitely, and which constitutes a substantial handicap to the individual. (Developmental Disabilities Act, 1969)

The concept of developmental disability has brought to light the needs of children and adults with many different handicapping conditions. Since developmental disabilities usually surface during infancy and early childhood, most definitions are concerned with children. The definition appears to exclude people whose disability is not associated with impaired neurologic function. In practice, developmental disabilities may connote only mentally retarded persons or may include children with moderate hearing and sight loss, learning disabilities, and psychological disturbance (Hobbs, 1975). The scope of developmental disabilities depends in large measure on the definitions used in a given survey (Robinson & Robinson, 1976). As Suran and Rizzo note, "there is no single consistent and universally accepted method of describing the different kinds of special children. Educators, social workers, physicians, psychologists, biomedical scientists, and others are all involved in helping the special child; and professionals in each of these areas tend to use a slightly different framework for classifying special children" (1979, p. 6).

In the United States perhaps one in five children will develop an identifiable condition that can potentially inhibit development (Suran & Rizzo, 1979). Excluding learning, behavioral, and emotional disorders and juvenile delinquency, about 13%, or 7,067,500 children in 1978) would fall under a more restricted definition of developmental disability (Suran & Rizzo, 1979). A still more exclusive group consists of mentally retarded people, who constitute 3% of the population (Office of Mental Retardation Coordination, 1972; Craig, 1976). Applying even this restrictive standard to the 1980 census, nearly 7 million people in the United States are developmentally disabled. In any case, developmentally disabled people are a significant minority.

DIAGNOSIS AND LABELING

Field observations and controlled investigations reveal different perceptions of developmental disabilities labels by parents, teachers, and human service workers (Foster, Ysseldyke, & Resse, 1975; Wadsworth & Checketts, 1980). Data on labeling effects should caution the professional against stereotyping any client (Carroll & Reppucci, 1978). Extreme caution should be exercised if clients are diagnosed in one place and subsequently moved to other contexts. The coming of multidisciplinary diagnostic centers means that developmentally disabled clients are labeled and treated at separate facilities (McGrath, O'Hara, & Thomas, 1976), and labeled diagnostic evaluations are often the beginning of interagency referral and treatment planning (Forness, 1979). Individual educational plans mandated under Public Law 94-142 are frequently based on the written testimony (Turnbull, Strickland, & Goldstein, 1978). Case reports usually precede clients and so can prophesy poor motivation, low achievement, and failure (Rosenthal & Jacobson, 1968; Lisbe, 1978). Such insidious and far-reaching effects demand accurate labels.

Truly objective labels are, of course, impossible. Diagnostic categories can only imprecisely describe handicaps unique to the individual (Nelson & Hays, 1979). Even correct diagnoses lose relevance when clients mature beyond the labeled condition. But casting off the developmental disabilities label is another matter. Because clients are dynamic and labels are not, the accuracy of the original diagnosis further erodes as a disability improves or worsens. Accurate labels therefore have two functions: they put the right client in the right program, and they keep the wrong client from entering the wrong program. A tragic example of the latter might be a deaf-blind person of normal intelligence who, due to a hurried or incomplete process, is diagnosed mentally handicapped, and then institutionalized.

Definitions, diagnoses, effects, and inaccuracies of clinical labels affect developmentally disabled persons' use of social networks. Precise definitions are salient because the homogeneous term "developmental disabilities" connotes a wide range of disorders. Handicaps lodged in behavior, genes, nutritional deficits, language, metabolism, motor functioning, neurology, and perceptual senses are mutually inclusive and not well defined. Labels fail to tell if clients are infants, children, adolescents, adults, or seniors. One diagnosis may obtain both for people who are visibly handicapped and for those who look perfectly normal. A single label can be handed to institutionalized clients and community dwellers. Clients totally dependent on artificial support and people entirely self-reliant may have the same diagnosis. Professionals thus are ill-advised to seek one kind of social network for all developmentally disabled clients.

SOCIAL NETWORKS

Adaptation involves interpersonal mechanisms that allow handicapped people to flourish at their full potential and to cope with stress (Stagner, 1981). Conceptually, social networks are a means of adaptation (Aldrich & Mendkoff, 1968; Coyne & Lazarus, 1980). Integral to the concept is that adaptation and stress are no different for disabled and nondisabled individuals (Price & Politser, 1980). Most people want to be in harmony with themselves, with others, and with the environment. Growing up and being independent are no less coveted by developmentally disabled people than by anyone else. What makes handicapped people special is that they enter the world with fewer resources for reaching these goals. As Haywood notes: "A defining characteristic of mental retardation is the relative dependency of many retarded persons" (1981, p. 191). Thus, developmentally disabled people may require special help and support as they encounter both the same difficulties as nonhandicapped people and obstacles unique to their particular disability.

For at least part of their lives, developmentally disabled people require help from formal institutions and trained professionals. Informal networks aside, handicapped people must often depend on recognized experts and organizations to achieve their goals. Although some people may wish for a return to a simpler time when social services meant food baskets from the church, the extraordinary needs of the handicapped cannot be met through informal helping alone.

The troublesome but necessary process of diagnosis and labeling must begin with professional skill, judgment, and insight. This process is set in motion when some part of the client's social network acts in response to its enduring commitment to the client. For example, parents whose children are developmentally delayed will most often turn to their pediatrician. Others may call directly to a child study clinic, like the University of Washington Child Development and Mental Retardation Center. The initial call to the intake social worker helps parents decide whether to wait a bit longer in hopes of developmental gains, or to arrange for diagnostic assessment. Families who proceed with evaluation gain a greater understanding of the child's development, often including a tentative or definitive diagnosis, and advice on treatment, remediation, and planning. In most instances they will meet with at least a half-dozen professionals from such specialities as nutrition, medicine, education, social work, psychology, and communication disorders in the course of their evaluation. Such services rendered to parents and their handicapped child cannot be supplanted by informal helping networks. On the other hand, professionals will be more effective as helping agents if they recognize, support, and enhance social networks that benefit the developmentally disabled (Newbrough, 1977).

The social support networks of developmentally disabled people are not unlike those of nondisabled persons. For those with developmental disabilities, as much as for any group, a social support network is a set of interconnected relationships that endures across many forms and provides daily, mutual reinforcement (see Chapter 1). No less certain is the reality that social support networks are at once especially important to handicapped people and particularly difficult for them to develop and maintain. This irony will surface as we discuss how supportive networks help developmentally disabled people adapt to the daily trials of living.

THE FUNCTION OF SOCIAL SUPPORT NETWORKS

We have noted that for at least part of their lives, and in varying degrees, handicapped people are more dependent than their nondisabled peers. Consider, at one end of the continuum, a mildly retarded person who may be labeled as mentally retarded solely because of academic limitations (Robinson & Robinson, 1976; Bogdan, 1980). During the school years the child is stigmatized as mentally retarded by the very educational system that claims to benefit him. Putting aside the question of what is the best form of education for such a child (Childs, 1981), it is nonetheless true that this individual will benefit from special help in acquiring basic academic skills. In addition, this young person may require special therapy, extra supervision, or even protection from playtime bullies. At the opposite end of the disability spectrum are profoundly retarded individuals who may exhibit virtually no skills in communication, self-help or even ambulation. A person with such a disability is totally dependent on others.

Both of these people will probably benefit from services provided by professionals and institutions. The mildly handicapped child receives special help from teachers, therapists, psychologists, and social workers who diagnose, plan, facilitate, teach, and train, usually within the context of the public schools. The profoundly handicapped person receives services from a variety of professionals and less highly trained care providers, and perhaps uses federal, state, and local resources from various governmental and private agencies. Both people benefit, of course, from the continuing commitment of their families, their primary social network.

These kinds of assistance are perhaps obvious; they are surely desirable and necessary. Most would agree that institutionalized supports (now referred to as a collective "safety net," as if to catch unfortunate souls just before they hit bottom) cannot replace informal network systems. To their credit, parents and professionals years ago came to realize the limitations and indeed the evils of policies that ignored the need of developmentally disabled people for informal social supports and society's ability to provide these supports. The movements to deinstitutionalize, mainstream, and provide access for handicapped people were not directed primarily at mobilizing informal social supports on behalf of those once relegated to backward, isolated schools, and circumscribed lives. Nevertheless, implicit in this shift in attitude and policy was the assumption that disabled people could and should have opportunities to become part of informal social networks.

As handicapped citizens increasingly mix with society as a whole, how do they rely on social support networks? The support networks of most developmentally disabled people are divided into contacts with handicapped people and nonhandicapped people. They may relate most easily to other disabled people, with whom they are likely to share common interests, experiences, and opportunities for contact (Hendrix, 1981). Developmentally disabled people also establish social support relationships with nonhandicapped people. Often the boundaries of these relationships are defined by the nonhandicapped, but this may vary according to the degree and nature of the handicapped person's disability. For example, vision-impaired people may socialize regularly and intimately with sighted people. In contrast, mentally retarded people may have only superficial social relationships with nondisabled people (Hendrix, 1981). Although many benefits accrue to those who develop support systems, the raison d'etre of networks is social contact with other people, be they disabled or nondisabled.

Social support networks also enable people with developmental disabilities to participate more fully in activities that nondisabled people take for granted. For example, developmentally disabled young adults in a local vocational training program often pair up as transportation buddies. As a pair, they are less likely to get on the wrong bus or to forget to get off at the right stop. For some developmentally disabled people, advocacy and political action are closely tied to social support networks. For them, the process of working with other like-minded persons may be at least as important as the goal of increased rights and benefits for the developmentally disabled population. Others with disabling conditions develop supportive networks that facilitate or enhance necessary treatments or services. Examples are home visits from physical therapists, homemakers, and social workers. The following section describes these and other social support networks involving developmentally disabled people, friends, relatives, professionals, and advocates.

DESCRIPTION OF SOCIAL SUPPORT NETWORKS

Social networks for developmentally disabled people and their families can be relatively formal support systems facilitated by professionals, or informal relationships maintained without help from practitioners. Families of developmentally disabled people, on their own initiative or in concert with helping professionals, have early recognized the potential of social support networks. For example, many parents who rear mildly handicapped children look back at the onset of school age as a benchmark when they were galvanized into expanding their social network. At this juncture parents face the painful reality that their child is different. They come to accept that special help is needed for their boy or girl who will not catch up as was once hoped. Parents see their child left out of games and sports that demand advanced understanding and coordination. Family members may fear such a child becoming a social outcast, rejected by agemates, and not always accepted by parents of younger children (Guralnick, 1978). They may fault the schools for providing inadequate instruction, therapy, or transportation. Not surprisingly, parents of developmentally disabled students may be drawn to other parents of handicapped children, who share similar feelings of disappointment, rejection, worry, and anger (Holland & Hattersley, 1980; Venters, 1981). Featherstone (1980) describes the sense of relief parents experience when they discover other parents with handicapped children. Such parents share a common bond that may have practical as well as emotional benefits (Bregman, 1980). Parents of developmentally disabled children may share transportation duties, resource information, and child care. Their collective efforts can lead to educational, recreational, and supportive services benefiting developmentally disabled children and their families.

A family whose child was evaluated at the University of Washington Child Development and Mental Retardation Center illustrates how informal bonds created by common circumstances can provide enduring social support for parents of disabled children. Ms. B. is a 35-year-old divorced mother of a mildly retarded 8-year-old boy. Years earlier, she was both shaken and relieved when told that her 4-year-old son was 18 months delayed in language, motor, and cognitive functioning. She at first refused to enroll him in a developmental preschool after seeing the wide range of handicapped children, most of whom seemed more markedly impaired than Jamie. Then one day as she was struggling to keep Jamie under control in the grocery checkout line, she traded empathic remarks with a couple whose mildly handicapped child was also grabbing for candy. Ms. B. disclosed that her son was a little slower than other children, and as a result was sometimes quite a handful. One comment led to another, and as the two families parted they exchanged phone numbers. Ms. B. was subsequently encouraged by Mr. and Ms. M. to visit the developmental preschool again, and she soon enrolled Jamie. In the months and years since then, these parents have confided in each other, traded child care, watched their children compete in Special Olympics, lent books on child development, provided rides for each other's children, and shared leadership positions on parent committees. Ms. B. looks on the Ms. as close friends and a principal source of social support. She recently remarked, "I don't know how I would have kept on trying if Judy and Ray weren't there to help."

If informal networks are the most typical, more structured social support systems have received more attention. Parent-to-parent groups sponsored by local associations for retarded citizens link new parents of Down's syndrome children with more experienced counterparts (Porter, 1978). New parents quickly learn that other normal, caring parents also give birth to Down's syndrome babies. They are told that the darkest moments are already past, that life does go on for parents who learn to take pride in small accomplishments. Later, new parents learn more about the causes of Down's syndrome, characteristics of such children, and how to obtain help through pediatricians, social workers, and developmental specialists.

A recently funded project at the University of Washington Child Development and Mental Retardation Center brings together fathers of young handicapped children and may serve as an example of nationwide efforts (Delaney, Meyer, & Ward, 1980). During Saturday morning groups, fathers of developmentally disabled preschoolers share common experiences and learn childrearing skills. A major thrust of the program is helping fathers—who often feel estranged from friends and family after the birth of a handicapped child—to develop and maintain social support networks. Encouraged by the group leaders, fathers learn to share help, guidance, and support with other fathers and with family and friends.

Groups that parents and family find most useful tend to endure. Two such formal groups have been meeting at one child development center for over five years. Parents of children with Prader-Willi syndrome meet monthly to discuss mutual concerns. Because this condition is characterized by uncontrolled appetite, participants share practical tips on controlling food intake (Leconte, 1981). Diet is also a principal focus at the monthly gathering of parents whose children have phenylketonuria (PKU). A rare condition, PKU is an inability to metabolize an amino acid (phenylalanine) found in most foods (Holm and Pipes, 1976). Children who do not maintain strict diets suffer mental retardation or epilepsy, while those who are maintained on the special diet have virtually normal development. Parents of such children soon learn how the cost, inconvenience, and taste of the food supplements, along with the child's inclination to eat forbidden foods, make diet maintenance a serious family challenge. During monthly get-togethers parents praise each other for their vigilance. Parents of younger children learn how older children's independence complicates dietary management. As with the Prader-Willi group, parents of PKU children receive advice from social work, nutrition, and medical staff, who urge all family members to cooperate with each other in their common goal. Practical outcomes of these networks have been the establishment of a group home for Prader-Willi young adults and the sharing of recipes using foods low in phenylalanine.

These programs are directed primarily at parents who must continually deal with the enormous responsibility of rearing a handicapped child. Because parents expend considerable effort in caring and seeking help for their developmentally disabled children, mothers and fathers have organized support networks that find services for handicapped people. In contrast to the parent-oriented programs already described, these formalized support systems have the stated purpose of helping developmentally disabled children and dependent adults. Doubtless, for many parents, the associations necessary to carry out the groups' activities become at least as important as the objectives that benefit the children. One organization that channels parents' desire for support and action is the Association for Retarded Citizens (ARC). Parent participation at many levels is required to carry out various activities of the local ARC chapters organized in communities across the nation. At the board level, parents can make policy for the association as a whole or invest their energies in board committees that deal with specific areas such as long-range planning, finance, program, and personnel. Other parents participate directly in the ARC service activities—parent-to-parent programs, information and referral, advocacy, grooming classes, activity clubs, and political action. Similarly, parents can become involved in associations on behalf of people with learning disabilities, autism, cerebral palsy, muscular dystrophy, and other disabling conditions.

Other formal organizations allow both parents and their developmentally disabled children to build social supports. The Special Olympics is a visible and clearly desirable program benefititing thousands of handicapped persons nationwide. Media coverage accurately portrays handicapped people competing against each other, meeting new friends, and joyfully accepting well-deserved praise from parents, officials, and onlookers. Not conveyed by print or picture are the enduring social networks generated during the planning, practice, fund-raising, and coordination before the event. Both parents and their developmentally disabled children benefit from the networks constituted during the Special Olympics. Another example of social support was demonstrated by 11 disabled persons who climbed 14,410-foot Mt. Ranier. Aided by professional guides, climbers with disabilities ranging from hearing and sight impairments to epilepsy scaled the peak in the summer of 1981. Most made the summit; all concurred that this victory was both real and symbolic. One year later, the same group of guides had a second attempt with a blind climber who had failed to complete the earlier climb (Gilje, 1982). Although weather forced the party off the mountain, the attempt is proof of the strength of social supports.

Still other informal social networks spin off from structured activities and interventions that are organized, directed, or facilitated by professional helpers. Consider, for example, an agency sponsoring a series of life skill workshops for developmentally disabled persons. Opportunities for informal bonds abound as participants congregate before and after the workshop, are gently pressed into role plays, ride together on the bus or with parents, and carry out real-life practice in tandem. In our own group training for mentally handicapped parents who have maltreated their children, we have encouraged using the social network as a necessary addition to teaching cognitive–behavioral skills. For example, transportation provisions forced clients to interact, as five parents were packed into a Volkswagen. The refreshment table provided not only sustenance, but a natural opportunity for fearful and uncomfortable parents to meet each other. Aware that social isolation is one element leading to child maltreatment (Young, 1976; Garbarino, 1977), group leaders continually encouraged parents to call each other between sessions. During role plays designed to let parents practice new ways of responding, participants were coaxed into relating to each other. Informal feedback suggests that these somewhat artificial efforts resulted in continued contact between the families well after the end of the training project.

We do not mean to overlook the ways in which developmentally disabled people form their own social support networks. Although the goals of mainstreaming are laudable, the normalization movement cannot ignore the reality that for many developmentally disabled children the preferred alternative is the opportunity to socialize and compete with children who are developmental peers. Early in life, most handicapped children come to understand that they are different. Many are drawn to other children with handicapped conditions. For handicapped children continually rejected by more able peers, other developmentally disabled playmates may be their only childhood buddies. Parents served by the Child Development and Mental Retardation Center tell of long-standing relationships between their own children and other handicapped peers, and this situation can be safely generalized (Baroff, 1974). Parents of children with more obvious handicapping conditions, such as those with moderate mental retardation, eventually come to accept that in many ways other children of like ability are appropriate playmates. For children with milder handicaps, the peer network may offer a series of sometimes painful encounters with peers who may accept or reject them (Haywood, 1981; Kingsley, Viggiano, & Tout, 1981). In time, such children learn to discriminate between the accepting playmate who overlooks or adjusts to developmental limitations and the competitive peer who reinforces and exaggerates the differences between them. To a developmentally disabled child, a peer network may be like some city streets, with dead ends, difficult turns, and occasional thoroughfares. Despite the periodic pain, these sometimes precarious and often circumscribed relationships are important threads in the handicapped child's social network.

As developmentally disabled youths grow older they encounter work and living environments that open up new sources of social support. Across North America, an array of structured work and living arrangements enables handicapped people to participate more fully in society (Baker, Seltzer, & Seltzer, 1974; Rusch & Mithaug, 1980). For example, a food service training program at the Child Development and Mental Retardation Center enables researchers to look closely at the social networks of a work setting (Moss, 1979). Designed to train developmentally disabled young adults in skills leading to competitive employment in restaurants, the program accepts only those who have been rejected by or have failed in other training programs. Hours before the start of work, some trainees congregate in the cafeteria. Many arrive in twos and threes on public buses, which run from the area where group homes are clustered. Most of the trainees sit drinking coffee, talking and joking with one another, eagerly awaiting a nod or greeting from agency staff and cafeteria supervisors. Their early arrival testifies to a sense of belonging for these young adults. Clearly, in this instance having a place to go is as important as the actual relationships that are part of that environment. The many network linkages become evident during the lunch period when trainees busy themselves clearing trays, carrying silverware, cleaning pans, stacking dishes, and replenishing steam tables. While learning these tasks, the young adults are gaining invaluable social skills as they interact with supervisors, co-workers, and customers. With stopwatches, counters, and point charts, the trainers track the clients' progress. Trainees learn through modeling, cuing, praising, and prompting behavior appropriate for a restaurant employee. The polite request, "Are you through, sir?" receives a reinforcing nod from the supervisor, even as joking with a fellow trainee earns a frown from the cashier. Thus, the trainee learns the limits of the various social relationships within the work setting.

For many developmentally disabled adults, the group home environment is the hub of the social support network (Landesman-Dwyer, Berkson, & Romer, 1979). Unlike homes created by nondisabled people, the group home environment is an artificial setting designed and operated for handicapped people. Such group residences are potentially rich sources of social support.

Group home staff have a supervisory and supportive role, setting limits and structure, offering advice and encouragement, and providing understanding and companionship. To increase and enrich social networks, group home associations may pool resources to obtain transportation, recreation, independence training, physical therapy, and social services for residents (Matson, 1980). Contact with biological parents is encouraged, as is participation in activities sponsored by church, YMCA, and service clubs. Outside experts occasionally provide training to staff and residents in areas of sexuality, rape prevention, music therapy, and first aid. Unfortunately, group home living often falls short of the ideal posed here. But, as these examples suggest, the possibilities exist for a varied tapestry of social supports within the structure of communal living facilities for developmentally disabled people. The continued cooperation of the parents and professionals ensures a good balance of both nurturance and expertise.

Finally, a relatively untapped source of social supports deserves mention. Hearing-impaired, cerebral palsied, autistic, and learning disabled people have formed self-help groups (Menolascino & Eaton, 1980). Advocacy, information and referral, and lobbying are key stated purposes of most such organizations. For example, People First is an organization founded by mentally retarded people for the purpose of informing policymakers about the needs of the handicapped. For many members, these worthy activities are secondary to the supporting network that forms when people band together to confront a nonhandicapped society. As Rhodes and Browning have observed, "such self-help organizations provide a community whereby persons with similar disability can establish a special peer relationship characterized by mutual exchange of trust and empathy, understanding of successes, joys, stresses, and hardships of life" (1977, p. 24).

In describing these social networks and the purposes they serve, we may have overstated the importance of organizations, agencies, and formalized groups. To be sure, many, perhaps most, developmentally disabled citizens rely on social support networks that differ little from the informal networks of nonhandicapped people. But, as we noted in the introduction, developmentally disabled populations depend on enriched sources of support. Thus, developmentally disabled individuals benefit from informal sources of social support, but they may also depend on more structured approaches to building social networks. The key is maintaining a balance of personalized caring (i.e., parental involvement) and professional expertise (i.e., the caseworker, therapist, or counselor).

BARRIERS TO SOCIAL SUPPORT NETWORKS

At the risk of blaming the victim, it is useful to point out that handicapped individuals' defining characteristics may prevent them from building and making full use of social networks. For example, Landesman-Dwyer, Sackett, and Kleinman (1980) found that even in the close quarters of a group home setting, mentally retarded residents had little social interaction. If social competence is an asset in forming support systems, then developmentally disabled individuals will be less successful in establishing such links. Physically disabled people may lack the energy to build and sustain networks requiring after-hours socializing or activity. Lethargy associated with retarded individuals (Robinson & Robinson, 1976) also may inhibit participation in social networks.

Reciprocity is often included in definitions of social support networks. Here, too, developmentally disabled individuals may fare poorly. In fact, it may be generally true that developmentally disabled people need more social supports but are less able to reciprocate in kind. Important exceptions to this tentative hypothesis abound, however. Consider the social worker with severe cerebral palsy whose humor, wit, and humanity more than replenish any well of support, or the mentally retarded busboy who, in return for hard work and a cheerful manner, asks only for an occasional smile. Still, the limitations of some handicapped individuals inhibit their participation in naturally formed reciprocal social networks.

Physical barriers and practical constraints inhibit developmentally disabled people from full participation in social networks. Sight-impaired individuals often are restricted to a daily routine of bus schedules and routes. Dropping by for coffee or stopping off for a beer may be possible only after complex logistical machinations. For people who walk with difficulty or must use a wheelchair, getting to and from a meeting, party, or restaurant is no small undertaking. Although some mildly retarded people gain driving privileges, most retarded individuals must rely on buses or rides from others (Birenbaum & Re, 1979). Inclement weather, only a nuisance to most people, precludes outings for many developmentally disabled people.

Fragmentation of the informal and formal social service system also militates against meaningful, enduring social supports. Service clubs dispense only a few dollars for each purpose, church auxiliaries have limited resources for any one family, and volunteers have limited time to donate. Fragmentation within the universe of developmentally disabled people has both beneficial and detrimental effects on enriched social supports. Even though most cerebral palsied people are retarded, cerebral palsy groups have maintained a separate identity from groups for retarded people. This separation has netted them resources not available to mentally retarded people. But, by maintaining their own identity and social service system, people with neuromuscular conditions have cut themselves off from other potential linkages. Similarly, parents whose handicapped children appear normal resist contact with families of Down's syndrome children. Parents of less handicapped children tend to want them placed in classrooms with higher functioning children and not with more disabled children. Although the issue of appropriate role models cannot be dismissed, parents who turn away from more handicapped children also turn away from potential sources of support.

Ironically, the normalization movement has reduced the depth and stability of the social networks of some developmentally disabled people. As Landesman-Dywer, Sackett, and Kleinman (1980) found, the smallest living environments are not necessarily the best settings for handicapped people. Like the melting pot theory, assumptions behind normalization may not always apply. As with many minority group members, developmentally disabled people may be most fulfilled when they are free to participate in the majority culture and maintain ties to their own culture. Normalization carried to an extreme could damage the fragile social support networks of developmentally disabled people who now depend primarily on other developmentally disabled people (Berkson & Romer, 1981).

A case example from the authors' practice is poignant testimony of the need for improved informal social supports.

A visit to a small house found a disabled mother and two young children. In the three years since multiple sclerosis left her largely homebound, she had seen her nearby parents only six times. Initial assessment revealed why this disabled woman's social network was limited to sporadic visitors from agencies, churches, service groups, and two close friends. Social Security and public assistance payments allowed for a run-down house, with inadequate plumbing, torn rugs, and broken furniture. The house reeked of urine, perhaps due to mishaps when the children carried the mother's bedpan from bedroom to bathroom. The children, out of sight and largely out of control of their mother, were bickering. Canned foods were mixed at the mother's bed and cooked in the kitchen by the 9-year-old daughter. Although this disabled woman was pleasant and very grateful for any help extended to her or the children, she was acutely aware that her physical and social needs far exceeded her ability to respond in kind. Sadly, over a period of months she and her children saw tens of visitors from agencies and churches troop through the home, putting in a few awkward hours or days before abandoning this "community project." This patchwork of social supports lacked planning, cohesion, continuity, and direction. Although perhaps better than no support, these tenuous relationships did not approach a stable social network. The enduring nature of a good social network was lacking.

As this vignette suggests, good intentions alone will not provide the informal social supports needed by developmentally disabled people. The next section discusses ways in which professionals can work together with developmentally disabled people and their families to develop and maintain social support networks.

DESIGNING SOCIAL NETWORKS

Through carefully planned efforts, social workers and other human service professionals can improve and expand the social networks of developmentally disabled people. Social network interventions designed for handicapped populations are more likely to succeed when negotiated with all who
will be affected. Therefore, clients and their caretakers, friends, teachers,
job supervisors, and co-workers are invited into planning sessions. Asking
for their input shows interest in these people's ideas and expands resources
in order to plan responsive networks (Scheinfeld et al., 1970). Together or
one-by-one the network participants analyze gathered information and
brainstorm ways to improve the client's social supports (Kazdin & Matson,
1981). In these meetings, workers note communication patterns, status differences, power and influence distributions, and who is willing and unwilling to lend a hand (Döhner & Angermeyer, 1981). The content and delivery
of the designed supports then simultaneously take form during the negotiations.

Whoever taps social networks for developmentally disabled clients should
be constructively oriented (Goldiamond, 1974). This orientation translates
into practice as worker, client, and others uncover potentially helpful networks. Professionals demonstrate how short- and long-term goals are reached
by collecting information on clients' thoughts, interactions, and surroundings (Schinke et al., 1981). Participants in the design write behavioral objectives to break large goals into small, reasonable ones, which they can
achieve within a brief time. For example, analytic data on Judi L., a blind
teenager, indicates that she never leaves home alone. Judi, her parents, and
the social worker negotiate a long-term goal for her to visit independently a
favorite aunt in a nearby city. A short-term goal is for Judi to go by herself
to a local shopping center and buy something for the trip. The client's
behavioral objective for the next week is to call a taxi; get a ride to the
shopping center; ask the driver to wait in front of the drug store; go in and,
with a clerk's assistance, purchase some toothpaste; and take the taxi home.
Over the next two weeks, her objective is to catch a bus to and from the
shopping center and purchase another item for the impending visit.

Social networks designed for special populations must engineer time off
for parents, siblings, and professional caregivers. If the load on those who
live and work with handicapped people gets too heavy or is not periodically
eased, family members and professionals undergo stress that soon touches
clients (Gath, 1977; Friedrich, 1979). The burnout phenomenon appears in
developmental disabilities caseworkers and is also expressed in the affect
and behavior of nonprofessionals who look after disabled people (Edelwich
& Brodsky, 1980; Pines & Maslach, 1980). Research on social networks for
families with exceptional children states: "Family involvement in the education of young children will work best when: (1) attention is paid to the

needs of all family members, not just the young child; and (2) explicit emphasis is placed upon linking the family and other social agencies and personnel in ways that utilize skills and aspirations of family network members and professionals for the futures of young children" (Berger & Fowlkes, 1980, p. 30).

IMPLEMENTATION

Social networks proposed for developmentally disabled people are put to use jointly by clients, professionals, and those from nontreatment milieus (Tharp & Wetzel, 1969; Schinke, 1981a). Mediators are clients' parents, siblings, acquaintances at school and work, caseworkers, and anyone contacted in analyzing the client's daily life. Goals and objectives agreed upon in the network design may implicate additional mediators such as grandparents, aunts, uncles, neighbors, ward attendants, custodial staff, food service workers, sales clerks, hairdressers, bus drivers, bartenders, police officers, pastoral counselors, and so on (Sussman & Burchinal, 1968). The social network is strengthened when all involved, professionals and nonprofessionals, view their relationship as a continuing partnership.

After clients and mediators review and react to the outlined design, workers redraft their plans and teach all involved to help make changes in clients' cognitions, interactions, and environments. A smooth learning process ensues when planned changes are explained and demonstrated by workers and rehearsed by clients and mediators. Workers review data behind network alterations, suggest a change strategy, and model each strategy's use. Clients and mediators discuss the demonstration and, if agreeable, rehearse how they can put the design into practice. Individual rehearsals are optimally accompanied by the worker's feedback, coaching, and reinforcement (Schinke & Wong, 1978; Schinke, 1981b). Modeling and rehearsal are illustrated as a retarded youngster learns to overcome his fear of going downtown in this example:

> *Worker* Rick, now I'll show you how I would change my thoughts by saying the things we talked about. I'll pretend I want to go to a downtown movie but I'm afraid of all the people. Listen to what I tell myself. "Oh, oh, I'm starting to get scared. I better stop worrying. I know, those people aren't interested in me. When I get on the bus, I'll sit by a window and won't look at the other people. When I get downtown I'll hurry to the theater. If I get in a crowd, I'll just move over to a store window and look inside."
> Now you say those same things. I'll stand beside you and tell you how you're doing. I'll touch your shoulder like this when you're doing well, and will whisper hints if you get stuck. All set?
>
> *Rick:* Uh, I guess so. [Clears his throat.] I'm pretending like I'm afraid to get on the bus, but then I tell myself to get on anyway.

Worker: Good so far, Rick. You've got the right idea. Listen to me say the thoughts again. [Repeats self-statements.] Now you try the thoughts again. Remember that you're just walking to the bus stop and you're thinking of all the people, and you can change your thoughts. Ready to go?

Rick: Yup. OK, I'm going to the bus stop and starting to get worked up. I better not do this. When I get on the bus I'll sit by a window and won't look at all the people. When I get off the bus I'll hurry to the theater. If I get into a crowd, I'll move to a store window and look inside.

Worker: Real fine that time Rick! Good work. You told yourself the right things, and your seemed pretty sure of yourself. Let's do it again. This time whisper exactly the same words.

Rick: [Repeats his self-statements quietly.]

Worker: Super! That time you even sounded more sure of yourself. All right, now say the same words silently inside your head. When you're done saying them, smile.

Rick: [Reflects for a moment, then smiles.]

Worker: Great! You're doing just fine. Let's practice some more so you think these words tomorrow when you go to the movie.

Modeling and rehearsals also enable developmentally disabled clients and their mediators to alter interpersonal and tangible networks (Spirito et al., 1981).

Homework moves network alterations into clients' daily routines. Homework is critical, since changes in systems of support cannot be accomplished through treatment per se. Available research removes any doubt that learning will not transfer and generalize by its own momentum (Russell, 1974; Wildman & Wildman, 1975; Keeley, Shemberg, & Carbonell, 1976; Marholin, Siegel, & Phillips, 1976; Stokes & Baer, 1977). Using the social network ensures the carry-over of positive changes through gradual tasks that handicapped clients complete at home, school, and job. Homework tasks are negotiated, rehearsed, and contracted well in advance of real-life performance. The case of Judi L. showed homework negotiation as Judi, her parents, and social worker planned her forays to the shopping center. Rick, the mildly retarded client, took homework planning a step further as he and the worker rehearsed his going downtown.

Homework contracting is depicted by another case from the authors' practice. At age 23, Nancy R. was afflicted with subacute sclerosing panencephalitis, a viral disease related to rubella (Farrell & Swanson, 1975). A college graduate and elementary school teacher, Nancy suffered the usual course of the nefarious disease. She had seizures, became visually impaired, nonverbal, incontinent, and unable to feed herself, and she was moved from her conjugal home to a private institution for full-time care. Gradually, Nancy fought off the worst of her symptoms and, with still limited motoric skills and a tested IQ of 63, went to live with her parents. The goals of this family were for Nancy to regain her former interests and capabilities.

Specific behavioral objectives were negotiated with the client and her parents, and community mediators were drafted to aid Nancy's rehabilitation. After everyone rehearsed changes to the client's networks, contracts were drawn up for all objectives. Nancy and her mediators projected the day, time, place, and responsible person for each homework task. The person responsible recorded quantitative data on Nancy's performance so others could monitor and reinforce her progress on all fronts. These oral agreements yielded a written contract in the form of weekly activity schedules, copied and disseminated to all parties. Completed schedules, as shown in Fig. 13-1, were an empirical base on which to negotiate, rehearse, and contract for future network changes.

The final chore of network implementation is to evaluate alterations in developmentally disabled clients' lives. Evaluation starts whenever social networks are implemented by juxtaposing baseline analysis data with subsequent information. More accurate evaluations of the client's changed social networks, however, need prior investment in a research design. Conventional designs include those suitable for single-case evaluation and those requiring control groups. Single-case designs examine the slope, drift, and level of data gathered before, during, and after network implementation (Glass, Willson, & Gottman, 1975; Elashoff & Thoresen, 1978; Kratochwill, 1978). Control-group designs compare before and after data for clients who learned new networks and for those who intentionally did not have intervention (Brunig & Kintz, 1977). Both paradigms separate the effects of treatment, time, client maturation, history, and other threats to internal and external validity (Kazdin, 1978; Kratochwill & Brody, 1978; Jayaratne & Levy, 1979; Schinke, 1979).

Evaluation findings are examined statistically, ideographically, and subjectively (Gottman & Leiblum, 1974; Kazdin, 1978). Subjective criteria weigh whether clients improved by their own standards, and if they gained in the eyes of family, friends, and professionals. To return to an earlier example, that of mildly retarded Rick who was a Prader-Willi client, postintervention analyses might reveal statistical significance as Rick's weight goes from 210 pounds at baseline to 195 pounds two months after he alters his cognitive network. Since a weight over 180 endangers his health, Rick, his family, and the worker will judge self-instructions successful when he loses another 15 pounds.

Evaluation reveals the effectiveness of the treatment and guides decisions about additional analysis, network design, and implementation. If evaluation proves them effective, networks are handed to clients and mediators. Evaluations not finding positive effects grant two options. Worker, client, and mediators can continue implementing networks to see if more treatment will produce an effect. This option appears sound if the network is expected to have a delayed action, or if workers have reason to think that client and mediators were lax in implementing the plan. The other option is to halt

ACTIVITY SCHEDULE

Name: Nancy R.   Effective Dates: From 10/8 To 10/14   (Responsible Mediator)

Time \ Day	Sunday	Monday	Tuesday	Wednesday	Thursday	Friday	Saturday
7:00 am	Dress (Nancy)		Dress (Nancy)		Dress (Nancy)		Dress (Nancy)
8:00							
9:00							
10:00		German (Ms. G.)	Math (Ms. M.)	Bible Lecture (Mr. C.)	German (Ms. G.)	Math (Ms. M.)	
11:00							
12:00 pm				Reading (Mrs. R.)			
1:00		Reading (Mrs. R.)	Crocheting (Ms. M.)		Reading (Mrs. R.)	Crocheting (Ms. M.)	
2:00		Craft Class (Staff)					
3:00			Reading (Mrs. R.)	Programmed Tapes (Nancy)	Programmed Tapes (Nancy)	Reading (Mrs. R.)	
4:00		Study/Review (Mrs. R.)	Study/Review (Mrs. R.)	Study/Review (Mrs. R.)	Study/Review (Mrs. R.)	Study/Review (Mrs. R.)	
5:00							
6:00							
7:00		Recreational Reading (Nancy)	Physical Exercise (Mr. R.)	Recreational Reading (Nancy)	Physical Exercise (Mr. R.)	Recreational Reading (Nancy)	
8:00							

Fig. 13-1. Illustrative activity schedule denoting activity, time, and responsible mediator for Nancy R.'s network implementation.

implementation and reanalyze the problem. The rationale in this case is that additional analysis will beget success. Before exercising the second option, professionals warn clients and mediators of the decision to stop the program as set up and poll each one on why networks are ineffective. The cycle of analysis, design, and implementation is repeated until everyone is confident that handicapped clients' networks will grow without extra assistance.

If the framework posed here seems a distant ideal, consider the reality of a current demonstration project. Extending Family Resources (Hamerlynck, Moore, & Barsh, 1981) is a project linking professionals, family, and friends into a network for children with neuromuscular disease. Project staff recognize that parents of developmentally disabled children need more support but have fewer supportive contacts than other parents. The authors of this model network argue that families need multiple sources of support to provide needed services and buffer the stresses of rearing a developmentally disabled child. As a first step, a social assessment helps professional staff and parents catalog existing social supports and define the family's unmet needs. Next, the nuclear family chooses its own network members. Project staff then train and contract with the network members, who in turn receive emotional and financial support, expert information, and advice. The family of the child maintains a log so that project staff can keep track of lifestyle changes resulting from the new extended network. One hope is that both parents and their handicapped children will benefit from new role models. The program is designed to extend the services of the agency, and to support rather than supplant professional services. Recruiting network members has been successful, but the outcome of this networking effort must await further data collection and analysis. The parent and professional are equally important members of the helping team.

CONCLUSION

Social network intervention with developmentally disabled clients embodies the person–environment fit sought by professional social workers (Collins & Pancoast, 1976). The science of using the social network therefore promises much to the human services, to family and friends of developmentally disabled citizens, and to disabled people themselves. To fulfill the promise, network analysts must know more about developmentally disabled clients' existing supports. Descriptive research is needed on strategies that help handicapped people cope with an alien world. Researchers are ignorant of how clients handle a barrage of confusing events, insensitive people, and physical barriers (Berger & Foster, 1976). No data exist on impromptu supports in families of developmentally disabled people. Original research should correlate the adaptive social networks of these families with their unique norms and interchanges (Rueveni, 1979).

Social network intervention with handicapped populations will benefit from more data on the acquisition of natural support systems. Attention should be given to studying the relative roles of vicarious learning, trial and error, positive reinforcement, and punishment as they explain social networks (Gresham, 1981). Both advantageous and deleterious networks ought to be examined. By cataloging and publishing their data, professionals can construct theory and methods to improve the social networks of developmentally disabled clients. Professionals should see the social network already existing as a web of potential allies, from parents and outward to friends, relatives, and helpful acquaintances. Characteristics of the social support network—its caring, its ongoing nature, its immediacy in the client's life—make it an ideal resource for professionals helping developmentally disabled people. We hope that the concepts presented in the foregoing pages will facilitate this process.

ACKNOWLEDGMENTS

The authors warmly thank Anna Bolstad, Lois Holt, and Aeolian Jackson. Funding was by Clipped Wings, United Airlines Stewardess Alumnae Incorporated, Seattle, Chapter; Grant 90CA902 from the National Center on Child Abuse and Neglect, Administration for Children, Youth, and Families, Office of Human Development Services; Maternal and Child Health Training Project No. 913 from the Bureau of Community Health Services, Health Services Administration; and Mental Retardation and Developmental Disabilities Branch Grant HD 02274 from the National Institute of Child Health and Human Development, National Institutes of Mental Health, United States Public Health Service, Department of Health and Human Services.

Afterword

Earlier in this volume we spoke of "Dearborn's Dictum": "If you want to understand something, try to change it." We think that the trend toward using social support systems in dealing with human service issues is a golden opportunity to profit from the wisdom in Dearborn's Dictum. As we try to help people by increasing their social resources, we are uncovering some very important basic information about the human condition, about human beings as social animals.

We are learning that social support is the glue that holds together human functioning. Without it the whole facade of social competence can come apart. With it, the best in human adaptability and judgment can proceed to deal with and even overcome the challenges people face in ordinary day-to-day life and in crises. This theme of social support as the common ground linking everyday coping and crisis management, the chronic and the acute, the normal and the troubled population, is central to this book.

A related theme is the constant interplay of the "formal" aid offered by the traditional helping professions through remedial, educational, counseling, and advocacy services with the aid provided by "informal" helpers—networks of family, friends, and neighbors. We have seen a growing recognition that aid need not take the form of an either–or situation: either formal or informal. Rather, it can and should be a collaborative effort. Each component in the total system is best adapted to meet some needs, and the two together are more than the sum of their parts in meeting the whole need of people for social support. The result, we believe, can be a more effective and compassionate response to people in need of help.

We began this book with five questions:

1. What problems in various areas of human service practices lend themselves to combined formal and informal helping strategies?
2. What research and practice demonstration projects currently exist and in what direction are they taking us?
3. What barriers and impediments exist in subfields of human services to implementing social support stratgies? What incentives and motivations?
4. What practical suggestions may be gleaned from current efforts at combined helping that will aid future practice applications?

5. What potential applications are there for social support interventions in the various subfields of human services?

We think that this book does much to answer these questions, and we believe that these answers bode well for the entire field of human services and the general improvement of the human condition.

We have identified problems and issues across a broad range of human service concerns that lend themselves to a combined formal–informal social support system approach. The convergence is quite astounding. From mental health to day care, from schools to services for the elderly, we find clear and often compelling relevance for social support system approaches. What is more, we suspect that better recognition of the everyday nature of still additional human service issues will allow us to see that social support system approaches have even greater applicability. This is encouraging. It is encouraging in part because it tells us that basic human resources—caring and "common sense"—are essential to a comprehensive approach to a humane society.

On the matter of research and practice demonstrations, we find that there is an exciting and convergent array of programs, projects, and studies going on throughout the North American continent and around the world. In the course of assembling the literally hundreds of references cited in our book we have been struck by the crescendo of validation for the fundamental axiom upon which the book is built: people help people. The many efforts to refine this principle through research and practical demonstration are providing more sophisticated guidelines for action and thought, but they are also providing a basic affirmation. We are encouraged by this.

When we look at barriers and incentives, we find that both exist. The culture that we operate in stresses individualism and specialization. Both can be barriers to social support system approaches if they lead to social isolation and rigid helper–client roles. On the other hand, there is growing practical incentive to proceed with the development and implementation of approaches that incorporate social support networks. Financial imperatives and the preponderance of research evidence come together to provide a strong incentive, and we think we see a pattern of action emerging, as reported in this book, as a response to that incentive. This is encouraging.

This book provides some of the practical suggestions that people will need to venture forth and try to work within the social support network approach. Of course, there is always ambiguity and uncertainty. Each situation has its own special character and there will never be a substitute for the skillful and insightful practitioner on the scene. But we think that the programs described here and the many detailed references cited in the text provide the motivated individual or agency with sufficient guidance to get started in the business of expanding formal services by complementing them with informal services. This is encouraging.

Finally, we believe that the social support network approaches described and analyzed in our discussions promise that most if not all subfields of human services can profit from efforts to combine formal and informal helping. We expect that research and programs will reach more and more subfields of human services as success breeds success, and demonstration in one area spawns programmatic development in another. This is encouraging.

The social support approach feels good humanistically as well as scientifically and financially. It arises from a fundamental respect for human competence. It capitalizes upon human concern for fellow humans. It resonates with a positive view of human nature. It emphasizes the virtues of cooperation, interdependence, and responsibility. It presupposes an active, moral human community. It feels good spiritually, and calls for the best in us.

Bibliography

Abels, S. L., & Abels, P. Social group work's contextual purposes. *Social Work with Groups*, 1980, *3*(3), 25–37.

Abelson, H., Cohen, R., & Schrayer, D. *Public attitudes toward marijuana. Part 1.* NJ: Response Analysis Corporation, 1972.

Abelson, H., Cohen, R., Schrayer, D., & Rappaport, M. *Drug experience, attitudes, and related behavior among adolescents and adults.* NJ: Response Analysis Corporation, 1973.

Abernathy, V. D. Social network and response to the maternal role. *International Journal of Sociology of the Family*, 1973, *3*, 86–92.

Adams, G. R. Runaway youth projects: Comments on care programs for runaways and throwaways. *Journal of Adolescence*, 1980, *3*, 321–334.

Adams, M., Caston, M., & Danis, B. A neglected dimension in home care of elderly disabled persons: Effect on responsible family members. Paper presented at the 32nd Annual Meeting of the Gerontological Society, Washington, DC, November 1979.

Addams, J. Charity and social justice. *Proceedings, national conference of charities and correction*, 1910, 3.

Akers, R. L., Krohn, M. D., Lanza-Kaduce, L., and Radosevich, M. Social learning and deviant behavior: A specific test of a general theory. *American Sociological Review*, 1979, *44*(4), 636–655.

Al-Anon Family Groups. *Alateen: Hope for children of alcoholics.* New York: Al-Anon Family Group Headquarters, 1973.

Albee, G. W. Primary prevention and social problems. In G. Gerbner, C. J. Ross, & E. Zigler (Eds.), *Child abuse: An agenda for action.* New York: Oxford University Press, 1980.

Albrecht, S. L. Correlates of marital happiness among the remarried. *Journal of Marriage and the Family*, 1979, *41*, 857–867.

Albrecht, S. L. Reactions and adjustments to divorce: Differences in the experiences of males and females. *Family Relations*, 1980, *29*, 59–68.

Aldrich, C. K., & Mendkoff, E. Relocation of the aged and disabled: A mortality study. In B. L. Neugarten (Ed.), *Middle age and aging.* Chicago: University of Chicago Press, 1968.

Aldrich, R. The influences of man-built environment on children and youth. In W. Michelson, S. Levine, & E. Michelson (Eds.), *The child in the city.* Toronto: University of Toronto Press, 1979.

Aleshire, D. O., & Strommen, M. P. Introducing innovations into volunteer organizations: Factors associated with readiness to change. *Innovations*, 1978, *2*(2), 23–27.

Alexander, B. K., & Dibb, G. S. Opiate addicts and their parents. *Family Process*, 1975, *14*, 499–514.

Alexander, L. B. Social work's Freudian deluge: Myth or reality? *Social Service Review*, 1972, *46*(4), 517–539.

Allen, V., & Feldman, R. Learning through tutoring: Low-achieving children as tutors. *Journal of Experimental Education*, 1974, *42*, 1–5.

Allen, W. R. Class, culture, and family organization: The effects of class and race on family structure in urban America. *Journal of Comparative Family Studies*, 1979, *10*, 301–311.

Allerhand, M. E., Weber, R., & Haug, M. *Adaptation and adaptability: The Bellefaire follow-up study.* New York: Child Welfare League of America, 1966.

Almy, M. Current structures of education and training in day care: Implications for child care education. Paper presented at the Initial Conference on Research Sequence in Child Care Education, Pittsburgh, PA, November 6–9, 1980.

Alwine, G. If you need love, come to us . . . An overview of a peer-counseling program in a senior high school. *The Journal of School Health,* 1974, *44,* 463–464.

American Psychiatric Association. *Diagnostic and statistical manual of mental disorders* (3rd ed.). Washington, DC: American Psychiatric Association, 1980.

Andrews, G., Tennant, C., Hewson, D., & Schonell, M. The relation of social factors to physical and psychiatric illness. *American Journal of Epidemiology, 1978, 108,* 27–35.

Anspach, D. F. Kinship and divorce. *Journal of Marriage and the Family, 1976, 38,* 323–330.

Apsler, R. People control the amounts of substances they use. *Journal of Drug Issues, 1979, 9,* 145–160.

Arling, G. The elderly widow and her family, neighbors, and friends. *Journal of Marriage and the Family, 1976, 38,* 757–768.

Aschenbrenner, J. *Lifelines: Black families in Chicago.* New York: Holt, Rinehart & Winston, 1975.

Asher, S. R., Oden, S. L., & Gottman, J. Children's friendships in school settings. In L. G. Katz (Ed.), *Current topics in early childhood education,* Vol. 1. Norwood, NJ: Ablex, 1977.

Ashery, S. Self-help groups serving drug abusers. In B. S. Brown (Ed.), *Addicts and aftercare.* Beverly Hills, CA: Sage, 1979.

Atkeson, M., & Forehand, R. Parents as behavior change agents with school-related problems. *Education and Urban Society, 1978, 10*(4), 521–540.

Attneave, C. Therapy in tribal settings and urban network intervention. *Family Process, 1969, 8,* 192–210.

Attneave, C. Social networks and clinical practice. In D. S. Freeman (Ed.), *Perspectives on family therapy.* Vancouver: Butterworth, 1980.

Auerbach, S. What parents want from day care. In S. Auerbach & J. A. Rivaldo (Eds.), *Child care: A comprehensive guide. Vol. 1. Rationale for child care services: Programs vs. politics.* New York: Human Sciences Press, 1975.

Auerswald, E. H. Families, change and the ecological perspective. *Family Process, 1971, 10,* 263–280.

Ayllon, T., Garber, S., & Pisor, K. The elimination of discipline problem through a combined school–home motivational system. *Behavior Therapy, 1975, 6,* 616–626.

Baekeland, F., & Lundwall, L. Dropping out of treatment: A critical review. *Psychological Bulletin, 1975, 82,* 738–783.

Bahr, S. J. Family determinants and effects of deviance. In W. R. Burr, R. Hill, F. I. Nye, & I. L. Reiss (Eds.), *Contemporary theories about the family,* Vol. 1. New York: The Free Press, 1979.

Baideme, S. M., Hill, H. A., & Serritella, D. A. Conjoint family therapy following divorce: Alternative strategy. *International Journal of Family Counseling, 1978, 6*(1), 55–60.

Bailey, J. S., Wolf, M. M., & Phillips, E. Home-based reinforcement and the modification of predelinquents' classroom behavior. *Journal of Applied Behavior Analysis, 1970, 3,* 223–233.

Baizerman, M., Thompson, J., & Stafford-White, K. An old, young friend. Adolescent prostitution. *Children Today, 1979, 10,* 20–24.

Bakan, D. *Slaughter of the innocents.* San Francisco: Jossey-Bass, 1971.

Baker, B. L., Seltzer, B. B., & Seltzer, M. M. *As close as possible: Community residences for retarded adults.* Boston: Little, Brown, 1977.

Baker, F. The interface between professional and natural support systems. *Clinical Social Work Journal, 1977, 5,* 139–148.

Baker, K., & Rubel, R. (Eds.) *Violence and crime in the schools.* Lexington, MA: D. C. Heath, 1980.

Ban, J., & Ciminillo, L. *Violence and vandalism in public education.* Danville, IL: Interstate Printers and Publishers, 1977.

Bandura, A. *Principles of behavior modification.* New York: Holt, Rinehart, & Winston, 1969.

Bandura, A. *Social learning theory.* Englewood Cliffs, NJ: Prentice-Hall, 1977.

Bandura, A., & Walters, R. H. *Social learning and personality development.* New York: Holt, Rinehart, & Winston, 1963.

Baran, A., Pannor, R., & Sorosky, A. D. Open adoption. *Social Work,* 1976, *21*(2), 97–100.

Barker, D. Comments on "The Spatial World of the Child." In W. Michelson, S. Levine, & E. Michelson (Eds.), *The child in the city.* Toronto: University of Toronto Press, 1979.

Barker, R. G., & Gump, P. V. *Big school, small school.* Stanford: Stanford University Press, 1964.

Barker, R. G., & Schoggen, P. *Qualities of community life: Methods of measuring environment and behavior applied to an American and an English town.* San Francisco: Jossey-Bass, 1973.

Barker, R. G., & Wright, H. F. *Midwest and its children: The psychological ecology of an American town.* Evanston, IL: Row, Peterson, 1954.

Baroff, G. S. *Mental retardation: Nature, cause, and management.* New York: John Wiley & Sons, 1974.

Barth, R. Home-based reinforcement of school behavior: A review and analysis. *Review of Educational Research,* 1979, *49*(3), 436–458.

Barth, R. P., Schinke, S. P., Liebert, M. A., & Maxwell, J. S. Distressing situations and coping responses for school-age mothers and mothers-to-be. Presented at the Biannual Western School-Age Parenthood Conference, Portland, OR, 1981.

Bassuk, E. L., & Gerson, S. Deinstitutionalization and mental health services. *Scientific American,* 1978, *238,* 46–53.

Bauer, J. The hot line and its training problems for adolescent listeners. *Adolescence,* 1975, *10,* 64–69.

Bawker, G. Stepparenthood: Stigma or challenge? *Stepparents Forum,* 1975 (November–December).

Beatrice, D. K. Divorce: Problems, goals and growth facilitation. *Social Casework,* 1979, *60*(3), 157–166.

Becerra, R., & Giovannoni, J. Information needs of low income minority parents with young children. In J. Spailing & I. Lewis (Eds.), *Information needs of parents with young children* Washington, DC: Administration for Children, Youth and Families (Grant No. 90-CW-062), 1980.

Becker, H. S. *Outsiders: Studies in the sociology of deviance.* New York: Free Press, 1963.

Beels, C. C. Social networks, the family, and the schizophrenic patient. *Schizophrenia Bulletin,* 1978, *4,* 512–521.

Behavior Associates. *Parents Anonymous self-help for child abusing parents project: Evaluation report.* Tucson: Behavior Associates, 1977.

Bellamy, A. Social support systems in the treatment programme of haemophilia in New South Wales, Australia. *Thrombosis and Haemostasis,* 1977, *38,* 364.

Belsky, J., Robins, E., & Gamble, W. Characteristics, consequences, and determinants of parental competence: Toward a contextual theory. In M. Lewis & L. Rosenblum (Eds.), *Social connections: Beyond the dyad.* New York: Plenum, 1982.

Belsky, J., & Steinberg, L. The effects of day care: A critical review. *Child Development,* 1978, *49,* 929–949.

Benjamin, L. S. Structural analysis of a family in therapy. *Journal of Consulting and Clinical Psychology,* 1977, *45,* 391–406.

Bennett, F. C., LaVeck, B., & Sells, C. J. The Williams elfin facies syndrome: The psychological profile as an aid to syndrome identification. *Pediatrics*, 1978, *61*, 303–306.

Berger, M., & Foster, M. Family-level interventions for retarded children: A multivariate approach to issues and strategies. *Multivariate Experimental Clinical Research*, 1976, *2*, 1–21.

Berger, M., & Fowlkes, M. A. Family intervention project: A family network model for serving young handicapped children. *Young Children*, 1980, *34*(4), 22–32.

Berger, P. L., & Neuhaus, R. J. *To empower people*. Washington, DC: American Enterprise Institute, 1977.

Berghorn, F. J., & Schafer, D. S. Support systems and the frail elderly. Presented at the 32nd Annual Meeting of the Gerontological Society, Washington, DC, November 1979.

Berk, L., & Berson, M. A review of the child development associate credential. *Child Care Quarterly*, 1981, *10*(1), 9–42.

Berkman, L. F., & Syme, S. L. Social networks, host resistance, and mortality: A nine-year follow-up study of Alameda County residents. *American Journal of Epidemiology*, 1979, *109*, 186–204.

Berkson, G., & Romer, D. A letter to a developmental disabilities administrator. In R. Bruinicks, C. E. Myers, B. B. Sigford, & K. C. Laking (Eds.), *Deinstitution and community adjustment of mentally retarded people* (Monograph No. 4). Washington, DC: American Association on Mental Deficiency, 1981.

Berleman, W. C. *Juvenile delinquency prevention experiments: A review and analysis*. National Institute for Juvenile Justice and Delinquency Prevention, Office of Juvenile Justice and Delinquency Prevention, Law Enforcement Assistance Administration, U.S. Department of Justice. Washington, DC: U.S. Government Printing Office, 1980.

Berman, W. H., & Turk, D. C. Adaptation to divorce: Problems and coping strategies. *Journal of Marriage and the Family*, 1981, *43*, 179–189.

Bernstein, B., Snider, D. A., & Meezan, W. *Foster care needs and alternatives to placement*. New York: New York State Board of Social Welfare, 1975.

Bernstein, S. (Ed.) *Explorations in group work*. Boston: Boston University School of Social Work, 1965.

Bertsche, J. W., Clark, F. W., & Iversen, M. A. *Using informal resources in child protective services*. Missoula: University of Montana School of Social Work, 1981.

Beyer, M. Continuing care for runaways. *Journal of Family Issues*, 1980, *1*, 300–302.

Biegel, D. E., & Naparstek, A. J. *Community support systems and mental health*. New York: Springer, 1982.

Billingsley, A., & Giovannoni, J. *Children of the storm*. New York: Harcourt Brace, 1972.

Bird, D. The key word is survival. *NASSP Bulletin*, 1977, *62*, 12–15.

Birenbaum, A., & Re, M. A. Resettling mentally retarded adults in the community—Almost 4 years later. *American Journal of Mental Deficiency*, 1979, *83*, 323–329.

Birren, J. E. *The psychology of aging*. Englewood Cliffs, NJ: Prentice-Hall, 1964.

Blau, Z. S. Structural constraints on friendships in old age. *American Sociological Review*, 1961, *26*, 429–439.

Blau, Z. S. *Old age in a changing society*. New York: Franklin Watts, 1973.

Blehar, M. Working couples as parents. *In Families today: A research sampler on families and children*. DHEW Publ. No. (ADM) 79-815, 1979.

Bloom, B. J., Asher, S. J., & White, S. W. Marital description as a stressor: A review and analysis. *Psychological Bulletin*, 1978, *85*, 867–894.

Bloom, W. A., & Sudderth, E. W. Methadone in New Orleans: Patients, problems, and police. In S. Einstein (Ed.), *Methadone maintenance*. New York: Marcel Dekker, 1971.

Blythe, B. J. Control of addictions. In S. P. Schinke (Ed.), *Behavioral methods in social welfare*. Hawthorne, NY: Aldine, 1981.

Boehm, R. G., & Larsen, R. D. *An evaluation of peer group counseling in Berrien County, Michigan.* Berrien County, MI: Berrien County Probate and Juvenile Court Services, 1978.

Bogdan, R. What does it mean when a person says "I am not retarded?" *Education and Training of the Mentally Retarded,* 1980, *15,* 74–79.

Bohannon, P. The six stations of divorce. In P. Bohannon (Ed.), *Divorce and after.* Garden City, NY: Doubleday, 1970.

Bohannon, P. *Stepfathers as parents.* DHEW Publication No. (ADM) 79-815. U.S. Department of Health, Education, and Welfare. Washington, DC: U.S. Government Printing Office, 1979.

Bolton, F. G. *The pregnant adolescent: Problems of premature parenthood.* Beverly Hills, CA: Sage, 1980.

Bond, G. R., Borman, L. D., Bankoff, E. A., Daiter, S., Lieberman, M. A., & Videka, L. M. Growth of a medical self-help group. In M. A. Lieberman & L. D. Borman (Eds.), *Self-help groups for coping with crisis: Origins, members, processes, and impact.* San Francisco: Jossey-Bass, 1979.

Bond, G. R., & Daiter, S. Participation in medical self-help groups. In M. A. Lieberman & L. D. Borman (Eds.), *Self-help groups for coping with crisis: Origins, members, processes, and impact.* San Francisco: Jossey-Bass, 1979.

Booth, C. Personal communication, 1981.

Borchert, J. *Alley life in Washington: Family, community, religion, and folklife in the city, 1850–1970.* Urbana, IL: University of Illinois Press, 1980.

Borman, L. D., & Lieberman, M. A. Conclusion: Contributions, dilemmas, and implications for mental health policy. In M. A. Lieberman & L. D. Borman (Eds.), *Self-help groups for coping with crisis: Origins, members, processes, and impact.* San Francisco: Jossey-Bass, 1979.

Boston Women's Health Book Collective. *Ourselves and our children.* New York: Random House, 1978.

Bott, E. *Family and social networks: Roles, norms, and external relationships in ordinary urban families.* London: Tavistock, 1957.

Bowerman, C. E. & Irish, D. P. Some relationships of step children to their parents. *Marriage and Family Living,* 1962, *24,* 113–131.

Bracey, D. H. *Baby pros: Preliminary profiles of juvenile prostitutes.* New York: John Jay Press, 1979.

Brandt, R. (Ed.). *Partners: Parents and schools.* Alexandria, VA: Association for Supervision and Curriculum Development, 1979.

Brandwein, R. A., Brown, C. A., & Fox, E. M. Women and children lost: The social situation of divorced mothers and their families. *Journal of Marriage and the Family,* 1974, *36*(3), 498–514.

Bregman, A. M. Living with progressive childhood illness: Parental management of neuromuscular disease. *Social Work in Health Care,* 1980, *5,* 387–408.

Brennan, T. Mapping the diversity among runaways: A descriptive multivariate analysis of selected social psychological background conditions. *Journal of Family Issues,* 1980, *1,* 165–189.

Brennan, T., Huizinga, D., & Elliott, D. S. *The social psychology of runaways.* Lexington, MA: D. C. Heath, 1978.

Bretherton, I. Young children in stressful situations: The supporting role of attachment figures and unfamiliar caregivers. In G. V. Coehlo & P. I. Ahmed (Eds.), *Uprooting and development.* New York: Plenum, 1980.

Briar, S., & Miller, H. *Problems and issues in social casework.* New York: Columbia University Press, 1971.

Brim, J. A. Social network correlates of avowed happiness. *Journal of Nervous and Mental Disease,* 1974, *158,* 432–439.

Brim, O. G. Macro-structural influences on child development and the need for childhood social indicators. *American Journal of Orthopsychiatry,* 1975, *45,* 516–524.

Brody, E. "Women in the middle" and family help to older people. Presented at the 33rd Annual Meeting of Gerontological Society, San Diego, CA, November 1980.

Brody, S., Poulshock, S. W., & Maschiochhi, C. F. The family caring unit: A major consideration in the long term support system. *The Gerontologist,* 1978, *18*(6), 556–566.

Bronfenbrenner, U. *Is early intervention effective?* Washington, DC: Department of Health, Education, and Welfare, Office of Child Development, Publ. No. (OHD) 75-25, 1974.

Bronfenbrenner, U. The origins of alienation. In U. Bronfenbrenner & M. Mahoney (Eds.), *Influences on human development.* Hinsdale, IL: Dryden Press, 1975.

Bronfrenbrenner, U. Unpublished lecture. Seattle: University of Washington, 1976.

Bronfenbrenner, U. *The ecology of human development.* Cambridge, MA: Harvard University Press, 1979.

Bronfenbrenner, U., Garbarino, J., & Moen, P. Families and communities. In R. Parke (Ed.), *Review of child development research,* Vol. 7. Chicago: University of Chicago Press, in press.

Brooks, K., & Edwards, F. The middle school in transition. *CPD Memorandum.* Center for Professional Development, College of Education, University of Kentucky, Lexington, Kentucky, 1978.

Broskowski, A., & Baker, F. Professional, organizational, and social barriers to primary prevention. *American Journal of Orthopsychiatry,* 1974, *44,* 707–719.

Brown, B. B. Social and psychological correlates of help-seeking behavior among urban adults. *American Journal of Community Psychology,* 1978, *6,* 425–440.

Brown, E. M. Divorce counseling. In D. H. L. Olson (Ed.), *Treating relationships.* Lake Mills, IA: Graphic Pub. Co. 1976.

Brown, G. W., Bhrolchain, M. N., & Harris, T. Social class and psychiatric disturbance among women in an urban population. *Sociology,* 1975, *9,* 225–254.

Brown, G. W., & Birley, J. L. T. Crises and life changes and the onset of schizophrenia. *Journal of Health and Social Behavior,* 1968, *9,* 203–214.

Brown, G., & Carlton, P. How to conquer stress when you can and cope with it when you can't. *National Elementary Principal,* 1980, *59,* 37–39.

Brown, G. W., & Harris, T. *Social origins of depression: A study of psychiatric disorders in women.* New York: Free Press, 1978.

Brown, P., & Manela, R. Client satisfaction with marital and divorce counseling. *The Family Coordinator,* 1977, *26*(3), 294–303.

Brown, S. Self-help. *Public Welfare,* 1981, *31*(1), 13–17.

Brown, W. Student to student counseling for academic achievement. *Personnel and Guidance Journal,* 1965, *43,* 811–817.

Brozan, N. Job loss: Ordeal at home. *New York Times,* July 20, 1981, p. B4.

Brunig, J. L., & Kintz, B. C. *Computational handbook of statistics* (2nd ed.). Glenview, IL: Scott, Foresman, 1977.

Bryant, H. D., Billingsley, A., Kerry, G. A., Leefman, W. V., Merrill, E. J., Senecal, G. R., Walsh, B. G. Physical abuse of children: An agency study. *Child Welfare,* 1963, *52,* 125–130.

Bryce, M., & Lloyd, J. C. (Eds.). *Treating families in the home.* Springfield, IL: Charles C. Thomas, 1981.

Budman, S. H. A strategy for preventive mental health intervention. *Professional Psychology,* 1975, *6,* 394–398.

Bureau of the Census, U.S. Department of Commerce. *Social indicators II.* Washington, DC: U.S. Government Printing Office, 1980.

Burgess, R. L., & Akers, R. L. A differential association-reinforcement theory of criminal behavior. *Social Problems*, 1966, *4*, 128–147.

Burke, R. J., & Weir, T. Giving and receiving help with work and non-work related problems. *Journal of Business Administration*, 1975, *6*, 59–78.

Burke, R. J., & Weir, T. Marital helping relationships: The moderation between stress and well-being. *Journal of Psychology*, 1977, *95*, 121–130.

Burke, R. J., & Weir, T. Benefits to adolescents of informal helping relationships with their parents and peers. *Psychological Reports*, 1978, *42*, 1175–1184.

Burke, R. J., & Weir, T. Helping responses of parents and peers and adolescent well-being. *Journal of Psychology*, 1979, *102*, 49–62.

Burke, R. J., & Weir, T. The importance of encouraging informal helping in our society. *Canada's Mental Health*, 1981, *29*(1), 3–5.

Burke, R. J., Weir, T., & Duncan, C. Informal helping processes in work settings. *Academy of Management Journal*, 1976, *19*, 370–377.

Burns, T. A structural theory of social exchange. *Acta Sociologica*, 1973, *16*, 183–208.

Burnside, I. M. Alzheimer's disease: An overview. *Journal of Gerontological Nursing*, 1979, *5*(4), 14–20.

Busby, D. Quoted in McHenry, S. Sister-to-sister: We're about navigating systems. *Ms.*, 1980, *9*(6), 63.

Butler, R. quoted in Hydtt, J. As lives are extended, some people wonder if it's really a blessing. *Wall Street Journal*, October 25, 1979.

Butler, R., & Lewis, M. *Aging and mental health*. St. Louis: C. V. Mosby, 1977.

Butterfield, W. H., & Werking, J. Behavioral methods in primary health care. In S. P. Schinke (Ed.), *Behavioral methods in social welfare*. Hawthorne, NY: Aldine, 1981.

Cabot, R. C. Report of the chairman of the Committee on Health. *Proceedings, National Conference of Charities and Correction*, 1915, 220.

Callan, D., Garrison, J., & Zerger, F. Working with the families and social networks of drug abusers. *Journal of Psychedelic Drugs*, 1975, *7*(1), 19–25.

Camara, K. A., Baker, O., & Dayton, C. Impact of separation and divorce on youths and families. In P. M. Insel (Ed.), *Environmental variables and the prevention of mental illness*. Lexington, MA. Lexington, 1980.

Campbell, D. T. On the conflicts between biological and social evolution and between psychology and moral tradition. *American Psychologist*, 1975, *30*, 1103–1126.

Campbell, R., & Chenoweth, B. Peer support systems. Presented at the 33rd Annual Meeting of the Gerontological Society, San Diego, CA, November 1980.

Cannon, I. M. *Social work in hospitals*. New York: Russell Sage, 1913.

Cannon-Bonventre, K., & Kahn, J. *The ecology of help-seeking behavior among adolescent parents*. Cambridge, MA: American Institutes for Research, 1979.

Cantor, M. Caring for the frail elderly: Impact on family, friends, and neighbors. Presented at the 33rd Annual Meeting of the Gerontological Society, San Diego, CA, November 1980.

Cantor, M. A. Life space and the social support system of the inner city elderly of New York. *The Gerontologist*, 1975, *15*(1), 23–27.

Caplan, G. *Support systems and community mental health*. New York: Behavioral Publications, 1974.

Caplan, G. *Principles of preventive psychiatry*. New York: Academic Press, 1964.

Caplan, G. Mastery of stress: Psychosocial aspects. *American Journal of Psychiatry*, 1981, *138*, 413–420.

Caplan, G., & Grunebaum, H. Perspectives on primary prevention: A review. *Archives of General Psychiatry*, 1967, *17*, 331–346.

Caplan, G., & Killilea, M. (Eds.). *Support systems and mutual help*. New York: Grune & Stratton, 1976.

Caplan, R. D. Organizational stress and individual strain: A social-psychological study of risk factors in coronary heart disease among administrators, engineers, and scientists. Unpublished doctoral dissertation, University of Michigan, 1971.

Caplan, R. D. Patient, provider, and organization: Hypothesized determinants of adherence. In S. J. Cohen (Ed.), *New directions in patient compliance*. Lexington, MA: D. C. Heath, 1979.

Caplan, R. D., Robinson, E. A. R., French, J. R. P., Jr., Caldwell, J. R., & Shinn, M. *Adhering to medical regimens: Pilot experiments in patient education and social support*. Ann Arbor, MI: University of Michigan, 1976.

Carbino, R. Developing a parent organization: New roles for parents of children in substitute care. In Maluccio, A. N. and Sinanoglu, P. (Eds.), *The Challenge of Partnership*, New York: Child Welfare League of America, 1981, pp. 165–189.

Carkhuff, R. R. *Helping and human relations*, Vol. 1. New York: Holt, Rinehart & Winston, 1969.

Carroll, C. F., & Reppucci, N. D. Meanings that professionals attach to label children. *Journal of Consulting and Clinical Psychology*, 1978, *46*, 372–374.

Carson, R. *Interaction concepts of personality*. Chicago: Aldine, 1969.

Cartwright, D. Achieving change in people: Applications of group dynamics theory. *Human Relations*, 1951, *4*, 381–392.

Cassel, J. The contribution of the social environment to host resistance. *American Journal of Epidemiology*, 1976a, *104*(2), 107–123.

Cassel, J. Psychosocial processes and "stress." *International Journal of Health Services*, 1976b, *4*, 471–482.

Catalano, R. *Health, behavior, and the community: An ecological perspective*. New York: Pergamon, 1979.

Cath, S. H. The institutionalization of a parent: A nadir of life. *Journal of Geriatric Psychiatry*, 1972, *5*, 25–46.

Cavan, A. *Liquor license: An ethnography of bar behavior*. Chicago: Aldine, 1966.

Cavior, E. C., Schmidt, A., & Karacki, L. *An evaluation of the Kennedy Youth Center differential treatment program*. Washington, DC: U.S. Bureau of Prisons, Research Office, 1972.

Cevaline, G. E. Drug use on high school and college campuses. *Journal of School Health*, 1968, *38*, 638–646.

Chambers, C. *Seedtime of reform*. Ann Arbor: University of Michigan Press, 1967.

Chambers, W. N., & Reiser, M. F. Emotional stress in the precipitation of congestive heart failure. *Psychosomatic Medicine*, 1953, *15*, 38–60.

Chapman, N. Working with the informal helping system: A way of supporting families of the elderly. Presented at the Worshop on Family Support Systems for the Elderly, Western Gerontological Society, Anaheim, CA, March 1980.

Chess, S., Korn, S. J., & Fernandez, P. B. *Psychiatric disorders of children with rubella*. New York: Brunner/Mazel, 1971.

Chestang, L. W. The delivery of child welfare services to minority group children and their families. In *Child welfare strategy in the coming years*. Washington, DC: U.S. Children's Bureau, 1978.

Ch'ien, J. M. Alumni associations of Hong Kong. In B. S. Brown (Ed.), *Addicts and aftercare*. Beverly Hills, CA: Sage, 1979.

Child care referrals for hospital workers. *The Children's Advocate*. Berkeley, CA, Children's Services, Jan.–Feb. 1981, p. 4.

Children's Bureau. *Migrant child welfare*. Washington, DC: U.S. Children's Bureau, 1977.

Children's Bureau. *Child welfare strategy in the coming years*. Washington, DC: U.S. Children's Bureau, 1978.

Children's Defense Fund. *Children out of school in America*. Washington, DC: Children's Defense Fund, 1974.

Children's Defense Fund. *Children without homes*. Washington, DC: Children's Defense Fund, 1978.

Childs, R. E. Perceptions of mainstreaming by regular classroom teachers who teach mainstreamed educable mentally retarded students in the public schools. *Education and Training of the Mentally Retarded*, 1981, *16*, 225–227.

Chiriboga, D. A., Coho, A., & Roberts, J. Divorce, stress, and social supports: A study in help-seeking behavior. *Journal of Divorce*, 1979, *3*, 121–135.

Christensen, L., & McDonald, D. Effect of a support system on single-parent families. *Psychology*, 1976, *13*(3), 68–70.

Churchill, S. R., Carlson, B., & Nybell, L. *No child is unadoptable*. Beverly Hills, CA: Sage Publications, 1979.

Clarke-Stewart, K. A. *Child care in the family*. New York: Academic Press, 1977.

Clavan, S., & Vatter, E. The affiliated family: A device for integrating old and young. *The Gerontologist*, 1972, *12*, 407–412.

Clincy, E. Adding up alternatives. In J. Rash & P. Markun (Eds.), *New views of school and community*. Arlington, VA and Washington, DC: National Association of Elementary School Principals and Association for Childhood Education International, 1973.

Cloward, R. Studies in tutoring. *Journal of Experimental Education*, 1967, *36*, 14–25.

Cloward, R. A., & Ohlin, L. E. *Delinquency and opportunity: A theory of delinquent gangs*. Glencoe, IL: Free Press, 1960.

Coates, R. B., Miller, A. D., & Ohlin, L. E. *Diversity in a youth correctional system: Handling delinquents in Massachusetts*. Cambridge, MA: Ballinger, 1978.

Cobb, S. Social support as a moderator of life stress. *Psychosomatic Medicine*, 1976, *38*, 300–314.

Cochran, M. M., & Brassard, J. A. Child development and personal social networks. *Child Development*, 1979, *50*, 601–616.

Cochran, M., & Woolener, F. *Programming beyond the deficit model: The empowerment of parents with information and informal support*. Ithaca, NY: Cornell University, 1980.

Coehlo, G. V., Yuan, T., & Ahmed, P. I. Contemporary uprooting and collaborative coping: Behavioral and societal responses. In G. V. Coehlo & P. I. Ahmed (Eds.), *Uprooting and development*. New York: Plenum, 1980.

Cohen, A. K. *Delinquent boys: The culture of the gang*. New York: Free Press, 1955.

Cohen, C., & Sokolovsky, J. Schizophrenia and social networks. *Schizophrenia Bulletin*, 1978, *4*, 546–560.

Cohen, C. & Sokolovsky, J. A reassessment of the sociability of long term skid row residents. *Social Networks*, 1981, *3*(2), 93–105.

Cohen, S. Peer modeling and normative influences in the development of aggression. *Psychological Reports*, 1971, *28*, 995–998.

Cohn, A. Essential elements of successful child abuse and neglect treatment. *Child Abuse and Neglect*, 1979, *3*, 491–496.

Coit, S. *Neighborhood guilds*. London: Swan Sonnenschein, 1892.

Cole, E. "Adoption Services Today & Tomorrow" in *Child Welfare Strategy in the Coming Years*, Washington, DC: U.S. Children's Bureau, 1978.

Coleman, J. *Social structures and social climates in high school, final report*. Chicago: University of Chicago, 1959.

Coleman, J., Bremer, R., Clark, B., Davis, J., Eichorn, D., Griliches, Z., Kett, J., Rydern, N., Doering, Z., & Mays, J. *Youth: Transition to adulthood*. Chicago: University of Chicago Press, 1974.

Colletta, N. D. Support systems after divorce: Incidence and impact. *Journal of Marriage and the Family*, 1979, *41*, 837–846.

Collins, A. Helping neighbors intervene in cases of maltreatment. In J. Garbarino, S. H. Stocking, & Associates, *Protecting children from abuse and neglect*. San Francisco, CA: Jossey-Bass, 1980.

Collins, A. H., & Pancoast, D. L. *Natural helping networks*. Washington, DC: National Association of Social Workers, 1976.

Collins, A., & Watson, E. *Family day care.* Boston: Beacon Press, 1976.

Colvin, B. K., Hicks, M. W., & Greenwood, B. B. Intrafamilial stress in stepfamilies: Research findings and theoretical implications. Paper presented at the National Council on Family Relations annual meeting, Milwaukee, WI, October 1981.

Combs, M. L., & Slaby, D. A. Social skills training with children. In B. B. Lahey & A. E. Kazdin (Eds.), *Advances in clinical child psychology,* Vol. 1. New York: Plenum, 1977.

Commission on Professional and Hospital Activities. *International classification of diseases: Clinical modification* (9th rev. ed.). Ann Arbor, MI: Commission on Professional and Hospital Activities, 1978.

Comptroller General of the United States. *Home health—The need for a national policy to better provide for the elderly.* U.S. General Accounting Office, 1977.

Coogler, O. J., Weber, R. E., & McKenry, P. C. Divorce mediation: A means of facilitating divorce adjustment. *The Family Coordinator,* 1979, *28*(2), 255–259.

Corporate day care: An idea comes of age. *Trenton Times,* Jan. 8, 1981, p. D3.

Costin, L. *Child welfare* (2nd ed.). New York: McGraw Hill, 1979.

Costin, L. B., Keyserling, M. D., Pierce, W. L., & Wadlington, W. *The challenge of child day care needs and improved federal and state approaches to day care standard setting and enforcement.* In Policy Issues in Day Care. Washington, DC: U.S. Dept. of H.E.W., 1977, pp. 133–137.

Cowen, E. L. Social and community intervention. *Annual Review of Psychology,* 1973, *24,* 423–472.

Cowen, E., Gesten, E. Boike, M., Norton, P., Wilson, A. & DeStefano, M. Hairdressers as caregivers: I: A descriptive profile of helpgiving involvements. Unpublished manuscript, University of Rochester, Rochester, New York, 1978.

Coyne, J. S., & Lazarus, R. S. Cognitive style, stress perception, and coping. In I. L. Kutash & L. B. Schlesinger (Eds.), *Handbook on stress and anxiety.* San Francisco: Jossey-Bass, 1980.

Craig, M. M., & Furst, P. W. What happens after treatment? A study of potentially delinquent boys. *Social Service Review,* 1965, *39*(2), 165–171.

Craig, P. A. Counting handicapped children: A federal imperative. *Journal of Educational Finance,* 1976, *1,* 318–339.

Craven, P., & Wellman, B. The network city. In M. P. Effrot (Ed.), *The community: Approaches and applications.* New York: The Free Press, 1974.

Cressey, D. Changing criminals: The application of the theory of differential association. *American Journal of Sociology,* 1955, *61,* 116–120.

Cronenwett, L. R., & Kunst-Wilson, W. Stress, social support, and the transition to fatherhood. *Nursing Research,* 1981, *30,* 196–201.

Croog, S. H. The family as a source of stress. In S. Levine & N. A. Scotch (Eds.), *Social stress.* Chicago: Aldine, 1970.

Croog, S. H., Lipson, A., & Levine, S. Help patterns in severe illness: The roles of kin network, non-family resources, and institutions. *Journal of Marriage and the Family,* 1972, *32,* 32–41.

C.S.C.—Directory of member agencies. Sacramento: C.S.C., 1982. (Available from C.S.C., 301 P Street #32, Sacramento, CA, 95814.)

Cumming, E., & Henry, W. E. *Growing old: The process of disengagement.* New York: Basic Books, 1961.

Curtis, W. Community human service networks: New roles for mental health workers. *Psychiatric Annals,* 1973, *3,* 23–42.

Curtis, W., & Simpson, D. D. Differences in background and drug use history among three types of drug users entering drug therapy programs. *Journal of Drug Education,* 1977, *7*(4), 369–379.

Curtis, W. R. Team problem solving in a social network. *Psychiatric Annals,* 1974, *4,* 11–27.

Curtis, W. R. From state hospital to integrated human service system. *Health Care Management Review*, 1976, Spring, 39–50.

D & SU we love you. Santa Clara, CA: Institute for the Community as Extended Family, Parents United, 1980.

Daley, M. R. Preventing worker burnout in child welfare. *Child Welfare*, 1979, *58*(7), 443–450.

Danish, S. Personal communication, 1981.

Danish, S. J., & D'Augelli, A. R. Promoting competence and enhancing development through life development intervention. In L. A. Bond & J. C. Rosen (Eds.), *Primary Prevention of Psychopathology*, Vol. 4. Hanover, NH: University Press of New England, 1980.

Danish, S. J., D'Augelli, A. R., & Hauer, A. L. *Helping skills* (2nd ed.). New York: Human Sciences Press, 1980.

Danish, S. J., Smyer, M. A., & Nowak, C. A. Developmental intervention: Enhancing life-event processes. In P. B. Baltes & O. G. Brim, Jr. (Eds.), *Life-span development and behavior*, Vol. 3. New York: Academic Press, 1980.

D'Augelli, A. R., & Vallance, T. R. The helping community: Promoting mental health in rural areas through informal helping. *Journal of Rural Community Psychology*, 1981, *2*, 3–16.

Davies, D. *Sharing the power.* Boston: Institute for Responsive Education, 1977.

Davies, D. *Federal and state impact on citizen participation in the schools.* Boston: Institute for Responsive Education, 1978.

Davies, L. J., & Bland, D. C. The use of foster parents as role models for parents. *Child Welfare*, 1978, *57*(6), 380–386.

Dean, A., & Lin, N. The stress-buffering role of social support. *Journal of Nervous and Mental Disease*, 1977, *165*, 403–417.

Deci, E. L. *Intrinsic motivation.* New York: Plenum, 1975.

Delaney, S. W., Meyer, D. J., & Ward, M. J. *Fathers and infants class: A model for facilitating attachments between fathers and their infants.* Seattle: University of Washington, Experimental Education Unit, 1980.

Della-Dora, D. Parents and other citizens in curriculum development. In R. Brandt (Ed.), *Partners: Parents and schools.* Alexandria, VA: Association for Supervision and Curriculum Development, 1979.

Dellworth, U., Moore, M., Mullich, J., & Leone, F. Training student volunteers. *Personnel and Guidance Journal*, 1974, *53*, 57–60.

deLone, R. *Small futures.* New York: Harcourt, Brace, and Winston, 1979.

Dembo, R., Schmeidler, J., & Koval, M. Demographic, value and behavior correlates of marijuana use among middle class youth. *Journal of Health and Social Behavior*, 1976, *17*, 177–187.

Denver apartment block pioneers 1-parent style. Dayton, Ohio, *Daily News*, December 24, 1979.

Derdeyn, A. P. Children in divorce: Intervention in phase of separation. *Pediatrics*, 1977, *60*(1), 20–27.

DeRios, D., & Smith, D. E. Using or abusing: An anthropological approach to the study of psychoactive drugs. *Journal of Psychedelic Drugs*, 1976, *8*(3), 263–266.

Desmond, D. P., & Maddux, J. F. Religious programs and careers of chronic heroin users. In R. Faukenberry (Ed.), *Problems of the 70s, drug solutions for the 1980s.* Proceedings of the National Drug Abuse Conference, New Orleans, 1979. Lafayette, LA: Endac Enterprises, Print Media, 1980.

Developmental Disabilities Services and Construction Act, 1969 (Public Law 91-517). Washington, DC: U.S. Government Printing Office, 1969.

Devereux, E. A critique of ecological psychology. Paper presented at the conference on Research Perspectives in the Ecology of Human Development, Cornell University, Ithaca, NY, August 1977.

Devin-Sheehan, L., Feldman, R., & Allen, V. Research on children tutoring children: A critical review. *Review of Educational Research*, 1976, *46*, 355–385.

DiMatteo, M. R., & Hays, R. Social support and serious illness. In B. H. Gottlieb (Ed.), *Social networks and social support*. Beverly Hills, CA: Sage, 1981.

Dobrof, R., & Litwak, E. *Maintenance of family ties of long-term care patients: Theory and guide to practice*. Washington, DC: National Institute of Mental Health, 1979.

Döhner, O., & Angermeyer, M. C. Gruppenarbeit mit Angehörigenpsychish Kranker. *Psychoterapie: Psychosomatik Medizinische Psychologie*, 1981, *31*, 70–73.

Dohrenwend, B. S., & Dohrenwend, B. P. Some issues in research on stressful life events. *Journal of Nervous and Mental Disease*, 1978, *166*, 7–15.

Dohrenwend, B. S., & Dohrenwend, B. P. Socioenvironmental factors, stress, and psychopathology. *American Journal of Community Psychology*, 1981, *9*, 128–159.

Dohrenwend, B. P., & Egri, G. Recent stressful life events and episodes of schizophrenia. *Schizophrenia Bulletin*, 1981, *7*, 12–23.

Dokecki, P. The liaison perspective on the enhancement of human development. *Journal of Community Psychology*, 1977, *5*, 13–17.

Dokecki, P., & Hutton, R. The liaison specialist. Paper presented at the 85th Annual Convention of the American Psychological Association, San Francisco, 1977.

Dole, P., Nyswander, M., & Warner, A. Successful treatment of 750 criminal addicts. *Journal of American Medicine Association*, 1968, *206*, 2701–2711.

Dono, J. E., Falbe, C. M., Kail, B. L., Litwak, E., Sherron, R. H., & Siegel, D. The structure and function of primary groups in old age. *Research on Aging*, 1979, *1*, 403–433.

Dougherty, A. M., & Dyal, M. A. Community involvement: Training parents as tutors in a junior high. *The School Counselor*, *27*, 1976, 353–356.

Dowd, J. J. Aging as exchange: A preface to theory. *Journal of Gerontology*, 1975, *30*, 584–593.

Dowd, J. *Stratification Among the Aged*. Monterey, California: Brooks Cole, 1980.

Dreyfus, E. A. Counseling the divorced father. *Journal of Marital and Family Therapy*, 1979, *5*(4), 79–87.

Drug Abuse Council. *The facts about drug abuse*. New York: Free Press, 1980.

Duberman, L. *The reconstituted family*. Chicago: Nelson-Hall, 1975.

Duhl, L. J. (Ed.). *The urban condition*. New York: Basic Books, 1963.

Dunham, W. H. *Sociological theory and mental disorder*. Detroit: Wayne State University Press, 1959.

DuToit, B. *Drugs, rituals, and altered states of consciousness*. Rotterdam: A. A. Balkema, 1977.

Eaton, W. W. Life events, social supports, and psychiatric symptoms: A reanalysis of the New Haven data. *Journal of Health and Social Behavior*, 1978, *19*, 230–234.

Eddy, W., Paap, S., & Glad, D. Solving problems in living: The citizen's viewpoint. *Mental Hygiene*, 1970, *54*, 64–72.

Edelbrock, C. Running away from home: Incidence and correlates among children and youth referred for mental health services. *Journal of Family Issues*, 1980, *1*, 210–228.

Edelwich, J., & Brodsky, A. *Burn out*. New York: Human Sciences Press, 1980.

Edmundson, E. D., Bedell, J. R., Archer, R. P., & Gordon, R. E. Integrating skill building and peer support in mental health treatment: The early intervention and community network development projects. In A. M. Jeger and R. S. Slotnick (Eds.), *Community mental health: A behavioral-ecological perspective*. New York: Plenum, 1982.

Egbert, L. D., Battit, G. E., Welch, C. E., & Bartlett, M. K. Reduction of postoperative pain by encouragement and instruction of patients, *New England Journal of Medicine*, 1964, *270*, 825–827.

Egeland, B., Breitenbucher, M., & Rosenberg, D. A prospective study of the significance of life stress in the etiology of child abuse. *Journal of Consulting and Clinical Psychology*, 1980, *48*, 195–205.

Ehrlich, P. Service delivery for the community elderly: The mutual help model. *Journal of Gerontological Social Work*, 1979, *2*(2), 125–137.

Eisenberg, L. A friend, not an apple, a day will help keep the doctor away. *American Journal of Medicine*, 1979, *66*, 551–553.

Eitinger, L. *Concentration camp survivors in Norway and Israel.* The Hague: M. Nijhoff, 1964.

Elashoff, J. D., & Thoresen, C. E. Choosing a statistical method for analysis of an intensive experiment. In T. Kratochwill (Ed.), *Single subject research: Strategies for evaluating change.* New York: Academic Press, 1978.

Elder, G. H. *Children of the great depression.* Chicago: University of Chicago Press, 1974.

Elder, G., & Rockwell, R. The life course and human development: An ecological perspective. Unpublished paper. Boys Town, NE: Boys Town Center for the Study of Youth Development, 1977.

Elliott, D. S., & Voss, H. L. *Delinquency and dropout.* Lexington, MA: Lexington Books, 1974.

Elliott, V. Economic impact of the use of day care centers upon the family. In L. F. Myers (Ed.), *The family and community impact of day care: Preliminary findings* (Pennsylvania Day Care Study). University Park, PA.: Institute for the Study of Human Development, CHSD Report No. 17, December, 1972.

Elmer, E. *Children in jeopardy.* Pittsburgh: University of Pittsburgh Press, 1967.

Emlen, A. If you care about children, then care about parents. Address to the Tennessee Association for Young Children, Nashville, TN, November 1977.

Emlen, A. *et al. Overcoming barriers to planning for children in foster care.* Portland, OR: Regional Research Institute for Human Services, Portland State University, 1977.

Empey, L. T. *American delinquency: Its meaning and construction.* Homewood, IL: Dorsey Press, 1978.

Empey, L. T., & Erickson, M. L. *The Provo experiment.* Lexington, MA: Lexington Books, 1972.

Empey, L. T. & Lubeck, S. G. *The Silverlake experiment: Testing delinquency theory and community intervention.* Chicago: Aldine-Atherton Press, 1971.

Empey, L. T., & Rabow, J. The Provo experiment in delinquent rehabilitation. *American Sociological Review*, 1961, *26*, 679–696.

Epstein, A. *Assessing the child development information needed by adolescents with very young children.* Washington, DC: Administration for Children, Youth and Families (Grant No. 90-C-1341), 1980.

Erickson, R., & Eckert, D. The elderly poor in downtown San Diego hotels. *The Gerontologist*, 1977, *17*, 440–446.

Erikson, E. *Childhood and society.* New York: Norton, 1950.

Erlandson, D., & Pastor, M. Teachers motivation, job satisfaction, and alternatives— Directions for principals. *NASSP Bulletin*, 1981, *65*, 5–9.

Etkin, L., & Snyder, L. A model for peer-group counseling based on role playing. *The School Counselor*, 1972, *19*, 215–218.

Everett, P. B., Hayward, S. C., & Meyers, A. W. The effects of a token reinforcement procedure on bus ridership. *Journal of Applied Behavior Analysis*, 1974, *7:* 1–10.

Fairchild, N. Home–school token economies: Bridging the communication gap. *Psychology in the Schools*, 1976, *13*(4), 463–467.

Fairweather, G. W. Experimental development and dissemination of an alternative to psychiatric hospitalization. In R. F. Munoz, L. R. Snowden, & J. G. Kelly (Eds.), *Social and psychological research in community settings.* San Francisco: Jossey-Bass, 1979.

Fairweather, G. W., Sanders, D., Maynard, H., & Cressler, D. *Community life for the mentally ill: An alternative to institutional care.* Chicago: Aldine, 1969.

Fallcreek, S. J., & Mettler, M. K. *A healthy old age: A sourcebook for health promotion with older adults.* Seattle: University of Washington School of Social Work, 1982.

Famiglietti, J., Fraser, M., & Newland, K. School–family delinquency prevention programs. *Social Work*, in press.

Family Advocacy Council: Therapeutic family home. Unpublished paper, 1979. (Available from Family Advocacy Council, 15 Western Prom, Auburn, ME, 04210.)

Fanshel, D. Parental visiting of children in foster care: Key to discharge? *Social Service Review*, 1975, *49*(4), 493–514.

Fanshel, D. Status changes of children in foster care. *Child Welfare*, 1976, *55*, 143–171.

Fanshel, D., & Shinn, E. *Children in foster care*. New York: Columbia University Press, 1978.

Faris, R. E., & Dunham, W. H. *Mental disorders in urban areas*. Chicago: University of Chicago Press, 1939.

Farrell, D. F., & Swanson, P. D. Infectious disease associated with myoclonus. In M. H. Sheldon (Ed.), *Myoclonic seizures*. Amsterdam: Excerpta Medica, 1975.

Fast, I., & Cain, A. C. The stepparent role: Potential for disturbances in family functioning. *American Journal of Orthopsychiatry*, 1966, *36*, 485–491.

Faulkner, A. The black aged as good neighbors. *The Gerontologist*, 1975, *15*(6), 554–566.

Fawcett, S. D., Mathews, R. M., Fletcher, R. K., Morrow, R., & Stokes, T. F. Personalized instruction in the community: Teaching helping skills to low-income neighborhood residents. *Journal of Personalized Instruction*, 1976, *1*, 86–90.

Featherstone, H. *A difference in the family*. New York: Basic Books, 1980.

Feldman, H., & Feldman, M. Preferences by low income women about day care. *Human Ecology Forum*, 1973, *4*, 16–18.

Felt, L. Opportunity structures and relative deprivation among the poor: The case of welfare careerists. Unpublished doctoral dissertation, Northwestern University, 1971.

Fiddle, S. Sequences in addiction. *Addictive Diseases*, 1976, *2*(4), 553–567.

Field, T. Interaction behaviors of primary vs. secondary caregiver fathers. *Developmental Psychology*, 1978, *14*(2), 183–184.

Fine, S., Knight-Webb, G., & Vernon, J. Selected volunteer adolescents in adolescent group therapy. *Adolescence*, 1977, *46*, 189–197.

Finkel, A. J. (Ed.). *Physicians' current procedural terminology* (4th ed.). Chicago: American Medical Association, 1977.

Finkelhor, D. *Sexually victimized children*. New York: Academic Press, 1979.

Finkelstein, N. W. Family centered group care. In A. Maluccio, & P. Sinanoglu (Eds.), *The challenge of partnership*. New York: Child Welfare League of America, 1981.

Finlayson, A. Social networks as coping resources: Lay help and consultation patterns used by women in husbands' post-infarction career. *Social Science and Medicine*, 1976, *10*, 97–103.

Fischer, C. S., Jackson, R. M., Stueve, C. A., Gerson, K., Jones, L. M., & Baldassare, M. *Networks and places: Social relations in the urban setting*. New York: Free Press, 1977.

Flanagan, J., Hindelang, M. J., & Gottfredson, M. R. *Sourcebook of criminal justice statistics—1979*. Washington, DC: U.S. Government Printing Office, 1980.

Flynn, R. J., & Nitsch, K. E. (Eds.). *Normalization, social integration and community services*. Baltimore: University Park Press, 1980.

Ford Foundation. *Ford Foundation Letter*, 1979, *10*(2), 1–8.

Forness, S. R. Developing the individual educational plan: Process and perspectives. *Education and Treatment of Children*, 1979, *2*, 43–54.

Foster, G. G., Ysseldyke, J. E., & Reese, J. H. "I wouldn't have seen it if I hadn't believed it." *Exceptional Children*, 1975, *41*, 469–473.

Fox, N. Attachment of kibbutz infants to mother and metapelet. *Child Development*, 1977, *48*(4), 1228–1239.

Frady, M. The buck stops here. (Review of *Governing America* by J. Califano). *New York Review of Books*, 1981, *28*(15), 15–20.

Frank, J. D. *Persuasion and healing*. Baltimore: Johns Hopkins, 1978.

Frease, E. The schools, self-concept, and juvenile delinquency. *British Journal of Criminology*, 1972, *12*, 133–146.

French, J. R. P. Person role fit. Unpublished manuscript, Institute for Social Research, The University of Michigan, Ann Arbor, 1973.

French, J. R., & Kahn, R. L. A programmatic approach to studying the industrial environment and mental health. *Journal of Social Issues*, 1962, *18*, 1–47.

French, J., Rodgers, W., & Cobb, S. Adjustment as person–environment fit. In G. V. Coeblo, D. Hamburg, & J. E. Adams (Eds.), *Coping and adaptation*. New York: Basic Books, 1974.

Freud, A. *Normality and pathology in childhood: Assessments of development*. New York: International Universities Press, 1965.

Freud, S. *An outline of psychoanalysis*. New York: Norton, 1963.

Friedman, S. Resident welcoming committee: Institutionalized elderly in volunteer services to their peers. *Gerontologist*, 1975, *15*(4), 362–367.

Friedrich, W. N. Predictors of the coping behavior of mothers of handicapped children. *Journal of Consulting and Clinical Psychology*, 1979, *49*, 1140–1141.

Froland, C. Talking about networks that help. In C. Froland & D. L. Pancoast (Eds.), *Networks for helping*. Portland, OR: Portland State University, Regional Research Institute, 1979.

Froland, C., Brodsky, G., Olson, M., & Stewart, L. Social support and social adjustment: Implications for mental health professionals. In Proceedings of the Conference on Networks, November, 1978, Portland, Oregon. (Available from Regional Research Institute, Portland State University, P.O. Box 751, Portland, OR 97207.)

Froland, C., & Pancoast, D. Networking: What's it all about? *Caring*, 1979, *5*, 1–5.

Froland, C., Pancoast, D., Chapman, N., & Kimboko, P. Professional partnerships with informal helpers: Emerging forms. Presented at the Annual Convention of the American Psychological Association, New York, NY, September 1979.

Froland, C., Pancoast, D. L., Chapman, N. J., & Kimboko, P. J. *Helping networks and human services*. Beverly Hills, CA: Sage, 1981.

Furstenberg, A. Lay consultation of older people: Differential use of support network members. Presented at the 33rd Annual Meeting of the Gerontological Society, San Diego, CA, November 1980.

Furstenberg, F., & Crawford, A. G. Family support: Helping teenage mothers to cope. In F. F. Furstenberg, Jr., R. Lincoln, & J. Menken (Eds.), *Teenage sexuality, pregnancy, and childbearing*. Philadelphia: University of Pennsylvania, 1981.

Furstenberg, F., & Spanier, G. Marital dissolution and generational ties. Unpublished manuscript, 1980.

Gad, M. T., & Johnson, J. H. Correlates of adolescent life stress as related to race, SES, and levels of perceived support. *Journal of Clinical Child Psychology*, 1980, *5*(2), 13–16.

Galaway, B. Contracting: A means of clarifying roles in foster family services. *Children Today*, 1976, *5*(4), 20–23.

Galaway, B. PATH: An agency operated by foster parents. *Child Welfare*, 1978, *57*(10), 667–674.

Galinsky, E., & Hooks, W. H. *The new extended family: Day care that works*. Boston: Houghton Mifflin, 1977.

Gallup, G. 12th annual poll of the public's attitude towards the public schools. *Phi Delta Kappan*, 1980, *62*, 33–46.

Gallup, G. 13th annual poll of the public's attitude toward the public schools. *Phi Delta Kappan*, 1981, *63*, 33–47.

Gambrill, E., & Stein, T. Decision making and case management: Achieving continuity of care for children in out-of-home placement. In A. Maluccio & P. A. Sinanoglu (Eds.), *The Challenge of partnership*. New York: Child Welfare League of America, 1981.

Garbarino, J. High school size and adolescent social development. *Human Ecology Forum*, 1973, *4*, 26–29.

Garbarino, J. A preliminary study of some ecological correlates of child abuse. The impact of socioeconomic stress on mothers. *Child Development*, 1976, *47*, 178–185.

Garbarino, J. The price of privacy: An analysis of the social dynamic of child abuse. *Child Welfare*, 1977, *56*, 565–575.

Garbarino, J. The price of privacy: An analysis of the social dynamic of child abuse. *Child Welfare*, 1977, *56*, 565–575.

Garbarino, J. Meeting the needs of mistreated youth. *Social Work*, 1980a, *25*, 122–127.

Garbarino, J. Some thoughts on school size and its effects on adolescent development. *Journal of Youth and Adolescence*, 1980b, *9*, 169–182.

Garbarino, J. Latchkey children. *Vital Issues*. 1980c, *30* (December), 1–4.

Garbarino, J., & Asp, C. *Successful schools and competent students*. Lexington, MA: Lexington Books, 1981.

Garbarino, J., & Bronfenbrenner, U. The socialization of moral judgement and behavior in cross-cultural perspective. In T. Lickona (Ed.), *Moral development and behavior*. New York: Holt, Rinehart, & Winston, 1976.

Garbarino, J., & Gilliam, G. *Understanding abusive families*. Lexington, MA: D.C. Heath, 1980.

Garbarino, J., & Plantz, M. *Urban children and urban environments*. New York: ERIC Institute for Urban Education, 1981.

Garbarino, J., & Sherman, D. High-risk neighborhoods and high-risk families: The human ecology of child maltreatment. *Child Development*, 1980a, *51*, 188–198.

Garbarino, J., & Sherman, D. Identifing high-risk neighborhoods. In J. Garbarino, S. H. Stocking, & Associates, *Protecting children from abuse and neglect: Developing and maintaining effective support systems for families*. San Francisco: Jossey-Bass, 1980b.

Garbarino, J., & Smyer, M. A continuum of care for the family: Balancing the needs of poor children and poor elderly. Presented at the 33rd Annual Meeting of the Gerontological Society, San Diego, CA, November 1980.

Garbarino, J., Potter, A., & Carson, B. Comparing adolescent versus child abuse cases. Unpublished manuscript, Center for the Study of Youth Development, Boys Town, NB, 1977.

Garbarino, J., Stocking, S., & Associates. *Protecting children from abuse and neglect: Developing and maintaining effective support systems for families*. San Francisco: Jossey-Bass, 1980.

Garduque, L., & Long, F. N. Fifty-state survey of family day care licensing practices. Manuscript in preparation, The Pennsylvania State University, University Park, PA.

Garrison, J. Network methods for clinical problems. E. M. Pattison (Ed.), *Symposium on clinical group methods for larger social systems*. Boston: American Group Psychotherapy Association, 1976.

Garrison, J., & Howe J. Community intervention with the elderly: A social network approach. *Journal of the American Geriatric Society*, 1976, *24*(7), 329–333.

Garrison, V. Support systems of schizophrenic and non-schizophrenic Puerto Rican women in New York City. *Schizophrenia Bulletin*, 1978, *4*, 561–596.

Garrison, V., & Podell, J. Community support assessment for use in clinical interviews. *Schizophrenia Bulletin*, 1981, *7*, 101–108.

Gartner, A., & Riessman, F. *Self-help in the human services*. San Francisco: Jossey-Bass, 1977.

Gasser, R., & Taylor, C. Role adjustment of single parent fathers with dependent children. *The Family Coordinator*, 1976, *25*, 439–444.

Gath, A. The impact of an abnormal child upon the parents. *British Journal of Psychiatry*, 1977, *130*, 405–410.

Gatti, F., & Colman, C. Community network therapy. *American Journal of Orthopsychiatry*, 1976, *40*, 608–617.

Gelfand, D. E., & Gelfand, J. R. Senior centers and support networks. In D. Biegel & A. Naparstek (Eds.), *Community support systems and mental health: Building linkages*. New York: Springer, 1982.

Genovese, R. G. A woman's self-help network as a response to service needs in the suburbs. *Signs*, 1980, *5*(3), S248–256.

Germain, C. Space: An ecological variable in social work practice. *Social Casework*, 1978, *59*, 515–522.

Germain, C. B. (Ed.). *Social work practice: People and environments*. New York: Columbia University Press, 1979.

Germain, C. B., & Gitterman, A. *The life model of social work practice*. New York: Columbia University Press, 1980.

Gersten, J. C., Langner, T. S., Eisenberg, J. G., & Simcha-Fagan, O. An evaluation of stressful life events in psychological disorder. *Journal of Health and Social Behavior*, 1977, *18*, 228–244.

Giarretto, H. Reply to letter from women molested as children. In *Institute for the Community as Extended Family, Child sexual abuse and training program: Exercises and conceptual material*. Santa Clara, CA: ICEF, 1978.

Giarretto, H. A comprehensive child sexual abuse treatment program. In P. B. Mrazek & C. H. Kempe (Eds.), *Sexually abused children and their families*. Oxford: Pergamon Press, in press.

Giarretto, H., Giaretto, A., & Sgroi, S. M. Coordinated community treatment of incest. In A. W. Burgess, A. N. Groth, L. L. Holstrom, & S. M. Sgroi (Eds.), *Sexual assault of children and adolescents*. Lexington, MA: Lexington Books, 1978.

Gilchrist, L. D., & Schinke, S. P. Counseling with adolescents about their sexuality. In C. S. Chilman (Ed.), *Social and psychological aspects of adolescent sexuality: A handbook for professionals in the human services*. New York: John Wiley & Sons, in press.

Gilchrist, L. D., Schinke, S. P., & Blythe, B. J. Primary prevention services for children and youth. *Children and Youth Services Review*, 1979, *1*, 379–391.

Gilje, S. Blind climber finds Rainier too tough, vows to try for a 3rd time. *Seattle Times*, June 28, 1982, p. 1.

Giovannoni, J. M., & Billingsley A. Child neglect among the poor: A study of parental adequacy in families of three ethnic groups. *Child Welfare*, 1970, *49*(4), 196–204.

Gladwin, T. Social competence and clinical practice. *Psychiatry*, 1967, *30*, 30–43.

Glass, G. V., Willson, V. L., & Gottman, J. M. *Design and analysis of time-series experiments*. Boulder, CO: Colorado Associated University Press, 1975.

Glasser, I. Prisoners of benevolence. In W. Gaylin, I. Glasser, S. Marcus, & D. Rothman (Eds.), *Doing good: The limits of benevolence*. New York: Pantheon, 1978.

Glenn, N. D., & Weaver, C. N. The marital happiness of remarried divorced persons. *Journal of Marriage and the Family*, 1977, *39*, 331–337.

Glick, P. C. Children of divorced parents in demographic perspective. *Journal of Social Issues*, 1979, *35*(4), 170–182.

Glick, P. C. Remarriage: Some recent changes and variations. *Journal of Family Issues*, 1980, *1*(4), 455–478.

Glueck, S., & Glueck, E. *Uravelling juvenile delinquency*. Cambridge, MA: Harvard University Press, 1950.

Gold, M. *Delinquent behavior in an American city*. Belmont, CA: Brooks/Cole, 1970.

Goldfried, M. R. Toward the delineation of therapeutic change principles. *American Psychologist*, 1980, *35*, 991–999.

Goldiamond, I. Toward a constructional approach to social problems. *Behaviorism*, 1974, *2*, 1–84.

Golin, N., & Safferston, M. *Peer group counseling: A manual for trainers*. Miami, FL: Dade County Public Schools, 1971.

Goodlad, J., & Klein, F. *Looking behind the classroom door*. Worthington, OH: Charles A. Jones, 1974.

Goodman, L. A. Some alternatives to ecological correlation. *American Journal of Sociology*, 1959, *64*, 610–625.

Goodsen, B. D., & Hess, R. D. *Parents as teachers of very young children: An evaluative review of some contemporary concepts and programs*. Washington, DC: Bureau of Education Personnel Development, Office of Education (ERIC Document Reproduction Service No. ED136967), 1975.

Gordon, I. *Baby learning through baby play*. New York: St. Martin's Press, 1970.

Gordon, I. *Child learning through child play*. New York: St. Martin's Press, 1972.

Gordon, I. The effects of parent involvement on schooling. In R. Brandt (Ed.), *Partners: Parents and schools*. Alexandria, VA: Association for Supervision and Curriculum Development, 1979a.

Gordon, I. Improving parents' skills. In A. Yahraes (Ed.), *Families today: Strengthening the family*. DHEW Publ. No. (ADM) 79-896, 813–835, 1979b.

Gore, S. The effects of social support in moderating the health consequences of unemployment. *Journal of Health and Social Behavior*, 1978, *19*, 157–165.

Gottlieb, B. H. Lay influences on the utilization and provision of health services: A review. *Canadian Psychological Review*, 1976, *17*, 126–136.

Gottlieb, B. The role of individual and social support in preventing child maltreatment. In J. Garbarino, H. Stocking, and Associates, *Protecting children from abuse and neglect*. San Francisco: Jossey-Bass, 1980.

Gottlieb, B. H. Preventive interventions involving social networks and social support. In B. H. Gottlieb (Ed.), *Social networks and social support*. Beverly Hills, CA: Sage, 1981.

Gottlieb, B. H., & Hall, A. Social networks and the utilization of preventive mental health services. In R. H. Price, & Politser, P. E. (Eds.), *Prevention in mental health*. Beverly Hills, CA: Sage, 1980.

Gottlieb, B. H., & Schroter, C. Collaboration and resource exchange between professionals and natural support systems. *Professional Psychology*, 1978, *9*, 614–622.

Gottlieb, B., & Todd, D. Characterizing and promoting social support in natural settings. In R. F. Munoz, L. R. Snowder, J. G. Kelley, & Associates. *Social and psychological research in community settings*. San Francisco: Jossey-Bass, 1979.

Gottlieb, D., & Chafetz, J. S. Dynamics of familiar generational conflict and reconciliation. *Youth and Society*, 1977, *9*, 213–224.

Gottman, J., Gonso, J., & Rasmussen, B. Social interaction, social competence, and friendship in children. *Child Development*, 1975, *46*, 709–718.

Gottman, J. M., & Leiblum, S. R. *How to do psychotherapy and how to evaluate it*. New York: Holt, Rinehart & Winston, 1974.

Gourash, N. Help-seeking: A review of the literature. *American Journal of Community Psychology*, 1978, *6*, 413–424.

Gove, W., & Greerken, M. The effect of children and employment on the mental health of married men and women. *Social Forces*, 1977, *56*(1), 66–76.

Granowsky, A., Middleton, F., & Mumford, J. Parents as partners in education. *The Reading Teacher*, 1979, *32*, 826–830.

Gray, H. D., & Tindall, J. A. *Peer power: Becoming an effective peer helper*. Muncie, IN: Accelerated Development Inc., 1978a.

Gray, H. D., & Tindall, J. A. *Peer counseling: An in-depth look at peer helping*. Muncie, IN: Accelerated Development Inc., 1978b.

Gray, K. *et al*. Reimbursing family/friends for home care: A demonstration project. Presented at the 33rd Annual Meeting of the Gerontological Society, San Diego, CA, November 1980.

Gresham, F. M. Social skills training with handicapped children: A review. *Review of Educational Research*, 1981, *51*, 139–176.

Grinnell, R. M., & Kyte, N. S. Modifying the environment. *Social Work*, 1974, *19*(4), 477–483.

Grinnell, R. M., & Kyte, N. S. Environmental modification. *Social Work*, 1975, *20*(4), 313–318.

Grinnell, R. M., Kyte, N. S., & Bostwick, G. J. Environmental modification. In A. Maluccio (Ed.), *Promoting competence in clients*. New York: MacMillan, 1981.

Grossman, H. J. (Ed.). *Manual on terminology and classification in mental retardation* (rev. ed.). Washington, DC: American Association on Mental Deficiency, 1977.

Grossnickle, R. A life support system for teachers. *Clearing House*, 1978, *54*, 135–137.

Grow, L. J. *Early childrearing by young mothers: A research study*. New York: Child Welfare League of America, 1979.

Gruber, A. R. *Children in foster care—Destitute, neglected, betrayed*. New York: Human Sciences Press, 1978.

Guerney, L., & Jordon, L. Children of divorce: A Community support group. *Journal of Divorce*, 1979, *2*, 283–294.

Guggenheim, F. G., & O'Hara, S. Peer counseling in a general hospital. *American Journal of Psychiatry*, 1976, *133*, 1197–1199.

Guillemin, J. *Urban renegades: The cultural strategy of American Indians*. New York: Columbia University Press, 1975.

Gump, P., & Adelberg, B. Urbanism from the perspective of ecological psychologists. *Environment and Behavior*, 1978, *10*, 171–191.

Guralnick, M. J. Promoting social interactions among children at different developmental levels: Processes and problems. Paper presented at the Annual Meeting of the Council for Exceptional Children, Kansas City, April 1978.

Gurin, G., Veroff, J., & Feld, S. *Americans view their mental health*. New York: Basic Books, 1960.

Guttman, D. Neighborhood as a support system for Euro-American elderly. In D. Biegel & A. Naparstek (Eds.), *Community support systems and mental health: Building linkages*. New York: Springer, 1982.

Hagestad, G. O., Smyer, M. A., & Stierman, K. Parent–child relations in adulthood: The impact of divorce in middle age. In R. Cohen, S. Wersman, & B. Cohler (Eds.), *Parenthood as an adult experience*. New York: Guilford Press, 1982.

Haley, J. *Leaving home: The therapy of disturbed young people*. New York: McGraw-Hill, 1980.

Hall, R. V., Panyan, L., Rabon, D., & Broden, M. Instructing beginning teachers in reinforcement procedures which impose classroom control. *Journal of Applied Behavior Analysis*, 1968, *1*, 315–322.

Hamburg, D. A., & Adams, J. E. A perspective on coping behavior: Seeking and utilizing information in major transitions. *Archives of General Psychiatry*, 1967, *17*, 277–284.

Hamerlynck, G., Moore, J. A., & Barsh, E. T. *Extending family resources*. Seattle: Spastic Aid Council, 1981.

Hamilton, G. *Theory and practice of social case work*. New York: Columbia University Press, 1951.

Hammer, M. Social supports, social networks, and schizophrenia. *Schizophrenia Bulletin*, 1981, *7*, 45–57.

Hammer, M., Makiesky-Barrow, S., & Gutwirth, L. Social networks and schizophrenia. *Schizophrenia Bulletin*, 1978, *4*, 522–545.

Hampden-Turner, C. *Sane asylum: Inside the Delancey Street Foundation*. New York: William Morrow, 1977.

Hancock, E. The dimension of meaning and belonging in the process of divorce. *American Journal of Orthopsychiatry*, 1980, *50*, 18–27.

Hansell, S., & Wiatrowski, M. D. Competing conceptions of delinquent peer relations. Center for Social Organization of Schools, John Hopkins University, Baltimore. Presented at the American Society of Criminology Annual Meetings, San Francisco, 1980.

Hansell, N., Wodarczyk, M., & Handlon-Lathrop, B. Decision counseling method. *Archives of General Psychiatry*, 1970, *22*, 462–467.

Harbin, H. T., & Maziar, H. M. The families of drug abusers: A literature review. *Family Process*, 1975, *14*, 411–431.

Harding, M., & Zinberg, N. The effectiveness of the subculture in developing rituals and social sanctions for controlled drug use. In B. DuToit (Ed.), *Drugs, rituals, and altered states of consciousness*. Rotterdam: A. A. Balkema, 1977.

Harrell, J. Substitute child care, maternal employment, and the quality of mother–child interaction. University Park, PA: Institute for Human Development, CHSD Report No. 23, April 1973.

Hartman, A. Diagrammatic assessment of family relationships. *Social Casework*, 1978, *59*(18), 456–476.

Hartup, W. W. Peer relations and the growth of social competence. In M. W. Kent & J. E. Roff (Eds.), *Primary prevention of psychopathology, vol. III: Social competence in children*. Hanover, NH: University Press of New England, 1979.

Hartup, W. W., Glazer, J. A., & Charlesworth, R. Peer reinforcement and sociometric status. *Child Development*, 1967, *38*, 1017–1024.

Hassall, E., & Madar, D. Crisis group therapy with the separated and divorced. *Family Relations*, 1980, *29*, 591–597.

Havighurst, R. J. A social-psychological perspective on aging. *The Gerontologist*, 1968, *8*(2), 67–71.

Havighurst, R. J., & Albrecht, R. *Older people*. New York: Longmans, Green, 1953.

Hawkins, J. D. Reintegrating street drug abusers: Community roles in continuing care. In B. S. Brown (Ed.), *Addicts and aftercare*. Beverly Hills, CA: Sage, 1979.

Hawkins, J. D., & Fraser, M. The social networks of drug abusers before and after treatment: Implications for drug abuse treatment. Paper presented at the International Congress on Drugs and Alcohol, Jerusalem, Israel, 1981.

Hawkins, J. D., & Wacker, N. Verbal performances and addict conversion: An interactionist perspective on therapeutic communities. *Journal of Drug Issues*, in press.

Hawkins, J. D., & Weis, J. G. *The social development model: An integrated approach to delinquency prevention*. Seattle, WA: National Center for the Assessment of Delinquent Behavior and Its Prevention, Center for Law and Justice, University of Washington, 1980.

Hawks, D. The epidemiology of narcotic addiction in the United Kingdom. In E. Josephson & E. Carrol (Eds.), *Drug use: Epidemiological and sociological approaches*. New York: Wiley, 1974.

Hawley, A. *Human ecology: A theory of community structure*. New York: Ronald Press, 1950.

Haynes, R. B., & Sackett, D. L. (Eds.). *Compliance with therapeutic regimens: Annotated bibliography*. Baltimore: Johns Hopkins University Press, 1976.

Hays, W. C., & Mindel, C. H. Extended kinship relations in black and white families. *Journal of Marriage and the Family*, 1973, *35*, 51–57.

Haywood, H. C. Reducing social vulnerability is the challenge of the eighties (Presidential address). *Mental Retardation*, 1981, *19*, 190–195.

Healy, W. *The individual delinquent*. Boston: Little, Brown, 1915.

Heath, D. Student alienation and school. *School Review*, 1970, *78*, 515–528.

Hever, R. F. A manual on terminology and classification in mental retardation. *American Journal of Mental Deficiency*, 1959, *64*, Monogr. Suppl. (rev. ed.), 1961.

Heifeisen, A. *Peer program for youth*. Minneapolis, MN: Augsburg, 1973.

Helfer, R., & Kempe, C. H. *Child abuse and neglect: The family and the community*. Cambridge, MA: Ballinger, 1976.

Heller, K. The effects of social support: Prevention and treatment implications. In A. P. Goldstein & F. H. Kanfer (Eds.), *Maximizing treatment gains: Transfer enhancement in psychotherapy*. New York: Academic Press, 1979.

Hendrix, E. The fallacies in the concept of normalization. *Mental Retardation*, 1981, *19*, 295–296.

Hepburn, J. R. Testing alternative models of delinquency causation. *Journal of Criminal Law and Criminology*, 1977, *67*, 450–460.

Herjanic, B., & Wilbois, R. Sexual abuse of children. *Journal of the American Medical Association*, 1978, *239*, 331–333.

Herlihy, B., & Herlihy, D. The loneliness of educational leadership. *NASSP Bulletin,* 1980, *64,* 7–12.

Herzog, E., & Sudia, C. E. Boys in fatherless families. DHEW Pub. No. (OCD) 72-33. Office of Child Development, U.S. Department of Health, Education, and Welfare. Washington, DC: U.S. Government Printing Office, 1971.

Hess, B. Friendship, In M. W. Riley, M. Johnson, & A. Foner (Eds.), *Aging and society, Vol. III: A sociology of age stratefication.* New York: Russell Sage Foundation, 1972.

Hess, R. D., & Camara, K. A. Post-divorce family relationships as mediating factors in the consequences of divorce for children. *Journal of Social Issues,* 1979, *34,* 79–96.

Hetherington, E. M. Divorce: A child's perspective. *American Psychologist,* 1979, *34,* 851–858.

Hetherington, E. M., & Parke, R. *Child psychology: A contemporary viewpoint.* New York: McGraw-Hill, 1979.

Hetherington, E. M., Cox, M., & Cox, R. Divorced fathers. *Family Coordinator,* 1976, *25,* 417–428.

Hetherington, E. M., Cox, M., & Cox, R. The aftermath of divorce. In J. H. Stevens & M. Mathews (Eds.), *Mother/child, father/child relationships.* Washington, DC: National Association for the Education of Young Children, 1978a.

Hetherington, E. M., Cox, M., & Cox, R. The development of children in mother headed families. In H. Hoffman & D. Reiss (Eds.), *The American family.* New York: Plenum, 1978b.

Hicks, D. J. Imitation and retention of film-mediated aggressive peer and adult models. *Journal of Personality and Social Psychology,* 1965, *2,* 97–100.

Hill, R. S. *The strengths of black families.* New York: Emerson Hall, 1972.

Hill, R. *Informal adoption among black families.* Washington, DC: National Urban League, 1977.

Hindelang, J. Causes of delinquency: A partial replication and extension. *Social Problems,* 1973, *20*(4), 471–487.

Hinkle, L. E. The effect of exposure to cultural change, social change and changes in interpersonal relationships on health. In B. S. Dohrenwend & D. P. Dohrenwend (Eds.), *Stressful life events.* New York: John Wiley, 1974.

Hirschi, T. *Causes of delinquency.* Berkeley, CA: University of California Press, 1969.

Hobbs, N. The process of reeducation. Unpublished manuscript, Nashville, TN: George Peabody College, 1964.

Hobbs, N. Helping disturbed children: Psychological and ecological strategies. *American Psychologist,* 1966, *21*(12), 1105–1115.

Hobbs, N. *The future of children: Categories, labels, and their consequences.* San Francisco: Jossey-Bass, 1975.

Hobbs, N. *Troubled and troubling children.* San Francisco: Jossey-Bass, 1982.

Hobson, P. The partnership with Title I parents. In R. Brandt (Ed.), *Partners: Parents and schools.* Alexandria, VA: Association for Supervision and Curriculum Development, 1979.

Hochschild, A. R. *The unexpected community.* Englewood Cliffs, NJ: Prentice-Hall, 1973.

Holahan, C. J., Wilcox, B. L., Spearly, J. L., & Campbell, M. D. The ecological perspective in community mental health. *Community Mental Health Review,* 1979, *4*(2), 1–9.

Holland, J. M., & Hattersley, J. Parent support groups for the families of mentally handicapped children. *Child: Care, Health and Development,* 1980, *6,* 165–173.

Hollis, F. *Casework: A psychosocial therapy.* New York: Random House, 1972.

Holm, V. A., & Pipes, P. L. Food and children with Prayda-Willi syndrome. *American Journal of Diseases of Children,* 1976, *130,* 1063–1067.

Holmes, T. H., & Rahe, R. H. The social readjustment rating scale. *Journal of Psychosomatic Research,* 1967, *11,* 213–218.

Horowitz, A. Sons and daughters as caregivers to older parents: Differences in role performance and consequences. Presented at the 34th Annual Meeting of the Gerontological Society, Toronto, November 1981.

Horowitz, A., & Shindelman, L. W. The impact of caring for an elderly relative. Presented at the Annual Meeting of the Gerontological Society, San Diego, CA, 1980.

Hotaling, G. T., Atwell, S. G., & Linsky, A. S. Adolescent life changes and illness: A comparison of three models. *Journal of Youth and Adolescence*, 1978, *7*, 393–403.

Howard, J. *Families*. New York: Simon and Schuster, 1978.

Howell, M. C. *Helping ourselves: Families and the human network*. Boston: Beacon, 1975.

Hubbell, N. Some things change—and some do not. In R. Brandt (Ed.), *Partners: Parents and schools*. Alexandria, VA: Association for Supervisor and Curriculum Development, 1979.

Hultsch, D. F., & Plemons, J. K. Life events and lifespan development. In P. B. Baltes & O. G. Brim (Eds.), *Life span development and behavior*, Vol. 2. New York: Academic, 1979.

Hunt, M., & Hunt, B. *The divorce experience*. New York: McGraw-Hill, 1977.

Hunter, R. S., & Kilstrom, N. Breaking the cycle in abusive families. *American Journal of Psychiatry*, 1979, *136*, 1320–1322.

Hurn, C. *The limits and possibilities of schooling—An introduction to the sociology of education*. Boston: Allyn and Bacon, 1978.

Hutchins, R. M. Foreword in M. Rosenheim (Ed.), *Pursuing justice for the child*. Chicago: University of Chicago Press, 1976.

Illich, I. *Toward a history of needs*. New York: Pantheon, 1977.

Indian Child Welfare Act of 1978. Oakland, California: American Indian Lawyer Training Program, 1979.

Information and Assistance Program, Elderly Services. Spokane, WA: Spokane Community Mental Health Center, December 1980.

Insel, P. M. Social climate of mental health. In P. M. Insel (Ed.), *Environmental variables and the prevention of mental illness*. Lexington, MA: Lexington, 1980.

Institute of Medicine. *Issues in adolescent health*. Washington, DC: National Academy of Sciences, 1978.

Ishisaka, A. American Indians and foster care: Cultural factors and separation. *Child Welfare*, 1978, *57*(5), 299–308.

Ishiyama, T. Self help models: Implications for drug abuse programming. In B. S. Brown (Ed.), *Addicts and aftercare*. Beverly Hills, CA: Sage, 1979.

Jarrett, M. Psychiatric social work. *Mental Hygiene*, 1918, *2*, 290.

Jayaratne, S., & Levy, R. L. *Empirical clinical practice*. New York: Columbia University Press, 1979.

Jeger, A. M., Slotnick, R. S., & Schure, M. Toward a "self-help/professional collaboration perspective" in mental health. In D. Biegel & A. Naparstek (Eds.), *Community support systems and mental health: Building linkages*. New York: Springer, 1982.

Jenkins, S. The tie that bonds. In A. Maluccio & P. Sinanoglu (Eds.), *The challenge of partnership*. New York: Child Welfare League of America, 1981.

Jenkins, S., & Norman, E. *Filial deprivation and foster care*. New York: Columbia University Press, 1972.

Jenkins, S. & Norman, E. *Beyond Placement: Mothers View Foster Care*. New York: Columbia, 1975.

Jensen, G. F. Parents, peers, and delinquent action: A test of the differential association perspective. *American Journal of Sociology*, 1972, *78*(3), 562–575.

Jessor, R., Chase, J., & Donovan, J. Psychosocial correlates of marijuana use and problem drinking in a national sample of adolescents. *American Journal of Public Health*, 1980, *70*(6), 604–613.

Johnson, B. *Marijuana users and drug subcultures*. New York: Wiley, 1973.

Johnson, H. C. Working with stepfamilies: Principles of practice. *Social Work*, 1980, *25*, 304–308.

Johnson, S. *Idle haven: Community building among the working class retired*. Berkeley, CA: University of California Press, 1971.

Johnson, S. Interim report of the Family Impact Seminar. Washington, DC: George Washington University, 1978.

Jonas, K., & Wellin, E. Dependency and reciprocity: Home health aid in an elderly population. In C. Fry (Ed.), *Aging in culture and society*. New York: Bergin, 1980.

Jones, L. W. *Informal adoption in black families in Lowndes and Wilcox Counties, Alabama*. Tuskegee, AL: Tuskegee Institute, 1975.

Jurich, A., & Jurich, J. The lost adolescent syndrome. *Family Coordinator*, 1975, *24*, 357–361.

Kadushin, A. *Child welfare services* (3rd ed.). New York: Macmillan, 1980.

Kahana, E., & Felton, B. Social context and personal need: A study of Polish and Jewish aged. *Journal of Social Issues*, 1977, *33*(4), 56–64.

Kahn, A. J. *Social policy and social services* (2nd ed.). New York: Random House, 1979.

Kahn, A., & Kamerman, S. *Social services in international perspective*. Washington, DC: U.S. Department of Health, Education and Welfare, Office of Planning, Research and Evaluation, 79 (HE 17.2: S. 1/4), 1979.

Kahn, R. L., & Antonucci, T. C. Convoys across the life course: Attachment, roles, and social support. In P. B. Baltes & O. G. Brim (Eds.), *Life span development and behavior, Vol. 4*. New York: Academic, 1980.

Kamerman, S. B., & Kahn, A. J. *Social services in the United States: Policies and programs*. Philadelphia: Temple University Press, 1976.

Kammeyer, K., & Bolton, C. Community and family factors related to the use of a family service agency. *Journal of Marriage and the Family*, 1968, *30*, 488–498.

Kandel, D. B. Adolescent marihuana use: Role of parents and peers. *Science*, 1973, *181*, 1067–1069.

Kandel, D. B. International influence on adolescent illegal drug use. In E. Josephson & E. Carroll (Eds.), *Drug use: Epidemiological and sociological approaches*. New York: John Wiley & Sons, 1974.

Kandel, D. B. Developmental stages in adolescent drug involvement. In D. J. Lettieri, M. Sayers, & H. Wallenstein Pearson (Eds.), *Theories on drug abuse*. Washington, DC: U.S. Government Printing Office, 1980.

Kandel, D. B., Treiman, D., Faust, R., & Single, E. Adolescent involvement in legal and illegal drug use: A multiple classification analysis. *Social Forces*, 1976, *55*(2), 438–458.

Kaplan, B., Fleisher, D., & Regnier, V. Helping networks. Presented at the 32nd Annual Meeting of the Gerontological Society, Washington, DC, November 1979.

Kaplan, D., & Mearig, J. S. A community support system for a family coping with chronic illness. *Rehabilitation Literature*, 1977, *38*, 79–82, 96.

Karraker, R. Increasing academic performance through home managed contingency programs. *Journal of School Psychology*, 1972, *10*(2), 173–179.

Kasarda, J., & Janowitz, M. Community attachment in mass society. *American Sociological Review*, 1974, *39*, 328–339.

Katz, A. H., & Bender, E. I. Self-help groups in western society: History and prospects. *Journal of Applied Behavioral Sciences*, 1976, *12*(3), 265–282.

Kazdin, A. E. Methodological and interpretive problems of single-case experimental designs. *Journal of Consulting and Clinical Psychology*, 1978, *46*, 629–642.

Kazdin, A. E., & Matson, J. L. Social validation in mental retardation. *Applied Research in Mental Retardation*, 1981, *2*, 39–53.

Keeley, S. M., Shemberg, K. M., & Carbonell, J. Operant clinical intervention: Behavior management or beyond? Where are the data? *Behavior Therapy*, 1976, *7*, 292–305.

Kellam, S. G., & Ensminge, M. E. Theory and method in child psychiatric epidemiology. In A. E. Slaby & B. Z. Locke (Eds.), *Studying children epidemiologically*, Vol. 1. New York: Neal Watson, 1980.

Kellams, D. The role of principals today. *NASSP Bulletin*, 1979, *63*, 88–96.

Kelly, J. G. The mental health agent in the urban community. *American Psychologist*, 1966, *21*, 535–539.

Keniston, K. *All our children: The American family under pressure*. New York: Harcourt Brace Jovanovich, 1977.

Kern, R., & Kirby, J. Utilizing peer helper influence in group counseling. *Elementary School Guidance and Counseling*, 1971, *6*, 70–75.

Keshet, H. F., & Rosenthal, K. Fathering after marital separation. *Social Work*, 1978, *23*, 11–18.

Kessler, M., & Albee, G. W. Primary prevention. *Annual Review of Psychology*, 1975, *26*, 557–591.

Kessler, S. Divorce adjustment groups. *The Personnel and Guidance Journal*, 1976, *54*(5), 250–255.

Kiesler, D. J. Some myths of psychotherapy research and the search for a paradigm. *Psychological Bulletin*, 1966, *65*, 110–136.

Kilmer, S. Infant-toddler group day care: A review of research. In L. G. Katz, M. Z. Glockner, C. Watkins, & M. J. Spencer (Eds.), *Current topics in early childhood education*, Vol. 3. Norwood, NJ: Ablex, 1979.

King, J. *The Probation and after-care service*. London: Butterworth, 1969.

Kingsley, R. E., Viggiano, R. A., & Tout, L. Social perception of friendship, leadership, and game playing among EMR special and regular class boys. *Education and Training of the Mentally Retarded*, 1981, *16*, 201–206.

Kinney, J., Madsen, B., Fleming, T., & Haapala, D. Homebuilders: Keeping families together. *Journal of Consulting and Clinical Psychology*, 1977, *45*, 667–673.

Kleiman, C. *Women's networks*. New York: Ballantine Books, 1980.

Kleiman, M. A., Mantell, J. E., & Alexander, E. S. Collaboration and its discontents: The perils of partnership. *Journal of Applied Behavioral Science*, 1976, *12*, 403–410.

Klein, M. Gang cohesiveness, delinquency and a street-work program. *Journal of Research in Crime and Delinquency*, 1969, *6*(2), 135–166.

Klentschy, M. An examination of sex-pairing effectiveness for reading tutoring. Paper presented at the meeting of the California Educational Research Association, San Diego, CA, 1971.

Koegel, R. L., & Rincover, A. Treatment of psychotic children in a classroom environment: Learning in a large group. *Journal of Applied Behavior Analysis*, 1974, *7*, 45–59.

Kogan, L., Smith, J., & Jenkins, S. Ecological validity of indicator data as predictors of survey findings. *Journal of Social Service Research*, 1977, *1*, 117–132.

Kompara, D. R. Difficulties in the socialization process of stepparenting. *Family Relations*, 1980, *29*, 69–73.

Koo, H. P., & Suchindran, C. M. Effects of children on women's remarriage prospects. *Journal of Family Issues*, 1980, *1*(4), 497–515.

Kornhauser, R. R. *Social sources of delinquency: An appraisal of analytic methods*. Chicago: University of Chicago Press, 1978.

Kratochwill, T. R. Foundations of time-series research. In T. Kratochwill (Ed.), *Single subject research: Strategies for evaluating change*. New York: Academic Press, 1978.

Kratochwill, T. R., & Brody, G. H. Single subject designs: A perspective on the controversy over employing statistical inference and implications for research and training in behavior modification. *Behavior Modification*, 1978, *2*, 291–307.

Kraus, A., & Lilienfeld, A. Some epidemiological aspects of the high mortality rate in the young widowed group. *Journal of Chronic Diseases*, 1959, *10*, 207–217.

Kraus, A. S., Spasoff, R. A., Beattie, E. J., Holden, D. E. W., Lawson, J. S., Rodenburg, M., & Woodcock, G. M. Elderly applicants to long-term care institutions. II. The application process; placement and care needs. *Journal of the American Geriatrics Society*, 1976, *24*, 165–172.

Kropotkin, P. *Mutual aid*. Boston: Extending Horizon Books, 1914.

Kroth, J. A. *Child sexual abuse: Analysis of a family therapy approach.* Springfield, IL: Charles C. Thomas, 1979.

Kuhn, T. S. *The structure of scientific revolutions,* 2d ed. Chicago: University of Chicago Press, 1970.

Kulka, R. A., & Weingarten, H. The long-term effects of parental divorce in childhood on adult adjustment. *Journal of Social Issues,* 1979, *35*(4), 50–78.

Kulys, R., & Tobin, S. Older people and their "responsible others." *Social Work,* 1980, *25*(2), 138–145.

Kurdek, L. A. An integrative perspective on children's divorce adjustment. *American Psychologist,* 1981, *36*, 856–866.

Kurdek, L. A. Blisk, D. and Siesky, A. Correlates of children's long-term adjustment to their parents' divorce. *Developmental Psychology,* in press.

Lahey, B., Gendrich, J., Gendrich, S., Schnelle, L., Gant, D., & McNee, P. An evaluation of daily report cards with minimal teacher and parent contacts as an efficient method of classroom intervention. *Behavior Modification,* 1977, *1*(3), 381–394.

Lahti, J. *A follow-up study of the Oregon project.* Portland, OR: Regional Research Institute for Human Services, Portland State University, 1978.

Laird, J., & Hartman, A. *A handbook of child welfare.* New York: Free Press, in press.

Lally, M., Black, E., Thornock, M., & Hawkins, J. D. Older women in single room occupant (SRO) hotels: A Seattle profile. *The Gerontologist,* 1979, *19*(1), 67–74.

Landesman-Dwyer, S., Berkson, G., & Romer, D. Affiliation and friendship of mentally retarded residents in group homes. *American Journal of Mental Deficiency,* 1979, *83*, 571–580.

Landesman-Dwyer, S., & Emanuel, I. Smoking during pregnancy. *Teratology,* 1979, *19*, 119–125.

Landesman-Dwyer, S., Sackett, G. P., & Kleinman, J. S. Relationship of size to resident and staff behavior in small community residences. *American Journal of Mental Deficiency,* 1980, *85*, 6–17.

Langlie, J. K. Social networks, health beliefs, and preventive health behavior. *Journal of Health and Social Behavior,* 1977, *18*, 244–260.

Langner, T. S., & Michael, S. T. *Life stress and mental health.* New York: Free Press, 1963.

Lathrop, J. C. Presidential Address. *Proceedings of the National Conference on Social Welfare,* 1919.

Lauer, B., Ten Broeck, E., & Grossman, M. Battered child syndrome: Review of 130 patients with controls. *Pediatrics,* 1974, *54*, 67–70.

Lawrence, T. S., & Vellerman, J. Correlates of student drug use in a suburban high school. *Psychiatry,* 1974, *37*, 129–136.

Lazarus, L. W., Stafford, B., Cooper, K., Cohler, B., & Dysken, M. A pilot study of an Alzheimer patients' relatives discussion group. *The Gerontologist,* 1981, *21*, 353–358.

Leavitt, S., Davis, M., Maloney, K. B., & Maloney, D. M. Parenting alone successfully: The development of a single-parent training program. In N. Stinnett, B. Chesser, & J. DeFrain (Eds.), *Building family strengths: Blueprints for action.* Lincoln, NE: University of Nebraska Press, 1979.

Lebowitz, B. Old age and family functioning. *Journal of Gerontological Social Work,* 1978, *1*(2), 111–119.

Leconte, J. M. Social work intervention strategies for families with children with Prader-Willi syndrome. In V. A. Holm, S. Sulzbacher, & P. L. Pipes (Eds.), *The Prader-Willi syndrome.* Baltimore: University Park Press, 1981.

Lee, G. R. Effects of social networks on the family. In W. Burr, R. Hill, F. E. Nye, & I. L. Russ (Eds.), *Contemporary theories of the family: Research-based theories,* Vol. I. New York: Free Press, 1979.

Leichter, J. J., & Mitchell, W. E. *Kinship and casework.* New York: Russell Sage Foundation, 1967.

Leighton, A. H. *My name is legion.* New York: Basic Books, 1959.

Lemert, E. *Social pathology.* New York: McGraw-Hill, 1951.

Lemon, B. W., Bengtson, V. L., & Peterson, J. A. An exploration of the activity theory of aging: Activity types and life satisfaction among in-movers to a retirement community. *Journal of Gerontology,* 1972, 27(4), 511–523.

Lenrow, P. Dilemmas of professional helping. In L. Wispe (Ed.), *Altruism, sympathy, and helping.* New York: Academic Press, 1978.

Lenrow, P., & Burch, R. W. Mutual aid and professional services: Opposing or complementary? In B. Gottlieb (Ed.), *Social networks and social support.* Beverly Hills, CA: Sage, 1981.

Leo, J. Getting tough with teens. *Time,* June 8, 1981, p. 47.

Leutz, W. N. The informal community caregiver: A link between the health care system and local residents. *American Journal of Orthopsychiatry,* 1976, 46, 678–688.

Levine, T. Community-based treatment for adolescents. *Social Work,* 1977, 22, 144–147.

Levine, T., & McDaid, E. Services to children in their own homes: A family based approach. Paper presented at the First Annual Symposium on Home Based Services to Children, University of Iowa, April 26, 1978.

Levinson, D. J., Darrow, C. N., Klein, E. B., Levinson, M. H., & McKee, B. *The seasons of a man's life.* New York: Knopf, 1978.

Levitt, J. L., & Reid, W. J. Rapid-assessment instruments for practice. *Social Work Research & Abstracts,* 1981, 17, 13–19.

Lewin, K. *Resolving social conflicts.* New York: Harper, 1948.

Lewin, K. *Field theory in social science.* New York: Harper & Row, 1951.

Lewis, D., & Sessler, J. Heroin treatment: Development, status, outlook. In Drug Abuse Council (Ed.), *The facts about drug abuse.* New York: Free Press, 1980.

Lewis, H. Informal support networks and the welfare state: Some ethical considerations. In D. Biegel & A. Naparstek (Eds.), *Community support systems and mental health: Building linkages.* New York: Springer, 1982.

Lewis, M., Bienenstock, R., Cantor, M., & Schneewind, E. The extent to which informal and formal supports interact to maintain the older people in the community. Paper presented at the 33rd Annual Meeting of the Gerontological Society, San Diego, CA, 1980.

Lewis, M., & Schaeffer, S. Peer behavior and mother–infant interaction in maltreated children. In M. Lewis & L. Rosenblum (Eds.), *The uncommon child: The genesis of behavior,* Vol. 3. New York: Plenum, 1981.

Liaison Task Panel on Psychoactive Drug Use/Misuse. Report to the President's Commission on Mental Health. Washington, DC: U.S. Government Printing Office, 1978.

Libertoff, K. Natural helping networks in rural youth and family services. *Journal of Rural Community Psychology,* 1980, 1, 4–17.

Lieber, L., & Baker, J. Parents Anonymous and self help treatment for child abusing parents: A review and an evaluation. *Child Abuse and Neglect,* 1977, 1, 133–148.

Lieberman, G. L. Children of the elderly as natural helpers: Some demographic differences. *American Journal of Community Psychology,* 1978, 6, 489–498.

Lieberman, M. A. The effects of social supports in responses to stress. In L. Goldberger & S. Breznitz (Eds.), *Handbook of stress.* New York: Free Press, 1982.

Lieberman, M. A., & Borman, L. D. *Self help groups for coping with crisis.* San Francisco: Jossey-Bass, 1979.

Lieberman, M. A., & Mullan, J. T. Does help help? The adaptive consequences of obtaining help from professionals and social networks. *American Journal of Community Psychology,* 1978, 6, 499–517.

Lieberman, M. A., & Glidewell, J. C. Overview: Special issue of the helping process. *American Journal of Community Psychology,* 1978, 6, 405–412.

Lindenthal, J., Thomas, C., & Myers, J. Psychological status and the perception of primary and secondary support from the social milieu in time of crisis. *Journal of Nervous and Mental Disease*, 1971, *153*, 92–98.

Lippitt, R., Watson, J., & Westley, B. *The dynamics of planned change.* New York: Harcourt Brace, 1957.

Lisbe, E. R. Professionals in the public schools. In J. S. Mearig & Associates (Eds.), *Working for children.* San Francisco: Jossey-Bass, 1978.

Litwak, E., & Szelenyi, I. Primary group structures and their functions: Kin, neighbors and friends. *American Sociological Review*, 1969, *34*, 465–481.

Lloyd, R. *For money or love: Boy prostitution in America.* New York: Vanguard, 1976.

Loewe, B., & Hanrahan, T. E. Five day foster care. *Child Welfare*, 1975, *54*(1), 7–18.

Longfellow, C. Divorce in context: Its impact on children. In G. Levinger & O. C. Moles (Eds.), *Divorce and separation: Context, causes, and consequences.* New York: Basic Books, 1979.

Longino, C., & Lipman, C. Married and spouseless men and women in planned retirement communities: Support network differentials. *Journal of Marriage and the Family*, 1981, 169–177.

Lopata, H. F. *Widowhood in an American city.* Cambridge, MA: Schenkman, 1973.

Lortie, D. *Schoolteacher: A sociological study.* Chicago: University of Chicago Press, 1975.

Low, A. A. *Mental health through will training.* Boston: The Christopher Publishing House, 1950.

Lowenthal, M. F., & Haven, C. Interaction and adaptation: Intimacy as a critical variable. *American Sociological Review*, 1968, *33*, 20–30.

Lowenthal, M. F., & Robinson, B. Social networks in social isolation. In R. Binstock & E. Shanas (Eds.), *Handbook of aging and the social sciences.* New York: Van Nostrand Reinhold, 1976.

Lowinson, J., & Langrod, J. Neighborhood drug treatment centers: Opposition to establishment. *New York State Journal of Medicine*, 72, 1975, 766–769.

Lowy, L. *Social work with the aging.* New York: Harper & Row, 1979.

Luborsky, L., Todd, T. C., & Katcher, A. H. A self-administered social assets scale for predicting physical and psychological illness and health. *Journal of Psychosomatic Research*, 1973, *17*, 109–120.

Lubove, R. *The professional altruist.* Cambridge, MA: Harvard University Press, 1965.

Lukoff, I. Issues in the evaluation of heroin treatment. In E. Josephson and E. E. Carroll (Eds.), *Drug use: Epidemiological and sociological approaches.* New York: Wiley, 1974.

Lukoff, I. Toward a sociology of drug use. In D. J. Lettieri, M. Sayers, & H. Wallenstein Pearson (Eds.), *Theory on drug abuse.* Washington, DC: U.S. Government Printing Office, 1980.

Maas, H., & Engler, R. *Children in need of parents.* New York: Columbia University Press, 1959.

McAdoo, H. P. Factors related to stability in upwardly mobile black families. *Journal of Marriage and the Family*, 1978, *40*, 761–778.

McAlister, A. L., Perry, C., & Maccoby, N. Adolescent smoking: Onset and prevention. *Pediatrics*, 1979, *63*, 650–658.

MacAndrew, C., & E. Edgerton. *Drunken comportment: A social explanation.* Chicago: Aldine, 1969.

McAuliffe, W. An exploratory study of self-help for treated addicts. Unpublished report, Boston: Harvard School of Public Health, 1981.

McCleary, L., & Thompson, S. *The senior high school principalship—Vol. III: The summary report.* Reston, VA: National Association of Secondary School Principals, 1979.

McClelland, D. C. Testing for competence rather than for "intelligence." *American Psychologist*, 1973, *28*, 1–14.

McCord, J. A 30-year follow-up study of treatment effects. *American Psychologist*, 1978, *33*, 284–289.

McCord, J., & McCord, W. The effects of parental role model on criminality. *Journal of Social Issues*, 1958, *14*, 66–75.

McCorkle, L. W. Group therapy in the treatment of offenders. *Federal Probation*, 1952, *16*, 22–27.

McCorkle, L., Elias, A., & Bixby, F. *The Highfields story: An experimental treatment project for youthful offenders*. New York: H. Holt, 1958.

McDill, E., Myers, E., & Rigsby, L. *Sources of educational climates in high schools*. Baltimore: Johns Hopkins University for U.S. Department of Health, Education, and Welfare, 1966.

MacDonald, W., Gallimore, R., & MacDonald, G. Contingency counseling by school personnel: An economical model of intervention. *Journal of Applied Behavior Analysis*, 1970, *3*, 175–182.

MacElveen, P. M. Social networks. In D. C. Longo & R. A. Williams (Eds.), *Clinical practice in psychosocial nursing: Assessment and intervention*. New York: Appleton-Century-Crofts, 1978.

McGoldrick, M., & Carter, E. Forming a remarried family. In E. Carter & M. McGoldrick (Eds.), *The family life cycle: A framework for family therapy*. New York: Gardner Press, 1980.

McGrath, F. C., O'Hara, D., & Thomas, D. *Graduate social work education in the university affiliated facility*. Miami, FL: University of Miami Mailman Center for Child Development, 1976.

McGuire, J. C., & Gottlieb, B. H. Social support groups among new parents: An experimental study in primary prevention. *Journal of Clinical Child Psychology*, 1979, *8*, 111–116.

McHenry, S. Sister-to sister: We're about navigating systems. *Ms*, 1980, *9*(6), 63.

Mackey, J. Youth alienation in post-modern society. *The High School Journal*, 1978, *61*, 353–367.

McKinlay, J. B. Social networks, lay consultation and help-seeking behavior. *Social Forces*, 1973, *51*, 275–292.

McLanahan, S. S., Wedemeyer, N. V., & Adelberg, T. Network structure, social support, and psychological well-being in the single-parent family. *Journal of Marriage and the Family*, 1981, *43*, 601–612.

Maddi, S. R. The search for meaning. *Nebraska Symposium on Personality*, 1970, *18*, 137–186.

Maddox, G. L. Themes and issues in sociological theories of aging. *Human Development*, 1970, *13*(1), 17–27.

Maddux, J. R., & Desmond, D. New light on the maturing out hypothesis in opiate dependence. Paper presented at the National Drug Abuse Conference, New Orleans, August 1979.

Make Today Count chapter celebrates 6th anniversary. *Make Today Count Newsletter*, June/July 1981, pp. 8–9.

Malcolm, P., & Young, I. Evaluation: Positive peer culture, instructional research report #1977-3. Omaha, NE: Omaha Public Schools, 1978.

Maluccio, A. N. (Ed.). *Promoting competence in clients*. New York: Free Press, 1981.

Maluccio, A., & Sinanoglu, P. (Eds.). *The challenge of partnership*. New York: Child Welfare League of America, 1981.

Malyon, A. K. The homosexual adolescent: Developmental issues and social bias. *Child Welfare*, 1981, *60*, 321–330.

Manpower Demonstration Research Corporation. *Summary and findings of the National Supported Work Demonstration*. Cambridge, MA: Ballinger, 1980.

Marascuilo, L., Levin, J., & James, H. Evaluation report for the Berkeley Unified School Districts remedial reading program sponsored under SB 28, September 15, 1969.

Marholin, D., II, Siegel, L. J., & Phillips, D. Treatment and transfer: A search for empirical procedures. In M. Hersen, R. M. Eisler, & P. M. Miller (Eds.), *Progress in behavior modification*, Vol. 3. New York: Academic, 1976.

Markun, P. Where it's happening. In J. Rash & P. Markun (Eds.), *New views of school and community*. Arlington, VA and Washington, DC: National Association of Elementary School Principals and Association for Childhood Education International, 1973.

Marlatt, G. A., Demming, B., & Reid, J. Loss of control drinking in alcoholics: An experimental analogue. *Journal of Abnormal Psychology*, 1973, *81*, 233–241.

Marmot, M. G., & Syme, S. L. Acculturation and coronary heart disease in Japanese-Americans. *American Journal of Epidemiology*, 1976, *104*, 225–247.

Martin, E. P., & Martin, J. M. *The black extended family*. Chicago: University of Chicago Press, 1978.

Martin, G. Power, dependence, and the complaints of the elderly: A social exchange perspective. *Aging: Human Development*, 1971, *2*(2), 108–112.

Maslow, A. *Motivation and personality* (2nd ed.). New York: Harper & Row, 1954.

Mason, D., Jensen, G., & Ryzewicz, C. *How to grow a parents' group*. Minneapolis, MN: International Childbirth Education Association, 1979.

Massachusetts Governor's Committee on Children and the Family—Report. Boston: State House, 1980.

Mather, H. G. Intensive care. *British Medical Journal*, 1974, *2*, 322.

Matson, J. L. A controlled study of pediatrician-skill training for the mentally retarded. *Behavior Research and Therapy*, 1980, *18*, 99–106.

Maultsby, M., Knipping, P., & Carpenter, L. Teaching self-help in the classroom with rational self-counseling. *The Journal of School Health*, 1974, *44*, 445–448.

Maybanks, S., & Bryce, M. (Eds.). *Home-based services for children and families*. Springfield, IL: Charles C. Thomas, 1979.

Meichenbaum, D. *Cognitive-behavior modification: An integrative approach*. New York: Plenum, 1977.

Meichenbaum, D., Bowers, K., and Ross, R. Modification of classroom behavior of institutionalized female adolescent offenders. *Behavior Research and Therapy*, 1968, *6*, 343–353.

Meiselman, K. C. *Incest—A psychological study of causes and effects with treatment recommendations*. San Francisco: Jossey-Bass, 1978.

Mellor, J., & Getzel, G. Stress and service needs of those who care for the aged. Presented at the 33rd Annual Meeting of the Gerontological Society, San Diego, CA, November 1980.

Menaghen, E. G. Seeking help for parental concerns: The middle years. *American Journal of Community Psychology*, 1978, *6*, 477–488.

Mendes, H. A. Single fatherhood. *Social Work*, 1976a, *21*(4), 308–313.

Mendes, H. A. Single fathers. *The Family Coordinator*, 1976b, *25*(4), 439–444.

Menolascino, F. J., & Eaton, L. F. Future trends in mental retardation. *Child Psychiatry and Human Development*, 1980, *10*, 156–168.

Messinger, L. Remarriage between divorced people with children from previous marriages: A proposal for preparation for remarriage. *Journal of Marriage and Family Counseling*, 1976, *2*, 193–200.

Messinger, L., Walker, K. N., & Freeman, S. J. Preparation for remarriage following divorce: The use of group techniques. *American Journal of Orthopsychiatry*, 1978, *48*, 263–272.

Metcalf, A. Social networks in families headed by a single working mother. Unpublished manuscript, University of Washington, School of Social Work, 1980.

Mettler, M. K., & Fallcreek, S. J. The community-based health promotion program: Social work and prevention. Paper presented at the National Association of Social Workers Professional Symposium, Philadelphia, November 1981.

Michelson, W., & Roberts, E. Children and the urban physical environment. In W. Michelson, S. Levine, & A. Spiva (Eds.), *The child in the city*. Toronto: University of Toronto Press, 1979.

Michigan State Department of Social Services, Demonstration project for the registration of family day care homes. Lansing, MI, May 1, 1977 (ERIC ED148486).

Miller, D., Miller, D., Hoffman, F., & Duggan, R. *Runaways—illegal aliens in their own land: Implications for service*. New York: J. F. Bergin, 1980.

Miller, G. A., Galanter, E., & Pribram, K. H. *Plans and the structure of behavior*. New York: Holt, 1960.

Miller, K., & Turner, D. Child development information utilization by reservation and urban Indian parents of very young children. In J. Sparling & I. Lewis (Eds.), *Information needs of parents with young children*. Washington, DC: Administration for Children, Youth, and Families, 1980.

Miller, P. M., & Ingham, J. G. Friends, confidants and symptoms. *Social Psychiatry*, 1976, *11*, 51–58.

Miller W. B. The impact of a community group work program on delinquent corner groups. *Social Services Review*, 1957, *31*(4), 390–406.

Miller, W. B. The impact of a total community delinquency control project. *Social Problems*, 1962, *10*(2), 168–191.

Mills, C. W. *The sociological imagination*. New York: Oxford University Press, 1959.

Minunchin, S., Rossman, B. L., & Baker, L. *Psychosomatic families: Anorexia nervosa in context*. Cambridge, MA: Harvard University Press, 1978.

Mitchell, J. *Social networks in urban situations*. Atlantic Highland, NJ: Humanities Press, 1969.

Mitchell, R. E., & Hurley, D. J. Collaboration with natural helping networks: Lessons from studying paraprofessionals. In B. Gottlieb (Ed.), *Social networks and social support*. Beverly Hills, CA: Sage, 1981.

Mitchell, R. E., & Trickett, E. J. Social network research and psychosocial adaptation: Implications for community mental health practice. In P. M. Insel (Ed.), *Environmental variables and the prevention of mental illness*. Lexington, MA: Lexington, 1980.

Mize, G. The influence of increased parental involvement in the educational process of their children. Madison, WI: Wisconsin Research and Development, Center on Cognitive Learning, University of Wisconsin, 1977.

Mizruchi, E. H., & Perrucci, R. Prescription, proscription, and permissiveness: Aspects of norms and deviant drinking behavior. In G. L. Maddox (Ed.), *The domesticated drug: Drinking among collegians*. New Haven: College and University Press, 1970.

Monahan, J. T., & Vaux, A. Macroenvironment and macrocommunity mental health. In P. M. Insel (Ed.), *Environmental variables and the prevention of mental illness*. Lexington, MA: Lexington, 1980.

Monk, A. Family supports in old age. *Social Work*, 1979, *24*(6), 533–538.

Moore, J. C. Parent choice of day care services: A statistical study of the amount and type of care used. Washington, DC: Day Care Council of America, Inc., July, 1980 (ERIC ED192871).

Moos, R. Evaluating and changing community settings. *American Journal of Community Psychology*, 1976, *4*, 313–326.

Morgan, R., & Toy, T. Learning by teaching: A student-to-student compensatory tutoring program in a rural school system and its relevance to the educational cooperative. *Psychological Record*, 1970, *20*, 159–169.

Morosan, E., & Pearson, R. E. Upon whom do you depend? Mapping personal support systems. *Canada's Mental Health*, March 1981, *26*, 5–6.

Morris, J. D., & Prescott, M. R. Adjustment to divorce through transactional analysis. *Journal of Family Counseling*, 1976, *4*(1), 66–69.

Morris, R. Attitudes toward delinquency by delinquents, non-delinquents, and their friends. *British Journal of Criminology*, 1965, *5*, 249–265.

Mosher, R., & Sprinthall, N. Psychological education: A means to promote personal development during adolescence. *The Counseling Psychologist*, 1971, *2*, 3–92.

Moss, J. W. *Post secondary vocational education for mentally retarded adults*. Reston, VA: Council for Exceptional Children, 1979.

Mowatt, M. H. Group psychotherapy for stepfathers and their wives. *Psychotherapy: Theory, Research, and Practice*, 1972, *9*, 328–331.

Myers, L. (Ed.). *The family and community impact of day care: Preliminary findings (PA Day Care Study)*. University Park, PA: Institute for the Study of Human Development, CHSD Report No. 17, December 1972.

Myllyluoma, J., & Soldo, B. Family caregivers to the elderly: Who are they? Paper presented at the 33rd Annual Meeting of the Gerontological Society, San Diego, CA, November 1980.

Nadler, R. Child abuse in gorilla mothers. *Caring*, 1979, *5*(3), 1–3.

National Academy of Sciences. *Toward a national policy for children and families*. Washington, DC: U.S. Government Printing Office, 1976.

National Center for Educational Statistics, U.S. Department of Education. *Digest of educational statistics, 1980*. Washington, DC: U.S. Government Printing Office, 1980.

National Center for Health Statistics. Births, marriages, divorces, and deaths for 1980. *Monthly Vital Statistics Reports*, 1981a, *29*(12), Washington, DC: U.S. Government Printing Office.

National Center for Health Statistics. Advance report of final divorce statistics, 1979. *Monthly Vital Statistics Reports*, 1981b, *30*(2), Washington, DC: U.S. Government Printing Office.

National Center on Child Abuse and Neglect. *Child abuse and neglect in residential institutions*. National Center on Child Abuse and Neglect, Department of Health and Human Services (Publ. #78-30160, OHDS). Washington, DC: U.S. Government Printing Office, 1978.

National Education Association, 1979 Teachers poll. *Today's Education*, 1979a, *68*, 10.

National Education Association. Trends. *Today's Education*, 1979b, *68*, 8.

National Institute of Drug Abuse. Nonresidential self-help organizations and the drug abuse problem: An exploratory conference. DHEW Publ. No. (ADM) 78-752. Washington, DC: U.S. Government Printing Office, 1978.

National School Public Relations Association. *Linking schools and the community*. Arlington, VA: National School Public Relations Association, 1977.

Natural Parent Newsletter, P.O. Box 5012, Postal Station B, Victoria, B.C., Canada, U8R 6N3, 1980.

Nayman, L., & Witkin, S. L. Parent/child foster placement: An alternative approach in child abuse and neglect. *Child Welfare*, 1978, *57*(4), 249–258.

Nelson, R. H., Singer, M. J., & Johnson, L. O. The application of a residential treatment evaluation model. *Child Care Quarterly*, 1978, *1*(2), 164–175.

Nelson, R. O., & Hays, S. C. Some current dimensions of behavioral assessment. *Behavioral Assessment*, 1979, *1*, 1–16.

Nettler, G. *Explaining crime*. New York: McGraw-Hill, 1974.

Nettleton, C., & Cline, D. Dating patterns, sexual relationships, and use of contraceptive of 700 unwed mothers during a two-year period following delivery. *Adolescence*, 1975, *10*, 45–47.

Networks for helping: Illustrations from research and practice. Proceedings of the Conference on Networks, Portland State University, Portland, OR, November 1978.

Neugarten, B. L., & Hagestad, G. O. Age and the life course. In R. H. Binstock & E. Shanas (Eds.), *Handbook of aging and the social sciences*. New York: Van Nostrand Reinhold, 1976.

Newbrough, J. R. Liaison services in the community context. *Journal of Community Psychology*, 1977, *5*, 24–27.

New York State Commission on Quality, Cost, and Financing of Elementary and Secondary Education. Final Report. Albany, NY: 1972.

Noblit, G. W. The adolescent experience and delinquency: School versus subcultural effects. *Youth and Society*, 1976, *8*, 27–44.

Norton, A. A portrait of the one-parent family. *National Elementary Principal*, 1979, *59*, 32–35.

Nuckolls, K. B., Cassel, J., & Kaplan, B. H. Psychosocial assets, life crises, and the prognosis of pregnancy. *American Journal of Epidemiology*, 1972, *95*, 431–441.

Nurco, D. N., & Makofsky, A. The self-help movement and narcotic addicts. *American Journal of Drug and Alcohol Abuse*, 1981, *8*(2), 139–151.

Nuttall, E. V. The support system and coping patterns of the female Puerto Rican single parent. *Journal of Non-white Concerns*, 1979, *7*, 128–137.

Nye, F. I. *Family relationships and delinquent behavior*. New York: Wiley, 1958.

Nye, F. I. Runaways: Some critical issues for professionals and society. *Cooperative Extension Bulletin*. Pullman, WA: Washington State University, 1980.

O'Brien, J., & Wagner, D. Help seeking by the frail elderly: Problems in network analysis. *The Gerontologist*, 1980, *20*(1), 78–89.

O'Brien, J., & Whitelaw, N. Analysis of community based alternatives to institutional care for the aged. U.S. DHEW, Final Report to Oregon State Program on Aging and AOA, 1973.

O'Brien, J., & Whitelaw, N. *Planning option for the elderly*. Portland, OR: Institute on Aging, Portland State University, 1978.

O'Donnell, J. A. *Narcotic addicts in Kentucky*. Washington, DC: U.S. Government Printing Office, Public Health Service Publ. No. 1881, 1969.

Office of Mental Retardation Coordination. Mental retardation resource book. DHEW Publ. No. OS 73-81. Washington, DC: Department of Health Education and Welfare, 1972.

O'Keefe, R. A. What Head Start means to families. In L. G. Katz (Ed.), *Current topics in early childhood education*, Vol. II. Norwood, NJ: Ablex, 1979.

Olsen, M. R. (Ed.). *Differential approaches in social work with the mentally disordered*. Birmingham, U. K.: British Association of Social Workers, 1976.

Opinion Research Corporation. *National statistical survey of runaway youth*. Princeton, NJ: ORC, 1976.

Orthner, D., Brown, T., & Ferguson, D. Single parent fatherhood: An emerging lifestyle. *The Family Coordinator*, 1976, *25*, 429–438.

Oshman, H. P., & Manosevitz, M. Father absence: Effects of stepfathers upon psychosocial development in males. *Developmental Psychology*, 1976, *12*, 479–480.

Pais, J., & White, P. Family redefinition: A review of the literature toward a model of divorce adjustment. *Journal of Divorce*, 1979, *2*, 271–282.

Pancoast, D. L. Finding and enlisting neighbors to support families. In J. Garbarino, S. H. Stocking, & Associates, *Protecting children from abuse and neglect*. San Francisco: Jossey-Bass, 1980.

Pargament, K. I. The interface among religion, religious support systems, and mental health. In D. Biegel & A. Naparstek (Eds.), *Community support systems and mental health: Building linkages*. New York: Springer, 1982.

Parks, A. Children and youth of divorce in Parent Without Partners, Inc. *Journal of Clinical Child Psychology*, 1977, *6*(2), 44–48.

Parks, C. M. The effects of bereavement of physical and mental health: A study of the medical records of widows. *British Medical Journal*, 1964, *2*, 274–285.

Patterson, G. R. "Interventions for boys with conduct problems: Multiple settings, treatments and criteria" Journal of Consulting and Clinical Psychology, 1974, Vol. 42, No. 4: 471–481.

Patterson, G. R., Reid, J. B., Jones, R. R. and Conger, R. E. *A Social Learning Approach to Family Intervention*/. Vol. 1. *Families with Aggressive Children*. Eugene, Ore.: Castilia Publishing Co., 1975.

Patterson, G. R., & Reid, J. B. Reciprocity and coercion: Two facets of social systems. In C. Neuringer & J. Michael (Eds.), *Behavior modification in clinical psychology*. New York: Appleton-Century-Crofts, 1970.

Patterson, S., & Brennan, E. Model helping roles for the older adults. Presented at the 33rd Annual Meeting of the Gerontological Society, San Diego, CA, November 1980.

Patterson, S., & Twente, E. *Utilization of human resources for mental health*. Lawrence, KA: University of Kansas School of Social Welfare, 1972.

Pattison, E. M. Clinical social systems interventions. *Psychiatry Digest*, 1977a, *38*, 25–33.

Pattison, E. M. A theoretical-empirical base for social system therapy. In E. F. Foulks, R. M. Wintrob, J. Westermeyer, & Favazzo (Eds.), *Current perspectives in cultural psychiatry*. New York: Spectrum, 1977b.

Pattison, E. M., Defrancisco, D., Wood, P., Frazier, H., & Crowder, J. A. psychosocial kinship model for family therapy. *American Journal of Psychiatry*, 1975, *132*, 1246–1251.

Pattison, E. M., Llasmas R., & Hurd, G. Social network mediation of anxiety. *Psychiatric Annals*, 1979, *9*, 56–67.

Pattison, E. M., & Pattison, M. L. Analysis of a schizophrenic psychosocial network. *Schizophrenia Bulletin*, 1981, *7*, 135–144.

Pearlin, L., & Johnson, J. Marital status, life-strains and depression. *American Sociological Review*, 1977, *43*, 704–715.

Pearlin, L. I., & Schooler, C. The structure of coping. *Journal of Health and Social Behavior*, 1978, *19*, 2–21.

Pecora, P. *Practice principles for foster family care*. Northwest Regional Child Welfare Training Center, Research Capsule #6. Seattle: University of Washington, School of Social Work, 1980.

Perkins, T. F., & Kahan, J. P. Empirical comparisons of natural fathers and stepfather systems. *Family Process*, 1979, *18*, 175–183.

Perlman, H. *Social casework: A problem solving process*. Chicago: University of Chicago Press, 1957.

Perry, C. L., Killen, J., Slinkard, L. A., & McAlister, A. L. Peer teaching and smoking prevention among junior high school students. *Adolescence*, 1980, *15*, 278–281.

Peters, D. L., & Kostelnik M. J. Current research in day care personnel preparation. In S. Kilmer (Ed.), *Advances in early education and day care*, Vol. 2. Greenwich, CT: JAI Press, 1981.

Peterson, P., Meriwether, C., & Buell, D. Final report: School Youth Advocacy Project 1975–76. Lansing, MI: Office of Evaluation Services, Lansing School District, 1976.

Peterson, R., & Becker, W. C. Family interaction and delinquency. In H. C. Quay (Ed.), *Juvenile delinquency*. Princeton, NJ: D. Van Nostrand, 1965.

Petty, B., Tamerra, P., & Campbell, R. Support groups for elderly persons in the community. *The Gerontologist*, 1976, *15*(6), 522–528.

Pfohl, S. The "discovery" of child abuse. *Social Problems*, 1977, *24*, 310–323.

Phillips, R. L. Role of lifestyle and dietary habits in risk of cancer among Seventh Day Adventists. *Cancer Research*, 1975, *35*, 3513–3522.

Pilisuk, M., Chandler, S., & D'Onofrio, C. Reweaving the social fabric: Antecedents of social support facilitation. Unpublished manuscript, Department of Applied Behavioral Sciences, University of California, Davis, 1979.

Pilisuk, M., & Froland, C. Kinship, social networks, social support, and health. *Social Science in Medicine*, 1978, *12B*, 273–280.

Pilisuk, M., & Minkler, M. Supportive networks: Life ties for the elderly. *Journal of Social Issues*, 1980, *36*(2), 95–116.

Pilisuk, M., & Parks, S. H. Structural dimensions of social support groups. *The Journal of Psychology*, 1980, *106*, 157–177.

Pincus, A. & Minahan, A. *Social work practice: Model and method.* Itasca, IL: Peacock, 1973.

Pines, A., & Maslach, C. Combating staff burn-out in day care center: A case study. *Child Care Quarterly,* 1980, *9,* 5–16.

Pink, W. T., & White, M. F. (Eds.). *Delinquency prevention: A conference perspective on issues and directions.* Portland, OR: Regional Research Institute, 1973.

P. L. 96-272, Adoption assistance and child welfare act of 1980. Washington, DC: U.S. Government Printing Office, 1980.

Platman, S. R. The chronically mentally impaired—Sharing the burden with the community. In D. Biegel & A. Naparstek (Eds.), *Community support systems and mental health: Building linkages.* New York: Springer, 1982.

Polak, P. R. A comprehensive system of alternatives to psychiatric hospitalization. In L. I. Stein & M. A. Test (Eds.), *Alternatives to mental hospital treatment.* New York: Plenum, 1978.

Polansky, N. Analysis of research on child neglect: The social work viewpoint. In Herner & Company (Eds.), *Four perspectives on the status of child abuse and neglect research.* Washington, DC: National Center on Child Abuse and Neglect, 1976.

Polansky, N. Chalmers, M. A., Buttenweiser, E. & Williams, D. P. *Damaged parents.* Chicago: University of Chicago Press, 1981.

Politser, P. E. Network analysis and the logic of social support. In R. H. Price & P. E. Polister (Eds.), *Evaluation and action in the social environment.* New York: Academic Press, 1980.

Polister, P. E., & Pattison, E. M. Community groups: An empirical taxonomy for evaluation and intervention. In R. H. Price & P. E. Polister (Eds.), *Evaluation and action in the social environment.* New York: Academic, 1980.

Polk, K., Frease D., & Richmond F. Social class, school experience and delinquency. *Criminology:* 1974, *12,* 84–96.

Polk, K., & Kobrin, S. *Delinquency prevention through youth development.* Washington, DC: Youth Development and Delinquency Prevention Administration, U.S. Department of Health, Education, and Welfare, 1972.

Poppenhagen, B., Mingus, J., & Rogers, J. Comparing perceptions of elementary junior high and senior high school principals on selected work related variables. *Journal of Educational Administration,* 1979, *18,* 69–87.

Porritt, D. Social support in crisis: Quantity or quality? *Social Science and Medicine,* 1979, 13A, 715–721.

Porter, F. *The pilot parent program.* Omaha, NE: Greater Omaha Association for Retarded Citizens, 1978.

Potter, B. R. Single parent families. In N. Stinnett, B. Chesser, & J. Defrain (Eds.), *Building family strengths: Blueprints for action.* Lincoln, NE: University of Nebraska Press, 1979.

Powell, D. R. Family–environment relations and early childrearing: The role of social networks and neighborhoods. *Journal of Research and Development in Education,* 1979, *13,* 1–11.

Powell, D. R. Individual differences in participation in a parent–child support program. Paper presented at a Conference on Changing Families, ETS, Princeton, NJ, November 1980.

Powell, D. R. Toward a socio-ecological perspective of relations between parents and child care programs. In S. Kilmer (Ed.), *Advances in early education and day care,* Vol. 2. Greenwich, CT: JAI Press, 1981.

Powell, D. R., & Eisenstadt, J. W. Parents' searches for child care and the design of information services. *Children and Youth Services Review,* in press.

Powers, E., & Witmer, H. *An experiment in the prevention of delinquency: The Cambridge–Somerville youth study.* New York: Columbia University, 1951.

Preble, E., & Casey J. Taking care of business: The heroin user's life on the streets. *The International Journal of the Addictions,* 1969, *4*(1), 1–24.

Prescott, E. Group and family day care: A comparative assessment. Pasadena, CA: Pacific Oaks College, 1972 (ERIC EE060945).

President's Commission on Law Enforcement and Administration of Justice. *Task force on juvenile delinquency.* Washington, DC: U.S. Government Printing Office, 1967.

President's Commission on Mental Health. *Report to the president* (Vol. 1). Washington, DC: U.S. Government Printing Office, 1978.

Price, R. H., & Politser, P. E. *Evaluation and action in the social environment.* New York: Academic, 1980.

Price-Bonham, S., & Balswick, J. O. The non-institutions: Divorce, desertion, and remarriage. *Journal of Marriage and the Family,* 1980, *42*(4), 959–972.

Proceedings of the conference on the care of dependent children. Washington, DC. U.S. Government Printing Office, 1909.

Rabkin, J. K., & Struening, E. L. Life events, stress, and illness. *Science,* 1976, *194,* 1013–1020.

Radelet, M. L. Health beliefs, social networks, and tranquilizer use. *Journal of Health and Social Behavior,* 1981, *22,* 165–173.

Ragozin, A. S. Attachment behavior of day care children: Naturalistic and laboratory observations. *Child Development,* 1980, *51,* 409–415.

Ransom, J. W., Schlesinger, S., & Derdeyn, A. P. Stepfamily information. *American Journal of Orthopsychiatry,* 1979, *49*(1), 36–43.

Raphael, B. Preventive intervention with the recently bereaved. *Archives of General Psychiatry,* 1977, *34,* 1450–1452.

Raschke, H. J. The role of social participation in postseparation and postdivorce adjustment. *Journal of Divorce,* 1977, *2,* 129–140.

Raschke, H. J., & Rashke, V. J. Family conflict and children's self-concepts: A comparison of intact and single parent families. *Journal of Marriage and the Family,* 1979, *41,* 367–375.

Ray, O. S. *Drugs, society, and human behavior.* St. Louis: C. V. Mosby, 1972.

Reed, S. What you can do to prevent teacher burnout. *National Elementary School Principal,* 1980, *59,* 67–70.

Reid, W. J., & Epstein, L. *Task centered casework.* New York: Columbia University Press, 1972.

Reid, W. J., & Epstein, L. (Eds.). *Task centered practice.* New York: Columbia University Press, 1977.

Reisman, D. A. *Richard Titmuss: Welfare and society.* London: Heineman, 1977.

Reiss, A. J. Delinquency as failure of personal and social controls. *American Sociological Review,* 1951, *16,* 196–207.

Reiss, A. J., & Rhodes, A. L. An empirical test of differential association theory. *Journal of Research in Crime and Delinquency,* 1964, *1,* 5–18.

Reiss, M. L., Piotrowski, W., & Bailey J. Behavioral community psychology: Encouraging low-income parents to seek dental care for their children. *Journal of Applied Behavior Analysis,* 1976, *9,* 387–397.

Rhodes, C., & Browning, P. Normalization at what price. *Mental Retardation,* 1977, *15,* 24.

Ricci, I. Divorce, remarriage and the schools. *Phi Delta Kappan,* 1979, *60,* 509–511.

Rich, D., Van Dien, J., & Mattox, B. Families as educators of their own children. In R. Brandt (Ed.), *Partners: Parents and schools.* Alexandria, VA: Association for Supervision and Curriculum Development, 1979.

Richardson, R. A. Assessing the interface between professional and public knowledge of family issues. Unpublished manuscript, The Pennsylvania State University, 1981.

Richmond, M. *Social diagnosis.* New York: Russell Sage, 1917.

Richmond, M. *What is social casework?* New York: Russell Sage, 1922.

Ricken, R. Teacher burnout—A failure of the supervisory process. *NASSP Bulletin*, 1980, *64*, 21–24.

Ridley, C. A., & Avery, A. W. Social network influence on the dyadic relationship. In R. L. Burgess & T. L. Huston (Eds.), *Social exchange in developing relationships.* New York: Academic, 1979.

Riessman, F. How does self help work? *Social Policy*, 1976a, *7*, 41–45.

Riessman, F. Self-care and self-help: Natural allies. In A. Fleugelman (Ed.), *The new games book.* New York: Doubleday, 1976b.

Rioux, W. *You can improve your child's school.* New York: Simon and Schuster, 1980.

Robertson, D. The effects of inter-grade tutoring experience on tutor attitudes and reading achievement. *Dissertation Abstracts International*, 1971, *32*, GA 3010.

Robins, N. *The Vietnam drug user returns.* Washington, DC: U.S. Government Printing. Office, 1973.

Robinson, B., & Regnier, V. Informal services provided by business and community organizations: An investigation of existing nonservice supports. Presented at the 33rd Annual Meeting of the Gerontological Society, San Diego, CA, 1980.

Robinson, B., & Thurnher, M. Taking care of aged parents: A family cycle transition. *The Gerontologist*, 1979, *19*(6), 586–593.

Robinson, N. M., & Robinson, H. B. *The mentally retarded child.* New York: McGraw-Hill, 1976.

Robinson, W. S. Ecological correlations and the behavior of individuals. *American Sociological Review*, 1950, *15*, 351–357.

Rock, M. Gorilla mothers need some help from their friends. *Smithsonian*, 1978, *9*(4), 58–63.

Rodes, T., & Moore, J. National Childcare Consumer Study, 1975. Washington, DC: Office of Child Development, 1975.

Rogers-Warren, A., & Warren, S. F. (Eds.). *Ecological perspectives in behavior analysis.* Baltimore: University Park Press, 1977.

Rogus, J., & Martin, M. The principal and staff development: Countering the school culture. *NASSP Bulletin*, 1979, *63*, 81–87.

Rohner, R. *They love me, they love me not.* New Haven, CT: HRAF Press, 1975.

Rohner, R., & Nielson, C. *Parental acceptance and rejection: Review of research and theory.* New Haven, CT: Human Relations Area Files Press, 1978.

Romero, D., & Thomas, S. Interactions between family and day care systems. East Lansing, MI: Michigan State University Computer Institute for Social Science Research, December, 1975 (ERIC ED182006).

Rooney, R. A task centered reunification model for foster care. In A. Maluccio & P. Sinanoglu (Eds.), *The challenge of partnership.* New York: Child Welfare League of America, 1981.

Rose, A. M. The subculture of the aging: A framework on social gerontology. In A. M. Rose & W. A. Peterson (Eds.), *Older people: Their social world.* Philadelphia: F. A. Davis, 1975.

Rosen, D. Social relationships and successful aging among the widowed aged. Unpublished doctoral dissertation, Brandeis University, 1973.

Rosenberg, M. *Society and the adolescent self-image.* Princeton, NJ: Princeton University Press, 1965.

Rosenblatt, A., & Mayer, J. Help-seeking for family problems: A survey of utilization and satisfaction. *American Journal of Psychiatry*, 1972, *128*, 1136–1140.

Rosenthal, R., & Jacobson, L. *Pygmalion in the classroom.* New York: Holt, Rinehart & Winston, 1968.

Rosow, I. *Social integration of the aged.* New York: Free Press, 1967.

Ross, B., & McKay, H. B. Adolescent therapists. *Canada's Mental Health*, 1976, *24*, 15–17.

Ross, H. The neighborhood family. *Aging*, 1978, 283–284 (May–June,) 27–32.

Ross, H., & Ross, M. S. The neighborhood family—Five years later, a program in preventive community health care of the elderly. Unpublished paper, 1979.

Rotenberg, M. Alienating-individualism and reciprocal-individualism: A cross-cultural conceptualization. *Journal of Humanistic Psychology*, 1977, *17*, 3–17.

Rothman, D. *The discovery of the asylum*. Boston: Little, Brown, 1971.

Rothman, D. *Conscience and convenience*. Boston: Little, Brown, 1980.

Rueveni, U. *Networking families in crisis*. New York: Human Sciences Press, 1979.

Rueveni, U. Networking families in crisis. *Journal of Personality Assessment*, 1980, *44*(6), 653–654.

Rufener, L., Rachal, J., & Cruze, A. Costs of drug abuse to society. In I. Leveson (Eds.), *Quantitative explorations in drug abuse policy*. New York: SP Medical and Scientific Books, 1980.

Ruffini, J., & Todd, H. F., Jr. A network model for leadership development among the elderly. *The Gerontologist*, 1979, *19*(2), 158–162.

Ruiz, P., Langrod, J., & Lowinson, J. Resistance to the opening of drug treatment centers: A problem in community psychiatry. *International Journal of the Addictions*, 1975, *10*(1), 149–155.

Ruopp, R. *Children at the center: Final report of the national day care study*. Cambridge, MA: Abt Associates, 1979.

Rusch, F. R., & Mithaug, D. E. *Vocational training for mentally retarded adults*. Champaign, IL: Research Press, 1980.

Russell, E. W. The power of behavior control: A critique of behavior modification methods. *Journal of Clinical Psychology*, 1974, *30*, 111–136.

Rutter, M. Maternal deprivation, 1972–1979: New findings, new concepts, new approaches. *Child Development*, 1979, *50*, 283–304.

Salts, C. J. Divorce process: Integration of theory. *Journal of Divorce*, 1979, *2*, 233–240.

Sampson, E. E. Psychology and the American ideal. *Journal of Personality and Social Psychology*, 1977, *35*, 767–782.

Samuels, M., & Samuels, D. *The complete handbook of peer counseling*. Miami, FL: Fiesta, 1975.

Sandler, I. N. Social support resources, stress, and maladjustment of poor children. *American Journal of Community Psychology*, 1980, *8*, 41–52.

Sandler, I. N., & Barrera, M. Social support as a stress buffer: A multi-method investigation. Paper presented at the meetings of the American Psychological Association, Montreal, Que., 1980.

Sandler, I. N., & Block, M. Life-stress and maladaptive children. *American Journal of Community Psychology*, 1979, *7*, 425–440.

Sarason, S. *The culture of the school and the problem of change*. Boston: Allyn & Bacon, 1971.

Sarason, S. B. *The psychological sense of community: Prospects for a community psychology*. San Francisco: Jossey-Bass, 1974.

Sarason, S. B., & Lorentz, E. *The challenge of the resource exchange network*. San Francisco: Jossey-Bass, 1979.

Sarri, R. Juvenile justice. In A. D. Kadushin (Ed.), *Child welfare strategy in the coming years*. Washington, DC: Department of Health and Human Services, 1980.

Saul, S., & Saul, S. Group psychotherapy in a proprietary nursing home. *The Gerontologist*, 1974, *14*(5), 446–450.

Scarpitti, F. R., & Stephenson, R. The use of the small group in the rehabilitation of delinquents. *Federal Probation*, 1966, *30*(3), 45–50.

Schafft, G. Nursing homes and the black elderly. Presented at the Annual Meeting of the Gerontological Society, Washington, DC, November 1979.

Scharse, R. Cessation patterns among neophyte heroin users. *International Journal of the Addictions*, 1966, *1*(2), 23–32.

Scheinfeld, D. R., Bowles, D., Tuck, S., Jr., & Gold, R. Parents' values, family networks, and family development: Working with disadvantaged families. *American Journal of Orthopsychiatry*, 1970, *40*, 413–425.

Schenk, Q. F., & Schenk, E. L. *Pulling up roots*. Englewood Cliffs, NJ: Prentice-Hall, 1978.

Schinke, S. P. Evaluating social work practice: A conceptual model and example. *Social Casework*, 1979, *60*, 195–200.

Schinke, S. P. (Ed.). *Behavioral methods in social welfare*. Hawthorne, NY: Aldine, 1981a.

Schinke, S. P. Interpersonal-skills training with adolescents. In M. Hersen, R. M. Eisler, & P. M. Miller (Eds.), *Progress in behavior modification*, Vol. 11. New York: Academic, 1981b.

Schinke, S. P., Blythe, B. J., Schilling, R. F., & Barth, R. P. Neglect of mentally retarded persons. *Education and Training of the Mentally Retarded*, 1981, *16*, 299–303.

Schinke, S. P., & Wong, S. E. Teaching child care workers: A behavioral approach. *Child Care Quarterly*, 1978, *7*, 45–61.

Schipp, W., & Vivian, P. *Foster care for gay youth*. Seattle, WA: The Shelter, 1982.

Schizophrenia Bulletin. 1978, *4*.

Schizophrenia Bulletin. 1981, *7*(1).

Schlesinger, B. Single-parent fathers: A research review. *Children Today*, 1978, *7*(3), 12–39.

Schmidt, M. Personal networks: Assessment, care, and repair. Presented at the 26th Annual Meeting of the Western Gerontological Society, Anaheim, CA, March 1980.

Schneider, J. W., & Conrad, P. In the closet with illness: Epilepsy, stigma potential and information control. *Social Problems*, 1980, *28*, 32–44.

Schofield, W. *Psychotherapy, the purchase of friendship*. Englewood Cliffs, NJ: Prentice-Hall, 1964.

Schreiber, S. T., & Glidewell, J. C. Social norms and helping in a community of limited liability. *American Journal of Community Psychology*, 1978, *6*, 441–453.

Schur, E. M. *Narcotic addiction in Britain and America*. Bloomington, IN: Indiana University Press, 1962.

Sebald, H. The pursuit of "instantness" in technocratic society and youth's psychedelic drug use. *Adolescence*, 1972, *7*, 343–350.

Seelbach, W. Gender differences in expectations for filial responsibility. *The Gerontologist*, 1977, *17*(5), 421–424.

Segal, S. P., & Aviram, C. *The mentally ill in community-based sheltered care: A study of community care and social integration*. New York: Wiley, 1978.

Select Committee on Aging. *Innovative developments in aging: Area agencies in aging*. U.S. House of Representatives, December 1979.

Seligmann, J. Burnt-out principals. *Newsweek*, March 1978, *91*, 76–77.

Severy, J. Exposure to deviance committed by valued peer group and family members. *Journal of Research in Crime and Delinquency*, 1973, *10*, 35–46.

Shanas, E. The family as a social support system in old age. *The Gerontologist*, 1979, *19*(2), 169–174.

Shaw, C. R., & McKay, H. *Juvenile delinquency in urban areas*. Chicago: University of Chicago Press, 1942.

Sheda, M., & Winger, J. Peer dynamics 1977–78 evaluation report. Lincoln, NE: Nebraska Department of Health, 1978.

Sherman, M. J., & Peterson, D. Multiple drug abuse patterns. In A. Schector, H. Alksne, & E. Kaufman (Eds.), *Drug abuse: Modern trends, issues and perspectives*. New York: Marcel Dekker, 1978.

Shinn, M. Father absence and children's cognitive development. *Psychological Bulletin*, 1978, *85*, 295–324.

Shipsey, M. Disability and physical handicap: Visual and auditory disorders. In (Ed.), *Encyclopedia of social work*, Vol. 1. Washington, DC: National Association of Social Workers Editor, 1977.

Short, J. R., Jr. Differential association and delinquency. *Social Problems*, 1957, *4*, 233–239.

Short, J. F., Jr. Differential association as a hypothesis: Problems of empirical testing. *Social Problems*, 1960, *8*, 14–25.

Shur, E. M. *Narcotic addiction in Britain and America*. Bloomington, IN: Indiana University Press, 1962.

Shyne, A. W., & Schroeder, A. G. *National study of social services to children and their families*. Washington, DC: National Center for Child Advocacy, 1978.

Silberman, C. *Crisis in the classroom— The remaking of American education*. New York: Random House, 1970.

Silberman, C. E. *Criminal violence, criminal justice*. New York: Random House, 1978.

Silverman, A. As parents grow older: A community-based intervention strategy. Presented at the 32nd Annual Meeting of the Gerontological Society, Washington, DC, November 1979.

Silverman, A., Kahn, B., & Anderson, G. A model for working with multigenerational families. *Social Casework*, 1977, *58*, 131–135.

Silverman, P. R. Mutual help. In R. Hirschowitz & B. Levy (Eds.), *The changing mental health scene*. New York: Spectrum, 1976.

Silverman, P. R. *Mutual help groups: Organization and development*. Beverly Hills, CA: Sage, 1980.

Silverman, P. R., & Associates. *Helping each other in widowhood*. New York: Health Sciences Press, 1974.

Simmons, G. S., Gumpert, J., & Rothman, B. Natural parents as partners in child placement. *Social Casework*, 1973, *54*(4), 223–232.

Simons, J. K. Background data for Aspen institute seminar, frontiers of corporate competition: Linkages between work and family. Washington, DC: Children's Defense Fund, 1981.

Simpson, D., Crandall, R., Savage, L., & Pavia-Krueger, E. Leisure of opiate addicts at posttreatment follow-up. *Journal of Counseling Psychology*, 1981, *28*(1), 36–39.

Sinanoglu, P. A. & Maluccio, A. N. (Eds.) *Parents of Children in Placement: Perspectives and Programs*, New York: Child Welfare League of America, 1981.

Siporin, M. Social treatment: A new-old helping method. *Social Work*, 1970, *15*(3), 13–26.

Skinner, B. F. *Science and human behavior*. New York: Macmillan, 1953.

Skinner, B. F. *Cumulative record*. New York: Appleton-Century-Crofts, 1959.

Sklar, L. S., & Anisman, H. Stress and cancer. *Psychological Bulletin*, 1981, *89*, 369–406.

Slatin, G. T. Ecological analysis of delinquency aggregation effects. *American Sociological Review*, 1970, *34*(6), 894–907.

Small, R., & Whittaker, J. K. Residential group care and home-based care: Toward a continuity of family service. In S. Maybanks & M. Bryce (Eds.), *Home-based services for children and families*. Springfield, IL: Charles C. Thomas, 1979.

Smart, R. G., & Fejer, D. Drug use among adolescents and their parents: Closing the generation gap in mood modification. *Journal of Abnormal Psychology*, 1972, *70*, 153–160.

Smart, R. G., Fejer, D., & White, W. Trends in drug use among metropolitan Toronto high school students: 1968–1972. *Addictions*, *20*, 62–72.

Smith, C., Farrant, M., & Marchant, M. *The Wincroft Youth Project: A social-work programme in a slum area*. London: Tavistock, 1972.

Smith, K., & Bengston, V. Positive consequences of institutionalization: Solidarity between elderly parents and their middle-aged children. *The Gerontologist*, 1979, *19*(5), 438–447.

Smith, L. Kinkeeping in the middle generation: The effects of role strain. Presented at the 32nd Annual Meeting of the Gerontological Society, Washington, DC, November 1979.

Smith, M. School and home: Focus on academic achievement. In A. Passow (Ed.), *Developing programs for the educationally disadvantaged*. New York: Teachers College Press, 1968.

Smith, M. J. The social consequences of single parenthood: A longitudinal perspective. *Family Relations*, 1980, *29*, 75–81.

Smith, S. M., Hanson, R., & Noble, S. Social aspects of the battered baby syndrome. *British Journal of Psychiatry*, 1974, *125*, 568–582.

Snyder, M., Davis, B., & Cohn, M. Primary prevention and the cooperative extension service: A pilot project. *Psychology Newsletter,* 1981, *14*(3), 4.

Sokolovsky, J., & Cohen, C. Being old in the inner-city: Support systems of the SRO aged. In C. Fry (Ed.), *Dimensions of anthropology and aging.* Brooklyn: Bergin, 1981.

Sokolovsky, J., Cohen, C., Berger, D., & Geiger, J. Personal networks of ex-patients in a Manhattan SRO hotel. *Human Organization,* 1978, *37,* 5–15.

Sorentino, A. The Chicago Area Project after 25 years. *Federal Probation,* 1959, *23*(2), 40–45.

Sorosiak, F. M., Thomas, E., & Balet, F. Adolescent drug use: An analysis. *Psychological Reports,* 1976, *38,* 211–221.

Sosa, R., Kennell, J., Klaus, M., Robertson, S., & Urrutia, J. The effect of a supportive companion on perinatal problems, length of labor, and mother–infant interactions. *New England Journal of Medicine,* 1980, *303,* 597–600.

Spanier, G. B. The changing profile of the American family. *Journal of Family Practice,* 1981, *13,* 61–69.

Spanier, G. B., & Castro, R. F. Adjustment to separation and divorce. An analysis of 50 case studies. *Journal of Divorce,* 1979, *2,* 241–253.

Spanier, G. B., & Furstenberg, F. F. Remarriage after divorce: A longitudinal analysis of well-being. Unpublished manuscript, 1981.

Spanier, G. B., & Glick, P. C. Paths to remarriage. *Journal of Divorce,* 1980, *3*(3), 283–298.

Spanier, G. B., & Hanson, S. The role of extended kin in the adjustment to marital separation. Paper presented at the annual meeting of the Southern Sociological Society, New Orleans, April 1978.

Speck, R., & Attneave, C. *Family networks.* New York: Vintage, 1973.

Speck, R. V., & Attneave, C. Social network intervention. In J. Haley (Ed.), *Changing families.* New York: Grune & Stratton, 1971.

Spergel, I. *Street gang work: Theory and practice.* Reading, MA: Addison–Wesley, 1966.

Spevak, M., & Pihl, R. Nonmedical drug use by high school students: A three year survey study. *International Journal of the Addictions,* 1976, *11*(5), 755–792.

Spicer, J. W., & Hampe, G. S. Kinship interaction after divorce. *Journal of Marriage and the Family,* 1975, *37,* 113–119.

Spirito, A., Finch, A. J., Jr., Smith, T. L., & Cooley, W. H. Stress inoculation for anger and anxiety control: A case study with an emotionally disturbed boy. *Journal of Clinical Child Psychology,* 1981, *5,* 67–70.

Springle, H., & Van de Reit, V. The learning to learn program: A sequential approach to early childhood education and a study of its effectiveness. Palo Alto, CA: American Institute for Research in Behavioral Sciences, 1969.

Srole, L., Langner, T. S., Michael, S. T., Kirkpatrick, P., Opler, M. K., & Tennie, T. A. C. *Mental health in the metropolis.* New York: Harper, 1977.

Stack, C. B. *All our kin: Strategies for survival in a black community.* New York: Harper, 1974.

Stagner, R. Stress, strain, coping, and defense. *Research on Aging,* 1981, *3,* 3–32.

Stanton, M. D. Some outcome results and aspects of structural family therapy with drug addicts. In D. Smith, S. Anderson, M. Buston, T. Chang, N. Gottlieb, & W. Harvey (Eds.), *A multicultural view of drug abuse: The selected proceedings of the national drug abuse conference, 1977.* Cambridge MA: Schenkman, 1978.

Stanton, M. D. The client as family member: Aspects of continuing treatment. In B. S. Brown (Ed.), *Addicts and aftercare.* Beverly Hills, CA: Sage, 1979.

Stanton, M., & Todd, T. Structural family therapy with heroin addicts. In E. Kaufman & P. Kaufman (Eds.), *The family therapy of drug and alcohol abusers.* New York: Gardner, 1978.

Stanton, M. D., Todd, T. C., Heard, D. B., Kirschner, S., Kleiman, J. I., Mowatt, D. T., Riley, P., Scott, S. M., & Van Deusen, J. M. Heroin addiction as a family phenomenon: A new conceptual model. *American Journal of Drug and Alcohol Abuse,* 1978, *5*(2), 1–26.

Stearns, M. *Parent involvement in compensatory education programs.* Menlo Park, CA: Stanford Research Institute, 1973.

Stein, L. E., & Test, M. A. An alternative to mental hospital treatment. In L. I. Stein & M. A. Test (Eds.), *Alternatives to mental hospital treatment.* New York: Plenum Press, 1978.

Stein, T. J., Gambrill, E. D., & Wiltse, K. T. *Children in foster homes—Achieving continuity of care.* New York: Praeger, 1978.

Steinberg, L. The changing role of parent groups in educational decision making. In R. Brandt (Ed.), *Partners: Parents and schools.* Alexandria, VA: Association for Supervision and Curriculum Development, 1979.

Steinberg, L., & Green, C. How parents may mediate the effect of day care. Paper presented at the meeting of the Society for Research in Child Development, San Francisco, March 1979.

Steinberg, L. D., Greenberger, E., Jacobi, M., & Garduque, G. Early work experience: A partial antidote for adolescent egocentrism. *Journal of Youth and Adolescence,* in press.

Steiner, G. *The futility of family policy.* Washington, DC: The Brookings Institution, 1981.

Steinitz, L. The church as family surrogate for the elderly. Presented at the 33rd Annual Meeting of the Gerontological Society, San Diego, CA, November 1980.

Stephens, D. In-home family support services: An ecological systems approach. In S. Maybanks & M. Bryce (Eds.), *Home based services for children and families.* Springfield, IL: Charles C. Thomas, 1979.

Stephens, J. Romance in the SRO: Relationships of elderly men and women in slum hotels. *The Gerontologist,* 1974, *14,* 279–282.

Stephens, R., Blau, Z. S., Oser, G. T., & Millar, M. D. Aging, social support systems and social policy. *Journal of Gerontological Social Work,* 1978, *1*(1), 33–45.

Stephenson, R. M., & Scarpitti, F. *Group interaction as therapy: The use of small groups in corrections.* Westport, CT: Greenwood Press, 1974.

Steritz, S., & Blank, M. *Readings in psychotherapy with older people.* Bethesda, MD: National Institute of Mental Health, 1978.

Stern, P. N. Stepfather families: Integration around child discipline. *Issues in Mental Health Nursing,* 1978, *1,* 50–56.

Stierlin, H. *Separating parents and adolescents: A perspective on running away, schizophrenia, and waywardness.* New York: Quadrangle, 1974.

Stokes, J., & Greenstone, J. Helping black grandparents and older parents cope with child rearing: A group method. *Child Welfare,* 1981, *50*(10), 691–701.

Stokes, T. F., & Baer, D. M. An implicit technology of generalization. *Journal of Applied Behavior Analysis,* 1977, *10,* 349–368.

Strand, R. Who cares for the children? A study of child care in Olmstead County, Minnesota, 1970. Minneapolis, MN: Synergistic Systems, 1970.

Straus, M. A. Stress and physical child abuse. *Child Abuse and Neglect,* 1980, *4,* 75–88.

Straus, M. A., Gelles, R. J., & Steinmetz, S. K. *Behind closed doors: Violence in the American family.* Garden City, NY: Doubleday, 1980.

Streiner, D. L., Norman, G. R., McFarlane, A. H., & Roy, R. G. Quality of life events and their relationship to strain. *Schizophrenia Bulletin,* 1981, 7, 34–42.

Streit, F., Halsted, D., & Pascale, P. Differences among youthful users/nonusers of drugs based on their perceptions of parental behavior. *International Journal of the Addictions,* 1974, 9, 749–755.

Streit, F., & Oliver, H. The child's perception of his family and its relationship to drug use. *Drug Forum,* 1972, *3,* 283–289.

Strong, C. The relationship of life event interpretations to helping interactions: A case study. *American Journal of Community Psychology,* 1978, 6, 455–464.

Sullivan, H. S. *The interpersonal theory of psychiatry.* New York: W. W. Norton, 1953.

Sulzbacher, S. I. Psychotropic medicine with children an evaluation of procedural basis in results of reported studies. *Pediatrics,* 1973, *51,* 513–517.

Sundberg, N. D., Snowden, L. R., & Reynolds, W. M. Toward assessment of personal competence and incompetence in life situations. *Annual Review of Psychology*, 1978, *29*, 179–211.

Suran, B. G., & Rizzo, J. V. *Special children: An integrative approach*. Glenview, IL: Scott Foresman, 1979.

Sussman, M. The development and effects of a model for training peer group counselors in a multi-ethnic junior high school. Unpublished doctoral dissertation, University of Miami, 1973.

Sussman, M. The family life of old people. In R. Binstock & E. Shanas (Eds.), *Handbook of aging and the social sciences*. New York: Van Nostrand Reinhold, 1976.

Sussman, M. B., & Burchinal, L. Kin family network: Unheralded structure in current conceptualizations of family functioning. *Marriage and Family Living*, 1962, *24*, 231–240.

Sutherland, E. *Principles of criminology* (4th ed.). Philadelphia: Lippincott, 1947.

Sutherland, E. *The Sutherland papers*, edited by A. K. Cohen, A. R. Lindesmith, & Karl Schuessler. Bloomington, IN: Indiana University Press, 1956.

Synge, J. *The Aran Islands*. Oxford: Oxford University Press, 1979 (originally published, 1907).

Tait, C., & Hodges, E. *Delinquents, their families and the community*. Springfield, IL: Charles C. Thomas, 1962.

Tannebaum, D. People with problems: Seeking help in an urban community. Toronto: University of Toronto, Center for Women and Community Studies, 1975.

Taylor, D. A., & Alpert, S. W. *Continuity and support following residential treatment*. New York: Child Welfare League of America, 1973.

Tec, N. The peer group and marijuana use. *Crime and Delinquency*, 1972a, *18*, 298–309.

Tec, N. Socio-cultural context of marijuana. *International Journal of the Addictions*, 1972b, *7*(4), 655–669.

Tec, N. Parent–child drug abuse: Generational continuity or adolescent deviancy. *Adolescence*, 1974, *9*(35), 351–364.

Tharp, R. C., & Wetzel, R. J. *Behavior modification in the natural environment*. New York: Academic Press, 1969.

Thomas, D. School site management in Salt Lake City schools. Presentation to Washington Safe Schools Project. Salt Lake City, UT: Salt Lake City School District, 1979.

Thompson, D. In California: Unswinging singles. *Time Magazine*, June 15, 1981, p. 8.

Thoresen, K., Thoresen, C., Klein, S., Wilbur, C., Becker-Haven, J., & Haven, W. Learning house: Helping troubled children and their parents change themselves. In J. Stump-hauzer (Ed.), *Progress in behavior therapy*, Vol. 2. Springfield, IL: Charles C. Thomas, 1977.

Thornburg, H. Peers: Three distinct groups. *Adolescence*, 1971, *6*, 59–76.

Tietjen, A. M. Integrating formal and informal support systems: The Swedish experience. In J. Garbarino, H. Stocking, and Associates, *Protecting children from abuse and neglect*. San Francisco: Jossey-Bass, 1980.

Titmuss, R. M. *Commitment to welfare*. London: Allen & Unwin, 1968.

Titmuss, R. M. *The gift relationship*. London: Allen & Unwin, 1971.

Titmuss, R. M. *Social policy*. London: Allen & Unwin, 1974.

Tobin, S., & Neugarten, B. Life satisfaction and social interaction in the aging. *Journal of Gerontology*, 1961, *16*(4), 344–346.

Toby, J. Social disorganization and stake in conformity: Complementary factors in the predatory behavior of hoodlums. *Journal of Criminal Law, Criminology and Police Science*, 1957, *48*, 12–17.

Todd, D. M. Contrasting adaptations to the social environment of a high school: Implications of a case study of helping behavior in two adolescent subcultures. In J. G. Kelly (Ed.), *Adolescent boys in high school: A psychological study of coping and adaptation*. Hillsdale, NJ: Lawrence Erlbaum, 1979.

Tolone, W. L., & Dermott, D. Some correlates of drug use among high school youth in a midwestern rural community. *International Journal of the Addictions*, 1975, *10*(5), 761–777.

Tolsdorf, C. C. Social networks, support, and coping: An exploratory study. *Family Process*, 1976, *15*, 407–417.

Toseland, R., Decker, J., & Bliesner, J. A community outreach program for socially isolated older people. *Journal of Gerontological Social Work*, 1979, *1*(3), 211–225.

Touliatos, J., & Lindholm, B. W. Teachers' perceptions of behavior problems in children from intact, single-parent, and step-parent families. *Psychology in the Schools*, 1980, *17*(2), 264–269.

Trimble, D. A guide to the network therapies. *Connections*, 1980, *III*(2), 9–21.

Trovato, J., & Bucher, B. Peer tutoring with or without home-based reinforcement, for reading remediation. *Journal of Applied Behavior Analysis*, 1980, *13*(1), 129–141.

Trower, P., Bryant, B., & Argyle, M. *Social skills and mental health*. London: Methuen, 1978.

Turkat, D. Social networks: Theory and practice. *Journal of Community Psychology*, 1980, *8*, 99–109.

Turnbull, A. P., Strickland, B., & Goldstein, S. Training professionals and parents in developing and implementing the IEP. *Education and Training of the Mentally Retarded*, 1978, *13*, 414–423.

Turner, J. C., & TenHoor, W. J. The NIMH Community Support Program: Pilot approach to a needed social reform. *Schizophrenia Bulletin*, 1978, *4*, 319–348.

Turner, J. T., Kimbrough, W. W., & Traynhan, R. N. A survey of community perceptions of critical life situations and community helping sources as a tool for mental health development. *Journal of Community Psychology*, 1977, *5*, 225–230.

Unger, D. G., & Powell, D. R. Supporting families under stress: The role of social networks. *Family Relations*, 1980, *29*(4), 566–575.

United States Bureau of the Census. Household and family relationships. *Current Population Reports*, Series P-20, No. 352. Washington, DC: U. S. Government Printing Office, 1980.

United States Department of Health, Education, and Welfare. *Child sexual abuse—Incest, assault and sexual exploitation*. Washington, DC: U. S. Government Printing Office, 1979a.

United States Department of Health, Education, and Welfare. Public Health Service. *Healthy people: The Surgeon General's report on health promotion and disease prevention*. Washington, DC: U. S. Government Printing Office, 1979b.

Vaillant, G. E. A 20 year follow-up of New York narcotic addicts. *Archives of General Psychiatry*, 1973, *29*, 237–241.

Van Houten, T., & Golembiewski, G. *Adolescent life stress as a predictor of alcohol and/or runaway behavior*. Washington, DC: National Youth Work Alliance, 1978.

Vaughn, C. E., & Leff, J. P. Patterns of emotional response in relatives of schizophrenic patients. *Schizophrenia Bulletin*, 1981, *7*, 43–44.

Venters, M. Familial coping with chronic illness: The case of cystic fibrosis. *Society, Science, and Medicine*, 1981, *15*, 289–297.

Veroff, J. B. The dynamics of help-seeking in men and women: A national survey study. *Psychiatry*, 1981, *44*, 189–200.

Vinter, R. *Readings in group work practice*. Ann Arbor, MI: Campus Publishers, 1967.

Visher, E. B., & Visher, J. S. *Stepfamilies: A guide to working with stepparents and stepchildren*. New York: Brunner/Mazel, 1979.

Voeller, B. (Executive Director of National Gay Task Force), Personal communication, 1981.

Wadsworth, R. D., & Checketts, K. T. Influence of religious affiliation on psychodiagnosis. *Journal of Consulting and Clinical Psychology*, 1980, *48*, 234–240.

Wagner, D., & Chapman, N. Informal group interaction, informal supports and neighborhood environments: Perspectives on the frail, urban elderly. In Proceedings of the Conference on Networks, Portland, OR, November 1978. (Available from the Regional Research Institute, Portland State University, P.O. Box 751, Portland, OR 97207.)

Wagner, D., & Gleeson, D. Late life frailty: Social networks. Presented at the 33rd Annual Meeting of the Gerontological Society, San Diego, CA, November 1980.

Wagner, H. The increasing importance of the peer group during adolescence. *Adolescence*, 1971, *6*, 53–58.

Wagner, P. S. Psychiatric activities during the Normandy offensive, June 10–Aug. 20, 1944: An experience of 5,203 neuropsychiatric casualities. *Psychiatry*, 1946, *9*, 341–364.

Wahler, R. The insular mother: Her problems in parent–child treatment. *Journal of Applied Behavior Analysis*, 1980a, 13(2), 207–219.

Wahler, R. G. The multiply entrapped parent: Obstacles to change in parent–child problems. *Advances in Family Intervention, Assessment and Theory*, 1980b, *1*:29–52.

Wahler, R. G., Afton, A. D., & Fox, J. J. The multiply entrapped parent: Some new problems in parent training. *Education and Treatment of Children*, 1979, *2*(4), 279–286.

Wahler, R. G., Leske, G., & Rogers, E. S. The insular family: A deviance support system for oppositional children. In L. A. Hamerlynck (Ed.), *Behavioral systems for the developmentally disabled: I. School and family environments*. New York: Bruner/Mazel, 1979.

Walberg, H., Bole, R., & Waxman, H. School-based family socialization and reading achievement in the inner city. *Psychology in the Schools*, 1980, *117*, 509–514.

Waldorf, D. Rock bottom. In *Careers in dope*. Englewood Cliffs, NJ: Prentice-Hall, 1973.

Waldorf, D., & Biernacki, P. The natural recovery from opiate addiction: Some preliminary findings. *Journal of Drug Issues*, 1981, *2*(1), 61–74.

Walker, F. C. "Cultural and ethnic issues in working with black families in the child welfare system." In Sinanoglu, P. A. & Maluccio, A. N. (Eds.) *Parents of Children in Placement: Perspectives and Programs*. New York: Child Welfare League of America, 1981, pp. 133–149.

Walker, K. N., MacBride, A., & Vachon, M. L. S. Social support networks and the crisis of bereavement. *Social Science and Medicine*, 1977, *11*, 35–41.

Wall, J., Hawkins, J., Lishner, D., & Fraser, M. Juvenile delinquency prevention: A compendium of thirty-six program models. National Institute for Juvenile Justice and Delinquency Prevention, Office of Juvenile Justice and Delinquency Prevention, Law Enforcement Assistance Administration, U. S. Department of Justice. Washington DC: U.S. Government Printing Office, 1981.

Wallerstein, J. S., & Kelly, J. B. The effects of parental divorce: The experiences of the preschool child. *Journal of the American Academy of Child Psychiatry*, 1975, *14*, 600–616.

Wallerstein, J., & Kelly, J. Divorce counseling: A community service for families in the midst of divorce. *American Journal of Orthopsychiatry*, 1977, *47*, 4–22.

Wallerstein, J. S., & Kelly, J. B. *Surviving the breakup: How children and parents cope with divorce*. New York: Basic Books, 1980.

Wandersman, L., Wandersman, A., & Kahn, S. Social support in the transition to parenthood. *Journal of Community Psychology*, 1980, *8*, 332–342.

Warren, D. Support systems in different types of neighborhoods. In J. Garbarino, H. Stocking, and Associates, *Protecting children from abuse and neglect*. San Francisco: Jossey-Bass, 1980.

Warren, D. I. *Helping networks*. Notre Dame, IN: University of Notre Dame Press, 1981.

Warren, D., & Warren, R. *The neighborhood organizer's handbook*. Notre Dame, IN: University of Notre Dame Press, 1977.

Watson, E. W., Maloney, D. M., Books, L. E., Blase, K. B., & Collins, L. B. *Teaching family bibliography*. Boys Town, NE: Father Flanagan's Boys Home, Youth Care Department, Child Care Assistance Program, 1980.

Weeks, H. *Youthful offenders at Highfields*. Ann Arbor, MI: University of Michigan Press, 1958.

Weeks, H., & Smith, M. Male and female broken home rates by types of delinquency. *American Sociological Review*, 1940, *5*, 601–609.

Weingarten, H. Remarriage and well-being. National survey evidence of social and psychological effects. *Journal of Family Issues*, 1980, *1*, 533–560.

Weinman, B., & Kleiner, R. The impact of community living and community member intervention on the adjustment of the chronic psychotic patient. In L. I. Stein & M. A. Test (Eds.), *Alternatives to mental hospital treatment*. New York: Plenum, 1978.

Weinraub, M., Brooks, J., & Lewis, M. The social network: A reconsideration of the concept of attachment. *Human Development*, 1977, *20*, 31–47.

Weis, J. G. Comparative analysis of social control theories of delinquency. In *Preventing delinquency: A comparative analysis of delinquency prevention theory* (Vol. 1 of 9). National Institute for Juvenile Justice and Delinquency Prevention, U.S. Department of Justice. Washington, DC: U.S. Government Printing Office, 1977.

Weis, J. G., Hall, J., Henney, J., Selderstrom, J., Worsley, K., & Zeiss, C. *Peer influence and delinquency: An evaluation of theory and practice*, Part I and II. National Institute for Juvenile Justice and Delinquency Prevention, Office of Juvenile Justice and Delinquency Prevention, Law Enforcement Assistance Administration, U.S. Department of Justice. Washington DC: U.S. Government Printing Office, 1981.

Weis, J. G., & Hawkins, J. *Preventing delinquency: The social development approach*. National Institute for Juvenile Justice and Delinquency Prevention, Office of Juvenile Justice and Delinquency Prevention, Law Enforcement Assistance Administration, U.S. Department of Justice. Washington, DC: U.S. Government Printing Office, 1982.

Weis, J. G., & Henney, J. Crime and criminals in the United States. In E. Bittner & S. L. Messinger (Eds.), *Criminology review yearbook*, Vol. 2. Beverly Hills, CA: Sage, 1980.

Weis, J. G., Sakumoto, K., Sederstrom, J., & Zeiss, C. *Jurisdiction and the elusive status offender: A comparison of involvement in delinquent behavior and status offenses*. National Institute for Juvenile Justice and Delinquency Prevention, Office of Juvenile Justice and Delinquency Prevention, Law Enforcement Assistance Administration, U.S. Department of Justice. Washington DC: U.S. Government Printing Office, 1979.

Weiss, N. S. Marital status and risk factors for coronary heart disease: The United States Health Examination Survey of Adults. *British Journal of Preventive Medicine*, 1973, *27*, 41–43.

Weiss, R. *Marital separation*. New York: Basic Books, 1975.

Weiss, R. S. The fund of sociability. *Transaction*, 1969, *6*(9), 36–44.

Weiss, R. S. The contributions of an organization of single parents to the well-being of its members. *The Family Coordinator*, 1973, *22*, 321–326.

Weiss, R. S. The provisions of social relationships. In Z. Rubin (Ed.), *Doing unto others*. Englewood Cliffs, NJ: Prentice-Hall, 1974.

Weiss, R. S. Growing up a little faster—Experience of growing up in a single-parent household. *Journal of Social Issues*, 1979, *35*(4), 97–111.

Wellman, B. The community question: The intimate networks of East Yorkers. *American Journal of Sociology*, 1979, *84*, 1201–1231.

Wellman, B. Applying network analysis to the study of support. In B. Gottlieb (Ed.), *Social networks and social support*. Beverly Hills, CA: Sage, 1981.

Wellman, B., & Leighton, B. Networks, neighborhoods, and communities: Approaches to the study of the community question. *Urban Affairs Quarterly*, 1979, *14*, 363–390.

Wells, L., & MacDonald, G. Interpersonal networks and post-relocation adjustment of the institutional elderly. *The Gerontologist*, 1981, *21*(2), 177–183.

Wentowski, G. Old age in an urban setting: Coping strategies, reciprocity, and personal networks. Presented at the 33rd Annual Meeting of the Gerontological Society, San Diego, CA, November 1980.

West, H. J. Adolescent drug attitudes: A seven year study on marijuana and LSD. *Dissertation Abstracts International*, 1975, *35*(9-A), 5944.

Westermeyer, J., & Pattison, E. M. Social networks and mental illness in a peasant society. *Schizophrenia Bulletin*, 1981, *7*, 125–134.

White, L. Sex differential in the effect of remarriage on global happiness. *Journal of Marriage and the Family*, 1979, *41*, 869–876.

White, R. W. Motivation reconsidered: The concept of competence. *Psychological Review*, 1959, *66*, 297–333.

White, S. W., & Bloom, B. L. Factors related to the adjustment of divorcing men. *Family Relations*, 1981, *30*, 349–360.

Whittaker, J. K. *Social treatment*. New York: Aldine, 1974.

Whittaker, J. K. *Caring for troubled children: Residential treatment in a community context.* San Francisco: Jossey-Bass, 1979.

Whittaker, J. K. Community support systems for troubled children and youth: A preliminary concept paper. Prepared for the National Institute of Juvenile Justice and Delinquency Prevention, March 1980.

Whittaker, J. K. Family involvement in residential treatment: A support system for parents. In A. Maluccio and P. Sinanoglu (Eds.), *The challenge of partnership*. New York: Child Welfare League of America, 1981.

Who knows? Who cares? Forgotten children in foster care. Report of the National Commission on Children in Need of Parents. New York: Child Welfare League of America, 1979.

Wilcox, B. Life event recency and social support as mediators of the relationship between stressful life events and psychological adjustment. Unpublished doctoral dissertation, University of Texas at Austin, 1979.

Wildman, R. W., II., & Wildman, R. W. The generalization of behavior modification procedures: A review—with special emphasis on classroom applications. *Psychology in the Schools*, 1975, *12*, 432–448.

Wilkinson, R. *The prevention of drinking problems. Alcohol control and cultural influences*. New York: Oxford University Press, 1970.

Willems, P. Sense of obligation to high school activities as related to school size and marginality of student. *Child Development*, 1967, *38*, 1247–1260.

Willner, A. G., Braukman, C. J., Kirigin, K. A., Fixsen, D. L., Phillips, E. L., & Wolf, M. M. The training and validation of youth preferred social behaviors. *Journal of Applied Behavior Analysis*, 1977, *10*(2), 219–231.

Wilson, K., Zurcher, L. A., McAdams, D. C., & Cartis, R. L. Stepfathers and stepchildren: An exploratory analysis from two national surveys. *Journal of Marriage and the Family*, 1975, *37*, 526–536.

Wiltse, K. *Education and training for child welfare services*. Unpublished manuscript, University of California, Berkeley, School of Social Welfare, 1981.

Wing, J. K., & Olsen, M. R. (Eds.). *Community care for the mentally disabled*. London: Oxford University Press, 1979.

Winick, C. The life cycle of the narcotic addict and of addiction. *U.S. Bulletin on Narcotics*, 1964, *16*(1).

Wispe, L. (Ed.). *Altruism, sympathy, and helping: Psychological and social principles*. New York: Academic Press, 1978.

Wolf, K., & Kerr, D. Companionship therapy in the treatment of drug dependency. In B. S. Brown (Ed.), *Addicts and aftercare*. Beverly Hills, CA: Sage, 1979.

Wolf, M. M. *Social validity: The case for subjective measurement*. Paper presented to the Division of The Experimental Analysis of Behavior, American Psychological Association, Washington, DC, 1976.

Wolfenden Committee. *The future of voluntary organizations*. London: Croom Helm, 1978.

Wolfensberger, W. *Normalization*. Toronto: National Institute on Mental Retardation, 1972.

Wolfensberger, W. Research, empiricism and the principle of normalization. In R. J. Flynn & K. E. Nitsch (Eds.), *Normalization, social integration and community services*. Baltimore: University Park Press, 1980.

Wolff, T. Undergraduates as campus mental health workers. *Personnel and Guidance Journal*, 1969, *48*, 294–304.

Wolins, M. (Ed.). *Successful group care: Explorations in the powerful environment.* Chicago: Beresford Book Service, 1974. (Originally published by Aldine.)

Wooden, K. *Weeping in the playtime of others.* New York: McGraw Hill, 1976.

Woody, J. D. Preventive intervention for children of divorce. *Social Casework,* 1978, *59*(9), 537.

Woolsey, S. H. Pied piper politics and the child-care debate. *Daedalus,* Spring, 1977, 127–145.

York, J., & Calsyn, R. Family involvement in nursing homes. *The Gerontologist,* 1977, *17*(6), 500–505.

York, P., & York, D. *Toughlove: A self-help manual for parents troubled by teenage behavior.* Sellersville, PA: Community Service Foundation, 1980.

Young, C. E., Plantz, M. C., & Giles, D. E. Natural networks: Help-giving and help-seeking in two rural communities. *American Journal of Community Psychology,* 1982, in press.

Young, M. *Lonely parents: Observations by public health nurses of alienation in child abuse.* ERIC Document Reproduction Service No. ED 134 894, 1976.

Young, M., & Kopp, C. Handicapped children and their families: Research directions. Unpublished paper, University of California, Los Angeles, 1980.

Zelnik, M., Kim, Y. J., & Kantner, J. F. Probabilities of intercourse and contraception among U.S. teenage women, 1971 and 1976. *Family Planning Perspectives,* 1979, *11*, 177–185.

Zimmer, A., Gross-Andrew, S., & Frankfather, D. Incentives to families caring for disabled elderly: Research and demonstration project to strengthen natural support systems. Paper presented at the 30th Annual Meeting of the Gerontological Society, San Francisco, CA, 1977.

Zinberg, N. E., & Harding, W. Control and intoxicant use: A theoretical and practical overview. *Journal of Drug Issues,* 1979, *9*(2), 121–143.

Zinberg, N. E., Harding, W., & Winkeller, M. A study of social regulatory mechanisms in controlled illicit drug users. *Journal of Drug Issues,* 1977, *7*(2), 117–133.

Zitner, R., & Miller, S. *Our youngest parents: A study of the use of support services for adolescent mothers.* New York: Child Welfare League of America, 1980.

Author Index

Italic numbers indicate page where complete reference is given.

Hawkins, J., 334, 337, 351, 352, 358, 362, 363, 368, 370, *428*, *433*, *452*, *453*
Hawks, D., 357, *428*
Hawley, A., 9, *428*
Haynes, R., 109, *428*
Hays, R., 123, 128, *420*
Hays, S., 386, *439*
Hays, W., 304, *428*
Haywood, H., 394, *428*
Haywood, S., *421*
Healy, W., 48, *428*
Heard, D., 357, 368, 373, *448*
Heath, D., 255, *428*
Heifeisen, A., 270, *428*
Helfer, R., *428*
Heller, K., 20, 72, 128, *428*
Hendrix, E., 389, *428*
Henney, J., 333, *453*
Henry, W., 136, 137, *418*
Hepburn, J., 341, *428*
Herjanic, B., 318, *428*
Herlihy, B., 259, 275, *429*
Herlihy, D., 259, 275, *429*
Herzog, E., 230, *429*
Hess, B., 243, *428*
Hess, R., 139, 142, 350, *525*, *429*
Hetherington, M., 177, 228, 229, 230, 242, 267, 269, *429*
Hever, R., 384, *428*
Hewson, D., *410*
Hicks, D., *429*
Hicks, M., 232, 233, 304, *418*
Hill, H., 239, *410*
Hill, R., 172, 182, *429*
Hindelang, R., 333, 334, 341, 357, 358, *422*, *429*
Hinkle, L., 44, *429*
Hirschi, T., 334, 337, 338, 341, 357, 358, *429*
Hobbs, N., 35, 41, 185, 385, *429*
Hobson, P., *429*
Hochschild, A., 137, 141, *429*
Hodges, E., 336, *450*
Hoffman, F., *438*
Holahan, C., 36, *429*
Holden, D., *432*
Holland, J., 390, *429*
Hollis, F., 34, *429*
Holm, V., 392, *429*
Holmes, T., 89, *429*
Hooks, W., 208, *423*
Horowitz, A., 143, 144, *429*, *430*
Hotaling, G., 301, *430*

Howard, J., 26, *430*
Howe, J., *424*
Howell, M., 304, 321, *430*
Hubbell, N., 260, 261, 262, *430*
Huizinga, D., 311, *413*
Hultsch, D., 89, 219, *430*
Hunt, B., 228, *430*
Hunt, M., 228, *430*
Hunter, R., 24, *430*
Hurd, G., 85, 87, 88
Hurley, D., 64, 65, *438*
Hurn, C., 255, *430*
Hutchins, R., 38, *430*
Hutton, R., *420*

Illich, I., 106, *430*
Ingham, J., 108, *438*
Insel, P., 78, *430*
Irish, D., 234, *413*
Ishisaka, A., 172, *430*
Ishiyama, T., 368, *430*
Iverson, M., 184, *412*

Jackson, R., *122*
Jacobi, M., *449*
Jacobson, L., 386, *444*
James, H., 268, *437*
Janowitz, M., 76, *431*
Jarrett, M., 34, 48, *430*
Jayaratne, S., 401, *430*
Jeger, A., 102, *430*
Jenkins, S., 26, 169, 181, *430*, *432*
Jensen, G., 117, 118, 127, *430*, *437*
Jessor, R., 357, *430*
Johnson, B., *430*
Johnson, H., *430*
Johnson, J., 227, 229, 234, 301, 316, *423*, *441*
Johnson, L., 176, *439*
Johnson, S., 22, *430*
Jonas, K., 154, 158, 159, *431*
Jones, L., 172, *422*, *431*
Jones, R., 338, *440*
Jordan, L., 237
Jordon, L., *427*
Jurich, A., 316, *431*
Jurich, J., 316, *431*

Kadushin, A., 167, 168, 169, 182, 185, *431*
Kahan, J., 233, *441*
Kahana, E., 160, *431*
Kahn, A., 14, 29, 30, 32, 44, 84, 194, 200, *431*

Subject Index